Breaking the Barriers
to Higher Economic Growth

Breaking the Barriers
to Higher Economic Growth

Better Governance and Deeper Reforms
in the Middle East and North Africa

 **THE WORLD BANK**

Mustapha Kamel Nabli

© 2007 The International Bank for Reconstruction and Development / The World Bank
1818 H Street NW
Washington DC 20433
Telephone: 202-473-1000
Internet: www.worldbank.org
E-mail: feedback@worldbank.org

2 3 4 5 11 10 09 08

Cover photo: © Henk Badenhorst/iStockphoto

Library of Congress Cataloging-in-Publication Data

Breaking the barriers to higher economic growth : better governance and deeper reforms in the Middle East and North Africa / Mustapha Kamel Nabli ... [et al.].
   p. cm.
 ISBN 978-0-8213-7415-3
1. Middle East—Economic conditions. 2. Africa, North—Economic conditions. 3. Middle East—Economic policy. 4. Africa, North—Economic policy. 5. Economic development—Political aspects—Middle East. 6. Economic development—Political aspects—Africa, North. 7. Macroeconomics. I. Nabli, Mustapha K.
 HC415.15.B74 2008
 338.956—dc22

            2007047530

Contents

Preface

The world's attention to the countries of the Middle East and North Africa[1] (MENA) region has often been dominated and held captive by headline issues. Much of that attention has centered on instability and uncertainty in the region, supported through coverage of both recent and long-standing conflicts. More recently intermixed with this perspective on the region is the world's growing attention to rising oil prices, from which another picture of the region emerges— one of strategically well-positioned oil producing economies with rapidly expanding wealth (and influence).

But little of the international coverage devoted to the region considers the broad range of development challenges facing this diverse group of countries. Providing quality jobs to a rapidly increasing labor force and reducing poverty, promoting the private sector, expanding gender equity, improving education access and quality, and effectively managing scarce water resources and finite oil wealth are only a few of the challenges facing the countries of this region. Because the MENA region's development challenges are multiple and complex, meeting them requires ambitious and coherent policy and institutional reforms. Through knowledge sharing and policy-relevant research, the World Bank's Middle East and North Africa region's Office of the Chief Economist has sought over the last few years to deepen understanding of these issues and help promote effective strategies for confronting these challenges. This book presents some of the work undertaken in this context.

The greatest challenge on which this book centers is that of implementing a comprehensive reform agenda to "break the barriers" to higher economic growth and create needed job opportunities. It is an agenda that requires realigning the MENA economies, to move from public sector-dominated to private sector-driven economies, from closed economies to more open economies, and from oil-dominated and volatile economies to more stable and diversified economies. The central message from this body of work is that deeper economic reforms are needed to attain higher growth rates and that better governance is key in achieving the required progress on reform. In Part I of this book, we explore two major themes related to the economic reform and growth nexus. First, we attempt to understand the factors which caused the growth collapse of the 1980s and the failure of reforms undertaken since then to spur a growth revival until the early 2000s. Second, we delve into the domain of the political economy of reform, in order to understand the reasons behind MENA's slow progress with implementing economic reforms. The core of this work points to the central role that public governance has played in hindering the region's progress with implementing the extensive reform agenda. In "Long-Term Economic Development Challenges and Prospects for the Arab Countries" I provide a broad overview of the development challenges in the region, examining the constraints of the old models of development and defining the set of transitions that constitute the contours of a new development model. In "Reform Complementarities and Economic Growth in the Middle East and North Africa," (with Marie-Ange Veganzonès-Varoudakis) a quantitative analysis of the relationship between economic reforms and economic growth in the Middle East and North Africa region is undertaken, in an effort to understand whether the anemic growth over the 1990s was the result of insufficient economic reforms or a poor growth dividend from reform. "After Argentina: Was MENA Right to Be Cautious?" looks at Argentina's experience with reform and its subsequent economic crisis and draws lessons for MENA on the strategic directions with respect to speed, consistency and scope of reforms so as to avoid such crises. In "Restarting Arab Economic Reform," the difficulties with implementing deeper economic reform are explored, and the reasons behind the stalled reform agenda in the region and ways in which to move it forward are discussed. In "Democracy for Better Governance and Higher Economic Growth in the MENA Region?" (with Carlos Silva-Jáuregui) we review the literature on the relationship between economic growth and democracy, and explore the implications for MENA, in order to understand whether democratic development could help or hinder a stronger economic performance in the MENA region, and under what conditions democracy leads to better governance. Finally, in "The Political Economy of Industrial Policy in the Middle East and North Africa," (with Jennifer Keller, Claudia Nassif, and Carlos Silva-Jáuregui) the specific topic of the region's experience with industrial policy is explored, to understand the political economy factors behind the persistence of a traditional model of government intervention, and to discuss the likely direction of new models of "industrial policy" in the region.

A central motivation for the economic growth agenda in the MENA region is the challenge it has been facing over the last two decades—and which it will continue to face over the next two decades—in terms of job creation. This challenge is unprecedented in the world and throughout history, with the region experiencing rates of growth of the labor force of 3–4 percent a year over several decades. The members of MENA's labor force, of which a growing proportion are women, are better educated than their parents and increasingly aware of economic opportunities worldwide, and they have greater expectations for good jobs. In Part II, the extent of this development challenge is explored, along with the links between labor market outcomes and various reforms. The first paper on "The Macroeconomics of Labor Market Outcomes in MENA: How Growth Has Failed to Keep Pace with a Burgeoning Labor Market" (with Jennifer Keller) reviews the trends and developments in labor markets in MENA over the 1990s and analyzes the links between these disappointing outcomes and the weak economic growth experience (which is the subject of Part I) and private investment (which is the subject of Part III). In "Challenges and Opportunities for the 21st Century: Higher Education in the Middle East and North Africa," the labor/education relationship is addressed, looking at ways in which the MENA region can best improve the social and private returns from its higher education systems in an increasingly globalized world. In "Labor Market Reforms, Growth and Unemployment in Labor-Exporting Countries in the Middle East and North Africa," (with Pierre-Richard Agénor, Henning Tarp Jensen, and Tarik Yousef) a quantitative assessment is made of the impact of labor market reforms in a typical labor-exporting MENA country on growth, real wages, and unemployment. Finally, in "Economic Reforms and People Mobility for a More Effective EU-MED Partnership," (with Ishac Diwan, Adama Coulibaly, and Sara Johansson de Silva) the developments in labor markets in the Southern Mediterranean countries are linked to the potential for managed migration and people mobility with the European Union (EU), and the role it may play in supporting the reform agenda in these countries.

The overall thrust of the analysis in Parts I and II points to one critical message: In order to break the barriers to higher growth and meet the employment challenge, the power of the private sector in MENA countries needs to be unleashed—through greater openness and integration with the world economy and greater competitiveness. Part III of the book looks in more detail at a number of issues relating to trade reform, the enhancement of competitiveness, and the growth of private investment in the region. In "Cruise Control, Shock Absorbers, and Traffic Lights: The Macroeconomic Road to Arab Competitiveness," I discuss the key macroeconomic policy elements needed for a supportive business environment in MENA, a business environment that facilitates long-term planning, promotes investment and knowledge transfer, and supports the efficient allocation of resources throughout the economy. In "Trade, Foreign Direct Investment, and Development in the Middle East and North Africa," (with Farrukh Iqbal) we discuss how the limited progress in trade reform and weak foreign direct investment, in interaction with a weak domestic investment climate, contributed to the region's weak growth performance. In "Making Trade Work for Jobs: International Evidence and lessons for MENA," (with Dipak Dasgupta, Christopher Pissarides, and Aristomene Varoudakis) the relationship between international trade and employment in manufacturing is examined, to analyze the prospects for stepping up employment growth in the region through trade and investment policy reform. In "Exchange Rate Management within the Middle East and North Africa Region: The Cost to Manufacturing Competitiveness," (with Jennifer Keller and Marie-Ange Veganzonès-Varoudakis) the repercussions from exchange rate misalignment in the region are discussed, and the reasons behind the region's continued reliance on fixed exchange rates analyzed. Further exploration of the costs of exchange rate misalignment is presented in "How Does Exchange Rate Policy Affect Manufactured Exports in MENA Countries?" (with Marie-Ange Veganzonès-Varoudakis). In "Public Infrastructure and Private Investment in the Middle East and North Africa," (with Pierre-Richard Agénor and Tarik Yousef) we assess quantitatively the impact of public infrastructure on private capital formation in three MENA countries: Egypt, Jordan, and Tunisia. Finally, Part III concludes with a paper on "Governance, Institutions, and Private Investment: An Application to the Middle East and North Africa," (with Ahmet Faruk Aysan and Marie-Ange Veganzonès-Varoudakis) which assesses the critical roles that poor governance and weak institutions have played in determining the region's low levels of private investment.

While major economic and political developments have an impact on the short-term policies and priorities for the MENA region, the core of the development agenda for the next two or three decades remains largely intact. The challenges of achieving significantly higher economic growth, of reducing poverty, of improving the quality of education and skills, of creating the hundreds of millions of good jobs for a rapidly growing male and female labor force, of building strong businesses and a healthy private sector, remain through the vicissitudes of oil price fluctuations, conflict, and political turmoil. It is hoped that the collective thinking represented in this book contributes in some modest way to highlighting and meeting these challenges.

Mustapha K. Nabli

---

1. The World Bank formally defines the Middle East and North Africa region as including the following countries: Egypt, Lebanon, Jordan, Tunisia, Morocco, Djibouti, and West Bank and Gaza (classified as resource-poor labor-abundant economies); Iran, Iraq, Algeria, Syria and Yemen (classified as resource-rich labor-abundant economies); and Saudi Arabia, United Arab Emirates, Kuwait, Qatar, Bahrain, Oman, and Libya (classified as resource-rich labor-importing economies).

Acknowledgments

This book includes many of the papers and speeches I have published and pre-sented over the last few years in various fora as Chief Economist for the Middle East and North Africa (MENA) region at the World Bank. The Office of the Chief Economist is responsible for monitoring, analyzing, and reporting on the MENA region's economic developments, presenting new research, and enriching the knowledge and policy debate among development practitioners, both within the MENA region and worldwide.

My greatest debt and gratitude goes first to Jennifer Keller, who in addition to co-authoring a few of the papers, has diligently and efficiently put together this volume. She also helped me draft and provided background work for many of the other papers and speeches included. The book is also the result of the collective effort of my colleagues who co-authored many of the papers, including Pierre-Richard Agénor, Ahmed Faruk Aysan, Adama Coulibaly, Dipak Dasgupta, Ishac Diwan, Farrukh Iqbal, Henning Tarp Jensen, Claudia Nassif, Christopher Pissarides, Sara Johansson de Silva, Carlos Silva-Jáuregui, Aristomene Varoudakis, Marie-Ange Veganzonès-Varoudakis, and Tarik Yousef. Finally, I am grateful to the wonderful research assistance of Paul Dyer, Manuel Felix, Adama Coulibaly, Nihal Bayraktar, and Claudia Nassif, which has enabled this work.

Part I

Growth, Reform, and Governance

Long-Term Economic Development Challenges and Prospects for the Arab Countries

Mustapha K. Nabli

It is a challenge to talk about an Arab economy and to explore its prospects. The countries that compose the Arab world are a diverse set in terms of size, geography, level of income, natural resource endowments, economic structure, human capital and skills, social structures, economic policies and institutions, and more. Yet, the economic similarities among the countries in the Arab world abound. The region has been linked by a common resource base. Oil provided the basis for rapid economic and social development throughout the region—not only for oil-producing economies but for resource-poor Arab economies as well, through labor remittances and aid flows. The common resource base also includes the shared lack of water resources, with water per capita in the Arab countries the lowest in the world. The region has been linked by policy, with similar models of economic development adopted by Arab countries at the time of their independence. Almost all adopted, since the 1950s and 1960s, models of development based upon state-led planning, with social policies designed for redistribution and equity.

With these strong similarities in terms of economic policy, natural resources, and the shared production base for economic growth and development, it is not surprising, then, that many of the development challenges facing the Arab countries today are also similar. Almost all have confronted stag-

---

Presented at Second Arab Thought Foundation Conference "The Prospects of the Arab Future"; Beirut, Lebanon; December 4–6, 2003. Originally titled "Long-Term Economic Development Challenges and Prospects for Arab Countries."

nant growth since the decline in oil prices, and despite some measured economic reforms in most of the economies, growth has remained weak throughout the region. All have been affected by regional conflicts and instability, either directly or through association, deterring investment. And almost all of the Arab states are facing one of the most pressing development problems to date: a burgeoning problem of unemployment, the result of both shrinking prospects for the main modes of employment creation in the past; labor migration and public sector employment; and a rapidly expanding labor force.

The Arab region faces a growing realization that the development paths of the past are no longer capable of achieving national objectives. The problem of insufficient job creation in the Arab region is mounting, and without fundamental transitions in the Arab economies to ensure greater and sustainable job creation, the employment challenge will worsen rapidly and dramatically.

Over the next pages, we will articulate the broad course of action needed in the Arab economies.[1] First we describe the development challenges facing the Arab world, in particular the challenge of employment creation. Next, we examine the constraints of the old development model in the region in terms of meeting these development challenges. Then we propose a set of transitions that constitute the contours of a new development model. Finally, we outline the fundamental changes needed for making this transition, including improved governance, higher-quality education, and greater gender equality. The concluding section makes a few observations about feasibility and issues of implementation.

A Central Challenge in the 21st Century: Employment

The Arab region faces many economic challenges as it enters the 21st century. There is the challenge of water scarcity, and its implications for the availability of this vital resource to its citizens and for development prospects. There is the environmental challenge and the sustainability of the use of natural resources, including soil degradation and deforestation, desertification, the preservation of sea coasts, and deep-sea resources. There are issues of poverty and exclusion. There is the issue of population growth, which has slowed dramatically in many countries, but remains high for many. But perhaps there is no more pressing economic challenge for the Arab world today than that of employment, on which this paper will focus.

A generation disappointed…One of the striking characteristics about the Arab world[2] is the youth of its population. Two-thirds of the population is under the age of 30, making it the second youngest region of the world behind Sub-Saharan Africa. As a comparison, in Europe those under 30 constitute only a third of the population. In East Asia and the Pacific, only half. The Arab world is a world of burgeoning youth, increasingly educated, with higher expectations than the generation before. Yet, at the same time, this group, which represents the new face of the Arab region, faces growing disappointment in the job market.

Labor market outcomes in the Arab region have steadily worsened over the last two decades. With the unemployment rate increasing since the mid-1980s, unemployment now averages over 15 percent of the labor force, by official figures. Actual unemployment is probably much higher.

And unemployment falls disproportionately on the Arab region's youth. First-time job seekers make up more than 90 percent of all unemployed in Egypt, and almost two-thirds of the unemployed in Yemen and the United Arab Emirates.

These are workers coming into the labor force with substantially higher levels of education than the generation before them: 20 years ago, the average level of education in the Arab world was about two years; today, that level is around fve years.[3] But unemployment has increasingly prevented those educational advancements from realizing economic returns in the labor market.

The Arab labor market is not only young, it is increasingly feminized, and the poor labor market outcomes that characterize the Arab region particularly affect women. While Arab women have the lowest labor force participation rates in the world, their engagement in the labor force has grown considerably over the last decades. But as their numbers increase, they are finding increasingly fewer job opportunities.

Unemployment rates average 30 percent higher for women than their male counterparts. The gender gap in unemployment is particularly great in coun-

Figure 1.1. Current Unemployment Rates in Arab Economies

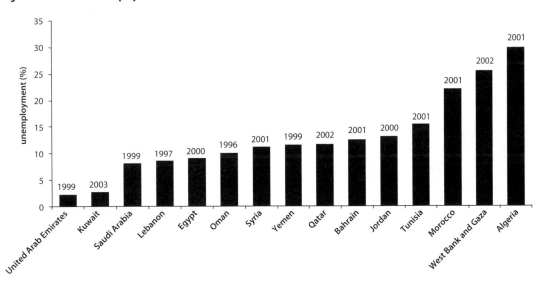

Source: Compiled by World Bank staff from ILO and country sources.
Note: Data include most recent estimates available for each country; rates in the GCC countries are for nationals only.

Figure 1.2. First-Time Job Seekers as a Proportion of Total Unemployed

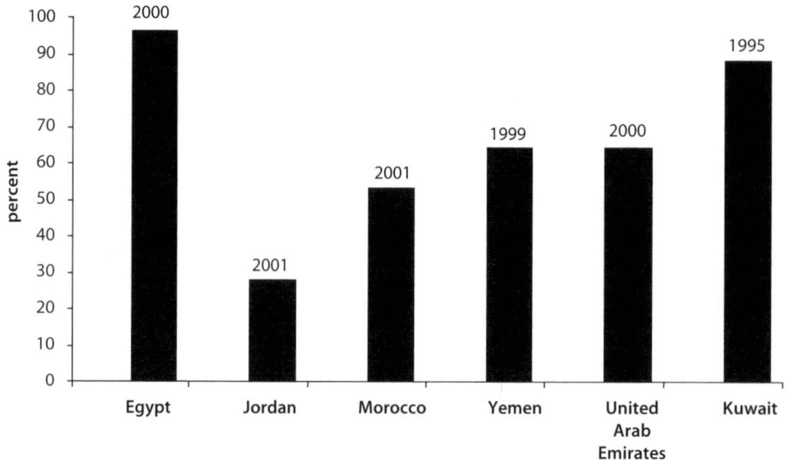

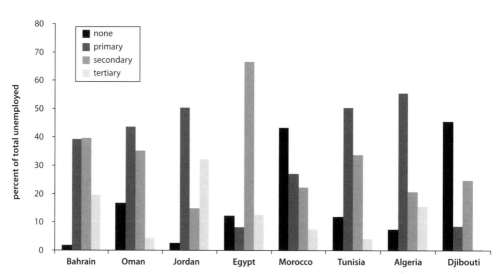

Sources: ILO 2003a, except for Kuwait: Population Census 2001; and for Jordan: AREUS 2001.

tries like Bahrain, Syria, Egypt, and Saudi Arabia, where the unemployment rate among women is two to three times that of males. Along with many other factors that have altogether discouraged the involvement of Arab women in the labor force, the poor prospects they face in the labor market have undoubtedly deterred their participation.

Poor labor market outcomes are not limited only to unemployment, but also to the poor wage prospects for the employed. Worker productivity, the basis for real wage growth, has increased only marginally over the last decade,

Figure 1.3. Distribution of Unemployed by Level of Education

Sources: ILO 2002, except for Bahrain: ILO 2003a; for Egypt: ELMS, 1998; for Morocco: LSMS 1999.

Figure 1.4. Female Labor Supply in Arab States, 1950–2020

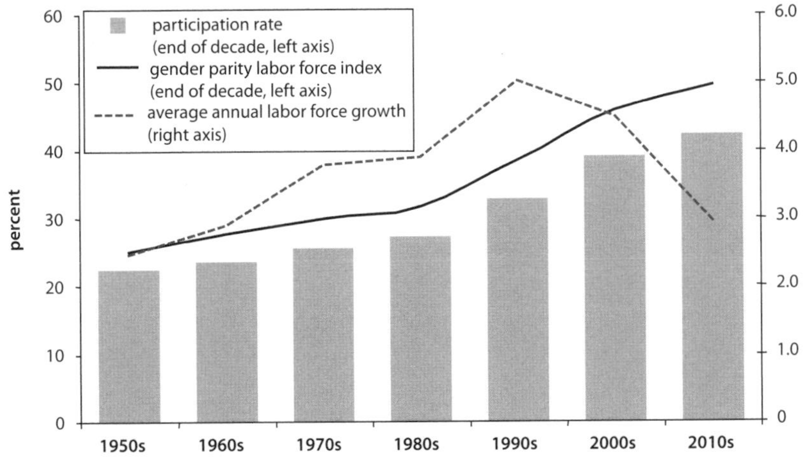

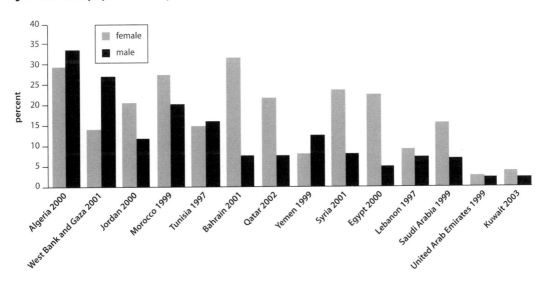

participation rate
(end of decade, left axis)
gender parity labor force index
(end of decade, left axis)
average annual labor force growth
(right axis)
percent
60
50
40
30
20
10
0
6.0
5.0
4.0
3.0
2.0
1.0
0
1950s
1960s
1970s
1980s
1990s
2000s
2010s

Sources: ILO 1996; UN 2002.

remaining far below that in East Asia and the Pacific, South Asia, and Latin America and the Caribbean. As a result, real wages have stagnated or declined in half the Arab countries since the 1980s, and only increased weakly in most of the other Arab countries.

Unprecedented labor market challenges to come. Beyond the poor job prospects that have characterized the Arab region over the past two decades, there is also the knowledge that labor market pressures will only build over the

Figure 1.5. Unemployment Rates by Gender in Arab Countries

female
male
percent
40
35
30
25
20
15
10
5
0
Algeria 2000
West Bank and Gaza 2001
Jordan 2000
Morocco 1999
Tunisia 1997
Bahrain 2001
Qatar 2002
Yemen 1999
Syria 2001
Egypt 2000
Lebanon 1997
Saudi Arabia 1999
United Arab Emirates 1999
Kuwait 2003

Sources: 1. Algeria, Jordan, Syria, Egypt, West Bank and Gaza, Yemen: ILO 2003b; 2. Tunisia, INS 2001; 3. Bahrain, Qatar, Saudi Arabia, Kuwait, UAE: Girgis, Hadad-Zervose, and Coulibaly 2003; 4. Morocco, LSMS 1999; 5. Yemen: NPPS 1999.

next two decades. A legacy of high population growth rates in the Arab region between 1950 and1990, which peaked at 3.2 percent a year in 1985, has translated into some of the most intense pressures on labor markets observed anywhere in the world in the post-WWII period. The current labor force is growing by a rate of 3.3 percent per year. That translates into some 37 million new workers entering the labor force between 2000 and 2010, swelling the total labor force by close to 40 percent in a span of only 10 years. Between 2000 and 2020, the labor force in the Arab states will have expanded by some 75 percent. In the span of 20 years, 74 million new jobs will need to be created, just to absorb the growing labor force.

Job creation must be even higher, if the region is to address the current unemployment problem. If the Arab region is to accomplish the more ambitious goal of absorbing these unemployed workers, in addition to the new entrants to the labor force, close to 90 million new jobs will need to be created by the end of the next decade, well over double the number of jobs that currently exist in the Arab world.

Under any comparison, the Arab region faces an unprecedented challenge in development. These labor market pressures would be a development challenge for any country. But for the Arab region, the need for accelerated job creation comes just as two of the Arab region's major sources of employment creation over the past four decades, public sector employment and labor migration, are providing fewer and fewer jobs.

Figure 1.6. Labor Force Growth in Developing Regions, 1970–2010

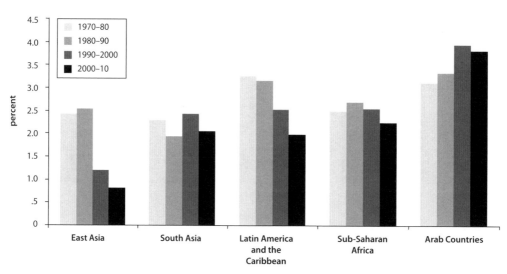

Source: ILO 1996.
Note: Arab countries include members of the League of Arab States except Comoros, Djibouti, Mauritania, Somalia, and Sudan.

Figure 1.7. Average Annual Growth in the Labor Force of Arab Countries, 1970–2010

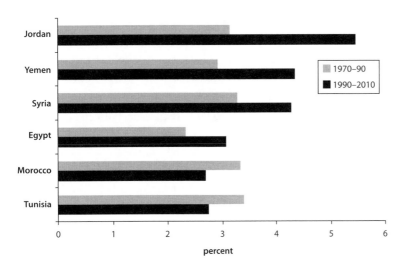

Source: ILO 1996; UN 2002.

Constraints of the Old Development Model

Employment creation in the Arab region has been greatly influenced by the historical model of development adopted throughout the Arab region. In part to correct for a legacy of inequities and poverty during the first half of the 20th century, at the time of independence the political actors of the Arab region adopted models of development based on strong governments, central planning of economic and social priorities, and wide-scale policies for redistribution and equity. This strategy included nationalization of many private assets, state planning, industrial development through protected local markets, and vast resources directed to social development and large-scale public sector employment.

Early positive results. Early on, this model had strong payoffs. The region as a whole benefited from oil, either directly (for oil-producing economies) or through aid and labor remittances. With oil and oil-related revenues, in addition to directing large resources toward public infrastructure, the Arab economies directed vast resources toward education, with the resulting average level of education of the adult population increasing from less than a year in 1960 to more than three years in 1985. Fueled by improvements in basic education and heavy investments in health care, health indicators also improved significantly, and poverty was substantially reduced.

Significant costs. But the model also has had strong implications for the economic orientation of the Arab economies, on governance, and on employment creation. Economically, heavy protection and regulation of industry, along with overvalued and uncompetitive exchange rates, provided marked disincentives for the growth of a tradable goods sector in the Arab states. Oil resources relieved many governments of the need to tax their citizens, and allowed governments to redistribute substantial resources through vast welfare and social services systems. At the same time, this system of pervasive redistribution of wealth reduced demands from Arab citizens for accountable and inclusive public institutions. Arab governance mechanisms lacked transparency, reflected in limited access to government information and carefully monitored freedom of the press. They lacked contestability, as reflected in some of the most centralized governments of all developing countries. And they lacked inclusiveness, as reflected in rural-urban inequalities in access to public services, gender inequalities in voice and participation in society, and nepotism or patronage determining who received public services or access to lucrative business opportunities and who did not.

The private sector that emerged under this model, developing under the patronage of governments, flourished not so much by being dynamic in a competitive environment, but often by supplying protected domestic markets and generally "living off the state." Despite high growth rates during the oil boom years, investments in the Arab region became progressively unproductive. Though still positive, total factor productivity growth was cut in half in the Arab region from the 1960s to the 1970s.

The model also had significant implications on employment creation. Along with vast social welfare systems, Arab governments redistributed resources through public sector jobs. Governments became the employer of choice throughout the Gulf Cooperation Council (GCC), and while oil revenues were high, nationals entering the labor force could be hired almost exclusively by the public sector. Even in the non-oil-producing economies, aid flows and labor remittances from citizens working in the Gulf permitted the public sector to grow to unprecedented levels.

A major source of employment in the region also came in the form of labor migration, with large numbers of Arab laborers working in other countries in the Gulf. At the peak of the oil boom in the early 1980s, some 3.5 million Arab migrant workers were employed in the Gulf states. During 1973-1984, official remittances totaled almost US$22 billion in Egypt, US$8.2 billion in Morocco, and US$6.5 billion in Jordan. This provided an enormous buffer to any lack of job opportunities at home.

The oil price collapse and a decade of crisis. When oil prices collapsed in the mid-1980s, government revenues throughout the region felt the blow, beginning with the oil producers, but with the nonoil producers close behind. Although cushioned by extensive external assistance, the flow of resources to the public sector slowed considerably and government expenditures on social systems and physical capital shrank. For the region as a whole, public fixed investment was cut heavily, and growth in physical capital stock per laborer declined by more than 60 percent from the 1970s.

Facing declining public revenues, governments struggled to maintain their redistributive commitments. The fiscal strains contributed to large macroeconomic imbalances. Productivity growth, already declining by the 1970s, plummeted over the 1980s. Growth collapsed under the multiple blows of declining public spending, an unattractive private investment climate, and continuing losses in efficiency. Economic growth per capita averaged only 0.7 percent per year.

At the same time, and for the first time, unemployment began to emerge as a serious problem in the Arab states. With reduced public sector revenues, guaranteed employment in the public sector was no longer possible. Labor migration opportunities were also diminished. Lower oil prices, rapidly rising domestic supplies of national labor, and competition from lower-cost labor elsewhere in the world all worked to dampen the GCC demand for labor from the rest of the Arab region.

Initial efforts at reform. The lack of economic growth and deteriorating budget deficits prompted several of the economies to undertake programs of macroeconomic stabilization and structural reform aimed at encouraging private sector development, so it would become an engine for growth and employment creation. Macroeconomic stabilization was broadly achieved, but the pace of structural reform differed markedly throughout the region.

• A group of resource-poor countries, including Tunisia, Morocco, and Jordan, implemented earlier and more intensive reforms toward more open, private sector-led economies than the rest of the Arab countries. Tunisia

Figure 1.8. GDP per Capita Growth in Developing Regions, 1970–2000

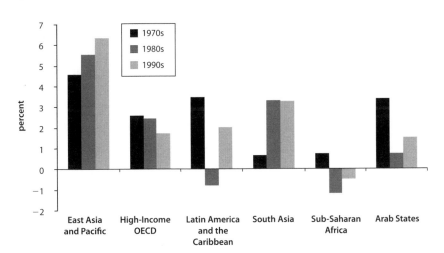

Note: Arab States include all MENA countries except Iran, plus Sudan.

introduced, as early as the 1970s, an "offshore" export-processing platform to facilitate trade, and both Morocco and Tunisia joined the General Agreement on Tariffs and Trade. Reforms also included exchange rate liberalization, tax reforms, trade and financial sector liberalization, and privatization. All three signed Euro-Med agreements in the 1990s, and Jordan signed a free trade agreement with the United States. In general, the reform effort has been steady in these countries, and without policy reversals.

- Other resource-poor countries, including Egypt and Lebanon, have pursued reform more slowly and sporadically. Despite early reforms in Egypt, and aggressive macroeconomic stabilization in the 1990s, reforms were partially reversed with escalating behind-the-border trade restrictions and significant exchange rate overvaluation. More recently, reforms have resumed, especially with the signing of a Euro-Med agreement in 2001. Lebanon, with a legacy of destroyed physical and economic infrastructure and weaker institutions, had to contend with large macroeconomic imbalances.

- Another set of countries with significant oil resources and large populations, including Algeria, Syria, and Yemen, also pursued reforms later, more gradually, and more sporadically than the early reformers. Algeria, with macroeconomic imbalances stemming from the collapse in oil prices, aggressively pursued macroeconomic stabilization, but structural reforms have been far more limited. Trade reforms initiated in the early 1990s were reversed in 1998, and then taken up again in 2001 with the signing of a Euro-Med agreement. Reforms in key areas such as the financial sector and privatization remain limited. In Syria, the trade and investment liberalization begun in 1991 was not sustained. While there has been modest progress in exchange rate unification and private sector regulatory reforms, broader structural reforms have been limited. And in Yemen, macroeconomic stabilization reforms have not been accompanied by more aggressive reforms to diversify the economy, despite relatively open trade policies. The investment climate remains poor, reflecting weak rule of law and property rights, ineffective regulatory frameworks, and security problems.

- The six GCC economies—Bahrain, Kuwait, Oman, Qatar, Saudi Arabia, and the United Arab Emirates—have long maintained an open trade system with free movement of capital and advanced financial systems. As oil prices deteriorated, most countries cut expenditures, but aggregate budget deficits have generally increased. Some of the smaller GCC countries have encouraged growth in selected sectors such as entrepot trade (United Arab Emirates), financial services, and tourism (Bahrain and United Arab Emirates). Oman has made substantial efforts to broaden private sector participation and improve the investment climate, with privatizations and changes in its foreign capital investment law. In Saudi Arabia, reforms have progressed more slowly. The public sector still dominates economic activities; and government revenues remain dependent on oil.

Failure of growth to improve. In general, the structural reform agenda in the Arab region, despite its intentions, has been cautious, selective, and often subject to pause and to reversals. The reform agenda avoided most governance reform or the opening of the political space needed for any type of deeper reforms that depend on the compliance and participation of the social groups whose well being the reforms are intended to improve. As a result, the reform effort stopped short of providing a substantially improved climate for growth and investment, and the recovery in growth over the 1990s was weak, with per capita GDP growing by an average of only 1.5 percent per year.

Declining employment opportunities from the old model. Now, as the Arab region faces an unprecedented challenge in job creation over the next two decades, the major sources of employment creation of the past are quickly dwindling. The public sector can no longer be the employment outlet it has been in the past. Most branches of public sectors are already overstaffed, by as much as a third or more in some countries. More important, the public sector, with the marked change in fiscal circumstances throughout the region, cannot act as a refuge to vast numbers of unemployed.

The Arab countries' development has relied heavily on three financial sources: oil, aid inflows, and workers' remittances. These three sources provided an essential supply of public revenues and private earnings, and supported the large-scale public sector employment policies of the past. But all three of these revenue sources are under greater pressure.

Figure 1.9. GDP per Capita Growth in the Arab World, 1970–2000

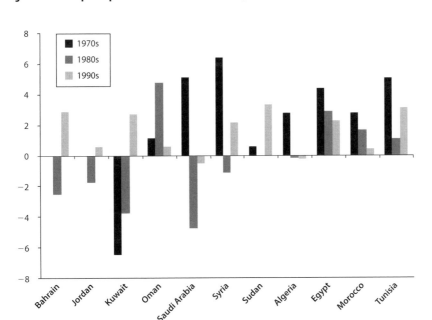

Oil revenues will decline for all countries in the Arab region, continuing the pattern of the past two decades. Known oil resources will be depleted in some countries of the region, such as Algeria, in about four decades, while in some others, such as Egypt and the Republic of Yemen, much sooner. Exports will fall as domestic energy consumption ratchets up and the population grows. With declining oil production, the decline in per capita oil rents will be steeper than in the past two decades.

Aid flows are expected to similarly decline, except in temporary periods of strategic importance and conflict resolution. Finally, labor remittances are not projected to increase significantly, a result of deteriorating prospects for labor migration.

Prospects for another major source of employment creation—labor migration—are also diminished. Throughout the 1970s and 1980s, labor migration provided a critical employment outlet for workers in many of the non-oil-producing Arab economies. In the mid-1980s, close to 10 percent of the Egyptian and almost 15 percent of the Yemeni labor forces were employed abroad, primarily in the Gulf. The last decade, however, has seen a rapid deceleration in the net outflow of Arab workers to other countries in the region. Migration has slowed to the GCC countries of the region.

Combined, the region's traditional sources of job creation are fast dwindling, just as the need for job creation is accelerating.

Three Major Economic Realignments Are Required

If the region is to ensure that the rapidly expanding labor force has both suf-

Figure 1.10. Per Capita Oil Exports in Arab Countries, 1980–2000 (US$)

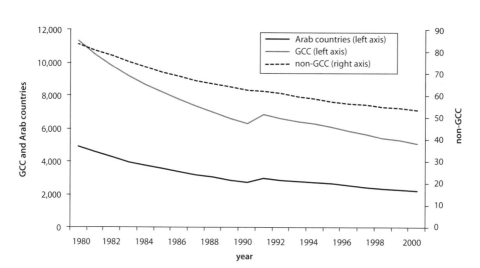

Source: Oil exports, COMTRADE 2002; population, WDI 2002.

Figure 1.11   Aid to GDP Ratio in Arab Countries, 1980–2000

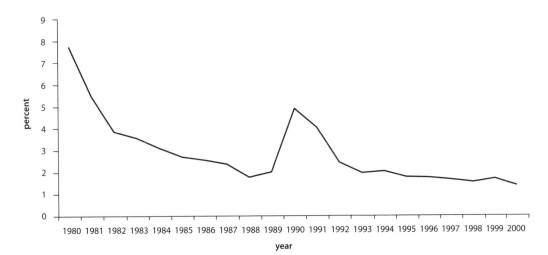

Figure 1.12.   Worker Remittances as Percentage of GDP, Egypt and Morocco: 1970–2000

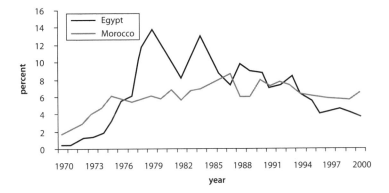

ficient employment opportunities and the prospects for real wage growth, GDP growth in the region will need to double from its average of 3 percent per year over the late 1990s to 6-7 percent a year for a sustained period. This is an enormous growth challenge, but tantamount to meeting the enormous labor market challenge ahead.

To meet the growth and employment challenges, the Arab countries must address a set of long-standing policy and institutional challenges to complete three fundamental and interrelated realignments in their economies:

• From public sector-dominated to private sector-dominated economies
• From closed economies to more open economies
• From oil-dominated and volatile economies to more stable and diversified economies.

Expanding the Role of the Private Sector in the Arab Economies

The private sector's contribution to value added in the Arab region is low compared to that in other regions, and while most Arab countries attempted to expand private sector activity since the late 1980s, it increased only marginally over the 1990s. The scope for private sector expansion is very large in the Arab region, but it requires a conducive economic and political environment.

Improving the investment climate. Firm startups and operations in the Arab world are significantly hindered by the time and financial costs of regulatory and administrative barriers. For new firms, the costs of complying with regulations as a proportion of gross national income are twice what new firms face in Eastern Europe, and five times what firms face in East Asia, Latin America, and the Caribbean. Other costs are also high, from licenses to domestic taxation, import duties, and regulations that slow customs clearance.

World Bank Investment Climate Surveys reveal that potential investors in the Arab world are significantly hindered by obstacles to entry, including cumbersome licensing processes, complex regulations, opaque bidding procedures, and official acceptance of uncompetitive practices. In Morocco, about half the firms say they have had to hire intermediaries or maintain full-time staff to deal with the bureaucracy. In Jordan, a potential investor interested in registering a new firm has to wait three months, with half of that time spent on a single procedure—inspection by the ministry concerned.

Figure 1.13. Private Sector Contribution to GDP in Arab Countries

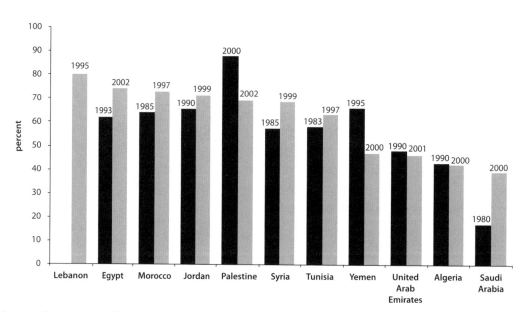

Source: Assaf and Benhassine 2003.

Businesses are further handicapped by judicial systems that facilitate neither restructuring of viable businesses nor closure of nonviable ones. The Arab region compares poorly with other regions in the complexity and time needed to initiate and complete a legal claim. Unpredictability of enforcement is an even more serious problem. Nearly half the surveyed firms expressed concern over the unpredictability of the legal system.

Improving key finance and infrastructure for business. Weaknesses in infrastructure and in the financial system are yet another burden on business operations. According to World Bank Investment Climate Assessments, almost half the private businesses in the region complain that infrastructure is a moderate to major obstacle to conducting business. Telecommunications and transport, two backbone services, are significantly underdeveloped. With public banks dominating the banking system in many countries, and favoring state enterprises, larger industrial firms, and offshore enterprises, smaller firms have a hard time getting the startup and operating capital they need.

Accelerating privatization. Finally, several strategic services for the private sector—banking, telecommunications, and transportation—remain under public ownership in most Arab countries. Privatizations in the 1990s focused on manufacturing firms, only recently extending to selected services such as telecommunications. And even where privatization of services is advancing, regulatory arrangements often remain weak.

Integrating with the World

The limited integration of Arab economies. The Arab region has largely missed out on the trends of global trade integration. The region's trade integration, measured by the ratio of trade to GDP, fell from about 92 percent of GDP in 1980 to about 70 percent in 1985, and it remains around 65 percent today. The region's oil resource boom helped it realize high initial export-to-GDP ratios, but with the windfall revenues invested at home in infrastructure and services (and not in tradables), the export-to-GDP ratio steadily declined.

The scope for expanding trade for the Arab countries is significant. Exports other than oil are about a third of what they could be, given the characteristics of the region in terms of endowments, size, and geography. Manufacturing imports are one half of what they could be. Foreign direct investment could be five to six times higher.

Arab country trade is marked by both a high degree of product and geographic concentration. Although the share of fuels in total exports has fallen, fuels still constitute the most significant exports for the region. In 1978, 76 percent of merchandise exports were fuels. By 2001, that share had only fallen to 58 percent. The manufacturing sectors of most Arab countries are small by

Figure 1.14 Arab Nonoil Export Potential

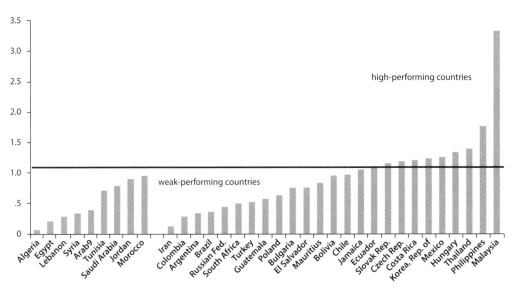

Note: Regression is based on 42 countries, but values for 8 low-income countries, including Yemen, are not reported because of negative values. Arab9 = Algeria, Egypt, Jordan, Lebanon, Morocco, the Republic of Yemen, Saudi Arabia, Syria, and Tunisia.

international standards—almost half the typical levels in other lower-middle-income economies. Some of the resource-poor countries, including Tunisia and Morocco, have seen a large fall in their trade product concentration, comparable with Chile or Malaysia, and countries like Lebanon and Jordan, already well diversified, have seen further declines in concentration. But the diversification by labor-abundant, resource-rich economies (Algeria, Egypt, Syria) was limited, and for the major oil producers—Libya, the GCC economies—there has been little improvement in diversification.

Barriers to integration. Several factors have hindered Arab integration into the world. The trade regimes in the Arab states are among the most protective in the world. Tariffs remain high and dispersed. Nontariff barriers, including lengthy processes to comply with customs and quality control standards, are still widespread. The trade-impeding effect of these barriers has been compounded by often persistent overvaluation of exchange rates.

In addition, behind-the-border constraints are considerable. Transport, logistics, and communication costs are high, effectively raising the costs of trade. Add to that an investment climate that generally discourages the start-up of small and medium firms, often critical to success in trading.

Removing the barriers to trade. The Arab region needs to significantly increase the speed of integration into the global economy, reducing the level of tariff protection, dismantling inefficient nontariff barriers, and removing the behind-the-border constraints to trade that have raised the costs of trade and have discouraged both domestic and foreign investment. Real exchange rates, which have been significantly overvalued in the Arab region for the last two decades, need to be corrected as well.

The imperative for trade reform is high. The costs of wait-and-see policies are also becoming increasingly expensive for global trade integration. The region faces intensified competition in world markets, at both the skill-intensive and the labor-intensive ends, affecting important industries and activities such as textiles and garments, light engineering, and manufacturing. On the skill-intensive end, two major competitive threats are the upcoming accession of some Eastern European countries to the European Union and Turkey's customs union agreement with the European Union, the Arab region's major export market. Other regional groupings and free trade agreements also present challenges. Both the Europe and Central Asia and the Latin America and Caribbean regions, two middle-income regions with labor skill profiles similar to the Arab region, have enjoyed faster trade reforms and integration with global markets in recent years, and are rapidly gaining market share as the Arab world lags behind. A mismatch between the skills required by firms and the skills produced by an education system still organized to turn out new government employees intensifies the competitive problem.

Labor-intensive products and manufactures are also facing a new challenge from low-wage, high-productivity countries such as Bangladesh, China, India, Indonesia, and Vietnam. That competition will escalate with the abolition in 2005 of quota preferences in textiles and garments, important to the region's manufacturing employment and export earnings. These labor-intensive sectors, employing more than a million workers, have been among the few in which the Arab region has been gaining market share—partly because of the protected quota markets in the European Union. Adjusted for labor productivity, labor costs in the garments sector in Arab counties are significantly higher than in populous countries of Asia, but lower than in Eastern European countries. The longer the region delays trade and related reforms, the more disadvantaged exporters will be in facing these competitive pressures.

How Arab trade can flourish. The future for Arab trade will involve specialization in manufacturing, cutting up the production chain, and permitting finer gradations of specialization within that chain among skills, labor costs, and productivity. Small, resource-poor countries in the region stand to benefit from such production chains, and given their size, the prospects are virtually unlimited in world markets. Larger countries will also benefit from such specialization. Their larger domestic markets, and proximity to major international markets, will drive a much larger range and scale of domestic manufacturing possibilities.

The role of regional trade agreements. Regional trade agreements can be an important anchor for reforms. Trade with Europe, the natural geographic partner of the Arab region, falls far short of its potential. Agreements with the EU could provide immediate and expanded access to its markets for agriculture, as well as increased temporary migration, funds for managing transition costs, and more efficient rules of origin.

At the same time, however, the Arab countries need to maintain open access to world markets, anchoring their trade and investment reforms in a multilateral framework, such as the WTO, to give them greater credibility. Only half of the Arab population lives in a WTO member country—the lowest share of all developing regions. This is partly due to the disproportionate share of Arab countries under trade and foreign investment sanctions. But it is also by choice. Arab countries have generally opted for preferential trading arrangements with the EU, which have immediate appeal because of geographic proximity and EU financial and technical support. In addition, primary oil exporters with little other trade are wary of bringing their oil trade under the WTO.

But speeding up WTO accession processes is necessary. The transition process for the Arab region depends upon signals. The enhanced credibility of government policies that are bound as commitments to the WTO gives the world's investors the greatest degree of confidence in the permanence of the reform process.

Limited intraregional trade and scope for expansion. There have been many attempts to foster intraregional integration among Arab countries over the last half century. But they have mostly failed to produce enhanced trade within the region. Intraregional exports among Arab countries remain of the order of 8-9 percent since the 1980s, compared to 22 percent for the ASEAN (Association of Southeast Asian Nations), and 25 percent for MERCOSUR (Argentina, Brazil, Uruguay). Many factors prevent an enabling environment for trade among the Arab economies. They include restrictions on imports—either directly through customs or more indirectly through the financial sector, but they also include a host of factors that prevent this facilitating environment for regional trade. There are a variety of infrastructure issues, such as inadequate telecommunications, as well as trade-chilling contingent protection and obstacles created by frontier frictions, such as frontier red tape and differences in national product standards. The Arab region needs to work to eliminate these inhibiting factors to trade, and allow Arab exports to the region to at least be on a level playing field with exports from the rest of the world.

The potential for increased intraregional Arab trade and investment is large and could be a source of increased investment, production and employment. The recent Pan-Arab Free Trade Area Agreement improves on past efforts and opens new opportunities. But its impact is likely to be limited for the reasons discussed above, and because it remains restrictive on trade in agriculture and services. In addition, the rules of origin remain loosely defined, leaving open the possibility that they will continue to be used to protectionist effect.

It is important to notice, however, that even a successful process of intraregional integration is unlikely to be a substitute for increased integration with the world economy at large. Analysis and lessons from international experience show that intraregional integration is best and most successful if it is pursued within a broader agenda of openness with the rest of the world. In addition, even integrated, the Arab economy would remain a relatively small player, and would not be able, with an intraregional focus only, to harvest the opportunities of the global economy in terms of production, technology, and investment.

Managing Oil Resources

In addition to greater private sector participation and openness, diversification out of oil will involve fundamental changes in institutions managing oil resources and their intermediation to economic agents.

Economic diversification requires proper fiscal policy and public expenditure management in addition to measures to expand globally competitive private businesses outside the oil sector. That means setting up institutions and fiscal rules that insulate public expenditures from oil price volatility, and save oil revenues so that they can continue to benefit citizens when oil resources decline. That also means improving the efficiency of public expenditures through better systems of budgeting that emphasize performance and accountability.

Diversifying productive activities is a growing priority, not only for countries whose known oil reserves will soon be depleted, but for all oil producers. Diversification is essential if the region is to ensure vital public expenditures. Per capita exports of hydrocarbon products have been declining across the region, with falling real prices, rising domestic demand for energy, and rapid population growth. Governments will need to develop new sources of revenue to ensure the efficiency of public expenditures.

Diversification is also critical for job creation. The labor force is rapidly expanding, in far greater numbers than the public sector can afford to employ, especially given the declining oil revenues. Significantly greater job opportunities need to be created in the Arab economies. To do that, the region must diversify into a broad range of productive activities, which can provide the basis for substantially greater employment. This diversification will not only create the needed new jobs, it will also provide substantially greater protection to the labor force from commodity price shocks.

A Transition Depending upon Improved Governance, Higher-Quality Education, and Gender Equality

The three realignments—key for managing the region's employment challenge—cannot be accomplished by policy change alone. Fundamental to each transition is improved governance, across the board. Each transition implies deep changes in the role of government and strong improvements in its effectiveness. The governance agenda is not a separate challenge, to be worked on at its own pace. It is a complementary and reinforcing agenda to reform efforts—in private investment, trade, and economic diversification—that change governance mechanisms, thereby improving capacity and incentives within government, while fostering a larger role for civil society in governance. While better governance cannot guarantee optimal economic policies, it is indispensable to guard against persistently poor policies and to ensure that the good policies needed to meet the Arab region's growth potential enjoy legitimacy and are implemented faithfully and with celerity.

The fundamental governance challenges are to strengthen the incentives, mechanisms, and capacities for more accountable and inclusive public institutions, and to expand allegiance to equality and participation throughout society. Those good governance mechanisms are first steps in improving economic policies that are themselves instruments for improving the climate and incentives for efficient growth.

To improve the region's governance, both governments and the people must commit publicly to formulating and implementing a broad program of inclusiveness and accountability of government, and increased transparency and contestability in public affairs. Such programs would vary across countries, but the process of formulating these programs should itself set high standards for including all segments of society, and for making all deliberations public to ensure maximum transparency.

Enhancing inclusiveness. The first step to enhanced inclusiveness is to adopt laws and regulations that secure access to widely accepted basic rights and freedoms, including participation and equality before the law, particularly for women. Broader public consultation, greater freedom for the media, fewer restrictions on civil society, more equitable channels of access to social services, and an end to discriminatory laws and regulations are examples of measures that secure inclusion. They need to be supplemented with strong monitoring to ensure that public officials treat all citizens equally.

Enhancing accountability. But a particular focus must rest on putting in place better systems of accountability, especially transparency and contestability. External and internal accountability are related; the former is critical for providing incentives for governments to strengthen their structures of internal accountability, so action is needed on both fronts. External accountability, to help citizens participate in and monitor government, can come from actions at both the national and local levels. Such measures include greater freedom of information and public disclosure of government operations, including data on government quality; wider public debate by an independent and responsible media and by representative civil society groups; and regular and competitive elections with external oversight to ensure they are fair and open. At the local level, external accountability can come from providing citizens with effective feedback mechanisms on public agencies, expanding choices in public service delivery, devolving responsibilities to empowered local communities, and by actively soliciting the participation of community empowerment organizations.

Enhancing internal accountability is about creating mechanisms and incentives within government to ensure effective functioning in the public interest. At the national level, it involves strengthening the checks and balances within government, in particular increasing the independence and capacity of the legislative and judicial branches, and installing independent oversight agencies like ombudsmen. Within the executive, it involves reforming public administration, strengthening the performance orientation of government budgets, enhancing the service orientation of the civil service, augmenting the capacity of local governments, and ensuring the independence of regulatory bodies.

Enhancing quality education also critical. The transition to more market-driven, globally oriented economies requires continuing progress in widening and deepening the stock of human capital, and more critically, changes in the qualitative outputs of the region's educational systems. Firm surveys in both labor-abundant and labor-importing countries in the region suggest that lack of skills is an important constraint in hiring. Qualitative deficiencies in education have resulted from a variety of factors, including overly centralized management of education, little assessment of performance, and promotion based on seniority rather than performance.

Improving the relevance of the region's educational outputs must be partly addressed from within the educational sector, but it will be partly accomplished by the transitions themselves. The past policies of ensuring public sector employment to those with higher or intermediate education, with little attention to content or quality, has resulted in Arab individuals seeking higher degrees that bear little relation to the skills needed by either the private sector or for the efficient functioning of the public sector. As the private sector's role in the economy expands, more appropriate signals will be sent to students of the types of education in need, and the types of education that will be rewarded.

Greater openness will also foster improvements in education. Greater openness fosters competition, encourages modern technology, increases the demand for highly skilled labor, and promotes learning by doing. Openness obliges industries to confront their inefficiencies. To compete successfully, industries must adapt, thereby creating demand for the new skills and trades to do so.

Greater economic participation by women needed. The success of these transitions hinges also on progress in enhancing gender equality. Progress on bridging the gender gap in education and health in the region has been substantial. But this has not translated into a commensurate increase in women's participation in the labor force. The participation of women in the labor force in the Arab region, at less than 33 percent, is the lowest in the world (compared to 45 to 75 percent in other parts of the world). This is partly the result of a range of civil, commercial, labor, and family laws and practices in the region that discourage women from entering the labor force.

At this time of exceptional demands on Arab economies to create jobs, there has been little incentive to improve economic opportunities for women, with some arguing that greater participation by women in the labor force would exacerbate unemployment among men in the current climate of slow growth and rising unemployment. But there is no empirical evidence to suggest this. International experience shows that in the long run, greater labor force participation by women is not associated with higher total unemployment rates.

The region needs to be able to draw on all of its talents and human capital. Women's greater participation in the labor force improves the overall growth of the region. With the highest economic dependency rates in the world (that is, each working person supporting two nonworking dependents, a burden that is double what is observed in East Asia), the Arab region is missing opportunities for increased welfare of families and society. Higher female labor force participation, in line with what would be expected given female education, age structure, and fertility rates, could allow family incomes to increase by 15-30 percent in most countries. In addition, this participation enhances the flexibility of families to adapt to changing economic conditions.

The agenda for addressing gender disparities includes the need for realigning legal provisions that fail to give effect to the recognition of equal rights under constitutions in most countries. It would also mean ensuring a supportive infrastructure that facilitates women's participation in the public sphere, as well as continued attention to education, particularly in areas that provide better market skills. Finally, it would involve reforming the labor laws and regulations that raise the cost of women's labor relative to that of men, and serve as disincentives to private employers' demand for female labor.

An Ambitious, but Feasible Agenda for the Arab Region

Large growth and employment gains. The impact of an integrated package of policy realignments that improves the business and investment climate for the private sector, and fosters integration with the world economy, is potentially very large. Based on the experience of comparable countries, output per laborer could increase by some 2–3 percent a year, with greater integration into the global economy. Using similar international evidence of high-performing countries, it is estimated that improving the institutions of accountability and public administration could boost output growth per capita by 0.8 and 1.3 percent a year. Increasing the participation of women in the labor force to levels comparable to the highest performers in the region may add 0.7 percent or more to GDP growth per capita.

While these effects are not additive, and reflect changes in policies and institutions that are not exclusive, a conservative estimate of the sum of these projected effects, taking into account overlap in the channels through which the policy changes operate, would be an increase in output growth per laborer of 2.5–3.5 percent a year.

The suggested economic transformation and deep reforms would generate millions of new jobs, and more productive jobs in traded sectors across manufacturing and services. For instance, the Arab region's share of nonoil merchandise exports in total exports averages only 6 percent, versus more than 20 percent in East Asia and the Pacific. Bridging only half that gap, with associated increases in domestic and foreign private investment, would create more than 4 million new jobs over the next five years. That is equivalent to cutting the unemployment rate by 4 percentage points of the labor force. The broader reform agenda would bring even larger benefits.

Feasibility. The underlying concern for many Arab countries is whether this broad transformation of their economies is even feasible. But the experience of countries around the world provides evidence that such a transformation is possible. Around the world, many countries have faced labor market crises and responded to the political challenges with reforms. Governments have reduced the scope of state intervention in markets, reorganized regulatory frameworks, and undertaken wide-ranging economic restructuring, including the large-scale privatization of public enterprises, while trying to preserve important aspects of social welfare, as well as wage and employment protections.

In some postsocialist states of Eastern and Central Europe, these transitions were facilitated by the urgency of establishing new systems of economic and political governance. Elsewhere, policy makers have advanced economic reforms within stable policies. In several Latin American countries, for example, politicians and reformers effectively navigated complex political environments containing entrenched, often competing interests. Despite the presence of supporters of the status quo, governments built effective reform coalitions and successfully re-regulated economies around market-based principles. Arab countries have also undertaken selective reforms, with positive, if limited, effects on economic performance.

The challenges confronting Arab governments do not arise from a lack of information about what needs to be done. Pathways to reform are much better mapped today than they were only two decades ago. Past decades have produced extensive knowledge about what works in development strategies and policy reform, and what does not.

A new path for greater employment and a new social contract. The limitations of past approaches to reform are visible in the deteriorating conditions in Arab labor markets. The old model that guided the region's development for the last 40 years no longer provides the needed employment opportunities. To ensure that the citizens of the Arab world have these opportunities as the need for jobs accelerates, the region must shift to market-based strategies of growth, which can provide the substantially higher growth rates to ensure better labor market outcomes. It involves fundamental transitions in each of the economies.

A new social contract as the basis for more productive relations among the state, labor, and the private sector. The new social contract would balance the needs for market flexibility with the rights of workers, would link reform to the principles of poverty reduction, income equality, and income security. It would restructure the rigid, exclusionary, and inefficient aspects of the old social contract. The exact agenda, the sequencing and emphasis will vary from country to country.

Need to link economic and political reform. Moving the reform program beyond its current limits requires reviving national conversations about labor market reform, restructuring redistributive programs, and redefining the terms of the new social contract. The top-down approach to economic reform—which has prevailed—sidesteps the need for political reform to secure the legitimacy of reform and the credibility of government commitment. It is no longer adequate. The strong preference of Arab governments for political and social stability has been often advanced as a justification for not proceeding with the strong and deep reform agenda that is needed for Arab economies to regain dynamism and meet their challenges. But today the costs of maintaining a nonviable status quo are becoming severe, and may undermine that much valued stability, as stresses in the labor markets continue to build. At the same time the need to establish consensus around a new social contract is critical. Political reform, which would strengthen political inclusiveness and accountability, becomes critically linked to economic reform.

The transition may be costly and needs to be managed. The impact of these transitions would be an improved business and investment climate, higher growth, and, most important, substantially greater opportunities for employment, improved standards of living, and lower poverty for the Arab region. But costs of transitions are likely, and may be significant. They may entail greater insecurity and job losses for some groups. Some economic sectors may be negatively affected. Inequality may increase as wages and returns to education become more market oriented. These risks highlight the need for careful design and sequencing of reform, and the development of mitigating strategies. Careful monitoring and early corrections are needed, but without backtracking and stop-and-go policy change.

External versus internal responsibilities. Embarking on such an ambitious agenda for political and economic reform is challenging by any measure. But the biggest challenge is for societies to own such a vision and to develop the confidence that they can achieve it. Pessimism in the region is pervasive. It is pessimism about the region's trading potential. It is fear about competing in world markets. It is pessimism about the capacity to innovate. It is pessimism about markets and the private sector. It is pessimism about the ability to develop an inclusive and accountable governance. But it is unfounded pessimism. In recent history, countries of the region have been able to achieve much, and to change when they mustered the will for doing so. Their histories have shown time and again that it can achieve success, and it can harness progress. Pessimism has to be replaced by ambition and confidence. The main responsibility for meeting the challenges is internal. It has to be with the governments and the people of the region.

There is no doubt that external factors and interference have contributed to the poor state of the region. Violence and conflict have severely impeded the pace of reform. Persistent regional conflict has large neighborhood effects that have spilled throughout the region, making it less attractive and more costly for business and investment, both domestic and foreign. Conflicts have drained resources to less productive uses in the military and for security. They have undermined the development of good governance. External partners bear a responsibility for helping the region establish regional stability and security. But the central responsibilities remain within the region itself.

Notes

1. The material draws on the diagnosis and conclusions from four major regional reports produced by the World Bank on the occasion of the World Bank–International Monetary Fund Annual Meetings in Dubai in September 2003. The reports address the issues of trade and investment, governance, gender, and employment.

2. The countries included in the Arab region for the purposes of this paper are those that are part of the MENA region according to the World Bank. They include Algeria, Bahrain, Djibouti, Egypt, Iraq,

Jordan, Kuwait, Lebanon, Libya, Morocco, Oman, Palestine, Qatar, Saudi Arabia, Syria, Tunisia, United Arab Emirates, and Yemen. Data for Iraq and Libya are often missing, and these two countries are generally not included in the analysis, save for population or labor force figures. In addition, four Arab countries not included in the MENA region, Comoros, Mauritania, Somalia, and Sudan, are included only in Arab totals for population and labor force figures. In 2000, the total population of the Arab region was estimated at 287 million people. GDP per capita averages US $1,850, ranging from a low of US$315 in Yemen and Sudan, to a high of US$13,900 in Kuwait.

3. Computed from Barro-Lee Educational attainment database, including Algeria, Bahrain, Egypt, Iraq, Jordan, Kuwait, Syria, and Tunisia.

•

2

Reform Complementarities and Economic Growth in the Middle East and North Africa

Mustapha Kamel Nabli
Marie-Ange Véganzonès-Varoudakis*

This paper explores the relationship between economic reforms and econom-ic growth in the Middle East and North Africa (MENA) region. Despite apparent reforms starting in the mid-1980s, the growth performance of the region has often been disappointing. Since the large fall in international oil prices in the mid-1980s, most MENA economies have experienced a marked slowdown and/or macroeconomic crisis. In spite of a small recovery of GDP per capita in the 1990s (from 1 percent in the 1980s to 1 percent in the 1990s) the MENA region is, for the second decade, the most slowly growing region in the world (see Dasgupta et al., 2004).

As a possible explanation, we try to understand in this paper whether the growth performance of the region has been disappointing because MENA economies have lagged behind in terms of reforms, or because the growth divi-dend of the reforms has been small. We illustrate that both explanations are rel-evant. On the one hand, economic reforms have been insufficient to boost the growth performance of the countries. This is the case for macroeconomic reforms during the 1980s, and for structural reforms during the entire period. On the other hand, our estimations reveal a low impact of some economic reforms. This is the case when structural reforms are implemented in a volatile

*Centre d'Etudes et de Recherches sur le Développement International and Centre National de la Recherche Scientifique, Université d'Auvergne, France.

Published in *Journal of International Development*, January, 2007, Vol. 19. Reprinted by permission from John Wiley and Sons; see page 17–54.

macroeconomic environment (which corresponds to the situation of the MENA countries in the 1980s) and when macroeconomic reforms are implemented without a sufficient level of structural reform (as observed during the 1990s). This result has been obtained by the introduction of a multiplicative term in our growth equation. It illustrates the complementarities between economic reforms as elaborated by Mussa (1987) and by Williamson (1994), and brings new empirical evidence to the subject of economic policy and economic growth.

A first critical step for the paper has been to measure the economic reform effort of the countries. The originality of our approach has consisted in generating aggregated reform indicators using principal component analysis. This methodology permits the aggregation of basic indicators in a more rigorous way than would a subjective scoring system (see, for example, the rating system elaborated by the International Country Risk Guide, ICRG). It also avoids multicollinearity problems when estimating an equation that includes several disaggregated indicators. Furthermore, the use of panel data estimation techniques has allowed some comparative analysis among the different regions, as well as among the MENA countries.[1] In addition to economic reforms, the link of human capital and physical infrastructure to economic growth has also been discussed.

The paper is organized as follows. The second section presents the aggregated indicators of economic reforms, human capital, and physical infrastructure, and summarizes the progress of these indicators in the MENA region. Our analysis is based on a panel of 44 developing countries over 1970–80 to 1999.[2] In the third section, we estimate a growth equation that includes the different composite indicators. We verify that economic reforms, human capital, and physical infrastructure have had a positive influence on the growth pattern of our sample of countries. The fourth section quantifies the contribution of economic reforms, human capital, and physical infrastructure to the economic growth of the MENA region. We illustrate that the lack of reforms has had a negative influence on the growth accomplished by the MENA economies. The last section offers conclusions.

Indicators of Economic Reforms, Human Capital, and Physical Infrastructure

MENA countries differ considerably among themselves, as well as with regard to the rest of the world. This is, in particular, the case in terms of economic reforms, physical infrastructure, and human capital. These differences have been assessed using various indicators that have been aggregated by means of principal component analysis. This method has been used to generate five aggregate indicators (see details on methodology in Nagaraj et al., 2000; appendix 2).[3]

In this section, we present succinctly the five composite indicators. More details on their composition and evolution are given in Appendices 2.3–6. The objective of this section is to highlight the MENA economic strengths and weaknesses that support the empirical analysis developed in the rest of the paper. A more in-depth analysis on economic reforms and their historical context in MENA can be found in the abundant literature on the subject (see in particular Safadi, 1998; Hoekman and El-Din, 2000; Hakimian and Nugent, 2004).

Macroeconomic Reforms

The first composite indicator of macroeconomic stability (MS) is based on:

- Inflation (p) and public deficit as percentage of GDP ($PubDef$), which can be disruptive to investment and growth if they lead to unsustainable macroeconomic imbalances (see Fischer, 1993; De Gregorio, 1992)
- Foreign exchange parallel market's premium (lBmp, in logarithm) as a proxy of various distortions in the economy that can also lead to macroeconomic instability.[4]

In MENA, macroeconomic stability clearly improved in the 1990s compared to the 1980s, when economies faced great instability (see figure 2.1).[5, 6] Our results confirm the findings of several studies on the subject (see in particular Iqbal, 2001). In some countries, however, macroeconomic reforms could have shown better progress compared to the rest of the world (with the exception of Latin America, where stability was not achieved in the 1990s). Efforts still need to be made, in particular, in Iran, Syria, and Algeria (see appendix 3 for more details).

External Stability

The second composite indicator of external stability (ES) is represented by:

- External debt as percentage of GDP ($DebExGdp$), as well as of exports of goods and services ($DebExX$), which represent the risk to an economy of

Figure 2.1. Macroeconomic Reform Indicators

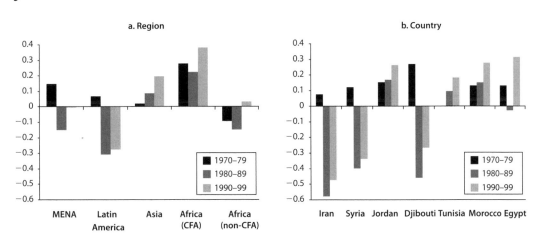

Source: Authors' calculations.

encountering difficulties in reimbursing its debt and facing a financial crisis

- Current account in percentage of exports of goods and services (*CurAcX*), which gives another signal of the fragility of the external position of the country.

MENA countries performed rather poorly in term of external stability, behind Latin America and Asia (see figure 2.2).[7] This is largely the result of the unsustainable level of foreign debt, which indicates that a significant scope for debt reduction exists in the region (see figure 2.11 in appendix 4). Debt reduction is a concern shared by the majority of MENA countries in our sample; however, Syria, Jordan, and, to a lesser extent, Morocco need special attention (see figure 2.12 and a more indepth analysis in appendix 4).

Structural Reforms

The third composite indicator of structural reforms (*SR*) includes an indicator of trade policy (*TradeP*) calculated as the ratio of imports plus exports to GDP, from which has been deducted the "natural trade openness" of the economies calculated by Frankel and Romer (1999),[8] as well as the exports of oil and mining products, which introduce a bias in the sample due to natural resource endowment. This indicator is based on the fact that trade reforms can be at the origin of economies of scale and of productivity gains as a result of increased competitiveness and increased access to larger markets (Balassa, 1978; Feder, 1983).

Private credit by deposit money banks and other institutions (in percentage of GDP, *PCrBOG*), as a proxy for the development of the banking system, can have a positive effect on productivity owing to a better selection of investment projects and to higher technological specialization through a diversification of risks (see Levine, 1997, for a synthesis).

Figure 2.2. External Stability Indicators

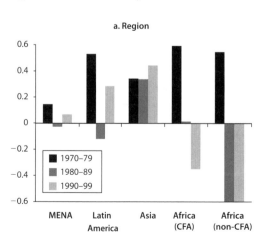
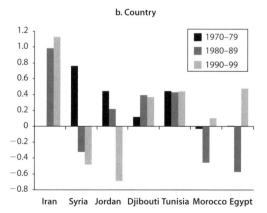

Source: Authors' calculations.

In terms of structural reforms, MENA seems to perform relatively well compared to the rest of the world (see figure 2.3). This result is largely the result of the apparent high financial depth of the MENA economies. Financial development, however, is usually not considered satisfactory in MENA (see appendix 5 for a discussion). This is also the case for trade openness, which has on average been particularly low across the region. This makes of structural reform a sector with a large potential for improvement in MENA (see figures 2.14a and 2.15a, and appendix 5 for a more in-depth analysis).

Human Capital

The fourth composite indicator of human capital (*MH1*) is represented by the logarithm of:

- The infant mortality rate (*lMort*) as a proxy of the health conditions of the population,
- The number of years of primary schooling of the population (*lH1*).

Both health and education increase the productivity of physical capital and can be at the origin of positive externalities (Lucas, 1988; Psacharopoulos, 1988; Mankiw et al., 1992).[9]

In MENA, human capital improved significantly throughout the period. Progress was among the best across regions (see figure 2.4a). Good performances are noticeable everywhere (see figure 2.4b). MENA human capital development, however, still lags behind that of Asia and Latin America. This means that a large potential gain can be expected from an increase of health and education in the region.

Figure 2.3. Structural Reform Indicators

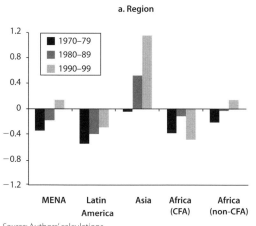
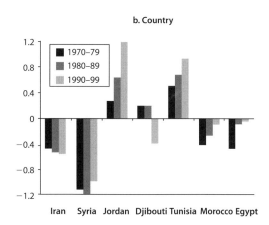

Source: Authors' calculations.

Figure 2.4 Human Capital Indicators (reduced[a])

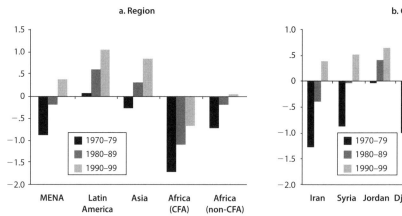
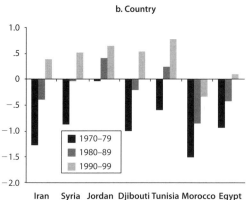

Source: Authors' calculations.
a. This indicator includes infant mortality and primary schooling only.

Core Infrastructure

The fifth composite indicator of physical infrastructure (*Phys*) is based on the logarithm of:

- The density of the road network (*lRoads*, in km per km^2)
- The number of telephone lines per 1000 people (*lTel*).

The complementarities among physical infrastructure and physical and human capital lead to higher productivity and increase the incentive to invest (see Barro, 1990; Aschauer, 1989; Murphy et al., 1989).

Despite real progress throughout the period, MENA's endowment in infrastructures has remained insufficient (see figure 2.5). The road network has

Figure 2.5. Physical Infrastructure Indicators

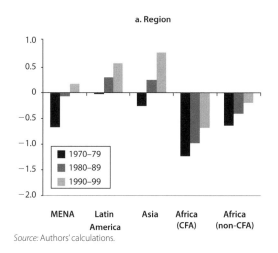
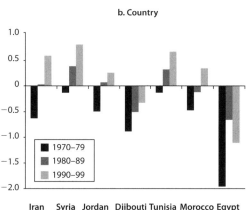

Source: Authors' calculations.

Figure 2.6. GDP per Capita Growth Rates (%)

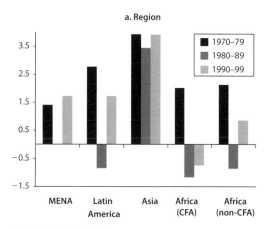
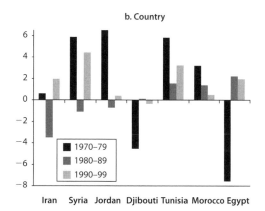

Source: Authors' calculations.

Figure 2.7. GDP per Capita (international dollars)

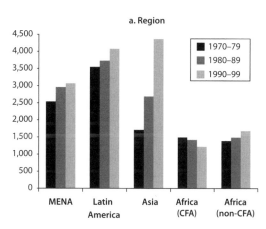
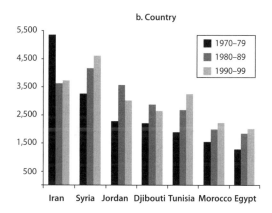

Source: Authors' calculations.

been very deficient (see figure 2.20 in appendix 7), and the telephone network also inadequate compared to Latin America and Asia (see figure 2.21 in appendix 7). Actually, closing the gap with more advanced developing countries constitutes a significant challenge for MENA (see appendix 7 for a more detailed analysis).

Growth Diagnostic for Our Sample of MENA Countries

Despite the noticeable progress in various areas of reform, MENA growth performance has shown disappointing results. Although growth improved almost everywhere during the 1990s, MENA results have been largely surpassed by the Asian economies, where GDP growth rates reached 4 percent a year on average (1.7 percent in MENA; see figures 2.6 and 2.7).

These low growth performances explain why MENA GDP per capita increasingly lags behind that in Asia and Latin America (see figure 2.7a).

Economic Reforms, Human Capital, Physical Infrastructure, and Growth

In this section, we address the link between economic reforms and economic growth by estimating a conditional convergence equation [Equation (1)] inspired by Barro and Sala-I-Martin (1995). In this equation, the long-run GDP per capita growth rate [$\Delta\ln(y_{i,t})$] depends on the logarithm of the initial level of the GDP per capita [$\ln(y_{i,\,t-1})$] and on a set of other variables. These variables aim at explaining the differences across countries in the long-term level of GDP per capita. In our case, we have added—in addition to the ratio of investment to GDP, which represents the increase in the productive capacities of the economy—the composite economic reform indicators, as well as the physical infrastructure and human capital indicators[10, 11]:

$$\Delta\ln(y_{i,t}) = c + a^*\ln(y_{i,t-1})+b^*\ln(Inv_{i,t})+d1^*(MS_{i,t})+d2^* \\ (ES_{i,t})+d3^*(SR_{i,t})+e1^*(Phys_{i,t})+e2^*(MH1_{i,t})+ \varepsilon_{i,t} \tag{1}$$

with: $y_{i,t-1}$ = GDP per capita of the previous period
$Inv_{i,t}$ = investment ratio to GDP
$MS_{i,t}$ = macroeconomic stability indicator
$ES_{i,t}$ = external stability indicator
$SR_{i,t}$ = structural reform indicator
$Phys_{i,t\,=}$ physical infrastructures indicator
$MH1_{i,t\,=}$ human capital indicator
c = intercept, a, b, d_1 to d_3, e_1 to e_2, = parameters, t= time index and ε_t =error term.

A variant of this equation was introduced: two multiplicative terms (MS^*SR and ES^*SR) to capture for the possible complementarities amongst reforms [Equation (2)]. This case has been developed by Mussa (1987) and Williamson (1994), who have elaborated, in particular, the idea that structural reforms are not efficient if the economy is not stable. This situation was observed on several occasions during the 1980s and the 1990s in various Eastern European and Latin American countries. In these countries, the introduction of structural reforms, such as trade and financial liberalization, in an unstable macroeconomic environment resulted in economic crisis. The multiplicative term also allows capture of the possible reverse effect: of the efficiency of external and macroeconomic stability increases with the level of structural reforms. This could be relevant to the MENA economies in which structural reforms have generally been insufficient.

$$\Delta \ln(y_{i,t}) = c + a^* \ln(y_{i;t-1}) + b^* \ln(Inv_{i,t}) + d1^*(MS_{i,t}) + d2^*(ES_{i,t}) + d3^*(SR_{i,t}) \\ + d4^*(MS_{i,t^*}SR_{i,tt}) + d5^*(ES_{i,t^*}SR_{i,t}) + e1^*(Phys_{i,t}) + e2^*(MH1_{i,t}) + \varepsilon_{i,t} \quad (2)$$

The first step in the econometric analysis was to estimate the degree of integration of the variables entering Equations (1) and (2). Co-integration of series is actually required if Equations (1) and (2) have to be estimated with the standard methods.

Table A5-1 in appendix 9 provides the results of the Augmented-Dickey-Fuller (ADF) test of the series entering the two equations. We used the Im et al. (1997) methodology, which provides critical values of ADF tests in the case of heterogeneous panel data. The results indicate that series are generally stationary at the 1 percent level (5 percent in the case of human capital). This allows running Equations (1) and (2) using the standard methods.[12]

Equations (1) and (2) have been estimated for our unbalanced panel of 44 developing countries. The regressions have used the White estimator to correct for the heteroscedasticity bias. To control for sample heterogeneity, country dummy variables have also been introduced. These variables reflect differences in the quality of institutions or in different endowments of natural resources,[13] which can be at the origin of large discrepancies in the "natural propensity" to grow. This hypothesis is supported by the data, as shown by the value of the Fischer tests of equality of the intercepts across countries, as well as by the value of the Hausman tests as far as the random hypothesis is concerned.[14] Results are presented in table 2.1.

The results of the estimations show that the relationship between GDP per capita growth rates and its determinants is consistent with the theory. Increases in the investment ratio, macroeconomic and external stability, struc-

Table 2.1. Estimate Results of the Growth Equations (1) and (2) Dependent Variable $\Delta \ln(y_t)$

Independent variables	Eq1	Eq2
$\ln(y_{t-1})$	−0.17 (8.62)***	−0.17 (8.96)***
$\ln(inv_t)$	0.065 (5.27)***	0.066 (5.38)***
$MS_t^{(1)}$	0.004 (1.76)*	0.028 (2.76)**
$ES_t^{(1)}$	0.03 (5.3)***	0.027 (3.95)***
$SR_t^{(2)}$	0.015 (2.05)**	0.011 (1.56)
$MS_t^{(1)} * SR_t^{(2)}$		0.027 (2.65)**
$ES_t^{(1)} * SR_t^{(2)}$		0.006 (0.69)
$Phys_t^{(2)}$	0.03 (2.07)**	0.031 (2.07)**
$MH1_t$	0.018 (1.70)*	0.016 (1.66)*
Adjusted R^2	0.29	0.30
Fischer test	4.1	4.3
Hausman test	56.2	67.0

Source: Authors' estimations.

Note: Student t statistics are within brackets. The number of observations used in the regressions is 589. Data have been compiled from World Development Indicators, Global Development Finance, Global Development Network,, and Live Data Base (World Bank).
(1): one lag; (2): two lags; (*) indicates significance at 10 percent; (**) indicates significance at 5 percent; (***) indicates significance at 1 percent.

tural reforms, physical infrastructure, and human capital lead to higher growth rates.[15]

The impact of most variables on growth is, however, not instantaneous. This is the case with macroeconomic and external stability, as well as with structural reforms (respectively one and two lags). This means that structural reforms need some time (two years, according to our estimations) to materialize into growth. As expected, the effects of macroeconomic and external reforms are faster (one year). The same conclusions can be drawn for human capital and physical infrastructure (no lag and two lags, respectively).[16]

Another, and even more interesting, feature can be observed in the estimation of Equation (2), which corroborates the sequencing of reforms developed by Mussa (1987) and Williamson (1994): the introduction of the multiplicative term MS^*SR (macroeconomic multiplied by structural reforms) turns out to be significant, while the structural reforms indicator alone (SR) is no longer significant (see table 2.1). This result highlights the complementarities between macroeconomic stability and structural reforms, as explained below.

On one hand, the efficiency of structural reforms depends on success in stabilizing the economy. In other words, reforming the economy materializes into growth if applied in a stable macroeconomic environment. In an increasingly volatile environment, a high level of structural reforms increases the disruptive effect of macroeconomic instability. This means that structural reforms should take place at least at the same time as macroeconomic reforms, if not after.

On the other hand, the opposite is partly true. If stabilization programs make more progress when the economy is reformed, and if the growth outcome of macroeconomic stabilization is linked to the level of the structural reforms (through the multiplicative term MS^*SR), then macroeconomic reform materializes into growth even in the absence of structural reforms (through the MS index alone). This is not the case of structural reforms that do not materialize into growth in an unstable macroeconomic environment (the coefficient of structural reforms alone not being significant). This stresses the importance of macroeconomic reforms for the growth prospects and the reform processes of the countries. This result clearly shows that macroeconomic stability remains a priority for the government to address, and that reforming the economy should not be undertaken prior to stabilizing.

Estimation of Equation (2) also reveals, in another way, the critical role of macroeconomic stability in the growth performances of the economies. The coefficient of the macroeconomic reform index is higher and more significant than when estimating Equation (1) (see table 2.1). The coefficient of the multiplicative term is of the same magnitude as that of the macroeconomic reforms index alone. This means that both effects are similarly significant. This will be illustrated in the next section, when calculating the contribution of each reform indicator to the economic growth of our sample of countries.

This result, however, does not hold for external stability for which the multiplicative term (ES^*SR) is not significant. The absence of correlation between external stability and structural reforms could be interpreted as an indication that structural reforms are not undertaken unless the external environment has been adjusted. This is because our indicator of structural reforms incorporates improvement of trade reform, which is unlikely to be sustained in the presence of external unbalance. These results show that external stability remains an important initial condition for reforming the economy, as well as for the growth prospects of the countries (the external stability index alone being still significant; see table 2.1).

Finally, the robustness of our estimations can be evaluated by the fact that the coefficients of the other variables are similar in both estimations. In the rest of this document, we will focus on the results of Equation (2), which give a more complete picture of the relation between reform and growth.

Assessing the Impact of Economic Reform, Human Capital, and Physical Infrastructure on the Growth Performance of the MENA Region

As noted above, the use of aggregate indicators of economic reform, human capital, and physical infrastructure overcomes the difficulties of estimating the impact of a large number of indicators that may have collinear relationships. This method allows for subsequent calculations of the contribution of the initial indicators to the growth performance of the countries. The calculation is based on the estimated coefficients of the aggregate indicators in the regression, as well as on the weights of each principal component in the aggregate indicator combined with the loadings of the initial variables in each principal component (see appendix 10 for more details on the methodology).

Table 2.2 presents the long-term coefficients/elasticities of the initial reform indicators (see tables A11-1 and A11-2 in appendix 11 for the short-term coefficients/elasticites). A number of conclusions can be drawn from these calculations.

Physical Infrastructure and Human Capital

A first set of conclusion shows that improvements in human capital and physical infrastructure present a strong and approximately equal potential impact on growth. In both equations, primary education, the road network, and the health conditions of the population show strong elasticities. These variables appear to be key factors in the growth prospects of our sample of countries. Although studies on the impact of core infrastructure rarely use physical indicators (such as the road or the telephone network),[17] our results are quite in line with the findings of some authors who have followed the same approach.[18]

These coefficients/elasticities have been used to calculate the contribution of the different factors to the growth performances of the region. As shown,

Table 2.2. Long-Term Coefficients/Elasticities

Index	Variables	Equation (1)	Equation (2)
MS alone**	P	−0.004	−0.025
	ln(Bmp)	−0.004	−0.029
	PubDef	−0.056	−0.443
ES	DebExX	−0.101	−0.089
	DebExGni	−0.003	−0.003
	CurAccX	0.453	0.396
SR alone***	TradeP	0.332	0.230*
	PCrBOG	0.363	0.252*
Phys	ln(Roads)	0.149	0.145
	ln(Tel)	0.106	0.104
MH1	ln(Mort)	−0.147	−0.123
	ln(H1)	0.169	0.142

Source: Authors' calculations.
*Not significant.
**In Equation (2), macroeconomic reforms impact growth through two channels: one is direct; the other depends on the level of structural reforms. Elasticities/coefficients have not been calculated in this last case, due to the difficulties linked to the multiplicative term ($MS*SR$). Nevertheless, the global impact of macroeconomic reforms will be assessed for our different countries/groups of countries through their contribution to growth (see below).
***As for macroeconomic reforms, because the impact of structural reforms depends on the level of macroeconomic stability, the coefficient/elasticity of the multiplicative term (MS*SR) has not been calculated. The contributions, however, will be presented in the section on contributions.

MENA's development effort in health and education has been consequential. It can be calculated that improvement in primary schooling contributed an annual average of 0.3 to 0.4 points of GDP per capita growth rate during the period. For the amelioration of health conditions, the contribution is even higher (0.8 and 0.5 points in the 1980s and the 1990s, respectively; see table 2.3).

Globally, improvements in human capital have explained between 0.9 and 1.1 points of growth per capita per year since the beginning of the 1980s. This means that, without progress in human capital, GDP per capita annual growth rate would have been -1.1 percent in the 1980s (instead of 0 percent)

Table 2.3. Contribution of Human Capital— MENA Region

MENA Years	%	Primary education	Health	Total contribution	Growth of GDP per capita
1980–89	Annual growth rate	2.8	−6.3		0
1990–99		2.3	−4.5		1.7
	Elasticity	0.14	0.12		Without H
1980–89	Contribution to	0.4	0.8	1.1	−1.1
1990–99	growth	0.3	0.5	0.9	0.8

Regional summary Years	MENA	Asia	LA	ACFA	ANCFA
1980–89	1.1	0.7	0.8	0.7	0.6
1990–99	0.9	0.7	0.7	0.6	0.4

Source: Authors' calculations.

and 0.8 percent in the 1990s (instead of 1.7 percent; see table 2.3). This contribution is even higher in the case of Iran, Syria, and Algeria, because of the initial gap in primary schooling compared to more advanced MENA countries (1.2 to 1.3 in the 1980s and 0.9 to 1.2 in the 1990s; see table A12-4 in appendix 12). These results clearly highlight the strong contribution of human capital to the growth performances of the economies.

The contribution of infrastructure to growth also appears to be substantial. This has been the case despite MENA's relatively low level of infrastructure. This result is mainly the result of the rapid increase in the number of telephone lines, which annually has accounted for 0.7 points of GDP per capita growth rate.[19] Globally, from the beginning of the 1980s, physical infrastructure has annually contributed from 1.0 to 1.4 points of the GDP per capita growth rate (see table 2.4). This contribution has even been higher in Iran and Syria (around 1.8 and 1.5, respectively; see table A12-5 in appendix 12). This result also implies that infrastructure and primary education constitute a potentially important source of growth for MENA, because the region lags in comparison to more advanced developing economies (such as Asia and Latin America) in these two fields of activity.

The importance of human capital and physical infrastructure for the growth performance of the other regions is also illustrated in tables 2.3 and 2.4. The rapid progress of MENA health conditions accounts for a higher contribution of human capital in that region. Closing the gap in education and infrastructure with more advanced regions remains, however, a concern for MENA.

Macroeconomic Stability and Structural Reforms

As far as macroeconomic stability is concerned, our calculations also stress the significance of this factor for the growth prospects of our sample of economies. As noted above, one part of this effect is direct. The other part

Table 2.4. Contribution of Physical Infrastructure—MENA Region

MENA Years	%	Tel lines	Roads networks	Total contribution	Growth of GDP per capita
1980–89	Annual growth rate	7.2	3.0		0
1990–99		7.5	1.8		1.7
	Elasticity	0.10	0.15		Without *Phy*
1980–89	Contribution to	0.8	0.6	1.4	−1.4
1990–99	growth	0.8	0.3	1.0	0.7

Regional summary Years	MENA	Asia	LA	ACFA	ANCFA
1980–89	1.4	1.5	0.9	0.4	0.6
1990–99	1.0	1.1	0.8	0.9	0.8

Source: Authors' calculations.

depends on the level of structural reforms. Table 2.5 summarizes these two effects, from which several conclusions can be drawn.[20]

During the 1980s, macroeconomic volatility in MENA was disruptive to growth. This was mainly the result of the sharp increase in the foreign exchange parallel market premium in some MENA countries (Iran, Algeria, and Syria).[21] Inflation and public deficit increased moderately, but stayed at a relatively high level (especially in Iran and Syria, as well as for inflation in Algeria). Both the direct and indirect effects contributed negatively, and with the same magnitude, to growth (0.6 to 0.7 points per year of GDP per capita growth, for a total of 1.3 points). This means that the negative effect of macroeconomic instability more than compensated for the positive impact of human capital or physical infrastructure (see tables 2.3 and 2.4). This negative contribution was even higher in Iran and Syria (2.6 and 2.4, respectively).

This finding stresses again the importance of macroeconomic stability for the growth prospects of our sample of economies. In Latin America, inflation and public deficit, as well as public deficit and foreign exchange parallel market premiums in non-Communauté Francophone d'Afrique (CFA) countries, contributed to the economic turmoil of the period (1.4 to 0.3 points, respectively, of the GDP per capita growth rate; see table 2.5 and figures 2.8 to 2.10 in appendix 3).

In the 1990s, this situation reversed, and economic stabilization contributed positively to MENA growth performance. Progress, however—which essentially concerned the public deficit—could have been more significant. The contribution of improved macroeconomic conditions reached only 0.4 points of GDP for the two effects (0.2 for the direct, 0.2 for the indirect). This can be explained by several factors.

First, the macroeconomic stability of the MENA economies, whatever the level, could have been further improved. This is the case for the foreign exchange parallel market premium in Iran, Algeria, and Syria; as well as, to a lesser extent, for inflation in Iran, Algeria, Egypt, Syria; and public deficit in Tunisia and Morocco.

Second, our analysis has shown that structural reforms in MENA have always lagged behind the experiences of more dynamic region such as Asia, particularly in the 1990s. This lack of economic reform has already been commented on in the literature. It has often been attributed to political economic considerations (see, for example, Hoekman and Kheir El Din, 2000, and Hakimian and Nugent, 2004).[22] In fact, the slow pace of structural reform has been an important factor limiting the benefits of macroeconomic stabilization.[23] The case of the MENA countries thus illustrates the complementarities between macroeconomic stability and structural reforms. These results also confirm that both macroeconomic stability and structural reforms have still to progress if MENA wants to catch up with more advanced developing countries.

Table 2.5. Contribution of Macroeconomic Stability—MENA Region

MENA Years	%	p	bmp	Pubdef	Total contribution	Growth of GDP per capita
1980–89	Annual growth rate	0.4	22	0.03		0
1990–99		−0.2	2.6	−0.6		1.7
	Coef/elasticity	−0.025	−0.029	−0.443	*MS* alone	With[2]/without[3] *MS*
1980–89	Contribution to	−0.01	−0.6	−0.01	−0.7	0.7
1990–99	growth	0.01	−0.1	0.26	0.2	1.5
	Coef/elasticity	−0.024	−0.028	0.427	*MS*SR*[1]	With[2]/without[3] *MS*SR*
1980–89	Contribution to	−0.01	−0.6	−0.01	−0.6	0.6
1990–99	growth	0.01	−0.1	0.25	0.2	1.5
					Total	With[2]/without[3]*MS*
1980–89	Contribution to	−0.02	−1.2	−0.03	−1.3	1.3
1990–99	growth	0.01	−0.15	*0.5*	0.4	1.3

Regional summary Years	MENA	Asia	LA	ACFA	ANCFA
1980–89	−1.3	0.1	−1.4	0.05	−0.3
1990–99	0.4	0.5	0.8	0.2	1.0

Source: Authors' calculations.
[1] Without change in *SR*.
[2] With *MS* in the case of a negative impact on growth.
[3] Without125 *MS* in the case of a positive impact.

Conversely, the contribution of structural reforms—0.2 points in GDP per capita growth rate during the two subperiods, despite the low level of reforms and the macroeconomic instability of the 1980s (see table 2.6)—stresses that reforming the economy is potentially a key factor for the growth prospects of the MENA region. This is confirmed by the strong contribution of structural reforms to the growth performances of the Asian countries (0.7 to 0.9 points; see table 2.6), as well as by the experience of Tunisia and Jordan (0.5 to 0.7 points; table A12-3 in appendix 12). The important gap between MENA and Asia shows that this factor constitutes another important potential source of growth for the region.

External Stability

As for macroeconomic stability, the external instability of the 1980s strongly contributed to the economic turmoil of the period. The increase in the debt ratio led to an average deterioration of 1 percentage point in the annual GDP per capita growth rate (see table 2.7). This deterioration was even greater in Syria (2.4 points: table A12-2 in appendix 12). Globally, imbalances in external stability cost the MENA countries an average of 1 percentage point per year in GDP per capita growth rate. This means that the growth performance of the region could have reached one percent on average per year (instead of 0 percent).

Table 2.6. Contribution of Structural Reforms (Structural Reforms*Macroeconomic Stability: $SR*MS^{(1)}$)—MENA Region

MENA Years	%	$TradeP*MS^{(1)}$	$PCrBOG*MS^{(1)}$	Total contribution	Growth of GDP per capita
1980–89	Annual growth rate	−0.1	0.8		0
1990–99		0.7	0.01		1.7
	Coefficients	0.24	0.27		Without *SR*
1980–89	Contribution to	−0.03	0.2	0.2	−0.3
1990–99	growth	0.2	0.0	0.2	1.5

Regional summary Years	MENA	Asia	LA	ACFA	ANCFA
1980–89	0.2	0.9	0.2	0.1	0.2
1990–99	0.2	0.7	0.3	−0.3	0.3

Source: Authors' calculations.
a. Without change in macroeconomic reforms.

During the 1990s, the process of debt reduction contributed positively to the growth performance of the region (0.2 point per year in GDP per capita). This low contribution, however, and the gap with other regions (Asia in particular) indicate that debt reduction still represents an important potential source of growth.

Special attention needs to be drawn to the current account balance. The strong long-term coefficient potentially makes of this variable a key factor that can lead to large variations in the rate of growth of the economies. This was the case in the 1990s, when improvement in the current account position contributed substantially to the growth performance of the region (0.8 point of GDP per capita growth rate). This improvement was even higher in Egypt (1.3 points) and Iran (1 point). During this period, MENA showed the best performance among the regions. Table 2.7 also confirms that external stability

Table 2.7. Contribution of External Stability—MENA Region

MENA Years	%	*DebX*	*DebGNP*	*CurAcc*	Total contribution	Growth of GDP per capita
1980–89	Annual growth rate	9.9	3.8	−0.3		0
1990–99		−1.8	1.4	2.1		1.7
	Coefficients	−0.089	−0.003	0.396		With/without *ES*
1980–89	Contribution to	−0.9	−0.01	−0.1	−1.0	1
1990–99	growth	0.2	−0.004	0.8	1.0	0.7

Regional summary Years	MENA	Asia	LA	ACFA	ANCFA
1980–89	−1.0	0.2	−1.4	−1.0	−1.9
1990–99	1.0	0.5	0.9	−0.9	−0.2

Source: Authors' calculations.

has constituted a key factor in explaining the growth achievements of all the regions in our sample.

Summary

Table 2.8 summarizes the global impact of economic reforms, human capital, and physical infrastructure on the growth performances of our sample of countries. In the 1980s, macroeconomic and external instability contributed significantly to MENA's low growth performances. These factors contributed to lowering the annual GDP growth rate by 2.2 percentage points. Growth could have reached 2.2 percent per year (instead of 0 percent) if no degradation of macroeconomic and external conditions had occurred. This negative contribution was even stronger in the case of Syria (5.4 points) and Iran (2.6 points for macroeconomic stability alone; see table A12.6 in appendix 12).

As far as positive contributions are concerned, human capital, physical infrastructure, and, to a lesser extent, structural reforms contributed during the same period to a 2.7 percent annual average GDP per capita growth rate. This positive influence more than compensated for the negative impact of macroeconomic and external instability. This positive contribution was even higher in the case of Tunisia, Iran (3.1 points), and Syria (2.8 points).

In the 1990s, economic reforms, and growth in human capital and physical infrastructure, together explain the improvement in the economic situation of MENA. Human capital and physical infrastructure still contributed the most (1.9 percent in GDP per capita growth rate), followed by macroeconomic and external stability (1.4 points in GDP per capita growth rate).[24] This finding reflects the efforts of the MENA countries to reform their economies. Reforms, however, have still lagged behind Asia and Latin America. Indeed, the low level of structural reforms, the still high debt ratio, the foreign

Table 2.8. Total Contributions—Summary MENA Region

| % Years | Contribution to growth | | | |
	MS + ES	H + Phy + SR	Investment	Total
1980–89	−2.2	2.7	−0.3	0.1
1990–99	1.4	2.1	−0.1	3.4

Regional summary	MENA	Asia	LA	ACFA	ANCFA
Total contribution to growth					
1980–89	0.1	3.6	−1.0	0.2	−1.0
1990–99	3.4	3.6	3.5	0.4	2.4
GDP per capita growth rate					
1980–89	0	3.4	−0.8	−1.2	−0.9
1990–99	1.7	3.9	1.7	−0.8	0.9

Source: Authors' calculations.

exchange parallel market premium in some countries, the insufficient development of infrastructure and primary schooling compared to Asia and Latin America, as well as the high potential of reforms, highlight the urgent need for MENA to accelerate the reform agenda in the region.

Conclusion

The empirical analysis carried out in this paper has clearly underlined the importance of economic reforms, human capital, and physical infrastructure to improve the growth prospects of the economies. These factors have been shown to have a powerful impact on growth. They have greatly contributed to the growth process in our sample of MENA countries. An original contribution of this paper has been to also bring to light new empirical evidence on the subject of economic reforms and economic growth. Our quantitative analysis has revealed the complementarities across macroeconomic reforms and structural reforms, as elaborated by Mussa (1987) and Williamson (1994). These complementarities have greatly contributed to the low growth performance of our sample of MENA countries.

During the 1980s, macroeconomic volatility in MENA was disruptive to growth. In the 1990s, this situation was reversed and economic stabilization contributed positively to MENA's development. Our empirical analysis shows, however, that although most MENA countries implemented better macroeconomic policies in the mid-1980s or in the 1990s, consolidating macroeconomic stability is still a priority for the success of structural reforms, as well as for successful competition with more successful developing countries.

The region is also concerned with achieving progress in structural reforms, which have always lagged behind faster-growing countries in terms of trade openness and financial development. In the 1990s, the slow pace of these reforms limited the benefits of macroeconomic stabilization. In fact, and as illustrated by our econometric results, improving trade openness and financial development would strongly contribute to the economic growth of MENA countries, in addition to facilitating the integration of the region into the world economy.

As for macroeconomic and structural reforms, external stability has been identified as another factor affecting growth performances in MENA. The external instability of the 1980s strongly contributed to the economic turmoil of the period. In the 1990s, the renegotiation of the external debt helped to improve the growth process in the region. The gap in terms of external debt and the significant scope for debt reduction indicate, however, that this still represents a potentially important source of growth for the future.

The last set of conclusions concerns the substantial role of human capital and physical infrastructure, improvements that have greatly contributed to MENA growth performances. Progress achieved in the health, education, and infrastructure sectors has been substantial in MENA. The level of education, however, remains lower than in other regions—such as Asia and Latin America—and the amount of infrastructure equipment available is still insufficient. The development gaps in education and infrastructure represent areas of potentially strong improvement in the region's growth prospects. This is particularly true in the current context of economic reform and integration into the world's global economy, particularly with the European Union. In fact, a more qualified labor force and an adequate level of infrastructure are essential for the success of economic reforms in MENA, as well as to stimulate and develop international competitiveness.

Notes

1. The comparative advantage of panel data regressions compared to time series estimation techniques can also be seen in:

a. The double dimension (time series-cross-section), which improves estimates by adding information

b. The country dummy variables, which generally ask for an important number of degree of freedom, and which add precision to the results of the estimations.

2. Among these countries, 16 are African countries (7 CFA and 9 non-CFA), 12 are Latin American countries, 9 are Asian countries, and 7 are MENA countries (see appendix 1 for the list of countries). These economies have been selected based on their level of income per capita. To preserve the coherence of the sample, we have chosen mostly intermediate-income countries that are comparable with MENA economies.

3. As part of our empirical work, we have tried, without success, to introduce in the principal component analysis the ratio of current account balance to GDP as a component of the macroeconomic stability index, exchange rate stability as part of the external stability, cumulative privatization receipts as a factor in the structural reforms, and real exchange rate misalignment processed by Nabli and Véganzonès-Varoudakis (2002). Other interesting indicators had to be ignored because of lack of information. This has been the case with the ratio M2 to GDP, the import cover of international reserves, the ratio of short-term to total debt, and net international liquidity as months of import cover, which could have reinforced the external stability index. Similarly, the structural reform index could not benefit from information on mean tariff rates, or highest marginal individual and corporate taxes.

4. The *Bmp* indicator is traditionally a measure of the distortions on the capital markets, which can hinder the mobilization of resources for investing, especially in tradable goods. This indicator is also used as a proxy for real exchange rate (*RER*) misalignment, and particularly for *RER* overvaluation. In fact, many governments, to ration scarce foreign exchange to the private sector, use exchange controls. The excess of foreign exchange demand arising from the official exchange rate being kept below its market clearing level leads to an overvaluation of the currency (see Pinto, 1990, for an analysis of the various foreign exchange markets' distortions captured by *Bmp*).

5. We have listed the MENA economies in decreasing order of welfare. The first countries presented in the graphs are the ones that exhibited higher GDP per capita in the 1970s.

6. As a result of the methodology of calculation of principal component analysis, the level and sign of the aggregate indicators have no particular interpretation. These indicators have to be read as follows:

a. A rise in the indicator indicates progress in reform. Conversely, a deterioration denotes a regression.

b. The intensity of reforms is measured as the difference of the indicator across countries and between periods. In the last section, we will use the annual growth rate of the composite, as well as of the initial indicators, to measure their impact on growth.

7. These results are partly due to the exclusion of the Gulf economies, in which the average debt ratio has been lower.

8. The "natural openness" of the economy is calculated by Frankel and Romer (1999) by taking into account the size and the distance of the markets of the countries.

9. We have also processed a more complete human capital indicator (H) that includes, as well, secondary and superior schooling (see appendix 2, table A2.4.a). This indicator does not give better results when estimating the growth equation. We will, however, give some details on the outcomes in secondary and superior education in Appendix 6.

10. It is worth noting that the reduced form used here (which includes the ratio of investment to GDP) is derived from a log-linear approximation around the steady state of a Solow (1967) type growth model. This model has been extended by several authors, by incorporating other explanatory variables in order to better explain the residual of the equation (the technical progress—see Mankiw, Romer, and Weil, 1992, as far as human capital is concerned). In this paper, we have chosen the same approach. We should, however, point out that reforms also materialize into growth by increasing the investment ratio. This should be kept in mind when analyzing our estimation results, which, in this context, may have underestimated the impact of reforms on growth.

11. This method, consisting of directly introducing the initial reform indicators into the regressions, has been tried with less success. Because of the correlation of the disaggregated variables, the significance of some of the variables turned out to depend on the specification of the model. These initial tests have not been reported here because of the large number of combinations.

12. This is also the case because our sample is sufficiently "big," with T (number of time periods) and N (number of countries) being large enough (see Im, Pesaran, and Shin, 1997). In this case, despite the presence of the lag variable $y - 1$, which is correlated with the constant terms, the distributions of the tests tend to converge.

13. This applies in particular to the oil-producing and mining economies in our sample.

14. Other estimations have consisted in testing the heterogeneity of the estimated relationship across regions. We have in particular tested the difference of slope of the economic reforms, human capital, and physical infrastructure indicators.

15. The coefficient of macroeconomic stability in Equation (1), and of human capital in Equations (1) and (2) are significant at the 10 percent level.

16. The lag of the reform variables also corrects for the potential bias due to the possible endogeneity of the right-hand variables. In this case, the reverse causality that might exist is not supposed to bias the value of the estimated coefficients.

17. Most of them employ aggregated indicators such as public investment.

18. Comparisons among studies are, however, also difficult because of the differences in indicators and/or of specifications used.

As far as the road network is concerned, Pouliquen (2000)—in his study of Indian infrastructure at the village level—found a short-term elasticity of 0.07 for the 1971-1981 period (here 0.03). Nagaraj, Varoudakis and Véganzonès (2000) obtained an elasticity of 0.05 at the Indian States level studied from 1970 to 1994, and Véganzonès (2001) found an elasticity of 0.06 for a panel of 87 countries during 1970-1995. Conversely, Nagaraj, Varoudakis and Véganzonès (2000) have come out with a long-term elasticity of 0.34 and Véganzonès (2001) of 0.16 (here 0.15). The impact of the development of the telephone network has been evaluated by, among others, Canning (1999) for a large sample of countries during 1965-1990, using cross-countries regressions. Canning has estimated a short-term elasticity of 0.013 (here 0.019) and a long-term elasticity of 0.15 (here 0.10). Véganzonès (2001) has obtained a short-term elasticity of 0.007 and a long-term one of 0.18. As far as education is concerned, Benhabib and Spiegel (1994) have estimated cross-countries regressions for the 1965-85 period. They have obtained a short-term elasticity of 0.01 for total education (here 0.025 for primary education) and a long term one of 0.04 (here 0.14). Véganzonès (2001) has found a short-term elasticity of 0.01 for primary education and a long-term one of 0.19. Infant mortality is an indicator rarely used in the growth literature, which focuses more on life expectancy. Nagaraj, Varoudakis, and Véganzonès

(2000) have estimated a short-term elasticity of 0.06 (here 0.02) and a long-term elasticity of 0.38 (here 0.12). Véganzonès] (2001) has obtained a short-term elasticity of 0.02 and a long-term one of 0.37. Our comparisons are constrained by the indicators and/or specifications chosen. Other close interesting results can be found, for example, in Grace and others (2001), Bougheas, Demetriades, and Mamuneas (2000), and Easterly and Levine (1997 and 2000).

19. The strong impact of the amelioration of the telephone network-which is, however, in line with the finding of other studies-may also be explained by the fact that this indicator, along with the road network, possibly captures the impact of other infrastructures.

20. As far as coefficients/elasticities are concerned, our results have also been compared to those of other studies. In the case of inflation, Barro (1996)—who studied a panel of 110 countries for three sub-periods between 1965 and 1990—found a short-term coefficient of 0.006 (here 0.005). Guillaumont, Guillaumont-Jeanneney, and Varoudakis (1999) have estimated a short-term coefficient of 0.006 and a long-term one of 0.14 (here 0.025) for a panel of 44 African countries studied on a five-year average basis during 1960–95. In the case of public deficit, the same authors found a short-term coefficient of 0.06 (here 0.08) and a long-term one of 0.14 (here 0.43). For the black market exchange rate premium, Easterly and Levine (1993), as well as Easterly, Kremer, Prichet and Summer (1993), obtained a short-term coefficient of 0.004 (here 0.005) for a panel of 115 countries studied during the 1960s, 1970s, and 1980s.

21. This indicator is considered here as a proxy of various distortions in the economy.

22. In the 1960s, most MENA governments implemented an import substitution strategy which isolated the countries from outside competition. Although this was also the case in a majority of developing countries, in MENA this policy was reinforced in the 1970s and in 1980s. The abundance of foreign reserve from oil revenues, as well as from workers' remittances and Arab assistance, encouraged the governments to assume a still more assertive role in the economy. In the 1990s, this policy was progressively reverted in the non-oil-producing countries, as a result of the growing imbalances in the government budget and in the balance of payments. The pace of reform was, however, slow in the oil-producing countries. The political instability and the rigidities of the economies explain also why this process has always remained less intensive in the region.

23. The same conclusions can be drawn for CFA Africa.

24. The relatively high potential growth of the 1990s (3.4 percent compared to 1.7 observed), contrary to the 1980s, shows that some adverse factors to growth have not been taken into consideration in our regressions. These factors could be political stability or quality of governance institutions, as developed recently in the literature (see, for example, Knack and Keefer, 1995, Acemoglu, Johnson and Robinson, 2001, and Rodrik, Subramanian and Trebbi, 2002. Some authors have in particular pointed out that the MENA deficit in "good" institutions—(essentially political rights, civil liberties, quality of administration and corruption)—have significantly contributed to the slow economic activity of the region (see El Badawi, 2002 and the World Bank, 2004).

References

Acemoglu, D., S. Johnson, and J. A. Robinson. 2001. "The Colonial Origins of Comparative Development: An Empirical Investigation." *American Economic Review* 91(5): 1369–401.

Aschauer, D. A. 1989. "Is Public Expenditure Productive?" *Journal of Monetary Economics* 23: 177–200.

Balassa, B. 1978. "Exports and Economic Growth—Further Evidence." *Journal of Development Economics* 5: 181–189.

Barro, R. J. 1990. "Government Spending in a Simple Model of Endogenous Growth. *Journal of Political Economy* 98(5, part II): S103–S125.

———. 1996. "Determinants of Economic Growth: A Cross-Country Empirical Study." Working Paper Series, No 5698. National Bureau of Economic Research, Washington, DC (August).

Barro, R. J., and X. Sala-I-Martin. 1995. *Economic Growth*. New York: McGraw-Hill.

Benhabib, J., and M. M. Spiegel. 1994. "The Role of Human Capital in Economic Development: Evidence from Aggregate Cross-Country Data." *Journal of Monetary Economics* 34(2): 143–173.

Bougheas, H., P. O. Demetriades, and T. P. Mamuneas. 2000. "Infrastructures, Specialization and Economic Growth." *Canadian Journal of Economics* 33(2): 506–522.

Canning, D. 1999. "Telecommunications, Infrastructures, Human Capital and Economic Growth." Discussion Paper No 55. Consulting Assistance on Economic Reform II, Cambridge, the Harvard CAER II project consortium, September.

Dasguptta, D., J. Keller, and T. G. Srinivasan. 2004. "Reforms and Elusive Growth in the Middle East—What Happened in the 1990s?" In *Trade Policy and Economic Integration in the Middle East & North Africa: Economic Boundaries in Flux*, ed. by H. Hakimian and J.B. Nugent. London: Curzon-Routledge.

De Gregorio, J. 1992. "The Effects of Inflation on Economic Growth: Lessons from Latin America." *European Economic Review* 36(2/3): 417–425.

Easterly, W., and R. Levine. 1993. "Is Africa Different? Evidence from Growth Regressions." Internal document. World Bank, Washington, DC (April).

———. 1997. "Africa's Growth Tragedy: Policies and Ethnic Divisions. *Quarterly Journal of Economics* 50(3): 112–120.

———. 2000. "It's Not Factor Accumulation: Stylized Facts and Growth Models." *IMF Seminar Series* No. 2000–12: pp. 1–52. International Monetary Fund, Washington, DC (March).

Easterly, W., M. Kremer, L. Prichet, and L. Summer. 1993. "Good Policy or Good Luck: Country Growth Performance and Temporary Shocks. *Journal of Monetary Economics* 32: 459–483.

El Badawi, I. A. 2002. "Reviving Growth in the Arab World." Working Paper Series, 0206. Arab Planing Institute, Safat, Kuwait.

Feder, G. 1983. "On Exports and Economic Growth." *Journal of Development Economics* 12(1/2): 59–79.

Fischer, S. 1993. "The Role of Macro-economic Factors in Growth." Working Paper N. 4565. National Bureau of Economic Research, Washington, DC.

Frankel, J. A., and D. Romer. 1999. "Does Trade Cause Growth." *The American Economic Review* 89(3): 379–399.

Grace, J., C. Kenny, J. Liu, C. Qiang, and T. Reynolds. 2001. "Information and Communication Technologies and Broad-Base Development: A Partial Review of Evidence." World Bank, Washington, DC (February).

Hakimian, H., and J.B. Nugent. 2004. *Trade Policy and Economic Integration in the Middle East & North Africa: Economic Boundaries in Flux*. London: Curzon-Routledge.

Hoekman, B., and H. Kheir-El-Din. 2000. *Trade Policy Development in the Middle East and North Africa*. Washington D.C. and Cairo: World Bank and Economic Research Forum.

Iqbal, Z. 2001. *Macroeconomic Issues and Policies in the Middle East and North Africa*. Washington, DC: International Monetary Fund.

Im, K. S., M. H. Pesaran, and Y. Shin. 1997. "Testing for Unit Roots in Heterogeneous Panels." DAE Working Paper Amalgamated Series, No 9526, University of Cambridge.

International Country Risk Guide (ICRG). 1999. "Brief Guide to the Rating System." Political Link Service Group, New York.

Knack, S., and P. Keefer. 1995. "Institutions and Economic Performance: Cross Country Tests Using Alternative Institutional Measures." *Economics and Politics* 7(3): 207–27.

Levine, R. 1997. "Financial Development and Economic Growth: Views and Agenda." *Journal of Economic Literature* 35: 688–726.

Levine, R., and S. Zervos. 1993. "Looking at the Facts. What We Know about Policy and Growth from Cross-Country Analysis." Policy Research Working Paper No. 1115. World Bank, Washington, DC.

Lucas, R. E. 1988. "On the Mechanism of Economic Development." *Journal of Monetary Economics* 22: 3–42.

Mankiw, N.G., D. Romer, and D. N. Weil. 1992. "A Contribution to the Empirics of Economic Growth." *Quarterly Journal of Economics* 107(2): 407–427.

Murphy, K. M., A. Schleifer, and R. W. Vishny. 1989. "Industrialization and the Big Push." *Quarterly Journal of Economics* 106(2): 503–530.

Mussa, M. 1987. "Macroeconomic Policy and Trade Liberalization: Some Guidelines." *World Bank Research Observer* 57(6): 61–77.

Nabli, M. K. 2000. "From a Growth Crisis to Prospects for a Strong Growth Recovery in the MENA Region." Internal document, MNSED. World Bank, Washington DC.

Nabli M. K., and M-A Véganzonès-Varoudakis. 2002. "Exchange Rate Regime and Competitiveness of Manufacture Exports: The Case of MENA Countries." In *Trade Policy and Economic Integration in the Middle East & North Africa: Economic Boundaries in Flux*, ed. by H. Hakimian and J. B. Nugent. Curzon-Routledge: London.

Nagaraj, R., A. Varoudakis, and M. A.Véganzonès. 2000. "Long-Run Growth Trends and Convergence across Indian States: The Role of Infrastructures." *Journal of International Development* 12(1): 45–70.

Pinto, B. 1990. "Black Market Premium, Exchange Rate Unification and Inflation in Sub-Saharan Africa." *The World Bank Economic Review* 3(3): 321–338.

Pouliquen, L. 2000. "Infrastructure and Poverty." Internal document. World Bank, Washington, DC.

Psacharopoulos, G. 1988. *Economics of Education: Research and Studies.* Elmsford, NY: Pergamon Press.

Rodrik, D., A. Subramanian, and F. Trebbi. 2002. "Institutions Rule: The Primacy of Institutions over Geography and Integration in Economic Development. NBER Working Paper 9305, National Bureau of Economic Research, Cambridge, MA.

Safadi, R. 1998. *Opening Doors to the World: A New Trade Agenda for the Middle East.* Cairo: Economic Research Forum and American University Press.

Véganzonès-Varoudakis, M-A. 2001. "Infrastructures, Investissement et Croissance: Nouvelles E´Vidences Empiriques." *Revue d'Economie du De´veloppement* 4: 31–46.

Williamson, J. 1994. *The Political Economy of Policy Reforms.* Washington, DC: Institute of International Economics.

World Bank. 2004. "Better Governance for Development in the Middle East and North Africa: Enhancing Inclusiveness and Accountability." MENA development report. The World Bank, Washington, DC.

Appendix 1. Countries in the Sample

MENA	Africa		Asia	Latin America
	CFA	Non-CFA		
Algeria (DZA)	Burkina Faso (BFA)	Botswana (BWA)	Bangladesh (BGD)	Argentina (ARG)
Egypt, Arab Rep. (EGY)	Côte d'Ivoire (CIV)	Ghana (GHA)	Indonesia (IDN)	Bolivia (BOL)
Iran, Islamic Rep.(IRN)	Gabon (GAB)	Kenya (KEN)	India (IND)	Brazil (BRA)
Jordan (JOR)	Cameroon (CMR)	Madagascar (MDG)	Korea, Rep.(KOR)	Chile (CHL)
Morocco (MAR)	Gambia, The (GMB)	Mauritius (MUS)	Sri Lanka (LKA)	Colombia (COL)
Syrian Arab Republic (SYR)	Niger (NER)	Malawi (MWI)	Malaysia (MYS)	Costa Rica (CRI)
Tunisia (TUN)	Togo (TGO)	Nigeria (NGA)	Pakistan (PAK)	Ecuador (ECU)
		South Africa (ZAF)	Philippines (PHL)	Guatemala (GTM)
		Zambia (ZMB)	Thailand (THA)	Mexico (MEX)
				Peru (PER)
				Paraguay (PRY)
				Uruguay (URY)

Appendix 2. Principal Component Analysis*

The principal components of the basic indicators are extracted for each group of indicators from an annual panel of 44 countries over 1970–80 to 1999. The five composite indicators are constructed as the weighted sum of one or two principal components, depending on the explanatory power of each component. We chose the most significant principal components whose eigenvalues are higher than one. In this case, we explain around 70 percent of the variance of the underlying individual indicators (see tables A2.1 to A2.5). The weight attributed to each principal component corresponds to its relative contribution to the variance of the initial indicators (calculated from the cumulative R^2).[1] The contribution of each individual indicator to the composite indicator can then be computed as a linear combination of the weights associated with the one or two principal components and of the loadings of the individual indicators on each principal component (see below). The calculations show that all initial indicators contribute as expected to the composite indicators.[2]

Table A2.1. Macroeconomic Stability Variables

Component	Eigenvalue	Cumulative R^2	
P1	1.19	0.40	
P2	0.96	0.72	
P3	0.85	1.00	

Loadings	P1	P2	P3
P	0.48	0.86	0.19
IBmp	0.72	−0.16	−0.68
PubDef	−0.67	0.45	−0.60

MS=0.40/0.72*P1+(0.72−0.40)/0.72*P2

Table A2.2. External Stability Variables

Component	Eigenvalue	Cumulative R^2	
P1	1.92	0.65	
P2	0.81	0.92	
P3	0.25	1.00	

Loadings	P1	P2	P3
DebExX	0.92	0.03	0.37
DebExGni	0.73	0.60	−0.26
CurAccX	−0.71	0.67	0.21

ES=P1

*Source: Authors' calculations.

Table A2.3. Structural Reform Variables

Component	Eigenvalue	Cumulative R^2
P1	1.49	0.75
P2	0.51	1.00

Loadings	P1	P2
TradeP1	0.86	0.50
PCRBOG	0.86	−0.50
SR=P1		

Table A2.4.A. Human Capital Variables (complete)

Component	Eigenvalue	Cumulative R^2
P1	2.95	0.74
P2	0.50	0.87
P3	0.34	0.95
P4	0.19	1.00

Loadings	P1	P2	P3	P4
ln(Mort)	0.79	0.590	0.15	0.08
ln(H1)	−0.84	0.340	−0.43	0.04
ln(H2)	−0.91	−0.005	0.26	0.32
ln(H3)	−0.89	0.210	0.27	0.29
H=P1				

Table A2.4.B. Human Capital Variables (reduced)

Component	Eigenvalue	Cumulative R^2
P1	1.52	0.76
P2	0.48	1.00

Loadings	P1	P2
ln(Mort)	0.87	0.49
ln(H1)	−0.87	0.49
MH1=P1		

Table A2.5. Physical Infrastructure Variables

Component	Eigenvalue	Cumulative R^2
P1	1.42	0.71
P2	0.58	1.00

Loadings	P1	P2
ln(Roads)	0.84	0.54
ln(Tel)	0.84	−0.54
Ph7ys=P1		

Appendix 3. Macroeconomic Stability indicators

Most MENA countries adopted better macroeconomic policies—some in the late 1980s (Morocco, Tunisia, and Jordan) and others in the 1990s— after a decade of regression (Iran, Syria, Algeria, Egypt). In the 1990s, some MENA countries (Morocco, Tunisia, Jordan, and Egypt) undertook a level of macroeconomic reforms similar to the average in the South and East Asian economies.

In the 1990s, inflation was successfully contained (particularly in Morocco, Jordan, and Tunisia; figure 2.8b). Public deficit was reduced everywhere in the region (figure 2.9b) and the foreign exchange parallel market premium ended in the majority of countries in our sample (figure 2.10b).

Although MENA macroeconomic policy has globally improved, further progress in Tunisia and Morocco would have reduced the public deficit, which has been higher than the MENA average (3.4 percent and 2.8 percent of GDP, on average, in the 1990s; see figure 2.9b). In Iran and Algeria, the black market exchange rate (owing to capital controls and political instability) and inflation (which reached 20 percent in the 1990s) should have been better controlled (see figures 2.8b and 2.10b). This is also the case, to a lesser extent, for the foreign exchange parallel market premium in Syria and for inflation in Egypt.

Figure 2.8. Inflation (%)

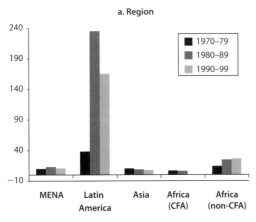
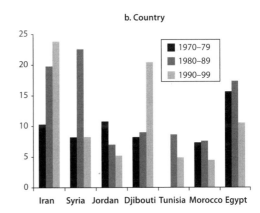

Source: Authors' calculations.

Figure 2.9. Public Deficit (% of GDP)

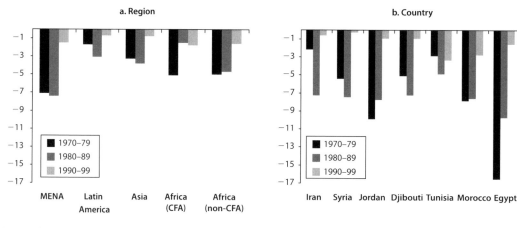

Source: Authors' calculations.

Figure 2.10. Black Market Premium (%)

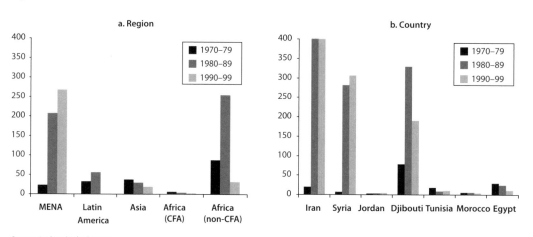

Source: Authors' calculations.

Appendix 4. External Stability indicators

In MENA, the level of foreign debt increased dramatically in the 1980s (see figure 2.11a and 2.12a, because of the high public investment ratio of the 1970s and 1980s (see appendix 8). The exceptions were Iran, and to a lesser extent, Tunisia and Algeria.[3]

In the 1990s, the MENA countries' external debt accounted for 60 to 70 percent of gross national investment (GNI) in Morocco, Egypt, Algeria, Tunisia (around 150 to 200 percent of exports), and more than 130 percent of GNI in Syria and Jordan (see figures 2.11b and 2.12b).[4] In the 1990s, Morocco and Egypt were the only two countries to reduce their external debt, following major debt forgiveness after the Gulf War.

These difficulties in containing the external debt have been partly compensated for by improvements in the current account balance. In fact, MENA countries are among the best performers from all regions (see figure 2.13a). Even though only a few MENA economies exhibited a positive balance in the 1990s—this was the case for Iran, Syria, and Egypt—efforts to reduce deficits are noticeable in almost every MENA country (except Jordan, see figure 2.13b).

Figure 2.11. External Debt (% of exports)

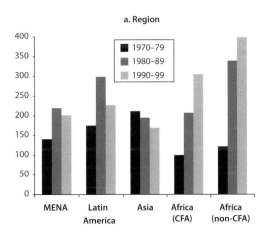

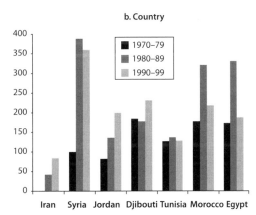

Source: Authors' calculations.

Figure 2.12. External Debt (% of GNI)

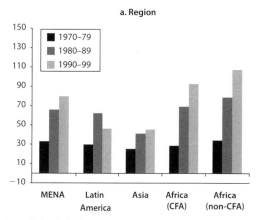
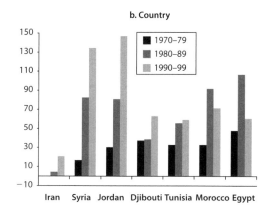

Source: Authors' calculations.

Figure 2.13. Current Account Balance (% of exports)

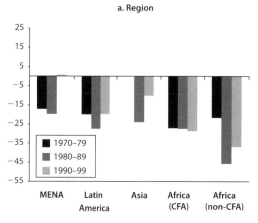
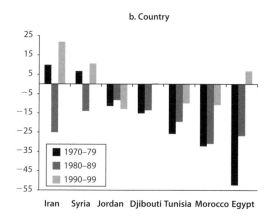

Source: Authors' calculations.

Appendix 5. Structural Reform indicators

The ratio of private credit as a share of total credit from banking systems and other institutions has averaged 35 percent during the 1980s and the 1990s. Financial depth has been particularly significant in Jordan and Tunisia (respectively 70 percent and 60 percent of GDP), but has improved almost everywhere—except in Egypt, Iran and Algeria in the 1990s (figure 2.14b). This achievement has been better only in Asia, where the financial ratio reached, on average, 60 percent in the 1990s (see figure 2.14a). Financial development has, however, been weaker in Syria, Algeria, and, to a lesser extent, Iran and Egypt in the 1990s (see figure 2.14b).

Our findings do not mean, however, that the MENA economies have benefited from a strong banking system or a developed Financial sector. In fact, other studies highlight the deficiencies of the financial sector as an effective means of boosting the development of the private sector and the growth prospects of the region (Nabli, 2000). In this context, our results might be due to the fact that the proxy used (PCrBOG) is unable to capture either the quality of the banking system (which could be better analyzed through other specific indicators),[5] or the development of the financial markets (which have also been deficient in the MENA economies).

Trade openness has often been particularly low in MENA—with a ratio, on average, of about 30 percent of GDP, compared to 45 to 70 percent in Asia[6]—and rather similar to that of Latin America (figure 2.15a). This is the case despite some exports diversification of the non-oil-producing countries in the 1990s, which explains why trade openness has been rather high in Jordan and Tunisia (around 60 percent of GDP; figure 2.15b). These countries (with Morocco) have been the most diversified in the region (table A5-1). Trade

Figure 2.14. Credit from the Banking System Indicator

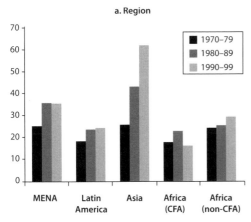

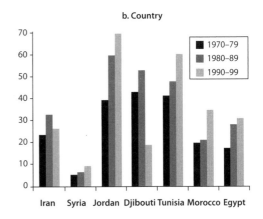

Source: Authors' calculations.

Figure 2.15. Trade Policy (excluding exports of oil and mining, % of GDP)

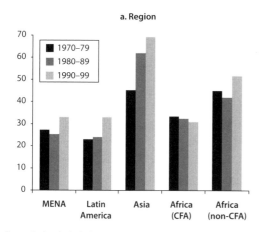

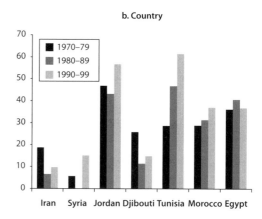

Source: Authors' calculations.

openness has remained weak in Iran, Syria, and Algeria (between 10 percent and 20 percent of GDP in the 1990s) due to the difficulties in moving from oil production and state-dominated management of the economies.[7] In these countries, the scope for improvement of trade policy is still very significant.

Table A5-1. Average Manufactured Exports of Selected MENA Countries

	Algeria		Egypt		Iran		Jordan		Morocco		Tunisia	
	%X	% GDP	% X	% GDP	%X	% GDP	%X	% GDP	%X	% GDP	%X	% GDP
1970–79	3	0.6	27	3.1	2.9	0.6	26	1.9	16	2.1	24	4.6
1980–89	1.5	0.3	19	1.5	4.0	0.3	43	5.4	39	6.0	49	12
1990–99	3.3	0.8	37	2.4	6.6	1.5	49	9.5	53	7.5	75	21

Source: Authors' calculations.
*For the first subperiod, four values were missing for Iran (1970, 1971, 1972, and 1973).
**As far as the thirrd subperiod is concerned, two values were missing for Iran (1991 and 1992) and one for Jordan (1996).

Appendix 6. Human Capital indicators

As far as human capital is concerned, one important area of success is the reduction of infant mortality. Mortality rates (which reached 30 per 1,000 in the 1990s) were cut by two-thirds compared to the 1970s. Levels are now in line with Asia and Latin America. In Egypt, the ratio of infant mortality fell sixfold during the same period. In this country, however, because of a high initial level, the ratio still surpasses the MENA average. Noticeable efforts were also made by Iran, Algeria, Tunisia, and Morocco (see figure 2.16).

In the field of education, results are more mitigated. Despite visible progress, the level of primary schooling has remained lower than in Asia, Latin America, and non-CFA Africa. Tunisia is the exception, with almost five years of primary schooling in the 1990s. Successful achievements were also realized in Jordan, Algeria, Syria, and Iran (about four years of schooling; see figure 2.17). On average, achievements were greater in secondary and superior education, where schooling was more in line with Asia and Latin America. The performance in Syria, Iran, Jordan, and Egypt has been above the MENA average, with 1.5 to 2 years, and 0.6 years of schooling, respectively (but only 0.15 for superior education in the case of Iran, see figures 2.18b and 2.19b).

Figure 2.16. Mortality Rate (per 1,000 population)

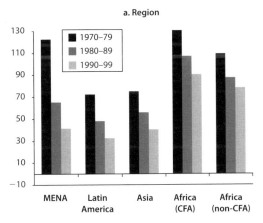
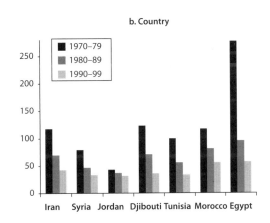

Source: Authors' calculations.

Figure 2.17. Primary Education (number of years of schooling of the population)

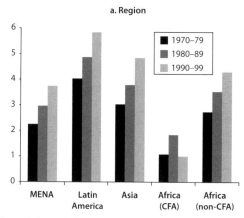
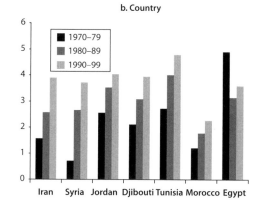

Source: Authors' calculations.

Figure 2.18. Secondary Education (number of years of schooling of the population)

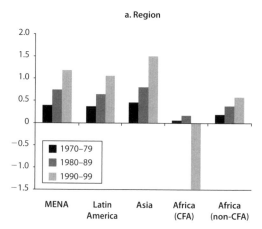
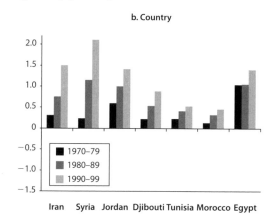

Source: Authors' calculations.

Figure 2.19. Tertiary Education (number of years of schooling of the population)

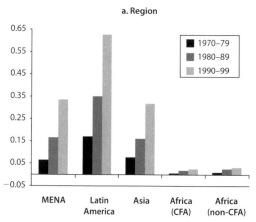
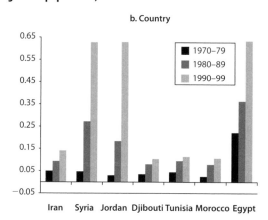

Source: Authors' calculations.

Appendix 7. Physical Infrastructure Indicators

Despite real progress throughout the period, MENA physical infrastructures remain on average insufficient. Iran, Syria, Tunisia, and to a lesser extent Morocco, however, show better achievements than other MENA economies (almost in line with Latin America and Asia; see figure 2.5).[8]

The road network, in particular, has been markedly insufficient, with a density as low as in CFA Africa. Although a majority of countries have progressively improved their road infrastructure, the level was still low in Jordan, Algeria, and Egypt in the 1990s. Better progress was made in Syria, Tunisia, Morocco, and Iran, where construction equipment was in some ways equivalent to that in Latin America (but worse than in Asia; see figure 2.20).

The same observation can be made for the telephone network. Despite real improvements in almost all MENA countries, the level of equipment has remained deficient compared to that in Latin America and Asia (but far better than in Africa). Only Iran, Syria, and Jordan have revealed a pattern similar to that in Latin America (see figure 2.21).

Figure 2.20. Road Network (km per km2)

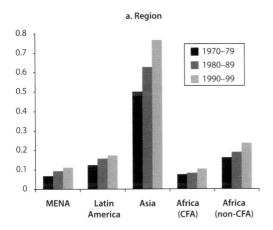
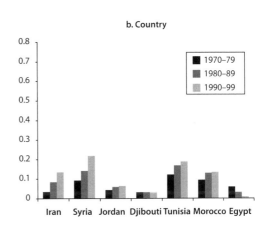

Source: Authors' calculations.

Figure 2.21. Telephone Network (number of lines per 1,000 people)

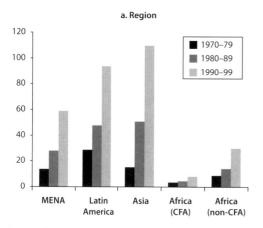

a. Region

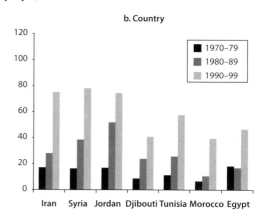

b. Country

Source: Authors' calculations.

Appendix 8. investment

Total investment in MENA has always remained rather dynamic compared to the rest of the world. At around 25 percent of GDP, total investment has been stronger than in Latin America and Africa, but inferior from the 1980s to Asia (figure 2.22a). This result is mainly the result of the high public investment ratio, private investment having conversely always been rather weak (Dasgupta, Keller, and Srinivasan, 2002).

In the 1970s, investment was particularly high in Egypt (more than 60 percent of GDP) and to a lesser extent, in Algeria and Jordan (35–40 percent of GDP). This situation can be explained by an abundance of liquidities resulting from the increase in oil revenues, workers' remittances, and the profusion of foreign capital. During this time, many countries were able to improve their physical infrastructure and human capital.

In the 1980s, because of the marked economic slowdown, many MENA economies faced overinvestment, in a context of macroeconomic imbalances and a growing debt burden.[9] Total investment was still high, around 30 percent of GDP in Algeria, Jordan, and Egypt (figure 2.22b), and public investment still more dynamic than private investment.

During the 1990s, many MENA countries were able to adjust their public investment ratio with some success, and total investment ranges from 20 to 30 percent of GDP. This has been done in a context of macroeconomic stabilization and structural reforms. Private investment remains, however, low compared to the need for productivity gains in the MENA economies.

Figure 2.22. Investment (% of GDP)

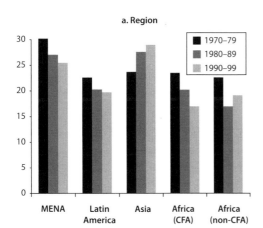

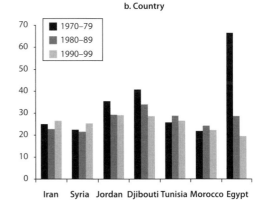

Source: Authors' calculations.

Appendix 9. Augmented Dickey-Fuller Test (ADF)

Table A9. Equations (1) and (2)

Variable	ADF statistic	$k^{(1)}$	Trend$^{(2)}$	Critical value$^{(3)}$	ADF test
Ln(y)	−3.22	1	Yes	−1.82*	I(0)
Ln(Inv)	−3.12	1	No	−1.82*	I(0)
MS	−3.19	1	No	−1.82*	I(0)
ES	−3.62	1	No	−1.82*	I(0)
SR	−1.86	1	No	−1.82*	I(0)
MH1	−1.76	1	No	−1.73**	I(0)
Phys	−6.58	1	No	−1.82*	I(0)

Source: Authors' calculations.
(1) k is the number of lags in the ADF test.
(2) The introduction of a trend when estimating Equations (1) and (2) shows, however, that this trend is not significant in the growth equation.
(3) Im, Pesaran, and Shin (1997) critical values (respectively *10% and ** 5% level).
Data have been compiled from World Development Indicators, Global Development Finance, Global Development Network, and Live Data Base (World Bank).

Appendix 10. Methodology of Calculation of the Coefficient/Elasticities of the Disaggregated Indicators

The impact of each disaggregated indicator can be computed as follows: Let P be the vector $(n*1)$ of the n principal components selected and δ the vector $(1*n)$ of their weights in the aggregate indicator. Furthermore, the n principal components are expressed as a linear combination of initial variables such that $P = AX$, X being the vector $(k*1)$ of k variables, and A represents the matrix $(n*k)$ of loadings assigned to them. The composite indicator is expressed as: $\delta P = \delta AX$. Denoting by γ the estimated coefficient for this indicator, the convergence equation can be written:

$$\ln(y_{ii,t}) - \ln(y_{i,t-1}) = \alpha_i - \beta \ln(y_{ii,t-1}) + \gamma \delta AX_{i,t} + \eta_{i,t} + u_{i,t} \qquad (3)$$

The vector $(1*k)$ (E), expressing the impact on growth of the original variables, can be calculated such that $E = \gamma \delta A$. These coefficients are estimated from Equations (1) and (2), as well as from the loadings summarized in Appendix 2. However, given the standardization procedure for the variables associated with the principal components method, the contribution of variations in level of each indicator to growth is expressed by the previously calculated coefficient (e_i), divided by the standard deviation for each variable $(e_i/\sigma i)$. The coefficients/elasticities of the long-run GDP per capita level with respect to different types of indicator is then obtained by dividing the impact coefficients by the convergence coefficient (β). Table 2.2 gives the long-term coefficients/elasticities for each indicator (see also table A11-1 and A11-2 in appendix 11 for intermediate calculations).

Appendix 11. Short- and Long-Term Coefficients/Elasticities of the Disaggregated Reform Indicators

Table A11-1. Equation (1)

Index	Variables	Short-term coefficients/elasticities		Long-term coefficients/ elasticities
		Standardized variables	Level variables	
MS	P	−0.0026	−0.0007	−0.004
	ln(Bmp)	−0.0013	−0.0007	−0.004
	PubDef	0.0006	0.0094	0.056
ES	DebExX	−0.027	−0.0172	−0.101
	DebExGni	−0.022	−0.0005	−0.003
	CurAccX	0.021	0.0770	0.453
SR	TradeP	0.013	0.0565	0.332
	PCRBOG	0.013	0.0618	0.363
Phys	ln(Roads)	0.025	0.0253	0.149
	ln(Tel)	0.025	0.0181	0.106
MH1	ln(Mort)	−0.0157	−0.0249	−0.147
	ln(H1)	−0.0157	0.0287	0.169

Source: Authors' calculations.

Table A11-2. Equation (2)

Index	Variables	Short-term coefficients/elasticities		Long-term coefficients/ elasticities
		Standardized variables	Level variables	
MS	P	0.0176	0.0044	0.026
ES	ln(Bmp)	0.0087	0.0050	0.029
SR	PubDef	0.0039	0.0637	0.375
Phys	DebExX	0.024	0.0154	0.091
MH1	DebExGni	0.020	0.0005	0.003
	CurAccX	0.018	0.0687	0.404
	TradeP	0.009	0.0414	0.244
	PCRBOG	0.009	0.0453	0.266
	ln(Roads)	0.026	0.0262	0.154
	ln(Tel)	0.026	0.0187	0.110
	ln(Mort)	0.0139	0.0222	0.130
	ln(H1)	0.0139	0.0255	0.150

Source: Authors' calculations.

Appendix 12. Contribution to Growth: MENA Countries' Experience

A12-1. Impact of Macroeconomic Stability

Years	(%)	MENA	Tunisia	Morocco	Algeria	Egypt	Jordan	Iran	Syria
1980–89	Contribution	−1.3	0.2	−0.01	−1.0	0.4	0.1	−2.6	−2.4
1990–99	to growth	0.4	0.4	0.70	0.8	1.3	0.6	0.3	0.6
1980–89	GDP per capita	0.0	1.6	1.40	0.1	2.2	−0.7	−3.5	−1.1
1990–99	growth rate	1.7	3.2	0.50	−0.3	1.9	0.4	2.0	4.4

Source: Author' calculations.

A12-1.a. Inflation

Years		MENA	Tunisia	Morocco	Algeria	Egypt	Jordan	Iran	Syria
1970s	Inflation	9	6	7	8	16	11	10	8
1980s	(%)	13	9	8	9	17	7	20	23
1990s	Average	11	5	4	20	13	5	24	8
1980–89	Annual	0.4	0.3	0.02	0.1	0.2	−0.4	0.9	1.4
1990–99	change	−0.2	−0.4	−0.3	1.1	−0.4	−0.2	0.4	−1.4
Total: p + p*SR									
1980–89	Contribution to	−0.02	−0.01	−0.001	−0.004	−0.01	0.02	−0.05	−0.07
1990–99	growth	0.01	0.02	0.020	−0.060	0.02	0.01	−0.02	0.07

Source: Authors' calculations.

A12-1.b. Black Market Exchange Rate Premium

Years		MENA	Tunisia	Morocco	Algeria	Egypt	Jordan	Iran	Syria
1970s	*bmp*	23.0	19.0	6.0	79.0	30.0	3.5	20.0	7.0
1980s	(%)	207.0	9.0	6.0	330.0	28.0	4.3	793.0	282.0
1990s	Average	268.0	5.0	4.0	191.0	13.0	4.5	1,349.0	307.0
1980–89	Annual	22.0	−7.3	0.5	14.0	−0.7	2.0	37.0	37.0
1990–99	growth rate	2.6	−4.9	−4.0	−5.5	−7.4	0.4	5.3	0.8
Total: bmp + bmp*SR									
1980–89	Contribution to	−1.2	0.4	−0.03	−0.8	0.04	−0.10	−2.1	−2.10
1990–99	growth	−0.1	0.3	0.20	0.3	0.40	−0.02	−0.3	−0.05

Source: Authors' calculations.

A12-1.c. Public Deficit

Years		MENA	Tunisia	Morocco	Algeria	Egypt	Jordan	Iran	Syria
1970s	Public deficit	−7.1	−2.9	−7.8	−5.1	−16.5	−9.9	−2.2	−5.4
1980s	(% GDP)	−7.8	−4.9	−7.6	−7.3	−12.5	−7.8	−7.3	−7.4
1990s	Average	−1.6	−3.4	−2.8	−0.9	−2.5	−0.9	0.6	−0.3
1980–89	Annual	0.03	0.2	−0.02	0.2	−0.4	−0.2	0.5	0.2
1990–99	change	−0.6	−0.2	−0.5	−0.6	−1.0	−0.7	−0.7	−0.7
Total PubDef + PubDef*SR									
1980–89	Contribution to	−0.03	−0.2	0.02	−0.2	0.4	0.2	−0.4	−0.2
1990–99	growth	0.5	0.1	0.4	0.6	0.9	0.6	0.6	0.6

Source: Authors' calculations.

A12-2. Impact of External Stability

Years	%	MENA	Tunisia	Morocco	Algeria	Egypt	Jordan	Iran	Syria
1980–89	Contribution to	−1.0	0.1	−0.8	0.1	−0.9	−0.4		−2.4
1990–99	growth	1.0	0.3	1.2	0.1	2.5	−1.1	0.6	0.8
1980–89	GDP per capita	0.0	1.6	1.4	0.1	2.2	−0.7	−3.5	−1.1
1990–99	growth rate	1.7	3.2	0.5	−0.3	1.9	0.4	2.0	4.4

Source: Authors' calculations.

A12-2.a. External Debt

Years		MENA	Tunisia	Morocco	Algeria	Egypt	Jordan	Iran	Syria
1970s	External debt	141	125	190	185	165	82		100
1980s	(% of exports)	219	139	300	178	350	136	42	389
1990s	Average	201	129	230	231	220	220	84	365
1980–89	Annual	9.9	1.4	11	−0.7	19	5.4		29.0
1990–99	change	−1.8	−1.0	−7	5.3	−13	8.4	4.2	−2.4
	LT Elasticity	−0.089							
1980–89	Contribution to	−0.9	−0.1	−1.0	0.1	−1.6	−0.5		−2.6
1990–99	growth	0.2	0.1	0.6	−0.5	1.2	−0.7	−0.4	0.2

Source: Authors' calculations.

A12-2.b. External Debt

Years		MENA	Tunisia	Morocco	Algeria	Egypt	Jordan	Iran	Syria
1970s	External debt	28	33	33	37	48	30		17
1980s	(% of GNI)	66	56	92	39	107	81	4	83
1990s	Average	80	59	72	63	61	147	21	135
1980–89	Annual	3.8	2.3	5.9	0.1	5.9	5.0		6.6
1990–99	change	1.4	0.4	−2.0	2.4	−4.6	6.6	1.6	5.2
	LT Elasticity	−0.003							
1980–89	Contribution to	−0.010	−0.01	−0.02	−0.0004	−0.02	−0.02		−0.02
1990–99	growth	−0.004	0.00	0.01	−0.0100	0.01	−0.02	0.00	−0.02

Source: Authors' calculations.

A12-2.c. Current Account Deficit

Years		MENA	Tunisia	Morocco	Algeria	Egypt	Jordan	Iran	Syria
1970s	Current account	−17	−26	−35	−24	−50	−11	26	−19
1980s	(% Exports)	−20	−20	−31	−14	−30	−8	−20	−14
1990s	Average	1	−15	−16	0	4	−16	4	4
1980–89	Annual	−0.3	0.6	0.4	1	2.0	0.3	−4.6	0.5
1990–99	change	2.1	0.5	1.5	1.4	3.4	−0.8	2.4	1.8
	LT Elasticity	0.396							
1980–89	Contribution to	−0.1	0.2	0.2	0.4	0.8	0.1	−1.8	0.2
1990–99	growth	0.8	0.2	0.6	0.6	1.3	−0.3	1.0	0.7

Source: Authors' calculations.

A12-3. Impact of Structural Reforms

Years	(%)	MENA	Tunisia	Morocco	Algeria	Egypt	Jordan	Iran	Syria
1980–89	Contribution to	0.2	0.6	0.1	−0.1	0.40	0.5	−0.05	−0.05
1990–99	growth	0.2	0.7	0.5	−0.8	−0.03	0.6	−0.10	0.40
1980–89	GDP per capita	0.0	1.6	1.4	0.1	2.20	−0.7	−3.50	−1.10
1990–99	growth rate	1.7	3.2	0.5	−0.3	1.90	0.4	2.00	4.40

Source: Authors' calculations.

A12-3.a. Trade Policy

Years		MENA	Tunisia	Morocco	Algeria	Egypt	Jordan	Iran	Syria
1970s	Trade openness	27	29	29	26	36	47	19	6
1980s	(% GDP)	26	47	31	11	41	43	7	3
1990s	Average	33	62	37	15	37	57	10	15
1980–89	Annual	−0.1	1.8	0.2	−1.4	0.4	−0.4	−1.2	−0.3
1990–99	change	0.7	1.5	0.6	0.3	−0.4	1.4	0.3	1.3
	LT Elasticity	0.24							
1980–89	Contribution to	−0.03	0.4	0.1	−0.3	0.1	−0.1	−0.3	−0.1
1990–99	growth	0.20	0.4	0.1	0.1	−0.1	0.3	0.1	0.3

Source: Authors' calculations.

A12-3.b. Financial Development

Years		MENA	Tunisia	Morocco	Algeria	Egypt	Jordan	Iran	Syria
1970s	Private credit	27	41	20	43	18	39	24	6
1980s	(% GDP)	35	47	21	52	28	59	33	7
1990s	Average	35	59	34	19	31	69	26	9
1980–89	Annual	0.80	0.6	0.1	1.0	1.1	2.0	0.9	0.1
1990–99	change	0.01	1.2	1.3	−3.3	0.3	1.0	−0.6	0.3
	LT Elasticity	0.27							
1980–89	Contribution to	0.2	0.2	0.03	0.3	0.3	0.5	0.2	0.02
1990–99	growth	0.0	0.3	0.40	−0.9	0.1	0.3	−0.2	0.10

Source: Authors' calculations.

A12-4. Impact of Human Capital

Years	%	MENA	Tunisia	Morocco	Algeria	Egypt	Jordan	Iran	Syria
1980–89	Contribution to	1.1	1.2	1.0	1.2	0.7	0.6	1.3	1.3
1990–99	growth	0.9	0.9	0.8	1.2	0.8	0.4	1.2	0.9
1980–89	GDP per capita	0.0	1.6	1.4	0.1	2.2	−0.7	−3.5	−1.1
1990–99	growth rate	1.7	3.2	0.5	−0.3	1.9	0.4	2.0	4.4

Source: Authors' calculations.

A12-4.a. Primary Education

Years		MENA	Tunisia	Morocco	Algeria	Egypt	Jordan	Iran	Syria
1970s	Primary Education	2.4	2.7	1.2	2.1	4.9	2.6	1.6	1.7
1980s	(number of years)	3.0	4.0	1.8	3.1	3.1	3.5	2.6	2.7
1990s	Average	3.7	4.8	2.3	3.9	3.6	4.0	3.9	3.7
1980–89	Annual	2.8	3.9	3.9	3.7	−4.4	3.2	4.9	4.6
1990–99	growth rate	2.3	1.8	2.4	2.5	1.3	1.4	4.1	3.4
	LT Elasticity	0.14							
1980–89	Contribution to	0.4	0.5	0.5	0.5	−0.6	0.4	0.7	0.6
1990–99	growth	0.3	0.2	0.3	0.3	0.2	0.2	0.6	0.5

Source: Authors' calculations.

A12-4.b. Infant Mortality

Years		MENA	Tunisia	Morocco	Algeria	Egypt	Jordan	Iran	Syria
1970s	Infant mortality	122	99	117	123	277	43	118	79
1980s	(/1000 population)	65	56	81	71	95	37	70	47
1990s	Average	41	33	56	36	57	32	43	34
1980–89	Annual	−6.3	−5.8	−3.7	−5.6	−10.7	−1.5	−5.2	−5.3
1990–99	growth rate	−4.5	−5.1	−3.8	−6.8	−5.1	−1.6	−4.9	−3.2
	LT Elasticity	−0.12							
1980–89	Contribution to	0.8	0.7	0.4	0.7	1.3	0.2	0.6	0.6
1990–99	growth	0.5	0.6	0.5	0.8	0.6	0.2	0.6	0.4

Source: Authors' calculations.

A12-5. Impact of Physical Infrastructures

Years	%	MENA	Tunisia	Morocco	Algeria	Egypt	Jordan	Iran	Syria
1980–89	Contribution to	1.4	1.3	1.0	1.0	1.0	1.6	1.8	1.5
1990–99	growth	1.0	1.0	1.3	0.5	−0.9	0.5	1.7	1.4
1980–89	GDP per capita	0.0	1.6	1.4	0.1	2.2	−0.7	−3.5	−1.1
1990–99	growth rate	1.7	3.2	0.5	−0.3	1.9	0.4	2.0	4.4

Source: Authors' calculations.

A12-5.a. Telephone Lines

Years		MENA	Tunisia	Morocco	Algeria	Egypt	Jordan	Iran	Syria
1970s	Telephone lines	14	11	7	9	9	17	17	16
1980s	(/1000 population)	28	26	11	24	17	52	28	39
1990s	Average	59	58	40	41	37	74	75	78
1980–89	Annual	7.2	8.1	4.7	10.0	6.8	11.2	4.9	8.5
1990–99	growth rate	7.5	8.1	13.1	5.5	8.2	3.6	9.8	7.0
	LT Elasticity	0.1							
1980–89	Contribution to	0.8	0.8	0.5	1.0	0.7	1.1	0.5	0.9
1990–99	growth	0.8	0.8	1.3	0.5	0.8	0.4	1.0	0.7

Source: Authors' calculations.

A12-5.b. Road Network

Years		MENA	Tunisia	Morocco	Algeria	Egypt	Jordan	Iran	Syria
1970s	Road network	0.068	0.121	0.094	0.032	0.025	0.043	0.035	0.092
1980s	(km/km2)	0.093	0.168	0.130	0.032	0.032	0.060	0.085	0.141
1990s	Average	0.111	0.188	0.133	0.030	0.009	0.065	0.135	0.218
1980–89	Annual	3.0	3.3	3.2	−0.1	1.8	3.2	8.9	4.2
1990–99	growth rate	1.8	1.1	0.2	−0.5	−11.3	0.8	4.6	4.4
	LT Elasticity	0.15							
1980–89	Contribution to	0.6	0.5	0.50	−0.01	0.3	0.5	1.3	0.6
1990–99	growth	0.3	0.2	0.03	−0.10	−1.7	0.1	0.7	0.7

Source: Authors' calculations.

A12-6. Contributions to Growth: MENA Countries Summary

Years	(%)	MENA	Tunisia	Morocco	Algeria	Egypt	Jordan	Iran	Syria
Macroeconomic stability									
1980–89	Contribution to	−1.3	0.2	−0.01	−1.0	0.4	0.1	−2.6	−2.4
1990–99	growth	0.4	0.4	0.70	0.8	13.0	0.6	0.3	0.6
External stability									
1980–89	Contribution to	−1.0	0.1	−0.8	0.1	−0.9	−0.4		−2.4
1990–99	growth	1.0	0.3	1.2	0.1	2.5	−1.1	0.6	0.8
Structural reforms									
1980–89	Contribution to	0.2	0.6	0.1	−0.1	0.4	0.5	−0.05	−0.05
1990–99	growth	0.2	0.7	0.5	−0.8	−0.03	0.6	−0.10	0.4
Human capital									
1980–89	Contribution to	1.1	1.2	1.0	1.2	0.7	0.6	1.3	1.3
1990–99	growth	0.9	0.9	0.8	1.2	0.8	0.4	1.2	0.9
Physical infrastructures									
1980–89	Contribution to	1.4	1.3	1.0	1.0	1.0	1.6	1.8	1.5
1990–99	growth	1.0	1.0	1.3	0.5	−0.9	0.5	1.7	1.4
Investment									
1980–89	Contribution to	−0.3	0.1	0.1	−0.3	−1.5	−0.24	−0.1	−0.03
1990–99	growth	−0.1	−0.1	−0.1	−0.2	−0.4	0.01	0.15	0.15
Total									
1980–89	Contribution to	0.1	3.5	1.4	0.9	0.1	2.2	0.4	−2.1
1990–99	growth	3.4	3.2	4.4	1.6	3.3	1.0	3.9	4.3
GDP per capita									
1980–89	Annual growth	0.0	1.6	1.4	0.1	2.2	−0.7	−3.5	−1.1
1990–99	rate	1.7	3.2	0.5	−0.3	1.9	0.4	2.0	4.4

Source: Authors' calculations.

Appendix Notes

1. In the case of macroeconomic stability, for example, the first component is weighted by 40/72 and the second by (72-40)/72, where 40 is the explanatory power of the first principal component and (72-40) the explanatory power of the second one. These coefficients are normalized by dividing by 72, which corresponds to the percentage of the variance of the initial indicators, explained by the two principal components selected.

2. For a better reading of the graphs and of the composite indicators, we have inverted the sign of the macroeconomic and external stability indexes. They can be interpreted as the efforts to reform the economy. The same thing has been done for the human capital indicator (see signs of the initial and composite indicators in tables A2.1 to A2.5)

3. Iran could not find long-term loans in the international market. Algeria and Tunisia followed a more cautious policy.

4. The case of Syria has to be treated with caution because of the Russian debt.

5. These indicators could, for example, be the nature and the quality of the loans, the ratio of reserves of the banks, or the percentage of loans through private banks. If such indicators were taken into consideration, the picture of the banking system would be different, with, in particular, a not always healthy sector, a very present State, and a slow pace of privatization (specifically in Algeria, Egypt, Tunisia, Iran, Syria; see Nabli, 2000).

6. Our trade openness indicator excludes the "natural" openness of the economy (see Frankel and Romer, 1999), as well as the exports of oil and mining products.

7. Trade policy should, however, be analyzed through other indicators, such as average tariffs and non-tariff barriers, which are not available on an yearly basis for a large sample of countries. By using these kinds of indicators from the mid-1980s and for a smaller sample of countries, Dasgupta, Keller and Srinivasan (2002) have shown that trade policy in MENA countries has historically been among the most restrictive in the world.

8. The analysis is, however, restricted by our limited number of indicators; that is to say the road network and the number of telephone lines per ,1000 population. Results would also have been different if we had included in our sample the Gulf economies, as well as other oil-producing countries.

9. Tunisia and Morocco offer a clear example of this situation. Despite a sharp economic slowdown during the 1980s, investment increased during this period.

3

After Argentina: Was MENA Right to Be Cautious?

Mustapha K. Nabli

Much has happened over the past few months to put the Middle East region into the spotlight of international attention. Perhaps most notable were the events following September 11. It is an increasing phenomenon that we see articles in the newspapers devoted to the region, sometimes looking to understand the causes of social exclusion, but almost always trying to understand better the region's economic and social structures. Our regional department in the World Bank is regularly called upon by some journalist seeking information about where the region stands in terms of economic growth, employment prospects, and political stability.

In this investigation, which has heightened of late, the progress that the region has made over the last decade, in terms of both achieving macroeconomic stability and initiating programs of structural reform, has become better known. Starting in the late 1980s, a handful of countries in the region—Morocco and Tunisia and, soon after, Jordan—embarked on programs of macroeconomic stabilization and policy reform. By the 1990s, nearly all of the non-Gulf Cooperation Council (GCC) countries in the region followed suit, as did several of the Gulf economies. The reasoning, of course, was to create an environment in which the private sector could emerge and become an engine for higher and sustainable economic growth—crucial for employment creation as well as for social cohesion. But at the same time, it must be conceded that the Middle East and North Africa region's (MENA) progress with structural reform has been incomplete. Financial sectors remain weak; trade

Speech at the Third Mediterranean Social and Research Meeting; Florence, Italy; March 2002.

liberalization remains incomplete, with continuing moderate to high protection levels; public ownership remains high; and the regulatory framework and supportive institutions for growth have not materialized.

As a result, the region has often been chastised by institutions such as the World Bank for not proceeding more quickly and deeply with its commitments to liberalization. But juxtaposed with this sense of frustration about the region's lack of continued progress with economic liberalization comes another event that has served in some circles to cast some doubt on what can be referred to as the "Washington Consensus" on economic reform programs: that being the recent crisis in Argentina. Until quite recently, Argentina was the darling of the international financial community. Within a single decade, it had embarked on an unprecedented effort, and had undone four decades of state interventionism. It deregulated most markets, but deregulation of labor markets was not deep enough. It privatized most state-owned enterprises, including difficult giants like the oil industry, railroads, and airlines. It radically reformed its social security system, substantially strengthened its financial sector, and swiftly aligned its economy to market forces. These policies revived the economy and brought stability to the country. But in a sudden shockwave, the country became engulfed in an unprecedented institutional, political, economic, and social crisis. Within a few days in December 2001, it changed presidents five times, its payment systems collapsed, it defaulted on its foreign and domestic debt, and it violated property rights. Argentina's real economy is imploding and the country's social fabric is being torn apart.

Looking at the current crisis in Argentina, the countries in the MENA region may be asking themselves: Were we right to be cautious? Did Argentina commit itself to an economic model that, in the end, suffers from some fatal flaws?

Before taking the Argentine crisis as confirmation of the need for guarded steps into economic liberalization and deregulation, one needs to look at its roots. I believe there are indeed lessons for the MENA economies from Argentina's example. Broadly, three factors, in combination, contributed to the collapse of the Argentine economy: first, a strict exchange rate rule that reduced competitiveness and the capacity to grow; second, a loose fiscal policy mix that generated an increase in public indebtedness; and third, a continuous weakening of the institutional environment. However, the collapse was not caused by liberalization of the economy. Liberalization strengthened the economy. It initially reduced economic imbalances, and the economy performed remarkably well until 1997. But as I intend here to speak to the MENA economies, if there is an additional lesson from Argentina regarding the role that liberalization played in the crisis there, it is that liberalization cannot be piecemeal. The liberalization process should present domestic enterprises with heightened competitive pressures, both international and domestic, but it should also allow them to respond —both positively to new opportunities and effectively to economic downturns. In Argentina, the lack of liberalization of labor markets reduced the economy's ability to adapt when it needed to adjust under reduced competitiveness abroad.

Let me take a few minutes to highlight the events that drove Argentina into crisis, and come back to these elements as they apply to lessons that can be taken by the economies of MENA. While all three of the factors I mentioned contributed in combination to the Argentine crisis, let me begin with the first factor:

The Exchange Rate Regime

To understand the story, we have to go back to the 1980s and early 1990s. In 1989, Argentina experienced hyperinflation at the same time as its first democratically elected president since the military dictatorship had to take an early leave. The incoming authorities at first failed with several stabilization attempts. But under very difficult circumstances, in 1991, the government made a radical change. It established a currency board that fixed the U.S. dollar price of the Argentine peso on a one-to-one basis, replacing its floating rate regime. This currency board, set up by law, provided a strong and reliable anchor. It succeeded in arresting inflation and providing price stability over the next 10 years.

Fixed exchange rate regimes require different preconditions from floating rates in order to be sustainable. Moreover, they also require a flexible economy that can swiftly adjust to exogenous shocks. During the late 1970s and early 1980s, Chile implemented a stabilization plan based on a fixed exchange rate. This plan failed, mainly because during its implementation the dollar appreciated substantially, and Chile could not withstand the appreciation of its own currency vis-à-vis the rest of the world.

On the other hand, a few years later, in 1985, Israel initiated a stabilization plan very similar to that of Chile and anchored its economy to the dollar through a fixed exchange rate. Israel's plan was successful, but this success was due in no small measure to the fact that in this period the dollar actually depreciated substantially.

The lesson of many experiments with fixed exchange rates is that most economies adjust better to real depreciation than to real appreciation of their currency.

During the 10-year period that Argentina kept its currency board, the U.S. dollar appreciated substantially, and Argentina's main trading partner, Brazil, devalued its currency by about 40 percent in real terms. Consequently, Argentina's multilateral real exchange rate appreciated substantially, and this disequilibrium required adjustment through deflation and unemployment.

During the early 1990s, the economy grew at very high rates, driven by a surge in capital inflows and the fact that the country was bouncing back from a deep crisis. In 1995, the economy suffered the "tequila effect" of the Mexican crisis, with a run on the banks and the sudden reduction in capital inflows. Later, in 1997, the Asian crisis led to a sharp fall in commodity prices. This meant that the Argentine equilibrium real exchange rate had depreciated. But instead of depreciating, the actual real exchange rate continued to appreciate, first because of the dollar's appreciation, and later because of the 1998 sharp depreciation of the Brazilian Real.

The exchange rate could not adjust to its new equilibrium value by nominal depreciation. It had to adjust through prices and quantities. Given the inflexibility of prices to downward pressures, the adjustment to lower nominal income had to be done through quantities, and real income took a dive.

It is at this point that the effects of the other factor propelling the crisis became evident:

Lack of Fiscal Discipline and Increasing Public Debt

A central issue in the crisis was the lack of fiscal discipline and its contribution to increasing public debt. During the years of massive privatization in Argentina, government expenditures were adjusted upward with the huge influx of privatization revenues (see figure 3.1). Between 1989 and 1994, for example, expenditures kept almost identical pace with overall revenues—including privatization proceeds. Once privatization revenues began to decline, however, an adjustment of spending never took place. Spending as a percentage of GDP remained almost unchanged between 1994 and 1997, despite the decline in overall revenues of about 1.5 percent of GDP.

The last three years of the Menem administration (1997-99) were characterized by excessive government spending, at both the federal and provincial levels. Government spending as a percent of GDP increased from 14 percent to 22 percent. At the time, the political system was split between the national

Figure 3.1. Government Spending as a Percentage of GDP and Revenues (including debt and privatization)

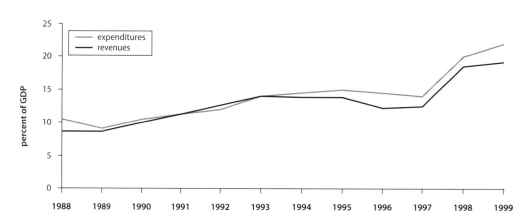

government (following a proprivatization, promarket policy) and the provincial governments (oriented to high-cost social programs). Because the provincial governors had direct control over national legislators, the Menem regime used revenues gathered from privatization and foreign investment to shower the provinces with money, to win their support for the national program.[1]

Lack of economic growth, combined with an expansion in government expenditures, generated a fiscal deficit that grew from 0.15 percent of GDP in 1994 to 2.4 percent in 2000. To achieve fiscal balance without distorting the economy, the government could have lowered its expenditures. Instead, it chose to finance the fiscal deficit by raising taxes and incurring additional debt in financial markets and with the IMF. Raising taxes proved to be a bad tactic; it generated more tax evasion and suffocated an already hobbled private sector.[2]

The extra tax burden and the reduction in credit to the private sector diminished the investment rate and reduced productivity. This, in combination with the loss of competitiveness, drove the economy into recession.

The recession led to double-digit unemployment. Early in 2000, the new government made the crucial mistake of increasing tax rates in the middle of a deep recession. Naturally, this exacerbated the recession, and instead of increasing fiscal revenues, the tax hikes reduced them. The higher fiscal deficit had to be adjusted with lower expenditures and financed with higher debt issues. Lower expenditures also worsened the recession. In this setting, the country debt became very risky, and interest rates on public debt soared.

With the soaring interest rates, the burden of the debt became unsustainable. The IMF and other international financial institutions (IFIs) continued supporting the currency board with huge multibillion-dollar loans. This did not solve the underlying disequilibria. By late 2001, the government had defaulted on its external debt held by domestic creditors, mainly banks and pension funds. It forced a swap of its high-yielding debt for new debt "guaranteed with future fiscal revenues" and yielding only 7 percent. The policy to restructure, on a "voluntary" basis, a good part of the domestic debt improved finances in the short term but complicated debt management for years to come, and signaled to the markets clear problems with Argentina's debt sustainability capacity, despite the seemingly comfortable levels in traditional debt indicators. The market interpreted this as a clear sign of unsustainability, which resulted in large withdrawals from the banking system.

The Central Bank issued a regulation putting a ceiling on interest rates. This was another element that helped to trigger the banking crisis. Banks had been paying a rate much higher than the new ceiling to keep deposits inside the system. The fixing of interest rates was the fatal blow to stability; a full-fledged currency crisis ensued. The flawed and time-inconsistent macroeconomic policy, the price fixing, a very weak president, and this not-so-"voluntary" debt swap with institutional investors and banks led to a run on

Figure 3.2. GDP Growth, 1988–2001

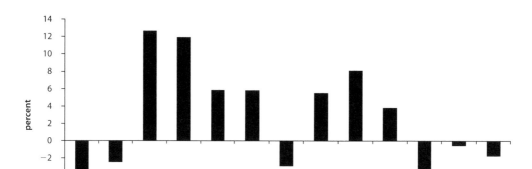

the banks and the collapse of the payment system. The financial fortress built over a decade was destroyed overnight.

Weakening of Institutional Environment

This component played a crucial role in destroying confidence in Argentina's economy and political institutions. It started gradually, during President Menem's unsuccessful attempt at reelection, which included a significant loosening of the fiscal stance. It was followed by the Alianza strategy, in 1999, to defeat Menem rather than govern. There followed a crisis in the senate in 2000, associated with the mild labor reform and the resignation of the Vice President in October 2000. This crisis tarnished the possibility of serious reform in the labor market in the future.

The weakest link was the fiscal regime that tied the federal government and the rest of the country together, which remained discretional and full of loopholes. Provincial governments depended upon on taxes raised at the federal level, while the municipalities depended upon taxes raised at the provincial level, with no balance between the political benefits of public services and the political costs of raising revenues. As the budget situation deteriorated, transfers from Buenos Aires to the provincial governments became a matter for day-to-day political bargaining.[3]

As the situation became increasingly complex, the rescue package from the IMF, in December 2000, gave some breathing room, but generated further (and excessive) loosening of the fiscal stance and culminated with the IMF losing confidence in Argentina's capacity to adjust.

The fiscal crisis, political mess, and debt overhang led the government to seek an orderly solution—restructuring public debt—but this proved impossible, as ordinary Argentines and foreign investors opted out of the system.

The market attempt at working out the money overhang led to the controversial decision to freeze the deposits. The public banks became a great liability as the crisis developed, pushing the country deeper into crisis, as the government lacked the political support to deal with them.

What can the MENA economies learn from the crisis in Argentina? Let's begin by talking about financial system, and the relationship between the financial system and macroeconomic fundamentals.

In 1999, Argentina had one of the strongest banking systems in Latin America. This was the result of several strategic decisions, including: requiring banks to hold capital ratios much higher than those demanded by the Basel Accord principles; imposing high loan-loss provisions and strict international accounting standards; actively favoring the entrance of large foreign banks; requiring that banks issue subordinated debt; demanding that banks be rated by international rating agencies; imposing reserve requirements higher than 20percent on liquid deposits, not withstanding their initial time structure; addressing the lack of a lender of last resort by buying insurance from international banks, in the form of contingent credit lines that would trigger in the case of a currency run.

During its convertibility experiment, Argentina increased its debt to the IFIs in an unprecedented way. In exchange for credit, the IFIs required and agreed with the government on the enactment of multiple and difficult measures to strengthen its capital markets. On every aspect related to capital markets, Argentina "went by the book" as written by the IFIs and, in this way, constructed a real financial fortress. However, one year later its banking system was on the brink of complete insolvency. The meltdown was instantaneous.

The question is "Why?" The answer is: economic shock resulting from the accumulation of disequilibria related to time-inconsistent macroeconomic policies and the loss of credibility in economic and political institutions. The "books" had left out a critically important chapter.

The lesson from this recent Argentine episode, as well as from others, is that microeconomic reform in the financial sector is very important, but not sufficient. No matter how strong the financial sector is; no matter how much expertise and confidence foreign banks may bring to the financial system, and how large their share of total lending; no matter how well the Basel regulations are put into place and enforced; if macroeconomic policies generate large disequilibria, they may lead to a real systemic implosion. This is a lesson that should be learned by other countries that are currently running significant macroeconomic imbalances.

Another lesson from the Argentine episode relates to the deleterious influence of government's debt finance on capital markets. Even during the exuberant period of the currency board experience and the substantial strengthening of the banking system, the Argentine stock exchange languished. The number of listed instruments was steadily reduced from 204 in 1989 to 125 in

1999. The number of listing companies also declined sharply. The pension reform provided funds that were mainly used for government debt and bank CDs. The stronger companies listed in foreign stock exchanges. Liquidity was substantially reduced.

The decline of the Buenos Aires Stock Exchange (BASE) during the 1990s can be directly related to the government's debt finance crowding out the private sector. During 1996-2000, as an average, 86 percent of net primary issues dealt through the stock exchange were fixed income instruments, and of those 76 percent were government issues. The overwhelming presence of the government was even more dramatic in relation to liquidity: More than 90 percent of trade was done on the Treasury's fixed income products.

Now, let me return to the MENA region, and look at what we have learned from the Argentine crisis. To begin, let's address the issue of a fixed exchange rate. In the MENA region, fixed exchange rates are still pervasive. In two-thirds of the economies of the MENA region, fixed exchange rate arrangements, whether explicit or implicit, are in place, despite the fact that worldwide, only half of economies operate under a de facto fixed exchange rate system (and only one-third have official fixed arrangements). The preoccupation with macroeconomic stability during the 1990s played a large role in maintaining nominally fixed and stable exchange rates, but it has meant that one important tool to make exports more profitable was surrendered.

There are many other reasons for the region continuing to rely on more rigid exchange rate arrangements, but both debt and oil play a role. By maintaining a fixed regime, and in particular an overvalued exchange rate, the governments in the region have an easy means to decrease their payments on foreign-denominated debt at the expense of domestic borrowers, who face tighter monetary policy, and of national industries whose competitiveness is weakened. In addition, the public sector's role as exporter of oil provides additional incentive to adopt a fixed regime, as it allows for directly subsidizing imports by the public sector.

But the lesson of Argentina on the fixed exchange rate should send a signal about what can happen when an overvalued rate is maintained, and what that implies for domestic industries and laborers. In Argentina's case, the fixed exchange rate contributed to reduce the competitiveness of the economy in a period of strong appreciation of the dollar. The devaluation of the Brazilian Real in 1999 deepened competitiveness problems from which the economy never recovered. The loss in competitiveness, and the sustained decline in real output since 1999, helped to destroy Argentina's credibility and increase its cost of capital. As the cost of capital increased, the needed downward adjustment on wages became too much to bear, particularly when labor market flexibility was weak. For each 1 percent increase in the interest rate, wages needed to decline by about 3 percent to maintain competitiveness. During 1990-98, the adjustment in unit labor costs came from increases in productivity that preserved the level of wages. Since 1999, the adjustments have come through reduction in labor costs and wages, which has depressed consumption. Since the tax structure of Argentina is based on indirect taxes, the reduction in consumption reduced tax receipts and deepened the fiscal imbalances, generating a fiscal crisis when government expenditures were impossible to contain.

What are the lessons that emerge on debt, in terms of its role in the Argentine crisis? The most important is that debt, even small debt, can become a major issue once credibility is lost. In Argentina's case, debt sustainability became an issue as the economy imploded, despite what we would term moderate levels of public debt. But when the spreads increased, the capacity to rollover or refinance public debt abroad vanished, forcing the government to impose a "voluntary" debt swap on domestic banks and other institutional investors. Although restructuring part of the debt improved finances short term, it also sent a powerful signal to markets of Argentina's debt sustainability, despite the appearance of comfortable debt levels by traditional indicators.

Within the MENA economies, outside of the Gulf economies, the size of public sector debt is substantially higher than that Argentina exhibited at the time of the crisis. At the time the crisis unfolded, public debt as a percentage of GDP was about 56 percent in Argentina. That compares to debt ratios of 85 percent in Egypt, over 60 percent in Algeria, Morocco, and Tunisia, over 100 percent in Jordan, and close to 170 percent in Lebanon. So, at the start, the MENA economies are saddled by extensively higher amounts of debt.

What is of greater importance than the debt level, however, is the maturity of these debts. It is not enough to comfort oneself into security by observing that the structure of debt is predominantly long term. Even long-term debt at some point becomes due. And when debt becomes due, the issue of credibility becomes important. If an event makes the payment of that debt impossible, then the economy must have credibility that the debt will be repaid, so that debt restructuring or rollovers can occur. In the case of Argentina, the lack of credibility put a complete halt to the possibility of rolling over the debt after the first "voluntary" debt swap. The problem was not how fast the debt was projected to grow, but that no one wanted to lend more resources to Argentina. The loss in the credibility of Argentina's capacity to repay its debt became an anchor in the crisis, and a run on the banking system by depositors occurred.

How is credibility maintained? In the case of Argentina, a decade of credibility was ultimately lost through reluctance to address serious reform of the labor market combined with the significantly loosened fiscal stance leading up to the 1999 elections.

What should the MENA countries learn from the Argentine crisis regarding the loss of credibility? There are many lessons, but they cannot be encapsulated into a few key economic indicators. Credibility is the fusion of many factors. Certainly, though, macroeconomic stability is vital, and upholding a tight fiscal stance sends a strong signal of the government's commitment to maintaining that stability. Most of the MENA economies, after deteriorating budget deficits in the early 1990s, embarked on programs of macroeconomic stabilization and structural reform designed to bring budgets back into balance. But several economies have also let their fiscal stance loosen since then. In Egypt, the near budget balance realized in 1997 turned to deficit again by 1998, which through the late 1990s averaged 4.6 percent of GDP. In Jordan, the budget surplus of 1 percent of GDP in 1995 also turned to deficit the following year, and by 1998 was close to 6 percent of GDP. In Algeria, the budget surplus of 3 percent of GDP in 1996 was followed by a budget deficit of 4 percent of GDP by 1998. While fiscal imbalances are not steadily growing in any countries in the region—which would send a signal of an impending crisis—we are seeing a laxness in maintaining fiscal determination that is simply unsafe given the levels of debt in the region.

Second, credibility cannot be bought through rhetoric. Markets are keenly observant of actions. When Egypt's progress in structural reform lagged, Standard and Poor's revised its outlook on the economy from stable to negative (though it did not adjust the country's risk rating), and Thomson Financial revised Egypt's sovereign risk rating outlook from positive to stable. While the comprehensive macroeconomic and structural reform programs espoused by many of the MENA economies in the early 1990s created an exuberant boost in their economic outlooks, markets will not wait forever. The MENA region must move beyond "stroke of the pen" reforms to the more serious, and challenging, issues that obstruct the development of a strong private sector. Unless the private sector begins to see itself as an independent source of growth and productivity in the economy, and society begins to underpin this change economically and politically, it is unlikely that any of the past economic reforms in themselves will be adequate.

It is not possible to go into detail about all of the issues that hinder the development of strong private sector-led growth in the region, but I will point out a few.

To begin, there is the size of the public sector. Governments may account for as much as 40-60 percent of gross domestic output and of employment in the region. This includes continuing high expenditures on military and social services, which account for the large size of the public sector. The big role of the state—a sector that essentially has low productivity and limited inherent potential for productivity gain—is a drag on growth in most economies in the region. Efforts to reduce the public sector through rationalizing public employment, improving performance through better incentives and institutions, and privatization of goods and services that could be produced more efficiently in the private sector have begun in many countries. But by and large, these efforts remain slow and halfhearted to date.

Second, there is the issue of trade reform. Trade policies in the region remain among of the most restrictive in the world. The degree and speed of integration into the world economy are low. Tariff rates remain high and the extent of nontariff barriers significant. A number of policy moves across the region are expected to lead to greater trade openness, stimulating integration and, it is hoped, growth. Most notable are the EU association agreements signed by Tunisia, Morocco, Jordan, and Algeria. This type of effort needs to be systematic.

Among the most important reforms is that of the banking sector. However, it is lagging, particularly as evidenced by the slow progress of privatizing state banks in countries including Algeria, Egypt, Tunisia, Iran, and Syria. While in a number of countries the banking sectors are relatively healthy, this is not the case in most, and financial sector development remains a principal constraint for the development of the private sector and for growth.

Finally, the region needs a virtual overhaul of its system of property rights, better legal systems, and improved contract enforcement mechanisms.

I will end this talk now, going back to where I started, and ask whether the MENA countries should be cautious, given the events in Argentina. The answer, of course, is yes. Yes, they should be cautious about the factors that precipitated the crisis in Argentina, including debt sustainability, fiscal determination, and exchange rate management. And in terms of reform, yes, there is a lesson of caution here for the MENA countries as well. But the caution does not suggest slowing the reform agenda in order to avert the type of crisis that Argentina is experiencing. If anything, the caution is that liberalization, whatever its speed, must be complete. The liberalization of one sector can be undone by the lack of liberalization of another sector. The elimination of trade barriers, for example, can be undermined if the financial sector is not liberalized, and if public sector banks control the financing of imports. Changes in the investment code are moot if labor laws impede the ability of firms to maintain competitiveness.

And so, I hope that the crisis in Argentina does serve some purpose for the countries of MENA in evaluating their steps forward, and that as a region, it renews its commitments to furthering and deepening the economic and structural reforms it began—so that higher and sustainable economic growth can be ensured, so that employment creation will meet the demands of a growing workforce, so that needs are met and opportunities expanded for the poor, and so that a crisis such as the Argentines are currently facing never occurs in the MENA region.

Notes

1. Mark Reutter; News Bureau; University of Illinois at Urbana-Champaign; December 21, 2001.

2. Ana I. Eiras and Brett D. Schaefer; Backgrounder; The Heritage Foundation; April 9, 2001.

3. Center for International Development. "The Grand Illusions." Andres Velasco. 2002.

4

Restarting Arab Economic Reform

Mustapha K. Nabli

Achieving greater international competitiveness often depends upon policy reform. Increasingly, the development community has come to appreciate not only the "what" of policy reform, but the "how." Economic policy reform is far from a straightforward undertaking. It is a deeply political issue. It affects the balance of power between actors in society; at its core, it involves finding the economic rents that have built up over the years and cutting them back; it attacks the economic privilege that some have enjoyed for generations. It is little surprise that carrying forward comprehensive economic reform is a profoundly difficult task.

This has been acutely apparent from the reform experience of the Arab region. Beginning in the mid-1980s, when several early reformers in the region—Egypt, Jordan, Morocco, and Tunisia—all implemented a broad range of macroeconomic policy and structural reform efforts, there was great optimism for change in the region. These hopes were heightened when other countries in the region successively followed suit. Now however, two decades after the nascent reform movement, and observing the subsequent slowdown in the pace of reform, and the inability to tackle deeper and more fundamental arrangements inhibiting growth, those in the development community must contend with the importance of the myriad forces *behind* policy reform.

In the following paper, I review the reform experience in the Arab region and discuss some of the factors which have inhibited the implementation of a deeper reform agenda. Among other factors, soft budget constraints and

Published in the *Arab World Competitiveness Report 2005*. Reprinted by permission from Palgrave Macmillan.

weaknesses in governance have both contributed to a lack of momentum in carrying forward the reforms needed for higher and sustained growth. The region's ability to continue to rely on oil, aid, and other strategic rents has allowed it to delay implementing deeper and more difficult reforms. Moreover, the lack of both accountable and inclusive governance mechanisms has prevented the emergence of coalitions for reform in the region, a central element of successful reform programs.

This paper first discusses the Arab reform agenda and the progress made to date. It then examines the reasons behind the stalled reform agenda in the region and ways in which to move the reform agenda forward. Concluding remarks are then presented.

The Arab Reform Agenda and Progress to Date

Four recent reports published by the World Bank[1] spell out fundamental transitions needed in the Arab economies to move to higher and more sustainable sources of growth, identifying three realignments in particular: a transition from public sector- dominated to private sector-led economies; from closed to more open economies; and from oil-dominated and volatile economies to more stable and diversified economies. Critical for completing these transitions will be better governance, improved quality of education, and greater gender equality throughout the region. As one of the reports points out, *few of these recommendations are new to the citizens or government of the region.*[2] The Arab reform agenda is well known. And the urgency for reform is growing.

One of the fundamental challenges facing the Arab world over the next two decades is job creation. In the next 10 years,[3] some 31 million new workers will have been added to the stock of Arab laborers, expanding the labor force by more than a third.[4] In the next 20 years, that figure grows to some 65 million new jobs needed, just to absorb the growing labor force, or an expansion in the labor force of almost 70 percent.

In addition, there are the region's unemployed, who constitute about 13 percent of the labor force. If the region is also to address job creation for the stock of unemployed, some 77 million new jobs will need to be created between 2004-24, almost doubling the number of jobs in the region.

To give perspective on these numbers, figure 4.1 presents the employment growth rates in several East Asian economies during periods of expansive job creation. Some of these countries managed the highest rates of sustained employment growth in modern history. In China, employment growth over the two decades between 1980 and 2000 averaged slightly over 40 percent. Korea's employment growth over the 1980s and 1990s was slightly less than 60 percent. Malaysia's employment growth was highest in East Asia over the 1980s and 1990s, with almost a 90 percent increase in jobs. These countries listed can be considered to have had some of the greatest spurts in employ-

Figure 4.1. Required Job Growth in Arab Region, versus International Experiences

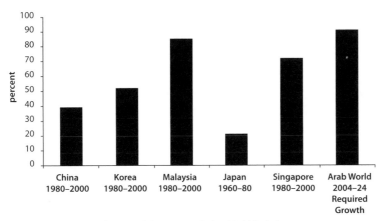

Source: World Development Indicators; U.S. Department of Labor; World Bank data.

ment growth over a sustained period of time. And the Arab region needs to do even better.

Add to these demographics that the traditional modes of employment creation in the region are fast coming to an end. Public sectors are unable to be the employment outlets they have been in the past. Labor migration prospects have diminished.

This is an extraordinary challenge that is facing this region. It is estimated that economic growth will need to average over 6 percent a year for a sustained period of time to create these kinds of employment levels.

It is against this backdrop that the state of economic reform in the region needs to be examined. We generally trace the Arab reform movement to the efforts by a handful of economies in the region in the mid to late 1980s toward macroeconomic stabilization and structural reform. Following the collapse in oil prices, and facing high debt, deteriorating budget deficits, and a lack of growth, a few countries—Morocco, Tunisia, and Jordan, and subsequently Egypt—adopted programs aimed at restoring macroeconomic balances and promoting the private sector as an engine for growth. By the late 1980s and early 1990s, most other countries in the region had followed suit, adopting some form of economic stabilization.

The macroeconomic stabilization achievements were non-negligible, as most Arab countries undertook better macroeconomic policies. Debt renegotiations and write-offs helped reduce the very large and unsustainable debt burdens and helped achieve improvements in the fiscal deficits. Continuing macroeconomic stabilization efforts have helped to contain inflation to less than 2 percent over the past three years, down from an average of 11 percent in 1991.[5] Fiscal deficits have been reduced by about two-thirds, and total external debt has declined from an average of 40 percent of gross national income in 1990 down to 28 percent in 2002,[6] with the largest declines achieved in Egypt, Morocco, Yemen, and Jordan. These achievements have largely been sustained when one looks at the standard indicators of macroeconomic stability. However, macroeconomic stability is not a foregone conclusion. Contingent liabilities have been building up in many of the Arab countries, related to the accumulating implicit debts from many sources, such as the pension systems, the banking sectors, the public enterprises, and a variety of explicit and implicit government guarantees. Thus, while macroeconomic stability has been broadly achieved, the fundamentals behind stability have, in some cases, weakened.

In terms of accompanying structural reforms, the results have been more mixed. A few early reformers have implemented more intensive reforms toward market-oriented, private sector-led economies, signing EU-Med agreements, implementing tax reform, undertaking trade and financial sector liberalization. Others have pursued reform more sporadically and slowly. Still others have made more modest progress. But by and large, the pace and intensity of the reform effort have been weak.

As evidence of this, some of the standard indicators of market-orientation or private sector development point to the Arab region remaining well below potential:

- The ratio of private investment to public investment hovers around 1.8, and has remained substantially unchanged since the early 1990s. In comparison, the private to public ratio averages 5 in East Asia.
- Arab manufacturing sectors are small—almost half the typical levels of other lower-middle-income economies.
- Trade integration—the ratio of trade to GDP—has actually declined over the last 25 years, averaging about 90 percent in 1980, compared with only 65 percent today.
- Exports other than oil are about a third of what they could be,[7] given the region's characteristics in terms of natural endowments, size and geography.
- Foreign direct investment could be five or six times higher.[8]

As a result, economic growth has lagged well below what is required to meet the region's employment challenge. Over the last decade, economic growth in the region has averaged about 3.7 percent per year[9]—less than two-thirds the rate needed over the next 20 years to meet the coming employment challenges.

The Failure to Sustain Deep Reforms

What has prevented a more intensive reform effort? There are certainly the regional security issues and conflicts which have been used to justify the maintenance of the status quo and the need to avoid risks of instability due to change and reform. And while there is a heated debate about the merits of such justifications, and it can be argued that such factors have played some role—which varies from country to country—in delaying reforms, there are two other major fundamental factors which stand out, and which are certainly more important.

The first has been the ability to continue to rely on oil and strategic aid to delay implementing a deeper economic reform agenda. The substantial revenues from oil, which declined throughout the 1980s and 1990s, remained significant, and have even spiraled upwards over the last several years, giving Arab leaders and the public a temporary sense of economic health (figure 4.2). This, along with foreign aid and strategic rents, has permitted Arab governments to adopt limited reforms and postpone the fundamental reforms needed for higher growth and employment creation.

There is a line of thinking that deep economic reform movements result only from fundamental *change,* either from leadership change (regime change, or a shift in governing coalition); or from dramatic economic change—in other words economic crisis. In many Latin American countries, for example, economic reforms were undertaken only when the "economic conditions had deteriorated sufficiently so that there emerged a political imperative for better economic performance."[10] Or, put another way, reform often is only adopted "once the possibilities of throwing money at the problem are foreclosed."[11] Indeed, the reform movement initiated in the Arab region was a direct consequence of the oil price collapse of the early 1980s.

There is certainly room for debate about whether crisis is necessary for reform, and there have been at least a few examples of gradualism in reform which were not driven by open crises—in China and Vietnam, to name two. But what is true is that the availability of a soft budget constraint in the region

Figure 4.2. Net Oil Export Revenues in Arab OPEC, Selected Years

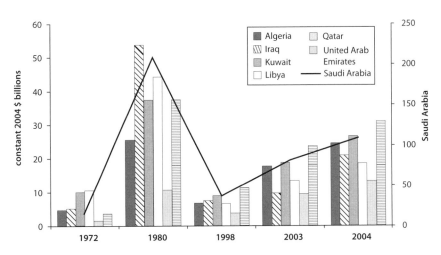

Source: U.S. Energy Information Administration.
Note: 2004 revenues based on estimated price per barrel of $39.

has delayed a change in the economic and social perspective needed to implement deeper reforms.

But the second and assuredly more important factor behind why reforms have stagnated has been the lack of coalitions emerging to press the government for deeper reforms and better policy choices. And underlying the lack of coalitions for change in the region are i) a resistance to reform by those included and protected by the status quo arrangements, and ii) an inability to mobilize and demand changes by those who might benefit from change.

The theory of collective action rests on the hypothesis that organized groups apply more pressure on politicians than unorganized groups.[12] Inherently, a central problem with successfully implementing reform is that those whose rents will be lost know who they are, but those who might benefit from reform are generally more dispersed and have a much vaguer notion of how economic reform will benefit them. Indeed, they may feel that they will lose with reform. In the Arab world, this situation is complicated by governance issues that further hinder the ability for potential beneficiaries of reform to band together for change.

Resistance by Those Protected by the Status Quo

Following independence, and in part to redress social inequity, a social contract between the government and the public developed throughout the Arab region, characterized by stateplanning, protection of local markets, and an encompassing view of the state in providing welfare, social services, and even employment. Economies became heavily protected and labor markets became highly regulated, with a strong emphasis on employment protection. Businesses developed under the patronage of governments, basically living off the state.

After the initial reforms in the 1980s and early 1990s, often undertaken under crisis conditions, and with economic conditions deteriorating or not improving, resistance to reform has deepened among those groups whom the social contract protects.

Internationally, one of the most effective lobbies for policy change is private business. Although the yardstick of firm preferences comes down to the ability to make profits, their interests are often closely aligned with those of society: greater profits can allow for greater job creation, growth, and poverty reduction.

But the private sector in most Arab economies is underdeveloped, with a predominance of small and family businesses. This is particularly evident in the manufacturing sector. In a recent paper,[13] we constructed an index of the lobby power of the manufacturing sector worldwide, estimated as an integrative of the size of the manufacturing sector in total exports and the concentration of manufacturing exports within the sector.[14] Thus, countries in which the manufacturing sector accounted for a large proportion of exports,

Figure 4.3. Manufacturing Export Lobby Power in Arab Region, Late 1990s

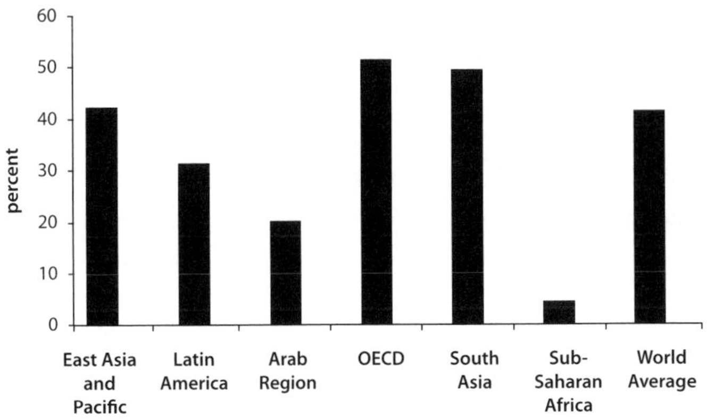

Source: Nabli, Keller, and Véganzonès, 2004.
Note: Regional averages weighted by national populations.

other things equal, would be expected to be better able to influence government policy. Likewise, the more concentrated the manufacturing sector, in terms of a few export categories, the more manufacturers could be expected to band together with a common interest to influence the government's policies. From these estimates, we found that in the Arab region, the lobby power of the manufacturing sector was lower than in any other region of the world but Sub-Saharan Africa, with a measured index of approximately 0.22 in the late 1990s,[15] compared with an average worldwide of 0.43, and lobby indices of over 0.4 in the OECD, South Asia, and East Asia.

The large-scale private sector, when it exists, is dominated by industries that benefit from the status quo, manipulating government policy for their own gain—the so- called state capture of government regulation. Actions range from persistent awarding of large public sector contracts to a few well-connected groups, to actual change in laws and regulations that lower the costs or increase the profitability of such groups.[16]

Internationally, trade unions have often proven instrumental in organizing support for comprehensive reform. In several Eastern European countries, for example, trade unions played an important role in designing and implementing large scale privatization programs. In the Arab world, independent trade unions are rare[17]—trade unions were banned in several GCC economies until recently, and in several other Arab countries, trade union membership is limited to a single national trade union. Throughout the Arab region, union activity is strictly controlled. As a result, without real independence from the political system, trade unions have not been effective in organizing the labor force to press for reform. At the same time, for those within the system, transitioning to a new development model implies abandoning the job security from which they benefited under the old social contract.

In reaction to these deep-seated fears, the intellectual climate and underlying ideologies in the Arab world have continued to be supportive of ideas which are not friendly to reforms that promote markets, integration in the world economy, a stronger role for the private sector, and less interference of government in the economic sphere.

Inability to Contest Policies by Those Who Would Benefit from Change

But additionally, the ability of those "outside the net" to contest for changes has been muted. Not all groups have been well represented in the region's social contract—indeed the region's development paradigm has suffered from great weaknesses in inclusiveness. Under-represented groups include the young and educated who are unemployed; small businesses and those young entrepreneurs who seek to enter protected markets but have difficulty accessing finance; consumers who pay high prices and get low-quality public services; small farmers, and so on. But these groups have not been able to unite for change.

The inability to form coalitions for change in the Arab region stems from two central problems. The first is the intrinsic logistical problem of potential beneficiaries of reform mobilizing for change when these groups are often dispersed. This is not a problem unique to the Arab world. Consumers, for example, are generally the primary beneficiaries of trade reforms that would allow for lower import prices, but it is intrinsically difficult for them to come together for change, and this is the case throughout the world. However, what exacerbates the problem in the Arab world is that the region's governance systems directly hinder groups from effectively uniting for change.

To unite for change, groups need certain central rights. They need access to information to formulate choices, they need the ability to mobilize, and they need the ability to contest policies that are poor. But these rights are not present in the region. Government information is not accessible by the public. Freedom of the press is carefully monitored and circumscribed in most countries. There are restrictions on civil society. There are restrictions on freedom of association. And the ability to contest government policies is weak.

More generally, the Arab region suffers from fundamental weaknesses in governance, in terms of both inclusiveness and public accountability. Inclusiveness reflects the notion that everyone who has a stake in development and wants to participate in governance processes can, on an equal basis with all others. Accountability reflects the notion that governance processes are known and can be contested.

In the Arab region, weaknesses in inclusiveness are reflected not only in differential business opportunities, with large or privileged firms being awarded contracts or favorable legislation, but also in rural dwellers having fewer public services; in gender inequalities in voice and participation; and in nepotism, tribal affinity, patronage, or money determining who gets public services and who does not. Weaknesses in accountability are reflected in limited access to government information, limited freedom of the press, and restrictions on civil society.

It is this combination—the entrenched interests and uncertainties of those "inside the net," combined with lack of information and an inability to mobilize and contest for better policies by those "outside the net"— that prevents deeper reform from taking place.

Moving the Reform Agenda Forward

Perhaps the central challenge to moving the economic reform forward is addressing the governance agenda. It cannot be viewed as a separate agenda. It is a complementary and reinforcing agenda—to reform efforts in private investment, trade, and economic diversification by changing governance mechanisms, thereby improving capacity and incentives within government— while fostering a larger role for civil society in governance. While better governance cannot guarantee optimal economic policies, it is indispensable to guard against persistently poor policies, and to ensure that the good policies needed to meet the Arab region's growth potential enjoy legitimacy and are implemented faithfully and with celerity.

The fundamental governance challenges are to strengthen the incentives, mechanisms, and capacities for more accountable and inclusive public institutions and to expand allegiance to equality and participation throughout society. Those good governance mechanisms are first steps in improving economic policies that are themselves instruments for improving the climate and incentives for efficient growth. Economic reform cannot proceed without reform of the incentive structure in which reforms are embedded.

Enhancing inclusiveness requires adopting laws and regulations that secure access to widely accepted basic rights and freedoms, including participation and equality before the law. Broader public consultation, greater freedom for the media, fewer restrictions on civil society, more equitable channels of access to social services, and an end to discriminatory laws and regulations are examples of measures that secure inclusion.

Enhancing accountability requires putting in place better systems of transparency and contestability, including greater freedom of information, public disclosure of government operations, wider public debate by an independent media and civil society groups, and regular and competitive elections. It involves strengthening the checks and balances within the government. It involves reforming public administration.

Early in the reform process and beginning in the 1980s, many of the Arab countries accepted an instrumental connection between economic and political reform. Governments recognized that they needed to secure popular support for market-oriented economic reforms, and so several countries initiated experiments in political reform, including increased opportunities for participation by opposition political parties, expanded civil liberties and freedom of the press, and increased participation in political life by civil society groups.

But these political openings have largely been reversed as Arab governments have sought to contain and manage the scope of political change. Constraints on civil society and non-governmental organization (NGOs), restrictions on the press, and other measures have restricted mobilization and autonomous collective action. As a result, Arab government have also seriously restricted the range of reforms that could be implemented. Reforms have been limited to those that could be implemented through top-down management, rather than those that would require the compliance and participation of social groups whose well-being might be adversely affected by reforms.

Now, opening up the political space for greater public participation in policy is needed to move further with the economic reform agenda. Greater voice in development is needed to take into account the needs and values of those who have been excluded from the Arab development model. It is equally important to ensure that in the transition to a new development model, the economic outcomes are socially acceptable among those who have benefited from the old social contract. The agenda is large. But without reforming the governance structure, economic reform cannot proceed forward.

Managing Comprehensive Reform Programs

In addition to the governance agenda, the international experience with economic reform can also provide some useful insights into managing comprehensive reform programs.

First, the region should look for ways to lock in reforms. This is where international agreements can play a role. Following the 1994 peso crisis, Mexico's reform program would undoubtedly have gone far off course had it not been for the North American Free Trade Agreement (NAFTA), which tied the continuation of Mexico's reform program to the international agreement. Similarly, the reform programs in the accession countries of Eastern Europe have undoubtedly been spurred forward by the desire for European Union membership.

The EU Association agreements could be a positive step in that direction, but they have not been able to act as the catalyst for change in the region originally envisaged. For a variety of reasons, the EU association agreements have not provided enough of a "carrot" for the Med partner countries to launch substantially deeper economic reforms. The main incentives of the EU agreements have been financial, and the trade incentives have been limited. Agricultural protection has been off limits, and many of the short-term adjustments in terms of barrier lower, meeting standardization requirements, and so forth have fallen to the Med countries. Combined with the problems with rights of migration, trade in services, restrictive rules of origin, and rights of establishment, the EU association agreements have fallen short of expectations.[18]

But with new members expanding the size and scale of the EU market, the potential gains for Arab countries is expanding as well. With this is mind, the region should look to strengthen these commitments, not only to realize the increasing trade benefits, but also to lock in reforms and enhance credibility for reform in general. The Euro-Med agreements will need to be improved by both sides to strengthen their potential. The new EU neighborhood approach is aiming at overcoming some of these limitations by linking the nature and scale of benefits to the scope and extent of reforms in the EU neighboring countries. The Arab countries should look to accelerate trade barrier reductions, liberalize services, and phase in domestic agricultural reforms. In turn, the EU could offer immediate expanded access to its markets for agriculture, as well as increased temporary migration, funds for managing transition costs, and more efficient rules of origin.[19] The region can also look to membership in the World Trade Organization (WTO) as a means to enhance credibility and lock in reform.

Second, the recent escalation of oil prices presents a valuable opportunity for the region in terms of adjustment. Oil has always been a double-edged sword for the region: the vast resources from oil, especially since the 1970s, contributed to tremendous gains in development. At the same time, the continued existence of these oil revenues has certainly diminished the urgency for reform and has contributed to procyclical fiscal policy. As a forthcoming World Bank study puts it,[20] a "tragedy of the commons" sets in during good times when government revenues are high—no claimant on the government's budgetary resources internalizes the need for fiscal solvency, and political imperatives thus cause the government to spend all of its resources in the boom, leaving little margin of solvency to draw upon in order to finance fiscal deficits when times are bad.

But now, with the region on the path of reform, it has an invaluable opportunity to buffer the adjustment costs of economic transition with these rising oil revenues. Several economies have already created oil stabilization funds to save windfalls and buffer against future oil price declines. But it may be more useful to earmark a proportion of the funds specifically for future economic transition costs, such as an expanded social safety net for job losses. Having these windfall revenues to draw on during the transition process gives the Arab region a significant advantage over other regions in terms of its ability to sustain reform.

Third, another feature the region has in its favor is that it is not in open crisis. To be sure, there are serious and compounding challenges that the region is facing, but it has not reached the precipice. It can reform ahead of crisis, and this substantially lowers the total costs of adjustment. In the next 10 years, if employment grows at the rates averaged during the last decade, unemployment will have grown to almost 25 percent[21] of the labor force. If the region initiates deeper, broad-based reforms then—with accompanying reductions in public sector employment, exposure of inefficient firms to greater competition, and reduced oil resources—all of the costs of adjustment will be borne at a time when it is significantly more difficult to handle them. So the region should look at this as an opportunity to embark on deeper reforms, at a time when the costs are more manageable and the resources exist to mitigate the adjustment.

Fourth, the region needs to look for ways to build upon successes. The international experience suggests that growth operates something like a snowball, requiring a moderate degree of success in several areas simultaneously to have impact. The economies of East Asia were characterized not only by the breadth of reforms undertaken, but also by the manner in which small successes were seized upon and developed. Several countries in the Arab region, in particular several of the smaller GCC economies, are notable for approaching reform in this more selective fashion—selective not because the reforms undertaken were easier, but because they aimed at creating momentum behind some specific agenda which might help to pilot and build up support for the broader reform agenda. Bahrain, for example, has implemented several economic and political reforms, in an aim to position itself as a financial and economic hub in the region. The United Arab Emirates has targeted the growth of entrepot trade. But in most countries, while successes abound, they have tended to be isolated and have not spilled over, creating positive feedback loops of cumulative successes.

Finally, there are the issues of capacity to implement reforms. It is not enough to make decisions about reform and to design the best policies. These policies have to be implemented by government and administrative structures which are competent and not corrupt. This cannot happen when high level government officials and bureaucrats are badly paid, with much lower salaries than can be obtained in the most common private sector activity. This cannot happen when civil servants who are called on to implement new types of rules and regulations are not well trained and remain with their old mindset of control and red tape. This cannot happen when government officials are selected and rewarded according to their loyalties to political patrons rather than their competence and performance. These problems are pervasive in all Arab countries, and building and enhancing the governments' capabilities to implement reforms is critical in the coming period.

Concluding Comments

Reform in the Arab region has moved to a new path The "what" of policy reform is well mapped, based on vast international experience. The "how" of policy reform is a road much less traversed. The Arab region has a large economic reform agenda ahead if it is to meet its employment and development challenges. Reforms initiated in the past have stalled, primarily the result of deeply entrenched interests of those benefiting from the status quo, and lack of information and inability to mobilize among those who would benefit from reform. For the Arab reform agenda to proceed forward, it is clear that the region must address critical governance issues that hinder these effective coalitions for change to unite.

Notes

1. World Bank, 2003a, 2003b, 2003c.

2. World Bank, 2003c.

3. Arab labor force and employment statistics calculated for the period 2004-14.

4. Arab labor force and employment statistics computed for Algeria, Bahrain, Egypt, Jordan, Kuwait, Lebanon, Morocco, Oman, Qatar, Saudi Arabia, Syria, Tunisia, United Arab Emirates, West Bank and Gaza, and Yemen.

5. Inflation figures for Algeria, Bahrain, Egypt, Jordan, Morocco, Syria, Saudi Arabia, and Tunisia.

6. Weighted average of external debt/GNI for Algeria, Egypt, Jordan, Lebanon, Morocco, Syria, Tunisia, Yemen, Kuwait, Oman, and Saudi Arabia.

7. World Bank, 2003a.

8. World Bank, 2003a.

9. Real growth of GDP for Egypt, Morocco, Tunisia, Jordan, Algeria, Syria, Yemen, Iran, Saudi Arabia, Kuwait, Oman, Bahrain, and the United Arab Emirates.

10. Krueger, Anne, 1993.

11. Koromzay, Val, 2004.

12. Keefer, Philip (2004).

13. Nabli, Keller, and Véganzonès, 2004.

14. Measured at the 4-digit ISIC.

15. Regional averages weighted by GDP.

16. World Bank, 2003b.

17. According to the International Confederation of Free Trade Unions, the Middle East region remains the most repressive in the world in terms of labor rights.

18. Alfred Tovias; 2000.

19. World Bank, 2003a.

20. Ibid, 2004.

21. Ibid, 2003c.

References

Keefer, Philip. 2004. "What Does Political Economy Tell Us About Economic Development—And Vice Versa?" Policy Research Working Paper #3250. World Bank, Washington, DC.

Koromzay, Val. 2004. "Some Reflections on the Political Economy of Reform." Presented at international conference on Economic Reforms for Europe: Growth Opportunities in an Enlarged European Union, Bratislava, Slovakia. March 18.

Krueger, Anne. 1993. *Political Economy and Policy Reform in Developing Economies*. Cambridge, MA: MIT Press.

Nabli, Mustapha, Jennifer Keller, and Marie-Ange Veganzones. 2004. "Exchange Rate Management within the Middle East and North Africa Region: The Cost to Manufacturing Competitiveness." Lecture and Working Paper Series No. 1. American University of Beirut: Institute of Financial Economics.

Tovias, Alfred. 2000. "The Political Economy of Partnership in Comparative Perspective." Jerusalem, Israel: The Hebrew University.

World Bank. 2004. *Economic Reforms and Growth Experiences: Lessons from the 1990s.* Washington, DC: World Bank.

———. 2003a. *Trade, Investment, and Development in the Middle East and North Africa: Engaging with the World.* MENA Development Report. Washington, DC: World Bank.

———. 2003b. *Better Governance for Development in the Middle East and North Africa: Enhancing Inclusiveness and Accountability.* MENA Development Report. Washington, DC: World Bank.

———. 2003c. *Unlocking the Employment Potential in the Middle East and North Africa: Toward a New Social Contract.* MENA Development Report. Washington, DC: World Bank.

5

Democracy for Better Governance and Higher Economic Growth in the MENA Region?

Mustapha K. Nabli
Carlos Silva-Jáuregui*

Democracy is valued in itself. The extent to which a citizen is able to live in an open society and participate in its democratic process affects directly his or her well-being. But democracy can also affect welfare indirectly, through its effects on other aspects of the social and economic interactions that influence the well-being of people.

Democracy can often positively affect the relative rights of social groups, such as gender-specific groups or minorities. In the economic area, democracy may affect the distribution of income, with democracies, for instance, tending to pay higher wages and improve human capital. It may affect volatility of incomes, with democracies tending to produce fewer recessions. Nobel Prize laureate Amartya Sen observes that famines have never occurred under democratic regimes (Sen 1999). Democracy may also affect the rate of economic growth.

To the extent that democratic development reinforces and is reinforced by these various positive effects, democracy will generally gain more acceptance and opposition to it will weaken. But what happens if there are trade-offs between democratic development and any of these positive social and economic effects? What happens in cases when a democratic process brings into power a government that is able to pursue policies that undermine gender

*World Bank.

Published in the proceedings of the International Economic Association World Congress 2006, Marrakesh, Morocco. Reprinted by permission from Palgrave MacMillan.

equality, or the rights of some minority group? What happens in situations where democratic development leads, for some reason, to a *reduction* in incomes or a reduction in the rate of economic growth?

In these situations, individuals and society may still value democracy despite the trade-offs. It is likely that most people today would go in such a direction. Society may also introduce checks and balances, and develop institutional mechanisms within the democratic process, which would reduce or eliminate the likelihood of a democratic process producing such negative outcomes.

In view of the complexity of the issues related to democratic development, the objective of this paper is to discuss only a limited topic: Does democracy tend to induce higher or lower economic growth? The aim is to help understand the links between democracy and economic growth. But it should be made clear that findings that show that democracy leads to less growth would not lead to any presumption that democracy should be sacrificed for the sake of growth. Such a choice needs to be made by a society (through a democratic process, preferably!) based on its special circumstances. On the other hand, a positive link reinforces the strength of arguments for democracy.

The paper will focus more specifically on the Middle East and North Africa Region (MENA),[1] given the recent emphasis on democratic development there. Actually, democracy has risen dramatically on the agenda for and in the MENA region and countries. It has become an explicit objective of foreign policy for the United States as well as the G8. Whether it is the primary objective, and whether it is being pursued effectively, are issues that are subject to much heated debate. But there is no doubt that promoting democracy has moved up high on the agenda of both the United States and the EU in the context of its European Neighbourhood Policy. Likewise, if not more important, there is increased domestic pressure for change from within the region. Civil society at large has been demanding more political openness over the last few years. This has been eloquently and forcefully expressed in the United Nations Development Programme (UNDP) Arab Human Development Reports.

The reasons for the recent drive for democratic change are varied and complex. For the foreign players, they may have to do with the possible or presumed links between the lack of democracy and "terrorism,"[2] or between democracy and "security of borders." For domestic actors, they may simply have to do with the people of the region aspiring for more empowerment and freedom after many decades, if not centuries, of political oppression. But the paper is not going to delve into those issues.

The paper does not look into the determinants of democratic development, either. For instance, there is a large literature and debate about whether economic growth fosters democratization, as first advanced by Lipset (1959). Most recently Friedman (2005) argues that over the long run a rising living standard fosters openness, tolerance, and democracy. He recognizes, however, that in the short run, economic growth makes more secure whatever political structure may be in place; while economic stagnation and crisis may undermine a nondemocratic regime. Also, in a recent review, de Mesquita and Downs (2005) argue that, while economic growth results in higher income and increases demand for democracy, it may also foster the ability of autocratic regimes to strengthen their power, as they are able to shape institutions and political events to their advantage. Acemoglu et. al. (2005) show that the strong cross-country correlation between income and democracy does not mean there is causality, and that this correlation can be explained by historical factors that jointly determine both economic and political development paths of various societies. In the most ambitious analytical undertaking to date, Acemoglu and Robinson (2006) develop a general framework using game theory for understanding how democratic development takes place and consolidates or not. This work shows that there are problems of simultaneity between democratic development and economic development that will be discussed when relevant. These issues go well beyond the scope of this paper.

This paper considers the possible effects of a "given" democratic process, without dwelling much on how it may have come about. Its scope is the relationship between "democratic development" and "economic growth." From an economic perspective, the objective is to determine whether there is a well-defined relationship (or lack thereof) between the two, and more specifically whether one should expect democracy to help or hinder a stronger economic performance in general, and in the context of the MENA region in particular.

The next section provides the general context for the democracy–growth linkages discussion in the MENA region—which has been characterized by the existence of a democracy deficit, as well as a growth deficit, for the last two decades. With this background, the third section reviews the empirical literature on the links between democracy and growth that focuses on direct links and uses mostly reduced-form type models, and concludes that the nature and strength of these links are at best ambiguous. More recent work on the relationship between democracy and growth, surveyed in the fourth section, pursues a more structural approach and looks at the intermediation channels and indirect links between democracy and growth, as well as the role of the nature of the democratic regimes. One main conclusion is that the effect of democracy on growth, especially in MENA, depends to a large extent on whether a democratic transition leads to better governance and, therefore, a better business climate and higher private physical capital accumulation. The fifth section explores the extent to which better governance is more likely to be achieved under democratic regimes or nondemocratic ones. The sixth section briefly discusses a different approach to looking at the links between democracy and growth by postulating that, while such a link may not be established systematically for any country at any time, it may be important for most MENA countries today. In this case, democratic reform may be needed to unlock the prevailing status quo— low public accountability and the main-tenance of prevailing economic policies and networks of privilege—in order to generate a great political and economic transformationthat could produce both more democracy and more economic growth in the region. The last sec-tion concludes that democratic development can be a strong lever for eco-nomic growth in the MENA region, and that these countries should strive for democratic regimes that are sustainable, in the sense of having characteristics that make them more likely to produce good governance. Good "quality democracy," which produces quality governance, improves the investment cli-mate and allows the emergence of a dynamic private sector that can con-tribute to meeting the current development challenges of the MENA region, which needs to achieve average growth rates of 6-7 percent per year in order to absorb the fast-growing, increasingly-educated, and feminized labor force. The main focus should be on the design of the appropriate democratic insti-tutionsthat (i) minimize imperfections in the political market, with more freedom of information and free press, adequate mechanisms to contain clientelism, and increased credibility of political promises; (ii) introduce safe-guards and effective checks and balances; (iii) increase the legitimacy of the democratic transformation; and (iv) in cases where there is significant ethnic and or religious fragmentation, minimize the risks of social conflicts.

The Democracy and Growth Deficits in the MENA Region

At this point, it is perhaps useful to further explain the context of the discus-sion of the links between democracy and economic growth in the MENA region. This context can be summarized by the existence of both a "democra-cy deficit" and a "growth deficit." Their simultaneous presence in practically all countries of the region (even though at different degrees) leads one to wonder whether any links exist between the two.

Before presenting the evidence about the democracy deficit, it is useful to provide some basic references about the definition of democracy.[3] At the most abstract level, democracy is a system of government (or of exercise of author-ity) in which effective political power is vested in the people, and where major decisions of government, and the direction of policy behind these decisions, rest directly or indirectly on the freely given consent of the majority of the adults governed. At the more practical level, democracy tends to be defined in procedural terms, as the body of rules and procedures that regulate the trans-fer of political power and the free expression of disagreement at all levels of political life. More concretely, it is defined as a political system where access to political power is regularly achieved through competitive, free and fair elec-tions. As stated by Schumpeter (1942), it is "...the institutional arrangement for arriving at political decisions in which individuals acquire the power to decide by means of a competitive struggle for the people's vote." (p.250).

Democracy Deficit in the MENA Region

Democracy has gained worldwide acceptance in recent decades. Without exception, all developed countries maintain democratic systems, and many developing ones are selecting their leaders through competitive elections, that is, moving toward more democratic political regimes. In a recent publication on lessons of the 1990s, the World Bank (2005a) points out that "...a striking phenomenon of the 1990s was the rise in the number of countries selecting their leaders through competitive elections. The number rose from 60 countries in 1989 to 100 in 2000. Among poorer countries (those with less than the median country's per capita income), the number nearly tripled, from 11 in 1989 to 32 in 2000; 15 percent of the poorer countries elected their governments in 1989 and 42 percent in 2000." This shows a remarkable move toward democracy, but one that did not spread to MENA as vigorously.

There is now a wide body of evidence on the "democracy gap or deficit" in the MENA region. It will suffice here to highlight some of this empirical evidence.

A first piece of evidence can be observed when using the well-known composite Polity index from the Polity IV dataset.[4] The composite Polity index (which ranges from −10 for the least democratic regimes to +10 for the most democratic regimes) shows that the MENA region has consistently lagged behind the rest of the world, suggesting that there is a persistent democracy deficit in the region (figure 5.1). The MENA democracy deficit has existed over the last 40 years, with the average regime in MENA remaining authoritarian, according to this metric (negative values for the Polity index). While the Organisation for Economic Co-operation and Development (OECD) countries have been consistently democratic, other regions in the world were traditionally not very democratic. The Polity index shows, however, a clear tendency toward democratization in developing countries outside MENA starting around 1977. Developing countries (other than MENA) have their average Polity index turning positive by 1991, with a gain of 7 points (30 percent of the scale) during the period 1977-2002.

As figure 5.2 shows during the 1960s, on average, the democracy level of countries in MENA and other developing regions was declining. The democracy gap between MENA and other regions remained, however, relatively stable, with a small declining trend during the period covering the mid-1960s and the mid-1970s. The democracy gap reached its lowest point around 1977. Since then, the gap has increased steadily, accelerating around 1990 as the Soviet Bloc disintegrated and new democracies emerged, particularly in Central and Eastern Europe. Since 1994, there has been a decline in the democracy gap between MENA and other developing regions, but the gap still remains significantly above the level attained in the 1970s. The democracy gap between MENA and the OECD countries increased steadily until 1988, when the average OECD Polity index reached its high plateau. At that point, the gap

Figure 5.1. Democracy Trends in MENA and Other Regions

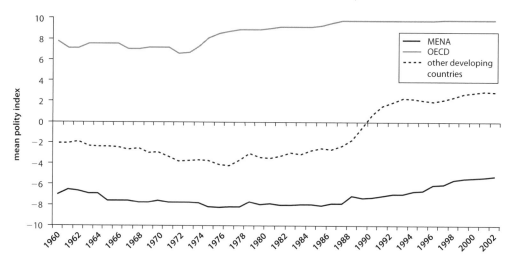

Source: Mean Polity Index 1960-2003.

was almost 17.5 points, or 88 percent of the scale. Since then the gap between MENA and the OECD countries has declined as gradual progress toward democratization has taken place in MENA. Nonetheless, the gap remains at 15 points, or 75 percent of the scale, above the levels attained in the 1960s.

A second piece of evidence comes from analyzing the trends in the Freedom House Political Rights index. This alternative measure of democracy has been used by several scholars (Acemoglu and Robinson 2006; Barro 1999).

Figure 5.2. Democracy GAP between MENA and Other Regions

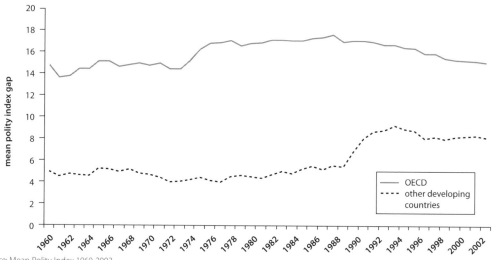

Source: Mean Polity Index 1960-2003.

The original Freedom House index ranges from 1 to 7, with 1 representing the most political freedom and 7 the least. We use the transformed Freedom House index (Acemoglu and Robinson 2006), which, following Barro (1999), is supplemented with data from Bollen (1990, 2001) for 1960 and 1965, normalized and transformed to lie between 0 and 1, with 0 corresponding to the least democratic set of institutions and 1 to the most.[5] This facilitates comparison with the other indicators of democracy used in the paper.

Figure 5.3 plots the normalized Freedom House Political Rights index since 1950. The index confirms the low level of democracy in the MENA region, and a growing democracy gap with OECD and other developing regions in the world. As the figure shows, the MENA region has a declining trend in the political rights index, losing ground particularly between 1960 and 1975, and between 1985 and 1990. The index reveals a small improvement in political rights in the period 1975-1980, at the height of the oil boom. The index also indicates little, if any, gain in political rights during the 1990-2001 period, contrary to the trends of the Polity index. This may indicate that while some elements of democratization were implemented, those related to political rights lagged.

An analysis of the democracy gap using the Freedom House index shows an increasing gap vis-à-vis OECD countries until the early 1990s. With respect to countries in other developing parts of the world, the democracy gap declined marginally during the 1960-1980 period. Since 1985, however, it has increased sharply, as other regions of the world have moved much more rapidly toward increasing political rights and advancing democratic reforms.

A third piece of evidence on the gap can be found in the work of Papaioannou and Siouroumis (2004), who constructed a complete dataset on

Figure 5.3. Freedom House Political Rights Index in MENA and Selected Regions

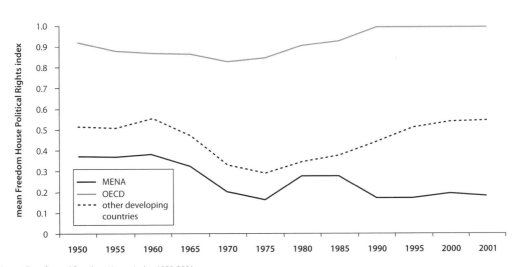

Source: Transformed Freedom House Index 1950-2001.

democratization in the world since the 1970s. The data used are wide-ranging, go beyond the various quantitative indicators, and use historical review of episodes. The authors find that 38 episodes of "full democratization" and 24 episodes of "partial democratization" occurred in the world over the last 30-40 years. None of these episodes took place in the MENA region.

A fourth piece of evidence on the "democracy deficit" is the absence of a positive correlation between democracy and level of income in the MENA region, unlike what is typically found for the rest of the world. Przeworski et al. (2000) found that democracies are more frequent in developed (wealthier) countries, while dictatorships are more frequent in poor countries. In typical charts showing the correlation between level of income and democratic development, MENA counties tend to cluster way below the line. In particular, the many oil producers tend to be less democratic than less wealthy countries. The Gulf Cooperation Council (GCC) countries have among the lowest scores in the region using the Polity IV index.

Driving the gap between MENA countries and the rest of the world are striking weaknesses in external accountabilities and in access to basic political and civic rights. The World Bank (2003e) constructed an index of public accountability (IPA). The IPA assesses the process of selecting and replacing those in authority. It measures the quality of governance according to the inclusiveness of access to basic political and civic rights, and the relative strength of external accountability mechanisms. It aggregates 12 indicators that measure the level of openness of political institutions in a country, and the extent to which political participation is free, fair, and competitive; civil liberties are assumed and respected; and the press and voice are free from control, violation, harassment, and censorship. It also captures the transparency and responsiveness of the government to its people, and the degree of political accountability in the public sphere.

All countries in the MENA region, whatever their income, score well below the world trend in the IPA (figure 5.4). Some richer MENA countries score especially low on the IPA—with scores equivalent to those in some of the poorest countries of the world. Oil seems to matter, as oil-exporting countries have the worst IPA scores.

Economic growth deficit in the MENA world

The recent history of economic growth in the MENA region can be easily understood . MENA's historical model of economic development was based on state-led development and central planning, economic and social policies designed for redistribution and equity, and a strong social contract between governments and the people they represented.

During 1965–85, economic growth per capita averaged 2.9 percent per year, second only to the East Asia and Pacific region (figure 5.5). Many factors contributed to this performance, including rapid progress in early-stage

Figure 5.4. Public Accountability and per Capita Incomes in MENA

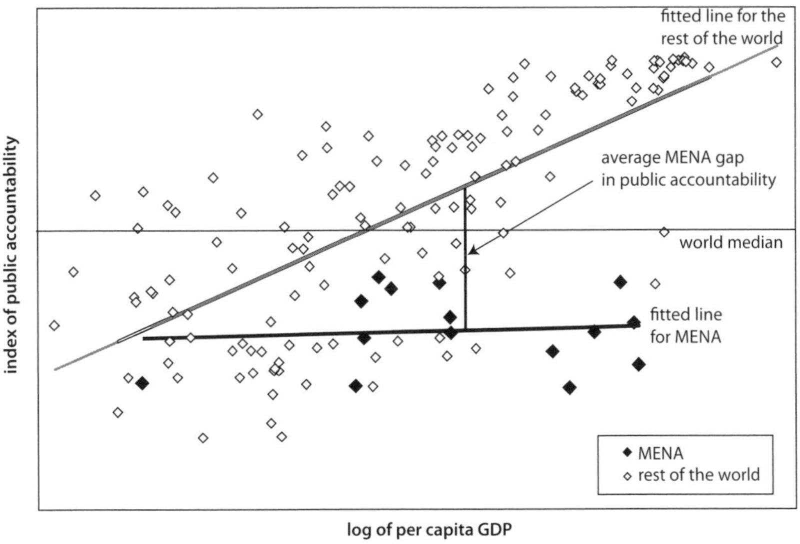

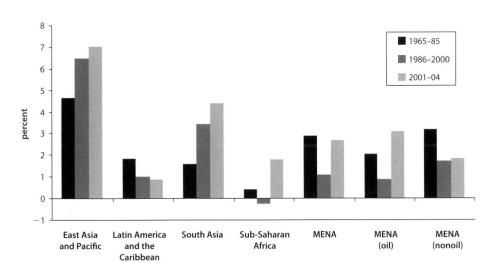

Figure 5.5. Average per Capita GDP Growth, 1965-2004

industrialization; high levels of public employment and spending, especially on infrastructure; trade protection for domestic producers; and rising oil prices that yielded large capital inflows, created jobs, and promoted remittance flows into non-oil-producing MENA states.

While this development model paid large dividends in the beginning, particularly with regard to improvements in social indicators, there were also sig-

Source: World Development Indicators 2005.
Note: MENA (oil producers) includes Algeria, Bahrain (1986–2004), Iran (1986–2004), Kuwait, Oman, Saudi Arabia, and UAE (1986–2004). MENA (nonoil producers) includes Egypt, Jordan, Lebanon (1986–2004), Morocco, Syria, Tunisia, and Yemen (1986–2004).

nificant costs. Centralized and hierarchical governments emerged in MENA, with limited transparency and contestability of representatives or policies. The MENA development model also created economies that had great difficulty adapting to shocks and economic change.

As early as the late 1970s, the economic systems that had developed in MENA—and that carried the people in the region through an unprecedented era of achievements—showed signs of cracking under stress. The high growth rates were becoming increasingly costly to achieve. Though investments were at record levels, with the rate of growth of physical capital per worker increasing by more than 80 percent in the 1970s over the 1960s, these investments were inefficient, delivering increasingly smaller growth payoffs. As a result of large inefficiencies, total factor productivity growth was lower than in any other region of the world, and turned negative during the 1970s.

The MENA region entered the 1980s with mounting evidence of strains and difficulties in sustaining the promise of continued prosperity. Facing declining public revenues after the oil shock in the mid-1980s, governments struggled to maintain their growth performance and redistributive commitments. With a public sector wage bill accounting for as much as 20 percent of gross domestic product (GDP), deficits mounted and debt grew at an alarming rate. The fiscal strains contributed to large macroeconomic imbalances. Productivity growth, already declining by the 1970s, plummeted to –1.5 percent a year on average over the 1980s. Real output growth collapsed under the multiple blows of declining public spending, in part a result of the negative oil shocks, an unattractive private investment climate, and continuing losses in efficiency. GDP per capita stagnated over the 1980s, growing an almost imperceptible 0.3 percent a year during the decade.

In the 1990s, several macroeconomic stabilization reforms were implemented, and they began to pay important dividends. By and large, MENA countries recovered from the instability of the 1980s. Inflation was brought under control, debt levels declined, and macroeconomic performance turned positive on average. These were fundamental preconditions for higher private investment and growth, but the strong growth rates needed to cope with the demographic transition in the region failed to materialize. Despite the mentioned reforms, the effort did not translate into the strong economic recovery that was anticipated. Though GDP growth improved compared to the crisis-ridden 1980s, per capita growth remained weak, averaging 1.5 percent per year in the 1990s. While the declines in productivity growth were arrested, productivity growth was close to 2 percentage points lower than the world average and 3.5 percentage points lower than East Asia—at about the same levels of investment.

With the coming of the new millennium, the region has experienced a new set of favorable conditions. As a result, the region has achieved exceptional growth over the last few years. Accelerating in the early 2000s, economic growth in the MENA region (excluding Iraq) averaged 5.1 percent a year over 2002-04, the strongest growth rate in a decade, and significantly higher than the average yearly growth during the 1990s. On a per capita basis, the MENA region's 3.2 percent average growth over 2002-04 was its strongest growth performance since the mid-1970s.

Despite the oil-driven growth boom, on a per capita basis the region's growth rate over the last few years continues to lag that of most other regions, a reflection of both the firming of GDP growth rates across developing regions and the MENA region's still-high population growth rate, which continues to be a key development challenge. At the regional level, per capita growth in East Asia and the Pacific, South Asia, and Europe and Central Asia all outpaced MENA's per capita GDP performance in both 2003 and 2004.

In sum, over the past two decades, the MENA region has experienced a growth deficit, with low per capita income growth. This growth performance has been weaker than that achieved by most other regions of the world, except for Sub-Saharan Africa.

Empirical Correlation and Direct Links between Democracy and Economic Growth

The previous discussion leads one to be tempted to hypothesize that there is a strong link between the low growth and the democracy deficit in the MENA region. This section more thoroughly reviews international experience regarding the empirical relationship between democracy and growth, and investigates how it applies for the MENA region. International experience, such as the economic success of many authoritarian regimes, including Singapore, South Korea, and Indonesia during the 1970s and 1980s, Chile in the 1980s, and China over the last 20 years, casts some doubt on the existence of any robust (positive) linear relationship between economic growth and democracy. Empirical studies using standard growth regression models and cross-country data have found mixed evidence for such direct links. Reviews of a large number of these studies (see Borner et al. 1995) found that only very few show any strong positive relationship, with most showing either insignificant results or even a negative link. Using the Freedom House indicator for democracy (electoral rights), Barro and Sala-i-Martin (2003) show that a nonlinear relationship may exist, similar to a Laffer Curve, in which democratization appears to enhance growth for countries that are not very democratic, but to retard growth for countries that have already achieved a high degree of democracy. Przeworski et al. (2000) analyzed the data over a long period of time and concluded that when countries are observed across the entire spectrum of conditions, total income grew at about the same rate for democratic and undemocratic regimes. However, they found that patterns of growth varied between democracies and nondemocracies, particularly in wealthy countries.

The history of the MENA region over the last 50 years shows limited experience with democracy and political openness. But while no country in the region has achieved a full transition to democracy, the degree of political openness, and the use of the election process to choose the government in power, have varied significantly over time and across countries. The high income growth rates achieved in the 1970s and early 1980s were not accompanied by any significant degree of political openness, while the growth collapse of the 1980s saw some degree of political liberalization in several MENA countries. During the 1990s, the experiences of low economic growth countries like Morocco were associated with gains in democratization, while higher-growth countries like Tunisia were increasingly autocratic. At the same time, Jordan experienced higher growth and political openness, while low growth and limited democratization were the norm in most Gulf countries. Overall, there was little correlation between changes in democracy and changes in income per capita during 1970-2003 in MENA and the rest of the world (figure 5.6). Countries that grow faster than others have not become more democratic.

The lack of strong empirical evidence of direct positive *links* between democracy and economic growth, which seems to apply for the MENA region as well, has led research to move in new directions for the study of the linkages between democratic and economic development. We look at some of them in the next section.

Figure 5.6. Democracy Growth and Income Growth, 1970–2003

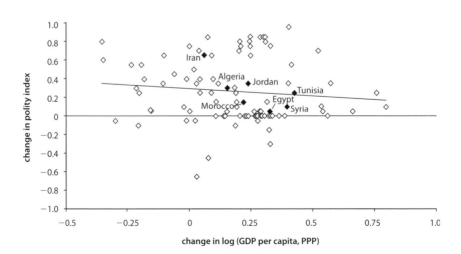

Structural Analysis of the Links between Democracy and Economic Growth

Indirect Links from Democracy to Economic Growth

Recent research has gone in three directions of study for the indirect linkages between democratization and economic growth.[6]

The first direction explores more carefully the theoretical and empirical links between democracy and economic growth, going beyond simple correlations and cross-country regressions, which considered only direct links. These studies look at the indirect effects of democracy on economic growth through a number of intermediation channels. They use structural models that involve income growth, democracy, and variables that represent such intermediation or transmission channels. Some of these channels show a negative impact of democracy on economic growth, whileothers show a positive link. A focus on the inefficiencies of representative government, using the "median voter model" or the public choice approach, would imply that democratic regimes result in larger demand for redistribution and prevalence of special interest politics. This may result in higher government consumption, higher taxation, more redistribution, and lower private investment. All these channels would imply lower growth rates.

But many other channels would lead one to expect a positive impact from democracy on economic growth. First, redistribution and higher taxation may result in higher human capital accumulation, through larger subsidies and dealing with capital market failures. Second, democracy deals better with economic instability, through better commitment achieved through the political process. Political instability is part of everyday life in democracies and does not affect economic growth as much as in the case of authoritarian regimes. In nondemocracies, any changes—or expectations of changes—in leadership negatively affect investment and growth: Whenever dictators are expected to be removed, growth declines sharply (Przeworski at al. 2000). Such nondemocratic regimes are successful only if they are stable. Shocks therefore have large negative impacts on economic growth. In addition, democratic regimes are better suited for both mediating conflicts among interest groups and responding to exogenous negative shocks. Countries with higher degrees of social and ethnic fragmentation and weak democratic institutions are found to have suffered the sharpest drops in GDP after shocks (Rodrik 1997, 1999).

Tavares and Wacziarg used a full system of simultaneous equations and panel data for the period 1970-89. They found that democracy fosters growth because it improves human capital accumulation and, in a weaker way, because it reduces income inequality. At the same time, they find that democracy hinders growth by reducing physical capital accumulation, and, in a less robust way, by increasing the government consumption to GDP ratio. However, no significant impact is found through the channels of political instability and policy distortions. The overall effect of democracy on growth is slightly *negative,* mainly through the large impact on the reduction in the rate of physical capital accumulation. In a similar vein, Feng (2003) conducts a wide-ranging empirical study of the impact of political institutions on economic growth. He finds that democracy has an insignificant direct effect on economic growth, but indirect effects that are strong and significant. These indirect channels include political instability, policy uncertainty, investment, education, property rights, and birth rates.

The second direction goes beyond cross-country analysis and intensively uses event analysis and differences in performance for before and after democratization episodes. Empirical findings from this analysis tend to show a positive impact of democratization on a given country's economic growth. From a theoretical standpoint, the evidence presented in this new branch of the democracy-growth nexus literature offers direct support for so-called development theories of democracy and growth that highlight the growth-enhancement aspects of the democratic process. From a policy perspective, the results suggest that democratic institutions, if properly introduced and adapted, can bring substantial growth benefits. They also suggest an important role for the international community—to help mitigate the transition costs, which can be high and can impede the consolidation of democratic rule.

To assess whether a successful democratic transition is associated with faster growth, Papaioannou and Siourounis (2004) first identify countries and the exact timing of permanent democratizations in the period 1960-2000. They employ an event study approach and analyze the evolution of GDP growth before and after such incidents of political modernization. Using a dynamic panel with annual observations, and econometric techniques that address concerns on shortcomings of previous research, the study reveals that conditional on various growth determinants, global shocks, and business cycle effects, permanent democratization is associated with approximately a 1 percent increment in real per capita growth. The analysis also reveals a J-shaped growth pattern. This implies that output growth drops during the democratic transition, but then fluctuates at a higher rate, suggesting a "short-run pain," resulting perhaps from to high transition costs and learning, followed by "long-run gain," resulting from higher growth after the consolidation of democracy. The effect is robust across various model specifications, panel data methodologies, alternative democratization dates, and the potential endogeneity of democratization. The methodology enables quantification of both the short- and the long-run correlations between political modernization and growth. The results favor the Aristotelian notion, recently put another way by Friedrich Hayek, that the merits of democracy will come in the long run.[7] That is, stable democracies can foster growth.

The Papaioannou and Siourounis work is related to a new wave of research that studies the effect of institutions on economic performance.[8] Their results suggest that, besides legal norms or property rights protection, the type and quality of political institutions correlate substantially with economic growth. The overall effect of democracy on growth is then positive in these studies.

The third direction of the literature goes beyond the general dualistic specification of political regimes as democratic or nondemocratic and explores a number of dimensions. A significant amount of work, mostly on advanced countries, looks at how the nature and rules of democratic regimes affect outcomes. Whether these regimes are presidential or parliamentarian, whether they use majoritarian or proportional representation, does matter for the way democracy affects economic outcomes.

In recent parallel studies, Persson (2004) shows that income gains following democratization are high when the transition leads to proportional representation (versus majoritarian) or when it leads to a parliamentary (versus presidential) system. Giavazzi and Tabellini (2004) document significant interactions between economic and political liberalization and show that countries experience substantial growth gains when they liberalize the economy first, and then the polity.

For developing countries, the focus has been on how imperfections in electoral markets tend to make democracy less effective in achieving good government than it is in advanced countries (World Bank 2005a). Imperfections in electoral markets—lack of voter information, the inability of political competitors to make credible promises, and social polarization—are important factors in understanding policy formulation and explaining differences in economic performance between rich and poor democracies. Voters in developing countries tend to be less informed, the role of media weaker, and campaign financing more prone to capture, which result in worse governance outcomes. At the same time, politicians tend to be less credible, and clientelism more pervasive, especially as the length of exposure to elections tends to be shorter. In addition, social polarization and ethnic fragmentation distort electoral processes.

The empirical findings from this strand of the literature tend to *condition* the possible impact of democratization on growth on how severe the political market imperfections are. Differences in economic performance across democracies can be explained by imperfections in electoral markets. Numerous imperfections in these markets make it difficult for citizens to hold politicians accountable for policies. Elected governments are most likely to make policies favouring narrow segments of the population, at the expense of the majority, when citizens do not have good information mechanisms, cannot trust promises made before elections, or are in societies that are deeply polarized. These factors are three of the most important political market imperfections that affect policy outcomes. In contrast, elected governments are most credible, and most likely to respect private property rights, when they confront checks and balances on their decision making. Thus, accountability becomes an essential component.

Informed voters are necessary for good political outcomes. Without information about what politicians are doing, and how their policies affect citizens' welfare, or about the attributes of political competitors, citizens cannot easily identify and reward high-performing politicians. As a result, bad performance is encouraged and bad political outcomes are likely to occur. In political markets, information about the characteristics of political competitors and government performance is key. Proxies like newspaper circulation are commonly used in empirical analysis for voter information, and reveal, controlling for income and other factors, that higher newspaper circulation is associated with lower corruption, greater rule of law, better bureaucratic quality, and greater secondary school enrolment (Keefer and Khemani 2005).

Credible commitments by politicians are also important for good governance outcomes. When challengers cannot make credible policy commitments, citizens have no reason to prefer them over incumbents. Even if incumbents do badly, citizens have no reason to believe that challengers will do better. This insulates incumbents from competition and diminishes pressure to perform. Politicians may only be able to make credible promises to some voters, generating clientelism and incentives to politicians to underprovide public goods and extract large rents.

Likewise, social polarization hinders the capacity for political systems to generate good outcomes. Social polarization undermines the accountability of government to citizens. In extreme cases, deep divisions among social groups hinder the capacity of one group to elect a representative of the other, irrespective of his or her characteristics, political platform, and qualities as a representative. Elected representatives from one group then have no incentive to address the concerns and solve the problems of citizens in the other, generating distortions in the provision of public goods. Empirical studies show that measures of ethnic tension are higher in poorer democracies that in rich ones. The consequences of social polarization can be worsened by all the factors that undermine voters' ability to hold politicians accountable.

Implications for MENA Countries?

What can be concluded for MENA countries from the previous brief survey? Does it mean that democratic reform is unimportant for economic growth? Since the survey shows a lot of uncertainty about the causal links from democracy to economic growth, MENA countries should not expect that the pursuit of democratization can in itself bring quick benefits in terms of economic growth. One can be tempted to conclude that the search for higher economic growth should focus more on traditional policy and institutional reforms within an existing political regime. In that case, striving for democratic development would be a different track, which should remain separate from the track of economic growth.

But such a conclusion is premature. In fact, the previous discussion suggests that there are some robust positive effects of democracy on growth, through higher human capital accumulation. But is such a link likely to be relevant and significant in MENA countries? There is a lot of empirical evidence that MENA countries have achieved strong gains in terms of human development during the last four to five decades—in the presence of nondemocratic regimes (World Bank 2006). Some of the most impressive improvements in human development indicators took place in the MENA region between 1960 and 2000, surpassing the performance of countries in other regions with similar purchasing power parity (PPP) income levels. For instance, as figure 5.7 shows, average years of education in MENA increased by more than 500 percent, and in the case of women by more than 800 percent, during the 1960-2000 period. Child mortality decreased from an average of 262 deaths per 1,000 births to an average of 47 deaths per 1,000 births during the same period. Life expectancy at birth improved from 47 to 68 years, a 45 percent increase.

Actually, one can argue that regimes in MENA did strive to buy the loyalty of citizens through strong redistributive programs such as free access to education and health care, public sector jobs, and lower prices for basic commodities. It is unlikely that the channel of increased investment in education will be important for increasing growth in MENA countries over the coming period. On the other hand, there is general recognition of the need for education reform, to improve the quality and adequacy of education in response to changing economic conditions. Governance mechanisms may turn out to be critical to the success of these reforms.

The previous analysis shows also that there are some robust positive effects of democracy on growth, through better commitments to policies with a more credible and predictable political process, and through better intermediation of conflicts. Such effects are likely to be relevant in many MENA countries and situations.

Figure 5.7. Human Development Indicators in MENA Improved Considerably

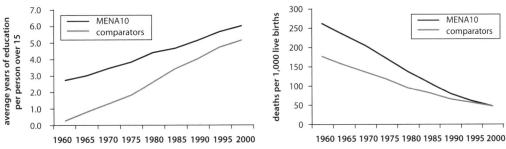

Source: World Bank (2006). MENA10 refers to Algeria, Egypt, Iran, Jordan, Lebanon, Libya, Morocco, Syria, Tunisia and Yemen. Comparators include 32 countries with similar income levels of MENA countries in PPP terms in 1980.

Another conclusion from this review is that for a number of other links from democracy to economic growth, the effects are largely contingent on whether a move toward more democratic government leads to better governance. In particular, there is uncertainty about the impact of democracy on capital accumulation and policy distortions. This uncertainty is most likely related to the extent to which democracy leads to more or less respect for property rights, to policies that favor broader or narrower interests, and to adequate or underprovision public goods; which in turn depends on the strength of politicians' credibility and the pervasiveness of clientelism.

The main general conclusion is that the net impact of democracy on growth depends on the severity of political market imperfections—in other words, whether democracy produces good governance and thereby enhances physical capital accumulation. This conclusion is strengthened by two additional and complementary findings from the literature on governance (without reference to democracy), which show direct, strong, positive links between good governance and economic growth, and between better governance and higher private investment. The latter linkage is particularly important for the MENA region.

Governance and Growth

The work of Buchanan, et al. (1980), Evans (1989, 1995), North (1981, 1990), and de Soto (1989) systematically linked country characteristics such as the security of property rights directly to the wealth of nations, improving the understanding of the effects of the nonpolicy characteristics of government performance on economic development and growth. The research stemming from this strand of the literature brought to the forefront the contribution of previously under-examined issues like the security of property rights, the rule of law, expropriation, bureaucratic quality, red tape, and the quality of regulation.

Both empirical evidence and theory support the influence of *individual* components of governance, rather than *aggregated* concepts of governance, on development and growth. Studies have found that some governance components have stronger links than others (Keffer 2004b). The security of property rights, the credibility of governments (see Knack and Keefer 1995, Acemoglu and Johnson 2005, Acemoglu, et al. 2001, Rodrik, et al. 2002, Hall and Jones 1999), and an honest and efficient bureaucracy emerge as the components with the best documented and strongest links to economic development and growth. On the other side, causality problems cloud estimates of the influence of bureaucratic capacity and corruption on development. In addition, analyses of voice and accountability, while the subject of substantial attention among researchers, have suffered from a lack of theoretical and empirical precision, which clouds interpretation.

The theoretical case for secure property rights is based on the basic idea that economic agents do not invest when the business environment is not right and they fear potential confiscation of their assets by government. Still, there are objections to the theoretical case linking the security of property rights to growth.[9] One relates to the fact that often, two important notions of property rights are confused: the *allocation* of property rights and the *security* of property rights. Democracy may render property rights less secure because the introduction of democracy creates opportunities for the poor to redistribute incomes away from the rich. However, it is not democracy, *per se,* that creates insecurity, but the transition to democracy. Once democracy is established, there is no reason to expect the distribution of property rights to change further.

Some contributions to the governance literature refer not only to the security of property rights, but also to the closely related (but somewhat broader) concept of "government credibility." This is the case with Knack and Keefer (1995), for example. Only credible governments can assure investors that their assets are safe from expropriation.

In the context of MENA, some empirical evidence shows that better governance may have a significant positive effect on economic growth. Weaker governance in MENA costs 1.0 to 1.5 percentage points in forgone annual GDP growth (World Bank 2003e). On average, improving the quality of institutions by one standard deviation—approximately equivalent to raising the average institutional quality in MENA to the average institutional quality of comparable East Asian countries (Indonesia, Malaysia, the Philippines, Singapore, Thailand, and Vietnam)—would have resulted in an increase of almost 1 percent in average annual GDP growth for the region as a whole. This figure would imply an income level that would have been 50 percent higher in a period of 40 years due to compounding. The gain in growth rate from better governance would have risen to a 1.5 percent difference for the MENA countries with substantial oil and gas revenues, implying an income level 81 percent higher in the same comparative period. Similar results have been found by Elbadawi (2002).

Governance and Private Investment

The influence of the quality of governance on growth works primarily through its effect on private businesses and their capacity to invest. Numerous studies (see World Bank 2003e) have documented the relationship between governance and private sector activity. Businesses react to the incentives, costs, and constraints that form their business environment. Those reactions are, in turn, influenced by the shaping and implementing of public policies.

Improved governance can produce better business climates that foster investment, productivity, and growth. It reduces the scope for arbitrary government policymaking, providing mechanisms that help countries minimize the persistence of policy distortions. By ensuring public accountability of politicians and bureaucrats, better governance also contributes to the effective implementation of economic policies that are conducive to growth.

Better governance also improves bureaucratic performance and pre-dictability, reducing uncertainty and the costs of doing business. This enhances the business environment. Better governance makes it easier to start new businesses and to run and expand existing ones. It lowers transaction costs at all levels (entry, operation, and exit), reduces information asymmetries between business and governments, and lowers uncertainties and unpredictability. It does so by protecting and enforcing property rights, curbing burdensome administrative and judicial rulings, reducing red tape, ensuring good regulatory quality, and improving access to affordable and reliable recourse to dispute resolution. By helping ensure more orderly public accountability processes, better governance also reduces political risk.

Better governance contributes to the effective delivery of public goods that are necessary for productive businesses. Firms operate in a commercial environment that depends on many key public goods. Better governance helps ensure that such goods are available in a timely, equitable, and cost-efficient manner. Public goods that are essential for a good business environment include appropriately regulated public utilities and natural monopolies, a stable and prudently regulated financial system, public safety and low crime, and good-quality health and education. Effective delivery of these and other public goods boosts the productivity of private investment and leads to faster growth and development.

A recent empirical study (Aysan, Nabli and Véganzonès-Varoudakis 2006) provides a quantification of the possible impact of better governance on private investment in a few MENA countries (Egypt, Iran, Morocco, Tunisia; figure 5.8). The study uses panel data and a simultaneous equation model for private investment and governance indicators to estimate this impact. They find that improved governance indicators, in terms of quality of public administration and public accountability, equivalent to one standard deviation of observed variability, would yield about a 3.5 percent increase in private

Figure 5.8. Private Investment in the MENA Region Remains Low

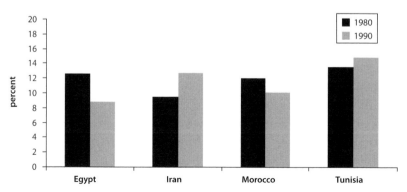

Source: Aysan, Nabli, and Véganzonès-Varoudakis (2006).

investment-to-GDP ratios. For MENA countries, this would have increased the ratio of private investment to GDP on average from 12 percent to 15.5 - percent—a significant impact.

Better Governance Is Critical—But How?

Governance is among the more elastic concepts in the social science and development lexicons (Keefer 2004a). Definitions tend to include the extent to which governments are responsive to citizens and provide them with certain core services, such as secure property rights and rule of law, and the extent to which public sector institutions and processes give government decision makers an incentive to be responsive to citizens.

Good governance requires inclusiveness, transparency, and accountability in the management of public affairs. The governance challenge in the MENA region is to strengthen the incentives, mechanisms, and capacities for more accountable and inclusive public institutions, and to expand allegiance to equality and participation throughout society. Those good governance mechanisms are first steps in improving economic policies that are themselves instruments for better economic growth.

The previous discussion makes a strong argument that democracy can have a positive impact on economic growth if it leads to better governance. But is democracy likely to generate good governance—and are there alternative paths to achieving good governance?

From Democracy to Better Governance?

Researchers have developed various arguments that link democracy to both greater and lesser quality of governance. The introduction of democratic institutions, in the form of more political and civil rights, and freedom of the press, among others, may or may not be associated with improved governance. On the one hand, democracies allow populations to peacefully and regularly oust inept, inefficient, and corrupt public administration and to retain more efficient, successful regimes, thus tending to make the quality of governance, on average, higher in the long run. On the other hand, a number of studies have noted that the proliferation of interest groups lobbying for power or rents under democratic institutions may lead to policy gridlock, pervasive clientelism, and lack of accountability. This could hinder growth prospects.

The empirical literature appears to confirm that stronger democratic institutions are positively associated with a higher quality of governance, as well as with its positive impact on growth (Rivera-Batiz 2002, Keefer 2004a). Stronger democratic institutions influence governance by constraining the actions of corrupt and inept officials. They also facilitate the activities of the press, which can monitor corruption and disseminate information on government officials to the public, so that they can be held accountable.

But research and experience have shown many situations where democracy is unlikely to produce better governance. For instance, it has been often observed that younger democracies are more corrupt, exhibit less rule of law and lower levels of bureaucratic quality. These young democracies spend more on public investment and government workers. The politicians are less credible (Keefer 2005), and the inability of political competitors to make credible promises to citizens leads them to underprovide public goods, overprovide transfers to narrow groups of voters, and engage in excessive rent seeking. Young democracies seem to require time to mature to generate the desirable results.

Democracy may also not lead to better governance and higher growth in MENA, because of the region's social cleavages and fragmentation, as discussed above in the context of the importance of political market imperfections.

The literature on these issues has shown that getting democracy right is indeed affected by the extent of social cleavages. Elbadawi (2004) tests for the impact of social cleavages on growth. In his model, social cleavages are measured by indexes of (ethnic, cultural, or religious) fractionalization and polarization. He finds that several MENA countries have highly ethnically and religiously fractionalized societies, including Djibouti, Jordan, Lebanon., Iraq, and Syria. Like other authors before (Alesina et al. 2003, Easterly and Levin 1997, and Rodrick 1998), Elbadawi finds that the conflict variable that measures the social cleavages in his model has a negative effect on growth. The conflict variable was highly significant in the case of ethnic fractionalization, and moderately significant in cases of language, religious, and dominant polarizations In all cases, it was negatively associated with long-term stability of growth. The results are much less robust in the case of the polarization-based conflict. However, ethnic and, especially, language polarizations were negatively and significantly associated with long-term growth stability.

This analysis indicates that relatively socially homogenous societies in MENA (Egypt and Tunisia) may be better suited to get good governance through democracy, while less homogenous societies in MENA (Iraq, Lebanon, Syria) may find it more difficult to achieve the needed sociopolitical consensus for good governance and good economic policy.

Should the Drive Be Just for "Better Governance"?

If there are risks that democracy does not lead to better governance, that is, more transparency, better voice and accountability, more secure property rights, less corruption, more efficient civil service, and more effective public service delivery, then what are the implications for the MENA region?

One possible implication may be that MENA countries should strive to achieve "better governance"—and not bother with seeking democracy. Countries should try to develop features of good governance such as secure property rights, rule of law, efficient and less corrupt government and public administration, predictable rules and laws, and so on. The economic success of authoritarian regimes, particularly in Asia, like China, Taiwan, Singapore, and South Korea, and even in some MENA countries, such as Tunisia and Egypt, that achieved relatively high rates of growth over the long run, suggests that this is possible, and that some adequate quality of governance can be secured under such regimes. Some even raise the question whether the very authoritarian discretion of such regimes actually helped growth, by enabling the leading parties to push through economic reforms that in a democratic setting might have been either slower, because of a need for consensus, or impossible to achieve. This argument would be even more compelling in situations where there is a high likelihood that democracy would not generate better governance because of significant social cleavages.

Many argue that this is not the case, and that democracy need not to be sacrificed on the altar of development. While East Asian countries have prospered under authoritarianism, many more countries have seen their economies deteriorate as a result of lack of democracy and accountability, for example, Zaire, Uganda, and Haiti. Such cases abound in MENA, with the examples of Iraq, Libya, and Syria. In addition, some of the most successful economic reforms of the 1980s and early 1990s were implemented under newly elected democratic governments in many regions, for instance, Latin America Countries (LAC) (Bolivia, Argentina, and Brazil), and Europe and Central Asia (ECA) (transition economies like Hungary, the Czech Republic, Poland, Slovenia, and Slovakia among others).

The critical question is whether "better governance" is more likely to emerge under democratic or nondemocratic regimes. Some of the previous discussion indicates that democracy leads to better governance, despite the risks faced by developing young democracies and countries with significant social cleavages. What about nondemocratic regimes? Are they able to produce governance systems that can enhance the quality of the business environment, leading to higher investment and sustained economic growth?

Rodrik (1999) and Rodrik and Wacziarg (2005) have argued that the performance record for democracies is even better than usually acknowledged. Claims that democratization leads to disappointing economic results are often used to justify calls to delay political reforms in poor, ethnically divided countries until they become "mature enough" for democracy. However, the hypothesis that democratization is followed by bad economic performance, particularly in poor, fractionalized countries, is not supported by their analysis.

In any case, the various cases of "enlightened dictatorship" appear to be the exception rather than the rule in the recent past. Authoritarian regimes may provide high-quality governance only randomly, and for each case of a nondemocratic regime that seems to produce better governance and growth outcomes, one can find many more cases of bad governance and dismal economic outcomes. In probabilistic terms, democracies appear to be more likely to generate better governance than nondemocratic regimes.

The Case of Oil-Producing Countries

Oil rents have shielded many MENA countries from economic crises, but they seem to have also helped to reduce the likelihood of the region becoming more democratic (Ross 2001). At the same time, the economic record of mineral-exporting countries over the past few decades, especially oil exporters, has been disappointing. Studies like Eifert et al. (2003) elaborate that this performance may be the result of poor public sector governance leading to poor oil revenue management. This phenomenon has sometimes been described as political Dutch disease, and was noticed by political scientists in the context of the MENA region. Several authors (Wantchekon 1999, Ross 2001, and Lam and Wantchekon 2002) find a positive correlation between resource dependence and authoritarian governments controlling for characteristics such as GDP, human capital, income inequality, and other possible determinants.

But can such regimes generate better governance in the absence of democracy? In fact, a recent study (Collier and Hoeffler 2005) finds major differences in the economic performance of autocracies and democracies when controlling for natural resource endowments. Richly endowed countries, such as oil producing countries, seem to perform better economically if they are not restrained by democratic institutions. The underperformance of oil-rich democracies is explained by economic policy choice, namely by the size and quality of investment. In view of the finding by Tavares and Wacziarg (2001) that democracies in general tend to under-invest in physical capital as they focus more on policies related to human capital development and a more equitable society, Collier and Hoeffler conclude that oil-rich democracies not only under-invest but also do so badly, since they face less financial, and consequently, political restraints. Resource-rich countries do not need to tax as much, which results in less scrutiny on their delivery of public services by their citizens. Therefore, the key argument is that resource-rich democracies need a distinctively different design that places more importance on checks and balances, that is, on instruments that rebalance how power is used, rather than on mechanisms that determine how power is achieved.

But empirical evidence shows that major oil-producing countries tend to have lower governance indicators. Though they seem to need more checks –and –balances, oil-reliant countries have the worst index of public accountability scores. Having substantial oil and gas revenues accrue directly to government budgets means that governments can maintain a deficient governance environment—as long as they do some redistribution and provide public goods to the population. In a situation of "no taxation, no representation," governments face little pressure to improve governance to increase economic development. Substantial revenue from natural resources relieves governments of the need to tax, thus reducing their obligation to be accountable. In addition, they are able to redistribute a significant share of their oil revenue through public employment and broad access to cheap public services. These two factors—no taxation and some redistribution—help mute demands for accountability (World Bank 2003e). While the presence of mineral wealth in a country may not be the cause for a governance deficit, it could make it more difficult for good governance institutions to emerge.

Eifert et al. (2003) reinforce this conclusion, and the importance of democracy for these countries. The study analyzes the oil-rich regimes of the world, and, depending on their characteristics, divides political systems into (i) mature democracies; (ii) factional democracies; (iii) paternalistic autocracies; (iv) reformist autocracies; and (v) predatory autocracies. The study concludes that mature democracies have clear advantages in managing oil revenues for the long term, because of their ability to reach consensus, their educated and informed electorates, and a level of transparency that facilitates clear decisions on how to use the oil revenues over a long-term horizon. Reformist and paternalistic autocracies lack transparency and face the risk of oil-led spending being the legitimizing force behind the state, which tends to foster corruption and creates problems with political transitions. These countries tend to be locked in high-spending patterns that are unsustainable in the very long term. Factional democracies lack an effective political system to create consensus among competing interests. Finally, predatory autocracies have short-term horizons and the characteristics of kleptocratic regimes that siphon money from state coffers, eventually drying up oil wealth.

The "Binding Constraint" to Growth Approach

The previous review of the links between democracy and economic growth has relied mostly on work that tries to find systematic relationships from cross-country comparisons. While such research finds complex relationships, and sometimes uncertain results, it tends to show the existence of a strong positive relationship between democracy and growth, especially if democratic institutions are designed in such a way as to lead to better governance, minimize the possible negative impact of political market failures, and avoid the risks from social cleavages.

But even using such an analytical framework to try to find systematic relationships between democracy and growth, Barro and Sala-i-Martin (2003) show that a nonlinear relationship may exist. Democratization appears to enhance growth for countries that are not very democratic, but to retard growth for countries that have already achieved a high degree of democracy. This finding, applied to MENA countries, would mean that democracy is important for growth, given their present low scores in democratic development.

A completely different approach to looking at the relationship between democracy and growth is to recognize that expectations of an overall systematic relationship between democracy and growth are ill placed. The impact of democratization on growth should be country- and time-specific; the static search for a stable relationship may be counterproductive.

One such alternative way to link democracy and economic growth is to use the recently-developed approach of "binding constraint" proposed by Hausmann, Rodrik, and Velasco (2004). This approach holds that constraints to growth are time- and country-specific. It rejects cross-country findings and one-size-fits-all solutions as useless tools for studying relationships between reforms and economic growth. In that framework, one has to ask the question: at a given time and in a given country, is the "democracy deficit," compared to other factors, the binding constraint of growth? For MENA countries, this could imply that democracy did not matter in the past but that it may be critical now. It may also imply that there is no general answer to this question for the region as a whole; one has to be country-specific.

The argument for the binding constraint approach for most countries in the region might go as follows. The low economic growth in the MENA countries is to the result of low private investment, which is itself to the result of weak investment climates and poor public sector governance. Major and credible reforms are needed, especially in terms of public sector governance and investment climate, in almost all countries of the region, in order to unlock the growth potential (see World Bank 2003a).[10] On the other hand, experience shows that after 20 years of attempts at reform, the depth and scope of such reforms, while they vary from country to country, remain limited. Political economy analysis suggests that political regimes, as they exist, have been unable to generate the required reforms (Nabli 2005). The existing political economy equilibrium favours the status quo: low public accountability and the maintenance of prevailing economic policies and networks of privilege. In such a situation, democratic reform may be able to unlock this state of affairs and generate a great political and economic transformation that could produce both more democracy and more economic growth in the region.

Conclusion: Striving for Democracy in the MENA Region?

Democratization yields benefits in the form of individual freedoms and empowerment that are valued independently of their consequences in terms of growth and material wealth. But democratization is also good because democracies can (a) yield long-run growth rates that are more predictable; (b) produce greater short-term stability; (c) handle adverse shocks much better; and (d) deliver better distributional outcomes.

Our review of the literature on the links between democracy and economic growth, and its application to the conditions of the MENA region, leads to the conclusion that MENA countries should strive for democratic regimes that are sustainable—in the sense of having characteristics that make them more likely to produce good governance. This means that democratic development requires going beyond an electoral process that guarantees free, open, and competitive elections. These formal democratic processes have to be complemented with a number of reforms that aim at (i) minimizing imperfections in the political market, with more freedom of information and free press, adequate mechanisms to contain clientelism, and increased credibility of political promises; (ii) introducing safeguards and effective checks and balances; and (iii) increasing the legitimacy of the democratic transformation. In cases where there is significant ethnic or religious fragmentation, or both, it is vital that the democratic institutions be designed so as to minimize the risks of conflict and emergence of unaccountable government.

These should help ensure or maximize the likelihood that democracy leads to better governance, and therefore to higher economic growth. In such a situation, one would not have to face short-term trade-offs between democracy and economic growth.

Such a conclusion is reinforced by the "binding constraint to growth" approach. Democracy may not be a "binding constraint" to growth, in the strict sense that if it were achieved today, it would result in higher economic growth in MENA countries. However, one can argue that progress in democracy is probably critical at this stage of the MENA world's history for achieving the required transformation, which would ensure better governance, more accountability, a better investment climate, and credible policies for increased private sector investment, employment, and growth.

Finally, one can argue that democracy can lead to better governance, and therefore, better economic policies and credible reforms, and that even the design of such economic reforms may in itself enhance democratic development. Producing a virtuous circle, where democratic development enhances governance and economic growth, will itself support consolidation of democratic development. For instance, more economic openness, which improves the relative incomes of the owners of human and physical capital, together with more economic equality, would enhance the development of democracy (Acemoglu and Robinson 2006).

Notes

1. The MENA region, in the World Bank definition, includes all Arab countries except Sudan, Somalia, Mauritania, and Comoros, plus Iran.

2. A recent paper by Gause (2005) reviews the question and challenges the view that promotion of democracy in the Middle East would stop generating anti-American terrorism.

3. The political regime universe has on one side democracy, and on the opposite side dictatorship (or authoritarian regimes). Dictatorships are defined here as regimes in which political rulers accede to power and maintain themselves in power by force. They use force to prevent societies from expressing their opposition to rulers' decisions. Because they rule by force, they are vulnerable to visible signs of dissent. These opposing political regimes represent different ways of selecting rulers, processing and resolving conflicts, and making and implementing public policy. In a sense, they are different ways of organizing political lives. As such, they are likely to impact people's lives and welfare in different ways.

4. The Polity IV index is produced by the Integrated Network for Societal Conflict Research Program of the University of Maryland's Center for International Development and Conflict Management (CIDCM)). Polity IV contains coded annual information on regime and authority characteristics for all independent states (with greater than 500,000 total population) in the global state system, and covers the years 1800-2003.

5. We thank Daron Acemoglu for providing the transformed Freedom House data.

6. Friedman (2005) provides a useful review and summary of the findings on this issue (Chapter 13).

7. Friedrich Hayek (1960) summarized this point by stating that "...it is in its dynamic, rather than in its static, aspects that the value of democracy proves itself. As is true of liberty, the benefits of democracy will show themselves only in the long run, while its more immediate achievements may well be inferior to those of other forms of government."

8. See Acemoglu et al. (2004).

9. In a recent study by Harber, Razo and Mauer (2003) on the politics of property rights, the authors challenge the idea that political stability and broader property rights are necessary for economic growth, based on Mexican historical evidence. They claim that economic growth does not always require a government that is constrained from preying upon property rights; it only needs a government that makes selective credible commitments to a subset of asset holders.

10. The Middle East and North Africa Region of the World Bank produced four major regional reports on the occasion of the World Bank-International Monetary Fund Annual Meetings in Dubai in September 2003. These reports-on trade and investment, governance, gender, and employment-are intended to enrich the debate on the major development challenges of the region at the beginning of the 21st century.

References

Aysan, A. F., M. K. Nabli, and M. A. Véganzonès-Varoudakis. 2006. "Governance and Private Investment in the Middle East and North Africa." Mimeo. World Bank, Washington, DC.

Acemoglu, D., and J. Robinson. 2006. *Economic Origins of Dictatorship and Democracy.* Cambridge, U.K.: Cambridge University Press.

Acemoglu, D., and S. Johnson. 2005. "Unbundling Institutions." *Journal of Political Economy* 113 (5): 949–95.

Acemoglu, D., S. Johnson, J. Robinson, and P. Yared. 2005. "Income and Democracy." Mimeo (February). Acemoglu, D., S. Johnson, and J. Robinson. 2004. "Institutions as the Fundamental Cause of Long-Run Growth." Paper prepared for the *Handbook of Economic Growth,* ed. Philippe Aghion and Steve Durlauf.

Acemoglu, D., S. Johnson, and J. Robinson. 2001. "The Colonial Origins of Comparative Development: An Empirical Investigation." *American Economic Review* 91: 1369–1401.

Alesina, A., A. Devleeschauwer, S. Kurlat, R. Wucziarg, and W. Easterly. 2003. "Fractionalization." *Journal of Economic Growth* 8: 155–94.

Barro, R. J., and X. Sala-i-Martin. 2003. *Economic Growth.* Cambridge, MA: MIT Press, 2nd edition.

Barro, R. J. 1999. "The Determinants of Democracy." *Journal of Political Economy* 107: S158–S183.

Barro, R. J. 1994. "Democracy and Growth." Working Paper 4909. National Bureau of Economic Research, Inc., Cambridge, MA.

Bollen, K. A. 2001. "Cross-National Indicators of Liberal Democracy, 1950-1990." Computer file, second ICPSR version. Chapel Hill, NC: University of North Carolina, Inter-university Consortium for Political and Social Research.

Bollen, K. A. 1990. "Political Democracy: Conceptual and Measurement Traps." *Studies in Comparative International Development* 25: 7–24.

Borner, S., A. Brunetti, and B. Weder. 1995. *Political Credibility and Economic Development.* London: Palgrave Macmillan.

Bourguignon, F., and T. Verdier. 2000. "Oligarchy, Democracy, Inequality and Growth." *Journal of Development Economics* (August) 62 (2): 285–313.

Buchanan, J. M., R. D. Tollison, and G. Tullock, ed. 1980. *Toward a Theory of the Rent-Seeking Society.* College Station, Texas: A & M University Press.

Collier, P. and A. Hoeffler. 2005. "Oil Democracies." Mimeo. University of Oxford, U.K., Department of Economics.

de Mesquita, Bueno B., and G. W. Downs. 2005. "Democracy and Development." *Foreign Affairs* (September-October) 84 (5).

de Soto, H. 1989. *The Other Path.* New York, NY: Harper and Row.

Easterly, W., and R. Levine. 1997. "Africa's Growth Tragedy: Policies and Ethnic Divisions." *Quarterly Journal of Economics* 111 (4): 1203–50.

Eifert, B., A. Gelb, and N. B. Tallroth. 2003. "Managing Oil Wealth." *Finance and Development* (40) 1. Washington, DC.

Elbadawi, I. A. 2004. "The Politics of Sustaining Growth in the Arab World: Getting Democracy Right." Lecture and Working Paper Series No. 2. American University of Beirut, Institute of Financial Economics.

Elbadawi, I. A., and S. Makdisi. 2004. "Democracy and Development in the Arab World." A program initiative from the International Development Research Center.

Elbadawi, I. A. 2002. "Reviving Growth in the Arab World." Working Paper Series 0206. Arab Planning Institute, Safat, Kuwait.

Evans, P. 1995. *Embedded Autonomy: States and Industrial Transformation.* Princeton, NJ: Princeton University Press.

Evans, P. 1989. "Predatory, Developmental, and Other Apparatuses: A Comparative Political Economy Perspective." *Sociological Forum* 4 (4): 561–87.

Feng, Y. 2003. *Democracy, Governance and Economic Performance: Theory and Evidence.* Cambridge, MA: MIT Press.

Friedman, B. M. 2005. *The Moral Consequences of Economic Growth.* New York, NY: Alfred A. Knopf.

Gause, F. Gregory III. 2005. "Can Democracy Stop Terrorism?" *Foreign Affairs* (September-October) 84 (5).

Giavazzi, F., and G. Tabellini, 2004. *Economic and Political Liberalizations.* Working Paper 10657. National Bureau of Economic Research, Cambridge, MA.

Haber, S., A. Razo, and N. Mauer. 2003. *The Politics of Property Rights: Political Instability, Credible Commitments, and Economic Growth in Mexico, 1876–1929.* Cambridge, U.K.: Cambridge University Press.

Hall, R. E., and C. I. Jones. 1999. "Why Do Some Countries Produce So Much More Output per Worker than Others?" *Quarterly Journal of Economics* 114 (1): 83–116.

Hausmann, R., D. Rodrik, and A. Velasco. 2005. *Growth Diagnostics.* Cambridge, MA: Harvard University Press.

Hayek, F. A. 1960. *The Constitution of Liberty.* Chicago, IL: The University of Chicago Press.

Keefer, P. 2004a. "Does Democracy Help?" Mimeo. Development Research Group, World Bank, Washington, DC.

_____. 2004b. "A Review of the Political Economy of Governance: From Property Rights to Voice." Mimeo. Development Research Group, World Bank, Washington, DC.

_____. 2005. "Democratization and Clientelism: Why Are Young Democracies Badly Governed?" Mimeo. Development Research Group, World Bank, Washington, DC.

Keefer, P., and S. Khemani. 2005. "Democracy, Public Expenditures, and the Poor: Understanding Political Incentives for Providing Public Services." *The World Bank Research Observer* 20 (1).

Knack, S., and P. Keefer. 1995. "Institutions and Economic Performance: Cross-Country Tests Using Alternative Institutional Measures." *Economics and Politics* 7 (3):207–28.

Lam, R., and L. Wantchekon. 2002. "Political Dutch Disease." Mimeo. New York University.

Lipset, S. M. 1959. "Some Social Requisites of Democracy: Economic Development and Political Legitimacy." *American Political Science Review* 53: 69–105.

Madison, J., A. Hamilton, and J. Jay. 1987. *The Federalist Papers.* London, U.K.: Penguin Classics.

Nabli, M. K. 2005. "Restarting the Arab Economic Reform Agenda." *The Arab World Competitiveness Report 2005.* World Economic Forum, Houndmills, Basingstoke: Palgrave Macmillan.

North, D. 1990. *Institutions, Institutional Change and Economic Performance.* Cambridge, U.K.: Cambridge University Press.

North, D. 1981. *Structure and Change in Economic History.* New York, NY: W.W. Norton.

Papaioannou, E., and G. Siourounis. 2004. "Democratization and Growth." London Business School, Economics Department Working Paper.

Persson, T. 2004. "Forms of Democracy, Policy and Economic Development." Working Paper. Institute of International Economics, Stockholm, Sweden.

Przeworski, A., M. E. Alvarez, J. A. Cheibub, and F. Limongi. 2000. *Democracy and Development: Political Institutions and Well-Being in the World, 1950–1990.* Cambridge, U.K.: Cambridge University Press.

Rivera-Batiz, F. L. 2002. "Democracy, Governance, and Economic Growth: Theory and Evidence." *Review of Development Economics* 6 (2): 225–47.

Rodrik, D. 2003. Growth Strategies. In *Handbook of Economic Growth*, ed. P. Aghion and S. Durlauf. North-Holland: Harvard University, John F. Kennedy School of Government, forthcoming.

Rodrik, D. 1999. "Institutions for High-Quality Growth: What They Are and How to Acquire Them." Paper presented at the International Monetary Fund Conference on Second-Generation Reforms, Washington, DC. November 8–9.

Rodrik, D. 1998. "Where Did All the Growth Go? External Shocks, Social Conflict, and Growth Collapses." Mimeo. Harvard University, John F. Kennedy School of Government, Cambridge, MA.

Rodrik, D. 1997. "Democracy and Economic Performance." Mimeo. Harvard University, John F. Kennedy School of Government, Cambridge, MA.

Rodrik, D. and R. Wacziarg, 2005. "Do Democratic Transitions Produce Bad Economic Outcomes?" Working paper. Center on Democracy, Development and the Rule of Law.

Rodrik, D., A. Subramanian, and F. Trebbi. 2002. "Institutions Rule: The Primacy of Institutions over Geography and Integration in Economic Development." NBER Working Paper 9305. National Bureau of Economic Research, Cambridge, MA.

Ross, M. 2001. "Does Oil Hinder Democracy?" *World Politics* 53: 325–61.

Sen, A. 1999. *Development as Freedom.* New York, NY: Alfred A. Knopf.

Schumpeter, J. A. 1942. *Capitalism, Socialism and Democracy.* New York, NY: Harper and Brothers.

Tavares, J. and R. Wacziarg. 2001. "How Democracy Affects Growth." *European Economic Review* 45: 1341–78.

Wantchekon, L. 1999. "Why Do Resource Abundant Countries Have Authoritarian Governments?" Working Paper 99: 12. Yale University, Leitner Center.

World Bank. 2003a. *Jobs, Growth, and Governance in the Middle East and North Africa. Unlocking the Potential for Prosperity.* Washington, DC: World Bank.

_____. 2003b. *Trade, Investment, and Development in the Middle East and North Africa: Engaging the World.* Washington, DC: World Bank.

_____. 2003c. *Unlocking the Employment Potential in the Middle East and North Africa: Toward a New Social Contract.* Washington, DC: World Bank.

_____. 2003d. *Gender and Development in the Middle East and North Africa: Women in the Public Sphere.* Washington, DC: World Bank.

_____. 2003e. *Better Governance for Development in the Middle East and North Africa: Enhancing Inclusiveness and Accountability.* Washington, DC: World Bank.

World Bank. 2005a. *Economic Growth in the 1990s: Learning from a Decade of Reform.* Washington, DC: World Bank.

_____. 2005b. *Middle East and North Africa: Economic Development and Prospects: Oil Booms and Revenue Management.* Washington, DC: World Bank.

_____. 2006. *Sustaining Gains in Poverty Reduction and Human Development in the Middle East and North Africa, Orientations in Development.* Washington, DC: World Bank.

6

The Political Economy of Industrial Policy in the Middle East and North Africa

Mustapha K. Nabli
Jennifer Keller*
Claudia Nassif *
Carlos Silva-Jáuregui*

The mainstream view on industrial policy has shifted back and forth over the past half century. During the 1950s and 1960s, industrial policy was widespread. Import substitution was a common strategy used to nurture "infant industries" throughout the developing world, including the Middle East and North Africa (MENA). A number of industrial and investment policies were used throughout the world to expand countries' industrial bases and develop key sectors.[1]

In some cases, industrial policy implemented over the 20th century seemed to yield astounding results, but perhaps nowhere more so than in a few high-performing East Asian economies. Interventions varied, including targeting and subsidizing credit to selected industries; keeping deposit rates low and maintaining ceilings on borrowing rates to increase profits and retain earnings; protecting domestic import substitutes; subsidizing declining industries-establishing and financially supporting government banks; investing in applied research; establishing firm- and industry-specific export targets; developing export marketing institutions; and sharing information widely between public and private sectors. Some industries were promoted while others were not.[2]

*World Bank.

Published as Egyptian Center for Economic Studies Working Paper no. 110; May 2006.

By the 1980s, however, views on industrial policy had decidedly changed. Growing evidence found that traditional approaches to industrial policy led to misallocation of labor and capital across industries and did not improve long-run growth in total factor productivity, but gave rise to rent seeking. Even among the high-performing economies of East Asia, it was argued that industrial policies—notwithstanding the contribution to the growth of the economies themselves—inflicted significant costs on the economies in the form of corruption and weak financial systems.[3] In Europe and the United States the practice of frequently "picking the loser" in declining industries such as agriculture, textile, steel, and shipbuilding reinforced this notion. Other factors contributed to industrial policy falling out of favor in most development circles, including the wide acceptance of the "Washington Consensus" reforms for Latin America, the fall of the Soviet Union, and an increasingly globalized economy.

The diverse experiences with industrial policy in different countries have shown that its outcome depends enormously on the national context, which determines how industrial policies are framed and implemented. Ultimately, the political economy will determine not only what types of industrial policy will be pursued, it may also determine whether a given set of strategic industrial policies will benefit one country, or specific economic groups therein, or whether it will harm another.

Despite these changing views of industrial policy, most of the countries in the MENA region continued to rely extensively on traditional industrial policy. Throughout the 1980s and 1990s, MENA countries maintained strong roles for the government and policies of significant government intervention in production and economic planning. During the same period, countries in Latin America, Europe and Central Asia that had broadly similar initial conditions undertook sweeping reforms of their economic structures and refocused their strategies into more coherent market-oriented policy packages to encourage private sector, export-led growth. The MENA economies made relatively less progress toward more market-oriented policies, and today governments in MENA are still actively implementing traditional industrial policies. More than in countries of other developing regions, these policies are characterized by vertical elements that protect selected industries and preserve existing market organizations. They include higher trade protection, higher public involvement in the production of goods and services, more control of strategic sectors like banking, and more price controls and subsidies.

In this paper, we examine the political economy and consequences of industrial policy in the MENA region. How can the particular features of MENA's industrial policy be explained? And why haven't industrial policies in MENA countries followed the evolutionary path of industrial policies of other countries? Unlike in many other regions, industrial policy in MENA developed within the context of the region's strong "social contract" between the government and its people. Although industrial development was an objective, it at times took a back seat to other goals such as social transformation and economic redistribution—which influenced not only the types and success of industrial policies adopted, but also the balance of power among interest groups. Political economy factors are central to understanding the industrial policy experience of the MENA region. These issues have scarcely been studied in the context of the MENA region, and this paper takes a broad regional and historical perspective, with the aim of providing a framework for examining them.

Section two of the paper provides the theoretical framework for understanding the industrial policy experience. Starting with a brief survey of the arguments used to justify industrial policy interventions, and drawing on various strands of the literature, it provides a review of various mechanisms and arguments to help understand the factors that determine the emergence and type of industrial policies observed and how they change. Using this framework, section three reviews the experience of MENA countries from the 1950s to the 1970s, and the emergence of state-dominated, vertical industrial policy, where traditional sector-selective and sector-specific policies have been used extensively.

Section four attempts to explain why industrial policy in MENA failed to change during the 1980s and 1990s. While most of the developing world has moved toward more market-oriented policies and production systems, dominated by the private sector and reliant on market signals, MENA has maintained many of the old-style industrial policies and the high level of state intervention that characterized much of the developing world in the past. Despite the mounting strains on MENA's economic development models, oil and strategic revenues, and the lack of a full-fledged economic crisis, have allowed the region to maintain industrial policies far longer than other regions. Equally important, the lack of interest groups to emerge and press for change has hindered the region's move toward more functional, market-friendly policies for growth—a phenomenon closely linked to the weaknesses in governance. In addition, during the initial industrialization stage, MENA countries used industrial policy to create new activities and support the development of new (infant) firms, but during the second stage (1980s-90s), industrial policy played a more passive role—that of preserving existing structures. From a political economy perspective, the preservation of structures can be explained by governments' desire to seek support to remain in power by continuing to offer rewards to supporters, in order to deter the formation of opposition groups.

The final section offers some concluding remarks on the likely direction of industrial policy in the region. As internal and external forces shape the way industrial policies can be used in the globalized economy, the MENA region's old style of industrial policy will need to adjust. The ultimate outcome will be largely determined by each country's initial conditions and individual political economy factors.

Understanding Industrial Policy

What exactly constitutes industrial policy? In the current vernacular, any policies or interventions that influence how industries expand are referred to as "industrial policies," but distinctions are made between "horizontal" industrial policies and "vertical" industrial policies. Interventions that are differentially applied across sectors of the economy are referred to as "vertical policy." Likewise, interventions applied across the board are referred to as "horizontal policy."

While vertical policies essentially target the economic output of specific industries and even firms, horizontal policies focus on improving the quality of inputs in the production process, which would presumably benefit all firms. Horizontal industrial policies often cited include promoting education and vocational training, building appropriate and efficient public infrastructure, encouraging international technology transfers, and fostering research and development.

Differentiating between policies that would benefit all firms and those that would benefit a select few may seem appealing, but it is not entirely accurate. Even horizontal policies may have substantially different impacts among sectors of the economy, and ultimately may be just as distortionary as vertical industrial policies. For example, if a government provides across-the-board energy subsidies (for example, in Iran) effectively lowering the unit price of energy for all consumers, it is technically a "horizontal" policy in that it is applied across sectors. However, it clearly affects firms differently, providing greater benefits to more energy-intensive (and often energy-inefficient) firms. Even a more "virtuous" horizontal policy, such as incentives for promoting education, will affect sectors of the economy differently depending on the education being promoted. Indeed, some firms may not benefit at all from a more educated workforce if education is not in line with the work of the firm. Thus, the line between "horizontal" and "vertical" industrial policy is often very difficult to distinguish. Despite these difficulties, this distinction is useful, especially from a political economy perspective, in order to try to understand the strong political appeal of vertical industrial policy compared to horizontal.

A useful starting point to understanding why countries primarily adopt vertical rather than horizontal policies is to examine some of the economic arguments behind both approaches. While the political economy may play a great role in determining the industrial policy approach adopted, economic justifications have provided a strong foundation for the road countries have traveled toward industrial development.

Economic Justifications of Vertical Industrial Policy

Industrial policy is traditionally justified by market failures that generate suboptimal outcomes in resource allocation. Once these market failures are identified, governments devise policy responses to cope with them in the form of industrial policy. Incentives and policies can also be used to compensate and correct government failures.

There have been a variety of economic justifications for the use of vertical industrial policy. Perhaps the most notable economic justification was the "infant industry" argument for selective protection. This dynamic comparative-advantage argument claims that protection is warranted for newly established firms and industries in countries where production costs may be initially higher than those of well-established competitors. If, over time, new domestic producers can reduce costs by learning by doing, then they can attain the production efficiency of their rivals. Without the initial protection, however, the domestic industry will never take off. The argument was used to curtail competition with both domestic and foreign firms. Many countries in MENA used this argument during the initial stages of industrialization after WWII, particularly regarding establishing trade barriers to protect their "infant" industries from competition from abroad.

But many other economic justifications for vertical industrial policy have been advanced as well. A second argument is that coordination problems of either upstream or downstream investments may hinder the development of otherwise competitive industries. This is exemplified by the development of the orchid industry in Taiwan,[4] where potential orchid growers contemplating investment in greenhouses needed to be assured that a variety of fixed investments were in place—including an electrical grid, irrigation, logistics and transport, and pest control measures. At the same time, all of these services had high fixed costs and were unlikely to be undertaken by the private sector without assurances that there were a sufficient number of greenhouses to demand their services. In this case, the Taiwanese government's upstream investments aimed to coax the downstream investments in greenhouses.

In the case of MENA, the argument has been used to support the creation of industrial zones (for example, in Morocco), or large investments in the water and irrigation sector to support agriculture (for example, in Egypt). In Jordan, a joint public-private initiative led to the establishment of "Cyber City" in 2003, which provides transportation, logistics, insurance, technology, and other commercial services to attract investments in the IT sector. In the service sector, specialized hubs have been created in the Gulf to support the development of financial services, education, health, trading, and transport. Qatar, for instance, is positioning itself to become a regional education and health services hub.

A third argument is based on information externalities that may restrict a country's capacity to determine which activities have costs low enough to be profitable. Unlike innovation, which can be protected with patents, the costs-(risks)-to-benefits ratio is high for starting a domestic industry that is already well established internationally. As Rodrik (2004) points out, entrepreneurs who figured out that Colombia was a good environment for flowers, Bangladesh for t-shirts, Pakistan for soccer balls, and India for software generated large social gains for their economies, but could keep very few of the gains for themselves. For this reason, selective government interventions may be required as a means of determining a country's areas of cost advantage. In MENA, information externalities arguments have been used in the development of export promotion agencies that played an important role in the Tunisian and Moroccan textile sectors.

The presence of market failures provides powerful arguments for governments to intervene, using vertical industrial policies to ensure that countries can determine their areas of advantage and generate spillovers to other sectors. In some instances, government failure, in the form of ineffective implementation of policies, leads to undesirable outcomes that have justified the implementation of compensatory industrial policies.

Despite theoretically sound arguments for vertical industrial policy, international success with industrial policy has been far from glowing, confirming that governments can "get it wrong." Well motivated or not, vertical industrial policies have often either prevented the emergence of dynamic, competitive enterprises or led to significant unintended consequences, not only when the policies were in place, but for a long period afterward.

The socialist industrial policy pursued by India in the 1950s included protectionist policies that increased the cost of unskilled labor. As a result, the country was shut out of the global market for manufacturing products with unskilled labor for many years after it ultimately opened up.[5] Korea's use of credit allocation as an industrial policy instrument is widely blamed for the financial system crisis that emerged in the late 1990s. Commercial banks were urged to lend to firms in preferred sectors or to the large and powerful conglomerates ("cronies"). Consequently, banks incurred weak balance sheets due to the low profitability of these firms. In addition, the policy nearly obviated bank skills for project monitoring and evaluation. As a result, the huge capital inflows that began in the mid-1990s were channeled through institutions that had suffered a serious erosion of skills and discipline.[6]

After Algeria nationalized nearly its entire economy in 1966, the government invested heavily in the creation of basic capital-intensive industries (for example, hydrocarbon, steel, plastic, and fertilizers) and in prioritized industries relevant to processing and import substitution (for example, construction materials, metal products, consumer goods). In many respects Algeria succeeded, and in less than a decade created a strong industrial base virtually from scratch. However, the rapid industrialization resulted in severe inefficiencies in the production capacity of various industries and generated fiscal imbalances in the mid-1970s, which constrained Algeria's ability to continue its expansionary industrial policy.[7]

In addition to possibly "getting it wrong," vertical industrial policy is subject to two potential (and common) damaging side effects: rent seeking and corruption. Wherever the government makes selective interventions that could contribute to the development of one sector or firm over another, there is the potential for interest groups to attempt to sway policy in their direction and utilize it for personal gain. The ability of countries to control corruption and rent seeking, in fact, is a key difference between countries in which industrial policy could be used effectively and those where the strategy floundered. However, the types of interest groups that emerge in a country, the mechanisms they can use to influence public policy, and how far they can shift industrial policy from "good" to "bad" can vary enormously from country to country. Attempting to deal with these government failures often leads to more selective policies, making industrial policies increasingly complex.

Economic Justifications of Horizontal Industrial Policy

While market failures, information asymmetries, externalities, and problems of coordination and learning are among the most commonly cited reasons for government intervention, addressing these issues from a horizontal policy perspective rather than a sector- or firm-specific one has been gaining acceptance by policy makers in the developing world.

Horizontal industrial policies may have many advantages over vertical policies. On one hand, horizontal policies tend to reduce the distortions generated by the use of vertical industrial policy. They approach industrial policy from an angle that is closer to competition policies, while still actively supporting the economy. Horizontal policies are applied across the board. As such, they tend to level the playing field across firms, industries and sectors, rather than giving a privileged position to some groups. Because of their "universal" nature, they also tend to reduce rent-seeking incentives and to limit corruption opportunities. This reduces the development of pressure and lobbying groups that seek to benefit from policies targeted to their interest. Horizontal industrial policies also increase transparency, by eliminating the need for backroom politics, and promote social cohesion as they can be seen as spreading the benefits across society as a whole instead of concentrating them within specific groups. In addition, they can promote efficiency and competition among firms, industries, and sectors in the economy, as each of these agents will have greater incentives to internalize the most from the horizontal policies.

On the other hand, horizontal industrial policies can serve to reduce the problem of state capture and government failure. Because these policies are applied across the board, they can eliminate some of the problems that help perpetuate the use of vertical policies. The distribution of benefits is more clearly defined with horizontal policies and the problems of non-neutrality are in principle eliminated (or at least reduced). However, it is important to note that while policies can be horizontal in design and nature, their effect may not be horizontal. The energy subsidy example above clearly indicates a case in which a horizontal policy may have a "vertical" outcome.

Finally, compared to traditional vertical policy, horizontal industrial policy adjusts more easily to changing market conditions, since its benefits are not captured by special groups, with vested interests, that would lobby to maintain the status quo. This builds a much needed dynamism in the policy itself, facilitating change and adjustment when needed.

Political Economy of Industrial Policy

The traditional approach to political economy posits that economic policies are shaped in the political market. The main actors in the market are interest groups or distributional coalitions who are rent seekers pursuing politically mediated gains. Any policy change is bound to produce winners and losers, who may or may not organize to block these policies and/or support other policies. Finally, policy makers mediate these pressures and determine their choices in view of their own objectives.

Sometimes policy makers may determine that it is in their interest to undertake fundamental policy reforms that may disrupt existing political coalitions and dislocate privileged economic actors. The old elites become losers in the reformed economic environment and a new set of winners emerges from the process. For example, reforms may aim at shifting the economic environment from cronyism, patronage, corruption, and rent seeking to transparency, accountability, and clear property rights. Such reform measures are risky because they disrupt the status quo and remove the dominant elites. In such situations reformers and policy makers distance themselves from prevailing interest groups, as they may be attempting to reach some longer-term objectives and mobilize alternative coalitions. The existing distributive coalitions do not shape policy reforms. The interests of winners and losers are essentially fixed by their position in the pre-reform political economy. Elites react to the reforms by attempting to block them or undermine the reform process to avoid losing their privileged position.[8]

So what influences the industrial policy choices countries make? Or more to the point, why, despite the frequent failures and the risks of vertical industrial policy, do political systems predominantly tend to produce and perpetuate vertical policies rather than horizontal? Despite the criticism leveled at selective policy interventions, most countries—both developing and developed—maintain something of a "halfway house" between mainstream free-market policy measures and vertical interventions to encourage specific industries. A number of arguments, rooted in the principles of collective action and interest groups, are relevant.

First, the benefits from horizontal policies tend to be diffused across groups and sectors, and it is not often easy to mobilize "winners" from horizontal policies. Take, for example, the case of education, skills development, and technological innovation policies. Although many businesses might benefit from skills upgrading, the extent to which a given firm could reasonably expect to benefit from across-the-board education policies might be small. In fact, a great deal of the resources might be devoted to the development of skills not used intensively in its own business. It is unlikely that collective action will emerge to support these generalized policies. On the other hand, within a particular sector, the types of skills used and technological knowledge needed are often highly specific. As a result, firms in a given sector are probably more likely to be able to develop lobbying power to pursue specific educational objectives.

Second, some of the most important horizontal policies are long term in nature; it often takes a long time for results to materialize. This is particularly the case with education and non-sector-specific research and development. Interest groups are unlikely to pursue and push such policies when the benefits to them are less visible and spread out over a long period of time. Therefore, it is up to governments to actively define and support such long-term development policies.

Third, in many instances, market and coordination failures are sector specific, and cannot be adequately addressed through horizontal approaches. Take the case of the tourism sector, in which coordination problems are pervasive. The emergence and/or expansion (new zones, new business niches) of the sector require coordination on a number of fronts: (i) development of basic infrastructure, such as zones with adequate water supply, sanitation, access to international transport, and similar core needs; (ii) development of specific technical and managerial skills; (iii) development of joint or support activities such as travel agencies, entertainment businesses, restaurants, and related activities; and (iv) information on markets, advertising, and opening of new markets. Given the number of factors that must come together for development of the sector, it is unlikely that market forces and mechanisms would be able to resolve all of the coordination problems. Typically, governments have to be involved. This was partly the case with the development of the tourism industry in Egypt when the government invested heavily in improving the tourism infrastructure near historic sites during the 1980s.[9]

Finally, arguments used by sector lobbies can often be couched in terms of benefits to other groups, such as workers and consumers, in strengthening their political power. Tariff protection for a specific sector is often couched in terms of domestic jobs protected. Protection of agricultural production and subsidies for European farmers are couched in terms of preserving the environment and livelihood of weak farmers. Protection of domestic production of many food products, such as meat, is couched in terms of health safety for consumers. These arguments cannot be made for blanket horizontal policies. They are intrinsically product- and sector-specific, and they have a powerful political thrust.

Lessons from reforms in the developing world (including the MENA region) indicate that in many instances, pre-reform elites are resilient. Privileged economic actors have been able to keep their positions after reforms. The process of reform has been one of reorganizing opportunities for rent seeking rather than eliminating them. Reforms have produced outcomes that continue to provide significant opportunities for privileged economic actors to capture rents from a set of regulatory arrangements and economic institutions.[10]

These lessons and experiences suggest that the effectiveness of political systems to generate welfare-enhancing policies would depend on a number of factors that can be usefully summarized as good governance. These factors include: (i) the extent to which policy makers are held accountable for the choices they make and the extent to which they pursue public vs. private interest; (ii) the transparency of the decision-making process and political influence; (iii) the ease with which interest groups can organize to pursue their interests openly; and (iv) the quality of information and analysis available to support and enlighten decision making.

The Emergence of State-Dominated Vertical Industrial Policy in MENA from the 1950s to the 1970s

Industrial policy in the MENA region developed to some extent as an offshoot of the region's social contracts that emerged in the 1950s. Partly to correct for a legacy of inequities and poverty in the region, the MENA countries adopted models of development based on heavy state intervention and redistribution. The social contract was designed to align with the norms and expectations of social groups to the legitimate claims they had on state resources, as well as to determine the demands state actors may legitimately make on society. It had a number of distinctive features, including institutional arrangements, public policies, legitimating discourses, and modes of state-society interrelations. Core attributes of the social contract—some of them directly linked with industrial policies of choice—included: (i) the preference of states over markets in managing national economies; (ii) a reliance on state planning in determining economic priorities; (iii) a penchant for redistribution and equity in economic and social policy; (iv) an encompassing vision of the role of the state in the provision of welfare and social services; and (v) a vision of the political arena as an expression of the organic unity of the nation, rather than as a site of political contestation or the aggregation of conflicting preferences.[11]

Another key marker in the rise of the interventionist-redistributive social contract and its associated industrial policy was the emergence of centralized, hierarchical, and tightly regulated corporatist structures of interest groups in the first decade after independence. These arrangements provided the blueprint for the organization of relations between the state and a wide range of stakeholders, including firms, laborers, students, and women, in addition to various professional associations. It was through these arrangements that corporatism created possibilities for agency, bargaining, and negotiation for the groups it was designed to contain; the so-called privileged networks that are the center of the new theories of political economy of reform. These structures also helped to determine the modalities of industrial policy used in the region, and facilitated state capture and corruption.

Institutionally and in terms of economic and social policies, these elements were consolidated through broadly similar strategies in a number of MENA states, including Algeria, Egypt, Iraq, Syria, and—to a lesser degree—Jordan, Morocco, Yemen, and Tunisia. These strategies included (i) the rise of a dominant single-party or ruling-party government; (ii) new, postindependence constitutions that enshrined interventionist and redistributive principles in the basic laws; (iii) a wave of agrarian reform programs to redress inequalities in the rural economy; (iv) the centralization of trade unions and professional associations; and (v) programs for state provision of social services, including education, housing, health care, food subsidies, and other benefits.

Understanding the reasons for the widespread "acceptance" of this type of state-dominated social contract in MENA countries is beyond the scope of this paper. However, it is clear that the political system underlying this social contract is different from the kind of governance structure that is typically assumed when arguments are made about the likely emergence of a vertical industrial policy. Such arguments assume a governance structure where political competition is prevalent, the market system is predominant, and there is a large degree of openness and availability of information and analysis. The different system prevalent in MENA would have significant implications for the type of industrial policies that emerged during the 1950s and 1960s. The attributes of the social contract and governance structure led to four mechanisms/features of this model, which modified and/or reinforced standard political economy arguments:

- First, sweeping nationalizations of industry, trade, and agriculture in the late 1950s and early 1960s produced a dramatic expansion in the scale of public sectors and reduced the role of the private sector; the relationship between state-owned enterprises and decision makers allowed them to influence policies more effectively.
- Second, the state captured (either wholly or predominantly) the banking and insurance sectors.
- Third, price controls and subsidies were chosen as the predominant mode of regulation based on the need to protect the poor and pursue a social agenda of redistribution.

- Fourth, the role of oil wealth—both oil resources for oil-producing economies, and oil-related revenues[12] for resource-poor economies— underwrote much of the region's emerging social contracts, and the public sector (both governments and state-owned enterprises) became a key vehicle for redistribution through employment. While this trend may be more apparent in the oil sectors, the role of the state in most of the MENA countries has been dominant, comparable at times to the command economies of the former Soviet bloc.[13] As a result of these trends, by the 1960s the commanding heights—the means of production—were mostly in the hands of the state in many MENA countries.

Within the predominant role of the state and the use of central planning as the main vehicle for resource allocation, these mechanisms and characteristics led to an industrial policy that was bound to be sectoral/vertical and highly preferential, thus creating an environment of "winners" and "losers."

The Public Enterprise Sector and Industrial Policy

To a large extent, industrial policy was structured to support public sector enterprises. This was partly the result of the waves of nationalization implemented in several countries of the region. Like many countries of the world that embraced the infant-industry concept in the 1950s, MENA implemented an inward-looking model with protection from external competition. Import tariffs, licenses, prohibitions and other forms of nontariff barriers were used as the direct instruments of choice to support public sector enterprises, but other policies supported public sector production (and employment), including credit rationing, subsidies, and foreign exchange policies.

The nature of public enterprises and their relation to decision makers made the pursuit of sectoral interests relatively easy and the implementation of incentive schemes straightforward, as most of the instruments could be shaped accordingly. MENA's trade policies of high import tariffs and nontariff barriers, which limited competition from abroad, echoed strategies adopted elsewhere, protecting industries that would, it was hoped, flourish and compete later on.[14] When, despite trade protection, these firms incurred losses, it was easy to cover them directly from the budget, or more commonly, from the banking system.

In situations where the private sector continued to play a role, it often faced distorted incentives and the negative impact of the presence of public enterprises, such as higher cost and lower quality. Under such circumstances, the only way for private businesses to pursue their interests was, in addition to dealing with externalities, to obtain specific incentives in the form of special protection, access to finance, or other subsidies. This process enhanced the vertical and complex nature of industrial policy.

Box 6.1. Industrial Policy in Tunisia

After gaining independence in 1956, Tunisia's manufacturing and mining sector was small, and in the years that immediately followed, there was little or no growth. Most Tunisian businessmen continued the long commercial tradition of the country, and there was no net inflow of capital from foreign industrial investors, partly as a result of uncertainty about the government's attitude to private investment and political tensions with France. In the late 1950s the government began to take steps to assure the industrial development of the country.

In the first half of the 1960s, the government launched an initiative involving a number of government offices and financial institutions, including the National Company for Investment (SNI), to establish several industrial enterprises that were either directly or indirectly controlled by the state. From 1959-60, the major share of industrial financing was provided by the government either directly, through equity participation, or indirectly through its banking and insurance subsidiaries lending or taking equity positions in industrial companies.

By the end of the 1960s virtually every industry was primarily controlled by the government. The tourism sector was the one area in which the government had been hesitant to invest, mostly because it regarded the investment potential as too risky and because there was considerable opportunity for private activities. Convinced that the tourism industry had great growth potential, the government actively promoted it with measures such as tax holidays for new hotels, a rebate on loan interest rates for tourism investments, preferred access to land, and subsidies for hotel construction. These policies led to high growth rates in the tourism sector, which developed into one of the main growth engines of the Tunisian economy during the 1970s.

Source: World Bank (1966, 1969, 1971, 1972).

Financial Sector and Industrial Policy

While this instrument of industrial policy is typically not available or of limited use in capitalist economies, it has emerged as one of the major mechanisms of sector-specific interventions in MENA countries. In combination with pension and social security funds, bank and nonbank financial institutions were used to collect sizable resources that were managed by the state. Savings were collected at low cost through administered interest rates that were usually negative in real terms. This generated implicit subsidies that were transferred to the privileged priority firms and sectors. Credit was directed by central bank command. Countries including Algeria, Egypt, Jordan, Morocco, and Tunisia created industrial development banks to provide foreign exchange loans for the imported capital goods necessary for investment. Government control of the banking systems made it possible to pursue vertical industrial policy. Resources of the banking system were directly allocated to selected activities, with quota allocations by sectors and preferential access by public enterprises. This is epitomized by Morocco, which created the Banque Nationale Pour le Développement Economique (BNDE) in 1959, with the sole purpose of providing loans to investment projects in selected industries that had experienced insufficient growth. In line with its mandate, the BNDE significantly contributed to the expansion of the tourism sector, the agrofood industry, and the textile industry. In addition, monetary policy was conducted through direct credit allocation and refinancing.

Consumer Subsidies and Industrial Policy

MENA countries also used subsidies as an active policy choice. In part, subsidies and other artificial supports were a necessary part of industrial policy in MENA because of the externalities of the instruments of redistribution. Administered prices prevailed throughout MENA economies and damaged the link between prices and production costs, making compensation mechanisms necessary.

Among initial subsidies, the most pervasive were for consumer goods, especially foodstuffs. These subsidies-cum-price-controls meant that specific sector policies were needed for agricultural and food products in order to compensate for the weakened production incentives. As a result, the agricultural sector required further policy instruments of trade protection, access to preferred bank financing and subsidies. The incentives were justified as critical for employment, protecting the poor and maintaining social peace.

Oil Wealth and Industrial Policy

In addition to supporting the social contract, in many MENA countries industrial policy developed in reaction to the influence of oil wealth. Recognizing the impact that Dutch disease had on the competitiveness of tradables, governments instituted a range of compensatory policies to mitigate the adverse effects. In a real sense, industrial development in the MENA economies could not take place without some direct government interventions. This is most obvious for the oil-producing economies, but even in the resource-poor economies of the region, the exchange rate appreciation that occurred from the massive inflow of aid and remittances contributed to the view that vertical industrial policies were needed for industrial development.

Additionally, the abundance of oil revenues has given rise to interest groups who have sought to retain a disproportionate flow of the rent and evaluate reform policies based on their capacity to be captured.[15] This has perpetuated and motivated the use of more vertical industrial policies.

The Economic "Outcomes" from MENA's Vertical Policies

Some of the economic costs of the industrial policies adopted in the MENA region have been widely acknowledged. The continued strategies of import protection and inward orientation in MENA have resulted in significantly weakened trade, with trade-to-GDP growth at about half of the world's pace since the 1980s. The region's exports are dominated by oil, with only the small number of resource-poor and labor-abundant economies developing fairly well-established nonoil export sectors. The entire MENA region, with a population close to 320 million, has fewer nonoil exports than Finland or Hungary, countries with populations of 5 and 10 million, respectively.[16]

Also, the region did not sustain high levels of productivity after the 1960s. MENA experienced two decades of strong economic growth during the 1960s and 1970s. In fact, MENA's economic growth performance in the 1960s was the strongest in the world. During the decade, productivity growth was strong, in part as a result of the industrial policies adopted, which allowed the region to utilize underused capacities and provide the early boost of industrialization. But by the 1970s, productivity deteriorated sharply as massive investments were generating increasingly poor payoffs in terms of growth. Over the 1970s and 1980s, productivity growth in the MENA region was negative.[17]

The MENA industrial policy strategy has also been less successful than expected. Egypt adopted an active industrial policy from the early 1960s until the early 1990s, when some elements of vertical interventions were phased out in the wake of structural reforms that did not prove very successful. One could argue that if industrial policy had been effective the Egyptian economy should be more diversified. A recent assessment of the impact of industrial policies in Egypt revealed, however, that this is not the case. In contrast, the manufacturing industry has become more concentrated over time, particularly between the 1980s and 1990s.[18]

Moreover, full employment—a virtual mainstay of the social contract—could not be maintained. Between the 1980s and 2000, the unemployment rate climbed from an average of less than 8 percent to 15 percent.[19] By 2000, the MENA region's unemployment rate was higher than every other region of the world except Sub-Saharan Africa.

Beyond the economic failures, the industrial policies adopted in MENA powerfully influenced the emergence and control of interest groups in the region, a fact that heavily contributed to the continued use of vertical policies well beyond their justification.

The Failure to Change Industrial Policy in the 1980s and 1990s

Deteriorating budget deficits and the lack of economic growth prompted a handful of economies in the region—including Jordan, Morocco, and Tunisia—to embark on programs of macroeconomic stabilization and structural reform in the mid-1980s. The programs aimed to restore macroeconomic balances and promote private sector-led development. By the late 1980s and early 1990s most governments followed suit, adopting some form of economic stabilization. Policies varied, but included cutting subsidies, reducing public spending, liberalizing trade, reforming exchange rate regimes, encouraging exports, easing restrictions on foreign investment, privatizing state enterprises, and strengthening the institutional foundations of a market-led economy, including consolidation of the rule of law. Many governments joined international trade-promoting institutions and signed trade agreements to spur the domestic economy.[20]

The use of vertical industrial policy diminished in MENA, but compared with other regions it has remained in place to a large extent. In the area of trade protection, tariffs in MENA countries have been slow to decline, in contrast to the rapid decrease observed in other developing countries. In 2004, half of the countries in the region had average tariff protection[21] higher than that of developing countries as a whole. Ranking countries worldwide according to average tariffs revealed that on average, MENA countries are in the bottom 35 percent in terms of tariff protection, second only to Sub-Saharan Africa[22] (see figure A1 in the Appendix).[23] Only in the last several years has the region achieved some progress in lowering barriers to trade. Nontariff protection—which can constitute a variety of measures, including quantitative restrictions, rules for valuations of goods at customs, rules of origin, and price control measures—has been reduced, but it is today still higher in MENA countries than in most countries of Latin America, East Europe, or South Asia. According to IMF classification, only three countries show a low incidence of nontariff barriers, namely Djibouti, Qatar, and the UAE, while all others show either an intermediate or high incidence, such as Syria, Iran, and Libya (see tables A1 and A2). Significant distortions in the tariff schedule continue to exist, especially in Iran, Syria, Tunisia, and Morocco (see table 6A.1).

Box 6.2. Financial Sector—Islamic Republic of Iran

The banking sector in Iran remains essentially dominated by the state. There are 10 large state banks in Iran. Six of them are general commercial banks that take deposits from the public and make loans to both the public and private sectors. The other four are specialist banks that lend to particular sectors: One lends exclusively to finance housing, a second lends to the agricultural sector, a third to industry and mining; the fourth specializes in export finance. These four specialist banks obtain most of their funds from the general commercial banks, the central bank, and other public sources.

The instruments that banks can use for borrowing and lending are governed by a 1982 law on Islamic banking. The rates of return on both loans and deposits set by the central bank have been generally less than the rate of inflation over the last decade. The controlled lending rates vary with the term and the sector receiving the loan. Every large loan must be approved by the central bank, which also sets the minimum percentages of each bank's loan portfolio that must be lent to various broad sectors such as housing, agriculture, exports, and state-owned enterprises.

Source: World Bank (2003e).

Inefficiencies and distortions of financial sector policies became apparent, and in many countries of the region, reforms have taken place to liberalize financial systems, and in a limited number of cases even privatize them.[24] In fact, the financial system might well be the policy sphere that has experienced the biggest reduction in government intervention. All countries, Syria and Iran aside,[25] unified their currency rates either before or in the early 1990s. Around the same time, most countries moved away from the administration of interest rates (see tables A3 and A4). But several MENA countries continue to use these distorted policies today. Access to credit by the private sector remains limited in Algeria, Iran, Libya, Qatar, Syria, and Yemen, where the private sector receives less than 35 percent of all domestic credit extended (see table 6A.5).

MENA countries also used subsidies as an active policy choice to support their industries (and consumers). Subsidies were greatly reduced as part of macroeconomic stabilization programs; cash subsidies to industries in particular were reduced by almost 50 percent. Nonetheless, the levels of subsidies remain high. Studies indicate that subsidies in the form of direct cash transfers to enterprises are significant in MENA countries, albeit not as high as the European Union or in Europe and Central Asia (see figure A2).[26] However, because of the difficulties of measuring subsidies (rates of effective protection and effective assistance are not easily available), cash transfers to industries may be only a weak proxy for the actual level of subsidies, which might be significantly higher.

Despite the MENA region's lack of success with industrial policy, transition from "bad" vertical industrial policies toward those that are more horizontal has proceeded slowly, especially in comparison to the transitions in other regions of the developing world, such as Latin America and the Caribbean, East Asia and the Pacific, and Europe and Central Asia. Several factors have contributed to this slow transition.

The first factor, perhaps ironically, has been the fact that the results of industrial policy have not been "bad enough." There is a line of thinking among those who study reform that deep economic reform movements only result from fundamental change, either from leadership change (regime change, or a shift in governing coalition), or from dramatic economic change—in other words economic crisis. In many Latin American countries, for example, economic reforms were undertaken only when the "economic conditions had deteriorated sufficiently so that there emerged a political imperative for better economic performance."[27] In other words, reform often is only adopted "once the possibilities of throwing money at the problem are foreclosed."[28] Crises elsewhere—Latin America in the early 1980s and Europe and Central Asia in the late 1980s—generated pressure for both political and economic change. As a result, countries in those regions moved from command to market economies with less state intervention.

Box 6.3. Strategic Crops in the Arab Republic of Syria

One example that illustrates how industrial policy is used as an instrument for achieving both economic as well as social objectives is agriculture policy in Syria. Agriculture plays a key role in Syria's economy by contributing substantially to domestic production, employment generation, and export revenues. As in many other countries in the world, the agriculture sector in Syria has been enjoying a high level of public protection and support. Interventions are targeted toward the crops that the government considers "strategic," namely wheat, barley, lentils, chickpeas, cotton, and sugar, either because they provide significant export earnings or ostensibly ensure food supply.

The case of cotton shows to what extent these interventions result in systemic distortions that are propagated throughout the economy. In order to protect farmers from price volatility, the government buys cotton from farmers above world market prices through its central marketing organization, which subsequently exports it. While this is done at world market prices, the domestic industry is required to purchase cotton at the state fixed price without the chance to obtain cheaper imported cotton (high duties are levied on cotton imports). Consequently, cotton-based textile manufacturing has been deprived from taking full advantage of the low wage level in Syria, which otherwise would have helped to develop a real comparative advantage in the textile industry. The government interventions in the agricultural sector have, thus, been counterproductive and hampered growth in the textile sector.

Source: FAO (2003) and World Bank staff.

The MENA region, although it has experienced a significant decline in growth and employment from the gradual exhaustion of its economic models, has not experienced economic crises in a systemic way.[29] The substantial revenues from oil, which declined throughout the 1980s and 1990s, have remained large (and of late increased significantly), giving MENA governments and the public a temporary sense of economic health. This, along with foreign aid and strategic rents, has permitted MENA governments to maintain damaging vertical industrial policies.

Second, the slow pace of change in industrial policy in the region reflects either a lack of power among those interest groups that might be instrumental in lobbying for a move toward more horizontal industrial policy, or the gradual creation of privileged networks that are influencing policy to retain their rent-seeking capacity.

The private sector, rather than challenge the status quo, has adapted to the prevailing industrial policy that has protected state-owned enterprises. Private sector activity is concentrated in a small number of large firms that have benefited from protective policies, along with a number of microenterprises, which account for a large percentage of employment but have little access to formal finance, markets, or government support programs. This behavior of the emerging private sector has reduced the likelihood of faster reform and policy change.

Trade unions, which could also be an effective vehicle for change, are tightly controlled in the region and lack real independence from the political system. Thus, trade unions have not been effective in organizing the labor force to press for reforms. Trade union membership as a share of employment in MENA averages about 9 percent, compared to 34 percent in the OECD, 43 percent in Europe and Central Asia, and 15 percent in Latin America and East Asia. Only South Asia and Sub-Saharan Africa have lower trade union membership.

The industrial export sector, which is highly competitive and would likely lobby for horizontal policies, is grossly underdeveloped and generally scattered among diverse product groups. A recent study examined the lobby power of the manufacturing sector[30] and found that MENA ranks last compared to the developing regions of the world (table 6.1).

Other groups that would benefit from more horizontal industrial policies that could stimulate growth and employment—the many young and educated who are unemployed,[31] small businesses and young entrepreneurs who seek to enter protected markets and have difficulty accessing finance, and small farmers—have limited ability to unite and lobby the government for change in industrial policy.

Table 6.1. Lobby Power of the Manufacturing Export Sector, 2001

Country/Region	Lobby power of the manufacturing sector
Bahrain	0.27
Algeria	0.01
Egypt	0.18
Iran	0.03
Jordan	0.14
Lebanon	0.35
Libya	0.00
Morocco	0.36
Oman	0.03
Qatar	0.06
Saudi Arabia	0.02
Syria	0.05
Tunisia	0.48
Middle East and North Africa	0.13
Sub-Saharan Africa	0.19
East Asia and the Pacific	0.34
Europe and Central Asia	0.42
Latin America and the Caribbean	0.31
South Asia	0.52
High-Income/OECD	0.51

Source: Nabli, Keller, and Véganzonès (2002).

To press for more horizontal policies, these groups require certain rights—access to information to formulate choices, the ability to mobilize, the ability to contest policies that are poor—which are only weakly present in the MENA region. Government information is not fully accessible to the public. Activities of the press are carefully monitored and freedom of the press circumscribed in most countries. There are restrictions on civil society, and the ability to contest government policies is weak. More generally, the MENA region suffers from fundamental weaknesses in governance, in terms of inclusiveness, public accountability, and strength of civil society. In a ranking of more than 142 countries according to some 19 indicators of governance (in terms of both the quality of public administration and public sector accountability), the MENA region on average ranked in the bottom third of countries worldwide—lower than every other region of the world (see table 6A.6). This has hindered the development of coalitions for change and helped perpetuate ineffective policies. Analysis suggests that the existing political economy equilibrium favors the status quo of little or no public accountability and maintaining prevailing economic/industrial policies and networks of privilege. In such a situation industrial policy reforms are likely to come slow. Democratic reform may be able to change this state of affairs and generate a great political and economic transformation that could produce more democratic governments, more effective policies and more economic growth in the region (Nabli 2005).

The move toward horizontal policies is far from straightforward. It affects the balance of power between actors in society; at its core it involves finding the economic rents that have built up over the years and cutting them back; and it attacks the economic privilege that some have enjoyed for generations. Thus, it is hardly surprising that MENA has found moving toward a more horizontal industrial policy a profoundly difficult task.

In many cases prereform economic elites have proven to be resilient to the reform process even when policy reforms were designed to reduce their rent-seeking opportunities—like those shifts aimed at moving toward horizontal industrial policy. The existing sectoral interests are better able to preserve their privileges, which leads to a passive industrial policy.[32] The governance structures did not help new pressure groups to emerge or move toward more effective reforms.

Where Does MENA Go from Here?

The claim that industrial policy is a thing of the past is largely exaggerated. Industrial policies continue to be used throughout the world, but their modalities and focus have been changing to reflect the reality of the new global economy and rapid technological change, as well as to acknowledge the costly mistakes made in the past with traditional industrial policy.

One of the greatest realizations is that vertical industrial policies almost always breed dependency. An "infant industry" seldom feels it has grown up and asks for government support to stop.[33] Because of this, the modalities of industrial policy have to change. At the same time, there is practically no country in the world without a foreign direct investment promotion policy or an export-oriented focus—a clear signal that industrial policy is alive and well.

The challenge for MENA in the 21st century is to recognize that the kinds of industrial policy needed in the current international setting are clearly different from the traditional forms of inward-looking, paternalist-state industrialization strategies of the past. What MENA needs is not more industrial policy but better, more sensible industrial policy. This may imply reducing the scope of intervention in the region. But it also implies moving away from vertical to horizontal policies, and from "choosing winners" (or more often "protecting losers") to policies that make sense in the current global environment. There is therefore a compelling argument for MENA to reconsider the types of industrial policies it uses. The rapid growth in information and communication technologies, the acceleration of technical change and the intensification of global integration require countries to focus on efficiency gains in the value chain. Economic development is increasingly linked to the economy's ability to acquire and adapt new technical and socioeconomic knowledge. Comparative advantages are coming less from abundant natural resources or cheaper labor, and more from technical innovations and the competitive use of knowledge. Moreover, the speed with which economies are able to disseminate and apply knowledge increasingly determines their level of competitiveness and their chances of succeeding in the global arena.

MENA countries, like other developing countries in the world, operate in an environment that is much different from two or three decades ago. The global crises of the 1980s and 1990s led to the tendency to impose greater discipline in national economies. External mechanisms, including multilateral, regional, and bilateral agreements, structural adjustment programs, and political pressure from the industrialized world, have all reduced the scope of industrial policies that MENA countries can use. Developing countries are members of a number of international organizations and have signed agreements that limit the countries' capacity to use distortionary policies to promote particular sectors. For example, the new formal trade rules under the auspices of the WTO limit selective interventions in trade; Basel core banking principles restrict direct lending; articles of agreement with international financial institutions impose market-driven procompetition policies in a large array of areas, eliminating or reducing food subsidies, trade distortions, restrictions on FDI, and regulating the use of monetary, foreign exchange, and fiscal policies; free trade agreements eliminate tariff barriers and nontariff barriers, enforce intellectual property rights, and regulate rules of origin and services; and codes of conduct increase transparency and accountability.

All these external pressures are shaping the changes in MENA's industrial policies.

Internal forces are also playing a role in reshaping MENA's industrial policies. Although the region has not suffered from the deep crises that forced other developing regions in the world to move rapidly out of their traditional industrial policies, the picture in the MENA region is not homogeneous. Wealth has allowed the oil-rich economies of the region to slow down the pace of reforms. However, in countries like Jordan, Morocco, and Tunisia, reforms have moved faster. Other internal forces are also putting pressure on the status quo. The growth and employment challenges that MENA countries are facing—in light of the region's demographic transition—are rapidly revealing the weaknesses of MENA's economic model. Industrial policies are failing to generate the promised results, and the social contract is not being honored. Several factors are intensifying the need for reform, including labor market pressures, rising expectations for improved standards of living, and the need for efficient production models that will allow the region to deal with competition from world markets.

In addition, the MENA region is facing sociopolitical pressures to improve inclusiveness and accountability, as well as to increase the transparency and contestability of public policy. These forces are manifested in public demands for greater individual and social freedoms, more democratization through open and fair electoral processes, greater female participation in the social sphere, better public services, and enhanced public sector governance. These internal forces are also shaping the path of MENA's reforms and the future of its industrial policies.

But how is MENA going to move from the policies of the past to the policies of the future? The processes that will determine the path of change are likely to depend on each country's initial conditions and individual political economy factors. All roads may lead to Rome, but which road each MENA economy takes is an open question. The priorities for change in policies, industrial or otherwise, vary with resource endowments, governance institutions, and reform progress to date, as will the paths to the target.

From the political economy point of view, differences in economic performance across countries can be explained by imperfections in electoral markets—such as uninformed voters, noncredible political competitors, and social polarization—which make it difficult for citizens to hold politicians accountable for policies and outcomes. These imperfections offer powerful insights into the development of particular (industrial) policies and the underperformance of many economies.

Clientelism is a dominant characteristic of public policy in many countries. One explanation for its existence derives from the struggle to make credible promises to citizens. Patron-client relations drive politicians to focus on targeted favors and goods rather than broad public goods and effective public policy: insofar as only clients believe patron promises (given the absence of well-developed political parties, for example), political competition mainly concerns targeted transfers to clients rather than public policy issues more generally (World Bank 2005c).

Given the complexity of MENA's political economy, political market incentives must be changed in favor of better policies. One avenue is through governance reform. The imperfections in political markets can be reduced, but require improving the availability of information, transparency, checks and balances, accountability, space for civil societies, and contestability of the political market. These elements are needed for improved governance and could increase the likelihood of effective design and implementation of public policies, including industrial policies, and that could lead to better economic outcomes for the region.

Notes

1. While the term "industrial policy" was originally used to describe policies relating specifically to the industrial sector, today the term has become more broadly recognized to include policies that encourage any sector (for example, agriculture or tourism) not only the industrial sector.

2. World Bank (1993).

3. Noland and Pack (2003, 2005).

4. Rodrik (2004).

5. As it turns out, the country found its niche in sunrise industries with high knowledge content. However, the best intentions with industrial policy have often produced the most disastrous outcomes.

6. Borensztein and Lee (2005) and Pack (2000).

7. World Bank (1975).

8. See, for example, Olson (1971, 1982) on collective action and rent-seeking behavior, North (1990) on economic institutionalism, Waterbury (1993) on public enterprise reform, and Hellman (1998) on "winners take all."

9. World Bank (1980).

10. This led Heydemann (2004) to propose a new approach to the political economy of policy reform that focuses on the so-called networks of privilege.

11. World Bank (2003a).

12. Including capital flows and labor remittances.

13. It is important to note that while socialist ideas had an important influence on the economic model implemented in the region, there is significant heterogeneity among countries and the economic polices they used in the past and continue to use today.

14. This was not a MENA-specific problem. Other regions that adopted these policies (for example,, Latin America and the Caribbean) experienced this problem as the domestic industry had less access- but particularly less incentive—to implement the latest technologies and management practices.

15. Auty (2004).

16. Muller-Jentsch (2005).

17. Nabli, Keller, and Véganzonès (2002).

18. Galal and El-Megharbel (2005).

19. World Bank (2003b).

20. World Bank (2003c).

21. Measured by unweighted average tariffs.

22. World Bank (2005b).

23. Ibid.

24. Jbili, Enders, and Treichel (1997).

25. Iran in the early 2000s.

26. Schwartz and Clements (1999).

27. Krueger (1993).

28. Koromzay (2004).

29. Some countries in the region, like Jordan, have experienced deep economic crisis and as a result have moved forward the reform agenda at a faster pace than the region's average.

30. Nabli, Keller, and Veganzones (2002). Lobby power is measured as an interactive between the size of manufacturing exports in total exports, and the share of manufacturing exports among the top four export categories at the three-digit ISIC.

31. Unemployment in the region, which averages about 15 percent of the labor force, is about two-three times higher for those under the age of 30.

32. As mentioned by Heydemann (2004), reforms in the MENA region as well as in other parts of the developing world have provided opportunities for the networks of privilege to survive. The elites continue to be elites in their sectors even after reform. In other regions privatization processes are good examples of where the networks of privilege exert their influence.

33. Krueger (1993).

References

Auty, Richard M. 2004. "Economic and Political Reform of Distorted Oil-Exporting Economies." Paper prepared for the workshop "Escaping the Resource Curse: Managing Natural Resource Revenues in Low-Income Countries," held at the Center for Globalization and Sustainable Development, Earth Institute at Columbia University. February 26.

Borensztein, Eduardo, and Jong-Wha Lee. 2005. "Financial Reform and the Efficiency of Credit Allocation in Korea." *Journal of Policy Reform* 8 (1): 55–68.

Creane, Susan, Rishi Goyal, A. Mushfiq Mobarak, and Randa Sab. 2004. "Financial Development in the Middle East and North Africa." IMF Working Paper 04/201. Washington, DC: International Monetary Fund.

FAO (Food and Agriculture Organization). 2003. "Syrian Agriculture at the Crossroads." *Agricultural Policy and Economic Development* 8. Rome, Italy: FAO.

Galal, Ahmed, and Nihal El-Megharbel. 2005. "Do Governments Pick Winners or Losers? An Assessment of Industrial Policy in Egypt." Working Paper 108. Cairo, Egypt: The Egyptian Center for Economic Studies.

Hellman, Joel S. 1998. "Winners' Take: The Politics of Partial Reform in Postcommunist Transitions." *World Politics* 50 (January): 203–234.

Heydemann, Steve. 2004. *Networks of Privilege in the Middle East: The Politics of Economic Reform Revisited.* New York: Palgrave Macmillan.

International Monetary Fund (IMF). 2005. *Annual Report on Exchange Arrangements and Exchange Restrictions.* Washington, DC: International Monetary Fund.

Jbili, Abdelali, Klaus Enders, and Volker Treichel. 1997. "Financial Sector Reforms in Morocco and Tunisia." Finance and Development IMF Working Paper 97/81. Washington, DC: International Monetary Fund.

Koromzay, Val. 2004. "Some Reflections on the Political Economy of Reform." Paper presented at international conference on "Economic Reforms for Europe: Growth Opportunities in an Enlarged European Union." Bratislava, Slovakia. March 18.

Krueger, Anne. 1993. *Political Economy of Policy Reform in Developing Economies*. Cambridge, MA: MIT Press.

Muller-Jentsch, Daniel. 2005. "Deeper Integration in Trade Services in the Euro-Mediterranean Region: Southern Dimensions of the European Neighborhood Policy." Draft working paper. Washington, DC: World Bank.

Nabli, Mustapha K., Jennifer Keller, and Marie-Ange Veganzones. 2002. "Exchange Rate Management within the Middle East and North Africa Region: The Cost to Manufacturing Competitiveness." Working Paper 2004:1. Beirut: American University of Beirut.

Nabli, Mustapha K. 2005. "Restarting the Arab Economic Reform Agenda." *The Arab World Competitiveness Report 2005*. World Economic Forum. Houndmills, U.K.: Palgrave Macmillan.

Noland, Marcus, and Howard Pack. 2003. *Industrial Policy in an Era of Globalization: Lessons from Asia*. Washington, DC: Institute for International Economics.

———. 2005. *The East Asian Industrial Policy Experience: Implications for the Middle East*. Washington, DC: Institute for International Economics.

North, Douglass C. 1990. *Institutions, Institutional Change and Economic Performance*. New York: Cambridge University Press.

Oliva, Maria Angels. 2000. "Estimation of Trade Protection in Middle East and North African Countries." IMF Working Paper 00/27. Washington, DC: International Monetary Fund.

Olson, Mancur. 1971. *The Logic of Collective Action: Public Goods and the Theory of Groups*. Cambridge, MA: Harvard University Press.

———. 1982. *The Rise and Decline of Nations. Economic Growth, Stagflation, and Social Rigidities*. New Haven, CN: Yale University Press.

Pack, Howard. 2000. "Industrial Policy: Growth Elixir or Poison?" *The World Bank Research Observer* 15 (1): 47–67. Washington, DC: World Bank.

Rodrik, Dani. 2004. "Industrial Policy for the Twenty-first Century." Unpublished paper. Harvard University, Cambridge, MA. Available at: http://ksghome.harvard.edu/~drodrik/UNIDOSep.pdf

Schwartz, Gerd, and Benedict Clements. 1999. "Government Subsidies." *Journal of Economic Surveys* 13 (2): 119–147.

UNCTAD (United Nations Conference on Trade and Development). 2005. Trade Analysis and Information System (TRAINS) database. Available at: http://r0.unctad.org/trains/

Waterbury, John. 1993. *Exposed to Innumerable Delusions: Public Enterprise and State Power in Egypt, India, Mexico and Turkey*. New York: Cambridge University Press.

World Bank. 1966. *Tunisia—Second Societe Nationale d'Investissement Project*. Staff appraisal report. Washington, DC: World Bank.

———. 1969. *Tunisia—Third Societe Nationale d'Investissement Project*. Staff appraisal report. Washington, DC: World Bank.

———. 1971. *Tunisia—Fourth Societe Nationale d'Investissement Project*. Staff appraisal report. Washington, DC: World Bank.

———. 1972. Tunisia—Fifth *Societe Nationale d'Investissement Project*. Staff appraisal report. Washington, DC: World Bank.

———. 1975. *Algeria—Industrial Credit Project*. Staff appraisal report. Washington, DC: World Bank.

———. 1990. *Egypt—Tourism Project*. Project completion report. Washington, DC: World Bank.

———. 1993. *The East Asia Miracle: Economic Growth and Public Policy*. New York: Oxford University Press.

————. 2003a. *Unlocking the Employment Potential in the Middle East and North Africa: Toward a New Social Contract.* MENA Development Report. Washington, DC: World Bank.

————. 2003b. *Trade, Investment, and Development in the Middle East and North Africa: Engaging with the World.* MENA Development Report. Washington, DC: World Bank.

————. 2003c. *Jobs, Growth and Governance in the Middle East and North Africa.* MENA Development Report. Washington, DC: World Bank.

————. 2003d. *Knowledge Economies in the Middle East and North Africa. Toward New Development Strategies.* Washington, DC: World Bank.

————. 2003e. "Iran: Medium Term Framework for Transition. Converting Oil Wealth to Development." Country economic memorandum. Washington, DC: World Bank.

————. 2005a. "Technology and Growth Series: Chilean Salmon Exports." PREM Notes 103. Washington, DC: World Bank.

————. 2005b. *MENA Economic Developments and Prospects 2005: Oil Booms and Revenue Management.* Washington, DC: World Bank.

————. 2005c. *Economic Growth in the 1990s: Learning from a Decade of Reform.* Washington, DC: World Bank.

World Economic Forum. 2003. *Arab World Competitiveness Report 2002–2003.*

Data Appendix

Figure 6A.1. Average Nominal Tariffs by Region, 1980–85

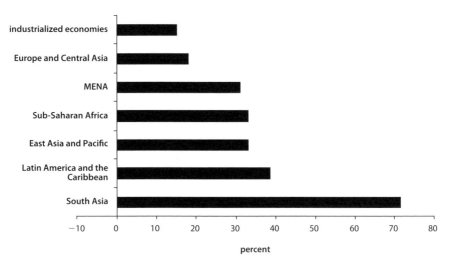

Source: World Economic Forum, Arab World Competitiveness Report 2002–2003.

Figure 6A.2. Cash Transfers to Industries (% of GDP)

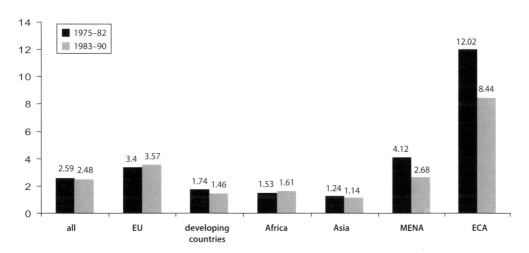

Note: Based on SNA database, national authorities, and authors' calculations. The category Developing Countries does not include Israel and South Africa, although they are included in their geographical country groups. Here, subsidies are defined as cash transfers to industries.

Table 6A.1. Current Average Tariffs and Standard Deviation for Selected Countries

	Average tariff	Standard deviation		Average tariff	Standard deviation
MENA			**High-Income**		
Algeria (2003)	18.63	10.37	European Union	4.4	5.5
Djibouti (2002)	30.71	7.65	Japan (2004)	3.13	7.06
Egypt (2002)	19.88	16.19	United States (2004)	3.7	11.27
Iran (2004)	19.88	20.14	**Africa**		
Jordan (2003)	13.7	16.1	Nigeria	27.21	23.51
Lebanon (2002)	6	10.75	South Africa (2001)	8.15	11.62
Morocco (2003)	28.87	20.25	**Asia (EAP + SA)**		
Saudi Arabia (2004)	6.11	6.65	China (2004)	10.46	7.92
Syria (2002)	14.64	21.6	India (2004)	29.02	13.79
Tunisia (2004)	25.96	26.81	Indonesia (2004)	7.05	15.53
Yemen (2000)	12.78	6.06	Malaysia (2003)	8.48	21.07
LAC			**Europe and Central Asia**		
Argentina (2004)	12.64	7.58	Hungary (2002)	9.5	13.49
Bolivia (2004)	9.28	2.5	Poland (2003)	13.39	32.14
Brazil (2004)	13.57	6.79	Russian Federation (2002)	9.62	5.13
Chile (2004)	5.99	0.71	Turkey (2003)	7.11	20.22
Mexico (2004)	17.43	14.99			

Source: UNCTAT (2005).

Table 6A.2. Ranking of Nontariff Measures, 1999

Low incidence	Intermediate incidence	High incidence
	Algeria	Syria
Djibouti	Egypt	Iran
Qatar	Jordan	Libya
U.A.E.	Kuwait	
	Lebanon	
	Morocco	
	Oman	
	Saudi Arabia	
	Tunisia	

Source: Oliva (2000), according to IMF classification.

Table 6A.3. Overview of Exchange Rate Systems in MENA Countries

Country	Exchange rate system	Exchange rate structure	Exchange tax/subsidy
Algeria	Managed Float	Unified	No/No
Djibouti	Currency Board	Unified	No/No
Egypt	Managed Float	Unified	No/No
Iran	Managed Float	Unified	No/No
Iraq	Peg	Unified	No/No
Jordan	Peg	Unified	No/No
Lebanon	Peg	Unified	No/No
Libya	Peg	Unified	No/No
Morocco	Peg	Unified	No/No
Saudi Arabia	Peg	Unified	No/No
Syria	Peg	Multiple	No/No
Tunisia	Managed Float	Unified	No/No
UAE	Peg	Unified	No/No
Yemen	Independent Float	Unified	No/No

Source: IMF (2005).

Table 6A.4. Overview of Interest Rates and Credit Controls in MENA

Country	Interest rate liberalized?	All credit controls removed?	Notes
Algeria	Yes, de jure.	Yes, de jure. Ceilings removed in 2000.	Interest rates were liberalized in 1990 (as well as deposit rates and ceilings on lending rates).
Bahrain	Yes	Yes.	
Djibouti	Yes	Yes	
Egypt	Yes, de jure.	Yes	Interest rates were liberalized in 1991.
Iran	No	No	Through the lending instruments of the state-owned banks, credit allocation is decisively used to support certain sectors in Iran's economy. The lending instruments that banks can use are governed by a 1982 law on Islamic banking with the rates of return on both loans and deposits set by the central bank, generally less than the rate of inflation over the last decade. The controlled lending rates vary with the term and the sector receiving the loan. Every large loan must be approved by the central bank, which also sets the minimum percentages of each bank's loan portfolio. The preferred sectors are, roughly speaking, agriculture and housing before export, industry, and trade and services.
Jordan	Yes	Largely. Preferential credit facilities remain for agriculture, handi-crafts and export sectors	In the early 1990s, Jordan fully liberalized interest rates. In 1993, the Central Bank of Jordan moved away from direct instruments of monetary control by issuing its own certificates of deposit to mop up excess liquidity. In 1996, the central bank's rediscount subsidies and preferential credit facilities were eliminated, except for small specialized banks that extended credit to the agricultural, handicrafts, and export sectors.
Lebanon	Yes	Yes	
Morocco	Yes	Yes	Steady steps of liberalization and elimination of credit subsidies since the1980s. Interest rates liberalized in 1991, full liberalization of ceilings, etc. by 1996.
Qatar	Yes	Yes	Specialized banks offer subsidized loans to small companies.
Saudi Arabia	Yes	Yes	

(Table continues on the following page.)

Table 6A.4. Overview of Interest Rates and Credit Controls in MENA (*continued*)

Country	Interest rate liberalized?	All credit controls removed?	Notes
Syria	No	No	Until interest rates were adjusted in 2003; the bank's discount interest had remained unchanged at 7-9 percent since 1981 (7 percent for the public sector) irrespective of liquidity conditions or inflation. As a result, real interest rates were negative in times of high inflation (over much of the 1980s and until 1995, when inflation averaged 19 percent), and very high for much of the rest of time, particularly in the late 1990s when prices were contracting. Lending priority is given to the public sector, with many loans often insufficiently serviced by public institutions. Private companies often find it difficult to obtain loans through the banks, and resort to the unofficial market (or offshore banks) where rates are often as high as 20 percent.
Tunisia	Partial. Some deposit rates remain regulated.	Yes, de jure. However, lending is still encouraged to certain sectors through preferential access.	Gradual liberalization except for interest rates on lending in priority sectors. In 1987, interest rates on short term deposits were liberalized. Lending rates, except for those to priority sectors, were allowed to be set freely within a set of 3 percentage points above TMM. In 1990, preferential rates for all priority sectors were increased, albeit only moderately for agriculture. In 1994 and 1996, interest rates were liberalized for all sectors.
UAE	Yes	Yes.	
Yemen	Partial	A minimum benchmark rate for saving deposits is set administratively.	

Source: Creane et al. (2004).
Note: Authors' notes based on various World Bank resources.

Table 6A.5. Share of Domestic Credit Directed to the Private Sector, 2003

Country	Share of domestic credit (%)	Region	Share of domestic credit (%)
Algeria	11.5	Middle East and North Africa	55.3
Iran	35.4	Latin America and the Caribbean	30.5
Syria	10.1	Europe and Central Asia	45.6
Yemen	6.9	Sub-Saharan Africa	73.8
Libya	18.0	High-income/OECD	123.0
Egypt	61.5	East Asia and the Pacific	137.9
Jordan	71.7		
Lebanon	82.0		
Morocco	55.1		
Tunisia	69.0		
Saudi Arabia	58.2		
United Arab Emirates	55.9		
Bahrain	65.4		
Oman	38.6		
Kuwait	73.8		
Qatar	30.5		
South Asia	31.7		

Source: World Bank World Development Indicators online (August, 2005).
Note: Regional averages weighted by total domestic credit.

Table 6A.6. Governance Indicators in MENA

Country	Quality of public administration	Public sector accountability	Overall governance
Algeria	44.1	42.3	42.5
Bahrain	..	37.2	..
Djibouti	..	..	..
Egypt	46.1	38.3	40.9
Iran	37.2	36.5	35.9
Iraq	..	..	..
Jordan	54.7	53.1	53.1
Kuwait	51.1	44.8	47.2
Lebanon	..	..	..
Libya	34.5	7.7	17.5
Morocco	57.8	47.9	51.1
Oman	51.7	32.8	40.6
Qatar	..	31.0	..
Saudi Arabia	50.8	21.0	32.6
Syria	37.0	25.8	29.7
Tunisia	58.4	37.1	44.3
United Arab Emirates	51.1	33.6	40.8
West Bank Gaza	..	..	..
Yemen, Republic	40.6	34.8	36.5
MENA	47.3	35.1	39.4
Sub-Saharan Africa	42.6	55.1	49.1
East Asia and the Pacific	43.1	57.3	50.6
Europe and Central Asia	49.0	69.5	60.3
Latin America and Caribbean	47.4	75.7	63.3
OECD	79.6	97.5	90.2
South Asia	47.2	58.2	52.9
LMIC (excluding MENA)	45.7	61.1	53.9

Source: World Bank staff calculations.
Notes: Governance indices range from 0 to 100; higher values reflect better governance standing compared with other countries. Regional and subregional aggregates are simple averages of relevant country values. The indices are constructed using principal component analysis (PCA), an aggregation technique designed to linearly transform a set of interrelated variables into a new set of uncorrelated principal components that account for all the variance in the original variables. LMIC refers to low- and middle-income countries.

Part II

Labor Markets and Human Capital

7

The Macroeconomics of Labor Market Outcomes in MENA

How Growth Has Failed to Keep Pace with a Burgeoning Labor Market

Jennifer Keller*
Mustapha K. Nabli

Perhaps the greatest single development issue facing the economies of the Middle East and North Africa (MENA)[1] is the challenge of employing its people in good jobs. While the region is heterogeneous in terms of developments in the labor market, the majority of the region has been characterized by high levels of unemployment, and in some cases by declining real wages, as well. The problem of job creation for the MENA region is enormous. A 2003 World Bank study on the region estimated that between 2000 and 2020, some 100 million new jobs will need to be created within the MENA countries, more than doubling the number of jobs in existence, if the region is to both absorb future labor force entrants and eliminate current unemployment.[2] To give some perspective on this challenge—a 100 percent increase in the number of jobs over two decades—one need only look at some of the countries in East Asia, which managed the highest rates of sustained employment growth in modern history. In China, employment growth over the two decades beginning in the late 1970s averaged 40 percent. Korea's employment growth over the 1980s and 1990s was slightly less than 60 percent. Malaysia's employment

*World Bank. The authors are grateful to Sebastien Dessus, Carlos Silva-Jauregui, Dipak Dasgupta, and Marie-Ange Véganzonès for their comments and suggestions.

Earlier version published as Egyptian Center for Economic Studies Working Paper 77, August 2002.

growth was highest in East Asia over the 1980s and 1990s, with a 90 percent increase in jobs.[3] These countries have experienced some of the greatest spurts in employment growth over a sustained period of time. And employment growth in the MENA region needs to exceed this pace.

Unemployment rates in the region are among the highest in the world, averaging 14.0 percent of the labor force.[4] The problem of unemployment affects virtually every country in the region, even several oil-exporting Gulf economies that traditionally had to import expatriate laborers to supplement the national work force. In a few countries, the unemployment rate reaches close to 20 percent or higher, including Algeria (23.7[5] percent), Morocco (19.3 percent), and the West Bank and Gaza (25.6 percent).

These high levels of unemployment imply a substantial loss of human capital to the economy. The MENA region has made considerable progress over the last decades in increasing access to basic education. The educational attainment of the adult population in MENA increased by an average of more than 5 percent a year between 1960 and 1990,[6] higher than any other region of the world. But just as these human capital achievements should be having their greatest payoff, in terms of economic growth, a considerable portion of these resources are left idle.

Much of the story behind the MENA region's lost decade of growth, and the consequences on the labor market, is understood. Declining oil prices had a major impact on the region, both for the oil-exporting nations and for much of the region, through the impact on remittances and external financial flows. Additionally, the region was marked by macroeconomic instability and structural inefficiencies that prevented the emergence of a strong private sector. At least half of the MENA economies suffered from some degree of macroeconomic instability during the 1985-95 period. Public sector ownership was extensive, yet while large investments were taking place with the oil windfalls, there were few policies in place to make these investments competitive. Trade regimes were protective. Regulation limited the entry of the private sector into most sectors. Financial sectors were geared to serving public enterprises, and institutions were not in place to facilitate a vibrant private sector. As a consequence, when oil prices collapsed, the engine for growth in the economies of MENA stalled, and there was limited ability to absorb the burgeoning labor force.

What was of far greater concern in MENA was that despite macroeconomic stabilization, and at least some structural reforms undertaken throughout most of the region over the late 1980s and early 1990s, a strong economic recovery remained elusive. GDP per capita growth over the region averaged 1.6 percent a year over the 1990s, higher than the anemic growth over the 1980s (averaging only 0.4 percent a year[7]), but hardly the rebound one would have desired following a decade of stagnation. Outside the Gulf economies, growth averaged a slightly higher 1.8 percent per year, far from robust. As a result, following two decades of poor or lackluster economic performance, by 2000 the MENA region faced unemployment rates averaging 15 percent of the labor force, higher than in every other region in the world but Sub-Saharan Africa. Improving labor market opportunities has become among the highest priorities for policy makers in the region.

In this paper, we analyze the major labor market trends that developed in the MENA region over the 1990s. We then examine the failure of growth to materialize following widespread structural reform throughout the region. By decomposing growth over the 1990s between factor accumulation and productivity growth, we find that productivity growth improved for the majority of countries in the region over the 1990s, with an average increase in TFP growth of 1.4 percent from the 1980s. At the same time, despite these positive improvements in productivity in MENA, economic growth remained anemic (with average growth in GDP per laborer over the 1990s virtually unchanged from the 1980s), in great part because of the collapse in investment that has occurred in virtually every economy in the region.

We then offer some reasons why private sector investment did not materialize as dynamically as hoped, despite widespread macroeconomic and structural policy reforms instituted throughout the region in the early part of the decade. Despite the region's achievements over the 1990s in terms of macroeconomic stabilization and policy reform, MENA's progress with structural reform has been incomplete. Financial sectors remain weak. Trade liberalization remains incomplete, with continuing high protection levels. Public ownership remains high. And, the regulatory framework and supportive institutions for private sector investment have not materialized.

Finally, we offer policy recommendations for improving labor market outcomes. Pushing forward with more complex and politically challenging "second-generation" reforms may be mandatory if the region is ever to ensure the higher and sustainable economic growth that is needed to ensure better labor market prospects in the region.

The Disappointing Labor Market Outcomes in MENA

According to national statistics, MENA's unemployment rates are among the highest in the world, averaging 14 percent of the labor force, second only to Sub-Saharan Africa (figure 7.1).[8] In a number of countries in the region, such as Algeria, Morocco, and the West Bank and Gaza, close to 20 percent or more of the labor force are without jobs.

Unemployment in the region worsened throughout the 1990s, contributing to the high unemployment rates currently observed. Table 7.1 compares labor force growth to employment growth over the 1990s. Because of discouraged workers leaving the labor force, it is not always possible to interpret employment growth's outpacing labor force growth as necessarily a reduction

Figure 7.1. Worldwide Comparison of Unemployment Rates, 2004[a]

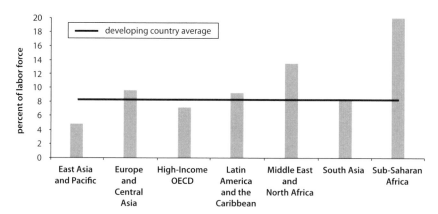

Source: World Bank data.
a. Or most recent year available.

in "unemployment." However, when the labor force growth exceeds the growth of employment, it is indicative of worsening unemployment. From that table, the rate of growth of the labor force exceeded the rate of growth of employment in Algeria, Iran, Egypt, and Morocco, which together account for approximately 70 percent of the entire region's labor force, and in which current unemployment rates now average 15 percent. In Tunisia and Jordan, where the rate of unemployment was already moderately high, the rate of growth of employment remained about on par with the rate of growth of the labor force.

Worker productivity—which over the long term forms the basis for increases in real wages—has generally increased throughout MENA, but remains low by international standards (table 7.2). Over the last decade, the growth of GDP per worker was lower in the MENA region than any other region of the world but Europe and Central Asia (heavily influenced by Russia), averaging only 0.5 percent a year. Productivity actually declined over the 1990s in Algeria, Saudi Arabia, and Jordan.

Table 7.1. Labor Force Growth versus Employment Growth over the 1990s

Country	Labor force growth (%)	Employment growth (%)	Time period	Unemployment (latest year available)	Size (labor force as % of total regional labor force)
Algeria	3.8	2.2	1989–2000	23.7	11
Iran	2.2	1.9	1991–2000	13.2	21
Egypt	2.8	2.4	1988–2000	9.9	26
Morocco	2.5	1.8	1987–2000	19.3	12
Tunisia	2.8	2.8	1989–2000	14.3	4
Jordan	5.5	5.9	1990–2001	14.5	2

Source: World Bank staff estimates from country sources.

Table 7.2. Employment, Growth, and Productivity Growth in MENA versus Other Regions, 1990–2004[a]

Country	Employment growth (%)	GDP growth (%)	Time period	Worker productivity growth (%)
Algeria	4.2	2.5	1990–2004	−1.6
Iran	3.0	4.2	1990–2002	1.2
Egypt	2.9	4.3	1992–2003	1.5
Morocco	2.1	2.6	1990–2001	0.5
Tunisia	3.0	5.0	1989–2000	2.0
Jordan	5.9	5.1	1990–2001	−0.7
Syria	3.7	4.6	1991–2002	0.8
Saudi Arabia	5..7	2.7	1990–2000	−2.0
MENA				**0.5**
East Asia and Pacific (including China)				8.0
EAP (excluding China)				2.5
Latin America and the Caribbean				0.8
Europe and Central Asia				0.2
South Asia				4.5
High-Income/OECD				1.5
World (excluding China)				2.4

Source: MENA employment growth: World Bank staff estimates from country sources; GDP: World Bank World Development Indicators; Employment outside of MENA economies: World Development Indicators, International Monetary Fund International Financial Statistics online.
Note: Worker productivity growth calculated as log growth of GDP/laborer for the period noted.
a. Or closest year available.

Understanding the Poor Labor Market Outcomes in MENA

Under most comparisons, MENA's labor market outcomes over the 1990s were disappointing. Why weren't enough jobs created? Why were laborers who found jobs unable to watch their wages grow?

The simplest answer is that economic growth has been insufficient, given the region's labor force growth. Labor force growth in MENA is exceptional, the result of both rapid population growth and increasing rates of labor market participation (particularly for females). At an average rate of growth of 3 percent a year, MENA's labor force is growing at a higher rate than in any other region of the world.

At the same time, before the recent upturn in growth from rising oil prices, the region's labor force growth was barely matched by economic growth. High labor force growth, of course, need not be an automatic recipe for poor labor outcomes. It could very easily contribute to high GDP growth, as was the case in East Asia during its high-growth years. But, in MENA, high labor force growth rates have been accompanied by only marginal growth of real output. In table 7.3, labor force growth rates and real GDP growth rates in East Asia in the 1970s are compared with labor force growth rates and real GDP growth

Table 7.3. Labor Force Growth and Real GDP Growth

MENA 1990s versus East Asia in the 1970s (%)

Country/Region	Labor force growth	GDP growth	GDP per worker growth
MENA, 1990–2000	**3.1**	**3.6**	**0.4**
Algeria	4.1	1.7	−2.3
Iran	2.9	4.0	1.1
Syria	4.3	5.1	0.8
Yemen	4.0	5.5	1.5
Egypt	2.9	4.5	1.6
Jordan	7.0	5.1	−1.8
Lebanon	3.2	10.3	6.9
Morocco	2.4	2.2	−0.2
Tunisia	3.1	4.7	1.6
Bahrain	3.5	4.6	1.1
Kuwait	0.4	3.4	3.1
Oman	4.2	4.6	0.4
Saudi Arabia	2.3	2.7	0.5
United Arab Emirates	6.3	3.2	−2.9
East Asia, 1970–80	**3.1**	**7.8**	**4.6**
Hong Kong	4.2	9.3	4.9
Indonesia	2.9	7.9	4.9
Korea	3.1	7.2	4.0
Malaysia	3.5	7.8	4.1
Singapore	4.4	8.9	4.3
Thailand	3.4	6.9	3.4

Source: World Bank, World Development Indicators.

rates of MENA economies in the 1990s. There is no difference between the two regions' labor force growth—both were exceptionally high, at 3.1 percent a year, on average.

The real difference between the regions, of course, is that East Asia's labor force growth was accompanied by enormous increases in real output not witnessed in the MENA economies. Real GDP growth in East Asia averaged 7.8 percent a year between 1970 and 1980—more than double its labor force growth rate for the same period. In MENA, in comparison, economic growth during the 1990s has only averaged about 3.6 percent a year —only marginally higher than the growth rate of its labor force, and implying virtual stagnation in productivity per potential laborer for the region as a whole.

To better understand the importance of the growth of output per laborer in improving labor market outcomes, we can refer to the simple accounting framework below. Creating employment for those who want to work is equivalent to increasing the ratio of employed persons to the total labor force (c). Increasing productivity (the basis for wage growth, at least over the long term) is equivalent to increasing output per employed person (b). The sum of these two objectives results in growth in output per laborer (a). The higher the real output per laborer growth, in turn, the greater is the scope for the economy to either reduce unemployment and/or increase productivity (and wages). In short, output per laborer growth provides a snapshot of the labor market outcomes that will arise.[9] Strong growth means that there is room for both unemployment reduction and wage increases. In MENA, output per laborer growth has been only 0.4 percent per year on an average basis. As a result, almost any reductions in unemployment have had to come at the expense of wages. There has been limited scope for simultaneously lowering unemployment and realizing real wage increases.

$$\text{Growth } \frac{\text{Output}}{\text{Labor Force}} \quad = \quad \text{Growth } \frac{\text{Output}}{\text{Employment}} \quad + \quad \text{Growth } \frac{\text{Employment}}{\text{Labor Force}}$$

$$\text{(a)} \quad = \quad \text{(b)} \quad + \quad \text{(c)}$$

Output per laborer has grown in MENA at an average annual rate of only 0.4 percent a year, with actual deteriorations in output per laborer in Algeria, Jordan, Morocco, and the United Arab Emirates. In only five countries—Yemen, Egypt, Lebanon, Tunisia, and Kuwait—did output growth per laborer exceed 1.5 percent a year (and the strong growth in output experienced in Lebanon was primarily the result of massive reconstruction efforts that took place following the 15-year civil war; the strong growth in output per laborer in Kuwait, meanwhile, reflects the growth rebound following the first Gulf War).

Does high growth guarantee good labor market outcomes? No. It is possible that employment problems will still persist with high economic growth, if that growth is primarily capital-intensive (rather than employment-intensive). Looking at the MENA economies, however, there does not appear to be an issue with past growth being employment-unfriendly. On the contrary, for the countries in which there exist both employment growth and economic growth estimations (table 7.2), the employment elasticity of output growth averaged 0.7 over the 1990s. As a comparison, during the height of their employment creation in the high-performing East Asian economies, the employment elasticity of growth rarely exceeded 0.6. The process by which output growth in MENA has led to employment (or more accurately, with which employment has expanded strongly despite low levels of growth) is a reflection of the nature of employment creation in the region, where public sector employment has been used to as a refuge for large portions of the labor force. While this type of employment creation is unlikely to be sustainable over the longer term (and employment will inevitably have to emerge from the private sector), there is still little evidence that the MENA region's growth has a poor employment-generating capacity.

But more important, what is clear is that employment cannot emerge without growth. High employment growth cannot coexist over a sustainable period with low levels of economic growth. Paramount to improving the region's labor market outcomes, then, is improving the region's growth prospects.

In the end, policy makers should have two basic goals for what happens in labor markets: (i) that those who want to work can find work, and (ii) that wages increase. In MENA, lack of growth of output per laborer has prevented both goals from transpiring simultaneously in the majority of countries. If one goal has been achieved (such as a reduction in unemployment), it has had to come at the expense of the other (real wage loss).

The story of employment outcomes in MENA is clear from an arithmetic standpoint: Output growth has been insufficient. With output growth just keeping pace with growth in the labor force, it is impossible to achieve simultaneous objectives of growth in wages and reduction in unemployment. Within MENA, that tradeoff is apparent—the region has, as a whole, experienced slight or no reductions in unemployment rates over the last decade, but output per worker has declined as well. If the region wants to achieve both higher employment growth and higher wages, much higher output growth will be required. It is well established, and backed by a wealth of empirical evidence, that rapid output growth brings with it rapid growth in employment. Periods of buoyant GDP expansion are almost invariably associated with rising job numbers while, conversely, slowdowns bring growing unemployment.[10]

What Explains MENA's Poor Growth Performance?

Over the last decade, MENA countries took a number of steps to overcome the macroeconomic imbalances and structural impediments that prevailed throughout the 1980s. Starting in the late 1980s, several countries in the region—Morocco and Tunisia, and soon after, Jordan and Egypt—embarked on extensive programs of macroeconomic stabilization and policy reform. By the 1990s, nearly all of the non-Cooperation Council for the Arab States of the Gulf (GCC) countries in the region followed suit, as did several of the Gulf economies. While there was considerable variance among economies in terms of both the speed and depth of these reforms, the overall change in policy throughout the region would seem to have been a significant step forward in creating an environment in which the private sector could emerge and become an engine for higher and sustainable growth. Despite this, strong growth failed to emerge.

In order to understand why, we have examined the region's economic growth in a growth accounting framework, in which economic growth occurs as the result of factor accumulation (either physical or human) and increases in total factor productivity (see Annex for methodology and description of the data).

Total factor productivity (TFP) growth is something of a mixed bag. It is the residual of what cannot be explained by investments, if we assume those investments (both physical and human) earn a reasonable rate of return. TFP growth is often thought of as "technical progress," but in fact, as the residual of a growth-accounting estimation, it not only embodies the differences across countries in their progress in the adoption of better technology, but also reflects a host of nontechnological differences, including changes in the use of both capital and labor, changes in schooling quality, and changes in the overall efficiency with which factors are allocated in the production process. Our interest is to explore how MENA's overall growth has improved or deteriorated since it began its structural reform process, to better understand what has prevented the region from achieving the rates of growth needed to improve its labor market outcomes.

In the MENA region, accumulation and productivity have often gone in opposite directions, such as during the period of massive public sector investments. Examining growth alone will mask these very different effects, and the somewhat anemic growth that has characterized the region since reform may be more a reflection of significantly lower investments than of continuing poor productivity performance.

In table 7.4, estimates of total factor productivity growth over the 1960-2000 period are presented by region and decade. TFP growth has been calculated as the simple residual between output growth and the growth of factor inputs (capital and labor), assuming those factors earn a reasonable rate of return.[11] From that table, MENA economies exhibited a pattern of high TFP growth in the 1960s, declining dramatically over the 1970s and continuing to decline throughout the 1980s.[12] Understanding these developments, however, requires a more detailed look at growth, accumulation, and productivity.

In the 1960s, MENA's economic growth performance was the highest in the world, averaging 6.3 percent per year (4.2 percent per year per laborer). Beginning in the 1960s, the region began a two-decade period of massive public investment in infrastructure, health, and education, which in this early period of development was able to translate into high growth. In addition to high levels of accumulation spurring growth, TFP growth over the 1960s was also high, with large-scale public investments in critical infrastructure generating a significant growth response.

This is not to say that all of the investments undertaken during the 1960s were exceptionally productive. Along with investments in large infrastructure projects, the regional also invested heavily into protected state industries. But in the 1960s, even the region's overall strategy of industrial and agricultural protectionism, supported by trade barriers and encouraged by publicly subsidized energy, water, and agrochemicals, was initially successful, as it allowed the region to utilize underused capacities and provide the early boost to industrialization.

In the 1970s, going by growth figures alone, MENA was still in the middle of a growth "heyday," with GDP growth averaging 5.8 percent a year. But the underlying conditions spurring growth in the 1970s represented a serious and negative departure from the previous decade of high growth and productivity.

Table 7.4. GDP per Laborer Growth and Growth of Accumulation and Productivity by Region, 1960–2000ª (%)

Region/country	Average annual GDP per laborer growth	Average annual growth of human capital per laborer	Average annual growth of fixed capital per laborer	Average annual TFP growth
Sub-Saharan Africa				
1960s	1.6	0.2	5.0	−0.5
1970s	1.1	0.5	2.9	−0.3
1980s	0.2	0.6	1.3	−0.7
1990s	0.5	0.5	0.8	−0.1
East Asia and Pacific				
1960s	2.0	0.9	1.2	1.0
1970s	3.8	0.9	5.2	1.2
1980s	6.1	1.0	6.0	3.1
1990s	7.2	0.7	8.5	3.3
Latin America and the Caribbean				
1960s	2.8	0.6	3.1	1.2
1970s	2.9	0.7	3.9	0.9
1980s	−1.7	0.9	0.2	−2.3
1990s	0.8	0.9	0.7	0.0
Middle East and North Africa				
1960s	4.2	0.6	4.6	2.0
1970s	2.6	1.1	7.2	−1.0
1980s	0.2	1.4	1.9	−1.5
1990s	0.6	1.3	-0.5	0.0
High-income/OECD				
1960s	4.3	0.5	5.7	1.7
1970s	1.9	1.4	3.7	−0.4
1980s	1.9	0.3	2.4	0.7
1990s	1.6	0.6	2.3	0.3
South Asia				
1960s	2.3	0.6	4.1	0.3
1970s	0.7	0.9	1.9	−0.7
1980s	3.4	0.9	3.2	1.6
1990s	3.1	0.9	3.7	1.1
World				
1960s	2.8	0.7	3.4	1.0
1970s	2.4	1.0	4.0	0.2
1980s	3.3	0.8	3.6	1.3
1990s	3.8	0.8	4.5	1.5
World (minus China)				
1960s	3.2	0.6	4.6	1.0
1970s	1.9	1.1	3.8	−0.3
1980s	1.9	0.7	2.7	0.4
1990s	1.9	0.8	2.7	0.4

a. Regional averages weighted by initial period population. Eastern Europe included in world averages.

To begin, the 1970s were marked by an increase in the rate of physical capital accumulation per laborer of more than 50 percent, and almost a doubling of the rate of human capital accumulation per laborer. Over the 1970s, the MENA region realized the highest rate of growth of physical capital per laborer in the world and the second highest rate of growth of human capital per laborer in the world. Despite this immense increase in accumulation, on a per laborer basis, growth actually declined, on average by 1.6 percent per year. Thus, the 1970s represented two large and yet conflicting growth dynamics for the region, where investments were being undertaken in record levels (all things equal, increasing the region's growth potential) at the same time as the investments were having increasingly poor payoffs, in terms of growth (figure 7.2).

While MENA's investments in needed infrastructure during the 1960s generated a significant payoff in terms of a growth response, by the 1970s, the public sector's sphere of comparative advantage in investment began to shrink, and the limits of the MENA region's strategy of protection of both public and private industries began to be realized.

The first countries to experience the pattern of higher levels of accumulation partnered with declining productivity were the oil-producing economies. Saudi Arabia saw a four-fold increase in the rate of growth of fixed capital per laborer—with physical capital per laborer increasing by an average of 18 percent a year over the 1970s (versus 3.5 percent a year over the 1960s). Despite this, total factor productivity growth plummeted from an average of 4.5 percent per year to negative 0.8 percent a year. In Algeria, despite doubling the rate of growth of human capital accumulation and a four-fold increase in the rate of growth of fixed capita per laborer, TFP growth went from around 2.1

Figure 7.2. Growth of Output versus Growth of Factor Inputs per Laborer, 1960s versus 1970s

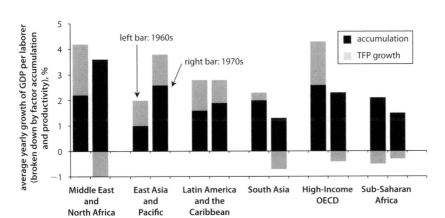

Source: See Annex.
Note: GDP growth equals bar length when TFP growth positive. Otherwise, GDP growth can be determined by taking accumulation and deducting that portion of growth lost t o negative TFP growth.

percent a year over the 1960s to negative growth of about 0.1 percent a year over the 1970s. And in Iran, despite a 50 percent increase in the rate of growth of human capital per laborer over the 1970s (and relative maintenance of the growth of fixed capital per laborer), the average growth of TFP over the decade fell by more almost 8 percentage points (averaging 2.3 percent a year over the 1960s and negative 5.5 percent over the 1970s).[13] Nonoil economies, on the other hand, by and large maintained positive productivity growth over the 1970s—the limits of state-led planning and investment not being felt until the following decade.

By the 1980s, as international oil prices slumped in the wake of global over-production, the region's economic gains became unsustainable and much of the region witnessed slow, or even negative, per laborer growth rates. By the 1980s, most of the nonoil economies in the region saw TFP growth turn negative. With eroding macroeconomic balances and growing debt burdens, and despite both heavy external assistance (which permitted spending for several more years) and a strong social contract (which hindered the government's abilities to retract from commitments), investments declined dramatically, with the rate of growth of the physical capital stock per laborer declining by almost three-quarters from the previous decade (figure 7.4).

The decline in accumulation was almost without exception, with every country in the region but Egypt and Kuwait experiencing a dramatic downturn in accumulation between the 1970s and 1980s (and in Kuwait, factor accumulation did not exactly grow, but rather the negative accumulation per

Figure 7.3. Growth of Output versus Growth of Factor Inputs per Laborer: MENA Economies, 1960s versus 1970s

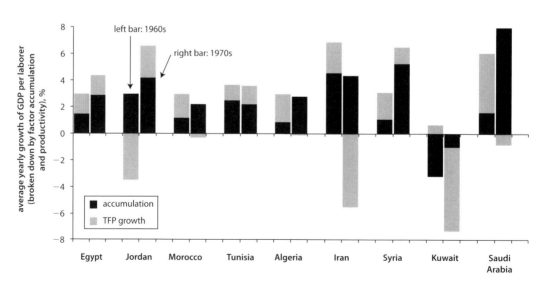

Source: See Annex.
Note: GDP growth equals bar length when TFP growth positive. Otherwise, GDP growth can be determined by taking accumulation and deducting that portion of growth lost t o negative TFP growth.

Figure 7.4. Growth of Output versus Growth of Factor Inputs per Laborer: MENA Economies, 1970s versus 1980s

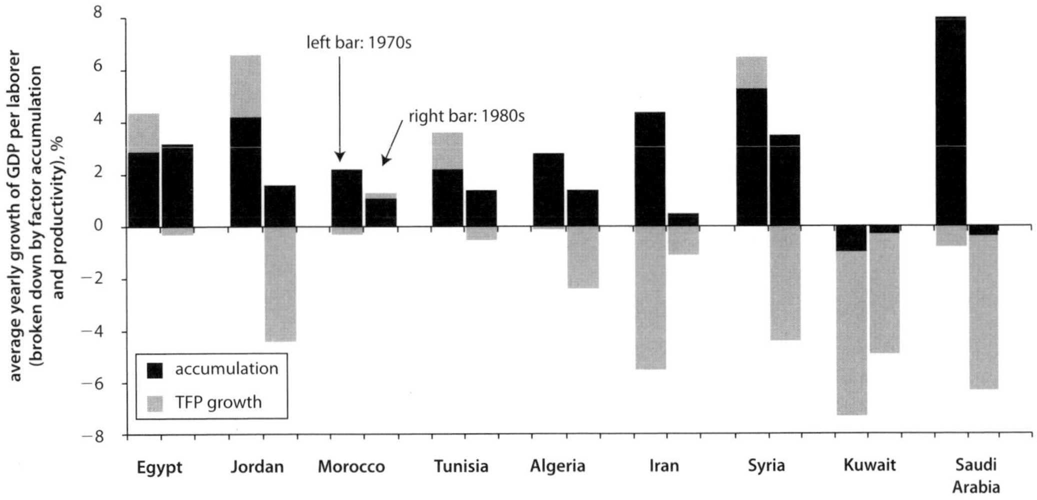

Source: See Annex.
Note: GDP growth equals bar length when TFP growth positive. Otherwise, GDP growth can be determined by taking accumulation and deducting that portion of growth lost t o negative TFP growth.

laborer that characterized the 1970s merely slowed over the 1980s), and almost every economy experiencing a like decline in TFP. Only Morocco, Iran, and Kuwait saw actual improvements in total factor productivity between the 1970s and 1980s (although for Iran and Kuwait, this improvement in TFP growth was only a reflection of continuing TFP declines slowing over the 1980s). Negative productivity growth was most prevalent in the oil-producing economies of the region—within the GCC economies as well as Algeria. Because our TFP estimates are a reflection of factor efficiency, the degree to which capital is underutilized will be heavily reflected in the ensuing TFP growth measurements. This feature is of particular importance for these economies, since, as oil prices collapsed in the 1980s, there was a significant effort on the part of oil producers to prop up oil prices by holding down production. Nevertheless, even in the non-oil-producing economies, there were widespread declines in productivity for almost every country. With both massive declines in accumulation and corresponding declines in TFP for most countries, the MENA region experienced a collapse of economic growth per laborer.

By the late 1980s, the "lost decade of growth" prompted a handful of countries in the region—Morocco and Tunisia, and soon after, Jordan, to embark on programs of macroeconomic stabilization and policy reform. By the 1990s, nearly all of the non-GCC countries in the region followed suit, as did several of the Gulf economies. The reasoning, of course, was to create an environment in which the private sector could emerge and become an engine for higher and sustainable economic growth, crucial for employment creation.

How did the region fare over the 1990s? To understand the developments over the 1990s, we turn to a growth decomposition. In table 7.5, we present the MENA region's changes to accumulation, productivity, and growth over the decade. For clarity, the table does not present GDP and TFP growth over the 1990s, but rather the change in average GDP, factor, and TFP growth between the 1980s and 1990s (thus if an economy moved from an average GDP per laborer growth of 2 percent a year in the 1980s, to 5 percent a year over the 1990s, the change in GDP growth per laborer over the decade is 3 percent).

The countries are presented in order of the change in their average TFP growth per laborer between the 1980s and 1990s. At the top of the list of improved productivity growth is Saudi Arabia, which stemmed the enormous productivity declines (averaging minus 5.9 percent a year) that characterized the 1980s. Also exhibiting strongly improved productivity relative to the 1980s is Syria, which in the 1990s benefited from both increased oil production and agricultural performance, an aid windfall during the Gulf War (which allowed it to undertake key growth-enhancing infrastructure investments, such as the purchase of power stations and a telephone network), as well as some limited liberalization reforms. And three of the four countries[14] we would term the 'early reformers' (specifically, Jordan, Tunisia, and Egypt) also experienced improvements in their average TFP growth between the 1980s and 1990s.

Overall, TFP growth in the region actually improved in all but one economy (Morocco, which suffered from recurring droughts over the 1990s). At the same time, however, as a result of large declines in accumulation within most of MENA (particularly accumulation of physical capital), the improvements in factor allocation and efficiency have not translated into significant increases in GDP growth.

What are the implications of this exercise? The message that emerges in terms of the region's failure to improve its labor market outcomes is that

Table 7.5. Change in MENA's per Laborer GDP Growth, Factor Accumulation, and TFP Growth between 1980s and 1990s (%)

Country	Change in GDP per laborer growth: 1990s versus 1980s	Change in HK per laborer growth	Change in K per laborer growth	Change in TFP growth
Saudi Arabia	6.7	−0.5	0.8	6.8
Syria	1.7	−0.7	−7.8	5.3
Jordan	2.3	−0.6	−3.0	3.9
Kuwait	3.1	−0.5	1.6	2.8
Iran	1.7	0.4	0.6	1.3
Tunisia	0.8	0.2	−1.1	1.1
Egypt	−1.3	−0.5	−5.2	1.0
Algeria	−1.3	−0.3	−3.8	0.4
Morocco	−1.5	0.1	−0.6	−1.4

improving the region's labor market outcomes must come from substantial increases in investment. Improving employment creation in the region can come from only two sources: enhancing the employment-creation capacity of growth (the employment elasticity), or higher economic growth itself.

Let's consider the first notion—that improving labor market outcomes could be achieved through increasing the employment intensity of growth. Employment elasticities reflect the percent change in employment that is associated with some percent change in real output. International evidence would suggest that the long-run elasticity of output with respect to employment falls somewhere between 0.4 and 0.8. In countries that are highly capital-intensive, employment elasticity is likely to be closer to 0.4, while in labor-intensive production structures, employment elasticity is likely to be closer to 0.8. In our estimates, we assume an employment elasticity of 0.7, which is relatively healthy by international standards, and is unlikely to be improved. In table 7.6, we estimate the level of output growth necessary to create sufficient jobs to fully absorb the growing labor force, given relatively high rates of employment creation.[15] We then compare that GDP growth rate with the observed growth rate over the 1990s. The difference reflects the gap between needed growth and observed growth.

In four cases (Egypt, Tunisia, Kuwait, and Iran) the rates of growth that were observed were sufficient, under optimistic employment generation assumptions, to create the levels of employment to meet the growth of the labor force, without any increases in either productivity or capital accumulation. For the other countries in the region, however, the needed increases in output growth in order to reach growth levels consistent with the desired rates of employment growth are substantial: in Jordan, output would have needed to grow by almost 3 percent more a year, and in Algeria, by more than 4 percent more a year.

Table 7.6. GDP Growth Consistent with Desired Employment Creation Rates, 1990–2000 (%)

Country	Needed employment growth over 1990s (= labor force growth)	GDP growth consistent with that of employment growth	Observed GDP growth	GDP growth gap
Egypt	2.9	4.2	4.5	0
Jordan	5.6	8.0	5.1	2.9
Morocco	2.4	3.5	2.2	1.2
Tunisia	3.1	4.4	4.7	0
Algeria	4.1	5.8	1.7	4.1
Iran	2.9	4.1	4.0	0.1
Syria	4.3	6.2	5.1	1.0
Kuwait	0.4	0.5	3.4	0
Saudi Arabia	2.3	3.2	2.7	0.5

Thus, even with employment-intensive growth, the level of economic growth itself has prevented the employment creation rates needed to absorb the growing labor force. The remaining potential for improving employment creation in the region, then, is higher economic growth. We saw, throughout the 1990s, a substantial improvement in the region's productivity growth. While there is always potential for even greater productivity improvements, there are also limits to what can be achieved. With economic growth so substantially below what would be needed to be consistent with full labor absorption, the considerable improvement in economic growth rates must come primarily from substantial increases in investment.

Over the 1990s, however, almost every economy in MENA experienced an actual decline in the amount of physical capital per laborer, and the region went from increasing its physical capital per laborer by 1.9 percent a year in the 1980s to experiencing actual declines in physical capital per laborer of 0.5 percent a year in the 1990s (Table 4). MENA stands at the bottom in terms of physical capital accumulation during this period.

Interpreting the Decline in Investment

It is difficult to definitively interpret the substantial declines in accumulation throughout the 1990s, without reliable investment data, broken down between the public and private sectors. Public sector investments have almost certainly dropped off. So, in the midst of an overall factor accumulation deterioration, it is possible that private sector factor accumulation is actually improving, but not sufficiently to counteract the large declines in public investment.

However, it is also possible that while productivity and factor allocation efficiency have improved significantly over the 1990s, they have failed to generate a comparable private sector investment response. Understanding the lack of increased private investment is complex. Much of the private sector investment that occurred in the 1980s in the region was domestically demand-driven. The private sector developed under the patronage of governments. It flourished not so much by being dynamic in a competitive environment, but often by supplying protected domestic markets and generally "living off the state." Thus, the investments that took place by the private sector during the 1980s were largely focused on serving the domestic market rather than on export expansion. For example, the share of construction in value added during the 1980s, at 7.1 percent (relative to a world average of 5.6 percent), suggests that a larger than average share of the region's investment constituted new buildings rather than retooling or investments in (new or high-tech) sectors (see table 7). Over the 1990s, we saw a decline in share of construction in value added (table 7.7), which may signal a change in the types of investment the private sector is undertaking. So, even while we saw declines in private sec-

Table 7.7. Share of Construction in Value Added, 1980s and 1990s (%)

| Country | Share of construction in value added | | |
	1980s	1990s	Change
Algeria	13.7	10.5	−3.2
Egypt	5.0	5.0	0.0
Iran	6.9	3.8	−3.1
Jordan	7.6	5.1	−2.5
Kuwait	3.5	3.3	−0.2
Morocco	5.9	4.7	−1.2
Oman	5.2	3.2	−2.0
Saudi Arabia	11.7	8.9	−2.9
Syria	5.9	4.1	−1.8
Tunisia	5.2	4.5	−0.8
Regional Average[a]	7.1	5.3	−1.8
World Average[a]	5.6	5.7	0.1

a. Unweighted average.

tor investments over the 1990s, it could be the case that the investments currently taking place are more externally demand-driven and, hence, over the long term, more sustainable.

Then there is the possibility that private sector investment, in addition to dropping off in the domestic demand markets, has not significantly improved in the tradable goods sectors, either. Why would the reform process, which has clearly produced an impact on the region's productivity, fail to generate a private sector investment response in the external-oriented sectors? While the comprehensive macroeconomic and structural reform programs espoused by many of the MENA economies created an exuberant boost in their economic outlooks, most of the region has failed to complete the reform process. Reforms have generally been limited to the "stroke of the pen" type, easily executed but in the absence of other, more serious, and challenging reforms, with limited effect.

Policy Implications

Understanding why private investment has failed to respond to the improved productivity and reforms in the region is essential for realizing the rates of investment necessary for high and sustained economic growth. In order to significantly increase the growth of private investment in the region, the private investment climate must be improved. While this paper cannot definitely establish the chief factors that have inhibited an enabling private investment climate, several likely possibilities are offered.

To begin, the region has substantial work to do in terms of creating an enabling macroeconomic environment through exchange rate management. The preoccupation with macroeconomic stability during the 1990s often relied on maintaining nominally fixed and stable exchange rates by virtually all countries in the region (Algeria, Tunisia, Yemen, and more recently Iran and Egypt are notable exceptions), which has meant that one important tool to make exports more profitable was surrendered. This is the opposite of the policies that the successful exporting countries such as the "East Asian Tigers" have pursued over the last three decades. We know from experience that growing export of manufactured and nontraditional goods also creates dynamism in the domestic economy with very significant spillover effects. The issue now is to find ways to "exit" the pegs, in an orderly manner, to push economic growth.

Next, there is the size of the public sector. On average, the public sector accounts for about 50 percent of GDP and about a third of employment in the region.[16] The large role of the state—a sector that essentially has low productivity and limited inherent potential for productivity gain—is a drag on growth in most economies in the region. Efforts have begun in many countries to reduce the public sector through rationalization of public employment, to improve its performance through better incentives and institutions, and to privatize production of goods and services that could be produced more efficiently in the private sector. But, by and large, these efforts have been slow and half-hearted to date.

Third, the private sector is deterred from development because of the systems of governance that pervade the region. The World Bank's report on governance in the MENA region[17] highlights the major governance challenges. On the administrative side, MENA countries fall short of other countries at similar income levels. In areas such as the efficiency of the bureaucracy, the rule of law, the protection of property rights, the level of corruption, the quality of regulations, and the mechanisms of internal accountability, MENA countries have, individually and on average, lower levels of quality of administration in the public sector than would be expected for their incomes.[18]

But even more important, countries across the region exhibit a pattern of limited government accountability and inclusiveness, reflected in an index of public accountability. In the area of openness of political institutions and participation, respect of civil liberties, transparency of government, and freedom of the press, the MENA region falls far short of the rest of the world.

Fourth, there is the issue of trade reform. Trade policy in the region remains among the most restrictive in the world, with low level and speed of integration into the world economy. Tariff rates remain high and the extent of nontariff barriers large. A recent evaluation of the trade policy within the MENA region, relative to other regions, found MENA economies to be among the most restrictive in the world, second only to Sub-Saharan Africa and South Asia.[19] The importance of export orientation in growth is well established in the empirical literature. High and sustainable growth simply does not occur without a substantial outward orientation. A number of policy moves across the region are expected to lead to greater trade openness, stimulating integration, and, it is hoped, growth. Most notable are the EU Association Agreements on preferential trade (currently in force in Jordan, Egypt, Algeria, Lebanon, the West Bank and Gaza, Tunisia, and Morocco, and with an agreement signed by Syria in 2004).

Among the most important but lagging reforms is that of the banking sector. While the economies in the GCC, Jordan, and Lebanon have fairly sophisticated financial sectors, with high bank and nonbank financial sector development and generally good regulation and banking supervision, much of the region's private sector still has limited access to market finance. Banks dominate the financial system, but in general they play a limited role in financial intermediation. Much of the banking sector remains primarily in government hands, inextricably linked to state-owned enterprises (SOEs), and subject to government intervention in its lending and credit allocation policies to SOEs. This intervention has led to a crowding out of the private sector where it is permitted to operate, especially in Algeria, Libya, Syria, and Yemen.[20]

And finally, the region needs a virtual overhaul of its system of property rights, as well as better legal systems and improved contract enforcement mechanisms.

Unless the private sector begins to see itself as an independent source of growth and productivity in the economy, and society begins to underpin this change economically and politically, it is unlikely that any of the past economic reforms in themselves will be adequate. The public sector's role in improving labor market outcomes in the region is important, but unlike in the 1960s and 1970s, better labor market outcomes cannot be guaranteed through public employment. The government's role has distinctly changed. Now the public sector must find ways to improve the investment climate and promote economic growth, which remains the single most important way to ensure better labor market outcomes in the future.

Notes

1. The countries of the Middle East and North Africa region included in this analysis (depending upon data availability) are: Morocco, Algeria, Libya, Tunisia, Egypt, Jordan, Lebanon, Syria, Iran, Iraq, Yemen, Bahrain, Kuwait, Oman, Qatar, Saudi Arabia, the West Bank and Gaza, and the United Arab Emirates.

2 .World Bank 2003.

3. World Bank World Development Indicators database (April 2004 update).

4. 2005 estimate, based upon unemployment data for Algeria, Morocco, Tunisia, Egypt, Iran, Jordan, Lebanon, Syria, West Bank and Gaza, Yemen, Bahrain, Kuwait, Oman, Qatar, Saudi Arabia, and West Bank and Gaza.

5. Unemployment in Algeria was close to 30 percent in 2002. With recent rising oil revenues and as part of the country's Economic Recovery Program, however, large-scale temporary employment schemes have dramatically lowered the rate of official unemployment (to 23.7 percent currently), although the longer-term sustainability of these jobs is questionable.

6. Based upon growth in average educational attainment of the adult (15+) population between 1960-90 in Algeria, Bahrain, Egypt, Iran, Jordan, Kuwait, Morocco, Saudi Arabia, Syria, and Tunisia. Educational attainment data from Barro and Lee (2000). Regional average population weighted.

7. Based on GDP per capita growth in constant US$ for Algeria, Bahrain, Egypt, Iran, Jordan, Kuwait, Morocco, Oman, Qatar, Saudi Arabia, Syria, Tunisia, and the United Arab Emirates (does not include Lebanon, Libya, Djibouti, Iraq, or Yemen, due to data availability for both periods). GDP per capita weighted by population for regional average.

8. This estimate does not include Iraq, where as much as 50 percent of the workforce may be unemployed.

9. Of course, over the short term, wages may not move in tandem with worker productivity increases. Additionally, employment growth may arise without real output growth. But over the long run, sustainable increases in employment and wages depend upon increases in real output per laborer.

10. Boltho and Glyn, 1995.

11. In our case, the elasticity of output with respect to capital is exogenously assumed to be 0.4, which is based upon both international evidence and our own estimations.

12. See Bosworth, Collins and Chen (1995) for similar findings.

13. See Annex Table 1.

14. Jordan, Morocco, Tunisia, and Egypt, which all embarked upon structural reform programs from the mid-1980s to early 1990s.

15. Of course, the process is circular: Just as employment creates output growth, output growth in some sense "creates" employment, in that—in order to sustain that level of output growth—it requires continuing increases in employment. Thus, rather than think of growth generating employment, we can think of certain levels of output growth consistent with a given level of sustainable employment creation.

16. World Bank 2005.

17. World Bank 2003b.

18. World Bank 2003b.

19. As measured by average tariffs on imports. From World Bank, 2005.

20. World Bank, 2005.

References

Barro, Robert J., and Jong-Wha Lee. 2000. "International Data on Educational Attainment: Updates and Implications." CID Working Paper No. 42. Center for International Development at Harvard University.

Boltho, Andrea, and Andrew Glyn. 1995. "Can Macroeconomic Policies Raise Growth?" *International Labor Review* 134 (4–5): 451–70.

Bosworth, Barry, Susan M. Collins, and Yu-chin Chen. 1995. "Accounting for Differences in Economic Growth." Paper prepared for conference on "Structural Adjustment Policies in the 1990s: Experience and Prospects," organized by the Institute of Developing Economies, Tokyo, Japan.

Easterly, William, and Ross Levine. 2001. "It's Not Factor Accumulation: Stylized Facts and Growth Models." *World Bank Economic Review* 15 (2): 177–219.

Fajnzylber, Pablo, and Daniel Lederman. 2000. "Economic Reforms and Total Factor Productivity Growth in Latin America and the Caribbean, 1990–95: An Empirical Note." World Bank Working Paper 2114. The World Bank, Washington, DC.

Griliches, Zvi. 1979. "Issues in Assessing the Contribution of Research and Development to Productivity Growth." *Bell Journal of Economics* 10 (1): 92–116.

Griliches, Zvi, and Frank Lichtenberg. 1984. "R&D and Productivity Growth at the Industry Level: Is There Still a Relationship?" In *R&D, Patents, and Productivity,* ed. Zvi Griliches. Chicago, IL: University of Chicago Press.

Islam, Nazrul. 1999. "International Comparison of Total Factor Productivity: A Review." *Review of Income and Wealth* 45 (4).

Lefort, Fernando, and Andres Solimano. 1994. "Economic Growth after Market-Based Reform in Latin America: The Cases of Chile and Mexico." World Bank Macroeconomics and Growth Division Working Paper. World Bank, Washington, DC.

Nehru, Vikram, and Ashok Dhareshwar. 1993. "A New Database on Physical Capital Stock: Sources, Methodology, and Results." *Revista de Análisis Economico* 8 (1): 37–59.

Rama, Martin. 1998. "How Bad is Unemployment in Tunisia? Assessing Labor Market Efficiency in a Developing Country." *World Bank Research Observer* 13 (1): 59–77.

World Bank. 2003. *Unlocking the Employment Potential in the Middle East and North Africa: Towards a New Social Contract.* MENA Development Report. World Bank. Washington, DC.

———. 2003b. *Better Governance for Development in the Middle East and North Africa: Enhancing Inclusiveness and Accountability.* MENA Development Report. World Bank. Washington, DC.

———. 2004. World Development Indicators database. April 2004 update.

———. 2005. *MENA Economic Developments and Prospects 2005: Oil Booms and Revenue Management.* World Bank, Washington, DC.

Annex: Measuring Growth, Accumulation, and TFP Growth

To examine how the MENA region's growth has changed since it began its comprehensive structural reform process, we made simple calculations of the change in rate of accumulation and total factor productivity growth.

TFP growth is the residual of what cannot be explained by investments if we assume those investments (both physical and human) earn a reasonable rate of return. TFP growth is often thought of as "technical progress," but in fact, as the residual of a growth accounting estimation, it not only embodies the differences across countries in their progress in the adoption of better technology, but also reflects a host of non-technology-related differences, including changes in the utilization of both capital and labor, changes in schooling quality, and changes in the overall efficiency with which factors are allocated in the production process. Because of the many other factors that can potentially affect the growth residual, much empirical work has focused on reducing those elements of the residual (TFP) which do not reflect actual shifts in technology-related opportunities in the economy. For example, adjustments for the business cycle have been introduced to account for the short-term fluctuations in capacity utilization (Griliches 1979; Lefort and Solimano 1994; Fajnzylber and Lederman 2000). An alternative procedure employed by Griliches and Lichtenberg (1984) has been to estimate growth over five-year periods, and to allow the TFP series only to increase or stay constant (resetting any values to the previously observed peak level), to maintain the assumption that "true" productivity can only improve and that measured reductions in TFP can only reflect short-term fluctuations.

For our purposes, we have adopted a more casual approach about our measurements. Our interest is to explore how MENA's overall growth has improved or deteriorated since it began the structural reform process. In the end, growth will be determined by accumulation of both physical and human capital, as well as the overall manner in which those factors are put to production. For the MENA region, things such as improved capacity utilization of capital and human capital by the region are precisely the elements we believe may be heavily affected by structural reform, and thus we would like to have this effect reflected in our estimates. At the same time, as we discuss in the subsequent section, we have controlled for global shocks.

Under many circumstances, the environment created to encourage investment would also correspond to an environment in which those investments could be productive. But in the MENA region, accumulation and productivity have often gone in opposite directions, such as during the period of massive public sector investments, which yielded rates of return well below international norms. Examining growth alone will mask these very different effects, and the somewhat anemic growth that has characterized the region since reform may be more a reflection of significantly lower public investments than of continuing poor productivity performance. From the standpoint of evaluating the impact of the region's structural reform, it is precisely TFP growth which we would expect to be most influenced by changes in national policies that enhance the efficiency of capital and labor.

Data and Methodology

TFP growth estimates were made utilizing panel data of capital stock accumulation, human capital stock accumulation, and GDP growth from 1960 to 2000. Estimates of the physical capital stock for a sample of 83 economies from 1960 to 1990 come from Nehru and Dhareshwar (1993[1]), which was created by a perpetual inventory method from investment rates from 1950 forward, with initial assumptions about the capital/output ratio, and assuming a common fixed annual geometric depreciation rate of 0.04. These capital stock data were extended to 2000 using the growth rates of constant price local currency investment from the World Bank's World Development Indicators database,[2] and applying similar assumptions on the depreciation rate. Capital stock estimates for another 12 economies, including 4 economies in the MENA region of particular interest to us, were created according to a similar methodology, using investment rates from 1960 forward.

Real GDP in constant local currency also come from World Bank data. The human capital-augmented labor stock was estimated, using both labor force estimates from the World Bank's World Development Indicators, and estimates of the educational attainment of the adult population from Barro and Lee.[3] The functional form of human capital-augmented labor has been assumed as

$$H = L\, e^{(r\, *\, S)}$$

where L is the labor force, S is the average years of schooling of the adult population, and r is the rate of return to schooling. According to international evidence, a reasonable approximation of that rate of return is 10 percent, which we have assumed for the purposes of our analysis.

TFP growth was calculated over 10-year periods from 1960 to 2000, rather than on an annual basis, to minimize the error that is inherent in current capital stock measurements. National accounts would attribute any investment expenditures made over the year, even the last day of the year, to that year's capital stock. However, it is unlikely that that investment expenditure would contribute to economic growth immediately, but rather would only create the potential to contribute to growth into the future. To reduce this lag effect that physical capital exhibits, we calculated TFP growth based on 10-year averages.

Production was assumed to follow a Cobb-Douglas specification with constant returns to scale between physical and human capital-augmented labor:

$$Y_t = A\,(t) * K_t^{\alpha} {}^* H_t^{(1\,-\,\alpha)}$$

where Y is output, A is an index of total factor productivity, and K and H are the stocks of physical and human-augmented labor, respectively. Dividing both sides by the work force, taking logs, and first-differencing, growth of output per laborer can be related as follows:

$$\ln (y_i / y_{i-1,}) = \alpha \ln (k_t / k_{t-1}) + (1 - \alpha) \ln (h_t / h_{t-1}) + \ln (A_t / A_{t-1})$$

To determine the coefficients on capital and human capital-augmented labor, α and $(1 - \alpha)$, the average annual rate of GDP per capita growth over the decade, was regressed on average growth of physical capital per worker and human-capital per worker with a least squares trend over the entire period of availability (1960–2000).

From our estimation, the elasticity of output of physical capital was estimated to be 0.49, somewhat higher than the average estimated coefficient from previous research, but within the range of accepted parameters. This may be due to the inclusion of several more developing countries than in the original Nehru-Dhareshwar physical capital stock dataset, made possible using World Bank data. At the same time, our purpose here is not to break new ground in measuring TFP, but to evaluate the region's performance in factor allocation and efficiency. Thus, we have calculated the TFP using three distinct calculations of factor shares—$\alpha k=0.3$, $\alpha k=0.4$, and $\alpha k=0.5$—to check the sensitivity of the region's growth performance to the assumptions made on the output elasticities. The resulting sets of TFP growth estimations for the full sample of countries are presented in Annex Table 1. Within the text of the paper, TFP calculations are based on an elasticity of capital assumption of 0.4 across countries. Regional averages were calculated by weighting growth rates by initial population.

Annex Table 1. TFP Estimates under Various Assumptions on Elasticity of Output with Respect to Physical Capital (α), 1960–2000

Region	Country	Decade	TFP (α = 0.3)	TFP (α = 0.4)	TFP (α = 0.5)
Africa	Botswana	1960s	..	..	..
Africa	Cameroon	1960s	−0.66	−0.95	−1.24
Africa	Ghana	1960s	−2.14	−2.37	−2.60
Africa	Kenya	1960s	1.34	1.45	1.56
Africa	Lesotho	1960s	−2.38	−4.38	−6.37
Africa	Malawi	1960s	0.10	−0.72	−1.53
Africa	Mali	1960s	0.62	0.42	0.21
Africa	Mauritius	1960s	0.01	0.26	0.50
Africa	Mozambique	1960s	1.58	1.16	0.73
Africa	Rwanda	1960s	..	..	..
Africa	Senegal	1960s	−0.37	−0.34	−0.31
Africa	Sierra Leone	1960s	1.26	0.66	0.07
Africa	South Africa	1960s	2.43	2.10	1.77
Africa	Sudan	1960s	−2.99	−3.76	−4.52
Africa	Tanzania	1960s	3.16	2.98	2.81
Africa	The Gambia	1960s	..	..	..
Africa	Togo	1960s	1.61	0.47	−0.67
Africa	Uganda	1960s	0.33	0.07	−0.18
Africa	Zambia	1960s	0.54	0.46	0.37
Africa	Zimbabwe	1960s	3.32	3.39	3.45
E. Asia	China	1960s	1.06	1.13	1.19
E. Asia	Indonesia	1960s	0.73	0.73	0.72
E. Asia	Korea, Rep. of	1960s	1.74	0.90	0.07
E. Asia	Malaysia	1960s	0.78	0.21	−0.37
E. Asia	Papua New Guinea	1960s	3.94	3.62	3.31
E. Asia	Philippines	1960s	0.40	0.09	−0.23
E. Asia	Singapore	1960s	2.04	0.75	−0.53
E. Asia	Taiwan, China	1960s	1.84	0.87	−0.10
E. Asia	Thailand	1960s	2.36	1.33	0.31
ECA	Bulgaria	1960s	..	..	..
ECA	Hungary	1960s	3.50	3.44	3.39
ECA	Portugal	1960s	3.33	2.66	1.98
ECA	Romania	1960s	..	..	..
ECA	Turkey	1960s	..	..	..
LAC	Argentina	1960s	0.66	0.39	0.12
LAC	Bolivia	1960s	0.40	0.03	−0.34
LAC	Brazil	1960s	1.61	1.33	1.05
LAC	Chile	1960s	1.48	1.26	1.04
LAC	Colombia	1960s	2.40	2.23	2.05
LAC	Costa Rica	1960s	1.20	0.91	0.62
LAC	Dominican Republic	1960s	0.68	0.62	0.56
LAC	Ecuador	1960s	0.81	0.62	0.43

(Table continues on the following page.)

Annex Table 1. (*continued*)

Region	Country	Decade	TFP ($\alpha = 0.3$)	TFP ($\alpha = 0.4$)	TFP ($\alpha = 0.5$)
LAC	El Salvador	1960s	0.56	0.35	0.14
LAC	Guatemala	1960s	1.62	1.40	1.17
LAC	Guyana	1960s	0.95	0.82	0.69
LAC	Honduras	1960s	0.86	0.63	0.39
LAC	Mexico	1960s	1.52	1.14	0.76
LAC	Nicaragua	1960s	1.51	1.08	0.65
LAC	Panama	1960s	2.62	1.97	1.31
LAC	Paraguay	1960s	0.69	0.50	0.30
LAC	Peru	1960s	1.34	1.22	1.09
LAC	Uruguay	1960s	0.52	0.59	0.66
LAC	Venezuela	1960s	1.86	1.92	1.99
MENA	Algeria	1960s	2.16	2.08	2.00
MENA	Bahrain	1960s	..	..	..
MENA	Egypt	1960s	1.81	1.52	1.23
MENA	Iran	1960s	3.29	2.34	1.39
MENA	Jordan	1960s	−2.97	−3.49	−4.02
MENA	Kuwait	1960s	−0.16	0.72	1.61
MENA	Morocco	1960s	1.98	1.84	1.71
MENA	Saudi Arabia	1960s	4.85	4.53	4.20
MENA	Syria	1960s	2.11	2.04	1.98
MENA	Tunisia	1960s	1.64	1.24	0.83
OECD	Australia	1960s	1.27	0.98	0.69
OECD	Austria	1960s	3.04	2.20	1.37
OECD	Belgium	1960s	2.26	1.90	1.55
OECD	Canada	1960s	1.94	1.78	1.63
OECD	Denmark	1960s	1.39	0.73	0.07
OECD	Finland	1960s	2.06	1.67	1.28
OECD	France	1960s	2.40	1.76	1.11
OECD	Greece	1960s	4.13	3.17	2.22
OECD	Iceland	1960s	0.69	0.46	0.24
OECD	Ireland	1960s	2.20	1.67	1.15
OECD	Israel	1960s	3.30	3.06	2.81
OECD	Italy	1960s	3.00	2.42	1.84
OECD	Japan	1960s	4.95	3.64	2.34
OECD	Netherlands	1960s	0.27	0.00	−0.26
OECD	New Zealand	1960s	0.88	0.69	0.50
OECD	Norway	1960s	1.26	1.17	1.07
OECD	Spain	1960s	3.30	2.58	1.86
OECD	Sweden	1960s	2.00	1.56	1.12
OECD	Switzerland	1960s	0.67	0.24	−0.18
OECD	United Kingdom	1960s	0.94	0.44	−0.07
OECD	United States	1960s	0.79	0.72	0.64
S. Asia	Bangladesh	1960s	1.27	1.08	0.89
S. Asia	India	1960s	0.52	0.20	−0.13
S. Asia	Myanmar	1960s	0.43	0.32	0.20

Region	Country	Decade	TFP ($\alpha = 0.3$)	TFP ($\alpha = 0.4$)	TFP ($\alpha = 0.5$)
S. Asia	Pakistan	1960s	0.81	−0.20	−1.22
S. Asia	Sri Lanka	1960s	1.25	1.20	1.15
Africa	Botswana	1970s	9.21	8.86	8.52
Africa	Cameroon	1970s	2.01	1.35	0.68
Africa	Ghana	1970s	−2.18	−2.15	−2.11
Africa	Kenya	1970s	3.09	3.10	3.11
Africa	Lesotho	1970s	6.05	5.57	5.10
Africa	Malawi	1970s	0.60	−0.03	−0.66
Africa	Mali	1970s	1.66	1.59	1.52
Africa	Mauritius	1970s	1.10	1.11	1.12
Africa	Mozambique	1970s	−3.64	−3.74	−3.84
Africa	Rwanda	1970s	0.42	−0.03	−0.47
Africa	Senegal	1970s	−1.26	−1.24	−1.21
Africa	Sierra Leone	1970s	−0.19	−0.22	−0.25
Africa	South Africa	1970s	0.41	−0.06	−0.52
Africa	Sudan	1970s	−0.82	−1.14	−1.46
Africa	Tanzania	1970s	−0.06	−0.36	−0.67
Africa	The Gambia	1970s	..	..	..
Africa	Togo	1970s	−1.42	−2.14	−2.85
Africa	Uganda	1970s	−10.30	−10.18	−10.06
Africa	Zambia	1970s	−1.92	−1.76	−1.61
Africa	Zimbabwe	1970s	−0.44	−0.60	−0.75
E. Asia	China	1970s	1.83	1.47	1.12
E. Asia	Indonesia	1970s	1.45	0.77	0.09
E. Asia	Korea, Rep. of	1970s	−1.41	−2.32	−3.23
E. Asia	Malaysia	1970s	1.11	0.51	−0.10
E. Asia	Papua New Guinea	1970s	−0.37	−0.50	−0.63
E. Asia	Philippines	1970s	0.29	0.03	−0.22
E. Asia	Singapore	1970s	0.96	0.00	−0.96
E. Asia	Taiwan, China	1970s	2.11	1.05	−0.01
E. Asia	Thailand	1970s	1.28	0.69	0.10
ECA	Bulgaria	1970s	..	..	..
ECA	Hungary	1970s	2.67	2.07	1.47
ECA	Portugal	1970s	0.23	0.03	−0.18
ECA	Romania	1970s	..	..	..
ECA	Turkey	1970s	0.06	−0.49	−1.03
LAC	Argentina	1970s	−0.04	−0.30	−0.56
LAC	Bolivia	1970s	1.96	2.09	2.22
LAC	Brazil	1970s	3.20	2.58	1.96
LAC	Chile	1970s	−0.05	0.10	0.25
LAC	Colombia	1970s	0.80	0.77	0.76
LAC	Costa Rica	1970s	−0.71	−1.04	−1.36
LAC	Dominican Republic	1970s	1.32	0.75	0.18
LAC	Ecuador	1970s	1.00	0.84	0.68
LAC	El Salvador	1970s	−2.21	−2.54	−2.87

(Table continues on the following page.)

Annex Table 1. (*continued*)

Region	Country	Decade	TFP (α = 0.3)	TFP (α = 0.4)	TFP (α = 0.5)
LAC	Guatemala	1970s	1.17	0.91	0.65
LAC	Guyana	1970s	−1.47	−1.43	−1.39
LAC	Honduras	1970s	0.77	0.56	0.36
LAC	Mexico	1970s	0.71	0.44	0.17
LAC	Nicaragua	1970s	−4.10	−4.25	−4.40
LAC	Panama	1970s	−1.62	−1.97	−2.32
LAC	Paraguay	1970s	2.68	2.10	1.53
LAC	Peru	1970s	−0.96	−0.91	−0.86
LAC	Uruguay	1970s	1.60	1.43	1.27
LAC	Venezuela	1970s	−3.72	−3.49	−3.25
MENA	Algeria	1970s	0.28	−0.14	−0.55
MENA	Bahrain	1970s	..	..	..
MENA	Egypt	1970s	1.98	1.51	1.04
MENA	Iran	1970s	−4.72	−5.52	−6.33
MENA	Jordan	1970s	3.18	2.38	1.58
MENA	Kuwait	1970s	−6.95	−6.33	−5.72
MENA	Morocco	1970s	0.04	−0.32	−0.68
MENA	Saudi Arabia	1970s	0.82	−0.83	−2.48
MENA	Syria	1970s	2.12	1.17	0.22
MENA	Tunisia	1970s	1.61	1.43	1.25
OECD	Australia	1970s	0.04	−0.19	−0.42
OECD	Austria	1970s	1.22	0.71	0.20
OECD	Belgium	1970s	1.88	1.50	1.13
OECD	Canada	1970s	−0.53	−0.53	−0.53
OECD	Denmark	1970s	−0.51	−0.81	−1.11
OECD	Finland	1970s	0.95	0.71	0.47
OECD	France	1970s	0.21	−0.15	−0.51
OECD	Greece	1970s	0.62	0.18	−0.26
OECD	Iceland	1970s	2.01	1.83	1.65
OECD	Ireland	1970s	1.57	1.14	0.71
OECD	Israel	1970s	0.72	0.49	0.25
OECD	Italy	1970s	1.55	1.22	0.89
OECD	Japan	1970s	0.09	−0.63	−1.35
OECD	Netherlands	1970s	0.21	0.01	−0.19
OECD	New Zealand	1970s	−1.85	−1.84	−1.83
OECD	Norway	1970s	1.43	1.30	1.17
OECD	Spain	1970s	0.21	−0.21	−0.63
OECD	Sweden	1970s	−1.15	−1.21	−1.27
OECD	Switzerland	1970s	−1.55	−1.71	−1.87
OECD	United Kingdom	1970s	0.09	−0.16	−0.40
OECD	United States	1970s	−1.13	−1.02	−0.90
S. Asia	Bangladesh	1970s	−2.11	−1.93	−1.75
S. Asia	India	1970s	−0.64	−0.76	−0.87
S. Asia	Myanmar	1970s	1.88	1.78	1.67
S. Asia	Pakistan	1970s	0.58	0.42	0.25
S. Asia	Sri Lanka	1970s	0.09	−0.33	−0.75

Region	Country	Decade	TFP ($\alpha = 0.3$)	TFP ($\alpha = 0.4$)	TFP ($\alpha = 0.5$)
Africa	Botswana	1980s	4.04	3.66	3.28
Africa	Cameroon	1980s	−1.56	−2.15	−2.74
Africa	Ghana	1980s	−0.37	−0.07	0.24
Africa	Kenya	1980s	0.96	1.17	1.39
Africa	Lesotho	1980s	0.98	0.51	0.04
Africa	Malawi	1980s	−0.35	−0.19	−0.03
Africa	Mali	1980s	−1.87	−1.86	−1.84
Africa	Mauritius	1980s	3.03	3.01	3.00
Africa	Mozambique	1980s	−1.32	−1.32	−1.33
Africa	Rwanda	1980s	−3.22	−3.77	−4.31
Africa	Senegal	1980s	0.45	0.45	0.45
Africa	Sierra Leone	1980s	−1.13	−1.03	−0.93
Africa	South Africa	1980s	−2.64	−2.47	−2.31
Africa	Sudan	1980s	−1.01	−1.09	−1.18
Africa	Tanzania	1980s	−0.14	−0.05	0.04
Africa	The Gambia	1980s	−1.91	−2.29	−2.67
Africa	Togo	1980s	−2.36	−2.31	−2.26
Africa	Uganda	1980s	0.40	0.75	1.10
Africa	Zambia	1980s	−0.74	−0.22	0.30
Africa	Zimbabwe	1980s	−1.16	−0.73	−0.30
E. Asia	China	1980s	4.40	3.92	3.45
E. Asia	Indonesia	1980s	1.06	0.37	−0.32
E. Asia	Korea, Rep. of	1980s	2.09	1.40	0.71
E. Asia	Malaysia	1980s	0.20	−0.24	−0.69
E. Asia	Papua New Guinea	1980s	−1.67	−01.61	−1.55
E. Asia	Philippines	1980s	−2.12	−2.23	−2.33
E. Asia	Singapore	1980s	1.81	1.28	0.75
E. Asia	Taiwan, China	1980s	3.92	2.30	2.49
E. Asia	Thailand	1980s	2.63	2.19	1.74
ECA	Bulgaria	1980s	−0.02	−0.32	−0.63
ECA	Hungary	1980s	0.92	0.54	0.16
ECA	Portugal	1980s	1.05	0.86	0.66
ECA	Romania	1980s	0.52	0.92	1.31
ECA	Turkey	1980s	1.35	1.21	1.08
LAC	Argentina	1980s	−3.43	−3.29	−3.16
LAC	Bolivia	1980s	−1.95	−1.59	−1.24
LAC	Brazil	1980s	−2.42	−2.38	−2.34
LAC	Chile	1980s	0.66	0.72	0.78
LAC	Colombia	1980s	−0.75	−0.75	−0.75
LAC	Costa Rica	1980s	−1.64	−1.59	−1.54
LAC	Dominican Republic	1980s	−1.80	−2.08	−2.37
LAC	Ecuador	1980s	−1.19	−1.17	−1.14
LAC	El Salvador	1980s	−2.87	−2.69	−2.51
LAC	Guatemala	1980s	−1.67	−1.59	−1.51
LAC	Guyana	1980s	−4.09	−3.94	−3.79
LAC	Honduras	1980s	−1.77	−1.58	−1.39

(Table continues on the following page.)

Annex Table 1. (*continued*)

Region	Country	Decade	TFP ($\alpha = 0.3$)	TFP ($\alpha = 0.4$)	TFP ($\alpha = 0.5$)
LAC	Mexico	1980s	−3.04	−2.92	−2.80
LAC	Nicaragua	1980s	−4.59	−4.48	−4.38
LAC	Panama	1980s	−2.69	−2.46	−2.23
LAC	Paraguay	1980s	−1.91	−2.20	−2.49
LAC	Peru	1980s	−3.70	−3.66	−3.62
LAC	Uruguay	1980s	−1.96	−1.76	−1.55
LAC	Venezuela	1980s	−1.68	−1.50	−1.33
MENA	Algeria	1980s	−2.45	−2.40	−2.36
MENA	Bahrain	1980s	−5.28	−5.24	−5.20
MENA	Egypt	1980s	0.01	−0.31	−0.63
MENA	Iran	1980s	−1.26	−1.10	−0.93
MENA	Jordan	1980s	−4.45	−4.43	−4.41
MENA	Kuwait	1980s	−5.12	−4.61	−4.10
MENA	Morocco	1980s	0.29	0.21	0.13
MENA	Saudi Arabia	1980s	−6.41	−5.88	−5.35
MENA	Syria	1980s	−3.92	−4.42	−4.92
MENA	Tunisia	1980s	−0.45	−0.54	−0.64
OECD	Australia	1980s	0.11	−0.05	−0.21
OECD	Austria	1980s	0.81	0.58	0.36
OECD	Belgium	1980s	0.70	0.55	0.40
OECD	Canada	1980s	−0.21	−0.33	−0.46
OECD	Denmark	1980s	0.05	−0.03	−0.11
OECD	Finland	1980s	0.06	0.03	−0.01
OECD	France	1980s	0.99	0.70	0.42
OECD	Greece	1980s	−1.41	−1.42	−1.42
OECD	Iceland	1980s	−0.11	−0.17	−0.23
OECD	Ireland	1980s	1.34	1.16	0.99
OECD	Israel	1980s	1.05	0.98	0.92
OECD	Italy	1980s	0.46	0.32	0.19
OECD	Japan	1980s	1.23	0.87	0.51
OECD	Netherlands	1980s	−0.27	−0.26	−0.24
OECD	New Zealand	1980s	−0.43	−0.50	−0.58
OECD	Norway	1980s	−1.26	−1.08	−0.90
OECD	Spain	1980s	0.67	0.48	0.29
OECD	Sweden	1980s	0.84	0.65	0.46
OECD	Switzerland	1980s	0.22	0.05	−0.12
OECD	United Kingdom	1980s	1.02	0.85	0.68
OECD	United States	1980s	1.36	1.15	0.94
S. Asia	Bangladesh	1980s	−0.19	−0.53	−0.87
S. Asia	India	1980s	2.33	2.10	1.87
S. Asia	Myanmar	1980s	−2.13	−2.24	−2.35
S. Asia	Pakistan	1980s	1.21	1.13	1.05
S. Asia	Sri Lanka	1980s	0.08	−0.44	−0.96
Africa	Botswana	1990s	−0.05	−0.39	−0.74
Africa	Cameroon	1990s	−1.21	−0.95	−0.69

Region	Country	Decade	TFP ($\alpha = 0.3$)	TFP ($\alpha = 0.4$)	TFP ($\alpha = 0.5$)
Africa	Ghana	1990s	0.34	0.16	−0.03
Africa	Kenya	1990s	−1.64	−1.43	−1.22
Africa	Lesotho	1990s	0.18	−0.35	−0.88
Africa	Malawi	1990s	1.90	2.15	2.39
Africa	Mali	1990s	1.66	1.66	1.66
Africa	Mauritius	1990s	1.74	1.39	1.03
Africa	Mozambique	1990s	2.48	2.24	2.01
Africa	Rwanda	1990s	−1.75	−1.75	−1.76
Africa	Senegal	1990s	0.18	0.10	0.01
Africa	Sierra Leone	1990s	..	..	″
Africa	South Africa	1990s	−1.29	−1.09	−0.88
Africa	Sudan	1990s	..	..	..
Africa	Tanzania	1990s	0.41	0.50	0.59
Africa	The Gambia	1990s	−1.31	−1.38	−1.45
Africa	Togo	1990s	−0.26	0.04	0.33
Africa	Uganda	1990s	3.52	3.43	3.33
Africa	Zambia	1990s	−1.42	−0.92	−0.43
Africa	Zimbabwe	1990s	−1.05	−1.15	−1.25
E. Asia	China	1990s	5.54	4.64	3.75
E. Asia	Indonesia	1990s	−0.76	−1.22	−1.68
E. Asia	Korea, Rep. of	1990s	0.90	0.23	−0.44
E. Asia	Malaysia	1990s	1.35	0.74	0.13
E. Asia	Papua New Guinea	1990s	2.04	2.22	2.41
E. Asia	Philippines	1990s	−0.83	−0.83	−0.83
E. Asia	Singapore	1990s	2.31	1.85	1.40
E. Asia	Taiwan, China	1990s	2.19	1.43	0.66
E. Asia	Thailand	1990s	0.23	−0.40	−1.03
ECA	Bulgaria	1990s	−1.38	−1.38	−1.38
ECA	Hungary	1990s	0.03	−0.11	−0.24
ECA	Portugal	1990s	0.18	−0.05	−0.29
ECA	Romania	1990s	−0.27	0.30	0.87
ECA	Turkey	1990s	−0.81	−0.95	−1.09
LAC	Argentina	1990s	1.98	2.01	2.05
LAC	Bolivia	1990s	0.75	0.78	0.82
LAC	Brazil	1990s	−0.04	0.01	0.06
LAC	Chile	1990s	2.24	1.81	1.37
LAC	Colombia	1990s	−1.06	−1.10	−1.15
LAC	Costa Rica	1990s	1.10	0.91	0.72
LAC	Dominican Republic	1990s	1.76	1.47	1.18
LAC	Ecuador	1990s	−1.23	−1.06	−0.90
LAC	El Salvador	1990s	0.27	0.25	0.22
LAC	Guatemala	1990s	0.32	0.34	0.35
LAC	Guyana	1990s	..	..	..
LAC	Honduras	1990s	−1.37	−1.45	−1.54
LAC	Mexico	1990s	−0.06	−0.11	−0.17
LAC	Nicaragua	1990s	−0.49	−0.20	0.09

(Table continues on the following page.)

Annex Table 1. (*continued*)

Region	Country	Decade	TFP ($\alpha = 0.3$)	TFP ($\alpha = 0.4$)	TFP ($\alpha = 0.5$)
LAC	Panama	1990s	1.00	0.73	0.45
LAC	Paraguay	1990s	−1.22	−1.34	−1.45
LAC	Peru	1990s	−0.31	−0.20	−0.10
LAC	Uruguay	1990s	1.27	1.19	1.11
LAC	Venezuela	1990s	−1.79	−1.44	−1.08
MENA	Algeria	1990s	−2.38	−1.99	−1.60
MENA	Bahrain	1990s	0.23	0.36	0.49
MENA	Egypt	1990s	0.58	0.73	0.88
MENA	Iran	1990s	0.02	0.16	0.31
MENA	Jordan	1990s	−0.81	−0.55	−0.29
MENA	Kuwait	1990s	−2.10	−1.79	−1.49
MENA	Morocco	1990s	−1.14	−1.15	−1.15
MENA	Saudi Arabia	1990s	0.47	0.88	1.28
MENA	Syria	1990s	0.68	0.89	1.10
MENA	Tunisia	1990s	0.51	0.55	0.59
OECD	Australia	1990s	1.00	0.85	0.69
OECD	Austria	1990s	0.68	0.47	0.26
OECD	Belgium	1990s	0.63	0.45	0.27
OECD	Canada	1990s	0.70	0.60	0.50
OECD	Denmark	1990s	1.52	1.33	1.13
OECD	Finland	1990s	1.05	1.04	1.04
OECD	France	1990s	−0.19	−0.27	−0.36
OECD	Greece	1990s	0.35	0.37	0.39
OECD	Iceland	1990s	0.57	0.53	0.49
OECD	Ireland	1990s	3.97	3.83	3.68
OECD	Israel	1990s	0.46	0.21	−0.05
OECD	Italy	1990s	0.12	0.03	−0.05
OECD	Japan	1990s	−0.53	−0.80	−1.06
OECD	Netherlands	1990s	1.16	1.04	0.92
OECD	New Zealand	1990s	0.66	0.62	0.57
OECD	Norway	1990s	2.32	2.26	2.20
OECD	Spain	1990s	0.01	−0.14	−0.29
OECD	Sweden	1990s	−0.29	−0.20	−0.11
OECD	Switzerland	1990s	−0.39	−0.52	−0.65
OECD	United Kingdom	1990s	0.82	0.65	0.48
OECD	United States	1990s	0.95	0.75	0.56
S. Asia	Bangladesh	1990s	0.87	0.45	0.02
S. Asia	India	1990s	1.42	1.16	0.90
S. Asia	Myanmar	1990s	3.40	2.97	2.54
S. Asia	Pakistan	1990s	0.92	0.69	0.46
S. Asia	Sri Lanka	1990s	1.38	1.13	0.87
Africa		1960s	−0.01	−0.49	−0.97
E. Asia		1960s	1.07	1.04	1.01
ECA		1960s	3.42	3.07	2.72
LAC		1960s	1.46	1.20	0.94
MENA		1960s	2.36	1.96	1.55

Region	Country	Decade	TFP ($\alpha = 0.3$)	TFP ($\alpha = 0.4$)	TFP ($\alpha = 0.5$)
OECD		1960s	2.18	1.67	1.15
S. Asia		1960s	0.62	0.27	−0.09
World		1960s	1.28	1.01	0.74
World (excluding China)		1960s	1.37	0.97	0.56
Africa		1970s	−0.07	−0.31	−0.55
E. Asia		1970s	1.61	1.18	0.76
ECA		1970s	0.58	0.08	−0.42
LAC		1970s	1.23	0.91	0.59
MENA		1970s	−0.35	−0.96	−1.56
OECD		1970s	−0.17	−0.39	−0.62
S. Asia		1970s	−0.57	−0.66	−0.76
World		1970s	0.52	0.22	−0.07
World (excluding China)		1970s	0.01	−0.26	−0.53
Africa		1980s	−0.62	−0.70	−0.77
E. Asia		1980s	3.58	3.08	2.59
ECA		1980s	0.95	0.89	0.83
LAC		1980s	−2.37	−2.29	−2.22
MENA		1980s	−1.39	−1.44	−1.48
OECD		1980s	0.92	0.71	0.50
S. Asia		1980s	1.79	1.56	1.33
World		1980s	1.62	1.34	1.07
World (excluding China)		1980s	0.58	0.39	0.19
Africa		1990s	−0.07	−0.11	−0.15
E. Asia		1990s	4.11	3.32	2.54
ECA		1990s	−0.57	−0.55	−0.54
LAC		1990s	0.02	0.03	0.04
MENA		1990s	−0.22	−0.03	0.15
OECD		1990s	0.45	0.28	0.11
S. Asia		1990s	1.39	1.11	0.83
World		1990s	1.88	1.51	1.13
World (excluding China)		1990s	0.55	0.37	0.18

Appendix Notes

1. Nehru and Dhareshwar, 1993.

2. In the case of MENA economies, where there were inconsistencies, the World Bank MENA regional database investment series was preferred.

3. Barro and Lee, 2000. Educational attainment data (available until 1999) were extended to 2000 assuming constant growth between 1995-2000.

•
•

8

Challenges and Opportunities for the 21st Century: Higher Education in the Middle East and North Africa

Mustapha Nabli

Good morning. It is a privilege for me to be here today to address this distinguished group, on the opening day of a conference that has tremendous importance for the Middle East and North Africa region, from my point of view. Particularly because this conference on tertiary education in the region comes at a time in which new research is changing the way in which we view the importance of higher schooling.

Over the last decade, the focus of development practitioners on educational priorities has undergone significant change. Until the beginning of the 1990s, many economists, including those within my own institution, maintained that developing economies should give highest priority to improving access to primary and secondary education. They generated the greatest rates of return, and thus justified government investment and relatively high Bank intervention in these levels. More than a decade of empirical analyses seemed to demonstrate that higher education offered lower private and social returns than basic education. Considering that higher education absorbs considerably higher investment, a powerful justification was provided for focusing public educational investment at the basic level. This justification was further reinforced by the obvious gains in social equity associated with such a strategy. As

---

Speech at the Conference on Higher Education in the Middle East and North Africa: Challenges and Opportunities for the 21st Century; Institut du Monde Arabe; Paris, France; May 23, 2002.

a result, there has been a preference for basic education in the developing world. In contrast, higher education was relegated to a relatively minor place on the development agenda.

But over the 1990s, we have seen more and more literature challenging the old orthodoxy that basic education should be the focus in the education strategies of developing economies. We now understand, as I am sure my colleagues at this conference will better argue, the critical importance of having a solid base of higher education in every economy—no matter what the level of income—to support its development strategy. Economic development is increasingly linked to a nation's ability to acquire and apply technical and socioeconomic knowledge. Highly skilled workers, and the capacity for technological innovation dissemination, are a foundation of economic development, not only for economies moving to a higher-technology production base, but of equal importance for low- and middle-income economies to obtain increased returns from their large stock of low- or unskilled labor. Comparative advantages come less and less from abundant natural resources or cheaper labor, and more and more from technical innovations and the competitive use of knowledge.[1] My colleague, Jamil Salmi, will be expanding upon this theme this afternoon. Prosperity in agriculture is more and more dependent upon technological innovations and their diffusion. Labor-intensive industries that cannot modernize with new technologies find themselves increasingly unable to compete.

The strategies of the East Asian economies demonstrate the importance of higher education with other educational advancements in promoting growth. The mainstay of their success stories has been the acquisition of foreign technology and production methods, which were adapted and improved upon by well-educated nationals. Rapid growth of labor-intensive manufacturing was made possible, with a highly trained set of individuals to put in place the structures to achieve greater productivity. Agricultural productivity was improved through adaptive local research. In countries without a sufficient stock of higher-educated nationals—Indonesia, Malaysia, Singapore, and Thailand—there was heavy reliance on multinational corporations that substituted foreign for missing local skills.

And the empirical evidence has materialized to support this notion. The pursuit and use of higher education is a critical factor affecting economic growth. In fact, at least some empirical studies have shown that among low- and middle-income economies, an increase in the educational stock at higher education levels promotes as much growth, or more rapid growth, than the same amount of increase in educational stock at lower levels does.

But, despite these new findings, what remains troubling in my mind is that the MENA region has been unable to realize the gains from its substantial investments in education. This applies not only to higher education but to lower levels of education, as well. Despite really extraordinary progress over the last decades in increasing the level of education throughout the region, the pay-offs have been very disappointing from an international context.

And what I would like to talk about today is how the MENA region can best improve the social and private returns from its higher education systems—in an increasingly globalized world. We often spend great amounts of time discussing how educational systems should be adapted to meet the needs of a more globalized world; how universities must better equip students to respond to new educational demands and opportunities; how organizations of higher learning need to meet better the growing demand among learners for improved accessibility and convenience, lower costs, direct application of content to work settings, and greater understanding of the dynamic complexity, and often interdisciplinary nature, of knowledge; how education needs to foster greater flexibility, so that workers can adjust to new market demand; how education needs to be more responsive to private sector needs; how skills need to be made more relevant. Indeed, these are important issues.

But we often approach the issue of educational reform from an internal point of view, asking how institutes or organizations of learning can adapt to meet better the demands of development. What is more rarely discussed is how the ability for educational systems to adapt to new demands and opportunities is fundamentally affected by policies outside of the educational sector.

There is a large body of literature that has focused on estimating the relationship between human capital and growth. From these studies, we have increasingly realized that the relationship depends strongly on the national context, which determines whether skilled labor is effectively utilized in productive activities. Unlike physical capital, human capital responds to incentives that increase its own private return, but sometimes the higher private rate of return is not derived from growth-enhancing activities, but rather from rent seeking.[2]

What I would like to focus my talk on today is the emerging consensus that the ability for an economy to leverage its stock of human capital is intrinsically determined by policies that fall outside the traditional area of education reform. Education can only be internationally competitive if work is. And so, key to honing the higher education sector to becoming more internationally competitive are identifying and removing those barriers to the productive use of education in the economy. Education and its use in the economy is a virtuous circle—if competitive, relevant skills are demanded and rewarded in the economy, and there will be increased demands on the educational sector to respond. But sustainable improvements to the higher educational system, by changes in its supply, cannot be achieved if, in the end, there are few incentives in place for its productive use.

What are the factors that inhibit the demand for more "productive" skills—meaning skills that not only garner private returns, but that also are productively utilized in the economy?

To begin, what is probably the most obvious, and has been most greatly explored in the development literature, is the degree of public sector employment. The MENA region maintains one of the highest levels of public sector employment in the world, and civil service employment as a proportion of total employment is the highest in the world. In the mid-1990s, civil service employment, including in health and education, accounted for 17.5 percent of total employment in the region. In comparison, civil service accounted for 16 percent of total employment in Eastern Europe and the former Soviet Union, 6.3 percent in Asia, 6.6 percent in Africa, and 8.9 percent in Latin America and the Caribbean. Still, these figures do not tell the entire story. The majority of MENA's civil service employment is not in the health and education sectors but in government administration. In fact, some 10.5 percent of employment in the MENA region is in government administration. That compares with 4.2 percent in Eastern Europe and the former USSR, 4 percent in Asia, 4 percent in Africa, and 5.4 percent in Latin America and the Caribbean.

Until recently, public sector employment was almost a guarantee in the region for persons with higher or intermediate education. As a result, individuals have often sought higher degrees—with little attention to content or quality. Public sector employment is characterized by a large number of workers possessing education that bears little relation to the skills needed by either the private sector or for the efficient functioning of the public sector. Most public sector jobs are protected, so there is a large element of rent seeking on the part of those who secure them.

In many countries in the region, new graduates have either obtained or queued for government jobs, giving rise to a very unusual pattern of unemployment. Unemployment in the region is almost always highest precisely for those individuals with advanced educations. Obviously, this should raise significant alarm for policy makers when addressing higher education reform, if investments in higher education go unused.

What has been the cost of an overstaffed public sector? A recent study examined the relationship between public sector employment and economic growth. Generally, cross-country growth studies are based upon explanations of economic growth by increases in factors of production and TFP—that portion of economic growth that cannot be explained by accumulation. But not all factor accumulation goes toward growth. One could argue that human capital that is diverted to the administrative civil service does not. In this particular study, the authors deducted the proportion of human capital diverted to the administrative civil service from the country's human capital stock, and ran traditional growth regressions. Then, from those estimates, they could calculate how much more growth countries would have realized if the human capital diverted to public administration had gone into the productive economy.[3] From this calculation, it was estimated that for the MENA region, the loss of GDP growth between 1985 and 1995, strictly as a result of public administration employment, was some 8.4 percent—or close to 1 percentage point per year.[4]

But there are other factors relevant to the region that have prevented the application of education to productive use. One factor that has been the subject of recent cross-country exploration is the degree of openness. When studies have examined the relationship between openness and human capital on total factor productivity, they have found that outward-oriented economies experience higher total factor productivity, but over and above the positive effect of openness. Rather, outward orientation is critical for allowing human capital to have a positive impact on economic growth. The effect of the stock of human capital on total factor productivity is conditional on the degree of openness.[5]

Greater openness fosters competition, encourages modern technology, increases the demand for highly skilled labor, and promotes learning by doing. Openness obliges industries to confront their inefficiencies. To compete successfully, industries must adapt, thereby creating demand for the new skills and trades to do so. More specific mechanisms associated with trade liberalization provide incentives for maximizing the private rate of return to education through growth-enhancing activities. Too little openness, therefore, does not allow a country to benefit as greatly from its investments in human capital. Human capital investment without liberalization of the external sector may lead to the underutilization of human capital.[6]

What is the dynamic influence that trade exerts over the use of human capital? One recent study points to three possible avenues: First, the contact of trade—the trading technology itself—is skil-intensive. Trade needs packaging and paperwork that conforms to international standards. It requires knowledge of international markets. It requires knowledge of distribution channels, legal requirements, government regulations, and import restrictions. The process of trade requires skills that only educated labor can have.

Second, traded goods are usually of higher skill content than those produced and consumed at home, especially for developing countries, since they must compete with foreign suppliers. Once trade has been liberalized, and the protective barrier of tariffs and direct restrictions has been lifted, home producers need to invest in new technology to compete in the global marketplace. Opening firms to competition provides the incentives for the efficient use of existing knowledge, the creation of new knowledge, and the flourishing of entrepreneurship.

Third, the exposure to the foreign markets that trade brings enhances the knowledge of domestic producers of superior technologies. Such technologies are usually complementary to skills, because of the abundance of skilled labor in more advanced countries. Their importation increases the wage premium paid to skilled labor in developing countries, and so encourages the redeployment of skilled labor to trade-related activities.[7]

And so, I would argue today that, along with discussing policy options for improving the relevance of higher education in MENA, at least some attention needs to be paid to removing the barriers that insulate the region from globalization, so that the incentive structure for educational attainments to have their greatest effect on economic and social development is in place.

Trade policy in the region remains one of the most restrictive in the world, with low level of and speed of integration into the world economy. Tariff rates remain high and the extent of nontariff barriers large. A number of policy moves across the region are expected to lead to greater trade openness, but the region's progress has been uneven, and in many cases has been superficial at best. But among the positive moves is the EU association agreements signed by Tunisia, Morocco, Jordan, Algeria, Egypt, and Lebanon. These policy moves are expected to stimulate integration, and, one hopes, compel workers to articulate better their demands of the educational system, based upon expected returns from productive activities.

In addition to creating economies more open to trade to compel their potential workforce to seek more relevant skills, more effective use of education in the region hinges upon developing a dynamic information infrastructure to facilitate the effective communication, dissemination, and processing of information. At first sight, this factor may seem to lie squarely within educational sector reform. Indeed, much of it is. But, as the focus of my talk is to detail the factors prohibiting the productive use of, and thereby qualitative demands for, higher education, the lack of a well-developed information infrastructure and the other dimensions of the knowledge economy also impact the way in which education is used.

To begin with, knowledge allows industries to tap into more efficient production methods, and in doing so, to better identify skill needs. As a result, with a keener sense of the precise skills needed to operate effectively, their ultimate workforce has a greater potential for efficiently using educational attainments.

In addition, the vast availability of knowledge allows workers to discern better what skills are demanded in the market. This is of immense importance to sustainable improvements in the higher education sector. Perfect information, in which market opportunities and returns for the skilled labor market are known, provides the ultimate guide for how the higher education system must respond.

And finally, knowledge is key to integration. Developed countries are moving quickly toward integrated "knowledge-based economies," in which knowledge, information, and communication technologies are becoming keys to competitiveness and engines for social and economic development. Not participating in the knowledge revolution presents the risk to the region of being further marginalized. As the knowledge gap between developed and developing economies widens, the potential for successfully competing in the global economy shrinks. This is a risk that is all too dangerous for a region that has embraced global integration less than enthusiastically. If this fundamental tool for being internationally competitive is not widely available, the potential for reverting to inward-oriented strategies is great.

I would point to a final feature of the MENA economies that undermines the efficient use of education, and that is the myriad governance issues that impede efficient business operations, private investment, and entrepreneurship and provide an enabling environment for rent seeking. While the comprehensive macroeconomic and structural reform programs espoused by many of the MENA economies in the early 1990s created an exuberant boost in their economic outlooks, the MENA region must move beyond "stroke of the pen" reforms to the more serious, and challenging, issues that obstruct the development of a strong private sector. Unless the private sector begins to see itself as an independent source of growth and productivity in the economy, and society begins to underpin this change economically and politically, the region will continue to find its educational enhancements underused.

In closing, I want to say that I sincerely welcome this conference on higher education in MENA, as it gives us the opportunity to explore the multiple dimensions of education and its applications. But I would add a caveat as we explore the many layers of educational reform. Improving access to and content of higher education in MENA is of critical importance in the region's economic and social development. But greater investment in higher education is not a magic bullet. While expansion in higher education is important in the context of economic growth, the economic context in which these services are provided is equally important. Human resource development policy must be designed in conjunction with an overall development strategy, to allow education to find its most effective use in the pursuit of higher economic growth, the expansion of employment opportunities, and the reduction of poverty.

Thank you.

Notes

1. Jamil Salmi June 2000. "Tertiary Education in the Twenty-First Century: Challenges and Opportunities." Human Development Department LCSHD Paper Series No. 62. World Bank.

2. Christopher Pissarides. "Human Capital and Growth: A Synthesis Report." OECD Development Center Technical Paper No. 168; 2000.

3. Letting the human capital stock diverted to public administration realize the same rates of return as the human capital stock not in public administration.

4. Ibid.

5. Stephen M. Miller and Mukti P. Upadhyay. "The Effects of Openness, Trade Orientation, and Human Capital on Total Factor Productivity." *Journal of Development Economics*, Vol. 63. 2000.

6. Ibid.

7. Pissarides, 2000.

9

Labor Market Reforms, Growth, and Unemployment in Labor-Exporting Countries in the Middle East and North Africa

Pierre-Richard Agénor*
Mustapha K. Nabli
Tarik Yousef†
Henning Tarp Jensen††

As in other developing regions in the post-World War II era, the demographic transition in the Middle East and North Africa region has given rise to rapid labor force growth. But with an average growth rate above 3 percent since the 1960s, no other region comes close to the magnitude and persistence of MENA's labor market pressures. And while employment growth was relatively strong in the 1970s, it failed to keep pace with the expansion of the labor force during the 1980s and 1990s. As a result, MENA recorded some of the highest unemployment rates among developing regions in the 1990s. Recent estimates indicate that unemployment rates range from about 2.3 percent in the United Arab Emirates to close to 29.8 percent in Algeria (see World Bank 2004). For the region as a whole, the unemployment rate is currently estimated at 15 percent of the labor force.[1] Based on current trends in job creation, the prospects for absorbing new entrants into labor markets, as well as those currently unemployed, are rather bleak. With the labor force growing in the

*World Bank. †Georgetown University. ††University of Copenhagen, Denmark. The authors are grateful to various colleagues for helpful comments on a preliminary version.

Published in *Journal of Policy Modeling* 29, (2007). Reprinted with permission from Elsevier Limited; see pages 277–309.

present decade at 3.4 percent per annum, the average unemployment rate for the region could reach 22 percent by 2010.

Low output growth is often the "proximate" cause for the rise in unemployment. Following the oil bust in the late 1980s, the region experienced a weak recovery in the 1990s due to the protracted pace of policy reforms. But there are also structural reasons for unemployment that were not addressed by policy makers in the past decade. MENA countries exhibit rigidities in educational systems, wage setting, and regulatory regimes due to the dominance of the public sector in labor markets. Although rates of human capital accumulation have remained steady, MENA has reaped less than its potential in terms of economic growth and job creation. Government legislation on hiring and firing, minimum wages, and collective bargaining agreements, as well as employment guarantees in the public sector, have interfered with the efficient functioning of the labor market.[2] In normal times, the impact of some of these structural rigidities may well be mitigated by the existence of large informal sectors. However, in periods of significant structural changes, they could turn into binding constraints on the expansion of output and employment. In such conditions, reforming the labor market becomes an important element of any reform program aimed at stimulating growth and promoting job creation.

Accordingly, the purpose of this paper is to offer a quantitative analysis of the impact of labor market reforms on growth, real wages, and unemployment in labor-exporting MENA countries.[3] We begin with a brief overview of the main features of the labor market in five labor-exporting MENA countries, namely, Algeria, Egypt, Jordan, Morocco, and Tunisia.[4] The next section presents a quantitative framework that captures many of these features (such as a large informal urban sector, active trade unions, public sector employment, and international labor flows), as well as other important structural features of these countries, such as an unfunded pension system.[5] Following is a discussion of the calibration procedure and parameter values. Finally, we present simulation experiments focusing on four types of individual policy shocks: a reduction in payroll taxation on unskilled labor, reductions in public sector wages and the size of the government workforce, higher employment subsidies to the private sector, and a reduction in the bargaining power of trade unions.

We also consider a "composite" reform package, involving a cut in payroll taxes and public sector employment, as well as a reduction in unions' bargaining strength. The extent to which high payroll taxes have tended to discourage the demand for (unskilled) labor has been an important policy issue in MENA countries in general. Our framework allows us to consider the implications of both revenue- and budget-neutral changes in these taxes, and the various channels through which they affect job creation and unemployment. The concluding section summarizes the results and draws together the main policy lessons of the analysis. It emphasizes the need for an overall package of reforms, involving not only labor market policies but also other structural measures, to foster sustained growth in output and employment in labor-exporting MENA countries.

Some Basic Facts

The functioning of the labor market in MENA countries in general, and labor-exporting countries in particular, has been reviewed in a number of recent contributions.[6] Here we briefly review some of the salient features of this market (as summarized in figure 9.1), in order to motivate the specification of the model developed in the next section.

Fundamentally, the labor market in labor-exporting MENA countries can be characterized as consisting of three segments: the rural sector, which continues to employ a sizable proportion of the labor force in many countries; the informal urban sector, characterized mostly by self-employment and a limited proportion of hired labor, a high degree of wage flexibility, low employment security, and no enforcement of labor regulations; and the formal (public and private) urban sector, where workers are hired on the basis of explicit contracts and the degree of compliance with labor regulation (particularly in the public sector) is relatively high.

The informal sector accounts for a large fraction of the labor force. Estimates of informal employment range from a low of 42 percent of nonagricultural employment in Syria to a high of 55 percent in Egypt. Although moderate compared to other developing regions, these estimates are high given the large share of public sector employment. In most labor-exporting MENA countries, the public sector is the dominant employer in the formal sector (see Abrahart, Kaur, and Tzannatos 2002). When measured as a percentage of nonagricultural employment, the public sector is the highest among developing regions. Governments are often considered as "employers of first resort," especially for people with middle and higher education levels. The perpetuation of employment guarantees in government hiring, and mismatched wage expectations resulting from generous public sector compensation and benefits policies, have contributed to the continued preference for public sector jobs.

Although open unemployment has increased in recent years, underemployment remains pervasive.[7] Open and disguised unemployment (which affects disproportionately the young and women) amount to anywhere between 25 and 60 percent of the labor force in some countries. A large majority of the openly unemployed have secondary or postsecondary degrees, but open unemployment is also becoming more widespread among unskilled workers. Part of this unemployment is "queueing" or "wait" unemployment, resulting from public sector hiring and wage-setting practices, as shown for

Figure 9.1. Labor-Exporting MENA Countries: Economic and Labor Market Indicators

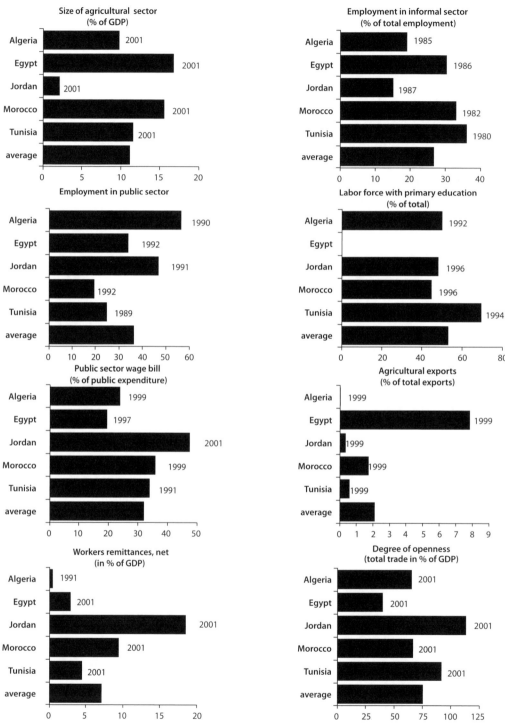

Note: Years are given next to bars.

instance by Assaad (1997) in the case of Egypt. The unemployed are essentially those who would have had a chance at a formal job in the public sector in the past and continue to have expectations of acquiring such a job. Those with no education must either accept whatever employment is available to them, no matter how casual, or create their own jobs in order to survive.

Labor market regulations, including restrictions on hiring and firing, as well as minimum wage legislation, are widespread in the region. In all labor-exporting MENA countries (except Jordan), there is a minimum wage regulation, although its impact on wage formation is not always clear.[8] In Egypt and Tunisia, compliance with minimum wages is mostly limited to the public sector. In recent years, high unemployment in Morocco has led authorities to allow the private sector to hire workers at wages below the minimum rate. Restrictions on layoffs in the formal sector (and often, generous severance payments) make firing redundant workers difficult in most labor-exporting MENA countries. In practice, however, the enforcement of the law is weak; compliance with existing regulations is limited to the formal sector. Thus, although labor market regulations may be pervasive on paper, their impact is mitigated by weak enforcement and the existence of large informal sectors.

Wage determination often departs from market-clearing mechanisms as a result of legal restrictions, the existence of labor unions, and imperfectly competitive wage-setting behavior by firms. Wages in agriculture and the urban informal sectors tend to be highly flexible. In contrast, some urban formal sectors show rigid systems that are characterized by segmentation and binding institutional constraints.[9] In most countries, civil service pay remains a point of reference for public enterprises and many large firms in the formal private sector. This "leadership effect" of public wage settlements is a source of downward rigidity in wage behavior in the private sector. Among nonwage labor costs, social security contributions (which are typically shared between employers and employees) are particularly significant. In Algeria, contributions to the social security system alone constitute more than 36 percent of total labor costs.

With the exception of Jordan, where collective bargaining is practically nonexistent, labor unions in Algeria, Egypt, Morocco, and Tunisia play a significant role in collective bargaining at the national level (see for instance Assaad and Commander (1994) for Egypt). This occurs despite the fact that actual unionization rates are relatively low in most of these countries (except Egypt) and union membership tends to be primarily in the public sector. The trade union movement is usually highly centralized, except in Morocco; its influence on wage formation is often through the political process (by lobbying to secure increases in minimum wages, for instance) rather than through industrial action, such as strikes and other forms of work disruptions. Through their influence on political parties, unionized workers are also able to exert considerable pressure to maintain job security.

Finally, international migration flows are an important source of foreign exchange and income for all of these countries. In the 1970s and 1980s, the peak years of oil-led growth in the region, the Gulf countries experienced unprecedented labor force growth, driven primarily by the large number of immigrants seeking work from the labor-exporting MENA economies, especially Egypt and Jordan. During the same period, millions of migrants from Morocco, Tunisia, and, (to a lesser extent) Algeria sought work in Europe. The 1990s witnessed a sharp fall in the outflows of workers from the sending countries in the region even though remittances remained an important source of income (see figure 9.1). These flows play a significant role in the adjustment of the domestic labor market, in ways that we discuss more specifically below.

A Formal Framework

We now describe a quantitative framework to analyze the impact of labor market reforms in labor-exporting MENA countries.[10] The model captures many of the structural features of the labor market highlighted in the foregoing discussion. In this section, we briefly summarize the main features of the model (focusing on the production structure, the labor market, and the pension system), with a complete list of equations provided in Appendix 9.A, and variable definitions in Appendix 9.B.

Production

The composition of output and the structure of the labor market are summarized in figure 9.2. The basic distinction on the production side is that between rural and urban sectors. The rural sector (or agriculture) produces only one good, which is sold both on domestic markets and abroad. Urban production includes both formal and informal components; in addition, the formal urban economy is separated between production of a private good and a public good. Land available for production in agriculture is in fixed supply. Gross output in the rural sector, as well as in all other sectors, is given by the sum of value added and intermediate consumption (Equation A1). Value added is assumed to be produced with a Cobb-Douglas function of a composite factor, defined as a function that depends on the number of unskilled rural workers employed in agriculture and the economy-wide stock of public physical capital (Equation A2).The presence of public physical capital in the production function of the agricultural good is based on the view that a greater availability of public physical capital in the economy (roads, storage facilities, power grid, and the like) improves the productivity of large-scale producers and other production units in agriculture, because it facilitates not only trade and domestic commerce but also the production process itself. For simplicity,

Figure 9.2 A Stylized View of the Labor Market in Labor-Exporting MENA Countries

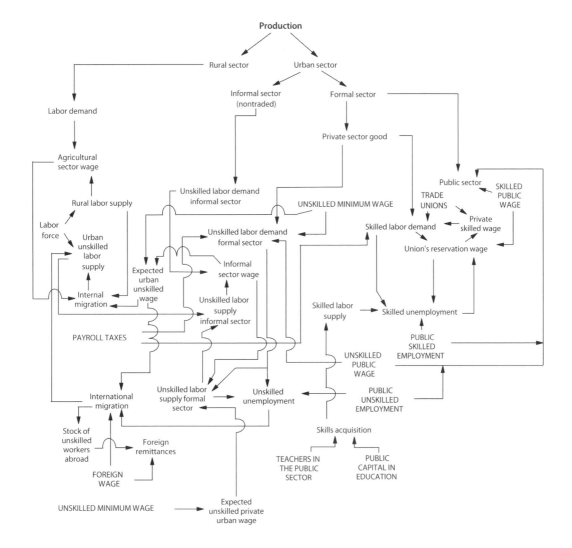

the area of land allocated to production is normalized to unity. Agricultural production exhibits decreasing returns to scale in the remaining (composite) input.

Value added in the informal economy is given as a function of the number of unskilled workers employed there, with decreasing returns to scale (Equation A4). Value added in the public sector is generated by combining skilled and unskilled labor using a CES function (Equation A5). Employment levels of both categories of workers are treated as exogenous.

Private formal production uses as inputs skilled and unskilled labor, as well as physical capital. Skilled labor and private physical capital have a higher degree of complementarity (lower degree of substitution) than physical capital and unskilled workers. In order to account explicitly for these differences in the degree of substitutability among inputs, we adopt a nested production structure. At the lowest level, skilled labor and private capital are combined to form a composite input with a low elasticity of substitution between them (Equation A8). At the second level, this composite input is used together with unskilled labor to form a second composite input (Equation A7). The elasticity of substitution between the first composite input and unskilled workers is taken to be higher than between skilled employment and private capital. The final layer combines the second composite input and the stock of government capital as production inputs (Equation A6).

The Labor Market

Unskilled workers in the economy may be employed either in the rural economy, U_R, or in the urban economy, U_U, whereas skilled workers are employed only in the urban formal sector.

Agriculture and Internal Migration The demand for labor in the agricultural sector, U_A^d, can be derived from profit maximization as

$$U_A^d = \left(V_A^{1+\frac{\rho_{XA}}{1-\eta_{XA}}} \frac{1-\eta_{XA}}{w_A} \cdot \frac{\beta_{XA}}{\alpha_{XA}^{\rho_{XA}}} \right)^{\frac{1}{1+\rho_{XA}}}, \text{ where } w_A = \frac{W_A}{PV_A}, \tag{1}$$

where V_A is value added in the agricultural sector, W_A denotes the nominal wage, and PV_A is the value-added price (net of input costs) in the agricultural sector.

Nominal wages in agriculture adjust to clear the labor market. Let U_R^s denote labor supply in the rural sector; the equilibrium condition is thus given by

$$U_R^s = U_A^d \left(V_A, \frac{W_A}{PV_A} \right). \tag{2}$$

Over time, U_R^s grows at the exogenous population growth rate, g_R, net of worker migration to urban areas, MIG:

$$U_R = U_{R,-1} \left(1+g_R \right) - MIG \tag{3}$$

In the spirit of Harris and Todaro (1970), the incentives to migrate are taken to depend negatively on the ratio of the average expected consumption wage in rural areas to that prevailing in urban areas. Unskilled migrant workers may be employed either in the private formal sector, in which case they are paid a minimum wage, W_M, or they can enter the informal economy and receive the market-determined wage in that sector, W_I. When rural workers make the decision to migrate to urban areas, they are uncertain as to which type of job they will be able to get, and therefore weigh wages in each sector by the probability of finding a job in that sector. These probabilities are approximated by prevailing employment ratios. Finally, migrants consider what their expected purchasing power in rural and urban areas will be, depending on whether they stay in the rural sector and consume the "typical" basket of goods of rural households, or migrate and consume the "typical" urban basket of goods.

The expected, unskilled urban real wage, Ew_U, is thus a weighted average of the minimum wage in the formal sector and the going wage in the informal sector, deflated by the urban consumption price index, P_{URB}:

$$Ew_U = \frac{\theta_U W_{M,-1} + \left(1 - \theta_U\right) W_{I,-1}}{P_{URB,-1}}, \tag{4}$$

where θ_U is the probability of finding a job in the urban formal sector, measured by the proportion of unskilled workers in the private formal sector, relative to the total number of unskilled urban workers looking for a job in the urban formal sector, U_F^s, net of government employment, U_G, in the previous period:[11]

$$\theta_U = \frac{U_{P,-1}}{U_{F,-1}^s - U_{G,-1}}. \tag{5}$$

In the rural sector, the employment probability is equal to unity, because workers can always find a job at the going wage. Assuming a one-period lag, the expected rural consumption real wage, E_{wA}, is thus

$$Ew_A = \frac{W_{A,-1}}{P_{R,-1}},$$

where P_R is the rural consumption price index.

The migration function can therefore be specified as

$$MIG = U_{R,-1} \lambda_m \left[\sigma_M \ln\left(\frac{Ew_U}{Ew_A} \right) \right] + \left(1 - \lambda_m\right) \frac{U_{R,-1}}{U_{R,-2}} MIG_{-1}: \tag{6}$$

where $0 < \lambda_m < 1$ measures the speed of adjustment and $\sigma_M > 0$ the elasticity of migration flows with respect to expected wages. This specification assumes that costs associated with migration or other frictions may delay the migration process, introducing persistence in migration flows.

The Urban Sector. The public sector employs an exogenous number of unskilled workers, U_G, at the nominal wage rate W_{UG}, whereas the demand for unskilled labor by the formal private sector is determined by firms' profit maximization subject to the given minimum wage, W_M. Both wages are assumed to be fully indexed on the urban formal price index, P_F

$$W_{UG} = \omega_{UG} P_F, \quad W_M = \omega_M P_F, \tag{7}$$

where ω_M and ω_{UG} measure exogenous real wages.

Labor demand by the formal private sector is determined by firms' profit maximization. We assume also that firms pay a payroll tax, at the rate $0 < ptax_U < 1$ on unskilled labor. This tax is proportional to the wage bill, $W_M U_P$. Firms also receive a nominal employment subsidy on unskilled labor of $ES_U < W_M$ per worker. Unskilled labor demand by the private sector is thus given by

$$U_P^d = T_1 \left(\frac{PT_1}{(1 + ptax_U) W_M - ES_U} \frac{\beta_{XP1}}{\alpha_{XP1}^{\rho_{XP1}}} \right)^{\sigma_{XP1}}, \tag{8}$$

where $\sigma_{XP1} = 1/(1 + \rho_{XP1})$ measures the elasticity of substitution between unskilled labor and the composite input.

We assume, as in Agénor (2002), that mobility of the unskilled labor force between the formal and informal sectors is imperfect, as a result of relocation and congestion costs. Migration flows are determined by expected income opportunities, again in line with Harris and Todaro (1970). Specifically, the supply of unskilled workers in the formal sector (including public sector workers), U_F^s, is assumed to change over time as a function of the expected wage differential across sectors, measured in real terms. Wage and employment prospects are formed on the basis of prevailing conditions in the labor market. Because there is no job turnover in the public sector (as noted earlier), the expected nominal wage in the formal economy is equal to the minimum wage, weighted by the probability of being hired in the private sector. Assuming that hiring in that sector is random, this probability can be approximated by the ratio between employed workers and those seeking employment during the previous period, $U_{P,-1}^d / (U_{F,-1}^s - U_{G,-1})$. The expected nominal wage in the informal economy, W_I, is simply the going wage, because there are no barriers to entry in that sector. Assuming a one-period lag, the supply of unskilled workers in the formal sector thus evolves over time according to

$$\frac{U_F^s}{U_{F,-1}^s} = \left\{ \frac{U_{P,-1}^d}{U_{F,-1}^s - U_{G,-1}} \left(\frac{W_{M,-1}}{W_{I,-1}} \right) \right\}^{\beta_F}, \quad \beta_F > 0, \tag{9}$$

where β_F is the elasticity of formal sector labor supply growth with respect to expected wages. The rate of unskilled unemployment in the formal sector, $UNEMP_U$, is thus given by

$$UNEMP_U = 1 - \frac{(U_G + U_P^d)}{U_F^s}. \tag{10}$$

From (A4), the demand for labor in the informal sector can be derived as

$$U_I^d = \beta_{XI}(V_I / w_I), \tag{11}$$

where V_I is value added in the informal sector and w_I the product wage, given by $w_I = W_I / PV_I$, with PV_I denoting the price of value added in the informal sector.

The supply of labor in the informal economy, U_I^s, is obtained by subtracting the unskilled labor supply in the formal sector, U_F^s, from the urban unskilled labor force, U_U:

$$U_I^s - U_U - U_F^s. \tag{12}$$

The informal labor market clears continuously, so that $U_I^d = U_I^s$. From equations (11) and (12), the equilibrium nominal wage is thus given by

$$W_I - \beta_{XI}\left(\frac{PV_I V_I}{U_I^s}\right). \tag{13}$$

The urban unskilled labor supply, U_U, grows as a result of "natural" urban population growth and migration of unskilled labor from the rural economy, as discussed earlier. In addition, a quantity *SKL* of urban unskilled workers acquires skills and leaves the unskilled labor force to augment the supply of skilled workers in the economy. We make the additional assumption that individuals are born unskilled, and therefore natural urban population growth (not resulting from migration or skills acquisition factors) is represented by urban unskilled population growth only, at the exogenous (gross) rate g_U. Finally, there are international migrations, the flow of which is measured by *IMIG*, and retirement from the urban labor force, measured by $\delta_{NP}^U U_U$, which is defined below. Thus, the urban unskilled labor supply evolves according to

$$U_U = \left(1 + g_U - \delta_{NP}^U\right) U_{U,-1} + MIG - SKL - IMIG, \tag{14}$$

where $\delta_{NP}^U \leq 1 + g_U$.

As noted earlier, the employment levels of both skilled and unskilled workers in the public sector are taken as exogenous. Given that some workers retire in every period, we have

$$U_G = \left(1 + g_{UG} - \delta_{NP}^U\right) U_{g,-1},$$

where $g_{UG} > 0$ is the exogenous growth rate of the unskilled labor force in the public sector.

The nominal wage that skilled workers in the public sector earn, W_{SG}, is also indexed on the urban formal consumption price index:

$$W_{SG} = \omega_{SG} P_F,\tag{15}$$

where ω_{SG} is an exogenous real wage.

To determine wages and employment for skilled labor in the private formal sector, we use the "right to manage" approach, in which firms bargain with trade unions over the nominal wage, WS, and set unilaterally the level of employment. In addition, we assume that private urban firms pay a payroll tax on the skilled labor wage bill, at the rate $0 < ptax_S < 1$, and receive a nominal employment subsidy of $ES_S < W_S$ per skilled worker. The demand for skilled labor, S_P^d, is therefore given by

$$S_P^d = T_{2KS}\left(\frac{PT_2}{(1 + ptax_S)W_S - ES_S} \cdot \frac{\beta_{XP2}}{\alpha_{XP2}^{\rho_{XP2}}}\right)^{\sigma_{XP2}}.\tag{16}$$

Following Booth (1995, pp. 124-26) and Layard, Nickell, and Jackman (1991, pp. 100-3), W_S is determined as follows. Assume that all private sector firms are unionized, or equivalently that all workers belong to a single (representative) union. Let Ω_S denote the union's reservation wage and $PROF_P$ firms' profits. Under the Nash bargaining approach, the bargained wage must solve, subject to (16),

$$\max_{W_s} N_S = \left[S_P^d(W_S - \Omega_S)\right]^\nu PROF_P,\tag{17}$$

where ν is a measure of the trade union's bargaining power. The bargained wage must therefore satisfy the first-order condition

$$\frac{\partial \ln N_S}{\partial W_S} = \frac{\nu \partial S_P^d}{S_P^d \partial W_S} + \frac{\nu}{W_S - \Omega_S} - \frac{S_P^d}{PROF_P} = 0,$$

because $\partial PROF_P / \partial W_S = -S_P^d$ by the envelope theorem (each firm will choose employment *ex post* such that W_S is equal to the marginal value product of skilled labor). This yields

$$\frac{\nu W_S}{W_S - \Omega_S} = \nu \varepsilon_{S_P^d / W_S} + \frac{W_S S_P^d}{PROF_P},\tag{18}$$

where $\varepsilon_{S_p^d/W_S} = -(\partial S_p^d/\partial W_S)(W_S/S_p^d)$ is the wage elasticity of the demand for skilled labor. The term on the left-hand side of this expression measures the proportional marginal benefit to the bargain from the proportional increase in the skilled wage. The benefit associated with a wage increase incurs only to the union, so it is weighted by the union's bargaining power, v. The first term on the right-hand side is the union's proportional marginal cost (the percentage reduction in employment due to the proportional increase in the wage), weighted by the union's bargaining power. The second term on the right-hand side represents the firm's proportional marginal cost. Condition (18) indicates therefore that the bargained wage is set such that the proportional marginal benefits to both parties from a unit increase in wages is exactly equal to the proportional marginal cost to each party.

The union's reservation wage, ΩS, is assumed to be related positively to skilled wages in the public sector, W_{SG}, and negatively to the skilled unemployment rate, $UNEMP_S$. Wage setting in the public sector is assumed to play a signaling role to wage setters in the rest of the economy. When unemployment is high, the probability of finding a job (at any given wage) is low. Consequently, the higher the unemployment rate, the greater the incentive for the union to moderate its wage demands and boost employment. The above expression can thus be rewritten as

$$\frac{W_S}{W_S - \Omega_0 UNEMP_S^{-\phi_1} W_{SG}^{-\phi_2}} - \varepsilon_{S_p^d/W_S} - \frac{W_S S_p^d}{vPROF_P} = 0,$$

where $\Omega_0, \phi_1, \phi_2 > 0$, and $UNEMP_S$ is defined below. Using the implicit function theorem, it can be established that lower unemployment, higher public sector wages, or an increase in the bargaining strength of the union, raise the level of wages in the private sector.

Given that firms are on their labor demand curve, open skilled unemployment may emerge. The rate of skilled unemployment, denoted $UNEMPS$, is given by the ratio of skilled workers who are not employed either by the private or the public sector, divided by the total (urban) population of skilled workers:

$$UNEMP_S = \frac{S - S_G^T - S_p^d}{S}, \tag{19}$$

where S_G^T is the *total* number of skilled workers in the public sector, engaged in both the production of public services, S_G, and education, S_G^E (see below):

$$S_G^T = S_G + S_G^E. \tag{20}$$

S_G^T grows over time according to

$$S_G^T = \left(1 + g_{SG} - \delta_{NP}^S\right)S_{G,-1}^T, \tag{21}$$

where $g_{SG} > 0$ is the exogenous growth rate of the skilled labor force in the public sector.

We assume that skilled workers who are unable to find a job in the formal economy opt to remain openly unemployed, instead of entering the informal sector (in contrast to unskilled workers), perhaps because of adverse signaling effects, as discussed by Agénor (2003).

The evolution of the skilled labor force depends on the rate at which unskilled workers acquire skills:

$$S = \left(1 - \delta_S - \delta_{NP}^S\right)S_{-1} + SKL, \tag{22}$$

where $0 < \delta_S < 1$ is the rate of "depreciation" or "de-skilling" of the skilled labor force.

Skills Acquisition. The acquisition of skills by unskilled workers takes place through a free education system operated by the public sector. Specifically, the flow of unskilled workers who become skilled, SKL, is taken to be a CES function of the "effective" number of teachers in the public sector, S_G^E, and the government stock of capital in education, K_E:

$$SKL = \left[\beta_E(\varphi S_G^E)^{-\rho_E} + (1 - \beta_E)K_E^{-\rho_E}\right]^{-\frac{1}{\rho_E}}, \tag{23}$$

where φ measures the productivity of public workers engaged in providing education. φ is assumed to depend on the relative wage of skilled workers in the public sector, W_{SG}, relative to the expected wage for that same category of labor in the private sector, which (in the absence of unemployment benefits) is given by one minus the unemployment rate, $1 - UNEMP_S$, times the going wage, W_S. Using the effort function derived by Agénor and Aizenman (1999) yields:

$$\varphi = 1 - \varphi_m \left[\frac{(1 - UNEMP_{S,-1})W_{S,-1}}{W_{SG,-1}}\right]^{\delta_E}, \quad \delta_E > 0, \tag{24}$$

where $0 < \varphi_M < 1$ denotes the "minimum" level of effort.[12]

International Labor Migration. As noted earlier, international migration is an important feature of the labor market in labor-exporting MENA countries. We assume here that migration involves only unskilled workers, and that potential migrants are in the urban sector (as captured in (14). Moreover, international migration flows are taken to be determined by two factors: the expected urban real wage for unskilled labor, Ew_u, given by (4), relative to the expected foreign wage measured in terms of the urban formal price index, Ew_{FOR}, defined as

$$Ew_{FOR} = \frac{ER \cdot W_{FOR,-1}}{P_{F,-1}},$$

with W_{FOR} denoting the foreign wage measured in foreign-currency terms, assumed exogenous, and with ER the exchange rate. Adopting a specification similar to (6), the migration function is specified as

$$IMIG = U_{U,-1}\lambda_{im}\left[\sigma_{IM}\ln\left(\frac{Ew_{FOR}}{Ew_U}\right)\right] + (1-\lambda_{im})\frac{U_{U,-1}}{U_{U,-2}}IMIG_{-1}, \tag{25}$$

where $0 < \lambda_{im} < 1$ measures the speed of adjustment, and $\sigma_{IM} > 0$ the elasticity of migration flows with respect to expected wages. Again, costs associated with migration (such as relocation costs) are assumed to introduce some degree of persistence. Remittances associated with international migration flows of unskilled labor are assumed to benefit unskilled households in the urban formal and informal sectors.[13]

The Pay-as-you-go Pension System

We assume that there is a pay-as-you-go pension system, whose current outlays to pensioners (retired workers in the urban formal sector, both public and private), denoted *PENSIONS*, are financed by payroll taxes on workers in the private formal sector and transfers from the government, *TRSOC*:[14]

$$PENSIONS = ptax_U U_P^d + ptax_S S_P^d + TRSOC. \tag{26}$$

Total pension outlays are given by the product of an average benefit, *BENEF*, which is fully indexed (with a one-period lag) on the price index for the urban formal sector, P_F:

$$BENEF = BENEF_{-1}(1 + \Delta \ln P_{F,-1}). \tag{27}$$

The number of pensioners at the current period, *NUMPEN*, consists of last period's "stock" (adjusted for a fixed mortality rate), plus the flow of skilled and unskilled workers retiring in each period, *NEWPEN*:

$$NUMPEN = (1 - \delta_N)NUMPEN_{-1} + NEWPEN,$$

where δ_N is the proportion of pensioners who die in each period. The number of new pensioners is defined as

$$NEWPEN = \delta_{NP}^{U}\left(U_{P,-1}^{d} + U_{G,-1}\right) + \delta_{NP}^{S}\left(S_{P,-1}^{d} + S_{G,-1}^{T}\right).$$

This equation indicates that at the beginning of each period, a fixed fraction δ_{NP}^{U} (respectively δ_{NP}^{S}) of employed unskilled (respectively skilled) workers retire from the formal sector labor force.

Thus, total pension outlays are given by:

$$PENSIONS = BENEF \cdot NUMPEN. \tag{28}$$

If we assume that the pension fund cannot borrow directly from the public, and that its accounts must be balanced, government transfers are determined from (26), given (28):

$$TRSOC = PENSIONS - ptax_U U_P^{d} - ptax_S S_P^{d}. \tag{29}$$

Alternatively, if government transfers are considered fixed, the budget constraint can be used to determine the pension benefit, *BENEF*, after dropping (27):

$$BENEF = \frac{ptax_U U_P^{d} + ptax_S S_P^{d} + TRSOC}{NUMPEN}.$$

Other Model Features

Components of supply and demand are described by equations (A37) to (A48). Both informal and public sector goods are nontraded. Total supply in each sector is thus equal to gross production (equations (A39) and (A40). Agricultural and private formal urban goods, by contrast, compete with imported goods. The supply of the composite good for each of these sectors consists of a combination of imports and domestically produced goods (equations (A38) and (A41).

For the agricultural and informal sectors, aggregate demand consists of intermediate consumption and demand for final consumption (by both the government and the private sector), whereas aggregate demand for the public and private goods consists not only of intermediate consumption and final consumption, but also of investment demand (Equations A42, A43, A44, and A45). Total demand for intermediate consumption of any good is the sum of intermediate consumption of this good over all production sectors (Equation A37). Government expenditure on any good (except informal good) is equal to a fixed share of total government expenditure (Equation A47). Household consumption of each good is the summation across all categories of households' consumption of this good (Equation A46). Consumption by individual households is derived from a Linear Expenditures System (LES). Total private investment by private urban firms consists of purchases of both public and urban formal private goods and services (Equation A48).

Regarding external trade, private firms in the urban formal sector allocate their output to exports or the domestic market according to a production possibility frontier/transformation function (Equation A9). Allocation of agricultural output to domestic consumption and exports occurs according to a production possibility frontier (Equation A3). Profit maximization requires firms to equate relative prices to the opportunity cost in production (Equation A49). Imports compete with domestic goods in the agricultural sector as well as in the private formal sector (Equations A38 and A41). Cost minimization requires the demand for imported vs. domestic agricultural and private urban goods to be a function of relative domestic and import prices (Equation A50).

Prices are defined in Equations A51 to A62. The value added price of output is given by the gross price net of indirect taxes, less the cost of intermediate inputs (Equation A51). The world prices of imported and exported goods are taken to be exogenously given. The domestic currency price of these goods is obtained by adjusting the world price by the exchange rate, with import prices also adjusted by the tariff rate (Equations A52 and A53). Because the transformation function between exports and domestic sales of agricultural and urban private goods is linearly homogeneous, the domestic sales prices are derived from the sum of export and domestic expenditure on agricultural and private goods divided by the quantity produced of these goods (Equation A54). For the informal and public sectors, the composite price is equal to the domestic market price, which is in turn equal to the output price (Equation A56). For the agricultural and private urban production sectors, the substitution function between imports and domestic goods is also linearly homogeneous, and the composite market price is determined accordingly by the expenditure identity (Equation A55). The nested production function of private formal urban goods is also linearly homogeneous; prices of the composite inputs are derived in similar fashion (Equations A60 and A61). The price of capital is constructed by using the investment expenditure identity, which involves public and private-formal urban goods (Equation A62). Finally, the consumption price indices for the rural, urban, and urban formal are given as weighted averages of composite good prices, with weights reflecting consumption patterns (Equations A57, A58, and A59).

Profits and income are defined in (A63) to (A70). Firms' profits in the informal and agricultural sectors are defined as revenue minus total labor costs (Equation A63). Profits of private-urban sector firms account for salaries paid to both skilled and unskilled workers (Equation A64). Firms' income in the agricultural and the informal sector is equal to their profits (Equation A65). But firms' income in the formal urban economy is equal to their profits minus corporate taxes and interest payments on foreign loans (Equation A66). Household income is based on the return to labor (salaries), distributed profits, and transfers. Households are defined according to their sector of occupation. There are four categories of households: rural, urban informal, urban formal, and capitalists. The rural household comprises all rural workers; the urban informal household consists of workers in the urban informal sector; and the urban formal household consists of urban formal sector employees (skilled and unskilled). Finally, there is a capitalist-rentier household, whose income comes from firms' earnings in the formal private sector. Households in the rural and informal urban economy own the firms in which they are employed—an assumption that captures the fact that firms in these sectors tend to be small, family-owned enterprises. Income of rural households is equal to the sum of value added from production and transfers from the government (Equation A67). Income of urban informal households also includes a fraction of foreign remittances from (unskilled) workers employed abroad (Equation A68). Income of urban formal households depends on government transfers and salaries, foreign remittances, and pension payments (Equation A69). Firms provide no source of income, because these groups do not own the production units in which they are employed. Firms in the private urban sector retain a portion of their after-tax earnings for investment financing purposes and transfer the remainder to capitalists. Thus, the capitalist-rentier household's income is the sum of transfer payments and distributed profits (Equation A70).

Consumption, savings, and investment are described in Equations A71 to A74. Each category of household saves a constant fraction of its disposable income, which is equal to total income minus income tax payments (Equation A71). The portion of disposable income that is not saved is allocated to consumption (Equation A72). The accumulation of capital over time depends on the flow level of investment and the depreciation rate of capital from the previous period (Equation A74). The aggregate identity between savings and investment implies that total investment must be equal to total savings, which is itself equal to firms' after-tax retained earnings, total after-tax household savings, government savings, and foreign borrowing by firms and the government (Equation A73). In the simulations reported later, this equation is solved residually for the level of private investment, which implies therefore that the model is "savings driven."

The government side is described in Equations A75 to A80. Government expenditures consist of government consumption, which only has demand-side effects, and public investment, which has both demand-and supply-side effects. Public investment consists of investment in infrastructure, education, and health. We define investment in infrastructure as the expenditure affecting the accumulation of public infrastructure capital, which includes (as noted earlier) public assets such as roads, power plants. and railroads. Investment in education affects the stock of public education capital, which consists of assets such as school buildings and other infrastructure determining skills acquisition, but does not represent human capital. In a similar fashion, investment in health adds to the stock of public assets such as hospitals, health clinics, and other government infrastructure affecting health. All value added in the production of public goods is distributed as wages. Thus, the current fiscal deficit is equal to tax revenue minus current household transfers, pension transfers, current expenditure on goods and services, wage expenditure, and interest payments on foreign public loans (Equation A75). Net government saving is equal to minus the overall government budget deficit and is obtained by adding public investment expenditure to the current fiscal deficit (Equation A76). Total tax revenues consist of revenue generated by import tariffs, sales taxes, income taxes (on both households and firms in the urban private sector) and payroll taxes net of employment subsidies (Equation A77). Government investment is the sum of investment in infrastructure, investment in health, and investment in education, which are all considered exogenous policy variables (Equation A78). Government investment increases the stock of public capital in either infrastructure, education or health. Accumulation of each type of capital is equal to the sum of the capital stock from the previous period and currentperiod investment minus depreciation of the capital stock from the previous period (Equation A79). Because we assume that only the private urban good is used for capital accumulation, we deflate nominal investment by the demand price for private goods to obtain real investment. Infrastructure and health capital affect the production process in the private sector, as they both combine to produce the stock of government capital (Equation A80).

Finally, the balance of payments is defined in Equations A86 to A88. The external constraint implies that any current account surplus (or deficit) must be compensated by a net flow of foreign capital, given by the sum of changes in foreign loans made to the government and to private firms (Equation A86). The flow of remittances is equal to the foreign wage, measured in foreign-currency terms, times the stock of domestic workers abroad (Equation A87). In turn, the stock of domestic workers abroad is the sum of new immigrants and the stock of domestic workers abroad from the previous period, minus attrition (Equation A88).

Calibration and Parameter Values

This section presents a brief overview of the characteristics of the data underlying the model's social accounting matrix (SAM) and discusses the parameter values.

The Social Accounting Matrix

The basic dataset consists of a SAM and a set of initial levels and lagged variables. The SAM encompasses 37 accounts, including; production and retail sectors (8 accounts); educational services (2 accounts); labor production factors and profits (5 accounts); enterprises (1 account), households (4 accounts), government current expenditures, taxes, and pensions (12 accounts); government investment expenditures (3 accounts), private investment expenditures (1 account), and the rest of the world (1 account).

The SAM dataset was derived to (i) reflect characteristics of a typical labor-exporting MENA country, and (ii) represent an equilibrium dataset, including a balanced government budget, a zero balance of payments (BoP), and zero net foreign borrowing. Nevertheless, the net factor service account of the BoP includes private and foreign interest payments reflecting past foreign borrowing. The characteristics of the SAM data can be summarized as follows. On the output side, agriculture and the informal sector account for respectively 12 and 35 percent of total output at producer prices. In contrast, private urban formal production accounts for almost 46 percent of total output. On the demand side, private current expenditures account for 64 percent of GDP, whereas government current expenditures and wages account for 11 percent of GDP. At the same time, total investment expenditures represent 22 percent of GDP, implying that our "prototype" labor-exporting MENA country is running a trade surplus equivalent to 2.8 percent of GDP.

Looking at the BoP, total net remittances to households amount to 1.2 percent of GDP. Together with the trade balance surplus, this is financing a deficit on the net factor services account amounting to 4 percent of GDP. This includes private foreign interest payments (-1.5 percent of GDP) and government foreign interest payments (-2.5 percent of GDP). The trade balance is dominated by nonagricultural imports and exports, with agricultural exports accounting for only 8 percent of total export earnings, and nonagricultural imports accounting for 92 percent of total import expenditures. The level of trade openness, measured by the ratio of the sum of imports and exports to GDP, amounts to a moderate 38 percent.

Looking at the government budget, indirect taxes in the form of production and retail level taxes (excluding payroll taxes) account for 84 percent of total government revenues. Household tax revenues, amounting to 13 percent of total government income, represent the largest revenue item among direct tax items, whereas enterprise taxes account for only 4 percent of revenues.

On the expenditure side, domestic transfers and foreign interest payments account for respectively 24 and 9 percent of the budget, whereas consumption and savings for investment purposes amount to respectively 40 and 27 percent of the budget. Overall, the government relies heavily on indirect taxes for revenue collection (as is common in developing countries), while at the same time allocating a significant fraction of its resources to investment.

Behavioral Parameters

Consider now the behavioral parameters of the model. In agriculture the Cobb-Douglas (share) parameter in the production of value added equals 0.8, whereas the CES substitution elasticity between rural labor and public capital equals 2/3. Public capital is aggregated from infrastructure and health capital using a substitution elasticity of 1/2. The informal sector only has one factor of production, unskilled labor, and the Cobb-Douglas (share) parameter also equals 0.8. In contrast, the private formal sector has a three-level nested production structure, with a bottom-level substitution elasticity of 2/3 between private capital and skilled labor, a middle-level substitution elasticity of 7/6 between the bottom level composite factor and unskilled labor, and a top level substitution elasticity of 5/6 between the middle-level composite factor and public capital. Finally, public sector value added is derived using CES aggregation of skilled and unskilled labor, with a substitution elasticity of unity.

Turning to the factor market and the wage bargaining equation for private sector skilled wages, elasticities with respect to skilled labor unemployment and public sector wages are set respectively at -2.0 and 2.0, whereas the wage elasticity of private skilled labor demand is -1.0. The parameter measuring the trade union's bargaining power is set at 0.7. Rural-urban and international migration elasticities with respect to relative expected wages are set respectively at 0.4 and 0.6, whereas persistence parameters for rural-urban and international migration are set respectively at 0.1 and 0.3. The formal-informal sector migration elasticity with respect to relative expected wages is 0.4. the elasticity of substitution between publicly employed teachers and public education capital in the skills-upgrading CES production function is 1/3, whereas the elasticity of teachers effort with respect to relative wages is 0.8.

The Armington elasticities for rural agricultural and urban formal sector goods imports are set respectively at 2/3 and 1.5. Similarly, the CET transformation elasticities for rural agricultural and urban formal sector goods exports are set respectively at 2/3 and 1.5. Finally, household minimum consumption levels amount to 10 percent of initial consumption levels.

Simulation Experiments

In what follows, we use the framework described above to analyze five types of labor market reforms: a reduction in payroll taxes on unskilled labor, assuming both neutral and non-neutral changes on the budget; reductions in public sector employment and wages; an active labor market policy, consisting of higher employment subsidies to unskilled workers in the formal private sector; and a reduction in trade unions' bargaining strength.[15] We also consider a composite reform package, which consists of a cut in payroll taxes and public sector employment, as well as a reduction in unions' bargaining power. In all of these experiments we use a savings-driven closure rule, and solve residually for private investment demand, using the aggregate savings-investment balance (equation (A73). This allows us to study the "crowding in" and "crowding out" effects of labor market policies through their impact on the government budget balance.

Reduction in Payroll Taxes on Unskilled Labor

The effects of a permanent, 5 percent reduction in the payroll tax rate on unskilled labor are illustrated in figure 9.3. In analyzing the impact of this policy measure on growth and employment, a key aspect involves evaluating its fiscal implications. For instance, assuming that the policy change must be neutral with respect to the budget deficit, what are the alternative options for offsetting the effect of a reduction in payroll taxation? To illustrate this type of interaction between labor market reforms and fiscal policy, we examine three alternative "closure" rules on the fiscal side. In the first, there is no offsetting change in revenue, and the government borrows domestically to balance its budget—implying therefore full crowding out of private investment, as implied by the aggregate savings–investment balance (equation (A73). In the second, the policy is budget-neutral, and the government raises sales taxes on the private, formal sector good to offset the increase in additional expenditures on transfers to the pension system. In the third, the policy is also budget-neutral, and the government offsets the reduction in payroll taxes by an increase in income taxes on capitalists and rentiers.[16] In all three cases, we assume that the accounts of the pension system are balanced through government transfers, as indicated in (29). Of course, even if the policy is budget-neutral in the sense described here, private capital formation may still be crowded out, as a result of general equilibrium effects leading to, say, smaller private savings relative to the baseline.

A number of results are common to all three payroll tax experiments. Reduced labor costs lead to increased employment of unskilled labor, as well as substitution away from skilled labor (and physical capital) in the private formal sector. A decrease in skilled labor wages—resulting from the rise in skilled unemployment, itself due to the reduction in the demand for that category of labor—partly offsets the initial tax-induced 5 percent increase in the differential between skilled and unskilled labor costs. The net increase in the labor cost differential amounts to around 3.8 percent in the longer term, suggesting a likely trend away from skilled labor toward unskilled labor even in the long run.

Figure 9.3 Simulation Results: Five Percentage Points Reduction in Unskilled Labor Payroll Tax Rate

Percentage deviations from baseline, unless otherwise indicated

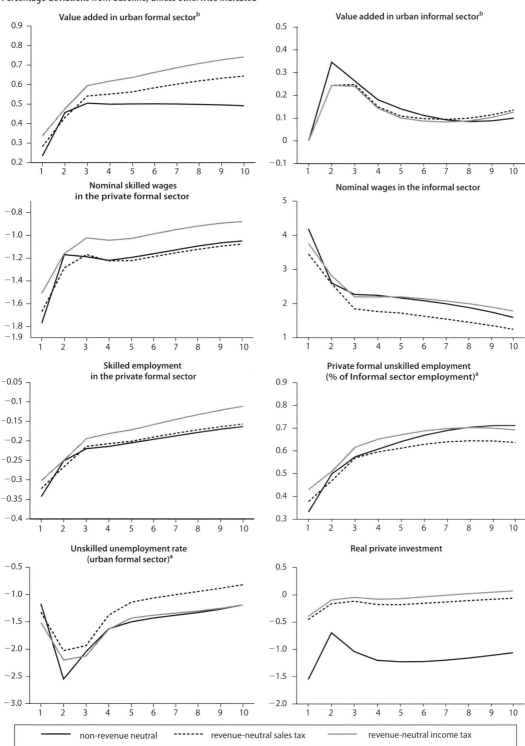

Note: a. Absolute deviations from baselines; b. Real terms.

The increase in unskilled employment is drawn partly from the pool of unemployed workers in the formal sector and partly from increasing migration from the informal sector. Increasing migration to the formal sector occurs against the backdrop of strongly increasing informal sector wages. The minimum wage increases over time as a result of full indexation on urban consumption prices, and higher demand in the formal sector for unskilled labor leads to a rise in the expected formal sector wage. Over time, the ensuing increase in the expected formal-informal sector wage differential leads to higher migration flows to the formal economy. This pushes the informal sector wage upwards. Employment in the informal sector also increases in the short run but tapers off in the medium to long term. The initial combination of reduced overseas and formal sector migration flows—a year after the shock and beyond—increases informal sector labor supply by 0.3-0.4 percent. However, although reduced migration overseas, due to increased domestic urban wages, continues to add workers to the informal sector labor force, the subsequent reversal of formal sector migration, coupled with migration outflows to the rural sector, leads to a gradual reversal of the initial increase in labor supply. The reduced supply of labor is matched by a reduction in demand due to the high informal sector wages. The mirror image of reduced informal sector employment is a gradual increase in rural employment. Accordingly, the cumulative effect of medium-term outward migration to rural areas, due to increasing agricultural wages, leads to a relatively strong expansion of labor supply in the rural sector.

At the aggregate level, the reduction in payroll taxes leads to a strong initial increase followed by a gradual decline in nominal GDP. In contrast, real GDP increases over time, indicating that the declining growth path for nominal GDP is a purely nominal phenomenon. The adjustment process involves a real exchange rate depreciation, which gradually raises exports and lowers imports in the long term. The increasing trade surplus is used to finance the net factor service income deficit, which rises due to declining migration overseas.

Whereas the growth paths of GDP and trade aggregates are relatively similar across payroll tax experiments, the growth paths of private consumption and investment are relatively sensitive—as could be expected—to whether or not there are offsetting changes in taxes. The growth paths of private consumption and investment are diverging strongly in the experiment, with a non-neutral budget closure. The ensuing budget deficit is financed through domestic borrowing, leading to crowding out of private investment and higher disposable household income, which translates into increased private consumption.

The strong crowding-out effect disappears when sales or income taxes are raised to pay for increased transfers to the pension system. However, differences persist. Sales taxes on formal sector goods raise the price of investment goods and intermediate inputs, which depresses (everything else equal) profits, savings, and private capital accumulation. In contrast, an increase in the tax rate on capitalists' income reduces household disposable income and private consumption, but allows for increased investment in the long term. Thus, the scenario where reduced payroll tax revenues and increased transfers to the pension system are offset by increased household income taxes, results in the highest long-term GDP growth rates.[17] Growth in the formal sector resulting from increased private capital accumulation is responsible for higher long-term aggregate growth in the latter scenario.

The impact on the government budget is of course related to the budget closure rule. Government transfers to the pension system will, in each case, increase by around 0.2 percent of GDP in the long run, due to the decline in own-financing, itself resulting from the reduction in payroll taxation. Without the introduction of alternative financing sources, this leads to a domestic borrowing requirement of 0.3 percent of GDP in the long term. In contrast, domestic borrowing is completely avoided in the long term if budget-neutral specifications with variable sales and/or income taxes are applied. Looking at the pension system, total pension payments increase the most when higher government transfers are financed by increased sales taxes on formal sector goods. The number of workers who qualify to enter the pension system rises (due to the expansion of formal sector employment) by around 0.5 percent in the long run, regardless of the budget closure. However, whereas the average benefit rate decreases by 0.4 percent— when increased government transfers are financed by higher income taxes or not financed by tax increases—it only falls by 0.1 percent when higher formal sector sales taxes lead to increases in prices of formal sector goods.

Cut in Public Sector Wages

We now examine the effects of wage reductions for both unskilled public workers and skilled public employees (excluding teachers). Results of a permanent 5 percent reduction in the wage rate for each labor category are summarized in figures 9.4 and 9.5.

The reduction in public sector wages leads, in both cases, to a reduction in the public sector borrowing requirement and to crowding-in of private investment. A reduction in unskilled wages in the public sector, by contrast, has little impact on growth in the long term. The main channel through which public sector wage reductions are transmitted is a reduction in aggregate demand, induced by lower government consumption expenditures, and an increase in total domestic savings (due to a reduction in the budget deficit only, because private savings fall concomitantly with income), and thus private investment. With employment in the public sector fixed, the expansion in investment demand leads to increased private sector employment of unskilled labor and a reduction in the unemployment rate. In turn, the reduction in unemployment (which raises the probability of finding a job in the private formal economy) leads to strong migration into the formal sector. The increased employ-

Figure 9.4 Simuation Results: Five Percentage Points Reduction in Public Sector Unskilled Labor Wage

Percentage deviations from baseline, unless otherwise indicated

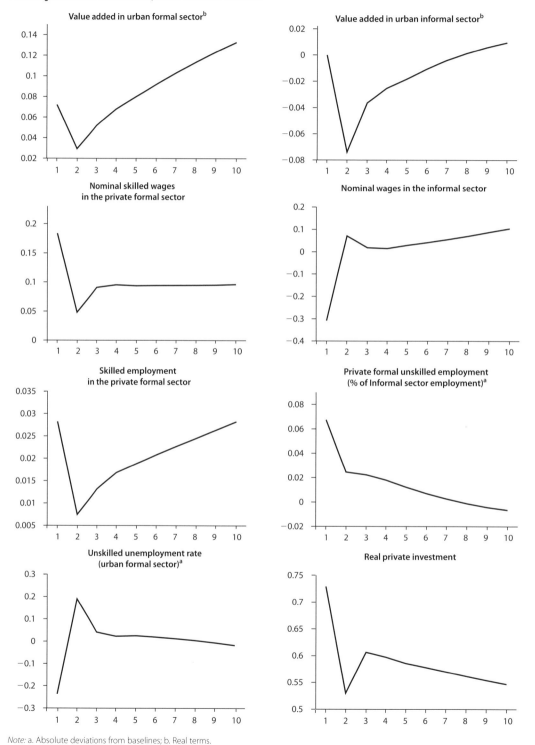

Note: a. Absolute deviations from baselines; b. Real terms.

Figure 9.5 Simuation Results: Five Percentage Points Reduction in Public Sector Skilled Labor Wage

Percentage deviations from baseline, unless otherwise indicated

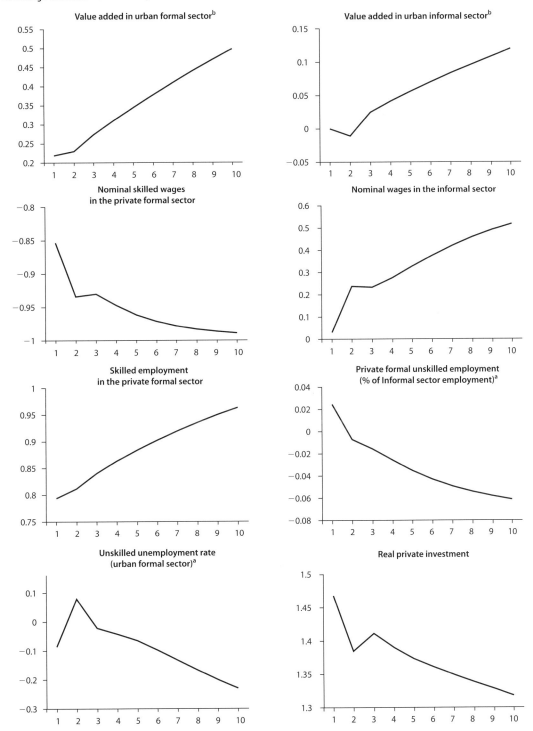

Note: a. Absolute deviations from baselines; b. Real terms.

ment and formal sector migration levels are, however, immediately reversed. The combination of declining demand for formal sector goods and increasing accumulation of capital lowers the demand for unskilled labor over time. Moreover, increasing informal sector wages and formal sector unemployment leads to outward migration from the formal sector. In the long term, employment levels are unchanged in every sector, and the higher level of production (in the formal sector) is entirely driven by increased private capital accumulation. Migration flows reverse themselves and unemployment rates remain unchanged at baserun levels. Looking at the pension system, overall pensions, including transfers from the government, remain unchanged. Accordingly, both the number of pensioners and the level of pension benefits are unchanged in the long term.

In contrast, a cut in skilled wages in the public sector has a relatively strong long-term impact on growth because of the leadership effect on private skilled wages. Reduced public sector wages spills over into lower private skilled wages and higher employment of that category of labor in the private sector. Combined with the cumulative effect of increased private investment, this leads to higher growth rates in the formal sector. At the same time, growth in the rural and urban informal sectors is driven by declining migration into the urban (formal) sector. The outward migration is driven by substitution of skilled for unskilled labor in private formal sector production, which leads to a declining formal-informal sector wage differential. In addition, an increase in the expected urban wage, due to increasing informal sector wages and a gradually declining unskilled unemployment rate, leads to a decline in international migration flows. The combination of declining international and formal sector migration leads to increasing labor supply in the urban informal sector, and, because of increasing rural wages, to further out-migration and higher labor supply in the rural sector.

Interestingly, a cut in public sector skilled wages leads to a long-term reduction in both skilled and unskilled formal sector unemployment rates. The reduction in unemployment among skilled workers results from increased formal sector employment. In contrast, the reduction in open unemployment among unskilled workers follows mainly from outward migration to the informal sector.

Looking at the current account, reduced international migration (resulting from the increase in the expected urban wage) leads to an increase in the net factor service account deficit. This is counterbalanced by an improvement in the trade balance, which comes about as a result of a small depreciation of the real exchange rate.

The pension system sees some minor changes in the long term, including a small increase in the number of retirees and a small decrease in the average pension benefit rate. The number of pensioners increases due to increased formal sector employment levels, while pension benefits decline because the strong supply response in the formal sector reduces formal sector prices. The overall effect is to leave overall pension payments, including government transfers to the pension system, unchanged in the long run. The main impact on the government budget is therefore to reduce the budget deficit through reduced consumption.

Public Sector Layoffs

The experiments of this section include public sector layoffs of both unskilled workers and skilled public employees (excluding teachers). Results of a permanent 5 percent reduction in the number of workers in each labor category are summarized in figures 9.6 and 9.7.

Reducing the size of public sector employment has the twin effects of increasing private capital accumulation and raising levels of employment in the private sector. Crowding-in of private investment is achieved because non-budget neutral layoffs turn into a smaller domestic government borrowing requirement. The increased private capital accumulation has a positive supply-side effect on formal sector output. Nevertheless, the net increase in relative demand for formal sector goods (resulting from higher private investment and lower private consumption), means that private formal sector employment levels also increases for both categories of workers.

Aggregate growth effects are absent in the case of unskilled labor layoffs. Real GDP declines in the short term, and returns to baserun levels in the longer run. Nevertheless, there is positive growth over time in every production sector other than public services, including the rural and urban informal sectors. Accordingly, while the aggregate growth impact is neutral in the long term, due to lower value added in the public sector, the growth path has a distinct upward trend toward the end of the 10-year horizon. Positive formal sector growth is particularly evident throughout the simulation period. Short-term growth is due to increased employment of unskilled labor in the private sector, whereas long-term growth is mainly driven by higher private capital accumulation. In fact, employment of unskilled labor in the private sector falls over time and returns close to baserun levels in the long term. At the same time, growth in the rural agricultural and urban informal sectors is driven primarily by increased labor supplies, due to the cumulative impact of outward migration from the urban (formal) sector. Outward migration is particularly strong because declining employment prospects lower the expected urban wage.

The unskilled unemployment rate increases sharply in the short term, because the rise in private sector employment is insufficient to absorb laid-off workers in the public sector. In the longer run, unskilled unemployment returns toward its baserun level, due to the cumulative effect of migration outflows into the urban informal and rural sectors. Accordingly, formal sector

Figure 9.6 Simuation Results: Five Percentage Points Reduction in Public Sector Unskilled Labor Employment

Percentage deviations from baseline, unless otherwise indicated

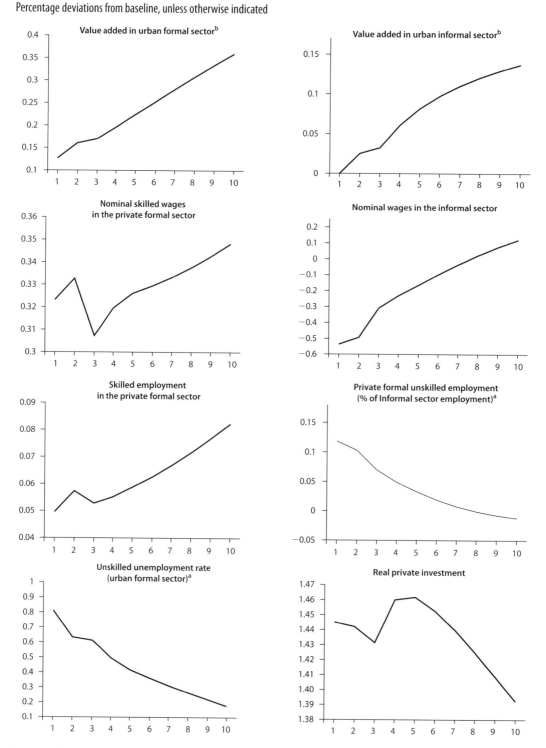

Note: a. Absolute deviations from baselines; b. Real terms.

Figure 9.7 Simuation Results: Five Percentage Points Reduction in Public Sector Skilled Labor Employment

Percentage deviations from baseline, unless otherwise indicated

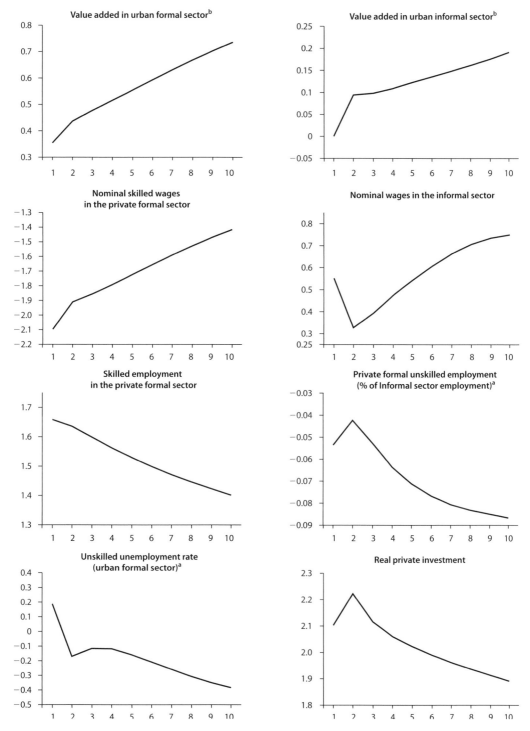

Note: a. Absolute deviations from baselines; b. Real terms.

employment of unskilled labor is reduced to baserun levels, whereas the supply of unskilled labor in the formal sector declines by more than 1 percent in the long term. International migration flows increase in the short term but move in the opposite direction in the longer term, due to higher domestic wages and lower unemployment levels.

In contrast to layoffs of unskilled government workers, layoffs of skilled public employees have markedly positive growth effects. Real GDP increases in both the short and the long term. Again, output growth occurs in all non-public sectors, but in contrast to the previous experiment involving unskilled labor layoffs, more balanced and stronger growth is recorded among the rural and urban informal and formal sectors. Strong formal sector growth is driven by increased employment of (skilled) labor in the short term. Thus, the short-term impact of skilled labor layoffs follows the pattern of unskilled layoffs. However, the long-term growth effect is driven by a combination of increased employment levels and private capital accumulation. Thus, the initial increase in the level of (skilled) labor employment persists in the long term, in contrast with the unskilled labor layoffs.

Growth in the rural and urban informal sectors is again driven by declining urban migration flows, resulting from layoffs of unskilled labor in the private sector. Sharply declining skilled labor wages (resulting from reduced union wage demands, due to increased unemployment among skilled workers) leads to increased substitution of skilled for unskilled labor in the private formal sector. The accompanying narrowing in wage differentials leads to declining urban (formal) migration and increasing rural and urban informal labor supplies. This leads to a decline in the open unskilled unemployment rate, and an accompanying increase in the expected urban formal sector wage, which partly reverses the strong initial reduction in migration from the formal sector. But high and increasing informal sector wages mean that formal sector migration remains lower in the long term.

In line with the previous experiment involving layoff of unskilled workers in the public sector, layoff of skilled workers leads to higher unemployment for that category of labor while reducing unemployment among unskilled workers. Moreover, the reduction in unskilled unemployment is magnified in the longer run by the fall in the supply of unskilled labor in the formal sector that is induced by migration flows. This long-term reduction is, however, markedly smaller than in the case of unskilled layoffs. The increase in informal and formal urban wages, combined with the declining open unemployment rate, means that international migration flows decline in the long run as well. The cumulative effect on the domestic workforce abroad again leads to an increasing deficit in the net factor services account over time. This is made up for by a moderate improvement in the trade balance, which comes about through a small real exchange rate depreciation.

The main impact of public sector layoffs on the government budget is to reduce current consumption and domestic government borrowing requirements. In contrast, transfers to the pension system remain relatively unchanged: Overall, pension payments decline by around 0.2 percent in the long run. In the case of unskilled layoffs, the decline in pension payments is due solely to a decline in the number of retirees. Layoff of unskilled workers results in the largest reduction in employment, and therefore results in the largest reduction in pensioners. In contrast, layoff of skilled workers leads to lower pension payments, partly because of declining numbers of retirees, and partly because of a declining average benefit rate. A stronger supply effect of skilled labor layoffs leads to declining formal sector prices and, accordingly, to an increasing pension benefit rate.

Subsidies to Private Employment

We now turn to an analysis of the impact of subsidies to employment of unskilled labor in the formal private sector under various government budget closures, including: (i) a non-neutral budget closure; (ii) a budget-neutral increase in sales taxes on private formal sector goods; and (iii) a budget-neutral increase in income taxes on capitalists. In each case, the increase in employment subsidy amounts to 5 percent of the base year private formal unskilled wage level. The simulation results are summarized in figure 9.8.

The employment subsidy for unskilled labor increases the differential between skilled and unskilled labor costs, in a manner similar to the 5 percent reduction in payroll taxes considered earlier. The only difference between the two sets of results comes from the fact that the payroll tax rate applies to the unskilled wage rate, while the employment subsidy does not. The unskilled wage rate is fixed in real terms, but variations in consumer prices in the formal sector lead to some variation in its nominal value. However, these wage changes have minimal impact on the results, which are therefore almost identical to the results of the payroll tax experiments.

In particular, the reduction in unskilled labor costs leads to a strong increase in formal sector employment and a decline in open unskilled unemployment. The increase in unskilled employment is the main engine for formal sector growth. Initial migration flows also fuel increases in labor supply in the informal sector. However, subsequent outward migration from urban to rural areas leads to an increase in rural labor supply, and the initial increase in informal sector labor supply therefore tapers off. In the long term, aggregate growth is driven equally by rural and urban formal sector growth when a non-neutral government budget closure is used. An increase in the public sector borrowing requirement leads to crowding out of private investment, reduced capital accumulation, and depressed formal sector growth. In contrast, urban formal sector growth is markedly stronger than rural agricultur-

Figure 9.8 Simulation Results: Five Percentage Points Increase in Unskilled Labor Employment Subsidy

Percentage deviations from baseline, unless otherwise indicated

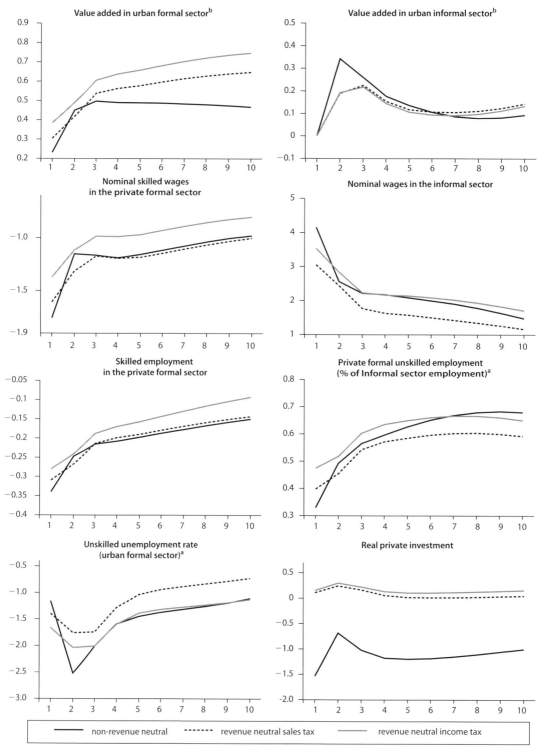

Note: a. Absolute deviations from baselines; b. Real terms.

al growth when employment subsidies are financed by higher income tax revenues. The domestic government borrowing requirement is eliminated and crowding out of investment is reversed, leading to slightly increased capital accumulation in the long term. Unemployment among skilled workers increases slightly, regardless of the government budget closure. In contrast, strongly increasing labor demand in the private sector reduces the unskilled unemployment rate, in spite of a sharp long-term increase in labor supply. The deficit of the net factor services account increases, due to the cumulative effect of reduced international migration, but a compensating improvement in the trade balance means that the current account balance is left essentially unchanged. Finally, pensions payments increase marginally, due to a relatively strong increase in the number of retirees (itself resulting from a rise in formal sector employment) and a smaller decline in the pension benefit rate (due to declining formal sector prices).[18]

Reduction in Unions' Bargaining Strength

We now turn our attention to a reduction in labor union bargaining strength. To do so we reduce the bargaining strength parameter, the coefficient v in Equation 17, from its initial level of 0.7 to a value of 0.6. The results are shown in figure 9.9.

The direct impact of the reduction in union bargaining power is to lower skilled wages and increase employment for skilled labor in the private sector. Increased production leads to lower formal sector goods prices and increased real demand for all goods, including agricultural and informal sector goods. The expansion of real private investment demand is particularly large. Increasing real demand, combined with a lower wage bill, raises firms' profits in the private formal sector. In turn, this boosts private savings and investment. The combination of higher skilled employment, capital accumulation in the private sector, and increased unskilled employment in urban informal and rural sectors leads to a rise in output, which persists in the long term. This growth scenario is therefore broad-based, in the sense that it stems from both rural and urban formal sector growth, and to a lesser extent from urban informal sector growth.

The sharp drop in skilled wages leads to strong substitution away from unskilled labor in the urban formal sector. Although the large initial decline in private formal unskilled employment is partly reversed over time, it remains below its baseline value in the long term, as a result of the permanent nature of the reduction in the wage differential. Growth in the formal sector is thus driven by increased employment of skilled labor and private capital accumulation. The strong initial substitution away from unskilled labor also leads to high unemployment in that category and a drop in expected urban wages. This leads to a marked initial decline in formal sector migration flows,

Figure 9.9 Simuation Results: Reduction in Labor Union's Bargaining Strength

Percentage deviations from baseline, unless otherwise indicated

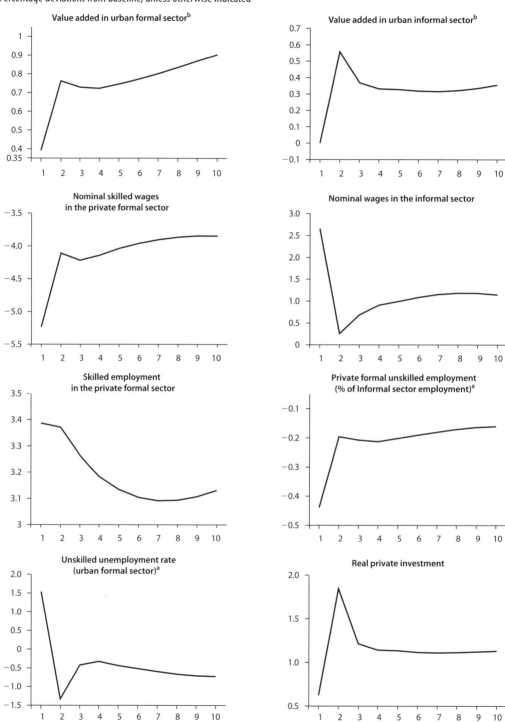

Note: a. Absolute deviations from baselines; b. Real terms.

and an equally large initial increase in labor supply in the informal sector. However, the strong migration response also reduces unemployment to below baserun levels. This increases the expected urban wage and, subsequently, leads to a reversal in the direction of formal sector migration flows. In the longer run, migration flows tend to increase labor supply in the urban informal sector at a constant rate, and labor supply in the rural sector at an increasing rate. This leads to relatively fast long-term growth in the rural sector, and slower, but robust, growth in the urban informal sector.

After an initial adjustment period, formal sector unemployment rates drop well below baserun levels and stay there in the long term. The reduction in skilled unemployment follows from increased employment of skilled labor in the private sector. In contrast, the long-term reduction in unskilled unemployment follows from a reduction in the formal sector supply of unskilled labor, itself resulting from reduced migration flows.

The international wage differential drops in the long term, leading to a decline in overseas migration flows. This contrasts with the long-term decline in migration between rural and urban areas, where a high degree of persistence implies weak migration flows, in spite of a long-term increase in the wage differential.

The decline in international migration leads to an increase in the net factor services income deficit. This reduction is counterbalanced in the long term by an improvement in the trade balance. The government budget is characterized by long-term declines in overall income- and expenditure-to-GDP ratios, and by a long-term decline in the domestic borrowing requirement, which allows for crowding-in of private investment. Government transfers to the pension system do not change significantly. Looking at the overall pension system, pension payments increase only slightly in the long run. An increase in the number of retirees is evened out by a drop in the pension benefit rate. The increase in the number of retirees follows from increased private sector (skilled) employment, whereas the reduction in the pension benefit rate follows from declining formal sector prices associated with the strong formal sector supply response.

A Composite Reform Program

Finally, we consider a composite, "realistic" package of policies, which combines reductions in payroll taxes on unskilled labor with a reduction in unions' bargaining strength, and a cut in unskilled employment in the public sector. We assume that the payroll tax on unskilled labor is reduced by 5 percent, the number of unskilled workers in the public sector is reduced by 5 percent, and that the bargaining strength of trade unions is reduced from an initial level of 0.7 to a "neutral" value of 0.6. We consider the three alternative budget closure rules specified above, but to save space we do not report the results graphically.

Given that the transmission channels of each of the individual components of the composite program have been described extensively in previous sections, we restrict our attention here to the impact and long-run effects of the program on growth and unemployment. Simulation results with a non-neutral public deficit closure do not show evidence of large nonlinear effects. Specifically, the impact and long-term effects on the growth rate of aggregate real value added amount to 0.2 and 0.9 percent, respectively. This is approximately equal to the sum of the growth rates derived from the individual simulations described earlier. Similarly, the impact and long-term effects on private formal sector employment are very close to linear, amounting to (minus sign)0.1 and 4.0 percent respectively for unskilled labor, and 3.2 and 3.1 percent, respectively, for skilled labor. Unskilled employment increases slightly by 0.2 percent when income taxes are used to keep the public deficit unchanged. Overall, although the simultaneous implementation of the individual components of the policy reform package above does bring some benefits (suggesting therefore that complementarity between labor market policies is desirable from an economic point of view, independently of other, political economy considerations) the impact of a "realistic" package of labor market reforms on growth and employment does not appear to be large. This has important implications for the design of adjustment programs in a region where the challenge is not only to reduce an existing high level of unemployment, but also to create sufficient jobs to absorb new entrants in the labor force.

Summary and Policy Lessons

The purpose of this paper has been to analyze the impact of labor market reforms on growth, real and relative wages, and the composition of employment and unemployment in labor-exporting MENA countries. We first provided a brief overview of the main features of the labor market in some of these countries. We then presented a simulation model, based on the IMMPA framework developed by Agénor (2003), Agénor, Izquierdo and Fofack (2003), and Agénor, Fernandes, and Haddad (2003), which captures many of these features (such as a large informal urban sector, a significant role of public sector employment and "leadership effects" of public sector wages, powerful trade unions, and international migration of labor) as well as other important structural characteristics of these countries (such as a pay-as-you-go pension system). After discussing the calibration procedure and our choices of parameter values, we presented and discussed a series of simulation experiments. We focused on a reduction in payroll taxation on unskilled labor, reductions in public sector wages and workforce, an increase in employment subsidies to the private sector, changes in the bargaining strength of trade unions, and a composite reform package involving several of these policies. In the case of payroll taxation, employment subsidies and the composite package, we considered both neutral and non-neutral changes. Specifically, we considered three alternative fiscal "closure" rules. In the first, we assumed no offsetting change in revenue, and the government borrows domestically to balance its budget—implying full crowding out of private investment. In the second and third, the policy is budget-neutral, and the government raises, respectively, sales taxes on the private, formal sector good, and income taxes on capitalist-rentier households, to cover increased expenditures (resulting from an increased deficit in the pension system and increased labor subsidy payments). Therefore, there is no crowding out of private capital formation in the second and third experiments.

There are a number of policy lessons that emerge from our results. For instance, we found that, regardless of how a cut in payroll taxes on unskilled labor is financed (either by borrowing from the private sector or by implementing revenue-neutral changes in sales or income taxation) reduced labor costs lead to increased employment of unskilled labor, as well as substitution away from skilled labor (and physical capital) in the private formal sector. A decrease in skilled labor wages—resulting from a rise in skilled unemployment—partly offsets the tax-induced increase in the differential between skilled and unskilled labor costs. The net increase in the labor cost differential is still very significant in the longer term, implying a strong substitution away from skilled labor toward unskilled labor, even in the long run. At the same time, our results showed that the overall rate of output growth varies significantly across experiments—essentially because the behavior of private investment depends very much (as could be expected) on whether or not there are offsetting changes in taxes. When the increase in the budget deficit resulting from a cut in the payroll tax is financed through domestic borrowing, private investment is crowded out; the lower rate of capital accumulation has an adverse effect on growth, and thus on the demand for both categories of labor. Thus, the indirect or "level" effect on the demand for unskilled labor may mitigate significantly the substitution effect triggered by the change in relative labor costs. The results associated with a reduction in trade unions' bargaining power in wage negotiations also indicate large long-term gains in overall employment associated with general equilibrium effects.

The main policy lessons of our simulation experiments can be summarized as follows. The first is that, in assessing the impact of labor market reforms on growth and unemployment, it is important to account not only for the direct (partial equilibrium) effects of these policies, but also for their indirect (general equilibrium) effects on income and aggregate demand (resulting from changes in the government budget). For instance, it has been argued that a policy of subsidizing employment in the private sector would help to reduce unemployment in MENA countries. A simple, partial equilibrium analysis of this policy is indeed unambiguous: by lowering the relative cost of unskilled labor, a subsidy leads to an increase in the demand for that category of labor, which may be particularly significant if wages are fixed (as a result, for example, of a binding minimum wage). As long as the increase in labor demand does not prompt greater participation in the labor force (that is, if unskilled labor supply is fairly inelastic), unskilled unemployment is thus likely to fall.

However, a partial equilibrium view can be misleading. The increase in subsidies must be financed, and this can occur in a variety of ways. Our experiments indicate that general equilibrium effects can be significant, even with a fairly neutral investment specification. Accordingly, if spending is kept constant, and the government chooses to let its fiscal deficit increase and borrow from the rest of the economy, this can have a large crowding-out effect on private investment, if private savings do not adjust quickly; the fall in investment may, over time, restrain the expansion of demand for all categories of labor—including unskilled labor. Thus, the longer-run effect of the policy on employment may be either nil or negative. Similarly, an increase in, say, taxes on capitalist-rentier households may restrain private capital formation and have an adverse effect on employment in the medium and the long run. More specifically, our general equilibrium analysis indicates that the overall impact of a change in payroll taxes on the demand for unskilled labor may be compounded or mitigated, depending on how the government chooses to adjust its tax and spending instruments to maintain a balanced budget. In the presence of large crowding-out effects on private investment (and possibly savings), the direct gains (in terms of higher employment) associated with a reduction in payroll taxes may be highly mitigated. Similarly, whether employment subsidies end up reducing open unemployment in the formal sector may depend on the extent to which a higher perceived probability of finding a job in that sector affects workers' decisions to remain in the informal sector.

The second policy lesson that our simulation results indicate is that a "piecemeal" approach to labor market reforms is unlikely to bring substantial benefits in terms of growth and employment. By contrast, a comprehensive approach will bring broad-based growth and reductions in both skilled and unskilled unemployment. The idea that labor market reform programs must be sufficiently broad (in the sense of covering a wide range of complementary policies) and deep (of substantial magnitude) to have much of an effect is emphasized by Coe and Snower (1997) and Orszag and Snower (1998). At the same time, however, although a "realistic" package of policies (which combines reductions in payroll taxes on unskilled labor, a reduction in unions' bargaining strength, and a cut in unskilled employment in the public sector) may have a significant impact on the composition of employment in labor-exporting MENA countries, fostering a sustained increase in growth rates and job creation in these countries may require a more comprehensive program of structural reforms—involving, in particular, financial sector reforms, privatization, and measures aimed at increasing private sector participation.

Notes

1. Youth unemployment ranges from 37 percent of total unemployment in Morocco to 73 percent in Syria, with a simple average of 53 percent for all countries for which data are available. Except in Jordan and Lebanon, first-time job seekers make up more than 50 percent of the unemployed (ILO 2003).

2. See for instance Pissarides (1993) and Pritchett (1999). In countries where wage levels fell in real terms during the 1990s, educated and experienced workers were affected the most, leading to a degradation of skills. Despite this, recent estimates suggest that returns on education are generally higher in the public sector than in the private sector at nearly all education levels but the university level (Assaad 2002 and World Bank 2004).

3. Our focus on labor-exporting MENA countries only is due to the fact that the characteristics of the labor market in these countries (as well as other structural economic features) differ significantly from those of the labor-importing countries of the region.

4. Yemen is also an important labor-exporting country in MENA, but due to the lack of reliable information on the labor market in that country we chose to exclude it from our review.

5. In principle, a rigorous analysis of pension systems and pension reform would require the use of an intergenerational framework, such as the OLG-CGE model discussed by Farmer and Wendner (1999), or more recently by Beetsma, Bettendorf, and Broer (2003); Cavalletti and Lubke (2002); and Fehr, Hans, and Erling Ateigum (2002). Our analysis should be viewed as an approximation only.

6. See Shaban et al. (2001) and World Bank (2004). A more detailed discussion of the features of the labor market in MENA countries is provided by Hollister and Goldstein (1994) and Salehi-Esfahani (2001). See also Agénor (1996, 2004) for a more general discussion of the features of labor markets in developing countries.

7. Published measures of unemployment mostly include unemployed workers looking for jobs in the formal sector, but not underemployed workers in the informal and rural sectors, that is, disguised unemployment. For the difficulty of measuring unemployment in MENA countries, see for instance Rama (1998) for Tunisia.

8. Said (2001) found no close correlation between minimum wages and unskilled wages in Morocco; and during the 1980s, real wages for these workers fell faster than the real legal minimum wage. However, other evidence, reviewed by Agénor and El Aynaoui (2003), suggests the minimum wage is binding in urban areas.

9. Labor market segmentation refers to a situation where observationally identical workers (that is, workers with similar qualifications) receive different wages depending on their sector of employment. It is a pervasive feature of labor-exporting MENA countries. Segmentation may be induced by various factors: government intervention in the form of minimum wages; trade unions, which may prevent wages from being equalized across sectors by imposing a premium for their members; and efficiency wages, resulting from nutritional factors, turnover costs or productivity considerations (see Agénor (1996, 2004). The first two sources of segmentation are incorporated in the model presented in the next section.

10. The model is based on the Integrated Macroeconomic Model for Poverty Analysis (IMMPA) framework developed by Agénor (2003), Agénor, Izquierdo and Fofack (2003), and Agénor, Fernandes, and Haddad (2003), modified to account for international labor migration (as in Agénor and El Aynaoui (2003) and a social security system.

11. Note that the specification of θU assumes complete job turnover outside the government sector every period.

12. Note that we do not explain endogenously the allocation of unskilled workers' time between production and learning-an important trade-off from the individual's point of view. Allocating more time to learning reduces the workers' current labor income, but enhances their human capital, thereby increasing their earnings in the future. To the extent that public capital in education enters as an input to the human capital production function, as in (23), it would also affect private decisions to accumulate human capital. See, for instance, Glomm and Ravikumar (1998) for a formal model of the labor-learning choice, which emphasizes, however, flow spending on education.

13. See Glystos (2002, 2003) for a discussion of the macroeconomic effects of foreign remittances in several MENA countries, including Egypt, Jordan, Morocco, and Tunisia.

14. Note that, in our model, only employers pay payroll taxes that serve to finance the pension system. In practice, workers also make significant contributions. However, we abstract from these contributions, given that the focus of our simulation experiments is on changes in payroll taxes paid by firms.

15. Results of all these experiments are summarized in Figures 9.3 to 9.9. A set of Excel sheets, containing more detailed results, are available upon request.

16. Of course, other offsetting changes, such as increases in direct tax rates on enterprises, or an increase in indirect taxes on urban goods, could also be considered.

17. Note that the model does not capture the disincentive effects of higher direct tax rates on labor supply (or participation rates). To the extent that these effects are large, the impact of higher output growth rates on unemployment would be ambiguous, because a reduction in labor supply (which would tend to lower unemployment) could be offset by large substitution effects toward physical capital.

18. A limitation of our analysis is that we do not account for the fact that employment subsidies may have unintended consequences, such as subsidized workers replacing unsubsidized ones, or employers firing subsidized workers once the subsidy period ends.

References

Abrahart, Alan, Iqbal Kaur, and Zafiris Tzannatos. 2002. "Government Employment and Active Labor Market Policies in MENA in a Comparative International Context." In *Employment Creation and Social Protection in the Middle East and North Africa*, ed. by Heba Handoussa and Zafiris Tzannatos. Cairo: American University in Cairo Press.

Agénor, Pierre-Richard. 1996. "The Labor Market and Economic Adjustment." *IMF Staff Papers* 43 (June): 261-335.

———. 2002. "Fiscal Adjustment and Labor Market Dynamics." Unpublished. World Bank, Washington, DC (October). Forthcoming, *Journal of Development Economics*.

———. 2003. "Mini-IMMPA: A Framework for Assessing the Unemployment and Poverty Effects of Fiscal and Labor Market Reforms." Policy Research Working Paper No. 3067. World Bank, Washington, DC (May).

———. 2004. *The Economics of Adjustment and Growth*. 2nd ed. Boston, MA: Harvard University Press.

Agénor, Pierre-Richard, Alejandro Izquierdo, and Hippolyte Fofack. 2003. "IMMPA: A Quantitative Macroeconomic Framework for the Analysis of Poverty Reduction Strategies." Policy Research Working Paper No. 3092. World Bank, Washington, DC (June).

Agénor, Pierre-Richard, and Karim El Aynaoui. 2003. "Labor Market Policies and Unemployment in Morocco: A Quantitative Analysis." Policy Research Working Paper No. 3091. World Bank, Washington, DC (June).

Agénor, Pierre-Richard, Reynaldo Fernandes, and Eduardo Haddad. 2003. "Analyzing the Impact of Adjustment Policies on the Poor: An IMMPA Framework for Brazil." Unpublished. World Bank, Washington, DC (June).

Assaad, Ragui. 1997. "The E_ects of Public Sector Hiring and Compensation Policies on the Egyptian Labor Market." *World Bank Economic Review* 11 (March): 85-118.

———. 2002. "The Transformation of the Egyptian Labor Market: 1988-98." In *The Egyptian Labor Market in an Era of Reform*, ed. by Ragui Assaad. Cairo: American University in Cairo Press.

Assaad, Ragui, and Simon Commander 1994. "Egypt." In *Labour Markets in an Era of Adjustment*, ed. by Susan Horton, Ravi Kanbur, and Dipak Mazumdar. Washington DC: World Bank.

Beetsma, Roel, Leon Bettendorf, and Peter Broer. 2003. "The Budgeting and Economic Consequences of Ageing in the Netherlands." *Economic Modelling* 20 (September): 987-1013.

Booth, Alison L. 1995. *The Economics of the Trade Union*. Cambridge, UK: Cambridge University Press.

Cavalletti, Barbara, and Eckhard Lubke. 2002. "Ageing Population and Pension Reform in Italy." In *Policy Evaluation with Computable General Equilibrium*, ed. by Amedeo Fossati and Wolfgang Wiegard. London: Routledge.

Coe, David T., and Dennis J. Snower. 1997. "Policy Complementarities: The Case for Fundamental Labor Market Reform." *IMF Staff Papers* 44 (March): 1-35.

Farmer, K., and R. Wendner. 1999. "The Use of Multi Sector OLG-CGE Models for Policy Analysis." Research Memorandum No. 99-03. Department of Economics, University of Graz (March).

Fehr, Hans, and Erling Ateigum. 2002. "Pension Funding Reforms in a Small Open Welfare State." In *Policy Evaluation with Computable General Equilibrium*, ed. by Amedeo Fossati and Wolfgang Wiegard. London: Routledge.

Glomm, Gerhard, and B. Ravikumar. 1998. "Flat-Rate Taxes, Government Spending on Education, and Growth." *Review of Economic Dynamics* 1 (January): 306-25.

Glystos, Nicholas P. 2002. "The Role of Migrant Remittances in Development: Evidence from Mediterranean Countries." *International Migration* 40 (March): 5-26.

———. 2003. "A Macroeconometric Model of the Effects of Migrant Remittances in Mediterranean Countries." In *Human Capital: Population Economics in the Middle East*, ed. by Ismail Siraguldin. London: I. B. Tauris Publishers.

Harris, John, and Michael P. Todaro. 1970. "Migration, Unemployment and Development: A Two-Sector Analysis." *American Economic Review* 60 (March): 126-43.

Hollister, Robinson G., and Markus P. Goldstein. 1994. *Reforming Labor Markets in the Near East: Implications for Structural Adjustment and Market Economies*. San Francisco, CA: ICS Press.

International Labor Organization. 2003. *Global Employment Trends*. Geneva: International Labor Office.

Layard, Richard, Stephen Nickell, and Richard Jackman. 1991. *Unemployment: Macroeconomic Performance and the Labor Market*. Oxford: Oxford University Press.

Norback, Pehr-Johan. 2001. "Cumulative Effects of Labor Market Distortions in a Developing Country." *Journal of Development Economics* 65 (June): 135-52.

Orszag, Mike, and Dennis Snower. 1998. "Anatomy of Policy Complementarities." *Swedish Economic Policy Review* 5 (Autumn): 303-51.

Pissarides, Christopher A. 1993. "Labor Markets in the Middle East and North Africa." Discussion Paper No. 5, MENA Region. World Bank, Washington, DC (March).

Pritchett, Lant. 1999. "Has Education Had a Growth Payo_ in the MENA Region?" Discussion Paper No. 18, MENA Region. World Bank, Washington, DC. (June).

Rama, Martin. 1998. "How Bad Is Unemployment in Tunisia? Assessing Labor Market Efficiency in a Developing Country." *World Bank Research Observer* (February): 59-77.

Said, Mona. 2001. "Public Sector Employment and Labor Markets in Arab Countries: Recent Developments and Policy Implications." In *Labor and Human Capital in the Middle East*, ed. by Djavad Salehi-Ishfahani. Reading, UK: Ithaca Press.

Salehi-Ishfahani, Djavad. 2001. *Labor and Human Capital in the Middle East.* Reading, UK: Ithaca Press.

Shaban, Radwan A., Ragui Assaad, and Sulayman Al-Qudsi. 2001. "Employment Experience in the Middle East and North Africa." In *Labor and Human Capital in the Middle East*, ed. by Djavad Salehi-Esfahani. Reading, UK: Ithaca Press.

Strand, Jon. 2003. "The Decline or Expansion of Unions: A Bargaining Model with Heterogeneous Labor." *European Journal of Political Economy* 19 (June): 317-40.

United Nations. 2003. *Arab Human Development Report.* Geneva: International Labor Office, UN.

World Bank. 2004. "MENA's Employment Challenge in the 21st Century: From Labor Force Growth to Job Creation." Unpublished. World Bank, Washington, DC (January).

Appendix A. List of Equations[*]

Production

$$X_j = V_j + X_j \sum_i a_{ij} \tag{A1}$$

$$V_A = \left[\alpha_{XA} \left\{ \beta_{XA} U_A^{-\rho_{XA}} + (1-\beta_{XA})K_G^{-\rho_{XA}} \right\}^{-\frac{1}{\rho_{XA}}} \right]^{1-\eta_{XA}} \tag{A2}$$

$$X_A = \alpha_{TA} \left\{ \beta_{TA} E_A^{\rho_{TA}} + (1-\beta_{TA})D_A^{\rho_{TA}} \right\}^{\frac{1}{\rho_{TA}}} \tag{A3}$$

$$V_I = \alpha_{XI} U_I^{\beta_{XI}} \tag{A4}$$

$$V_G = \alpha_{XG} \left\{ \beta_{XG} U_G^{-\rho_{XG}} + \left(1-\beta_{XG}\right)S_G^{-\rho_{XG}} \right\}^{-\frac{1}{\rho_{XG}}} \tag{A5}$$

$$V_P = \alpha_{XP} \left\{ \beta_{XP} T_1^{-\rho_{XP}} + \left(1-\beta_{XP}\right)K_G^{-\rho_{XP}} \right\}^{-\frac{1}{\rho_{XP}}} \tag{A6}$$

$$T_1 = \alpha_{XP1} \left\{ \beta_{XP1} T_2^{-\rho_{XP1}} + \left(1-\beta_{XP1}\right)U_P^{-\rho_{XP1}} \right\}^{-\frac{1}{\rho_{XP1}}} \tag{A7}$$

$$T_2 = \alpha_{XP2} \left\{ \beta_{XP2} S_P^{-\rho_{XP2}} + \left(1-\beta_{XP2}\right)K_P^{-\rho_{XP2}} \right\}^{-\frac{1}{\rho_{XP2}}} \tag{A8}$$

$$X_P = \alpha_{TP} \left\{ \beta_{TP} E_P^{\rho_{TP}} + \left(1-\beta_{TP}\right)D_P^{\rho_{TP}} \right\}^{\frac{1}{\rho_{TP}}} \tag{A9}$$

Employment

$$U_R = U_{R,-1}\left(1+g_R\right) - MIG \tag{A10}$$

$$U_A^d = \left(V_A^{1+\frac{\rho_{XA}}{1-\eta_{XA}}} \left(1-\eta_{XA}\right) \left(\frac{PV_A}{W_A}\right) \frac{\beta_{XA}}{\alpha_{XA}^{\rho_{XA}}} \right)^{\frac{1}{1+\rho_{XA}}} \tag{A11}$$

---

[*]Unless otherwise indicated, the indexes i and j, with $i, j = A, I, P, G$ refer to production sectors and $h = A, I, F, KR$ to households.

$$U_R^s = U_A^d \left(V_A, \frac{W_A}{PV_A} \right) \tag{A12}$$

$$U_P^d = T_1 \left(\frac{PT_1}{(1 + ptax_U)W_M - ES_U} \frac{\beta_{XP1}}{\alpha_{XP1}^{\rho_{XP1}}} \right)^{\sigma_{XP1}} \tag{A13}$$

$$\frac{U_F^s}{U_{F,-1}^s} = \left\{ \frac{U_{P,-1}^d}{U_{F,-1}^s - U_{G,-1}} \left(\frac{W_{M,-1}}{W_{I,-1}} \right) \right\}^{\beta_F} \tag{A14}$$

$$U_U = U_{U,-1} \left(1 + g_U - \delta_{NP}^U \right) + MIG - SKL - IMIG \tag{A15}$$

$$U_G = \left(1 + g_{UG} - \delta_{NP}^U \right) U_{G,-1} \tag{A16}$$

$$U_I^s = U_U - U_F^s \tag{A17}$$

$$S_P^d = T_2 \kappa_S \left(\frac{PT_2}{(1 + ptax_S)W_S - ES_S} \frac{\beta_{XP2}}{\alpha_{XP2}^{\rho_{XP2}}} \right)^{\sigma_{XP2}} \tag{A18}$$

$$UNEMP_S = 1 - \frac{(S_G^T + S_P^d)}{S} \tag{A19}$$

$$UNEMP_U = 1 - \frac{(U_G + U_P^d)}{U_F^s}. \tag{A20}$$

$$W_M = w_M P_F \tag{A21}$$

$$W_I = \beta_{XI} \left(\frac{PV_I V_I}{U_I^s} \right) \tag{A22}$$

$$W_{UG} = w_{UG} P_F \tag{A23}$$

$$\frac{W_S}{W_S - \Omega_0 UNEMP_S^{-\phi_1} W_{SG}^{\phi_2}} - \varepsilon_{S_P^d / W_S} - \frac{W_S S_P^d}{\nu PROF_P} = 0 \tag{A24}$$

$$W_{SG} = w_{SG} P_F \tag{A25}$$

$$MIG = U_{R,-1} \lambda_m \left[\sigma_M \ln\left(\frac{Ew_U}{Ew_A} \right) \right] + \left(1 - \lambda_m\right) \frac{U_{R,-1}}{U_{R,-2}} MIG_{-1} \tag{A26}$$

$$Ew_U = \frac{\theta_U W_{M,-1} + \left(1 - \theta_U\right) W_{I,-1}}{P_{URB,-1}} \tag{A27}$$

$$\theta_U = \frac{U_{P,-1}}{U^s_{F,-1} - U_{G,-1}} \tag{A28}$$

$$Ew_A = \frac{W_{A,-1}}{P_{R,-1}} \tag{A29}$$

$$IMIG = U_{U,-1} \lambda_{im} \sigma_{IM} \ln\left(\frac{Ew_F}{Ew_U} \right) + \left(1 - \lambda_m\right) \frac{U_{U,-1}}{U_{U,-2}} IMIG_{-1} \tag{A30}$$

$$Ew_{FOR} = \frac{ER \cdot W_{FOR,-1}}{P_{URB,-1}} \tag{A31}$$

$$SKL = \left[\beta_E \left(\varphi S^E_G \right)^{-\rho_E} + \left(1 - \beta_E\right) K^{-\rho_E}_E \right]^{-\frac{1}{\rho_E}} \tag{A32}$$

$$\varphi = 1 - \varphi_m \left[\frac{\left(1 - UNEMP_{S,-1}\right) W_{S,-1}}{W_{SG,-1}} \right]^{\delta_E} \tag{A33}$$

$$S^T_G = S_G + S^E_G \tag{A34}$$

$$S^T_G = \left(1 + g_{SG} - \delta^S_{NP}\right) S^T_{G,-1} \tag{A35}$$

$$S = \left(1 - \delta_S - \delta^S_{NP}\right) S_{-1} + SKL \tag{A36}$$

Supply and Demand

$$INT_j = \sum_i a_{ji} X_i \tag{A37}$$

$$Q_A^s = \alpha_{QA} \left\{ \beta_{QA} M_A^{-\rho_{QA}} + \left(1 - \beta_{QA}\right) D_A^{-\rho_{QA}} \right\}^{-\frac{1}{\rho_{QA}}} \tag{A38}$$

$$Q_I^s = X_I \tag{A39}$$

$$Q_G^s = X_G \tag{A40}$$

$$Q_P^s = \alpha_{QP} \left\{ \beta_{QP} M_P^{-\rho_{QP}} + \left(1 - \beta_{QP}\right) D_P^{-\rho_{QP}} \right\}^{-\frac{1}{\rho_{QP}}} \tag{A41}$$

$$Q_A^d = C_A + G_A + INT_A \tag{A42}$$

$$Q_I^d = C_I + INT_I \tag{A43}$$

$$Q_G^d = C_G + G_G + Z_P^G + INT_G \tag{A44}$$

$$Q_P^d = C_P + G_P + \left(Z_P^P + Z_G\right) + INT_P \tag{A45}$$

$$C_i = \sum_h C_{ih} = \sum_h x_{ih} + \frac{\Sigma_h cc_{ih}\left(CON_h - \Sigma_i PQ_i x_{ih}\right)}{PQ_i} \tag{A46}$$

$$G_j = gg_j \frac{NG}{PQ_j}, \quad \sum gg_j = 1, \text{for } j = A, G, P \tag{A47}$$

$$Z_P^j = zz_j \frac{PK \cdot Z_P}{PQ_i}, \quad \sum zz_j = 1, \text{for } j = G, P \tag{A48}$$

Trade

$$E_i = D_i \left(\frac{PE_i}{PD_i} \cdot \frac{1 - \beta_{Ti}}{\beta_{Ti}} \right)^{\sigma_{Ti}}, \text{ for } i = A, P \tag{A49}$$

$$M_i = D_i \left(\frac{PD_i}{PM_i} \cdot \frac{\beta_{Qi}}{1 - \beta_{Qi}} \right)^{\sigma_{Ti}}, \text{ for } i = A, P \tag{A50}$$

Prices

$$PV_i = V_i^{-1} \left\{ PX_i(1 - indtax_i) - \sum_j a_{ji} PQ_j \right\} X_i \qquad \text{(A51)}$$

$$PE_i = wpe_i ER, \ \text{for} \ i = A, P \qquad \text{(A52)}$$

$$PM_i = wpm_i (1 + tm_i) ER, \ \text{for} \ i = A, P \qquad \text{(A53)}$$

$$PX_i \frac{PD_i D_i + PE_i E_i}{X_i}, \ \text{for} \ i = A, P \qquad \text{(A54)}$$

$$PQ_i = \frac{PD_i D_i + PM_i M_i}{Q_i}, \ \text{for} \ i = A, P \qquad \text{(A55)}$$

$$PQ_i = PX_i = PD_i, \ \text{for} \ i = I, G \qquad \text{(A56)}$$

$$P_R = \sum_i wr_i PQ_i, \ \text{with} \ \sum_i wr_i = 1 \qquad \text{(A57)}$$

$$P_F = \sum_i wf_i PQ_i, \ \text{with} \ \sum_i wf_i = 1 \qquad \text{(A58)}$$

$$P_{URB} = \sum_i wu_i PQ_i, \ \text{with} \ \sum_i wu_i - 1 \qquad \text{(A59)}$$

$$PT_1 = \frac{T_2 PT_2 + \left[(1 + ptax_U) W_M - ES_U \right] U_P}{T_1} \qquad \text{(A60)}$$

$$PT_2 = \frac{PROF_P + \left[(1 + ptax_S) W_S - ES_S \right] S_P}{T_2} \qquad \text{(A61)}$$

$$PK = \frac{\sum_i PQ_i Z_i}{Z} = \frac{PQ_G Z_P^G + PQ_P Z_P^P}{Z} \qquad \text{(A62)}$$

Income

$$PROF_i = PV_i V_i - W_i U_i, \ \text{for} \ i = A, I \qquad \text{(A63)}$$

$$PROF_P = PV_P V_P - \left[(1 + ptax_U) W_M - ES_U \right] U_P \\ - \left[(1 + ptax_S) W_S - ES_S \right] S_P \qquad \text{(A64)}$$

$$YF_i = PROF_i, \ \text{for} \ i = A, I \qquad \text{(A65)}$$

$$YF_P = \left(1 - entax\right)PROF_P - IF \cdot ER \cdot FL_{P,-1} \tag{A66}$$

$$YH_A = \gamma_A TRH + PV_A V_A \tag{A67}$$

$$YH_I = \gamma_I TRH + PV_I V_I + (1 - \tau_F)ER \cdot REMIT \tag{A68}$$

$$YH_F = PENSIONS + \gamma_F TRH + \left(W_M U_P + W_{UG} U_G\right)$$
$$+ \left(W_S S_P + W_{SG} S_G\right) + \tau_F ER \cdot REMIT \tag{A69}$$

$$YH_{KR} = \gamma_{KR} TRH + \left(1 - re\right)YF_P \tag{A70}$$

Consumption, Savings, and Investment

$$SAV_h = sr_h \left(1 - inctax_h\right)YH_h \tag{A71}$$

$$CON_h = \left(1 - inctax_h\right)YH_h - SAV_h \tag{A72}$$

$$PK \cdot Z_P + PQ_P Z_G = re \cdot YF_P + \sum_h SAV_h - CDEF + ER\left(\Delta FL_P + \Delta FL_G\right) \tag{A73}$$

$$K_P = \left(1 - \delta_P\right)K_{P,-1} + Z_{P,-1} \tag{A74}$$

Government

$$-CDEF = TXREV - TRH - TRSOC - W_{SG}S_G^E$$
$$- NG - IF_G ER \cdot FL_{G,-1} \tag{A75}$$

$$-ODEF = -CDEF - PQ_P Z_G \tag{A76}$$

$$TXREV = \sum_{i=A,P} wpm_i tm_i M_i ER + ptax_U W_M U_P^d + ptax_S W_S S_P^d$$
$$+ \sum_i indtax_i PX_i X_i + entax \cdot PROF_P + inctax_R YH_R \tag{A77}$$
$$+ inctax_A YH_A inctax_F YH_F - ES_U U_P^d - ES_S S_P^d$$

$$PQ_P Z_G = I_{INF} + I_E + I_H \tag{A78}$$

$$K_i = \left(1 - \delta_i\right)K_{i,-1} + \frac{I_{i,-1}}{PQ_{P,-1}}, \quad \text{where} \quad i = INF, H, E \tag{A79}$$

$$K_G = \alpha_G \left\{\beta_G K_{INF}^{-\rho_G} + \left(1 - \beta_G\right)K_H^{-\rho_G}\right\}^{-\frac{1}{\rho_G}} \tag{A80}$$

Pension System

$$TRSOC = PENSIONS - ptax_U U_P^d - ptax_S S_P^d \tag{A81}$$

$$BENEF = BENEF_{-1}\left(1 + \Delta \ln P_{F,-1}\right) \tag{A82}$$

$$NUMPEN = \left(1 - \delta_N\right) NUMPEN_{-1} + NEWPEN \tag{A83}$$

$$NEWPEN = \delta_{NP}^U \left(U_{P,-1}^d + U_{G,-1}\right) + \delta_{NP}^S \left(S_{P,-1}^d + S_{G,-1}^T\right) \tag{A84}$$

$$PENSIONS = BENEF \cdot NUMPEN \tag{A85}$$

Balance of Payments

$$0 = \sum_{i=A,P} \left(wpe_i E_i - wpm_i M_i\right) + REMIT - IF \cdot FL_{P,-1} \\ - IF_G FL_{G,-1} + \Delta FL_G + \Delta FL_P \tag{A86}$$

$$REMIT = W_{FOR} FORL_{-1} \tag{A87}$$

$$FORL = \left(1 - \delta_{IMIG}\right) FORL_{-1} + IMIG \tag{A88}$$

Appendix B. Variable Names and Definitions[*]

Endogenous Variables

$BENEF$	Average pension benefit
C_i	Consumption of good i by the urban and rural private sector
C_{ih}	Consumption of good i by household h
CON_h	Total nominal consumption by household h
$CDEF$	Current public budget deficit
D_i	Domestic demand for good $i = A, P$
E_i	Export of traded goods for $i = A, P$
ES_S	Nominal employment subsidy on skilled labor in the private sector
ES_U	Nominal employment subsidy on unskilled labor in the private sector
Ew_U	Expected urban unskilled wage
Ew_A	Expected agricultural wage
$FORL$	Stock of domestic workers abroad
G_i	Government spending on good $i = A, G, P$
$IMIG$	International migration
INT_i	Intermediate good demand for good i
K_E	Public capital in education
K_G	Total public capital
K_H	Public capital in health
K_{INF}	Public capital in infrastructure
K_P	Private capital
M_i	Imports of good $i = A, P$
MIG	Migration to urban area
$NEWPEN$	Flow of skilled and unskilled workers retiring in each period
$NUMPEN$	Number of pensioners
$ODEF$	Overall budget deficit
P_F	Formal urban price index
P_R	Rural price index
P_S	Price index for skilled labor
P_{URB}	Urban price index
PD_i	Domestic price of domestic sales of good $i = A, P$
PE_i	Price of exported good $i = A, P$
$PENSIONS$	Total amount of pension paid to pensioners
PK	Price of capital
PM_i	Price of imported good $i = A, P$
PQ_i	Composite good price of good i
$PROF_i$	Profits by firms in sector $i = A, I, P$

---

[*]Unless otherwise indicated, the index $i = A, I, P, G$ refers to production sectors and $h = A, I, F, KR$ to households.

PT_1	Price of composite input T_1
PT_2	Price of composite input T_2
PV_i	Value added price of good i
PX_i	Sales price of good i
Q_i^s, Q_i^d	Composite supply and demand of good i
$REMIT$	Foreign currency value of the flow of remittances from abroad
S	Skilled workers
S_P^d	Demand for skilled workers in private urban formal sector
SAV_h	Saving by household h
sr_h	Saving rate for household h
SKL	New skilled workers
S_P	Skilled labor employed in private urban formal
T_1	Composite input from T_2 and unskilled labor
T_2	Composite input from capital and skilled labor
TRH	Transfers to households
$TRSOC$	Net government pension transfers
$TXREV$	Tax revenues
U_i	Unskilled labor employed in sector $i = A,I,P$
U_R	Unskilled workers in rural sector
U_R^s	Unskilled labor supply in the rural sector
U_U	Unskilled workers in urban sector
U_i^d	Demand for labor in sector $i = A,I,P$
U_F^S	Unskilled labor supply in the urban formal sector
U_I^S	Unskilled labor supply in the informal sector
$UNEMP_S$	Skilled unemployment rate
$UNEMP_U$	Unskilled unemployment rate in the formal sector
V_i	Value added in sector i
W_i	Nominal wage for labor employed in sector $i = A, I$
w_i	Real wage rate for unskilled labor employed in sector $i = A, I$
W_M	Minimum wage (unskilled labor in urban formal private sector)
w_M	Real minimum wage (unskilled labor in urban formal private sector)
W_S	Nominal wage rate for skilled worker in the private urban formal sector
w_S	Real wage rate for skilled worker in the private urban formal sector
W_{SG}	Nominal wage rate for skilled labor in the government sector
w_{SG}	Skilled wage in the public sector, real terms
W_{UG}	Nominal wage rate for unskilled labor in the government sector
w_{UG}	Unskilled wage in the public sector, real terms

x_{ih}	Subsistence level of consumption of good i by household h
X_i	Production of good i
YF_i	Income by firms in sector $i = A, I, P$
YH_h	Household income for household h
Z	Total investment demand
Z_i	Investment demand for good $i = P, G$
Z_P^i	Investment demand for good $i = P, G$ by formal private sector

Exogenous Variables

Name	Definition in text
$entax$	Corporate income tax
ER	Nominal exchange rate
Ew_{FOR}	Expected real foreign wage (in terms of domestic prices)
FL_i	Foreign loans to sector $i = G, P$
G_C	Government consumption
g_R	Population growth in rural economy
g_{SG}	Growth rate of the skilled labor force in the public sector
g_{UG}	Growth rate of the unskilled labor force in the public sector
g_U	Population growth in urban economy
I_E	Investment in education
IF	Foreign interest rate
IF_G	Interest rate on government foreign loans
I_H	Investment in health
I_{INF}	Investment in infrastructure
$inctax_h$	Income tax rate for h
$indtax_i$	Rate of indirect taxation of output in sector i
NG	Total government current expenditure on goods and services
$ptax_S$	Payroll tax for skilled labor in private urban sector
$ptax_U$	Payroll tax for unskilled labor in private urban sector
S_G	Skilled workers in public sector
S_G^E	Skilled labor in the public sector engaged in education
S_G^T	Total number of skilled workers in the public sector
tm_i	Import tariff for good $i = A, P$
U_G	Unskilled workers in public sector
W_{FOR}	Nominal foreign wage
wpe_i	World price of export for $i = A, P$
wpm_i	World price of import for $i = A, P$

Parameters

Name	Definition in text
a_{ij}	Input-output coefficient
α_G	Shift parameter in the public capital equation
α_{Qi}	Shift parameter in the total supply function of good $i = A, P$
α_{Ti}	Shift parameter in transformation function between exported and domestic production of good $i = A, P$
α_{Xi}	Shift parameter in production of good $i = A, P$
α_{XP1}	Shift parameter in composite input of unskilled and skilled/capital composite input
α_{XP2}	Shift parameter in composite input of skilled workers and private capital
β_E	Parameter determining the weight of skilled labor in production of education
β_F	Speed of adjustment for the supply of unskilled labor in the formal private sector
β_G	Share parameter in the public capital equation
β_{QA}	Shift parameter in agricultural composite good
β_{QP}	Shift parameter in urban composite good
β_{Ti}	Shift parameter between exported and domestic production of good $i = A, P$
β_{Xi}	Shift parameter in production of good $i = A, I, P$
β_{XP1}	Share parameter between unskilled and skilled/capital composite input
β_{XP2}	Share parameter between skilled workers and private capital
cc_{ih}	Shares of household h in consumption of good i
δ_E	Depreciation rate of education capital
δ_H	Depreciation rate of health capital
δ_{INF}	Depreciation rate of infrastructure
δ_{IMIG}	Rate of "attrition" of the stock of migrants
δ_{NP}^S	Rate of skilled retirement in the urban formal sector
δ_{NP}^U	Rate of unskilled retirement in the urban formal sector
δ_E	Sensitivity of skilled effort level to relative wages
δ_P	Depreciation rate of private capital
δ_S	Rate of "depreciation" or "de-skilling" of the skilled labor
$\varepsilon_{S_P^d/W_S}$	Wage elasticity of the demand for skilled labor
φ	Productivity of public workers engaged in providing education
φ_m	Minimum level of effort
η_{XA}	Coefficient of returns to scale in the agricultural value added function
γ_h	Share of transfers allocated to household h

gg_i	Share of government expenditure on good $i = A, G, P$
κ_S	Shift parameter for skilled private sector employment
λim	Speed of adjustment in the international migration equation
λm	Partial adjustment rate on migration
φ_j	Parameters determining the nominal wage rate for the skilled labor for $j = 1, 2$
re	Percentage of profits retained
ρ_E	Substitution parameter between skilled labor in production of education and educational capital stock
ρ_G	Substitution parameter in the public capital equation
ρ_{Qi}	Substitution parameter in total supply of good $i = A, P$
ρ_{Ti}	Substitution parameter between exported and domestic production of good $i = A, P$
ρ_{Xi}	Substitution parameter in production of good $i = A, P$
ρ_{XP1}	Substitution parameter between unskilled and skilled/capital composite input
ρ_{XP2}	Substitution parameter between skilled workers and private capital
σ_{IM}	Elasticity of international migration flows with respect to expected wages
σ_M	Elasticity of migration flows with respect to expected wages
σ_{QA}	Elasticity of agricultural composite good
σ_{QP}	Elasticity of private urban composite good
σ_S	Elasticity of saving rate to deposit rate
σ_{Ti}	Elasticity of transformation between exported and domestic production of good $i = A, P$
σ_{XP1}	Elasticity of substitution between unskilled workers and composite input of skilled workers and private capital
σ_{XP2}	Elasticity of substitution between skilled workers and private capital
τ_F	Fraction of remittances that are allocated to households in the formal sector
θ_U	Share of urban unskilled workers employed in formal sector
υ	Measure of the trade union's bargaining power
wf_i	Initial share of good i in consumption of formal sector goods
wr_i	Relative weight of good i in rural consumption
wu_i	Initial share of good i in urban unskilled workers' consumption
zz_i	Share of investment expenditure on good $i = G, P$

:

10

Economic Reforms and People Mobility for a More Effective EU-MED Partnership

Ishac Diwan*
Mustapha Nabli
Adama Coulibaly†
Sara Johansson de Silva†

Introduction

The new framework for partnership between the European Union (EU) and the Southern Mediterranean countries was launched at the Barcelona Conference in November 1995; the Extraordinary Conference held in Barcelona in November 2005 marked its 10th anniversary. The purpose of the initiative was to reinvigorate the partnership between the EU and the Southern Mediterranean (MED) countries, and work toward integration and convergence. The core mechanism for achieving these results has been the gradual establishment of a free trade area for industrial goods.

Other examples of regional partnerships, both involving the EU (the Central European countries that became members of the EU in 2004) and outside (the United States-Canada-Mexico NAFTA agreement) are evidence of the potential benefits from integration between richer and poorer areas. For the EU-MED Partnership, however, there has been little progress so far compared with what the agreements set out to achieve. Growth in the MED

*World Bank. †World Bank.

Published as "Rendre le Partenariat EU-MED plus effectif: Réformes et Mobilité de la Main d'œuvre," in *L'Union Européenne et le Moyen-Orient: Etat des Lieux.* Reprinted by permission from Bruylant, Presses Universitaires de Saint-Joseph.

countries is relatively modest, exports remain undiversified with limited non-mineral exports growth, and foreign companies still hesitate to invest in the region. At the same time, lack of growth and lack of job creation are giving rise to a serious economic, political and social crisis.

This paper argues that to reverse these negative trends, the EU-MED agenda needs to be enriched in two significant directions. First, there should be a clearer, much broadened agenda for supporting growth-enhancing structural reforms that complement trade liberalization. The second and parallel track focuses on the potential for including labor mobility between the EU and the MED countries on the agenda. Managed migration flows, by construction of limited magnitude, would explicitly address the critical political and social implications of the employment situation in the MED countries.

The EU-MED Agreements: Background

The EU-MED Partnership initiative following the 1995 Barcelona Conference led to new association agreements between the EU and each of the Arab Southern Mediterranean countries. Eight have been already signed: Tunisia (1995), Israel (1995), PLO for the benefit of the Palestinian Authority (1997), Morocco (1996), Jordan (1997), Egypt (2001), Algeria (1992), and Lebanon (2002). Negotiations are continuing with Syria (table 10.1).

The agreements have several intertwined purposes: to provide a framework for political dialogue between the EU and the MED region; to establish the conditions for gradual liberalization of trade in goods, services, and capital to promote trade and the expansion of economic and social relations between the EU and Mediterranean region; and to encourage regional integration within the Southern Mediterranean zone. The commitment to trade liberalization is intended to improve competitiveness by allowing for import competition and more effective resource allocation. It is also expected to attract foreign direct investment (FDI) into the MED region: firstly, since the main regulatory obstacles to FDI are removed, and secondly, since companies locating in the MED region benefit from geographic proximity to the EU and the lower labor costs in the MED region. The acceleration of trade and investment should result in economic integration and bring further benefits, including a much-needed revival of economic growth in the MED region.

Although the agreements' objectives are broad based, the central mechanism of the EU agreements is rather narrowly focused on establishing free trade areas, covering industrial products between the EU and each partner country within a 12-year period. Since manufacturing products from the MED countries already have access to the EU market, the agreement is in essence a means for gradually allowing EU manufacturing products into the MED markets. Further liberalization of agricultural goods and services is expected to proceed on a different time frame, following additional negotiations. A parallel financial instrument (MEDA) is used to support and facilitate

Table 10.1. Progress on the EU-Mediterranean Association Agreements [a]

	Conclusion of negotiations	Signature of agreement	Effectiveness date	End of transition period[b]
Tunisia	Jun 1995	Jul 1995	Mar 1998	2008
Israel	Sep 1995	Nov 1995	Jun 2000	2012
Morocco	Nov 1995	Feb 1996	Mar 2000	2012
PLO/PA	Dec 1996	Feb 1997	Jul 1997c	2009
Jordan	Apr 1997	Nov 1997	May 2002	2014
Egypt	Jan 2001	Jun 2001	June 2004	2016
Algeria	Dec 2001	Apr 2002	Sep 2005	2017
Lebanon	Jan 2002	June 2002	Mar 2003c	2015
Syria	In progress	..	..	..

a. As of October 2006. b. The date on which all tariffs on imported goods from the EU—as included in the agreements—will have to be dismantled. c. Interim agreement.

the adjustment process. This financial assistance is intended to complement the free trade agenda by supporting economic reforms and compensating for the socioeconomic costs of the transition to a market economy.[1]

The Achievements in Terms of Economic Integration and Convergence Have Been Limited

Regional integration, in particular between a developed and an underdeveloped area, can bring several political and economic gains (World Bank 2000). On the economic side, market enlargement could increase the incentives for domestic and foreign private investment through scale effects, and at the same time force firms to undertake efficiency improvements in response to increased competition. On the political side, regional commitments can provide a mechanism for increasing the credibility of economic and political reforms. It is also clear, however, that these benefits are far from automatic and that whether they materialize, and to what extent, will depend on the characteristics of both the partners and the agreement itself.

In this light, what has been achieved in the more than 10 years that have passed since the Barcelona Conference? It may seem early to assess achievements, since only two of the eight agreements became effective before the year 2000 (Tunisia, West Bank and Gaza), meaning that in most countries, reforms have just begun. However, we will argue that some assessment is already possible, for at least three reasons. First, a significant impact of the agreements should occur from the announcement effect, even before the agreements are fully implemented. Second, for some countries, some dismantling of the tariffs started even before the agreements became effective (Tunisia, Morocco), and financial assistance was also activated. Third, the experience of other countries, as highlighted below, shows that the effects of similar agreements can be significant in a relatively short time, in fact similar to the time that has passed since the beginning of the Barcelona process.

Unfortunately, the evidence so far points to limited success in achieving the objectives envisaged by the MED agreements. In the discussion following, we focus on the experience of four countries that have signed the agreements with the EU: namely, Tunisia, Morocco, Jordan, and Egypt. As we will see, even in countries where the positive effects should be most strongly felt, given the agreements that are in place, there has been little progress toward economic integration and convergence.

Contrary to their purpose, the agreements have not accelerated the process of economic integration. Generally, the export performance of the four MED countries has not improved since the mid-1990s: nonmineral exports as share of GDP have remained more or less stagnant and at low levels by international standards. Nor has there been a discernible change in trade flows: the four countries together provide less than 1 percent of total EU nonmineral imports, with virtually no increase in market share over the last decade. Foreign direct investment has fluctuated significantly between the years, largely because they have been concentrated on large and bulky infrastructure deals. With the exception of Jordan, however, inflows have not increased significantly (table 10.2).

Table 10.2. Lack of Economic Integration and Growth in the MED Countries, 1990–2000

	Egypt	Jordan	Morocco	Tunisia
Nonfuel merchandise exports, % of GDP				
1990–94	4.4	24.3	15.4	24.0
1995–99	2.9	24.2	19.9	26.6
2000–04	3.7	28.1	20.3	29.3
Nonfuel merchandise exports to EU (14), % of total EU (14) merchandise imports[a]				
1990–94	0.13	0.08	0.30	0.24
1995–99	0.11	0.09	0.36	0.27
2000–04	0.13	0.11	0.33	0.28
FDI, % of GDP				
1990–94	1.4	0.2	1.4	2.3
1995–99	1.1	2.3	0.1	1.9
2000–04	0.9	4.2	1.6	2.8
GDP per working age population, av. annual growth (%)				
1990–95	0.7	−1.2	−1.8	1.0
1995–00	2.8	−0.4	1.3	3.0
2000–04	0.8	2.3	2.4	2.3

Source: World Bank (2006).

a. EU (14) excludes countries that became members in 2004. In addition, Luxembourg is excluded for lack of data.

The lack of economic integration is mirrored in the comparatively weak growth rates in the MED countries. Generally, growth rates of GDP per working age population have been lower than in the EU. As a result, there has not yet been any discernible economic convergence between the two regions.

Yet, the potential rapid gains from integration between a large developed region and a less developed area are well illustrated elsewhere. Successful experiences with regional partnerships include the NAFTA trade liberalization agreement among the United States, Canada, and Mexico, which took effect in 1994. Another example are the (considerably broader) preaccession agreements between the EU and applicant countries in Central and Eastern Europe (CEE), who became members in 2004.

The lack of economic integration between EU and the MED countries stands in stark contrast to the cases of both Mexico-United States and the EU-accession countries. In the following discussion, we present information for Mexico and three of the CEE countries: namely the Czech Republic, Hungary, and Poland. Since the early 1990s, both Mexico and the three CEE countries have doubled their market share (that is, share of total imports) in the United States and EU respectively (figure 6.1). This was not a result of pure trade diversion, however: in Mexico, total nonfuel merchandise exports increased from less than 10 percent of GDP in 1990 to 25 percent of GDP by 2004, and over the same period, the three CEE countries almost doubled their share of nonfuel exports in GDP to nearly 50 percent. Foreign direct investment saw even more spectacular development (figure 6.2). Total FDI flows into Mexico increased from 1 percent of GDP in the beginning of the 1990s to almost 3 percent of GDP by the end of the decade. In the group of CEE countries, foreign direct investment increased more significantly, from around 1 percent of GDP to 5 percent of GDP on average, and reaching as high as 10 percent in the Czech Republic. As seen, the MED4 countries saw no comparable increase in either market share or investment.

A similar picture of the potential benefits from regional integration emerges from the accession process of Spain and Portugal, which became members of the European Union in 1985. Between 1980 and 1988, foreign direct investment more than tripled in Spain and Portugal and exports increased rapidly over the same period. As economic growth rates increased, Portugal and Spain began catching up with the rest of Europe (figure 10.3). Greece, which joined the EU in 1980, did not benefit as clearly from regional integration, however. The differences in outcomes are linked to the depth of the reforms which Spain and Portugal undertook in response to EU integration, but which Greece avoided.

In sum, it is clear that regional cooperation can deepen economic integration and lead to economic convergence, but this does not appear to be happening for the MED countries. The question is then how to explain the poor performance of the EU-MED integration process.

Figure 10.1. Nonfuel Merchandise Exports, Percent of Total EU (14) Merchandise Imports (MED4, CEE3) or U.S. Merchandise Imports (Mexico)

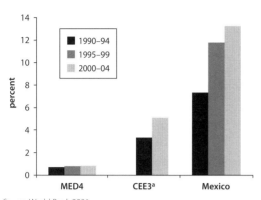

Source: World Bank 2006.
a. No data available for 1990–94.

Figure 10.2. FDI, Percent of GDP

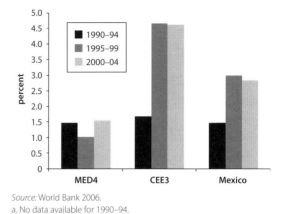

Source: World Bank 2006.
a. No data available for 1990–94.

Figure 10.3. GDP per Potential Worker as Percent of Italy's: Spain, Portugal and Greece, 1980–2004

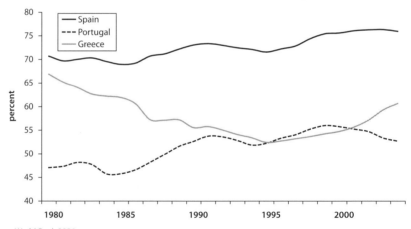

Source: World Bank 2006.

The Needed Agenda for Complementary Reforms Has Failed to Materialize

The lack of progress in economic integration and convergence, compared to the underlying objectives and initial expectations, clearly begs the question as to whether the EU-MED agenda in its current form is sufficient to deliver the desired results. The far more superior performance—in terms of concrete results and beneficial impact—of the NAFTA and EU preaccession agreements in the 1990s, suggests that a comparative exercise could be useful to evaluate the content and limitations of the EU-MED agenda as it stands. In particular, the NAFTA and preaccession agreements appear to offer a more complete form of integration and harmonization, whereas that complementary agenda of wider institutional reform and convergence is missing in the case of the EU-MED partnership.

The slow transition toward a well-functioning liberalized market has been a key factor in containing growth in the MED countries, in limiting the supply response of domestic firms and in reducing the region's attractiveness as a host for foreign direct investment, especially for exports-oriented companies. Although the four countries have launched reforms in several areas, considerable acceleration and widening of the reform agenda are required to catch up with other regions. Such growth-promoting structural reforms relate to the general business and investment climate, including reduction of the role of the state in economic activities. Broad liberalization of the domestic market also needs to be accompanied by improved competition policies, strengthened property rights, and other complementary reforms.

Although private investment and growth depend on reforms, the opposite also holds: without growth there will be no strong political constituency supporting a reform program. Economic policy reforms aimed at liberalizing the economy and opening up the sphere for private sector activities, will succeed only if indeed there is an adequate supply response from the private sector to replace the public sector as the main source of growth and employment. Thus, because of self-fulfilling expectations, only a credible reform process will generate the response necessary for its own success. Credibility will hinge on whether the private sector (domestic and foreign investors) believes not only that the reforms undertaken are sufficient to improve the economic environment, but also that they will not be reversed.[2]

Whereas the four MED countries succeeded in maintaining macroeconomic stability throughout the 1990s, they lag behind their comparators in both the scope and speed of structural reforms. Figure 10.4 shows two composite indices of progress on reforms for the MED countries and their comparators—here, Mexico and two CEE countries, Poland and Hungary (data are lacking for the Czech Republic for 1985–2001). One index relates to economic stability and comprises fiscal and current account balances, exchange rate black market premium, and inflation rates. The other refers to structural reforms and comprises tariff rates, tax rates, PPP distortions, and privatization revenues.[3]

As can be seen, the MED countries have been more successful than the comparator countries from the point of view of macroeconomic stability: they were more stable at the outset and have remained comparatively stable over time. However, with respect to structural reforms, the picture is very different: a difficult mix of an unfavorable starting point, in terms of the level of distortions present in the economy, and slow progress on removing those distortions, left the MED countries far behind Mexico and the CEE accession countries in the 1990s. The structural reform index for the MED countries not

Figure 10.4. Progress on Economic Stability Reforms (Left) and Structural Adjustment (Right), MED and Comparator Countries[a, b]

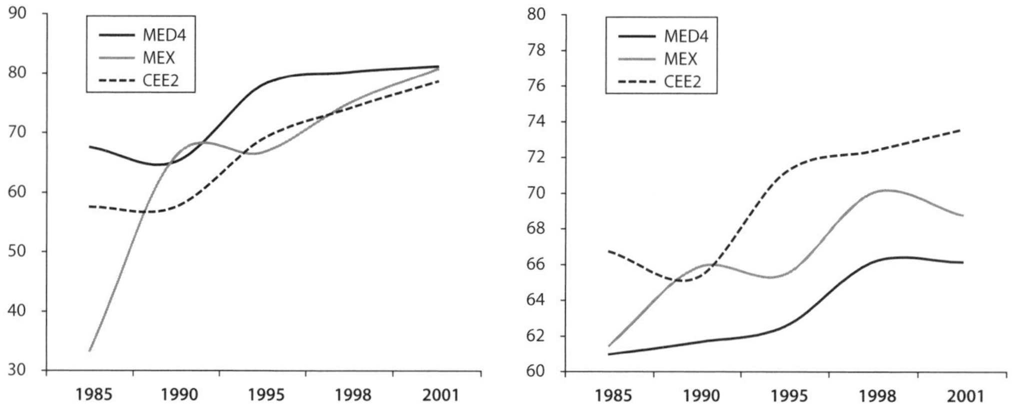

Source: World Bank 2003 employment study references.
a. The Economic Stability (ES) and Structural Reform (SR) indices are composite indices. The ES index is a weighted average of indices for fiscal and current account balances, exchange rate black market premium, and inflation rates. The SR index is a weighted average of indices for tariff rates, tax rates, PPP distortions and cumulative privatization revenues. The separate indices are calculated so that 100 = best value for all countries and all years 1985–1998. The larger the deviation from 100, the worse the reform performance of the specific country. To arrive at an average for each set of countries, the individual composite indices have been averaged (unweighted).   b. CEE2 = average for Poland and Hungary.

only starts at a lower level than the comparator countries, it also improves at a slower speed, further widening the gap.

For example, although average unweighted tariff rates for the MED countries were reduced by almost a third over the 1990s, they remained more than twice the level of those of Hungary, Poland, or Mexico. Mexico's tariff rates were more than halved between 1985 and 1998, and whereas tariff rates were not much more reduced in the CEE countries than in MED countries over the 1990s, they were already at a lower level from the outset.[4] Privatization proceeds, however, increased rapidly in the 1990s in the comparator countries, but remained relatively small in the MED countries.

What explains the lag in implementing economic reforms? The most compelling arguments are related to the motivations to undertake reforms within the specific social and political context facing the MED countries.

First, international experience shows that reforms are easier to launch in times of deep economic crisis when there are no alternatives left, for example, a situation with unsustainable economic imbalances, and when other resources have been depleted or become inaccessible. As we have seen, there has been no major stabilization crisis in the MED countries since 1985. Moreover, although aid inflows have fallen over time, they remain much higher than in other regions (figure 10.5). Combined with sizable fuel exports receipts, especially for Egypt, the continued availability of foreign resources may have reduced the incentive to foster economic reforms.

Further (and related), the very structure of the EU-MED agreements—a gradual and back-loaded trade liberalization scheme together with front-

Figure 10.5. Average Annual Inflows of Aid, US$ per Capita

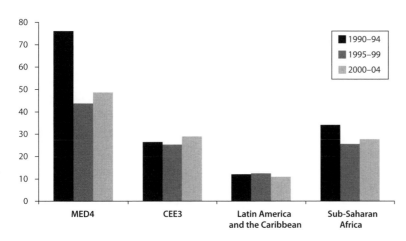

Source: World Bank 2006.

loaded financial assistance to support reforms—does not provide incentives to accelerate economic restructuring. The early financial assistance intended to ease the transition and implementation costs of reforms may instead delay them by providing alternative means for financing an inefficient economic structure. In addition, the reforms imposed by the agreements—dismantling of trade barriers for industrial goods—have a long implementation period on the part of the MED countries. Although other complementary reforms are included on the agenda, either for future negotiations (services and agricultural goods), or as areas for harmonization and cooperation (for example, product standards, competition policy, international property rights), there is no mechanism within the agreement that would ensure timely implementation and guarantee continued adherence.

Finally, the present political and social environment in MENA is proving a particularly difficult setting for launching reforms. The combination of low growth, high and increasing unemployment rates, and sometimes worsened poverty levels has resulted in a tense social climate where political survival may hinge on the state retaining its role as a guarantor of employment, and in which domestic and foreign private investors are deterred from investing because of social, political and economic uncertainty. The result is low growth and job destruction, which further increases the instability of these countries.

The high uncertainty surrounding the political situation as well as the reform agenda in the MED countries is a deterrent to private investment, whether foreign or domestic. There is strong evidence from MENA countries and elsewhere that uncertainty has an important negative impact on investment decisions (Sondergaard 2001). The irreversible nature of most investments will make investors hesitant to act in a high-risk environment—there is almost always the option to wait and see what happens today, and adjust the investment strategy so as to make an optimal investment choice tomorrow.

The contrast to the accession partnerships in this respect is telling (table 10.3). The preaccession strategy for the CEE countries was based on strict and detailed accession criteria and contained precise commitments on the part of the candidate country relating to a broad agenda, including democracy, macroeconomic stabilization, industrial restructuring, and the adoption of the *acquis communautaire*. The criteria included free movement of goods, services, capital, and labor (albeit with a transition period), and implied a complete overhaul of institutions, law, and regulations. Moreover, although the reform agenda was being complemented with financing along the way, these reforms were not parallel but preconditions for EU accession. The CEE countries therefore essentially faced a back-loaded process, in that the main benefit it provided came after reforms had been undertaken.

The comparison with NAFTA is, at first glance, less clearcut. Like the EU-MED agreements, NAFTA is limited to enforcing trade liberalization—although it included service liberalization early—and possible complementary reforms are on the agenda as areas for cooperation without any binding commitments regarding content, implementation, or timing. However, the Mexican accession to NAFTA was in large part the logical conclusion to, rather than the beginning of, a process of liberalization undertaken unilaterally by the Mexican government since the mid-1980s (Galal and Hoekman 1997). Thus, the purpose of the agreement was more to anchor the substantial achievements already made in liberalizing the Mexican economy than to actually initiate liberalization reforms, as has been the case with the EU-MED agreements. As mentioned earlier, Mexican tariffs have not fallen significant-

Table 10.3. The Complementary Reform Agenda Is Missing in the EU-MED Agreements

Reforms included in the agreements	EURO-MED	U.S.–Mexico NAFTA	EU accession
Free Movement			
Industrial goods	Yes	Yes	Yes
Agricultural goods	To be negotiated	Yes	Yes
Services	To be negotiated	Yes	Yes
Capital	No	No	Yes
Labor	No	No	Yes, with transition period
Complementary Reforms			
Competition Policy	Included as areas for cooperation and harmonization, but no mechanisms for implementation	Included as areas for cooperation and harmonization, but no mechanisms for implementation	Included as preconditions for accession
IPRs			
Privatization			
Company Law			
Financial Sector Reform			

ly during the 1990s, but in 1990 were already at half the level of (the average of) those of the MED countries in 1999. The difference between NAFTA and EU-MED distinguishes the role of a free trade agreement as an anchor to enhance the credibility of reforms already undertaken, from that of a vehicle for initiating reforms.

The Looming Social Crisis and the Labor Market in the MED Countries

At the same time, the comparatively weak economic performance in the MED countries poses a serious threat to political and social stability in the region. The combination of economic stagnation or recession, massive migration to urban areas, and a demographic transition that translates into a rapidly growing workforce, is increasing pressure on the labor market and, along with it, political and social unrest. Evidence from the region and elsewhere shows that from the perspective of political stability, the lack of job opportunities for the educated and politically vocal middle class is particularly serious.

30. Labor markets in the MED countries are characterized by low or no job creation and low turnover, and the trends are very worrisome. First, average overall unemployment rates are already reaching high levels and invariably increased over the 1990s (table 10.4). More important, the rate of unemployment is much higher among the young, the educated, and the new entrants to the labor market, and again, the tendency is worsening. In Egypt, for example, new labor market entrants made up around 70 percent of all unemployed in 1998, compared to 58 percent in 1988. Of these unemployed, first-time job-seekers, more than 90 percent had completed at least secondary education. More than 90 percent of all unemployed were aged between 15 and 30 years, and 80 percent of all unemployed had secondary education or more (Assaad 2000).[5] The picture is similar for the other MED countries.

These characteristics are all the more serious, given that the inflow to the formal labor market is bound to increase over the coming years. As in most developing countries, the urban population is still growing fast, rapidly increasing the supply of job seekers in cities: in Jordan and Morocco, urban population growth is almost 3 percent per year; in Morocco and Tunisia, it is many times higher than rural population growth (figure 10.6). Moreover, the combination of a demographic transition increasing the available workforce and improved access to education will further increase the share of educated new entrants in the labor market. In Egypt, the number of people in the labor force with at least secondary education increased, on average, by some 440,000 per year between 1988 and 1998. Measured as a percentage of total labor force, this is equivalent to an annual increase of 3 percent. At these arrival rates, the net addition to the Egyptian labor force in the coming years would consist entirely of mid- or highly skilled labor. Two-thirds of the Egyptian labor force would have at least secondary education by 2010, with

Table 10.4. Unemployment in MED Countries by Age and Level of Education

	Egypt (1998)	Jordan (2005)	Morocco[a] (2004)	Tunisia (2001)
Overall unemployment rate, 1988–89	5%	10%	16%	15%
Overall unemployment rate, latest available year	8%	15%	18%	15%
Youth unemployment rate	15%	39%	33%	35%
	(ages 15–19)	(ages 15–19)	(ages 15–24)	(ages 15–19)
	19%	29%	—	25%
	(ages 20–29)	(ages 20–24)		(ages 20–29)
Young unemployed by age group, % of total unemployed ages 15–64	84% (% unemployed ages 15–29)	81% (% unemployed ages 15–24)	60% (% unemployed ages 15–34)	—
Unemployed with secondary education or more, % of total unemployed	80%	35%	—	42%
Unemployment rate, economically active population with tertiary education	—	18%	26%[b]	—

Source: Egypt: Assaad (2000); Morocco: Direction de la Statistique; Jordan: Jordan Dept. of Statistics; Tunisia: IMF (2001), World Bank (2004).
Note: Latest available year 1998–2005. a. Urban areas. b. With diploma.

correspondingly high expectations of a payoff to their human capital investments (figure 10.7).

Traditionally, the public sector has constituted a major source of employment for the educated middle class in the MENA region. Up until the mid-1980s, the parallel expansion of the parastatal sector and of publicly provided services absorbed most of the skilled labor. As the economy slowed down—and with it, private sector job creation—the public sector continued to absorb the residual workforce, in effect acting as a form of unemployment insurance. By now it is clear, however, that the public sector can no longer sustainably absorb new cohorts of well-educated workers as it has reached its upper limits in absorbing fiscal resources (figures 10.8 and 10.9). Most countries are

Figure 10.6. Urban Population Growth High (Average Growth per Year, 2000–04, Urban and Rural Population)

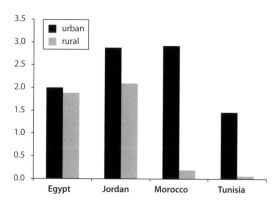

Source: World Bank 2006.

Figure 10.7. Increasing Share of the Labor Force Expects Payoff for Education (Egypt)

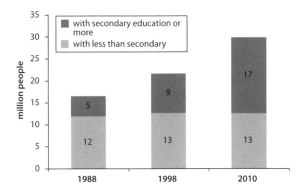

Source: Authors' estimates based on Assaad 2000.

Figure 10.8. Public Sector Absorbs Large Share of Employment and Resources

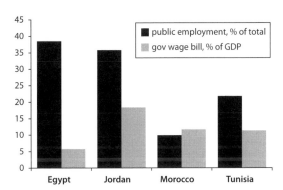

Source: World Bank 2006, World Bank 2003. Latest available 1997–2004.

Figure 10.9. Weight of Wage Bill High in MED Countries Compared to Other Regions

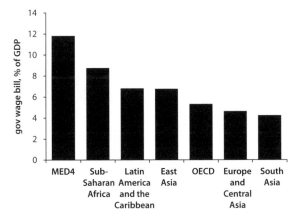

Source: World Bank 2006, World Bank 2003. Latest available 1997–2004.

faced with a pressing need for public workforce downsizing, and at any rate, expansion of the public sector is likely impossible.

New jobs for skilled (and unskilled) workers will consequently have to be created in the private sector. Yet the domestic private sector has so far failed to provide a source of employment growth—in large part because of persistent structural problems in the economies, including the strong presence of the state.

The cost of long-term youth unemployment and the resulting disillusionment of a whole generation could be very high. The region is already seeing a large exodus of highly skilled people. More important, social and economic malaise could in itself block the reform process necessary to reverse the negative trends. In this way, the political and social costs of high unemployment rates and worsening poverty trends limit the possibilities for public sector reform and wide-scale industrial restructuring. This status quo bias is exacerbated by the phenomenon of self-fulfilling expectations, which is creating a vicious negative growth circle. The high political uncertainty and instability deter private investment and increase capital flight, which further depresses growth rates, and thus further increases political instability and uncertainty.

New Directions for the Barcelona Framework

It is clear that the current framework for cooperation and integration between EU and the MED countries so far has not proved sufficient either to achieve the goals set out in the Barcelona agreements, or to mitigate the social and political tensions in the MED countries. Instead of contributing to growth and savings, the increasing workforce has become a barrier. Political and social phenomena are reducing the incentives for reform, making the countries unattractive for investment and unfit for productivity improvements.

Given this dire background, this paper proposes that the Barcelona framework be enriched along several dimensions. First, the constituency that should find it in its interest to support the EU partnership needs to be broader and stronger. In the present framework, one can hardly find groups within MED countries that can clearly identify benefits from the agreements for themselves. On the contrary, many see costs: the business sector, which has to adapt to European competition; the workers, who may bear some of the costs of adjustment to trade liberalization; and the young (and less young) population, who find it increasingly difficult to enter Europe because of more stringent entry requirements. Political support for the Barcelona agreements is weak.

Second, more credible mechanisms for anchoring the implementation of a broad and intense agenda for reforms complementary to trade liberalization should be developed, to make sure that the expected benefits from the agreements do actually materialize sooner rather than later. It is clear that financial support cannot be the only answer, even though it may be part of a larger package. On the contrary, as argued previously, merely providing financial flows could have a perverse effect on incentives to undertake reform.

In this respect, widening and accelerating the agenda for liberalization on agricultural trade is important for the agricultural constituency, and may play a role in helping reduce rural poverty. Yet this measure on its own is unlikely to be enough to reverse the trend of overall rural migration to the cities, for several reasons. First, productivity improvements in the agricultural sector in response to trade liberalization are more likely to actually reduce demand for labor. Second, the severe water shortage characteristic of most of the MED countries will limit the supply response from the rural sector. Third, competition from Poland and Hungary is also likely to limit demand from the EU for agricultural products from the MED countries.

Similarly, broadening the agenda to services liberalization may also increase the benefits of the agreements, in particular as its implementation would highlight the need for harmonization and reforms in a number of areas outside tariff reduction. However, risks remain that the complementary reform agenda does not materialize.

A more credible reform process would hence require a strong early commitment on the part of MED governments to carry out and maintain critical reforms in complementary areas such as public sector reform and financial sector modernization. These reforms should be accompanied by official support from the EU, a signal that would then further support the credibility of the reform program.

Third, labor mobility at present is not included in the partnership framework, nor is it on the agenda for negotiations. However, the strong links between labor market conditions in MENA on the one hand, and political resistance to growth-enhancing reforms on the other, suggest that migration could well be an important ingredient in improving the framework. Indeed, a well-designed significant program of managed migration from MED countries to the EU can be a major vehicle for achieving the objectives of the partnership. First, it would create an immediate constituency that benefits from the partnership. Second, it would help relieve socioeconomic and political pressures from unemployment in MED countries, and facilitate undertaking the complementary reform agenda. This would smooth the impact of the transition costs of trade liberalization, as well as the impact of the bulge in the demand for jobs over the coming 15–20 years that results from the demographic transition. Both factors would help support and enhance the reform agenda.

Intensified trade relations, as in the EU partnership, have been put forward as a substitute for interregional migration, and indeed as a means of containing mass migration from poorer to richer areas. First, from a purely theoretical perspective, factor endowment trade theory would suggest that trade in goods is indirectly trade in factors, including labor. Second, increased trade is expected to lead to higher growth, especially in poorer countries, which in turn leads to economic convergence, thereby reducing the incentives for migration in the first place.

Yet research on trade and migration shows that trade liberalization and migration controls are not necessarily substituting policies, at least not over the short term (Faini et al. 1999). In fact, historical evidence suggests the opposite: the globalization drives at the end of the 19th century and in the 20th century postwar period were accompanied by a surge in migration flows, as both labor and goods benefited from a decline in communication and transportation costs. High-income countries that liberalize trade with middle-income countries are not likely to have to fear massive migration flows. However, trade liberalization between high-income countries and significantly poorer countries may at least initially result in increased pressures for migration, if production is polarized and if migration previously has been repressed by financial constraints.

In the following discussion, we undertake to advance the debate by developing the arguments for increased movement of people between the MED countries and Europe.

People Mobility between EU and MED Countries as Part of the Solution

What are the possibilities for channeling migration in ways that maximize the potential current and future gains for the sending country and use the reduced labor market pressures to make a big push for reforms? Migration, and perhaps especially from Muslim countries, has a bad name in Europe. A variety of reasons explain the poor reputation: high overall unemployment rates in the EU; previous large waves of migrants, especially from the Maghreb (Morocco) region (to France, Italy, Spain) and Turkey (mostly to Germany), among whom unemployment rates are often higher than among nationals; high fertility rates among immigrant communities; continued flows of illegal immigration, among others. The strong tightening of migration policies in the 1980s and 1990s is evidence of the changing perception toward foreign labor. The debate over the perceived cost of opening the borders to workers from the EU accession countries in Central and Eastern Europe, and the imposition of a seven-year transition period for free movement of labor to this end, has highlighted the lack of a common agreed framework for migration within the EU. It has also revealed the tension surrounding the management of migration flows and the concerns of EU members—in particular in the Mediterranean area, which at present receives an important share of inflows from Maghreb. This paper, however, advances the benefits from a scheme with managed migration for mid-skilled labor: that is, with secondary education from the MENA region, which would differ from past waves of immigration.

Critics would argue that from the perspective of EU countries, opening the borders for workers outside the EU will put upward pressure on the already high unemployment rates in the EU, and especially in the countries which, for cultural and historical reasons, are most likely to be recipients of large-scale immigration. Indeed, unemployment rates in EU (15) averaged 8 percent between 2003 and 2005 and reached 10 percent in France, Germany, and Spain (OECD 2006). From the perspective of the MED countries, on the other hand, migration of skilled labor would imply losing its best workforce to foreign countries, at a time when capacity and skilled labor are considered key in improving international competitiveness and in the leveling of the private sector.

Yet several facts speak in favor of a deeper integration of labor markets between EU and the MED countries. First, whereas the present trade-focused format of the EU-MED agreements seems insufficient to lead to economic convergence, international and historical experience shows that migration can be a major force in bringing it about. A study by Taylor and Williamson (1994) suggests that migration between the old and the new world at the end of the 19th century was the main factor behind convergence in real wages, GDP-worker, and GDP-capita between Europe on the one hand and the United States and Australia on the other. In short, migration served to take off pressure on the labor markets in Europe and instead provide a much needed workforce in the new countries, with an impact on both GDP and the compensation of workers (figure 10.10).

More recently, migration within the Middle East and North Africa has also served as a means of convergence. Migration has provided a vehicle for distributing oil revenues within the region: millions of Egyptians, Palestinians,

Figure 10.10. Average Annual Growth Rates of United States and Italy between 1870–1910, with Migration (Actual) and Without Migration (Counterfactual)

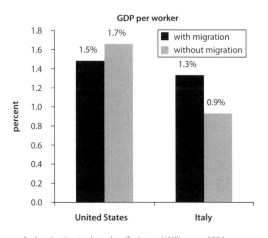
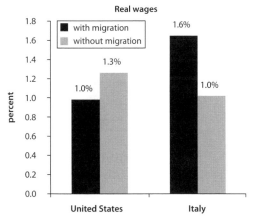

Source: Authors' estimates based on Taylor and Williamson 1994.

Yemenis, Syrians, Lebanese, and Jordanians have worked in the oil-producing Gulf countries for extended periods, sending home money to their families. Later on, many have returned home as investors or skilled and experienced labor. As shown in figure 10.11, GDP growth in these labor-exporting countries moved together with oil revenues and GDP growth in the Gulf countries during the 1970s, 1980s, and 1990s (except for the beginning of the 1980s), suggesting important spillover effects. With the Gulf war at the beginning of the 1990s, however, labor demand fell radically in the oil-rich economies, leading to a large involuntary return of workers. The shrinking labor market in the Gulf has been one key factor in pushing unemployment rates up in Jordan and Egypt, for example.

Further, some access to the EU labor market for the MENA countries, even if limited, could potentially bring important economic, political, and social gains for the sending countries. The risk for "brain drain" is a real and serious one, but the migration option must be contrasted with the current situation, where skills are not put to use. Long-term unemployment persistence, especially for new and well-educated entrants to the labor market, is at present both increasing frustration and eroding skills that are not maintained through on-the-job training. The resulting political and social tension is in turn hampering the investment climate and economic growth. All the while, labor skills are becoming obsolete.

Moreover, the lack of opportunities is already pushing highly skilled labor to leave the region, but to other regions such as the United States, Canada, or Australia. By way of illustration, out of the more than 50,000 Egyptians migrants that resided in the United States in 1990 (as recorded by the census),

Figure 10.11. Oil Revenues Trickle Down in the MENA Region

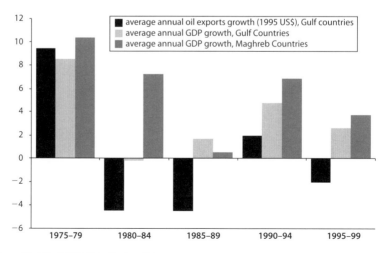

Source: World Bank 2006, United Nations 2001.

98 percent had completed secondary education and almost 80 percent had tertiary education (Carrington and Detragiache 1998).

Although geographical proximity to the EU area will induce emigration, it will also facilitate return migration. This is not necessarily the case for migrants who have taken the step to move to continents much further away from the MENA region. The more rooted immigrants become in the host country, the less likely they are to return home; and as immigrants lose their personal and professional ties to their home countries, the benefits associated with sending workers abroad will also weaken.

An appropriately managed migration to the EU area, in contrast, would bring important benefits in the form of foreign exchange savings (workers' remittances) and simultaneously provide better management and capitalization of human capital assets. Such a scheme, although focused and limited in size, would at the same time relieve some critical pressure on labor markets in the MENA countries. With several migrants returning home after a certain time spent in the EU, the region would also gain from upgrading skills and business connections.

Workers' remittances already make up an important source of balance of payments support in the Middle East and North Africa Region, and have, as shown in table 10.5, by far exceeded direct investment inflows in the four MED countries.

Migration can also provide the means for skilled labor to capitalize on investment in human capital already made, in a place where returns to education are higher, and to continue upgrading skills overseas. When conditions at home have improved, they can return home with accumulated savings as well as new skills. There is strong evidence that an important percentage of migrants do not lose their ties with their home countries but choose to return home after a certain time abroad. It has been estimated that of all U.S. immigrants, one-third return to live in their home country at some point during their lives, and 20 percent return within the first 10 years after arriving in the United States (Stalker 2000).

Returning migrants often bring back significant skills, experience, and connections within business networks in Europe or elsewhere, as well as savings

Table 10.5. Workers' Remittances and Foreign Direct Investment, Percent of GDP (Average)

	1990–94 Workers' remittances	FDI	1995–99 Workers' remittances	FDI	2000–04 Workers' remittances	FDI
Egypt	10.8	1.4	4.4	1.1	3.3	0.9
Jordan	15.5	0.1	20.2	2.3	19.4	4.2
Morocco	7.1	1.4	5.7	0.1	8.2	1.8
Tunisia	3.8	2.4	3.7	1.9	4.8	2.8

Source: World Bank 2006.

for investment. There are also indications that savings in the form of workers' remittances are more directly translated into growth than other forms of savings, since they tend to be used for productive investment to a higher degree. For example, a study of the use of international remittances by households in rural Egypt showed first, that a substantial share of migrant household incomes is spent on investment, and second, that the propensity to invest is larger than for nonmigrant households (Adams Jr. 1991).

Clearly, however, the propensity to return home to put savings and experience to use will depend on whether the work and investment climate in the home country improves or not. International experience shows that return migration is ruled by "push" factors—worsening labor market climate in host countries—but also to a large extent by "pull" factors, that is, increasing attractiveness of the home country (Dustmann 1996; Gmelch 1980).

The southern European countries' experiences of migration to northern Europe (primarily Germany, France, and Switzerland) indicate an inverse u-pattern in the propensity to migrate (figure 10.12). As work opportunities increased in the buoyant northern European economies in the 1960s, migration from Greece, Portugal, Spain, and Turkey rapidly took off, and fell together with the declining opportunities after the first oil shock. However, as the economies in Northern Europe improved in the 1980s, net migration from Southern Europe did not pick up, although there were still considerable gaps in real wages and incomes between the two regions. Although stricter immigration policies did play a role, it does not fully explain the trend toward return migration, since migrants from other countries continued to arrive in the northern European countries.

Empirical work suggests that the propensity to migrate in the southern European economies was determined by income disparities between the home and the host country and by the individual level of wealth of the potential migrant—that is, his resources for migration, but also by the strength of cultural and social ties to the home country (Faini and Venturini 1994). Hence, in a poor country migration is likely to initially increase with growth, as potential migrants acquire the financial means and the level of education necessary to go abroad. But as conditions at home improve, the incentive to migrate is reduced and some of the migrants return home to their preferred country of residence, becoming an important source of dynamism and a bridge between the two markets.

Similarly, it could be argued that the quality of investment made by returning migrants—in choice of sector, productive use, growth potential, and spillover effects—is likely to depend on opportunities for investment in the home country (Chandavarkar 1980). The quality of the investment climate at home will thus be important in determining not only the propensity to return, but also the productive use of remittances.

Figure 10.12. Migration Rates in Southern Europe, 1960–1988

(Migrants per 1,000 Inhabitants)

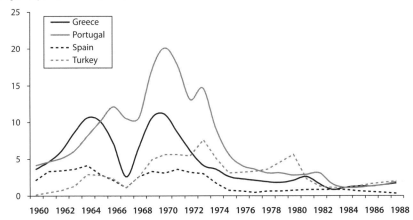

Source: Faini and Venturini 1994.

Finally, the willingness of political decision makers to undertake important but politically difficult economic reforms is likely to increase with migration. Outflows of workers would alleviate labor market pressures during structural reforms that may have a potentially negative bearing on the labor market, at least in the short run—including civil service reform, changes in the education system, and so forth. This can create a positive feedback loop, in which migration allows for a more decisive take on economic reforms without immediate large social costs, which in turn improves the investment climate and growth prospects, and thus attracts migrants back after a certain time.

Can the EU Cope?

However strong the arguments from the sending countries, a migration scheme that is costly to the recipient countries, especially from the prospect of labor market impacts, will not be politically feasible. The expected impact on the EU labor market of taking in more skilled migrants from North Africa is therefore a key issue in assessing the viability and applicability of a migration scheme. It is evident from the current debate on migration in Europe that the perception of migration as socially and economically costly for the host countries is widespread. As discussed previously, there are several counterarguments to increasing migration: high unemployment rates suggest that the EU labor markets can no longer absorb their own workforce, let alone take in foreign labor. This further increases already high levels of immigration that would lead to even higher unemployment, or a drop in real wages, or both; the EU needs to concentrate on accommodating workers from the accession countries in the CEE, rather than on nonmember countries (Maghreb) that have already been allowed their share of immigration for decades. As we will see, however, these arguments do not necessarily hold up to close scrutiny.

First of all, although the EU has received a large share of immigrants, the share of foreign-born labor force remains lower than in the United States and Canada. Yet unemployment rates in the United States and Canada have remained below those of the EU area. This could be due to a variety of factors, including differences in labor markets, migration types, and selection criteria, but the fact remains that the United States and Canada have managed migration flows and labor market pressures better.

Second, it is true that earlier waves of migration from the MENA region, and in particular from the Maghreb countries, have resulted in an important presence in several EU countries, especially Belgium, France, Italy, and Spain. During the industrial boom of the 1960s, several EU countries actively recruited workers from the Maghreb to occupy low-skill jobs in the industrial sector. As the recession hit Europe in the mid-1970s, migration policies took a sharp turn and access to the EU market for foreigners tightened considerably. However, as economic conditions subsequently worsened in the MENA region as well, in particular after the collapse in oil prices in the mid-1980s, there was still an important supply of migrants. With stricter migration policies, illegal immigration increased, in particular to the southern European countries, where the Mediterranean coast poses an obstacle to tight border entry control. With the exception of a sharp increase in Moroccan immigration to Italy and Spain (partly a reflection of regularization of existing illegal immigrants), there has been little or no increase of the share of North African immigrants since the mid-1980s (table 10.6). Immigrants from other countries have instead increased their presence in Northern Europe.

Table 10.6. Stock of Foreign Population by Nationality (Percent of Total Foreign), Selected EU Countries, Earliest and Latest Available Year[a]

As % of total foreign population	Belgium		France		Germany		Italy		Netherlands		Spain	
	1986	2001	1982	1999	1986	2002	1986	2001	1985	1998	1985	1998
Morocco	15	11	12	15	..	..	1	12	10	10	3	21
Algeria	1	1	22	15	..	..	..	..	..	..	..	..
Tunisia	..	..	5	5	..	..	1	3	1	0	..	..
Egypt	..	..	..	..	..	..	2	2	..	..	..	..
North Africa	*16*	*12*	*39*	*35*	*0*	*0*	*4*	*17*	*11*	*10*	*3*	*21*
Turkey	9	5	3	6	32	26	..	..	12	11	..	..
Poland	..	1	2	0	3	4	2	2	..	..	..	..
Other	75	82	56	59	65	70	94	81	77	79	97	79
Total foreign population	*853*	*846*	*3,714*	*3,263*	*4,513*	*7,336*	*450*	*1,363*	*1,217*	*1,675*	*539*	*1,109*

Source: OECD (2003).

1. Definitions of foreign population differ across countries. In the table above, the numbers refer to foreign population, except for the Netherlands, where it refers to the foreign-born population. For Italy and Spain, figures include results of regularization programs (Italy: in 1987–88, 1990, 1995; Spain: in 1991).

Third, demographic developments in the EU would in fact imply that increased workforce migration would be highly desirable. Under the prevailing pay-as-you-go social security system, a rapidly aging population is threatening to weigh heavily on future workers and taxpayers who will need to provide for retirees with increasing life expectancy. Short of an immediate and drastic change in fertility rates in the EU area, migration provides the only means of reinforcing the shrinking workforce. At present, the EU receives around 0.6 million migrants (on a net basis) every year. Demographic projections by the UN suggest that to keep the working-age population constant, another million people would need to enter the EU each year (UN 2000). To keep the ratio of old population to working population constant, that is, to ensure that each retiree can rely on the same number of workers, the region would need as much as 10 million additional immigrants per year (figure 10.13).

From the perspective of replacement migration: can and will the additional workforce needed be more than adequately provided by the accession countries in Central and Eastern Europe? The discussion regarding EU enlargement and labor mobility has revealed large differences in perception regarding the potential pool of immigrants from Central and Eastern Europe: whereas EU members fear mass immigration, the CEE countries appear to expect emigration to be more limited. Several characteristics that distinguish the CEE countries from MED countries speak in favor of the latter scenario. First, the CEE countries have already started their integration and convergence process, and the lion's share of migration might already have taken place at the beginning of the 1990s after the fall of the Iron Curtain. Net inflows from Poland to Germany, for example, declined from an average of 58,000 people per year in

Figure 10.13. European Union: Current Net Migration (1995–1999) and Projected Average Annual Net Migration Needs, 2000–30

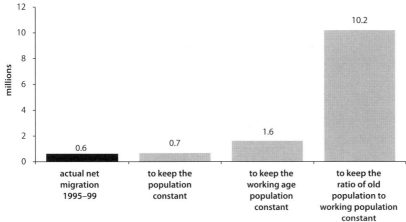

Source: Authors' estimates based on United Nations 2000.

Table 10.7. CEE Accession Countries: Labor Force Growth

	Labor force 2004 (million)	Growth rate p.a., 1999–2004	Share of EU (15) labor force, 2004
Czech Rep.	5.4	−0.1%	2.8%
Hungary	4.4	0.4%	2.3%
Poland	19.8	−0.2%	9.5%

Source: World Bank 2006.

1989–1991, to 15,000 in1999–2001 (OECD, 2003). Second, the accession countries are also at a much higher per capita income than the MED countries and, following the pattern of the southern European countries accession, improved living conditions at home are likely to dampen the tendency to migrate. As discussed earlier, evidence suggests that trade liberalization of high-income countries with middle-income countries tends to foster convergence and discourage migration. Third, their demographic structure is mirroring that of the EU, with shrinking working populations, reducing the number of workers who would or could migrate (table 10.7). Indeed, as shown above, the accession of Greece, Portugal, and Spain in the 1980s did not lead to mass immigration, in spite of widely held fears, but had almost an opposite effect. The accession process provided better conditions in the home countries, which led people to return home to take advantage of improved prospects.

A Managed EU-MED Migration Scheme—Mid-Skilled Labor in Search of Experience

The prospects of relatively limited migration flows from CEE accession countries would open the way for migration flows from the MENA region to the EU. However, these flows should be different from previous waves of legal migration of unskilled labor, or the illegal migration flows currently taking place. In line with changing characteristics and upgrading of the education level of the MENA labor force, the new form of migration flows would consist of middle-skilled labor going to work in the formal sector, with full economic and social rights.

Focusing on managed migration to the formal sector means that only labor with some skill proficiency will be targeted. In EU, comparatively high minimum wages topped with high social security contributions (often amounting to 100 percent of wages) result in a high minimum cost per worker. The high cost of labor implies in turn that only workers with higher productivity, that is, with some skill or education level, can get jobs in the formal sector.

In these circumstances the relative importance of MENA labor inflows will be of comparatively small and manageable magnitude. Concentrating on the MED countries—the most populous countries in the MENA region, except Iran—the potential pool of migrants would be limited to the labor force with mid- to higher skill level of education. Although the share is increasing rapidly, it remains small in absolute numbers compared to the EU labor force (table 10.8).

The goals of an EU-MED migration scheme would be threefold: first, to help tighten labor markets in MENA, especially for mid-skilled workers with at least secondary education; second, help ensure that returns to education are high; third, help produce experienced investors who, when returning to their home country, would have built networks within the EU for future use in their business activities.

The design of such a scheme should take into account previous experience from migration schemes, within and outside the EU, to minimize illegal immigration and maximize the benefits for both sending and receiving countries. It would need to ensure that workers from the MED countries are channeled to sectors where they are most needed, and where their ability to gain useful work experience and contacts is high. It will also be important to put in place mechanisms that facilitate and encourage voluntary return migration: for example, by increasing business opportunities in the sending countries over the long term. The migration scheme would thus be an integral part of the EU-MED agenda, complementing other areas for cooperation, including growth-enhancing economic reforms.

A survey of international experience of migration schemes, whether for temporary and permanent, high-skilled and low-skilled workers, presents mixed results (Coulibaly 20.

A managed migration scheme that responds to EU needs for mid-skilled and skilled workers, although ensuring positive returns to migration and education for MED economies, would therefore need to contain the following provisions:

- Focus on (i) mid-skilled labor (ii) on training experience in the EU, and on (iii) encouraging return migration.

Table 10.8. Pool of Potential Migrants from MED Countries

	A. Economically active population (millions)	B. Labor force with at least secondary education (millions)	C. Unemployed with at least secondary education (millions)
Jordan	1.8	0.6	0.1
Tunisia	3.3	1.2	0.2
Egypt	22.3	9.3	1.4
Morocco	11.0	1.8	0.3
TOTAL	38.4	12.0	2.0
% of EU(15) labor force	*21.1*	*6.6*	*1.1*

Source: Labor force and unemployment numbers—Egypt, Jordan: 2004 data from WDI 2006; Morocco: 2003 data from Direction de la Statistique; Tunisia: 2001 data from World Bank 2004, EU: 2004 data from WDI 2006. Shares for LF and U by education (applied to LF numbers in column A): Egypt: 1998 data from Assaad 2000; Jordan: 2005 data from Department of Statistics; Morocco: 1999 data from Boudarbat 2005; Tunisia: 2001 data from World Bank 2004.

- In the absence of a common EU migration policy, allow for bilateral arrangements, but with the support of a common EU Fund.
- Create an EU fund for cofinancing with the private sector. This fund would be used to support the financing of both training programs, and return migration-integration of graduating trainees or returnees. A three-year trainee program could be offered to selected graduates geared toward the industry and services sectors. A shorter training opportunity could be offered to interested workers as part of company transfers under an EU-MED Guest Worker Program. Trainees would be partly funded by the EU, and partly by the private sector in the respective countries. At the end of the training program, MED country nationals who receive a job offer should have the possibility to stay.
- Provide assistance on both sides of the Mediterranean to help manage these programs and assist trainees as well as returnees in their effort to adapt and reintegrate. This would include technical and financial assistance needed by returnees.
- Establish clear and accessible information channels for prospective EU employers and MED employees. This could include a virtual market that could allow for job and skills matching and training offers made by local or foreign employers.
- MED governments must engage their responsibility and pledge their direct participation in efforts to manage and indeed encourage return migration. In addition to active participation in the scheme management together with the EU (especially jobs and skills matching, and so on), these efforts need to focus on setting the ground rules for a friendly business environment with safety nets for returnees, and facilitating the readmission of their illegal immigrants.
- This framework could be augmented with easier entry for business visits and educational purposes, which would both encourage human capital development and strengthen the personal and professional links between the regions.

The scheme would in itself be time-limited, but with stronger emphasis both on encouraging voluntary return migration, and on providing the opportunity for qualified MED country nationals to remain working in EU after the trainee period. For example, the guest worker programs in Germany and Switzerland, as well as the foreign trainee program in Japan, largely failed as temporary schemes, as there were no mechanisms in place either to integrate these workers in their host country, or to encourage (or coerce them) to return. With a rapidly aging population, the EU may be obliged to adopt a more pragmatic approach to migration. Here, the EU countries may have something to learn from the experiences of other large labor-importing regions, including the United States, Canada, and Australia, where economic migration is still possible, and where programs appear better targeted to the needs of both sending and receiving countries.

Conclusions

The EU-MED partnership needs to be revitalized and broadened if it is to fulfill its purpose of encouraging economic growth and the process of integration between the two regions. In this paper, we have suggested that the broadening take place along two parallel and complementary tracks. First, reform efforts need to be intensified, to lay the groundwork for increased private investment, economic growth, and job creation in the MED countries. Second, allowing for limited economic migration flows between the regions would ease off the demographic pressure on labor markets in the MED countries, and thus indirectly ease some of the political and social tension that are blocking reforms.

There is a need to find mechanisms that enhance the credibility of the reform programs in the MED countries. The EU-MED agenda needs to go beyond trade. On the part of the MED countries, this will require a strong early commitment by undertaking reforms in critical areas, including public sector reform. EU support should accompany rather than lead these reforms. A credible program that results in both EU official support and private FDI would further support and facilitate the reform process, creating the positive credibility feedback loop that is missing at present.

A migration program that would open up the EU labor market for mid-skilled workers in MED countries could improve labor market conditions and increase public support for both the EU-MED agreement as such, and for reform efforts more generally. The risk of brain drain, although important, must be seen in the light of what is happening at present, when new labor market entrants see their skills eroding and where an exodus of skilled labor is taking place, but with less positive spillovers than under a managed migration scheme. When economic reforms at home deliver better conditions in due time, several of these migrants are likely to return home, bringing back savings, experience, and contacts and the potential to contribute further to economic growth. This would increase the potential gains for both recipient and sending countries, and strengthen the link between the two regions.

Notes

1. Under MEDA I (1995-1999), a total of €3 billion was committed with a payment ratio of about 30 percent. Since 2000, MEDA II has been implemented. Between 2000 and 2004, €3 billion was committed, with a 77 percent payment ratio.

2. See, for example, Rodrik 1989 or 1991.

3. Note that these indices refer to reform outcomes rather than reform efforts per se.

4. The EU-Med agreements are in fact by construction, leading to a transitional increase in effective trade protection in the MED countries as the initial stages of tariff dismantling focus on intermediate and capital goods.

5. The analysis in Assaad (2000) is based on the Egypt Labor Market Survey 1998 and the Labor Force Survey of 1988. To ensure comparability between the two surveys, the author uses an extended definition of the labor force, including all employment in subsistence agriculture, and defines unemployed as those seeking work. These definitions give rise to a lower unemployment rate than would otherwise be the case.

6. Several factors will motivate international (economic) migration, including wage differentials, preferences for the home country, and the cost of migration. In a very poor country, migration to a richer area may be attractive from the point of view of wage differentials. but may be contained simply by lack of resources. In higher middle-income countries, although prospective migrants have the resources to move abroad, the wage differentials may not be a sufficient incentive, especially not if the prospects for growth in the home country are good (Schiff 1996). The highest migration pressures could therefore come from lower middle-income countries where the financial constraint is less binding, but where the wage differential still provides an incentive.

Bibliography

Adams Jr., R. 1991. "The Economic Uses and Impact of International Remittances in Rural Egypt." *Economic Development and Cultural Change* 39: 695–722.

Assaad, R. 2000. "The Transformation of the Egyptian Labor Market: 1988–1998." Middle East and North Africa Region. World Bank, Washington, DC.

Boudarbat, Brahim. 2005. "Job Search Strategies and Unemployment of University Graduates in Morocco." EBRD. May 5.

Carrington, W., and E. Detragiache. 1998. "How Extensive is the Brain Drain?" *Finance & Development* (IMF) 36:46–49.

Chandavarkar, A. 1980. "Use of Migrants' Remittances in Labor-Exporting Countries." *Finance & Development*, IMF, 17:2: 36–39.

Coulibaly, A. 2001. "A Survey of the International Experience of Migration Schemes." Mimeo. Middle East and North Africa Region. World Bank, Washington, DC.

Dustmann, C. 1996. "Return Migration: the European Experience." *Economic Policy: A European Forum* 22: 215–50.

Faini, J., and A. Venturini. 1994. "Migration and growth: The experience of Southern Europe." CEPR Discussion Paper No. 964. CEPR, London.

Faini, R., J. de Melo, and K. Zimmermann. 1999. *Migration: The Controversies and the Evidence*. CEPR, London.

Gmelch, G. 1980. "Return Migration." *Annual Review of Anthropology* (9): 135–159.

Galal, A., and B. Hoekman. 1997. *Regional Partners in Global Markets: Limits and Possibilities of the Euro-MED Agreements*. Ed. CEPR, London.

IMF. 2001. *Tunisia: Article IV*.

Rodrik, D. 1989. "Promises, Promises: Credible Policy Reform via Signaling." *The Economic Journal* (99), 1989.

————. 1991. "Policy Uncertainty and Private Investment in Developing Countries." *Journal of Development Economics* 36 (2)..

Schiff, M. 1996. "North South Migration and Trade: A Survey." Working paper 1696, Research Department. World Bank, Washington, DC.

Sondergaard, L. 2001. "Private Investment in Egypt, Morocco and Tunisia." Mimeo, Middle East and North Africa Region. World Bank, Washington, DC.

Stalker, P. 2000. *Workers without frontiers: the impact of globalization on international migration*. ILO, Geneva.

Taylor, A., and J. Williamson. 1994. "Convergence in the Age of Mass Migration." NBER working paper 4711. NBER, New York.

World Bank. 2000. *Trade Blocs*. Washington, DC.

World Bank Employment Study. 2003. *Unlocking the Employment Potential in the Middle East and North Africa: Toward a New Social Contract*. MENA Development Report. World Bank, Washington, DC.

World Bank. 2004. Tunisia Employment.

United Nations. 2000. *Replacement Migration*. New York.

Data sources

World Development Indicators Database. 2006. World Bank, Washington, DC.

United Nations ComTrade Database. 2001. United Nations, New York.

Labor Statistics Database. 2001. International Labour Organization, Geneva.

Main Economic Indicators. 2006. Organisation for Economic Co-operation and Development.

Trends in International Migration. 2003. Organisation for Economic Co-operation and Development, Paris.

Part III

Trade, Competitiveness, and Investment

11

Cruise Control, Shock Absorbers, and Traffic Lights

The Macroeconomic Road to Arab Competitiveness

Mustapha K. Nabli

Good afternoon. I am sincerely happy to be here today to talk to this diverse and distinguished group. The topic of competitiveness, and a conference devoted exclusively to the subject, I think, is well overdue for the region. I also think it is a good omen that the meeting has been designated the "First Arab World Competitiveness Meeting," so I'm encouraged that we can anticipate sequels to this forum in the future.

This lunchtime dialogue has been set aside to discuss some of the macroeconomic drivers of competitiveness. I found myself uncomfortable with the term drivers, because I think it creates an inaccurate picture of the process by which an economy becomes internationally competitive.

The road to competitiveness is a long journey, and as such requires responsible macroeconomic policy and a supportive business environment to facilitate long-term planning, promote investment and knowledge transfer, and support the efficient allocation of resources to ensure that the drivers reach the intended destination.

And the drivers on this road trip to competitiveness are the firms— enterprises that find ways to create increasing value added, through their ability to invent products, adopt new technologies, and respond to changes in market conditions at home and abroad.

Speech for the first Arab World Competitiveness Meeting at the World Economic Forum; Geneva, Switzerland; September 9, 2002.

So let me build on this analogy of a road trip and focus on what I think are three of the key forces in the macroeconomic arena that determine whether the drivers on the road to competitiveness are best equipped to succeed on this challenging expedition of long drives, unexpected terrain, and the satisfaction of an ever-approaching destination.

In my mind, one of the central requisites for competitiveness is appropriate exchange rate management. In a sense, it is the choice between working the brake and gas pedals yourself to determine your speed—or relying on cruise control to do it for you.

And what are the pitfalls that can develop from inappropriate exchange rate management? The most important, in my mind, is an overvaluation of the currency. From almost all assessments of economic policy and performance throughout the world, it has been shown that best performers are countries that have maintained an "appropriate" exchange rate regime. In particular, countries that have been successful in promoting manufactured exports have avoided exchange rate overvaluation.

Profitability of production hinges on prices—prices of inputs that go into the production process, and the price that can be obtained in the market for output. Overvaluation is damaging to competitiveness because it artificially alters the price ratio between tradables and nontradables. So the producers of tradable goods find they are less able to compete with either imported goods or with other countries' exports.

Economies that, in reality, have cost advantages in labor and domestically produced inputs begin altering their production processes and substituting for capital equipment and imported inputs. And the greater the overvaluation that takes place, the more difficult it becomes for the existing drivers of competitiveness to maintain their competitive edge, and the more it discourages new drivers from getting on the road.

What has been the experience of the Middle East and North Africa region (MENA) with exchange rate management? In a recent paper I co-wrote, we examined this issue by looking at the degree of exchange rate misalignment in the region. What we found is discouraging. In the past three decades, MENA countries experienced substantial overvaluation of their exchange rate—around 29 percent a year from the mid-1970s to the mid-1980s, and 22 percent a year from the mid-1980s to 1999. Currency overvaluation has been prevalent in MENA for a long time, unlike in most other regions, and especially relative to trends in the past few years.

What accounts for the significant overvaluation that has prevailed in MENA? In my opinion, it is almost wholly the result of relying on fixed exchange rate regimes that no longer are appropriate for responsible economic management.

Prior to the late 1980s and early 1990s, most economies in MENA opted for a fixed exchange rate regime as the most effective strategy for combating high inflation.

The adoption of fixed exchange rates, either de facto or de jure, was successful in contributing to macroeconomic stability. However, once the immediate threats of inflation running out of control had been averted, only a handful of countries shifted to more flexible exchange rate arrangements.

From the battery of empirical investigations looking at the subject, a central piece of evidence has emerged: Exchange rates are overwhelmingly more likely to become overvalued under fixed systems than under more flexible ones.

In the analogy of the road trip, the choice of the exchange rate regime is akin to relying on cruise control to determine your speed of travel. While taking pressure off the driver of the vehicle, the cruise control option does not take into account weather conditions, the terrain of the road, or other vehicles in your path. If your foot is not free to access the gas and break pedals, you can't change gears, limiting your maneuverability options.

And so it has been in the MENA economies, having to adjust the exchange rate periodically as it has gotten off course. But these fixes are only temporary and do not wholly address the problem. Moreover, these ad hoc adjustments to the exchange rate discourage the entry of companies into the export market, since exchange rate volatility sends confusing signals to economic agents and raises the uncertainty of long-run investment in producing tradable goods.

My point: Keep your foot on the gas pedal. Choose an exchange rate system that will suffer from fewer limitations and distortions, so that economic agents—these drivers of competitiveness—know where their true cost advantages lie, and are able to make decisions based on those advantages.

The second issue on which I would like to focus is what I would compare to driving through rough and rocky terrain on the road to competitiveness: MENA countries have historically suffered from excessive volatility in output and external balances.

In the 1970s and 1980s, output was more volatile in MENA than in Latin America or in East Asia and the Pacific. And although volatility has fallen in the 1990s, it still exceeds, by far, the world average.

There are several reasons behind the high volatility in MENA. First, countries in the region remain relatively undiversified and dependent on a few export commodities that often experience strong fluctuations in relative prices. Oil prices in particular have tended to cause sharp fluctuations in fiscal and external accounts, either through direct dependence on oil revenues or through strong linkages between oil producers and other countries in the region through trade, financial and labor flows, including workers' remittances.

Moreover, several countries in the region are subject to frequent droughts, which in turn produce sharp cuts in rural incomes and agricultural production. Volatility is higher in agriculture than in any other sector, and agricultural volatility is the main force behind output fluctuations in many non-oil-exporting countries. Morocco, for example, experienced as many as five droughts in the 1990s, and booms and busts in total output were correlated directed with these droughts.

In addition, most countries in MENA are adversely affected by the instability of regional security, either directly, by association, or through the various economic linkages within the region. For those areas directly affected by conflict, the economic costs of an interrupted and damaged economic structure have been very high. But almost all countries have been affected by association, through lower tourism revenues, and more generally through lower confidence in their economies, bringing down private domestic investment and foreign direct investment, and so forth.

What is the cost of volatility to competitiveness? Perhaps the biggest cost is lower investment from domestic and external sources. An economic slowdown and drop in private consumption trigger a response by businesses to cut their expenses and investments to adapt to declining demand. Weaker business activity further dampens consumer confidence, exacerbating the recession. At the same time, the effect on investment is not altogether compensated for by a commensurate economic boom the following period.

In addition to capacity constraints, volatility dampens investment because economic agents cannot be certain that a recovery is sustainable. So businesses tend to adapt their investment decisions more to the downswing in the business cycle than the upswing. This dampening effect on investment, particularly foreign investment, makes competitiveness for existing companies in the region substantially more difficult, with fewer opportunities for information flows between economic agents, and thus fewer opportunities to tap into the technological, organizational, and managerial capabilities of other companies.

I compare the volatility in output growth and external balances to driving on a segment of the road that is full of potholes and fallen rocks. Volatility creates a lack of confidence in the road trip altogether. And while ensuring that the vehicle is equipped with the appropriate shock absorbers is a multistep process, including diversifying economic structures and stabilizing the security environment in the region, there are other steps that can be taken on the macroeconomic policy front to mitigate the effects of volatility.

In particular, monetary and fiscal (and even exchange rate) policies are often a transmission channel for external shocks. Weak policies amplify the impact of volatility as it is transmitted to the economy. In some MENA countries, procyclical fiscal policies have historically acted as an important amplifier of terms of trade shocks. The absence of mechanisms for intertemporal government smoothing of revenue shocks has in turn rendered government expenditures very volatile in the past, and although public expenditures volatility was reduced in the 1990s compared to earlier decades, it was still twice as high as output volatility.

There exist mechanisms that reduce both revenue uncertainty and the transfer of volatility from revenue to expenditure levels, some of which have been applied by natural resource-dependent countries. These include market-based options such as hedging and stabilization funds. The latter have been favored by developing countries like Venezuela (oil) and Chile (copper), and have recently been implemented by Algeria. These types of mechanisms need to be explored throughout the region.

More generally, my advice on volatility follows my road trip analogy. If the journey takes you through rough terrain, then you are better off insuring the proper mechanics are in place to handle it than to wait for an accident. And detours and bypasses, while not ideal, can still ensure that the trip is taken and the journey is completed.

Finally, I come to my third point about the road to competitiveness. In the long run, that road is built on raising productivity. Period. As has been the case since the industrial revolution at least, productivity is the fundamental source of competitiveness.

Our own institution recently looked at productivity growth in MENA over the past four decades—from the 1960s to the 1990s. What we found was interesting. While the region experienced negative productivity growth over both the 1970s and 1980s, there was substantial improvement in productivity growth in the 1990s. This is the good news.

The more disappointing news is that, despite this almost universal turn-around in productivity growth, it has failed to generate a comparable private sector investment response. In fact, investment per worker declined from the 1980s to the 1990s in 8 out of 10 countries. As a result, there has been no growth "pay-off" from the accumulation of productive, privately owned capital.

What is preventing the private sector from responding? Clearly, private investment depends on a host of factors. They encompass the range of reforms that are needed to create an environment in which private investments in value-creating industries can thrive. I will focus here on one area in particular. These are what I call the traffic signals on the road to competitiveness: that is, the systems of governance and the related matters of legal and regulatory reform.

To begin with, there is little doubt that the current systems of governance in MENA stifle the development of a private sector. Chief among the governance problems is the issue of state capture, where groups of influential businesses (whether public or private) exercise effective control over rules and regulations, and utilize them to profit at the expense of the rest of the private sector. Glaring examples of this are infrastructure and telecommunications, but the list extends to taxes, licensing, and manipulating the loopholes within the system.

The privileges extended to some elite firms prevent other entrepreneurs from entering and competing. But the damage extends beyond competition. The process of reform also suffers when time and resources are wasted on maintaining unfair advantages and restricting access to consumers. Rent-seeking behavior in government is rewarded, reformers are discouraged, and needed changes in governance are delayed, or worse, derailed altogether.

Related to this, there is the host of reforms that are needed in the area of the legal and regulatory framework. In many of the MENA economies, there are some reforms underway to revise and modernize company laws, investment codes, and customs and tax regulations. Some of these reforms are being considered in connection with accession to the World Trade Organization or European Union membership.

But as a whole, the business environment in MENA is plagued by burdensome regulations. In Egypt, entrepreneurs spend about 30 percent of their time resolving problems of regulatory compliance. In Morocco, it still takes up to six months to register a business.

Transparency of regulations is also a problem. In a survey of businesses in Lebanon, 62 percent of businesses admitted they had paid bribes to state employees. And 70 percent of respondents knew in advance how much they would have to pay to get a transaction through the bureaucracy.

To create an enabling environment for the private sector, the MENA region needs to insure that the road to competitiveness is not full of yield signs, red lights, and one-way streets. It needs to create the reforms that can eliminate the gridlock of honking cars and unnecessary U-turns that currently hinder the speed of the traveler, and hinder the rate of private sector growth.

So, these are just a few of the reforms that come to mind as being essential for making the road more attractive to domestic and foreign private investors.

In an age of instant communication and supersonic travel, the lure of the open road has been eclipsed by the conveniences of expediency. But economic competitiveness cannot be achieved through shortcuts or alternatives. A successful end must have a successful beginning, and a successful middle, as well. If this conference has established nothing else, it has confirmed the responsibility of macroeconomic policy to provide the essential background forces.

12

Trade, Foreign Direct Investment, and Development in the Middle East and North Africa

Farrukh Iqbal*
Mustapha Kamel Nabli

Even a casual observer of international development trends cannot fail to notice that, in the last two decades or so, the MENA region[1] has lagged most other regions of the world in both development outcomes (such as growth and employment) and international integration (such as trade and foreign investment). This paper argues that these two phenomena are linked, and that the region's weak development performance originated in part from its inability to engage substantially with the rest of the world at a time when such engagement was the main engine of rapid economic growth for a large number of developing countries.

The plan of the paper is as follows. In the next section, we review the development performance of the MENA region and show that it has been trapped in a slow growth and high unemployment situation since the early 1980s. In the following section, we review trade and foreign investment links and show that the region has not participated significantly in the huge growth of trade and investment flows that have taken place in the last two decades. In the fourth section, we connect these two sets of observations through a review of

*World Bank.

Prepared for the conference *The Middle East and North Africa Region: The Challenges of Growth and Globalization,* organized by the International Monetary Fund and held in Washington, DC, on April 7-8, 2004. This paper was drawn from *Trade, Investment, and Development in the Middle East and North Africa: Engaging with the World* (World Bank, 2003). The main authors of the report were Dipak Dasgupta and Mustapha Kamel Nabli. Reprinted by permission from the World Bank.

international evidence linking growth and employment to trade openness and investment climate. The review shows that openness and investment climate are complementary in their effect on development performance. Indeed, a good investment climate is a prerequisite for obtaining the full benefits of an open trade environment. We briefly assess the investment climate in the MENA region and conclude that, despite some improvements in the last two decades, the region still lags in this respect. Finally, in the last section, we simulate the expected impact on growth and employment of further trade and investment integration for the region.

MENA's Record in Growth, Employment, and Poverty

Figure 12.1 provides a view of growth performance in the MENA region between 1963 and 2000.[2] This extended perspective allows one to see both the oil-price-supported boom of the 1970s and the slow growth trend thereafter. For the past decade, the average growth rate of the region has been around 3.3 percent per annum. This translates into a per capita growth rate of around 1.2 percent.

Figure 12.2 provides a comparison of MENA's growth during the 1990s with that of other regions. The MENA region's per capita growth rate of 1.2 percent is worse than that of such regions as Latin America, South Asia, and East Asia. It is better only than that of Sub-Saharan Africa and the Europe/Central Asia region. The latter spent most the decade in the throes of

Figure 12.1. GDP Growth Rates for Selected MENA Countries (1963–2000)

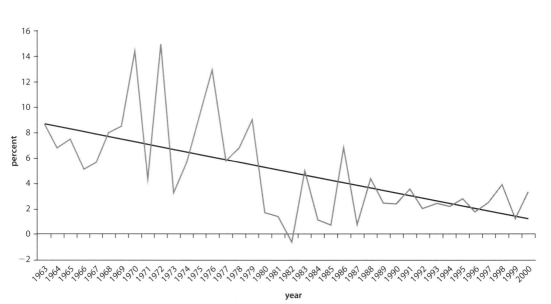

Note: Includes Algeria, Egypt, Kuwait, Oman, Morocco, Saudi Arabia, Syria, and Tunisia.

Figure 12.2. Comparative per Capita Growth Rates (1990–2000)

Source: World Bank, 2003, Appendix Table 1, p. 228.

a wrenching transition away from state-dominated economies. In recent years, however, several Eastern European countries have posted high growth rates and appear set to become much more integrated into the world trading and investment system. This observation applies in particular to such countries as Hungary, Poland, and the Czech Republic, which have been granted accession to the European Union.

Weak growth has been reflected as well in high unemployment. While there is a demographic aspect to this, in that the region's fertility rates have been relatively high, there is no denying that slow overall economic growth has meant that the demand for labor, especially in the private sector, has failed to keep pace with the large numbers of people joining the labor force. Figure 12.3 shows how serious the problem of unemployment has become in the region.

Figure 12.3. Unemployment Rates in MENA (1980–2000)

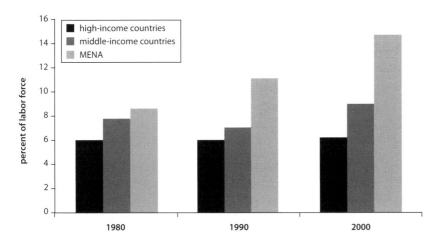

Table 12.1. Comparative Poverty Reduction Performance (1990-2000)

	$1 poverty index		$2 poverty index	
	1990	2000	1990	2000
East Asia	29.4	14.5	68.5	48.3
Europe/Central Asia	1.4	4.2	6.8	21.3
Latin America	11	10.8	27.6	26.3
MENA	2.1	2.8	21	24.4
South Asia	41.5	31.9	86.3	77.7
Africa	47.4	49	76	76.5

Source: Global Economic Prospects, World Bank, 2004.

The average unemployment rate is over 14 percent currently, with some countries, such as Algeria, reaching rates as high as 29 percent.

Finally, it is instructive to consider the region's performance in poverty reduction. Here the region appears to have done much better than its growth and employment situation would suggest (see table 12.1). Measured by the US$1 per person per day criterion, the region's poverty rate is around 2.8 percent currently. This is the lowest comparedwith other regions. Measured by the US$2 criterion as well, MENA fares comparatively well, although the absolute rate of poverty jumps to around 24 percent. However, the trend over time is not comforting. Between 1990 and 2000, there was an increase in poverty (by both criteria). If weak growth persists over the next decade or so, the poverty rate will continue to increase, and the region will begin to look much worse in comparison with its own past and with several other regions.

Trade and Foreign Investment Performance

Trade Performance

Overall trade. Countries in the region differ significantly in relative endowments of natural resources and labor. Some are resource-poor with abundant labor—Egypt, Jordan, Lebanon, Morocco, and Tunisia. Some are resource-rich with abundant labor—Algeria, Iran, Syria, and Yemen (as a special low-income case). And some are labor-importing and resource-rich—the GCC countries. Despite the diversity of country characteristics, trade outcomes are fairly common throughout the region. The past two decades have largely featured missed opportunities in trade integration—worse for the resource-rich and labor-abundant countries, and somewhat better among the resource-poor countries, with the GCC falling in between. The MENA region clearly failed to ride the wave of globalization that began in the mid-1980s. While world trade rose by around 8 percent in the 1990s, MENA's trade with the world rose by only 3 percent (figures 12.4 and 12.5).

Figure 12.4. Trade Performance of MENA Countries

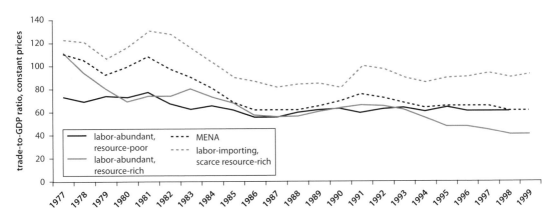

Source: World Bank, 2003, p.74.

Nonoil exports. A significant portion of the trade of the MENA region is made up of oil and oil-related products whose value fluctuates with the price of oil. To fully appreciate the role of policy in determining exports, it is necessary to focus on the performance of the nonoil component of exports. Figure 12.6 shows that while overall merchandise exports have fluctuated between 32 percent and 17 percent of GDP, most likely depending on the price of oil at any given time, nonoil exports have stayed at a steady and low rate of around 7 percent of GDP since the early 1980s. There is no evidence that the nonoil exports sector has grown systematically since the 1970s to offset the relative decline of oil exports and form a substantial new base of export earnings for the region. Whatever policies have been introduced over this period have clearly not succeeded in generating a higher ratio of nonoil exports.

Figure 12.5. Exports (as Percent of GDP) Middle East and North Africa

All Countries

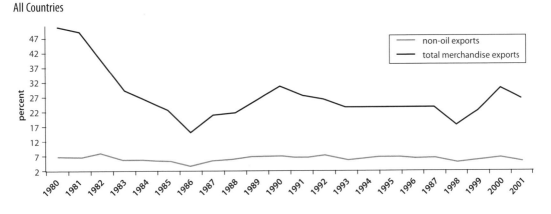

Figure 12.6. Comparative Nonoil Exports, 2000

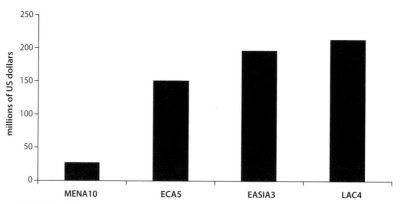

Source: World Bank, 2003, p.42.
Note: ECA5 is the Czech Republic, Hungary, Poland, Russia, and Turkey. EASIA3 is Indonesia, Malaysia, and Thailand. LAC4 is Bolivia, Chile, Mexico, and Brazil.

Another way to measure trade performance is to compare across regions. Figure 12.7 provides such a comparison in the case of nonoil exports. Total nonoil exports of the MENA region amounted to about $28 billion in 2000 (excluding re-exports). For a middle-income region with nearly 300 million people and with good resource endowments, this is a small fraction of potential. Finland, with 5 million people, has almost twice the nonoil exports of the entire MENA region. And Hungary and the Czech Republic, with populations

Figure 12.7. MENA Nonoil Export Potential, Conditioned on per Capita Incomes, Natural Resources, and Population, 2000

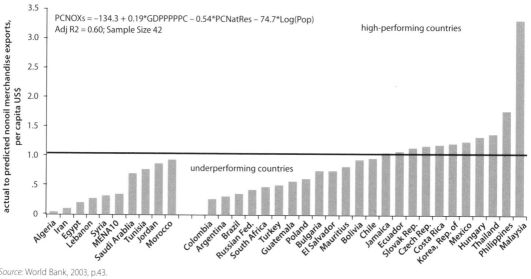

Source: World Bank, 2003, p.43.
Note: Regression is based on 42 countries, but values for 8 low-income countries (Bangladesh, Cameroon, Côte d'Ivoire, Ghana, India, Indonesia, Pakistan, and Yemen) are not reported because of negative values.

of about 10 million, each had greater nonoil exports than the region. Nonoil exports from the MENA region are vastly smaller than those from other sub-regions with similar populations and resource endowments. For example, a group of five Eastern European countries—the Czech Republic, Hungary, Poland, Russia, and Turkey, with a similar population of 270 million—had nonoil exports of $151 billion, five times more than MENA's. Three Southeast Asian countries—Indonesia, Malaysia, and Thailand—had nonoil exports of $197 billion, seven times more than MENA's. And four Latin American countries—Bolivia, Chile, Mexico, and Brazil—had nonoil exports of $213 billion, eight times more than MENA's .

Nonoil exports relative to potential. The analytical basis for such a comparison can be extended more carefully by conditioning per capita nonoil exports on per capita incomes (as a proxy for overall skills and institutional endowments that influence the capacity to export), and on natural resources endowments (measured by the value of resource-based exports, mainly oil and minerals) and population. For some 42 mostly middle-income countries (including the MENA countries), the results suggest a strong positive association of per capita nonoil exports with per capita incomes, a negative association with natural resource endowments and population size. That is expected, since higher skills and institutional endowments should support higher exports, while greater natural resource rents should appear in less intensity of effort to export non-natural resource exports. And larger countries tend to trade less. For the MENA countries, their nonoil exports are, on average, one-third of their predicted levels. Only Jordan and Morocco had exports close to what would be predicted. The world's three biggest underperformers are MENA countries (Algeria, Iran, and Egypt), and the other MENA countries are all also underperformers.

Manufactured imports relative to potential. Trade has impacts much bigger than those captured by export performance. When firms can get imported inputs at world prices and quality, the knowledge embodied in goods and services is transferred from the rest of the world to the domestic economies—the productivity and knowledge-enhancing spillover of trade. When consumers can buy goods and services produced more efficiently in the rest of the world, they benefit from lower prices and better quality. But the biggest benefit of trade is that it allows countries to specialize in the production of goods and services that rely most more intensively on their most abundant resource—for MENA, labor—and import more of its least abundant resource—for MENA, capital and, increasingly, knowledge-intensive goods and services. Barriers that impede trade therefore impede potential gains in knowledge, consumer welfare, and labor productivity.

The relative openness of countries to imports can be measured by comparing actual imports versus a predicted level of imports conditioned on per capita incomes (where a higher level of incomes should be associated with a higher level of imports) and population (to the extent that larger countries tend to trade less). For the same group of 42 mostly middle-income countries, per capita manufacturing imports in the MENA region were about half of their predicted levels in 2000, confirming again that the region trades far less than its potential (figure 12.8). Once again, Iran, Algeria, and Syria have extremely low actual levels of imports, implying relatively closed trade regimes. Others also fall surprisingly below predicted levels, including Egypt, Jordan, Saudi Arabia, Morocco, and Tunisia. Only Lebanon is more open than expected.

Trade in services. The MENA region has been losing world market shares in exports of services. In contrast, comparators in both East Asia and Pacific, and Eastern Europe and Central Asian regions, have more than doubled their world market shares (figure 12.9).

Tourism, the main service export of the MENA region, has fluctuated between 3 and 4 percent of GDP during the 1990s. Some other regions have done better. Eastern Europe and Central Asian region (ECA4), a competing destination for tourists from Europe, had a threefold increase in the share of tourism receipts to GDP, overtaking all other regions. Also, while world tourism trade has expanded fivefold in the last 20 years, MENA's market share has declined from 3.4 percent in 1987 to around 2.6 percent in 2000. But with a favorable endowment of world heritage sites and a home to some of the

Figure12.8. MENA's Import Potential, Conditioned on per Capita Income and Population, 2000

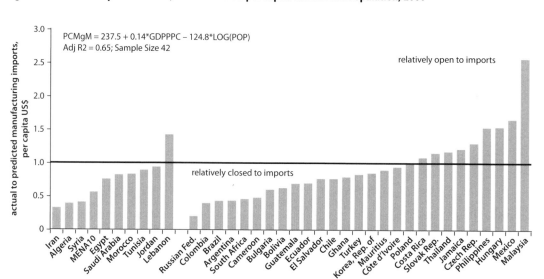

Source: World Bank, 2003, p.45.
Note: Regression is based on 42 countries; values for 6 low-income countries (Bangladesh, China, India, Indonesia, Pakistan, and Yemen) are not reported because of negative values.

Figure12. 9. MENA's Share of World Exports of Services

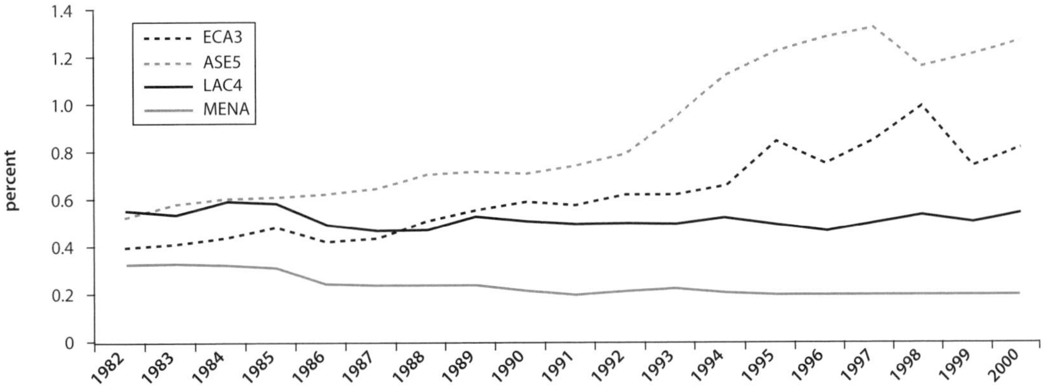

Source: World Bank, 2003, p.85
Note: ECA 4 is Czech Republic, Turkey, Poland, and Hungary. EA5 is China, Indonesia, Republic of Korea, Malaysia, and Thailand. LAC4 is Argentina, Brazil, Chile, and Mexico.

world's key religions and civilizations, the tourism potential of MENA region remains significant. Regional conflicts may have discouraged tourists from visiting in larger numbers, but infrastructure and marketing efforts have proved successful in some countries, such as Jordan.

Foreign Direct Investment (FDI) Performance

The MENA region is not well connected with global investment and production chains. This is evident from the limited role played in the region's economies by foreign direct investment and by trade in parts and components. Integration with global private capital flow markets has also been relatively stagnant, in sharp contrast to comparable country groups. Net FDI inflows to MENA (measured as a share of PPP GDP) were consistently less than half a percentage point of GDP for most of the period (figure 12.10). In the early 1980s this put MENA roughly on par with comparable groups. But in the next 15 years, the average of the other comparators had risen to between 1.0 to 2.5 percent, while MENA continued to trail at around 0.5 percent.

The MENA region, excluding the Gulf countries, received net inflows of FDI of about $2.2 billion in 2000—slightly more than 1 percent of the $158 billion to all developing countries, and one-sixth of their share (7 percent) in the GDP of all developing countries. The group of five Eastern European countries (Czech Republic, Hungary, Poland, Turkey, and Russia) together received some $19 billion, nine times more than MENA. The three East Asian countries (Malaysia, Philippines, and Thailand) received more than US$8 billion in inflows, four times more than MENA. And the group of four Latin American countries (Bolivia, Chile, Mexico, and Brazil) received about US$50 billion, more than 22 times the inflows to the MENA region. These compar-

Figure 12.10. Net FDI Flows to MENA and Other Regions

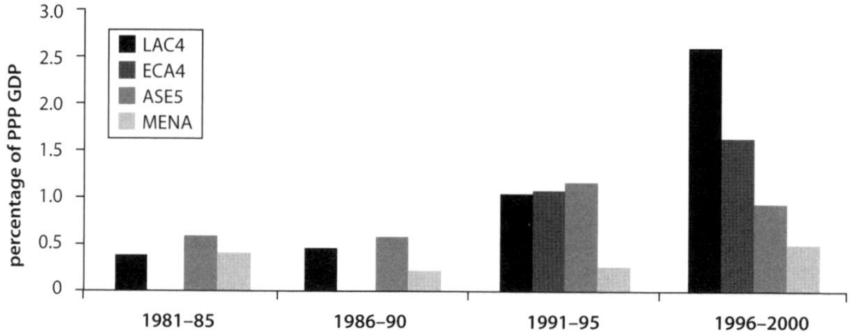

Source: World Bank 2003, p.80.
Note: ECA 4 is Czech Republic, Turkey, Poland, and Hungary. EA5 is China, Indonesia, Republic of Korea, Malaysia, and Thailand. LAC4 is Argentina, Brazil, Chile, and Mexico.

isons provide some indication of the huge potential for expanding inflows of FDI to the MENA region. A large part of these inflows came from (neighboring) high-income Europe. Egypt accounted for about half the MENA total (US$1.2 billion), and Tunisia and Jordan about a quarter each (US$750 million and US$560 million, respectively). The rest received very small amounts or even had significant outflows (Yemen).

Potential for foreign direct investment. The potential for higher inflows by country can be determined by conditioning FDI inflows on nonoil trade performance (measured by nonoil export to PPP GDP ratios), natural resources, and population. FDI inflows are known to be closely related to trade flows, so the predicted levels of FDI should be associated with trade. Natural resource endowments often also lead to higher levels of foreign investment, albeit of different types of flows. And size may matter, with larger countries expected to receive higher investment inflows (market-seeking investments); but because this is already accounted for by measuring FDI inflows relative to GDP, the residual population variable may or may not be significant. The results for 42 countries are largely in accord with expectations: trade and natural resources raise FDI flows, but size turns out to be a negative influence.

How do the actual inflows of FDI to MENA countries look in relation to expected inflows, once nonoil trade, natural resources, and population are factored in? First, only Jordan, Lebanon, and Tunisia (small resource-poor countries) do as well or slightly less well than expected (figure 12.11). Morocco is a surprise in how little it receives in FDI inflows (at least for 1998–2000); Egypt receives more, possibly given its larger size, but still well below expected levels. Second, among the countries with large natural resource endowments, Saudi Arabia is the only country that receives relatively high FDI, led by its oil sector. All the larger oil-producing countries

Figure 12.11.   Foreign Direct Investment Potential, Conditioned on Openness, Natural Resources, and Population, 2000

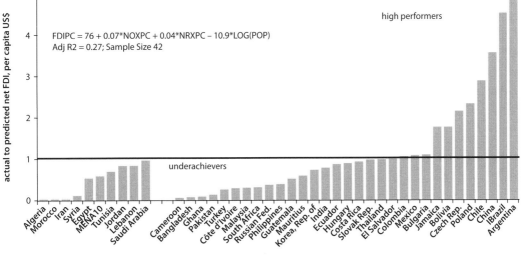

$$FDIPC = 76 + 0.07*NOXPC + 0.04*NRXPC - 10.9*LOG(POP)$$
Adj R2 = 0.27; Sample Size 42

Source: World Bank, 2003, p.49.

Note: Regression is based on 42 countries; values for 2 low-income countries (Indonesia and Yemen) are not reported because of negative values.

(Algeria, Iran, Syria, Yemen) receive very low FDI relative to expected levels. Third, for the MENA countries as a whole, FDI inflows are only about half what they should be. In comparison, Chile receives three times as much FDI as expected, and the Czech Republic twice as much. Others, such as China, Brazil, and Argentina, receive FDI inflows four to five times their expected levels. The FDI gap for MENA also shows investment climate barriers in these countries, since the gap in potential already takes into account their very low nonoil trade. If their nonoil trade were higher and if the investment climate were better, the region could expect FDI inflows at least four to five times the current level—or some 3 percent of GDP on average, compared with the current 0.5 percent of GDP.

MENA's Participation in Global Production Chains

The region as a whole has a very large negative trade balance with OECD countries in trade in parts and components (US$14 billion), with imports accounting for about 15 times the value of exports to these countries. In contrast, China and Malaysia have exports of parts and components to the OECD that are twice as large as their imports. The MENA region thus participates very little in global production sharing, exporting primarily low-value finished goods, and importing parts and components for an inefficient manufacturing base—typical of inward-looking, import-substitution economies (table 12.2).

Table 12.2. The Relative Importance of Parts and Components in MENA Countries

| Country | Value of parts and components in OECD trade ($ million) | | | | Share of parts and components in all manufacture (%) | | | |
| | Exports | | Imports | | Exports | | Imports | |
	1988	2000	1988	2000	1988	2000	1988	2000
Algeria	6	7	943	994	2.6	2.8	23.5	18.7
Bahrain	39	24	156	208	19.6	6.9	18.1	16.5
Egypt	19	54	1,279	2,142	4.3	3.1	23.5	24.7
Iran	8	18	941	1,311	1.7	2.2	21.1	25.6
Jordan	25	21	301	276	20.2	8.5	21.0	18.4
Kuwait	42	8	437	505	38.0	3.9	15.4	17.0
Lebanon	3	9	80	242	1.5	3.5	7.6	11.8
Libya	10	6	560	369	3.8	1.6	16.3	21.3
Morocco	33	105	421	1,231	2.1	2.5	14.4	19.2
Oman	22	45	208	330	8.3	14.0	15.2	18.8
Qatar	6	17	115	300	11.1	3.7	16.6	20.4
Saudi Arabia	73	213	1,941	3,298	3.6	7.1	13.5	19.0
Syria	1	9	148	338	4.5	2.7	16.2	21.5
Tunisia	72	332	330	859	5.5	7.4	15.8	14.4
United Arab Emirates	31	208	714	2,919	12.2	10.9	16.7	20.8
Yemen Rep.	2	1	61	105	47.0	6.7	15.5	19.6
MENA	391	1,078	8,635	15,430	5.2	5.7	17.1	19.9
Labor-abundant, resource-poor	151	521	2,411	4,751	4.2	4.7	18.6	19.3
Labor-abundant, resource-rich	17	35	2,094	2,748	2.4	2.5	21.4	21.9
Labor-importing, resource-rich	171	508	3,133	7,057	6.1	8.4	14.5	19.7
Memo Items:								
China	379	25,409	2,237	16,091	1.9	11.9	11.1	25.6
Japan	34,212	51,583	5,373	17,268	20.4	20.3	13.5	21.1
Republic of Korea	2,841	15,720	5,077	11,128	6.7	18.3	19.4	17.6
Malaysia	452	11,526	1,241	6,959	7.7	22.5	18.8	23.1
Singapore	4,425	9,584	4,492	10,877	32.8	23.4	25.1	22.9
Taiwan, China	5,231	21,369	4,265	11,208	11.5	24.3	17.2	17.1

Source: World Bank, 2003, p. 81.

Trade Policy, Investment Climate, and Growth Performance

Trade Protection

Of the many factors that affect trade outcomes, price-related ones are usually among the most important. The prices of tradable goods and services are strongly affected by tariff levels and non-tariff barriers, as well as by real effective exchange rates, which are themselves influenced by macroeconomic policies and conditions. In general, trade protection is high for the developing countries in MENA relative to their income levels. Comparing over regions and over time, we find that MENA trade barriers have been the slowest to come down, and there have been episodes as well of reversals in policy during the 1990s. Exchange rate misalignments, in several countries and over significant periods, have also affected trade performance.

High protection. Trade protection can be shown by a variety of measures reflecting tariff rates and the tariff equivalents of non-tariff barriers. Table 12.3 presents data for MENA and several comparator groups, using several different measures whose derivations are described in the notes to the table. All the measures show a similar ranking. Key results include:

- Average nontariff barrier protection is higher in MENA than in other lower-middle-income countries; indeed, it is higher than in all other regions of the world except Latin America.
- Average MENA trade protection, measured in terms of Anderson-Neary Ideal Measure, is one-quarter above the comparable average for lower middle-income countries; it is also higher than in all other comparator groups.

Table 12.3. Trade Protection Indicators for MENA

(Most recent year)

	Simple average	Weighted average	Standard deviation	NTB coverage	Anderson-Neary Ideal Measure
Algeria	22.4	15.0	14.3	15.8	20.0
Bahrain	8.8	..	..	..	..
Egypt	20.5	13.8	39.5	28.8	19.0
Iran	4.9	3.1	4.2	..	..
Jordan	16.2	13.5	15.6	0.0	..
Lebanon	8.3	12.0	11.2	..	22.2
Morocco	32.6	25.4	20.5	5.5	25.9
Oman	4.7	4.5	1.2	13.1	4.4
Saudi Arabia	12.3	10.5	3.1	15.6	11.0
Syria	21.0	..	..	..	..
Tunisia	30.1	26.3	12.6	32.8	19.2
MENA	**16.5**	**13.8**	**13.6**	**15.9**	**17.4**
ECA4	**12.9**	**7.2**	**18.3**	**12.4**	**3.5**
LAC4	**12.2**	**12.9**	**6.9**	**48.4**	**13.9**
EA5	**11.3**	**8.3**	**17.9**	**13.5**	**6.0**
LMIC	**15.3**	**12.5**	**15.0**	**13.4**	**13.2**

Source: World Bank, 2003, p.103.

Notes: Tariff rates used are most favored nation tariff rates. Nontariff barrier coverage refers to the number of tariff lines that have at least one nontariff barrier. The Anderson and Neary Ideal Protection Measure is the uniform tariff rate that must be applied to the free-trade regime, as a compensating variation to return welfare to most recent year of observation. The comparators are ECA4 (Czech Republic, Turkey, Poland, and Hungary), LAC4 (Argentina, Brazil, Chile, and Mexico) and EA5 (China, Indonesia, Thailand, Malaysia, and Republic of Korea). LMIC refers to lower-middle-income countries (with GNI per capita in the range $746-$2975). The comparator numbers are simple averages of the data for the respective countries they represent.

- Tunisia and Morocco have among the highest protection rates in MENA (and the world) despite several reform episodes since the early 1980s, while Egypt has the highest dispersion of tariff rates.
- On the positive side, Oman and Saudi Arabia, two oil-rich countries, have lower protection than the average for upper-middle-income comparators.

With respect to nontariff barriers, the typical experience in recent years is one of improvement. In Tunisia, extensive quantitative restrictions (affecting some 90 percent of domestic output) have progressively been reduced (textiles, passenger cars, agricultural products) in the 1990s. In Morocco, most quantitative restrictions have been eliminated. In Algeria, quantitative restrictions have been reduced, although temporary reversals occur and prior authorization lists still exist for some items. In Jordan, removal of quantitative restrictions was the main item of trade liberalization in 1988 and reduced coverage from 40 percent to 7 percent of production; most remaining quantitative restrictions have been eliminated since 1995. In Egypt, import licensing was eliminated in 1993 and the scope of quantitative restrictions progressively reduced. In Lebanon, some import licensing and multiple authorizations remain. Syria has several lists of goods with import eligibility requirements (public sector, private sector, and two negative or banned lists) with a general licensing requirement for all imports.

Exchange Rate Management

During the past three decades, many MENA countries experienced substantial overvaluation of their real exchange rate—around 29 percent a year from the mid-1970s to the mid-1980s, and 22 percent a year from the mid-1980s to 1999 (table 12.4). In general, the extent of overvaluation did not seem to have significantly decreased during the 1990s—contrary to the experience of Latin American, African, or Asian economies.

For the MENA region as a whole, exchange rate policy explains losses in competitiveness and in manufactured exports. Real exchange rate overvaluation has reduced, on average, the ratio of manufactured exports to GDP by 18 percent a year. Manufactured exports, which averaged 4.4 percent of GDP from 1970 to 1999, could have reached 5.2 percent of GDP if no overvaluation had taken place. These losses were more concentrated in the 1970s and 1980s than in the 1990s, due to the higher overvaluation of the currencies during those two subperiods.

Finally, a significant reason for the persistent misalignment and overvaluation of exchange rates is the prevalence of pegged or fixed exchange rate practices. Most MENA countries have had de facto or formal pegged nominal exchange rates, with only some recent changes towards floating exchange rates (as in Egypt in 2003). This is related to a general fear of floating. While there may have been gains in terms of reduced inflation, the tradeoff clearly has been to hurt GDP growth and exports.

Table 12.4. Average Exchange Rate Misalignment and Volatility

1975–80/84 (depending on country)	Misalignment (percent per year)	Volatility
MENA	29	7.9
Latin America	20	11.2
Africa (CFA)	61	12.7
Africa (non-CFA)	29	11.3
South Asia	43	13
South East Asia	10	5.4
1985–99	**Misalignment**	**Volatility**
MENA	22	12.4
Latin America	10	12.9
Africa (CFA)	28	14.5
Africa (non CFA)	13	16
South Asia	15	8.3
Southeast Asia	5	8.6

Source: Nabli and Véganzonès-Varoudakis, 2002.

The Critical Role of the Investment Climate

Trade barriers and overvalued exchange rates impede growth, in part by restricting domestic expansion into potential export areas, and in part by constraining the inward flow of knowledge embodied in new products and services. However, they are not the only such impediments. The process of growth via trade expansion involves a phase of investment supply response that is influenced by a broad range of considerations that are sometimes grouped together under the label "investment climate." They include the transaction costs encountered in trade-related business activities such as clearing goods from customs and shipping goods overseas, the expenses involved in routine business operations for telecommunications and electricity, and the burden of regulations involved in starting a business, hiring and firing labor, and closing down a business. They can also refer to aspects of governance, such as corruption, the strength of property rights, and adherence to the rule of law.[3]

Recent analyses suggest that openness to trade has limited or no impact on growth in economies with excessive regulations. Using indices of regulations derived from employment laws, industrial relations laws, and business registration and entry procedures, Bolaky and Freund (2003) show that the effect of trade on growth is more than halved in heavily-regulated economies. They conclude that the potentially beneficial effects of trade liberalization can be lost if labor laws prevent the sort of labor re-allocation to more productive sectors and firms that is necessary for productivity enhancement and growth to occur. Similarly, if it is very difficult to register new businesses, one would expect less investment response to new opportunities provided by trade liberalization.

A similar result, with somewhat broader implications, is found by Dasgupta and others (2003). They show that trade expansion adds significantly to employment in industry (a proxy for good jobs) only in countries where there are large foreign investment inflows (a proxy for investment climate). Thus, Figure 12.12 shows a higher elasticity of employment to trade openness among countries with relatively large investment inflows (left panel) but zero elasticity among countries with low inflows (right panel). These results may be interpreted to mean that countries with poor investment climates are unlikely to benefit significantly from trade openness.

The Investment Climate in MENA

International comparisons suggest that the MENA region lags most other regions in regard to investment climate considerations. The region tends to have relatively high transaction costs for starting, operating, and closing businesses. The following list provides a summary account of some relevant issues—for which more detailed information can be found in World Bank (2003).

Starting businesses. The cost of legally registering a new business is influenced by both the number of steps required and the number of days required to fulfill necessary procedures. When measured as a ratio of per capita income, this cost is higher in MENA than in most other regions.

Contract enforcement. When ranked along a procedural complexity index, the MENA region has the second highest score among seven regions for which the relevant data have been compiled (see World Bank, 2004). This index covers

Figure 12.12. Interaction between Trade Openness and Foreign Investment

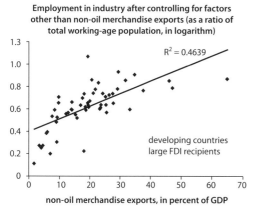
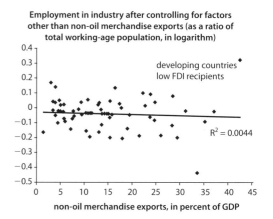

Source: Dasgupta and others (2003).

both the number of procedures required in contract enforcement actions and the number of days. Difficulties and delays in contract enforcement are often cited by foreign investors as a significant impediment to investment.

Air transport. Despite some progress, the regulatory reform of air transport in MENA is still at an early stage. Services remain largely provided by state-owned airlines and airports, with competition restrained by restrictive licensing regimes for domestic flights and international air service agreements. Efficiency indicators, such as freight and passenger capacity use, suggest that MENA carriers fall short of international standards by an estimated 15 to 20 percent.

Telecommunications. Many developing countries have liberalized their telecommunications sectors in the last two decades, with Latin America in the lead, closely followed by South Asia and East Asia and the Pacific. But regulatory reform in telecommunications has been slow in MENA, where markets remain on average less competitive than in other developing countries. Lower-cost telecommunications could help improve the weak position of MENA countries in global production networks, boosting the region's participation in global trade. Evidence from developing countries over the 1990s suggests that the share of manufactured exports in GDP increases with improvements in the overall quality of telecommunications.

Power. In MENA the power sector is still dominated by vertically integrated public monopolies with poor financial health, low operating efficiency, and extensive government interference. Regulatory frameworks are not characterized by independence, transparency, and accountability. Regulatory and operational functions are not sufficiently separated to assure potential private investors and new entrants that the future policy developments in the sector will be fair and competitively neutral. Until the end of the 1990s MENA's reform scorecard in the industry was very low, ahead only of Africa.[4]

Financial Services. Most MENA countries embarked on financial sector reform only in the 1990s, almost two decades after East Asia and Latin America. Banking systems were state-dominated and excessively regulated, and remain so in Algeria, Iran, and Syria, where state-owned banks still account for more than 95 percent of domestic bank assets. In some cases, state-owned banks have extended soft loans to loss-making public enterprises, creating contingent liabilities for the public sector and credit bottlenecks to private sector investment. Foreign bank presence remains limited.

Conflict and the Investment Climate

The investment climate of a country, or region, for that matter, is clearly affected not just by the domestic policy context discussed in the preceding sections but also by what one might call the geopolitical context. This is reflected most directly in the incidence of conflicts, wars, and politically inspired trade and investment barriers such as sanctions. The geopolitical context is likely to have been very important in shaping the manner and extent to which the MENA region has been able to participate in world trade and investment.

Persistent conflict reduces the scope for trade and investment and thus lowers growth. In the MENA region, frequent conflicts and militarization are related to the absence of a lasting peace settlement in the region, but also to several interstate and intrastate conflicts.[5] These events raise the risk perceptions and willingness to invest in the region among both domestic and foreign sources. A recent comparative study of conflict-affected developing countries and a control group of countries not affected (Gupta and others 2002) suggests that the numerous effects include slower GDP growth, falling trade, sharply reduced tourism, macroeconomic instability, large security expenditures, higher fiscal deficits and inflation, and the crowding out of education and health spending. The compounded effects appear to be a sharp slowdown in GDP growth in the preconflict stage (−1% GDP growth change) and an even sharper decline during conflict (−2%). Given the extent and duration of conflict in the MENA region, the effects are possibly even greater. Other research suggests strong contemporaneous negative spillover effects of conflict on neighbors—effects as dramatic as those of the conflict within a country, with the contiguity or nearness (length of common border) a key factor. These appear to work through general contagion as much as through other channels (such as trade or labor migration or capital flows). When conflict does end, there is a sharp rebound in economic activity (+3 percent GDP change)—signaling the positive effects that ending persistent conflict might have in the MENA region.

Potential Gains from Trade and Investment Climate Reforms

We have seen in earlier sections that the MENA region exhibits trade and investment integration ratios that are substantially below the potential levels estimated on the basis of their income and population levels. We have also seen that growth and employment can rise significantly if the investment climate is improved and more trade is enabled. In this section, we simulate the effect of the region's moving from its current level of trade and investment integration to a higher level.

We start with the assumption that the region achieves about half its trade and investment potential over 10 years. This would raise the nonoil export ratio of the region from about 6 percent of GDP to about 13 percent by the end of 10 years—reaching roughly half the average ratio of nonoil exports to GDP of all developing countries today. The nonoil export growth rate underlying this scenario is about 15 percent a year, nearly twice the expected world export growth, but the increase in MENA's share of that market remains very small because of the very low starting levels. Merchandise imports, now 20 percent of GDP, would also be expected to rise by about 7 percentage points over the decade (with incremental financing of additional imports from higher nonoil exports and higher FDI).

The effect would be to raise the merchandise trade ratio from about 46 percent of GDP (2003) to about 58 percent over a decade (2013) and nonoil merchandise trade from about 26 percent of GDP to about 39 percent. The 50 percen gain in the nonoil merchandise trade ratio over the decade would be a substantial gain—about half of the average (100 percent) increase for fast-integrating developing countries in the 1990s. FDI inflows are correspondingly assumed to rise by some 2.5 percent of GDP, and private productive investment rates (inclusive of FDI) by some 7 percent of GDP (from the current 12.5 percent of GDP to about 20 percent of GDP).

Impact on growth. These broad assumptions are useful for calibrating the likely impacts on growth and productivity with an aggregate source of growth model (table 12.5). The MENA region has three basic sources of growth other than exploiting oil (or other non-reproducible assets) more intensively: deepening capital investment per laborer; deepening human capital per laborer; and increasing total factor productivity. If policies are reasonably successful in achieving the trade and investment outcomes described above, and a reasonably modest turnaround in productivity growth of about 1.4 percent a year is achieved as a result of greater trade, the net effect would be to raise annual growth from about 1.4 percent per capita in the 1990s, to about 4 percent per capita in the coming decade. This is consistent with the experience of other countries in the world, where correspondingly faster growth was achieved with greater trade and investment orientation (Dollar and Kraay, 2001).

Table 12.5. Potential for Faster GDP Growth, Accumulation, and Productivity from Trade and Investment Climate Reforms in MENA, 2003–13

Percentage per annum per laborer, except when noted)

	Physical capital		Human capital		Total factor productivity		Growth of GDP per labor (labor force weighted)		Growth of GDP per capita	
	1990s	2003–13	1990s	2003–2013	1990s	2003–13	1990s	2000–13	1990–00	2003–13
MENA	−0.3	2.4	1.2	1.2	−0.2	1.4	0.7	3.0	1.4	4.3
East Asia	8.4	..	0.7	..	3.2	..	7.0	..	7.1	..
South Asia	3.3	..	0.9	..	0.9	..	2.7	..	3.2	..
OECD	2.0	..	0.6	..	0.4	..	1.6	..	2.1	..
World	4.8	..	0.7	..	1.6	..	3.9	..	4.7	..

Source: World Bank, 2003, p.52.
Note: All growth estimates by regions and world are labor force weighted. GDP per capita growth rates differ from GDP per-labor growth rates because of differences between labor force and population growth rates. ".." means not projected.

The 1990s were marked by a fall in capital per laborer in MENA, primarily because of low and falling rates of growth in private investment relative to the growth of the labor force. With gains in trade intensification and major improvements in the investment climate, faster growth in private domestic investment and foreign direct investment can be expected to lead to a significant improvement in capital deepening. Given a fast-expanding stock of labor force (of about 3.4 percent a year), achieving such gains will be difficult, but critical. Historically, capital per laborer increased in the region—by as much as 7.9 percent per annum in the 1970s (driven by public investment)—but slowed to 2.1 percent per annum in the 1980s and then collapsed to negative levels in the 1990s. Therefore, business climate reforms to elicit a more robust private investment response are likely to be central to the success of trade reforms in the MENA region. Moreover, the shift from public to private investment will be critical.

Improving total factor productivity (TFP) is also a key driver of growth. It is reasonable to hypothesize that the total factor productivity gains from opening trade and investment would be significant. Opening trade would improve productivity by encouraging shifts in resources to more productive and internationally competitive activities (the stock effect), by improving access to higher quality inputs, and by spillovers from FDI and greater competition. World Bank staff estimates suggest, for example, that fast-integrating countries obtained an additional 1 percent of GDP from productivity gains over the 1990s compared to only 0.6 percent among slow-integrating countries (World Bank, 2003, p.53). For the next decade, therefore, it is reasonable to assume that TFP gain of 1.4 percent per laborer will be achieved in the MENA region, reversing the negative TFP growth of the previous two decades, as the region's economies open up to trade and private investment.

Impact on employment. The employment effects of GDP growth at about 6 percent annual rate (resulting from faster trade integration and improvement in investment climate) are likely to be substantial. Faster GDP growth will itself generate equivalently faster growth in employment. However, assumed technological progress and productivity growth will mean that the gains will be distributed more widely, and that employment growth will therefore be at a slower pace. Moreover, likely real wage increases will also dampen employment growth as firms respond to higher wages. Offsetting these pressures will be greater labor-intensity of production driven by greater trade orientation of the production structure. The net effects of these factors is employment growth of up to 4.5 percent a year. This would be adequate to absorb the new entrants to the labor force and cut unemployment rates by half over the next decade.[6]

Exporting more merchandise goods and manufactures will create new jobs. Just over the next five years, if the MENA region can achieve15 percent real annual nonoil export growth for the region with improved policies, it would boost the region's nonoil exports to about US$60 billion from the present level of US$28 billion (excluding re-exports). This could directly generate some 2 million additional jobs in such nonoil export activities, and another 2 million indirectly, as domestic goods and services supply inputs to these activities, and from the multiplier effects on domestic final demand. So closing even a small part of the export gap could generate some 4 million jobs over five years from direct trade effects alone. This simplified projection abstracts from a much more complex set of factors, but the magnitude is indicative of the potential.

Examples abound of the effects of expanding trade on jobs. For Mexico, thanks to NAFTA and radical economic reforms, trade more than tripled, from $82 billion in 1990 to about $280 billion in 1999, making it the seventh largest trading nation in the world and resulting in a rapid pace of job creation in manufacturing. From 1994 to 1999, manufacturing employment grew at almost 16 percent per annum, at almost twice the pace recorded in the pre-NAFTA years of 1985-93. Job creation has also been strong in export-processing zones in Mauritius, the Dominican Republic, and El Salvador (Rama 2001). Indonesia is another country that saw a major trade and investment policy reform produce employment benefits in the mid-1980s. Manufactured exports and FDI boomed, as did manufacturing employment. Indonesia is especially relevant to some MENA countries in that it was a resource-dependent economy until the mid-1980s, when it found a new engine of growth in manufactured exports (Iqbal 2002). Within the MENA region, Tunisian exports of textiles and clothing have boomed in "offshore companies" that supply foreign markets, and employment in these industries increased steeply. Morocco is another example of a country that gained significantly from an initial burst of economic reforms in the early 1980s. Manufacturing sector employment and exports rose sharply in the early 1980s in response to a series of trade and investment liberalization measures (World Bank, 2003, p. 59). But the Moroccan boom faltered in the 1990s, as the impact of the initial reforms package dissipated and macroeconomic policies allowed the real effective exchange rate to appreciate, hurting both exports and employment in manufacturing.

Conclusions

The MENA region has been traveling along a slow growth and high unemployment trajectory over the past two decades. To pull out of this path, the region needs to make three shifts in its sources of growth: from oil to nonoil sectors, from public state-dominated to private market-oriented investment, and from protected import-substitution to export-oriented activities. Intensifying trade and private investment is at the core of all three shifts.

The region has good potential for expanding trade. Exports other than oil are a third of what they could be, given the characteristics of the region. Openness to manufacturing imports is half of what would be expected. Increasing its share of world trade is possible for at least three reasons. First, the present level of the region's presence in world markets is small; an increase is unlikely to be resisted among major trading partners. Second, competitiveness based on low wages is possible, since wages in the region are fairly low, in the bottom half of world wages. (However, for competitiveness to be sustainable, overall trade policy and investment climate considerations will have to be improved). And third, the region is close to a high-income region: across the Mediterranean is the EU, which can potentially be a source of high demand for certain regional products.

MENA countries also have great potential for attracting more investment from abroad and encouraging more private investment at home, both crucial for trade and development. If exports other than oil were higher, and in a better investment climate, domestic private investment in traded goods and services would be much higher. And the FDI inflows that the region could expect would be four to five times what they are today—some 3 percent of GDP, up from an average of 0.6 percent. On the other hand, the region remains subject to a geopolitical context featuring high levels of tension and conflict, which can discourage foreign investment and even trade.

Nevertheless, if only half the region's trade and private investment potential were realized over the next ten years, that would be enough to raise its per capita GDP growth from about 1 percent to about 4 percent a year—half from more private investment and half from the greater productivity that openness would encourage.

Expanding trade also holds the promise of substantial dividends in job creation, because export opportunities would add millions of jobs. For example, if the region can achieve faster nonoil export growth of about 15 percent a year over the next 5 years, it would probably be sufficient to generate some 4 million jobs or 4 percent of the labor force, directly and indirectly, in the export sectors alone. The employment effects are however, conditional on there being a more favorable investment climate in the region.

Notes

1. The term "MENA region" refers in this paper to Algeria, Djibouti, Egypt, Iran, Jordan, Lebanon, Morocco, Syria, Tunisia, Yemen, and the six GCC countries, namely, Bahrain, Kuwait, Oman, Qatar, Saudi Arabia, and the United Arab Emirates. In cases where data are available only for a subset of these countries, the relevant countries are identified in table or chart notes.

2. A consistent series starting in the 1960s could be obtained only for the eight countries noted in the figure. However, this set includes most of the bigger economies of the region, with the exception of Iran and Iraq. From what is generally known of their economic performance over this period, it is unlikely that their omission affects the conclusions drawn here.

3. A vigorous debate has arisen around the question of the direction of causality in the link between trade openness, institutional quality, and growth (see Frankel and Romer, 2002, Rodrik, Subramaniam and Trebbi, 2002 and Dollar and Kraay, 2003).

4. The ranking is based on the following six criteria: Is the existing electric utility functioning on commercial principles? Have laws been passed which would permit unbundling and/or privatization in part or in all of the industry? Is a regulatory body in place that is separate from the utility and ministry? Is there any private sector investment in the industry? Has the core state-owned utility been restructured? Have any of the existing state-owned enterprises been privatized?

5. The MENA region has seen a large number of conflicts in recent decades, including some 14 years of civil conflict affecting 8 major countries, and some 15 years of cross-border regional and international conflicts affecting 14 countries. Between 1945 and 1999, it had the second highest number of violent conflicts, compared with other regions (World Bank, 2003, p.91).

6. Note that this is consistent with an implied employment elasticity of about 0.7 with respect to GDP, which is also fairly uniformly noted in other regions such as Latin America and East Asia.

References

Bolaky, B., and C. Freund. 2003. "Trade, Regulations and Growth." Unpublished paper. World Bank, Washington DC.

Dasgupta, D., J. Keller, and T.G. Srinivasan. 2002. "Reforms and Elusive Growth in the Middle East—What Has Happened in the 1990s?" MENA Working Paper 25. World Bank, Washington, DC.

Dasgupta, D., M. Nabli, C. Pissarides, and A. Varoudakis. 2003. "Making Trade Work for Jobs: International Evidence and Lessons for MENA." MENA Working Paper 32. World Bank, Washington, DC.

Dollar, D., and Kraay, A. 2001. "Trade, Growth and Poverty." World Bank Policy Research Working Paper 2615. World Bank, Washington, D.C.

———. 2003. "Institutions, Trade and Growth." World Bank Policy Research Working Paper 3004. World Bank, Washington, D.C.

Frankel, J., and D. Romer. 2002. "Does Trade Cause Growth?" *American Economic Review* 89(3): 379-99.

Gupta, S., B. J. Clements, R. Bhattacharya, and S. Chakravarti. 2002. "Fiscal Consequences of Armed Conflict and Terrorism in Law and Middle Income Countries." Working Paper 02/142. International Monetary Fund, Washington DC.

Iqbal, F. 2002. "Deregulation and Development in Indonesia: An Introductory Overview." In F. Iqbal and W.E. James, eds., *Deregulation and Development in Indonesia*. Westport, Connecticut: Praeger Publishers.

Nabli, M., and M.Veganzones-Varoudakis. 2002. "Exchange Rate Regime and Competitiveness of Manufactured Exports: The Case of MENA Countries." MENA Working Paper 27. World Bank, Washington, DC.

Rama, M. 2001. "Globalization, Inequality and Labor Market Policies." Paper for Annual Bank Conference in Development Economics (ABCDE-Europe), Washington.

Rodrik, D., A. Subramaniam, and F. Trebbi. 2002. "Institutions Rule: The Primacy of Institutions over Geography and Integration in Economic Development." Unpublished. International Monetary Fund, Washington, DC.

World Bank. 2003. *Trade, Investment and Development in the Middle East and North Africa: Engaging with the World*. Washington, DC: World Bank.

———. 2004. *Doing Business in 2004: Understanding Regulation*. Washington, DC: World Bank.

13

Making Trade Work for Jobs

International Evidence and Lessons for MENA

Dipak Dasgupta*
Mustapha Kamel Nabli
Christopher Pissarides†
Aristomene Varoudakis††

Can trade expansion help MENA countries step up the pace of job creation? Despite the short-term costs of adjustment to trade liberalization, in a number of countries that have successfully integrated into global markets, export-led growth has eventually brought large employment dividends. The paper examines the medium-term relationship between international trade and employment in manufacturing in developing countries. Evidence from 59 developing countries, from the early 1960s to the late 1990s, reveals a positive medium-term association between employment in manufacturing and openness to trade, after controlling for other structural determinants of employment. By contrast, an opposite relationship is found in high-income countries. Countries in MENA find it difficult to make trade a driver of employment creation and growth, partly because MENA exports are concentrated in low value-added, slowly growing products, and partly because MENA trade is poorly linked to global production networks and Foreign Direct Investment

*World Bank. †London School of Economics. ††World Bank. The authors wish to thank Manuel Felix for providing excellent research support, Martin Rama for making available an international database on employment and labor market regulations, and T.G. Srinivasan for contributing data on trade. Comments from Farrukh Iqbal, Kiihiro Fukasaku, Douglas Lippoldt, Andrea Goldstein, and other participants in an OECD Development Center seminar are gratefully acknowledged.

Published in the MENA Working Paper series, no. 32, July 2003. Reprinted by permission from the World Bank.

(FDI) flows. Evidence suggests that while the impact of trade expansion on employment in manufacturing is highly significant in developing countries that are large FDI recipients, trade adds little to job creation in countries that receive small amounts of FDI. To meet the employment challenge, trade liberalization and companion policies would need to strengthen the investment climate and upgrade the quality of trade-related services to improve the attractiveness of MENA as a place to invest.

Introduction

Accelerating the pace of job creation is a key challenge in MENA. Across the region, unemployment is high and the working-age population is growing fast. Even though a young and fast growing labor force is a valuable asset for the future, it also presents a serious challenge: How to achieve faster, more labor-intensive growth, to accelerate job creation, and reduce the currently very high unemployment rates across the region? Past policies, relying on the expansion of public sector employment and the use of oil rents to stimulate domestic demand, migration and growth in agricultural employment, are running out of steam, calling for more innovative approaches to stimulate employment growth.

Can trade expansion help MENA countries step up the pace of job creation? In a number of countries that have successfully integrated into global markets, export-led growth has eventually brought large employment dividends. But evidence on the impact of trade on employment is not clearcut, because in developing countries, trade expansion usually relies on trade liberalization, which may hurt sheltered sectors in the short term and displace workers in import-competing industries. Moreover, the reforms that help expand trade are part of more comprehensive programs, aimed at improving competitiveness and economic efficiency, that may also entail adjustment costs. However, trade expansion holds the promise of substantial dividends in terms of job creation and income growth in the medium term. The delocalization of production in developing countries, in labor-intensive manufacturing such as textiles and clothing, footwear, and food processing, eventually spurs the demand for labor and boosts workers' earnings.

The paper examines the medium-term relationship between international trade and employment in manufacturing in developing countries. The analysis draws on a panel data set from 59 developing countries, spanning five-year periods from the early 1960s to the late 1990s. Evidence reveals a positive medium-term association between employment in manufacturing and openness to trade, after controlling for other structural determinants of employment. By contrast, the opposite relationship is found in high-income countries.

But countries in MENA find it difficult to make trade a driver of employment creation and growth. After controlling for other structural determinants of employment in manufacturing, evidence suggests that trade openness has contributed less to overall employment creation in manufacturing in MENA, compared to trends seen elsewhere in developing countries. This is so partly because MENA exports are concentrated in low value-added, slowly-growing products, and partly because MENA trade is poorly linked to global production networks and FDI flows (Nabli and De Kleine, 2000; Yeats and Ng, 2000; Petri, 1997a,b). Evidence indeed suggests that while the impact of trade expansion on employment in manufacturing is highly significant in developing countries that are large FDI recipients, trade adds little to job creation in countries that receive only small amounts of FDI.

To step up employment growth, MENA exports would need to be diversified away from raw materials and resource-based manufactures, toward high value-added, labor-intensive products, linked more closely with international production networks and global investment flows. The challenge is to bridge the "quality gap" in MENA trade, through deeper integration with trade partners and improved attractiveness to investment. To meet this challenge, trade liberalization will not be enough. Companion policies would be needed to strengthen the investment climate and relax the "beyond-the-border" constraints—especially in trade-related services—that increase the cost of doing business and limit the attractiveness of MENA as a place to invest.

The Employment Challenge in MENA

Accelerating the pace of job creation is a key policy challenge in MENA because unemployment across the region is among the highest in the world—at above 15 percent in most countries, and close to 30 percent in Algeria. High unemployment hinders the reduction of poverty, adds to inequality, and feeds social instability in an already fragile region. As a result of slow growth and the slack in the labor market, real wages fell by 30-50 percent in 1980-90, and have stagnated or fallen since. Projections suggest that the required employment growth in MENA, to reduce the unemployment rate by half over the next 15 years, would range between 4 and 5 percent per year—well above the average growth of 2.5-3 percent seen in the past (Figure 13.1.a; also see Dhonte et al., 2001).

Fast employment growth is needed not only because of high actual unemployment, but primarily because of the rapid growth of the working-age population. Although the growth of this population in Arab countries is projected to slow down somewhat over the next 15 years, it will remain significantly faster than in the rest of the world, adding to labor market pressures (figure 13.1.b). Moreover, reflecting the very low, but rising, participation rates of women, the labor force is likely to grow even faster in the years ahead. Thus, unless the pace of employment growth accelerates, unemployment could rise further across the region. According to estimates, 50 million new jobs need to be created over the next 10 years to employ expected additional job seekers.

This is four times more than Eastern Europe and Central Asia require, and about as much as in all of Latin America—a region three times bigger than MENA in terms of GDP. The employed workforce would need to rise by almost 60 percent in 10 years—an even stronger increase than in East Asia in its years of high growth.

The employment challenge is further complicated by important structural imbalances in MENA labor markets that heighten economic inefficiencies and exacerbate social tensions. First, unemployment is more severe among female workers, and is on the rise—exceeding by far levels seen in other middle-income developing countries (figure 13.1.c). This discourages the participation of women in the labor force—thus preventing a needed increase in the very low female participation rates—and denies MENA a significant part of its productive human resources. Second, compared to other middle-income countries, unemployment in MENA is much higher among skilled workers with secondary education, while unemployment of workers with higher education remains very high as well (figure 13.1.d). Thus, MENA countries are losing the benefit of substantial past investments in human capital—a sizeable opportunity cost in a context where the knowledge-based economy is becoming an increasingly strong driver of growth. The high rates of unemployment among the educated and female workers are also reflected in severe unemployment among the young and first-time job seekers.

Even more worrisome is the fact that in the face of sluggish job creation, continuing pressures from population growth, and structural imbalances in the labor market, the mechanisms that sustained employment in past are running out of steam. In MENA, public sector employment (in civil service and public enterprises) expanded rapidly in the 1970s and 1980s in response to the oil boom, because it was seen as a convenient means of redistributing income, providing a social safety net, and alleviating the pressures of the fast growing flow of new entrants into the labor market. Despite efforts to scale back public employment and pay in the 1990s, prompted by the reversal of the oil boom, both public sector employment and the wage bill remain higher in MENA than elsewhere in developing countries, and cannot be relied on to promote employment in the years ahead (Schiavo-Campo, de Tommaso, and Mukherjee, 1997; figure 13.2.a). If anything, public employment would have to be downsized, as in many MENA countries the wage bill in the public sector exceeds that in private sector manufacturing—contrary to patterns seen in other developing countries, including the economies in transition (figure 13.2.b).

Moreover, employment in agriculture, which still accounts for about 30 percent of jobs, on average, in MENA, is declining. If anything, the shift out of agricultural employment would further intensify pressures on the labor market. Migration has also provided substantial relief to MENA labor markets in the past. However, with slowing growth in high-income countries and tighter immigration controls, the pace of migration has considerably slowed. For

Figure 13.1. Accelerating Job Ceation in MENA—a Multifaceted Challenge

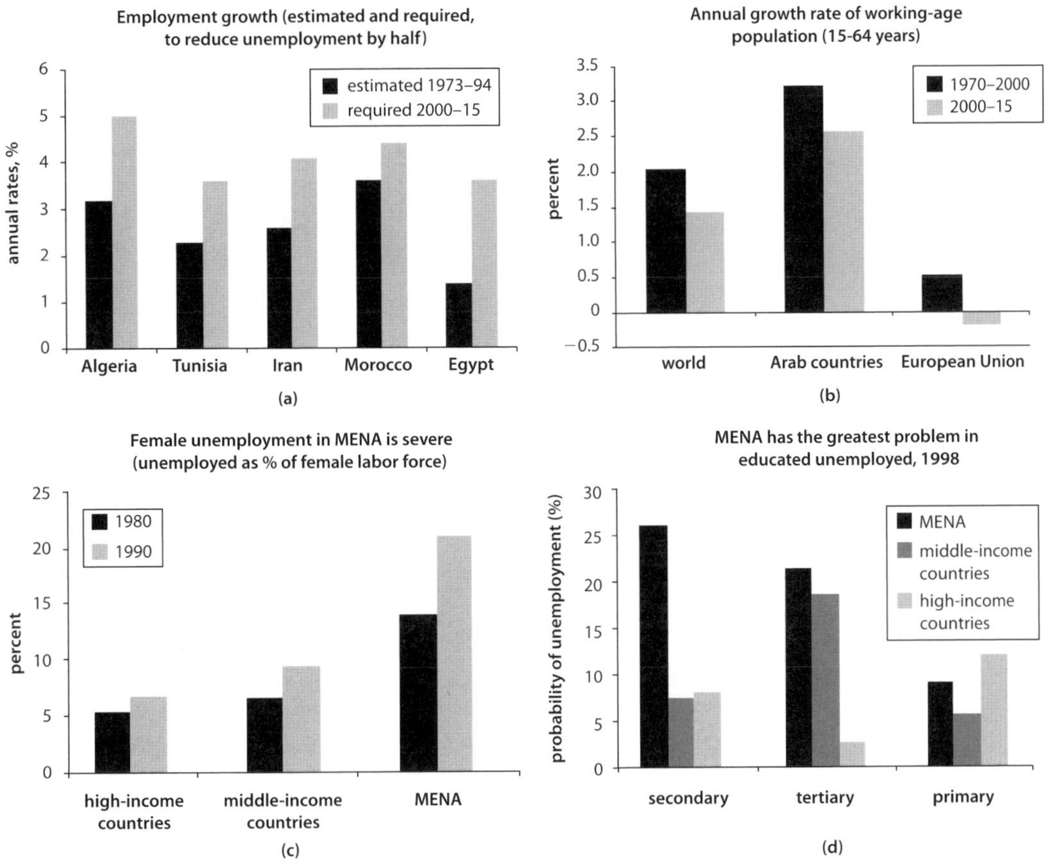
Employment growth (estimated and required, to reduce unemployment by half)
annual rates, %
estimated 1973–94
required 2000–15
Algeria
Tunisia
Iran
Morocco
Egypt
(a)
Annual growth rate of working-age population (15-64 years)
percent
1970–2000
2000–15
world
Arab countries
European Union
(b)
Female unemployment in MENA is severe (unemployed as % of female labor force)
percent
1980
1990
high-income countries
middle-income countries
MENA
(c)
MENA has the greatest problem in educated unemployed, 1998
probability of unemployment (%)
MENA
middle-income countries
high-income countries
secondary
tertiary
primary
(d)

Source: Authors' calculations; partly based on data from Dhonte et al. (2001).

example, Egyptian immigrant workers, which account for about 10 percent of the workforce, have been stagnant since 1997.

Can Trade Expansion Become an Engine of Job Creation?

World merchandise trade has grown rapidly during the 1990s, at an annual rate of about 9 percent, and is also expected to be a major engine of growth over the next ten to fifteen years (World Bank, 2001). Thanks to continued reforms that have enhanced competitiveness, developing countries are gaining strength in global nonenergy merchandise export markets, with their market share increasing more that 7 percent over the 1990s (figure 13.3.a). And despite still-high market access barriers for labor-intensive manufactures such as textiles and clothing, footwear, and food processing, developing countries' exports increased sharply in the 1990s, and their export market share now surpasses that of high-income countries.

Figure 13.2. Patterns in Public Sector Employment and Pay

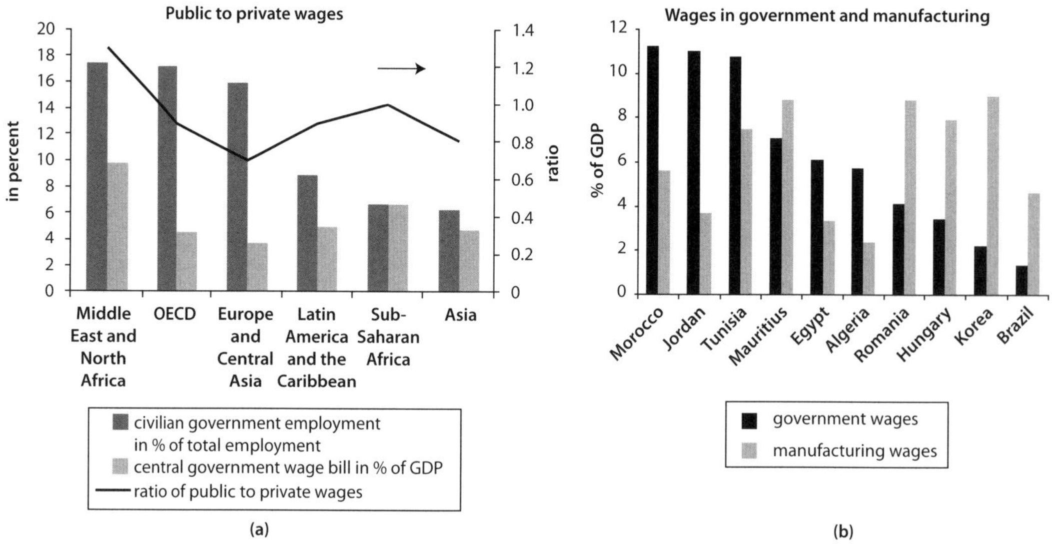

Source: Based on Schiavo-Campo, de Tommaso, and Mukherjee, 1997, and authors' calculations.
Note: Figure 13.2.a. refers to the early 1990s.

Trade expansion, especially in the form of rising exports, has been a major source of growth in developing countries. During each of the past two decades, developing countries which have had fast export growth—leading to an increase in the share of non-energy merchandise exports in GDP—have also had, on average, 1 percent higher real GDP growth (figure 13.3.b). Faster overall growth is in turn the prerequisite for accelerated job creation. And global trade in manufactures can be a major driver for employment growth in the years ahead, as it is expected to increase almost threefold by 2010, compared to the late 1990s. By contrast, trade in nonoil commodities is projected to double, and trade in fuels is expected to rise by only 50 percent (Riordan et al., 1997). Thus, from the demand side, there is ample room for further growth in MENA's non-energy exports, provided the region succeeds in meeting the challenge of increased competition in global markets.

However, MENA was bypassed by expanding global trade in the 1990s. Across the region, trade flows stagnated at about 40 percent of GDP on average, while in other developing regions trade expanded rapidly (figure 13.4.a). The trade performance of MENA countries is even weaker when non-hydrocarbon exports are considered separately. While a few countries, including—Bahrain, Morocco, Tunisia, Jordan, and the UAE, succeeded in diversifying their exports, non-hydrocarbon merchandise exports remained in a number of countries at very low levels, below 5 percent of GDP (figure 13.4.b). This is even more a concern in countries with a large labor force—such as Algeria, Egypt, and Iran—that face high and rising levels of unem-

Figure 13.3. Export Performance and Output Growth in Developing Countries

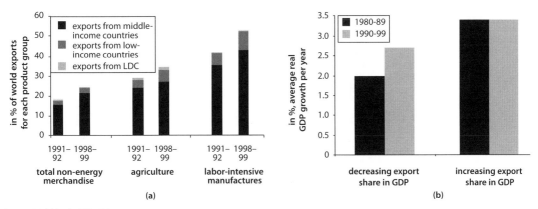

Source: World Bank, GEP 2002.

ployment, because the hydrocarbon sector and downstream industries contribute little to job creation.

The slow integration of MENA countries into global trade reflects bottlenecks in export capacity, but is also linked to the still-high levels of protection
of domestic markets. Despite some progress in the late 1990s in liberalizing
external trade regimes, partly in connection with the Association Agreements
with the EU and partly as a result of unilateral moves, the average level of tariff protection still remains higher in MENA than elsewhere in developing
countries—with the exception of South Asia (figure 13.5). Regions such as
Latin America, where trade protection used to be as high as in MENA, have
slashed tariffs by more than three times in a decade, while low-income
regions, such as Sub-Saharan Africa, have reduced tariffs to levels below those

Figure 13.4. Trade Patterns in MENA

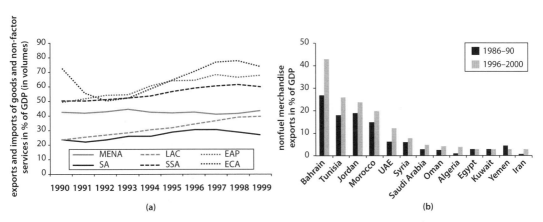

Source: Author's calculations.

Figure 13.5. MENA Markets Still Remain Highly Protected

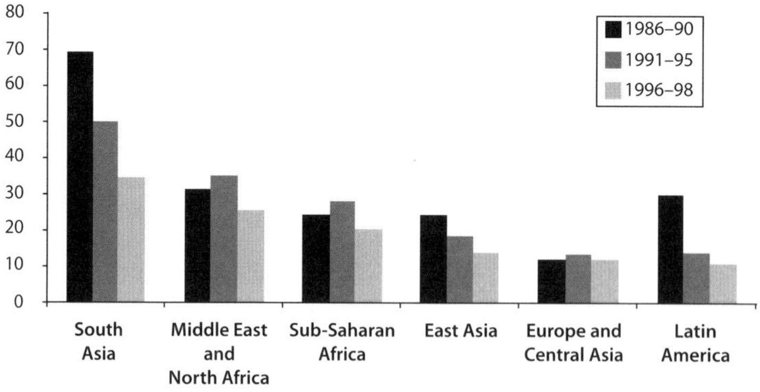

Source: Authors' calculations.

in MENA. Besides tariff barriers, "para-tariffs" are also widespread in MENA. They are often geared to raising revenues for the state, but they also, in effect, protect domestic companies (Zarrouk, 2000).

The delocalization of production of labor-intensive manufactures in developing countries has the potential to spur the demand for labor and boost workers' earnings. The most visible part of job creation, driven by exports of labor-intensive manufactures, has been associated with FDI—as for example in China's Eastern provinces, or in Mexico's Maquiladoras. Thanks to the NAFTA and radical economic reforms, Mexico's trade more than tripled, from US$82 billion in 1990 to about US$280 billion in 1999, making Mexico the seventh largest trading nation in the world. The pace of job creation has been particularly swift in manufacturing, shared most in the expansion of trade (figure 13.6.a). Job creation has also been strong in export processing zones in a number of developing countries—such as Mauritius, the Dominican Republic, and El Salvador (Rama, 2001).

Indonesia is an earlier (mid-1980s) example of a country that started a major trade reform effort, whichsubstantially reduced nontariff barriers and impediments to foreign investment. Manufactured exports and FDI boomed and were accompanied by rising manufacturing employment rates (figure 13.6.b). The Indonesia case is especially relevant to some MENA countries, since Indonesia was "single-engine" economy (oil and natural resources) until the mid-1980s, when it found a new engine of growth in the form of manufactured exports (Agrawal, 2002). In MENA, Tunisia is an example of successful diversification out of resource-based exports. Tunisian exports of textiles and clothing have boomed in the distortion-free environment for "offshore companies" that supply foreign markets, while employment in the offshore sector increased steeply.

However, trade expansion may occur in a number of different ways that affect employment differently—as a result of better access to foreign markets,

Figure 13.6. Examples of Trade Expansion and Job Creation in Manufacturing

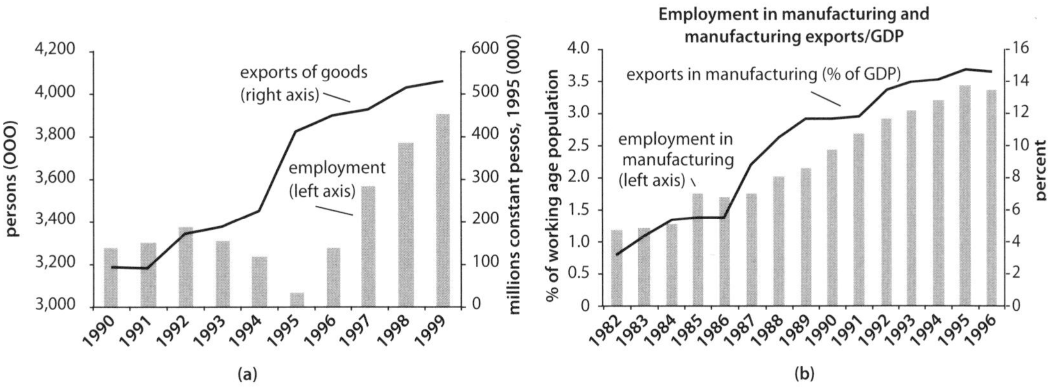

(a)   (b)

Source: Authors' calculations.

for example, or of lower international trade barriers or export-oriented FDI seeking to take advantage of an economy's comparative strengths. But, in most cases, sustained trade expansion follows domestic reforms that reshape taxes and incentives in the economy. Typically, such reforms call for lowering tariff protection and nontariff barriers, with the aim of reducing the anti-export bias of protective external trade regimes—especially in countries where narrow domestic markets cannot provide sufficient support for industrial growth. Trade liberalization reduces the anti-export bias, as it helps domestic producers purchase inputs at internationally competitive cost. By increasing the profitability of export sectors, trade liberalization helps shift resources to the uses that give countries the greatest comparative advantage.

Because the previously protected import-substitution sectors are likely to be capital-intensive, semiskilled (especially female) labor is likely to be underutilized. With sizeable amounts of labor remaining underemployed in the home, or queuing for public sector employment, trade liberalization is likely to have a net positive impact on employment in the medium term. But in developing countries, the fear is that massive trade liberalization would erode rents, expose inefficient industry to competition and cost jobs. Indeed, trade liberalization may disrupt job creation in the short term for a number of reasons:

- Lowering trade barriers may initially hurt sheltered domestic producers and displace unskilled workers in import-competing industries. Though import-competing industries are usually capital-intensive, in many middle-income countries—and also in MENA—industries intensive in unskilled labor are often protected disproportionately, because they face potentially stiff competition from lower-cost producers (Wood, 1997). For example, in Morocco, before trade liberalization, the nominal tariff and import license coverage in apparel and footwear was among the higher in manufacturing (Currie and Harrison, 1997). Similarly, in 1995, Egypt's import-weighted tariffs on textiles were about three times higher than average tariffs for the economy as a whole (Dessus and Suwa-Eisenman, 1998).

• Trade reallocates activity and labor across import-competing and export-oriented sectors. But while market exit of previously sheltered companies may be swift, business expansion takes time, and the timing of the net benefits will depend on the flexibility of product and labor markets, and on the availability of finance. Bottlenecks in access to credit or in availability of trade-related services (transport, communications) may tame the growth of export-oriented industries in the medium term. Moreover, the quality of the investment climate affects investment and, thus, job creation. In some cases, the investment climate may not be sufficiently attractive—so that export-oriented companies may lack incentives to expand and absorb labor released by the contracting, import-competing industries.

• Companion policies such as exchange rate management also affect the impact of trade policy reform. Exchange rate misalignment has been a factor in weak export performance in manufacturing in MENA (Nabli and Veganzones, 2002; Sekkat and Varoudakis, 2002). Morocco is a case in point: Over the 1980s, Morocco witnessed fast growth in exports and employment in manufacturing, supported by trade liberalization. However, over the 1990s, the growth in manufactured exports and employment ran out of steam, partly owing to deteriorating competitiveness (figure 13.7.a). The fixed exchange regime implemented in the 1990s helped achieve stabilization, but led to a 22 percent appreciation of the real effective exchange rate over the decade, which heightened competitive pressures on the tradable goods sector (figure 13.7.b). An association of textile producers reported the loss of 29,600 jobs in the textile industry (about 12 percent of employment in that industry) since 1999 (IMF, 2001).

Trade liberalization may thus typically lead to an increase in the rate of unemployment, which may take some time to reverse (figure 13.8.a). Although unemployment is generally trending downward in the medium term, its persistence will depend on market flexibility, exchange rate policy, and other reforms that may accompany trade liberalization. In the adjustment process, the impact of trade liberalization is difficult to single out, because other reforms—such as privatization of state-owned enterprises and reforms of bloated administrations and government agencies—are also likely to generate employment costs.

Job destruction has been particularly dramatic when trade policy reform has been associated with large-scale downsizing of state-owned enterprises, as

Figure 13.7. Growth of Manufactured Exports and Employment in Morocco

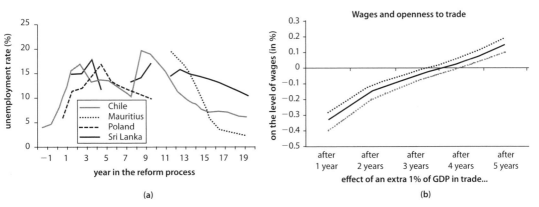

(a)

(b)

Source: Authors' calculations—based on IMF data on the real effective exchange rate,

in the transition economies where millions of workers had to be made redundant for the restructured enterprises to become profitable as private firms. For example, in Algeria, an estimated 500,000 workers—about 10 percent of the labor force—lost their jobs from 1995 to 1999 as a result of only partial restructuring of nonviable state-owned enterprises.

The increase in unemployment during the adjustment to trade liberalization may also be associated with a decline in real wage growth, as a result of the slack in the labor market (figure 13.8.a). But evidence on the net employment impact of labor market adjustment is mixed. In Mexico, Revenga (1997) found that even in the protected sectors, trade liberalization resulted in lower wages when rents were eroded, rather than lower employment. The wage reductions were uneven, but a feature of her microdata set was that it showed

Figure 13.8. Adjustment Costs of Trade Liberalization

(a)

(b)

Source: World Bank.

wage reductions, but no employment reductions—across the board. Experience in Morocco tells a similar employment story. Although experience across different occupations differed, trade liberalization surprisingly had no noticeable impact on either wages or employment. Currie and Harrison (1997), who studied a large microdata set for Morocco, concluded that the reduction in economic rents was absorbed by a reduction in profit margins and improvements in labor productivity, but not by less overall employment. In the medium term, as the labor-intensive, export-oriented sectors gain strength, the demand for labor increases, and leads to an increase in real wages. The net benefit to wage earners appears, on average, after the fourth year of the adjustment process (figure 13.8.b).

The Medium-Term Impact of Trade Expansion on Manufacturing Employment: Evidence from Developing and High-Income Countries

To assess the medium-term impact of trade expansion on employment, we examined evidence from both developing and high-income countries. The developing country sample includes 59 countries—containing about 140 observations, spanning five-year periods from the early 1960s to the late 1990s. The high-income country sample includes 22 countries and 135 observations of five-year periods, spanning the same period. In order to remove shortrun fluctuations, we averaged the data over five-year periods.

Casual inspections of the developing country sample reveals a positive medium-term association between employment in industry (as a share of the total working-age population) and openness to trade, but the association is at first sight weak, because there is considerable variation in employment outcomes across countries (figure 13.9). Cross-country differences in employment ratios in manufacturing reflect, indeed, a number of diverse factors apart from trade that may affect the demand (or the supply) of labor. Such factors may include the relative sizes of the primary and services sectors—which depend on the level of development; the overall level of production capacity and technical skills in manufacturing; the size of the informal economy (since the reported employment ratios capture employment in the formal sector); the level of real wages; and socioeconomic factors that affect the participation of women in the labor force.

To account for different structural factors that may affect employment in manufacturing, we estimated employment equations that include other determinants of the demand for labor, along with a variable for trade effects. The explained variable in the regressions presented in the tables below is employment in manufacturing as a percent of working-age population. A number of controls were used: (i) real labor costs per worker; (ii) a measure of total physical capital as a ratio to total employment; and, (iii) the real interest rate. The capital-to-employment ratio captures changes in manufacturing employment

Figure 13.9. Employment in Manufacturing and Trade Flows: Evidence from Developing Countries

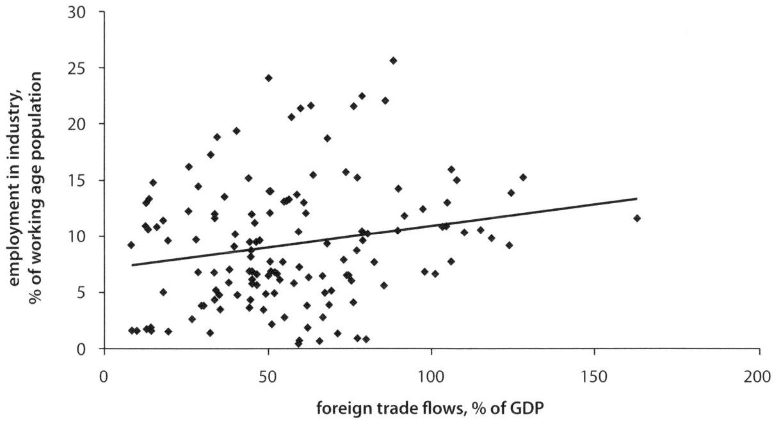

Source: Authors' calculations.

due to growth in production capacity, and to the shift of employment between sectors that accompanies economic development (e.g., from manufacturing to the services sector). All regressions are logarithmic (except for the real interest rate) and were run using fixed effects. Four different indicators of trade expansion were used: (i) total trade flows (the sum of exports and imports); (ii) total exports; (iii) merchandise exports; and (iv) merchandise exports excluding hydrocarbons. All four indicators are measured relative to GDP. While the three last indicators are proxies for export-led growth, the first indicator also accounts for import penetration, and thus also indirectly reflects the impact of trade liberalization (box 13.1).

The equation fits the data well, with real wages having a negative impact on employment in manufacturing and capital having a positive impact (table 13.1). The size and significance of the coefficients varies according to the different specifications. All else equal, a 10 percent increase in real labor costs lowers the industrial employment ratio by an estimated 2 to 3 percent on average. High real interest rates appear to also depress industrial employment—though in a statistically less robust way across the different specifications.

The findings suggest that trade expansion has a positive medium-term impact on employment in developing countries. All coefficients associated with trade expansion are statistically significant. This comes true for the various measures of export performance, but also for the broader measure of trade openness that accounts for import penetration. All else equal, a 10 percent increase in the share of nonoil merchandise exports in GDP is associated with an increase in the employment ratio in manufacturing of about 1.4 percent, while the same increase in the share of trade flows in GDP could raise the employment ratio by an estimated 2.3 percent.

Box 13.1. Measuring the impact of trade liberalization on employment

Employment effects are likely to be different when trade expansion is the result of a reform process that restructures implicit and explicit taxes and incentives in the economy. In developing and transition economies, trade expansion usually follows a reform process that may well have more important effects on employment than the growth of trade itself. Usually these other effects are more difficult to assess, and likely to be more diverse than the reallocation effects of trade. The diversity of the likely effects explains why the empirical literature has not reached a consensus about the overall effects of trade on labor market outcomes.

If trade liberalization follows other reforms, should one attribute the employment effects of the whole process to trade? In an ideal world, the answer is likely to be no. But in the real world of political economics, a country needs incentives to reform. The institutions that are dismantled in the reform process shield some sections of society; these sections are usually the ones with the power to stop the reform from taking place. The prospect of beneficial trade growth gives incentives to those in power to push through the reforms, and those that are hurt by the process to accept them.

In the statistical analysis, it would be difficult to describe the institutional framework of each country and measure the implications of its reform. There is very little in the literature on measures of institutional rigidity, and what there is usually applies to single points in time and to the richer countries that keep more complete statistical records. It is therefore not possible to disentangle the employment effects of institutional reform from those of the trade expansion that follows the reforms. But our usual measures of trade expansion may not be bad proxies for reform. A country that dismantles rigid institutions in labor markets when it liberalizes trade is likely to experience faster trade growth than one that keeps the rigid institutions. Trade growth in the statistical analysis picks up both the direct effects of trade and the indirect effects of reform. For this variable to be a good proxy, it has to bear a monotonic relation to the degree of reform. Although there is no research on this point, intuitively it makes sense. Trade growth normally requires restructuring of employment and countries with flexile labor markets are in a better position to take advantage of the new trade opportunities that liberalization offers.

The estimates also accounted for the fact that the measures of trade expansion are endogenous, which could be at the origin of some bias, in that both trade and employment in manufacturing could be affected by a common set of factors not included in the regression. One of the specifications (table 13.1, column 6) uses the black market premium, total world trade as a share of world GDP, and the country population as instruments for trade expansion. The results are consistent with the previous specifications, with total merchandise exports remaining a significant determinant of the manufacturing employment ratio. However, when instrumental variables are used, the significance of trade expansion is not always robust across specifications.

Table 13.1. Determinants of Employment in Manufacturing—Developing Countries

(Dependent variable: ratio of employment in manufacturing to working-age population) (Estimation period: 1960–95)

Explanatory variables	Employment in manufacturing and openness to trade in developing countries Explained variable: log of employment in manufacturing-to-working-age population ratio							
Log of trade-to-GDP ratio	0.229*				0.613**			
Log of trade-to-GDP ratio non-MENA countries							0.247**	
Log of trade-to-GDP ratio MENA countries							−0.04	
Log of exports-to-GDP ratio		0.202*						
Log of merchandise exports-to-GDP ratio			0.312**					
Log of merchandise exports non-MENA countries								0.343**
Log of merchandise exports MENA countries								0.054
Log of merchandise exports (excluding petroleum)-to-GDP ratio				0.143**		0.201*		
Log of labor costs in manufacturing	−0.187*	−0.192*	−0.271*	−0.216*	−0.339**	−0.301*	−0.198*	−0.266*
Log of total physical capital-to-total labor force ratio	0.15	0.159	0.396**	0.240**	0.257	0.319*	0.169*	0.370**
Real interest rate					−0.005*	−0.003		
Constant	0.589	0.764	−2.13	0.104	−1.228	−0.481	0.45	−1.845
Observations	140	140	110	134	102	96	140	110
Number of group (country)	49	49	49	45	44	40	49	49
R-squared	0.16	0.16	0.3	0.2	0.36	0.23	0.18	0.32

Source: Data on wages and employment are from Rama and Artecona (2000); data on total physical capital are from Sandeep Mahahjan (2001); data on merchandise exports including nonoil merchandise exports comes from UN Comtrade database; data on working-age population, exports, total population, GDP, total world trade come from World Development Indicators, World Bank.
Note: All figures are US $ based. Working-age population is defined as persons between 15 and 64 years old.
*significant at 5 percent; **significant at 1 percent.

The estimates suggest that the medium-term benefits of trade expansion in terms of employment could be substantial. In MENA, the share of nonoil merchandise exports in GDP was about 10 percent on average, against 23 percent in East Asia and the Pacific (regression sample statistics). Bridging just half of this gap in export performance could bring about an estimated 2 percent increase in industrial employment as a share of working-age population. This would be equivalent to a 4 percent decrease in the average unemployment rate, as participation in the labor force in MENA amounts to only about 50 percent of the working-age population.

Moreover, the full impact of trade expansion on manufacturing employment may be underestimated, because the data only account for formal employment in manufacturing. With the regulatory framework in the labor market unchanged, an increase in formal employment is likely to also have an impact on informal manufacturing employment. Higher employment and incomes in (formal and informal) manufacturing would also boost domestic expenditure in nontradables, so second-round multiplier effects from trade expansion could further contribute to economy-wide job creation.

It is noteworthy that trade has a different impact on manufacturing employment in high-income and developing countries. The results presented in table 13.2 and figure 13.10 suggest that, after controlling for other factors, trade has a negative impact on manufacturing employment in high-income countries. The results are statistically significant only for the trade-to-GDP ratio and total exports, but all coefficients signs are congruent across specifications. Indeed, in several high-income countries, trade intensification has gone in tandem with delocalization of production to developing countries, along with a shift towards areas of comparative advantage in higher-skill activities in services.

Given the trends of the variables used in the regressions, the story told by these estimates is consistent with the theoretical argument that in the medium to long run, capital growth increases the demand for labor, but is absorbed by wage growth, which offsets its impact on employment. In the economy as a whole, trade should have no role to play in an employment equation, but in a regression restricted to manufacturing it has a role. In high-income coun-

Table 13.2. Determinants of Employment in Manufacturing—High-Income Countries

(Dependent variable: ratio of employment in manufacturing to working-age population) (Estimation period: 1960–95)

Explanatory variables	Employment in manufacturing and openness to trade in developing countries Explained variable: log of employment in manufacturing-to-working-age population ratio			
Log of trade-to-GDP ratio	−2.59*			
	[2.22]			
Log of exports-to-GDP ratio		−0.267*		
		[2.29]		
Log of merchandise exports-to-GDP ratio			−0.24	
			[1.76]	
Log of merchandise exports (excluding petroleum)-to-GDP ratio				−0.121
				[1.14]
Real interest rate				
Log of labor costs in manufacturing	−0.447*	−0.443**	−0.261	−0.401**
	[3.88]	[3.84]	[2.02]	[3.03]
Log of total physical capital-to-total labor force ratio	0.297**	0.309**	−0.144	0.244**
	[3.69]	[3.76]	[1.20]	[2.80]
Constant	3.828**	3.434**	8.609**	3.491**
	[7.15]	[5.79]	[5.63]	[5.79]
Observations	135	135	60	121
Number of group (country)	22	22	21	20
R-squared	0.18	0.18	0.32	0.1

Source: Data on wages and employment are from Rama and Artecona (2000); data on total physical capital are from Sandeep Mahahjan (2001); data on merchandise exports including nonoil merchandise exports comes from UN Comtrade database; data on working-age population, GDP come from World Development Indicators, World Bank.

Note: All figures are US $ based. Working-age population is defined as persons between 15 and 64 years old.

*significant at 5 percent; **significant at 1 percent. Absolute value of t-statistics in brackets.

Figure 13.10.   Trade Expansion and Manufacturing Employment in Developing and High-Income Countries

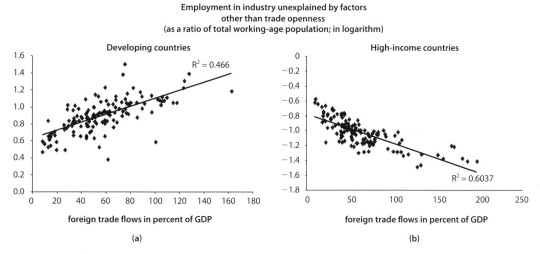

Employment in industry unexplained by factors
other than trade openness
(as a ratio of total working-age population; in logarithm)

(a)

(b)

Source: Authors' calculations.

tries, wage growth alone cannot explain the fall in manufacturing employment because wages are common across the whole economy. Trade expansion
lies behind the fall in manufacturing employment relative to employment
elsewhere.

The influence of trade expansion on the overall level of employment in
developing countries that dismantle trade barriers is different from its effect
on employment in developed countries. Trade barriers and other institutional rigidities have deadweight costs, in addition to disincentives that are associated with implicit and explicit taxes used to finance them. Removing costly
institutional structures increases national welfare, improves incentives, and
increases both the demand and supply of labor, by attracting more people of
working age into the labor force. Thus, in developing countries, trade expansion promotes manufacturing employment in the medium term, because it
allows these countries to take better advantage of their comparative advantage
in labor-intensive industries.

Why Has Trade Expansion Had a Weak Impact on Manufacturing Employment in MENA?

Despite the evidence presented so far, there is widespread sentiment that the
impact of trade expansion on manufacturing employment in MENA has been
weak. That perception is, indeed, confirmed by our estimates: As shown in
table 13.1, when estimated separately, the coefficients of trade in the employment equations turn out not to be significant for the MENA countries. This is
true not only for broad indicators of trade flows, but also for indicators of
export performance. To be sure, employment in manufacturing is higher in

countries with high nonoil merchandise exports (Tunisia, Morocco, Jordan) compared to countries with weak export performance (Algeria, Egypt). However, such differences are largely explained by country-specific factors (such as, for example, greater female participation in the labor force in Tunisia) and structural factors other than trade. The employment ratio responded only modestly to changes in the share of nonoil merchandise exports in GDP in both groups of MENA countries (figure 13.11). Empirical evidence suggests that, contrary to the experience elsewhere in developing countries, when such structural factors are accounted for, trade expansion did not have a significant impact on industrial employment in MENA.

What might be the reasons for the weak impact of trade on employment in MENA? A number of factors can be singled out. They are partly related to what might be called the "quality gap" in MENA trade, and partly to poorly performing labor market institutions that tame the medium-term benefits from increased trade openness while exacerbating the adjustment costs.

A number of attributes of MENA trade may account for the weak impact of trade on employment:

- Non-hydrocarbon exports are concentrated in resource-based, low value-added products, whose growth has only a weak impact on labor demand and employment (Petri, 1997). Moreover, in these sectors, world trade is growing slowly, so that MENA could not take advantage of the strong growth in world trade growth over the 1990s that gave an impetus to employment creation elsewhere in developing countries.

- In hydrocarbon-rich countries such as Algeria, exports of manufactures are concentrated in the downstream energy industries, which are capital-

Figure 13.11. Impact of Trade Expansion on Manufacturing Employment in MENA

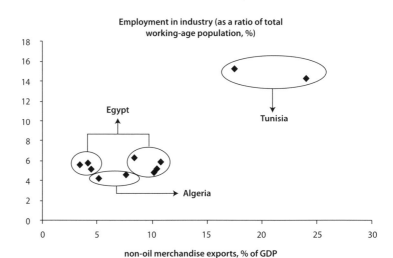

Source: Authors' calculations.

intensive and have only little impact on employment (for example, refined gas; fertilizers; plastics).

• MENA trade is poorly integrated into cross-border production-sharing networks, which have increasingly become a driver of growth in global trade (Humels et al., 2001; Yeats and Ng, 2000). MENA exports do not, thus, benefit from rapidly expanding vertical trade. As a result, FDI—the complement of increased participation in global production networks—remains limited. The weak responsiveness of foreign and domestic investment to trade liberalization tames the impact on job creation.

The functioning of the labor markets may also affect the impact of trade on job creation, because the net effect on employment depends on the response of wages to the reform process—and thus on the institutional rigidities in the labor market and the wage setting process. To give some examples, the reforms and trade expansion that accompanied Spain's transition to democracy in the late 1970s did not give rise to more employment because newly-emancipated trade unions claimed those benefits in the form of higher wages. The integration of eastern Germany into the western economy in the 1990s tells a similar story, as the newly liberated labor in the east sought to catch up with their western counterparts through overvalued wages (and their western counterparts supported the big wage rises to stop massive immigration).

In MENA, labor market rigidities are largely associated with the important role of public sector employment and pay, which sets the stage for real wage increases and employment conditions in the formal labor market. As shown in Figures 13.2.a. and 13.2.b., MENA is the developing region with the largest share of public sector employment and pay—by far larger than the share of manufacturing employment in total employment or of the share of manufacturing wages in GDP. The large share of public sector employment and pay makes MENA the only region where real wages in the public sector are, on average, higher than real wages in the private sector. Because of non-pecuniary benefits of public sector employment and job security, this leads to queuing for public sector jobs, and puts pressure on private-sector real wages in order to attract workers (especially skilled workers) when activity is expanding. The restrictive employment regulations in the private sector formal labor markets, and the high nonwage costs, may further tame the responsiveness of job creation to growing trade.

Among the above factors, our estimates highlight, in particular, the role of FDI as one explanation for the weak impact of trade on jobs in MENA. Indeed, in developing countries, the impact of trade expansion on employment is likely to be reinforced by capital flows. Trade liberalization allows large international corporations to take advantage of the cheaper labor in developing countries and locate processing plants in them, through direct investment. FDI flows into developing countries have been identified with higher wages and with more male/female wage equality. They increase the demand for labor in the receiving country by increasing the supply of capital. The impact of this on employment creation is likely to be greater than the impact of the demand-driven increase in labor demand because although the demand-driven increase may hit supply bottlenecks, the FDI-induced increase is not likely to. Indeed, the effect of more FDI on the domestic economy must be beneficial, unless the higher wages that they pay provoke comparability demands elsewhere in the economy, an argument that has not received support in the empirical literature.[1]

The estimates reported in table 13.3 confirm the critical role of FDI in job creation. They are similar to the estimates for developing countries reported in table 13.1, with the difference that the observations in the sample are split in two different groups: (i) a group of developing countries with large FDI inflows and, (ii) a group of small FDI recipients—the cutoff point being the overall sample median of 0.7 percent of GDP. While the impact of trade expansion on employment in manufacturing is highly significant in the group of large FDI recipients (figure 13.12.a), the estimated coefficients of trade turn out not to be significant in the group of countries that receive only small

Table 13.3. Determinants of Employment in Manufacturing in Developing Countries: The Role of Foreign Direct Investment

(Dependent variable: ratio of employment in manufacturing to working-age population) (Estimation period: 1990–95)

Employment in manufacturing and openness to trade in developing countries by foreign direct investment level							
Explanatory variables	Explained variable: log of employment in manufacturing-to-working age population ratio						
Log of trade-to-GDP ratio * high FDI	0.534**							
Log of trade-to-GDP ratio * low FDI		0.021						
Log of merchandise exports * high FDI			0.270*					
Log of merchandise exports * low FDI				0.309				
Log of exports of goods and services * high FDI					0.447*			
Log of exports of goods and services * low FDI						–0.013		
Log of merchandise exports excluding petroleum * high FDI							0.222*	
Log of merchandise exports excluding petroleum * low FDI								–0.017
Log of labor costs in manufacturing	–0.074	–0.377*	–0.054	–0.419*	–0.044	–0.383*	–0.079	–0.483**
Log of total physical capital-to-total labor force ratio	0.195	0.377*	0.305	0.573*	0.157	0.396*	0.323	0.496**
Constant	–2.172	–0.235	–2.414	–3.452	–1.208	–0.329	–2.328	–0.884
Observations	60	69	53	57	60	69	57	65
Number of group (country)	31	35	27	32	31	35	29	33
R-squared	0.38	0.19	0.36	0.3	0.35	0.19	0.28	0.26

Source: Data on wages and employment are from Rama and Artecona (2000); data on total physical capital are from Sandeep Mahahjan (2001); data on merchandise exports including nonoil merchandise exports comes from UN Comtrade database; data on working-age population, exports, total population, GDP, total world trade come from World Development Indicators, World Bank.
Note: All figures are US $ based. Working-age population is defined as persons between 15 and 64 years old.
*significant at 5 percent; **significant at 1 percent.

Figure 13.12. Quality of the Investment Climate as a Determinant of the Impact of Trade on Job Creation in Manufacturing

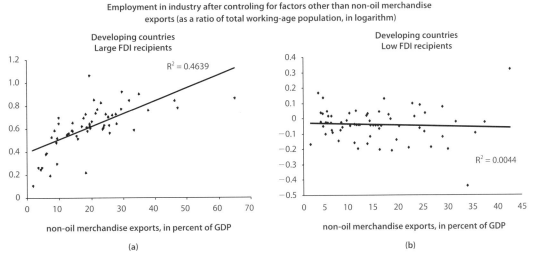

Employment in industry after controling for factors other than non-oil merchandise exports (as a ratio of total working-age population, in logarithm)

(a)

(b)

Source: Authors' calculations.

amounts of FDI (figure 13.12.b). This is true whatever the indicator of trade in the regressions.

But MENA countries have lagged considerably behind other developing regions in attracting FDI, which also explains the limited impact of trade expansion on job creation. MENA has missed in particular the surge in FDI to developing countries seen in the 1990s, with the share of FDI in GDP remaining compressed to 0.5 percent, against 2.5 percent, on average, in developing countries (figure 13.13). Moreover, the structure of FDI in MENA is highly skewed toward the hydrocarbon sector, thus contributing even less to job creation in manufacturing and in services. Reflecting the slow pace of restructuring and privatization of the business sector in MENA, and a weak investment climate, non-energy FDI stagnated over the 1990s, compared to the levels seen in lower middle-income countries in Latin America, Central and Eastern Europe, and East Asia (Nabli et al., 2000; Petri, 1997b; Council on Foreign Relations, 2002).

Rising to the Challenge: Strengthening the Investment Climate and Enabling Greater Participation in Global Production-Sharing Networks

To step up employment growth, MENA exports would need to be diversified away from raw materials and resource-based manufactures and toward high value-added, labor-intensive products, linked more closely with international production networks and global investment flows. International evidence reviewed in this paper suggests that, to achieve these goals, and provide a stimulus to employment creation, lowering the still high degree of trade protection

Figure 13.13. MENA's Share of the Surge in FDI to Developing Countries

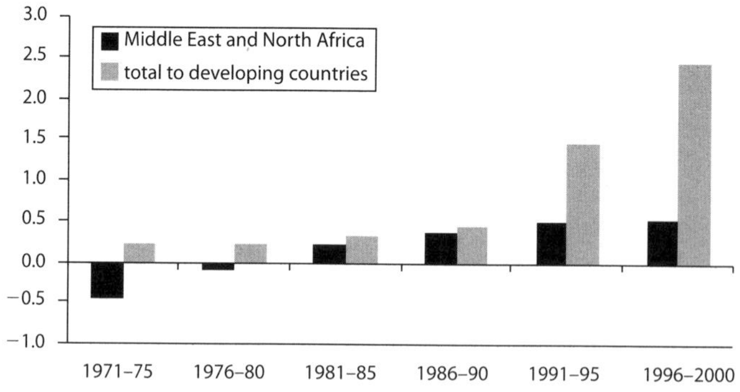

Source: Authors' calculations.

in MENA will not be enough. Companion policies would be needed to help bridge the "quality gap" in MENA trade, by strengthening the investment climate and relaxing the "beyond-the-border" constraints that increase the cost of doing business and limit the attractiveness of MENA as a place to invest.

Improving participation in global production-sharing is key, because a common pattern of integration in today's global economy is the increasing fragmentation of production chains across borders (Arndt and Kierzkowski, 1999). This is reflected in far above average growth of global trade in components and partially assembled manufactured goods (Yeats, 2000). Sharp reductions in the cost of moving goods across borders have enabled firms to better coordinate production in different locations, and have facilitated exporters' linkages with vertical production chains that stretch increasingly across borders (Hummels et al., 2001). Lower logistics costs have resulted from an accelerating "logistics revolution"—driven by the more widespread use of containers in trade; the adoption of "just-in-time" manufacturing techniques; enhanced supply-chain management; and more widespread use of information technology and the internet in logistics. Lower levels of trade protection have also facilitated the fragmentation of production across borders.

Given the increasing sophistication of the division of labor in the global economy, efficient trade-related services are becoming key in enabling producers at various stages of production chains to better coordinate their activities with intermediate input suppliers located in other countries. Speed, flexibility, reliability, and low cost of transport and information logistics are particularly adding value to companies participating in production chains around the globe. Slow or unpredictable delivery delays the response to new market opportunities and rapidly changing demand patterns, forcing customers to hold costly buffer stocks, and making supply chain management ineffective. Countries that have strengthened their positions in global production chains have improved their Information and Communication Technology (ICT) capabilities; lowered the cost of transport; and created more competitive finance and insurance markets. Better service delivery has greatly contributed to reducing the cost of doing business, thus improving the attractiveness of these countries to both foreign and domestic investment.

Because the location of manufacturing activities has become, competition to maintain positions has increased. A strong investment climate and logistical excellence are important parts of all success stories to date. Countries that have created more open, investment-friendly markets have been able to attract significant flows of FDI along with their integration into broader economic areas. But for this to happen, the reduction of trade barriers had to go in tandem with broader regulatory reform that improved the attractiveness to investment.

For example, the Central and Eastern European countries (CEECs) that gained EU accession status carried forward broad-based restructuring programs, while aligning their regulatory framework to the EU single market. More ambitious reformers, and countries that were more successful in integrating EU production networks, attracted massive FDI that boosted growth. By contrast, the Commonwealth of Independent States (CIS) countries lagged far behind in terms of industrial restructuring, trade expansion, and growth (World Bank, 2002b). Trade liberalization and regulatory reform in the CEECs under the European Association Agreements (EAAs) also spurred a deeper integration of these countries into the EU production-sharing networks. CEECs exports of parts have thus increased fourfold from 1993 to 1998—to about US$12 billion, or 14.2 percent of CEECs manufactured exports (Kaminski and Ng, 2001). The shares of parts in manufactured exports have thus approached those seen in more integrated countries in global production sharing, such as Malaysia and Mexico (about 19 percent in 1998).[2] Integration in EU production networks has been also a factor in attracting FDI—as evidenced by the positive correlation between FDI per capita and the share of parts in total exports (figure 13.14).

MENA countries are still poorly integrated in global production-sharing networks, as reflected by their small share of global FDI flows and trade. The share of components in manufactured exports remains far below that seen in other developing countries, such as Singapore, Malaysia, and Taiwan (Yeats and Ng, 2000). One exception is textile and clothing, especially reflecting Tunisia's strong position in EU companies' outsourcing chains.

Trade liberalization, especially in the countries that have signed the Association Agreements with the EU (Tunisia, Egypt, Morocco, Jordan, and most recently Algeria), will help MENA producers improve their competitiveness by purchasing inputs at internationally competitive cost. Moreover, MENA countries could be attractive locations for assembly operations due to low labor costs and a good quality of human resources. The decrease in tariffs on imported intermediate inputs, scheduled in the first stages of the Association Agreements, has the potential to increase trade in components across the

Figure 13.14. Integration into EU Trade Networks and FDI in the Central and Eastern European Countries

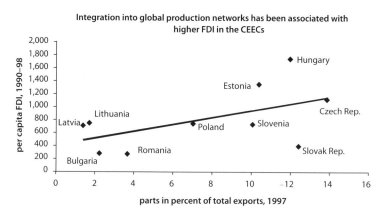

Source: Authors' calculations.

Mediterranean and facilitate the integration of MENA countries into EU production networks. The planed free trade zone with the EU thus provides a unique opportunity to MENA to attract more FDI, increase exports, and benefit from knowledge and technology spillovers. This could also help upgrade the quality of MENA exports toward more high value-added and technologically advanced products, as in the example of the economies in East Asia.

However, MENA has yet to rise to this challenge. Slow progress to date partly reflects heightened competition from the transition economies in Central and Eastern Europe. However, domestic weaknesses, due to the weak investment climate and the poor quality of backbone services that facilitate trade, dilute the potential advantages of MENA countries. Bottlenecks in transport logistics are particularly damaging, but they are not only limited to poor quality and high cost of transport and information services per se. Trade-related controls in MENA are associated with burdensome administrative procedures, and create red tape.

Creating an enabling environment for foreign and domestic investment would be key to reaping the benefits from further trade liberalization in MENA. In order to encourage transnational companies to extend their supply chains to MENA through partnerships with domestic companies or new investment, further progress in lowering trade barriers should go in tandem with complementary policies in other areas. In particular, trade logistics, transport, and information systems would have to become more flexible, reliable and sophisticated. This would require ambitious opening up of service markets to competition—supported by continuous efforts at public enterprise reform in network industries; privatization; and procompetitive regulation.

The stakes of more ambitious liberalization in services are high for a number of additional reasons:

- Inefficient and costly services, provided mostly by the public sector, raise the cost of MENA merchandise exports, limit attractiveness of investment, while also impeding trade expansion within the region.
- With the right enabling environment in place, liberalization of key services—such as, for example, telecommunications—may facilitate the development of export capacity in other services—especially in tourism-related services and the ICT sector.
- In addition to enhancing export capacity, liberalization in services can create more investment opportunities for the domestic private sector, and help attract more non-debt-creating foreign financing in the form of FDI. Stepped up investment can offset the short-term adjustment costs stemming from lower protection of import-competing industries.

Procompetitive reforms that facilitate entry by new firms can generate employment opportunities for skilled and unskilled workers who are now employed by governments in low-productivity jobs or in threatened import-competing private manufacturing (Council on Foreign Relations, 2002). Because services often cannot be traded, increasing access to service markets is likely to require the entry of foreign competitors through FDI. This will not only lead to the introduction of new technologies that improve efficiency and competitiveness, but also entail the hiring of domestic labor. By creating more opportunities for the employment of skilled workers, services liberalization would also help address the structural imbalances in MENA labor markets, especially the exceptionally high rates of unemployment for educated workers and the young.

Notes

1. There is some concern that the jobs created by FDI are also less secure, as financial crises or political uncertainties can lead to capital flight and job closures. However, experience since the Asian crisis has shown that FDI and the employment that it generated has been resilient to the financial crisis. FDI in 2001 was at about the same level as in 1997, despite the collapse of private debt and equity flows. See World Bank, 2002a.

2. The EU absorbs the lion's share of CEECs exports of parts—about 79 percent in 1998. At the same time, 82 per cent of CEECs imports of parts in 1998 originated in the EU. Germany has emerged as the main trading partner among EU countries, as it takes almost half of CEECs exports of parts. Among the CEECs, the Czech Republic, Hungary, Slovenia, Estonia, and Slovakia had the highest participation of parts in their trade.

References

Agrawal, N. 2002. "The Impact of Liberalization on Employment and Earnings in Indonesia." In F. Iqbal and W.E. James (eds.) *Deregulation and Development in Indonesia*, Westport, Conn.: Praeger Publishers. Arndt, S., and H. Kierzkowski. 2002. "Introduction." In S. Arndt and H. Kierzkowski, eds., *Fragmentation and International Trade*. Oxford and New York: Oxford University Press.

Council on Foreign Relations. 2002. *Harnessing Trade for Development and Growth in the Middle East*. Washington, DC: Council on Foreign Relations.

Currie, J., and A. Harrison. 1997. "Sharing the Costs: The Impact of Trade Reform on Capital and Labor in Morocco." *Journal of Labor Economics* 15: S44–S71.

Dessus, S., and A. Suwa-Eisenmann. 1998. "Trade Integration with Europe, Export Diversification, and Economic Growth in Egypt." Technical Paper No. 135. OECD Development Centre, Paris.

Dhonte, P., R. Bhattacharya, and T. Yousef. 2000. "Demographic Transition in the Middle East: Implications for Growth, Employment, and Housing." In Z. Iqbal, ed., *Macroeconomic Issues and Policies in the Middle East and North Africa*. Washington, DC: International Monetary Fund.

Hummels, D., J. Ishii, and K.-M. Yi. 2001. "The Nature and Growth of Vertical Specialization in World Trade." *Journal of International Economics* 54(1): 75–96.

International Monetary Fund (IMF). 2001. Staff Report. Article IV: Consultation with Morocco. June. Washington, DC: IMF.

Kaminski, B., and F. Ng. 2001. "Trade and Production Fragmentation: Central European Economies in EU Networks of Production and Marketing." Unpublished. World Bank, Washington, DC.

Nabli, M., and A. De Kleine. 2000. "Managing Global Integration in the Middle East and North Africa." In B. Hoekman and H. Kheir-El-Din, eds., *Trade Policy Developments in the Middle East and North Africa*. Washington, DC: World Bank Institute.

Nabli, M., and M.-A. Veganzones-Varoudakis. 2002. "Exchange Rate Regime and Competitiveness of Manufactured Exports: The Case of MENA Countries." MENA Working Paper No. 27. World Bank, Washington, DC.

Petri, A. 1997a. "Trade Strategies for the Southern Mediterranean." Technical Paper No. 127. OECD Development Centre, Paris.

———. 1997b. "The Case of Missing Foreign Investment in the Southern Mediterranean." Technical Paper No. 128. OECD Development Centre, Paris.

Rama, M. 2001. "Globalization and Workers in Developing Countries." Unpublished. June. World Bank, Washington, DC.

Revenga, A. 1997. "Employment and Wage Effects of Trade Liberalization: The Case of Mexican Manufacturing." *Journal of Labor Economics* 15: S20–S43.

Riordan, E.M., and others. 1997. "The World Economy and its Implications for the Middle East and North Africa, 1995–2010." In N. Shafik, ed., *Prospects for MENA Economies: From Boom to Bust and Back?* New York: St. Martin's Press.

Schiavo-Campo, S., G. de Tommaso, and A. Mukherje. 1997. "Government Employment and Pay in Global Perspective: A Selective Synthesis of International Facts, Policies and Experience." Unpublished. World Bank, Washington, DC.

Sekkat, K., and A. Varoudakis. 2002. "The Impact of Trade and Exchange-rate Policy Reforms on North African Manufactured Exports." *Development Policy Review* 20(2).

Wood, A. 1997. "Openness and Wage Inequality in Developing Countries: The Latin American Challenge to East Asian Conventional Wisdom." *The World Bank Economic Review* 11: 33–57.

World Bank. 2001. *Global Economic Prospects and the Developing Countries 2002*. Washington, DC: World Bank.

———. 2002a. *Global Development Finance 2002*, Washington, DC: World Bank.

———. 2002b. *Transition: The First Ten Years*. Washington, DC: World Bank.

Yeats, A. 1998. "Just How Big Is Global Production Sharing?" Policy Research Working Paper 1871. January. World Bank, Washington, DC.

Yeats, A., and F. Ng. 2000. "Production Sharing in East Asia: Who Does What, for Whom and Why?" Unpublished. World Bank, Washington, DC.

Zarrouk, J. 2000. "Para-Tariff Measures in Arab Countries." In B. Hoekman and H. Kheir-El-Din, eds., *Trade Policy Developments in the Middle East and North Africa*. Washington, DC: World Bank Institute.

14

Exchange Rate Management within the Middle East and North Africa Region

The Cost to Manufacturing Competitiveness

Mustapha Nabli
Jennifer Keller*
Marie-Ange Véganzonès†

Perhaps the greatest challenge currently facing the MENA region is the challenge of creating jobs. A recent World Bank report[1] estimates that some 100 million new jobs will need to be created in the next two decades to absorb both the current unemployed as well as the rapidly expanding labor force—more than doubling the current number of jobs today. If the region is to ensure that this labor force has both sufficient employment opportunities and the prospects for real wage growth, GDP growth in the region will need to more than double from its average of 3 percent per year over the late 1990s to 6-7 percent a year for a sustained period.

Making this possible will require a fundamental transformation in the region, from public sector-dominated economies to private sector-led economies, open to international trade, with competitive private sector industries other than oil becoming the engine for growth and employment creation. Supporting a competitive private manufacturing sector in MENA will

*World Bank. † Centre d'Etudes et de Recherches sur le Developpement International. Centre National de la Recherche Scientifique (CNRS), Université d'Auvergne. The authors are grateful to Pedro Alba, Dipak Dasgupta, Tarik Yousef, and Paolo Zacchia for their comments and suggestions, and to Paul Dyer and Adama Coulibaly for their analytical support.

Presented at the School of Oriental and African Studies (SOAS) Conference; London, July 2001.

require actions on numerous fronts, including governance, trade, and monetary and fiscal policy actions.

A requisite component of supporting private sector development in MENA will be appropriate exchange rate management. Evaluations of the economic policies in developing countries have demonstrated the importance of proper management of the real exchange rate (RER) in a country's performance. Empirical evidence consistently indicates that best economic performers are those countries that have maintained an "appropriate" RER.[2] Countries that have properly managed their RER (avoiding substantial RER appreciation) have been more successful in promoting manufacturing exports.[3] They have been more successful in attracting foreign direct investment.[4] And more generally, they have experienced higher growth.[5]

The Middle East and North Africa region has not followed the general trend worldwide in its choice of exchange rate regimes. Although over the past decades, countries have progressively adopted more flexible exchange rate regimes, the majority of the economies in the Middle East and North Africa continue to maintain de facto fixed exchange rate regimes. While about 65 percent of economies were operating under de facto fixed exchange rate regimes in 1974 (within MENA, the proportion was somewhat higher, at 77 percent), by the end of the 1990s, only 42 percent of economies outside of MENA had fixed exchange rate systems. Within MENA, however, that proportion was 60 percent.

What impact, if any, have fixed exchange rate regimes had on RER misalignment and, ultimately, the economic performances in the MENA region? In this paper, we calculate the level of exchange rate misalignment across a panel of countries over the 1970-1999 period, and show that the MENA region has suffered from substantial exchange rate overvaluation which, though highest over the 1970-1985 period, has persisted into the 1990s. It is estimated that over the 1985-1999 period, the degree of exchange rate overvaluation in MENA averaged some 22 percent, higher than for any other region but CFA Africa. We then calculate the effect that overvaluation of the exchange rate has had on the competitiveness of nonoil exports. It is estimated that the overvaluation of exchange rates has reduced the region's manufacturing exports—as a percentage of GDP per year—by about 18 percent over the 1970-1999 period.

Armed with this information, we discuss the empirical relationship between the extent of exchange rate misalignment and the choice of exchange rate regime. From our own calculations, the probability for fixed exchange rates to become overvalued is substantially higher than for floating regimes, and the probability for exchange rates under fixed regimes to become seriously overvalued (in excess of 25 percent) is almost twice as high as for flexible arrangements. We then discuss the reasons behind MENA's continued reliance on fixed exchange rate regimes. While the exchange rate choices in the region are poorly explained by most traditional models of exchange rate choice, they in part reflect the interests of the public sector as both producer of oil and holder of debt, both of which make the government likely to favor fixed exchange rates over floating ones.

Exchange Rate Management, Overvaluation, and the Costs to Competitiveness

MENA's exchange rate management has relied predominantly upon rigid exchange rates, though not necessarily "officially" fixed exchange rates.[6] In part, the reliance on fixed regimes was in response to the rapid inflation many economies experienced over the late 1980s and early 1990s. Most economies in MENA opted for a fixed exchange rate regime as the most effective strategy for combating high inflation.

This adoption of fixed exchange rates was successful in contributing to macroeconomic stability. However, once the immediate threats of high inflation had been averted, only a handful of countries shifted to more flexible exchange rate arrangements.

One of the arguments for countries that are not contending with high levels of inflation— and thus not necessarily requiring a monetary anchor— to adopt flexible exchange rate arrangements is that the real exchange rate is less likely to become overvalued. Overvaluation can negatively affect a country's economic performance through a variety of channels. Overvaluation reduces the profitability of tradables and, in turn, decreases exports. It leads to a reduction in economic efficiency and a misallocation of resources. By increasing uncertainty and raising the risk of macroeconomic collapse, misalignment can hinder economic growth through a deterioration of domestic and foreign confidence and investment, and can act as a catalyst for capital flight.[7]

Our own estimates suggest that fixed exchange rate regimes are substantially more likely to become overvalued than flexible regimes. We estimated the level of exchange rate misalignment for a panel of countries, measured as the percent difference between the real exchange rate (RER) and its equilibrium value (ERER).[8] The RER was modeled following the approach used by Edwards (1989) and extended by Elbadawi (1994) and Baffes, Elbadawi and O'Connel (1997).[9]

From these misalignment estimates, we find that over the 1974-99 period, the proportion of observations under fixed regimes which were even marginally overvalued was 88 percent, versus 76 percent of flexible exchange rate regimes. Moreover, the proportion of observations under fixed regimes that were seriously overvalued (in excess of 25 percent) was 50 percent, almost twice as high as for flexible regimes (28 percent).

This tendency for fixed exchange rates to become overvalued has impacted the MENA region significantly, with substantial overvaluation of the real exchange rate experienced over the past three decades—around 29 percent per year in the 1970s to the mid-1980s and 22 percent per year from the mid 1980s to 1999 (see table 14.1). In addition, this tendency has not significantly decreased—contrary to the Latin American, African, or Asian economies in our sample, which have in general chosen a more flexible exchange rate regime—with regular devaluation of their currency—as well as more consequent macroeconomic reforms.

Overvaluation and Manufactured Exports

What has been the cost of this greater degree of overvaluation in MENA to total exports and manufactured exports? To determine, the following model tests the effects of RER misalignment and volatility on the logarithm of total and manufactured exports to GDP ($\log(X_t)$):

$$\ln(X_t) = c + b_1. \ GDPgrTP_{i,t} + b_2. \ ln(TOTn_{i,t}) + b_3. \ ln(Inv_{i,t}) + b_4. \\ ln(Roads_{i,t}) + b_5. \ ln(H1_{i,t}) + b_6. \ RerVol_{i,t} + b_7. \ ln(RerMis_{i,t}) + \varepsilon_t.$$

where:

(i) $GDPgrTP_{i,t}$ = the rate of growth of GDP of country's trading partners (which can have a "pulling" effect on export growth);

(ii) $ln(TOTn_{i,t})$ = logarithm of terms of trade (in which improvements can increase the profitability of production for export);

(iii) $ln(Inv_{i,t})$ = logarithm of investment/GDP (which increases the overall production capacity, and thereby, export capacity);

Table 14.1. Average Misalignment and Volatility[a]

1975/80– 84 (in % per year)[b]	Misalignment	Volatility
MENA	29	7.9
Latin America	20	11.2
Africa (CFA)	61	12.7
Africa (non CFA)	29	11.3
South Asia	43	13
East Asia	10	5.4
1985–99 (in % per year)[b]	**Misalignment**	**Volatility**
MENA	22	12.4
Latin America	10	12.9
Africa (CFA)	28	14.5
Africa (non CFA)	13	16
South Asia	15	8.3
East Asia	5	8.6

a. Volatility is calculated as the coefficient of variation of the RER over a five-year period.
b. Depending on the countries.

(iv)   *ln(Roads $_{i,t}$)* = logarithm of lenth of roads (in km per km^2)

(v)   *ln(H1 $_{i,t}$)* = logarithm of the average number of years of primary schooling of adult population.

{Both (iv) and (v) capturing the availability of core physical and human
infrastructures}

(vi)   *RERVols = volatility of the RER, as a measure of volatility of relative
prices*[10] *(with RER*[11] *volatility increasing the uncertainty of export profitability)*

(vii) *RERMis* = RER misalignment, as a measure of the distortion of relative
prices (overvaluation hampers competitiveness and diverts investment
out of more productive tradable goods sectors).[12]

The equation was estimated on our panel of 53 countries over 1970/80 to
99. The results from our estimation are shown in table 14.2.

Table 14.2. Estimation Results of the Exports Equations

Dependent variables: ln(*Xmanuf$_t$*) and ln(*Xtot$_t$*)

Variable	Manufactured exports	Total exports
GDPgrTP $_{i,t}$	2.83	1.48
	(1.9)	(2.52)
ln(TOTn $_{i,t}$)	−1.4	0.1
	(0.81)	(2.49)
ln(Inv $_{i,t}$)	0.87	0.30
	(5.8)	(8.69)
ln(Roads $_{i,t}$)	0.08	0.10
	(1.4)	(3.48)
ln(H1 $_{i,t}$)	1.92	0.26
	(11.13)	(5.66)
RerVol	-0.27	-0.1
	(0.80)	(1.21)
Ln(RerMis)	−0.72	−0.10
	(5.75)	(2.75)
Year 1974	0.25	
	(1.65)	
Year 1975	0.34	
	(1.7)	
Intercept		-1.14
		(9.05)
Adjusted R^2	0.81	0.13
Fischer test	31.7	78.3
Haussmann test	12.4	0.20

*Note: Student t statistics are within brackets. The numbers of observations are 816 and 964. Cointegration of the variables
was tested using Im, Pesaran, and Shin (1997) critical values of ADF tests in the case of heterogeneous panel data. (see
table A-2 in Annex 2). The equations were estimated by using the fixed effect method in the case of manufactured exports
and the random effect method in that of total exports.*

Our estimations confirm a significant negative impact of ER mismanagement (in the form of overvaluation) on total and manufacturing export performance. According to our estimations, a 10 percent increase in the level of misalignment lowers the ratio of manufactured exports to GDP by 7.2 percent, and the ratio of total exports to GDP by 1 percent. Overall, for the MENA region, this RER overvaluation during the 1970-99 period reduced, on average per year, manufacturing exports to GDP by 18 percent.

In terms of individual countries in MENA, losses have been important in Jordan and Morocco in the 1970s and 1980s, because of the more diversified export base of these economies. This is also the case of Tunisia in the 1990s, despite a low level of overvaluation. In the major oil-exporting countries (Algeria and Iran), losses appear small because of the low level of manufactured exports (table 14.3). The large overvaluation, however, has certainly contributed to the low diversification of these economies.

Overall, overvaluation represents a large cost to the region. Developing a competitive private sector depends upon ensuring appropriate prices. Profitability of production hinges on prices: prices of inputs that go into the production process, and the price that can be obtained in the market for output. Overvaluation damages competitiveness because it artificially alters the price ratio between tradables and nontradables, and the region's producers of tradable goods find they are less able to compete with either imported goods or with other countries' exports.

Economies that, in reality, have cost advantages in labor and domestically produced inputs begin altering their production processes and substituting for capital equipment and imported inputs. And the greater the overvaluation that takes place, the more difficult it becomes for otherwise competitive firms

Table 14.3. Cost of Overvaluation on Manufactured Exports

(Selected MENA Countries)

	Algeria			Egypt			Iran		
	Mis (%)	ExpM (%)[a]	Cost[b]	Mis (%)	ExpM (%)[a]	Cost[b]	Mis (%)	ExpM (%)[a]	Cost[b]
1970–79	79	3	−1.7	15	27	−2.9	42	3	−0.9
1980–89	59	1.5	−0.6	22	19	−3	24	4	−0.7
1990–99	8	3.3	−0.2	19	37	−2.4	84	7	−4
1970–99	49	2.6	−0.8	15	27.6	−2.7	49	4.5	−1.8

	Jordan			Morocco			Tunisia		
	Mis (%)	ExpM (%)[a]	Cost[b]	Mis (%)	ExpM (%)[a]	Cost[b]	Mis (%)	ExpM (%)[a]	Cost[b]
1970–79	57	26	−10.5	49	16	−5.7		25	
1980–89	31	43	−9.4	8	39	−2.4	3	49	−1
1990–99	9	49	−3.1	1	53	−3.7	16	75	−8.7
1970–99	25	39.1	−7.7	21	36.1	−3.9	9	49.6	−4.8

a. ExpM: manufactured exports as percent of total exports.

b. Cost of overvaluation as percent of total exports.

to maintain their competitive edge, and the more it discourages new firms from entering the market. At a time when encouraging an export-oriented, nonoil private sector in MENA is critical, there is little room for excessive exchange rate overvaluation.

Exchange Rate Regime Choice

While fixed exchange rates significantly increase the incidence of overvaluation, and subsequently the cost to manufacturing exports, the question emerges, why does the region continue to rely upon rigid exchange rate arrangements? Is misalignment a justified cost that the MENA region must pay to maintain stability in other macroeconomic fundamentals? In other words, have MENA countries been choosing the appropriate exchange rate arrangements?

The question is complex. A great deal of research has been devoted to improving our understanding of how exchange rate regime choices are made, with two major branches of research emerging. The first branch has produced models of exchange rate choice based solely upon economic factors.[13] In this framework, the optimal regime could be determined as the one that minimizes fluctuations in output, the price level, or some other macroeconomic variable. The other branch of research has focused on the political economy. While there have been several arguments within this general framework, they have generally focused on the relationship between domestic political institutions and exchange rate decisions.[14]

But while both economic and political economic models have substantially improved our understanding of exchange rate choice across countries, traditional models have been less successful in explaining the de facto[15] exchange rate regime decisions within MENA. Standard models of exchange rate choice that incorporate both structural and political characteristics, when applied to MENA economies, result in incorrectly predicted exchange rate regimes twice as often as for non-MENA economies. In table 14.4, several conventional models of exchange rate regime choice are outlined, which incorporate a broad range of structural and political economy variables. In none of these standard models are the exchange rate regimes adopted in MENA as well predicted as for other countries. In most cases, the difference in the proportion of observations correctly predicted between non-MENA economies and MENA economies is substan'

Where do the standard models fail in predicting the exchange rate regimes within MENA? The majority occur for fixed exchange rate observations. Model A, for example, correctly predicts 31 percent of the MENA observations of floating regimes. On the other hand, it does not correctly predict any fixed regime observations (that compares with non-MENA economies, with 55 percent correct predictions for floating regime observations and 10 percent

Table 14.4. Correct Predictions of Exchange Rate Regime under Alternate Model Specifications[a]

Model	Independent variables[b]	Non-MENA		MENA	
		No. obs	% correct predictions[c]	No. obs.	% correct Predictions
A	Size, Openness, CVEX, CVGDP	895	37	106	16
B	Size, Openness, CVEX, CVGDP, CAPCONT, RESERVES, INFLAT	895	43	106	19
C	POLSTABLE, HISTGROW, Size, Openness, CVEX, CVGDP, CAPCONT, RESERVES, INFLAT	674	41	91	15
D	HISTGROW, Size, Openness, CVEX, CVGDP, CAPCONT, RESERVES, INFLAT	779	42	97	17

a. Dependent variable exchange rate regime arrangement (1=fixed; 0=floating). Probit estimation for the 1985-2000 period.

b. SIZE = lagged ratio of GDP in constant US$ to US. OPENNESS = average ratio of (imports + exports) / GDP for five years prior to observation year. CVEX = Coefficient of variation of exports for period (t-5) to (t-1). CVGDP = Coefficient of variation of GDP for period (t-5) to (t-1). CAPCONT = dummy variable for whether country had controls on movement of capital. RESERVES = lagged ratio of international reserves to imports. INFLAT = average inflation rate over five year period prior to observation year. POLSTABLE = lagged index of political stability (ICRG). HISTGROW = average lagged log growth, period (t-5) to (t-1). All estimations performed over the 1985-2000 period.

c. Exchange rate choice was modeled through probit estimation, with fixed exchange rates having a value of 1, and flexible regimes a value of 0. Probit estimations will produce a probability of adopting a fixed regime, ranging from 0 to 1. A fixed exchange rate regime was said to be correctly predicted if the estimated probability of adopting a fixed exchange rate regime was greater than 0.6. A flexible exchange rate regime was said to be correctly predicted if the estimated probability of adopting a fixed regime was less than 0.4. Estimated probabilities between 0.4 and 0.6 were categorized as not definitively predicted by the model.

correct predictions for fixed regime observations). Model B correctly predicts 31 percent of MENA's floating regime observations, but only 6 percent of its fixed regime observations (compared with 57 percent and 21 percent for non-MENA observations of floating and fixed regimes, respectively). Overall, and especially for the cases where fixed regimes have been adopted, according to traditional models for exchange rate choice, the MENA region isn't getting it right.

Why the MENA countries, which would be predicted along structural variables lines to adopt flexible regimes, have chosen to maintain fixed exchange rate arrangements may have something to do with the public sector's personal interests.

Recent research advances the proposition that countries with high unhedged foreign currency-denominated debt, and a correspondingly high exchange rate risk exposure (such as economies in the MENA region) have an incentive to peg (see Calvo and Reinhard, 2000; Hausman, Panizza, and Stein, 2000). For governments with high publicly guaranteed external debt, fixed regimes may be preferred as a means to better control the direction of temporary currency appreciation (or depreciation), since by allowing overvaluation of the currency, it permits at least a temporary reduction in foreign-denominated debt payments (albeit while sacrificing the competitiveness of some national industries in the process). Continued build-up of further debt, at the same time, allows an overvalued fixed exchange rate to be maintained, since it permits the government to continue to borrow foreign currency to sustain the current account deficit and meet the excess demand.

In addition, the public sector in many MENA economies (and most oil-based economies) has interest in its own business, namely the export of natural resources. Oil still represents the major source of income and a dominant source of foreign exchange for the oil-producing economies of MENA. Shares of oil in current total exports ranged from a high of more than 95 percent in Yemen, to a low of less than 1 percent in Jordan and Morocco in at the end of the 1990s. In 10 of the 16 countries of MENA listed below in figure 14.1, oil revenues account for more than 70 percent of total export revenues, and in 12 of the 16, it accounts for more than 45 percent of export revenue.

What is striking about oil economies, in general, is the reliance they have maintained on fixed exchange rate regimes. For economies in which over 50 percent of export revenue emanated from natural resource extraction in 1997, some 83 percent had fixed exchange rate arrangements in place. That compares with fixed exchanges rate regimes being adopted in only 38 percent of economies in which oil represented less than 25 percent of exports. Conventional economic models approach the desire for fixed or flexible regimes by agglomerating the interests of the tradable goods sector together. The problem with this approach is that the various industries within the exporting sector are assumed to have concurrent interests. There is reason to believe this may not always be the case.

Figure 14.1. Share of Oil in Total Exports, 1999

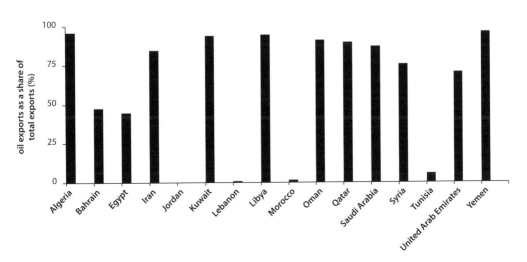

Source: United Nations CONTRADE data, as reported in WITS trade data warehouse.

The manufacturing sector, with relatively elastic worldwide demand, is likely to be more dependent upon competitiveness (and thus, more likely to lobby for floating exchange rates) than is the natural resources sector. Floating exchange rate mechanisms may entail greater short-term volatility, but better prevent long-term appreciation of the exchange rate. As a result, it allows exporters to better achieve external competitiveness through efficiency, by leaving to the market forces of supply and demand the exchange rate determination.

On the other hand, the natural resource extraction sector is assumed to face more inelastic demand and depend less upon imported raw materials. As a result, currency appreciation has weaker impact on profits (and depending upon the elasticity of demand, may result in even higher profits). Thus, the natural resource-exporting sector is more likely to prioritize stability in exchange rates, and the potential gains from currency overvaluation (under control of policy makers under a fixed regime, at least for the short-term), than the potential for competitiveness.

In an attempt to better understand the exchange rate regime decisions in MENA, we estimate exchange rate choice according to traditional models of exchange rate choice for a large sample of economies, but include public external debt and the divergent interests of the oil versus manufacturing sectors.

The Empirical Results. Several standard exchange rate regime choice models are augmented with proxies for the importance of oil revenues to the public sector, the importance of external debt payments to the public sector, and the ability of the manufacturing sector to lobby the government for flexible regimes. Debt payments are measured by the ratio of public external debt to GDP, lagged one period. The importance of the oil sector is captured as the value of oil exports to total exports, lagged one period. The lobby power of the manufacturing sector is measured as an interactive between the size of the manufacturing export sector in GDP and the concentration of manufacturing exports within the sector, with the expectation that larger or more concentrated manufacturing sectors (in terms of the industries represented) are more able to have an effective voice in influencing the government's exchange rate regime choice. The manufacturing lobby variable is also lagged a period.

Other variables include political stability, size, degree of openness, measures of external and domestic variability, inflation, reserves, and capital controls. Annex 3 provides a more detailed explanation of the variables included in the estimations, and the expectations about their influence on exchange rate regime choice.

To investigate whether the incorporation of additional explanatory variables significantly improves the predictive power of traditional models on the exchange rate regime choices within MENA, standard probit models of exchange rate choice are compared with augmented models (table 14.5), incorporating variables for external debt and for the interests of the oil sector versus the lobby power of the manufacturing sector. To avoid simultaneity problems, the oil sector and manufacturing sector variables are included in separate estimations.

By then comparing the predicted exchange rates from the models to the actual exchange rate choices in MENA and outside of MENA, versus models incorporating the public sector's and the manufacturing sector's interests, it is possible to measure the improvement of fit.

Table 14.5. Standard and Augmented Models of Exchange Rate Choice

Dependent variable: Exchange rate regime (1=fixed; 0=floating)

Independent variables	Model 1 (a)	Model 1 (b)	Model 1 (c)	Model 2 (a)	Model 2 (b)	Model 2 (c)	Model 3 (a)	Model 3 (b)	Model 3 (c)
Size	−4.97	−2.91	−4.32	−5.58	−3.13	−4.75	−4.76	−2.48	−4.17
	(−4.75)	(−2.75)	(−4.05)	(−4.80)	(−2.74)	(−4.12)	(−3.76)	(−2.23)	(−3.48)
Open	0.01	0.02	0.14	0.01	0.01	0.01	0.04	−0.00	−0.01
	(5.08)	(5.40)	(5.23)	(3.17)	(3.05)	(3.01)	(0.92)	(−0.15)	(−0.31)
CVEX	−0.12	0.25	−0.29	0.09	0.43	−0.09	0.12	0.99	0.39
	(−0.21)	(0.44)	(−0.50)	(0.16)	(0.72)	(−0.14)	(0.14)	(1.08)	(0.43)
CVGDP	0.37	0.30	0.40	0.81	0.62	0.80	0.71	0.56	0.89
	(0.79)	(0.63)	(0.84)	(1.65)	(1.24)	(1.61)	(1.04)	(0.80)	(1.30)
CAPCONT				0.23	0.23	0.20	0.44	0.13	0.02
				(2.35)	(2.37)	(2.04)	(0.38)	(1.09)	(0.17)
RESERVES				−0.15	0.53	0.10	0.34	0.84	0.56
				(−0.22)	(0.78)	(0.15)	(0.44)	(1.05)	(0.71)
INFLAT				−0.71	−0.80	−0.80	−0.81	−1.01	−0.96
				(−5.33)	(−5.73)	(−5.79)	(−5.02)	(−6.00)	(−5.71)
POLSTABLE							0.00	0.01	0.01
							(−0.40)	(2.13)	(1.63)
HISTGROW							0.04	−0.01	−0.03
							(−2.12)	(−0.30)	(−1.63)
OILX			0.50			0.57			0.83
			(2.90)			(3.22)			(4.07)
MANLOBBY		−1.53			−1.60			−2.16	
		(−6.97)			(−7.15)			(−7.06)	
PUBEXDEBT		0.00	0.08		0.06	0.14		0.27	0.39
		(0.05)	(1.08)		(0.89)	(1.98)		(2.28)	(3.16)
No. obs	1001	1001	1001	1001	1001	1001	765	765	765
MENA									
Proportion right	16	35	16	19	37	32	15	44	26
Proportion wrong	16	19	12	10	14	11	9	13	9
No prediction	67	45	73	71	49	57	76	43	65
NON-MENA									
Proportion right	36	49	41	43	57	46	41	61	52
Proportion wrong	13	15	16	11	17	14	13	14	15
No prediction	50	36	43	46	27	41	46	25	34

The incorporation of debt, combined with a measure of the interests of the oil sector or the lobby power of the manufacturing sector, significantly increases the predictive power of the exchange rate models under all three model classifications, not only for MENA economies, but for economies overall. The improvement in predictive power of these augmented models explain MENA's exchange rate arrangements is substantial, especially so for models incorporating the lobby power of the manufacturing sector.

Conclusions

Against the overall trend throughout the world, the majority of the MENA region has continued to maintain de facto fixed exchange rate arrangements. Empirical analysis suggests that fixed exchange rates are associated with greater levels of exchange rate misalignment in the form overvaluation, which, in turn, reduce competitiveness for nonoil exporters. In MENA, manufacturing exports—as a percentage of GDP per year—were reduced by some 18 percent over the 1970-99 period as a result of the region's substantial overvaluation of its currency. At a time when developing a strong, export-oriented private sector outside of oil is critical in MENA, there is no room for excessive currency overvaluation.

We find that MENA's choice of exchange rate regime—predominantly leaning toward rigid exchange rate arrangements—is less a reflection of structural characteristics of the economies than it is a reflection of the political economy. With a large public sector, which has individual interests as producer of oil and holder of external debt, the interests of the economy are often at odds with the interests of the political economy. If the manufacturing sector has enough power, however, it may lobby effectively for flexible exchange rate regimes.

Notes

1. Unlocking the Employment Potential in the Middle East and North Africa: Toward a New Social Contract; World Bank; 2003.

2. That is, its equilibrium real exchange rate value (ERER). See Williamson, 1985; Harberger, 1986; and Collins, 1997.

3. See Balassa, 1990, for empirical evidence among Sub-Saharan African economies.

4. Goldberg 1993; Goldberg and Kolstad 1995; and Cushman 1985; 1988.

5. Edwards, 1988; Cottani, Cavallo and Khan, 1990; and Ghura and Grennes, 1993.

6. In many cases of exchange rate systems officially classified as flexible, for example, there has been considerable "management" of the exchange rate. De facto exchange rate regimes, according to Levy-Yeyati/Sturzenegger (2000), are determined by looking at the actual behavior of three variables closely related to exchange rate behavior: exchange rate volatility, volatility of exchange rate changes, and volatility of reserves. External liabilities and government deposits were netted out from the reserves data, in order to consider only changes with a counterpart in monetary aggregates, an especially

important correction for both oil-producing countries and countries with large privatization programs. The LYS dataset of exchange rate regimes has subsequently been amended. This paper's analysis reflects use of the earlier de facto classification system, and will need to be revised.

7. In addition to misalignment, variability of the RER has been found to have negative consequences on growth (Ghura and Grennes, 1993; Grobar, 1993; Cushman, 1993; and Gagnon, 1993).

8. This estimate represents a new contribution to the study of exchange rate policy in MENA countries, since previous studies are sparse (Domac and Shabsigh, 1999; Mongardini, 1998; Sundararajan, Lazare and Williams, 1999).

9. This model estimates the RER as a function of both "fundamental" factors in the medium to long term (terms of trade, investment, capital flows, and trade openness) and less persistent factors in the short term (macroeconomic policies, nominal devaluations, and others). Following the estimation of the RER, the ERER could be computed. Using the estimated RER, the ERER is computed by eliminating the effects of transitory variables, and using estimates of "sustainable" values of the fundamentals.

10. Calculated as the coefficient of variation of the RER over an eight-year period. To compute this indicator, some economists use more or less sophisticated regression techniques, such as the variance of the residual of the regression of the RER on a time trend, or an ARCH modelization RER behavior. However, from an empirical point of view, all these various measures are highly correlated and the standard deviation or the coefficient of variation measures perform as well as more sophisticated ones (see Kenen and Rodrik, 1986 or Grobar, 1993).

11. In addition to misalignment, variability of the RER has been found to have negative consequences on growth (Ghura and Grennes ,1993; Grobar, 1993; Cushman, 1993; and Gagnon, 1993)

12. RER misalignment can also disrupt exports by increasing RER uncertainty. Our measure of RER misalignment comes from our estimation of the ERER (see previous section).

13. The earliest literature focused strictly on the structural characteristics of the economy, such as economic openness, country size, and labor mobility. From these characteristics, the optimal exchange rate arrangement is determined (Dreyer, 1978; Heller, 1978; Holden et al., 1979; Wickman, 1985; Savvides, 1990). Later research in this branch of the literature has focused on country-specific shocks emanating from both the international and domestic community (Fischer, 1977. Savvides, 1990).

14. Within that concentration, arguments have centered around policy discipline and credibility (Kydland and Prescott, 1977; Barro and Gordon, 1983; Flood and Isard, 1989; Giavazzi and Pagano, 1988; Rogoff, 1985), policy-making capability (Eichengreen, 1992; Simmons, 1994), and constraints on future governments (Rogowski, 1987; Edwards, 1996).

15. As opposed to the de jure classification of exchange rate regimes, we have examined the de facto classification of exchange rate regimes (Levy-Yeyati and Sturzenegger, 2000), which looks at the actual behavior of three relevant variables to exchange rate behavior: exchange rate volatility, volatility of reserves, and volatility of exchange rate changes. This new classification of exchange rate regimes refines the analysis substantially.

References

Balassa, B. 1990. "Incentive Policies and Export performance in Sub-Sahara Africa." *World Development* 18 (3).

Baffes, J., I. A. Elbadawi, and S.A. O'Connell. 1997. "Single-Equation Estimation of the Equilibrium Real Exchange Rate." Mimeo. Swarthmore College, Swarthmore, PA. May.

Barro, Robert J. and David B. Gordon. 1983. "A Positive Theory of Monetary Policy in a Natural Rate Model." *Journal of Political Economy* 104: 589–610.

Beveridge, S., and C. R. Nelson. 1981. "A New Approach to Decomposition of Economic Time Series into Permanent and Transitory Components with Particular Attention to Measurement of the 'Business Cycle.'" *Journal of Monetary Economics* (7).

Caramazza, Francesco, and Jahangir Aziz. 1998. "Fixed or Flexible? Getting the Exchange Rate Right in the 1990s," *Economic Issues* 13. International Monetary Fund, Washington, DC.

Clark, P. B. and R. MacDonald. 1998. "Exchange Rates and Economic Fundamentals: A Methodological Comparison of BEERs and FEERs." IMF Working Paper WP/98/67. International Monetary Fund, Washington, DC. May.

Cordon, M. 1984. "Booming Sector and the Dutch Disease Economies: Survey and Consolidation." *Oxford Economic Papers* 36 (3): 359–380.

Cottani, J. A., D. F. Cavallo, and M. S. Khan. 1990. "Real Exchange Rate Behaviour and Economic Performance in LDCs." *Economic Development and Cultural Change* 39.

Cuddington, J. T., and L. A. Winters. 1987. "The Beveridge-Nelson Decomposition of Economic Time Series—A Quick Computational Method." *Journal of Monetary Economics* (19).

Cushman, D. O. 1985. "Real Exchange Rate Risk, Expectations, and the Level of Direct Investment." *The Review of Economics and Statistics* 67: 297–308.

———. 1988. "Exchange Rate Uncertainty and Foreign Direct Investment in United States." Weltwirtschaftliches Archiv, *Review of World Economics* 124 (2): 322–336.

———. 1993. "The Effects of Real Exchange Rate Risk on International Trade." *Journal of International Economics* 15.

Dreyer, J. S. 1978. "Determinants of Exchange Rate Regimes for Currencies of Developing Countries: Some Preliminary Results." *World Development* 6: 437–45.

Domac, I., and G. Shabsigh. 1999. "Real Exchange Rate Behaviour and Economic Growth: Evidences from Egypt, Jordan, Morocco and Tunisia." IMF Working Paper WP/99/40. International Monetary Fund, Washington, DC. March.

Edwards, S. 1988. *Exchange Rate Misalignment in Developing Countries.* Baltimore, MD: The Johns Hopkins University Press.

———. 1989. *Real Exchange Rate, Devaluation and Adjustment: Exchange Rate Policy in Developing Countries.* Cambridge, MA: MIT Press.

———. 1992. "Oil and the Exchange Rates in Venezuela: Historical Experience and Policy Options." Mimeo. UCLA and NBER.

———. 1994. "Real and Monetary Determinants of Real Exchange Rate Behaviour: Theory and Evidence from Developing Countries." In *Estimating Equilibrium Exchange Rates,* ed. J. Williamson. Institute of International Economics, Washington, DC.

———. 1996. "The Determinants of the Choice Between Fixed and Flexible Exchange Rate Regimes." NBER Working Paper 5756. NBER, Cambridge, MA.

Elbadawi, I. A. 1994. "Estimating Long-Run Equilibrium Real Exchange Rates." In *Estimating Equilibrium Exchange Rates,* ed. J. Williamson. Institute of International Economics, Washington DC.

———. 2002. "Real Exchange Rates Policy and Non-Traditional Exports in Developing Countries." In *Non-Traditional Export Promotion in Africa: Experiences and Issues,* ed. G. Helleiner. Palgrave, New York.

Engel, R. F., and C W. J. Granger. 1987. "Cointegration and Error: Representation, Estimation and Testing." *Econometrica* (35).

Fischer, S. 1977. "Stability and Exchange Rate Systems in a Monetarist Model of the Balance of Payments." In *The Political Economy of Monetary Reform,* ed. R. Aliber. London: Macmillan Press.

Frieden, Jeffry A. 1991. "Invested Interests: The Politics of National Economic Policies in a World of Global Finance." *International Organization* 45: 425–51.

Funke, N. 1996. "Vulnerability of Fixed Exchange Rate Regimes." *Economic Studies* 26: 1. Organisation for Economic Co-operation and Development, Paris, France.

Gagnon, J. E. 1993. "Exchange Rate Variability and the Level of International Trade." *Journal of International Economics.*

Gelb, A., et al. 1988. *Oil Windfalls: Blessing or Curse?* New York, NY: Oxford University Press for the World Bank.

Ghura, D., and T. J. Grennes. 1993. "The Real Exchange Rate and Macroeconomic Performances in Sub-Saharan Africa." *Journal of Development Economics* 42.

Goldberg, L. S. 1993. "Exchange Rate and Investment in United States Industry." *The Review of Economics and Statistics* 75 (4). November.

Goldberg, L. S., and C. D. Kolstad. 1995. "Foreign Direct Investment, Exchange Rate Variability and Demand Uncertainty." *International Economic Review* 39 (4). November.

Gowa, J. 1983. *Closing the Gold Window.* Ithaca, NY: Cornell University Press.

Grobar, L. M. 1993. "The Effect of Real Exchange Rate Uncertainty on LDC Manufactured Exports." *Journal of Development Economics* 14.

Harberger, A. 1986. "Economic Adjustment and the Real Exchange Rate." In *Economic Adjustment Exchange Rates in Developing Countries,* ed. S. Edwards and L. Ahamed. Chicago, IL: University of Chicago Press.

Heller, H. R. 1978. "Determinants of Exchange Rate Practices." *Journal of Money, Credit, and Banking* 10: 308–21.

Holden, P., M. Holden, and E. Suss. 1979, "The Determinants of Exchange Rate Flexibility: An Empirical Investigation." *Review of Economics and Statistics* 61: 327–333.

Im, K. S., M. H. Pesaran, and Y. Shin. 1997. "Testing for Unit Roots in Heterogeneous Panels." DAE Working Paper Amalgamated Series No. 9526. Cambridge, U.K.: University of Cambridge.

Levy-Yeyati, E., and F. Sturzenegger. 2000. "Exchange Rate Regimes and Economic Performance." Draft mimeo. Buenos Aires, Argentina: Universidad Torcuato Di Tella.

Kenen, P. B., and R. Rodrik. 1996. "Measuring and Analysing the Effects of Short Term Volatility in Real Exchange Rates." *Review of Economics and Statistics* 68.

Kydland, F., and E. Prescott. 1977. "Rules Rather than Discretion: The Inconsistency of Optimal Plans." *Journal of Political Economy* 85: 473–91.

Mongardini, J. 1998. "Estimating Egypt Equilibrium Real Exchange Rates." IMF Working PaperWP/98/5. International Monetary Fund, Washington, DC. January.

Pinto, B. 1990. "Black Market Premia, Exchange Rate Unification and Inflation in Sub-Saharan Africa." *The World Bank Economic Review* 3 (3).

Razin, O., and S. M. A. Collins. 1997. "Real Exchange Rate Misalignments and Growth." NBER Working Paper No. 6174. NBER, Cambridge, MA. September.

Rizzo, Jean-Marc. 1998. "The Economic Determinants of the Choice of an Exchange Rate Regime: A Probit Analysis." *Economic Letters* 59: 283–87.

Rodrik, Dani. 1994. "Getting Intervention Right; How South Korea and Taiwan Grew Rich." NBER Working Paper Series No. 4964. NBER, Cambridge, MA. November.

Rogoff, K. 1985. "The Optimal Degree of Commitment to an Intermediate Monetary Target." *Quarterly Journal of Economics* 100: 1169–90.

Rogowski, R. 1987. "Trade and the Variety of Democratic Institutions." *International Organization* 41 (2): 203–33.

Savvides, A. 1990. "Real Exchange Variability and the Choice of Exchange Rate Regime by Developing Countries." *Journal of International Money and Finance* 9: 440–54.

Stein, J. L. 1994. "The Natural Exchange Rate of the U.S. Dollar and Determinants of Capital Flows." In *Estimating Equilibrium Exchange Rates,* ed. J. Williamson. Institute for International Economics, Washington, DC.

Sundararajan, V., M. Lazare, and S. Williams. 1999. "Exchange Rate Unification, the Equilibrium Real Exchange Rate, and Choices of Exchange Rate Regime: The Case of Islamic Republic of Iran." IMF Working Paper WP/99/15. International Monetary Fund, Washington, DC. January.

Wickman, P. 1985. "The Choice of Exchange Rate Regime in Developing Countries: A Survey of the Literature." *IMF Staff Papers* 32: 248–88. International Monetary Fund, Washington, DC.

Williamson, J. 1985. "The Exchange Rate System." Policy Analyses in International Economics, No. 5. Institute of International Economics, Washington, DC.

———. 1994. "Estimates of FEERs." In *Estimating Equilibrium Exchange Rates,* ed. J. Williamson. Institute for International Economics, Washington, DC.

Annex 14.1. Calculating RER Misalignment

Modeling the Long-Run Equilibrium of the RER

The long-run equation explaining the RER behavior is based on Edwards (1994), which has developed a dynamic model of RER determination for a small, open economy with a single nominal exchange rate system. The model allows for both real and nominal factors to play a role in the short run. In the long run, only real factors—the "fundamentals"—influence the ERER. In our case, the long-run relation is specified as follows[1]

$$\ln (e_t) = c + a_1.\ln(Inv_t) + a_2.\ln(Open_t) + a_3.\ln(TOT_t) + a_4.Capinf_t + \varepsilon_t. \quad (1)$$

with:

- $e_t =$ RER. This indicator is used as a proxy for the ratio of the price of nontradable goods (P_{Dt}) to the price of tradable goods ($P_{wt}.E_t0$, E_t. being the nominal ER in local currency/US\$ and P_{wt} the world prices);
- $Inv_t =$ Investment ratio to GDP;
- $Open_t =$ Indicator of trade openness, measured as the sum of import and export divided by GDP;
- $TOT_t =$ External terms of trade, measured as the ratio of export to import prices (in dollars);
- $Capinf_t =$ capital inflows calculated as the net change in reserves minus the trade balance scaled by GDP[2]
- $c =$ intercept, a_1 to a_4 = parameters, t = time index and ε_t = error term.

Following Edwards (1989), we assume that—in the long term—an increase in the investment rate results in an augmentation in the demand and in the relative price of nontradables—thus appreciating the real exchange rate. This assumption implies, however, that investment is predominantly constituted of nontradable products (such as services and construction) and not of tradable goods (such as equipment). It can also be due to the multiplier effect of the investment, which increases the aggregate demand for nontradable products, principally. Conversely, the RER is positively affected by trade restrictions, for which the ratio of imports plus exports to GDP is a proxy. The impact of the terms of trade on the RER is more ambiguous, since there are two opposite effects: An increase in the relative price of export goods to import goods leads to an appreciation of the RER if the income effect, which results in higher demand for nontradables, dominates the substitution effect—associated with a decline in the relative cost of imported intermediate goods used in the production process of nontradables. Finally, an increase in capital inflows, either officially or not, involves stronger demand for both tradable and nontradable goods. They, therefore, lead to a higher relative price of nontradables, and conversely appreciates the RER, as needed for domestic resources to be diverted toward production in the non-tradable sector to meet increased demand.

A complementary equation has been estimated in order to take more into consideration the characteristics of some MENA countries. The idea is that in a certain number of countries, including Egypt, debt relief should have led to an appreciation of the ERER. For this purpose we have added to equation (1) the ratio of the debt service to total external trade (imports + exports, DebtServ).

$$\ln(e_t) = c + a_1.\ln(Inv_t) + a_2.\ln(Open_t) + a_3.\ln(TOT_t) + a_4.Capinf_t + a_5.\ln(DebtServ_t) + \varepsilon_t. \qquad (2)$$

The existence of these long-term relationships implies that variables of Equations (1) and (2) are cointegrated. It is therefore required to determine the order of integration of the series. Table A-1 in annex 2 provides the results of the Augmented-Dickey-Fuller (ADF) tests of the data for our sample of 53 countries during 1970-80 (depending on the countries) to 1997. We used the Im, Pesaran, and Shin (1997) methodology—which provides critical values of ADF tests in the case of heterogeneous panel data. The results indicate that the series are stationary at either the 1 percent or 5 percent levels, when allowed to run Equations (1) and (2). We then used the Engel and Granger (1991) method to test for cointegration between the variables of Equations (1) and (2). Cointegration tests have been based on the residuals of the two equations. ADF tests conclude, still using Im, Pesaran, and Shin (1997) critical values, that residuals are stationary.

Hence, Equations (1) and (2) describe the long-run relationship between RER and a number of fundamental variables. The equations were estimated on an unbalanced panel of 51 countries, among which 17 are African countries (8 CFA and 9 non CFA), 13 Latin America countries, 10 Asian countries, 10 MENA countries, plus one country[3] (see annex 2 for the list of countries). The results of the regressions—using the White esti-mator to correct for the heteroscedasticity bias—are presented in table A1. The equations were estimated by using the fixed effect methodology.[4] The estimated regressions explain a fairly large amount of the observed varia-tion of the RER.

Estimated relationships between RER and its fundamentals are consistent with theory: An increase in investment and in capital income, or an improve-ment of the terms of trade, results in a RER appreciation, which indicates, in the latter case, that the income effect dominates the substitution effect. Conversely, the opening of the economy and the increase in the debt service lead to a RER depreciation.

Table 14A1. Estimation Results of the Cointegrating Equations (1) and (2)

Dependent variable: ln(e_t)

Variable	Eq (1)	Eq (2)
ln(Inv_t)	0.16	0.10
	(3.6)	(2.6)
ln($Open_t$)	-0.64	-0.72
	(12.5)	(13.7)
ln(TOT_t)	0.14	0.21
	(3.1)	(4.41)
$Capinf_t$	0.34	0.44
	(3.6)	(4.3)
ln($DebtServ_t$)		-0.18
		(9.9)
Adjusted R^2	0.61	0.65
Fischer test	28.3	25.7
Haussmann test	28	15.5

Source: Authors'estimations.
Note: Student *t* statistics are within brackets. The number of observations used in Equations (1) and (2) are respectively 1183 and 1062. Data have been compiled from WDI, GDF, GDN, and LDB World Bank databases.

Calculating RER misalignment

RER misalignment is measured as the ratio of the RER and its equilibrium value (ERER):

$$MIS = (RER / ERER)$$

Thus, when the RER is higher than its equilibrium value (when the currency is overvalued), misalignment takes a value greater than 1. But when the RER is lower than its equilibrium value (undervalued), misalignment takes a value less than 1.

The estimations of the long-term relationship between the RER and its fundamental determinants have been used to compute the ERER.[5] For this purpose, the "sustainable" or "equilibrium" values of the fundamental variables had to be assessed. The idea is that the deviation of the fundamental variables from their "equilibrium"—in addition to the variations of the short-term economic policy variables (see the estimation of the error correction model through Equation 4 in annex 3)—leads to a misalignment of the RER. The "permanent" values of the four fundamental variables, that is, Inv_t, $Open_t$, TOT_t, and $Capinf_t$,were computed using moving averages of the series over a three years period. This simple method was possible because our series were stationary.[6]

Following this methodology, excessive trade protection, unexpected appreciation of the terms of trade or increase in investment and capital flows, in comparison to the "normal" or long-term trend in the economy, lead to an overvaluation of the RER. It can also be shown from the estimation of the error correction model that in the short run, nominal devaluations (*Dev*), the black market premium (*BMP*), and inflation (*Infl*) explain the deviations of the RER from the ERER.

Annex 14.2. List of Countries in Estimations of Exports/GDP

| MENA | AFRICA | | ASIA | LATIN AMERICA |
	CFA	NonCFA		
Bahrain (BHR)	Burkina Faso (BFA)	Botswana (BWA)	**South East Asia**	Argentina (ARG)
Algeria (DZA)	Côte d'Ivoire (CIV)	Gambia, The (GMB)	Indonesia (IDN)	Bolivia (BOL)
Egypt (EGY)	Gabon (GAB)	Kenya (KEN)	Korea, Rep.(KOR)	Brazil (BRA)
Iran (IRN)	Cameroon (CMR)	Madagascar (MDG)	Malaysia (MYS)	Chile (CHL)
Jordan (JOR)	Gambia, The (GMB)	Mozambique (MOZ)	Philippines (PHL)	Colombia (COL)
Kuwait (KWT)	Niger NER)	Mauritius (MUS)	Thailand (THA)	Costa Rica (CRI)
Malta (MLT)	Senegal (SEN)	Malawi (MWI)	**South Asia**	Ecuador (ECU)
Morocco (MAR)	Togo (TGO)	Nigeria (NGA)	Bangladesh (BGD)	Guatemala (GTM)
Syria (SYR)		Tanzania (TZA)	India (IND)	Mexico (MEX)
Tunisia (TUN)			China (CHN)	Peru (PER)
OTHER COUNTRIES			Sri Lanka (LKA)	Paraguay (PRY)
Israel (ISR)			Pakistan (PAK)	Uruguay (URY)
				Venezuela, RB (VEN)

Annex 14.3. Modeling Exchange Rate Choice

In this paper, we empirically tested the hypothesis that for each economy, the public sector's determination of exchange rate regime is a decision-making process that weighs three factors: the overall structural characteristics of the economy, its personal interests in minimizing its current external debt payments and maximizing natural resources revenue (both better achieved under fixed exchange rates), and the degree to which lobby pressures by the manufacturing sector can sway the public sector. The greater the lobby power of the manufacturing sector, the more likely the public sector will be to adopt a floating exchange rate regime.

A central problem throughout the literature in the testing of models of exchange rate regime choice has been the utilization of de jure exchange rate regimes. Most empirical analysis has used the published exchange rate regimes from the IMF's *Exchange Arrangements and Exchange Restrictions: Annual Report*. The report classifies economies, according to their exchange rate arrangement, into three broad groups: (i) those whose currency is pegged to a single currency or currency composite; (ii) those whose exchange rate system has limited flexibility, in terms of a single currency or group of currencies; and (iii) those with more flexible exchange rate systems. Unfortunately, in many countries, exchange rates that are officially flexible have been subject to considerable official "management." Indeed, as Calvo and Reinhart (2000) and others have emphasized, many countries that claim to have floating exchange rates do not in practice allow the rate to float freely, but use interest rate and intervention policies to affect its behavior.

Within the approaches pioneered by Holden, Honden, and Suss (1979) to characterize the de facto exchange rate regimes economies employ, a major contribution was provided by Levy-Yeyati and Sturzenegger (2000, hereafter LYS), who developed a database of exchange rate classifications by looking at the actual behavior of the main relevant variables, as opposed to the traditional classification compiled by the IMF. The LYS classification is based on three variables closely related to exchange rate behavior to determine the de facto exchange rate regime: exchange rate volatility, volatility of exchange rate changes, and volatility of reserves. The empirical results from this paper were based on the original reclassification of exchange rates by LYS for their 2000 paper. That dataset has recently been amended, and the results from this paper will have to be revised.

Structural variables in the analysis include many of the variables suggested by the optimal currency areas (OCA) literature. Two of these are the country size and the degree of openness of the economy, with the expectation that smaller countries that are more open tend to favor fixed exchange rate regimes. In our estimations, size (SIZE) is measured by the log of GDP, relative to the United States, lagged one period, and openness (OPEN) is defined as the average share of exports to GDP for the five- year period prior to the observation year. In addition, the OCA literature would suggest that the vulnerability of an economy's output to shocks affects its choice of exchange rate regime. Thus, we have included two indices of the extent of external and domestic shock variability. The first, CVEX, is the coefficient of variation of real exports for the five-year period prior to the observation year. Likewise, CVGDP was constructed as the coefficient of variation of real GDP for the five-year period prior to the observation year. Each of these indicators was assembled from World Bank data.

Several control variables suggested by the literature were also included in our analysis. One, capital controls (CAPCONT) is suggested in the literature on capital liberalization and financial openness, with countries with capital controls more likely to have fixed exchange rates. If a government controls the movement of international capital, it can insulate itself from the international price movements and will be more able to maintain a pegged regime. A dummy variable was included if the country in question had controls on the international movement of capital, and the data were assembled from the IMF's *Annual Report on Exchange Arrangements and Exchange Restrictions.*

An additional control variable suggested by the political economy literature (Edwards 1996) is the historical rate of inflation. Theory would predict that countries with a history of rapid inflation will have a lower probability of maintaining a pegged regime, and will thus tend to favor the adoption of a more flexible system. In most other studies, the history of inflation is measured as the average rate of inflation for some period prior to the observation year. We constructed a slightly different index, INFLAT. This was constructed by taking the average rate of inflation over the five-year period prior to the observation, and determining the proportion of years in which inflation exceeded 30 percent. This was meant to better capture the variable which decision makers might consider important in determining their exchange rate regime.[xx] One might question whether a policy maker makes a serious distinction between whether his economy experienced average inflation rates of 140 percent a year versus 100 percent a year. Even taking logs of past inflation rates would retain these ordinal differences in the inflation rate, which from the point of view of a policy maker may lose their significance at some level of inflation. On the other hand, the past probability of the economy facing episodes of high or runaway inflation (above 20 percent a year, in our estimations) may play a serious role in considerations for exchange rate policy in the future.

In addition to these variables, we have incorporated variables that proxy the public sector's weight put on personal interests (in minimizing external debt payments and maximizing natural resource export revenue) versus its ability to be lobbied by the manufacturing sector. For the reasons given above, countries that have higher levels of external debt will have a greater tendency to opt for a fixed exchange rate regime over a floating one, since there is an economic pay-off to allowing the currency to become overvalued, in terms of lower foreign currency debt payments. In our estimations, we included PUB-XDEBT, which is the lagged value of public and publicly guaranteed external debt to GDP.

To measure the public sector's interest in petroleum revenues, we include the size of the petroleum sector (measured by its share of total exports), OILX, to measure the public sector's personal exporting interests, again lagged one period, and assembled using World Bank data. Lobby power in the manufacturing sector, MANLOBBY, is measured as an interactive between the share of manufacturing exports in GDP and the concentration of manufacturing exports among the top three products, constructed using data from the United Nations' COMTRADE (which allows for analysis of trade by commodity). Like the size of the petroleum sector in exports, the manufacturing lobby variable was lagged one period. Because of significant reporting errors on the part of some economies (particularly the GCC) in terms of exports, exports of oil, exports of manufacturing goods, and total exports (to determine shares in total exports) by each economy were recomputed by aggregating world imports from each economy in the various sectors as a share of total world imports from the economy in question.

Our estimations were performed over the 1985-1999 period.

Appendix Notes

1. The short-run dynamic of the RER has also been estimated through an error correction model Equation (4) in Annex 3. Results are shown in table A.3.

2. An increase in net capital inflows may result from (i) an autonomous augmentation in foreign aid, foreign voluntary lending, or FDI; (ii) an increase in borrowing due to the removal of domestic capital controls; (iii) a fall in the world interest rates; or (iv) an increase in public borrowing to finance the fiscal deficit.

3. The countries have been selected on the criteria of their level of income per capita. To preserve a kind of coherence in the sample, we have chosen (most of the time) intermediate income countries that would be comparable to the ones of the MENA region.

4. This is supported by the data, as shown by the Fischer test of equality of intercepts across countries, and is preferable to the random effect methodology, as revealed by the value of the Haussmann test.

5. In the rest of the document, it is Equation (2) that has to be used to calculate the misalignment.

6. Other trials consist of an "economic" determination of these "sustainable" levels, inspired by Edwards, 1988, which, for example, takes as sustainable value for openness the average of the three higher values of the variable, or in the case of capital inflows, zero, if the rate of growth of the economy is inferior to the international interest rate, which means, in this case, that that borrowing is not sustainable—did not give better results as far as misalignment is concerned. They are not presented here.

Our calculations of misalignment appear, however, in some cases, to underestimate the level of misalignment as generally perceived in the different countries. We thereby have adjusted our estimates by scaling them up, according to the difference between our calculations of ERER and its level in periods in which the actual RER was considered to be at the equilibrium. The RER was considered to be close to its equilibrium in periods following devaluations and structural adjustment, where the balance of payment was also close to the equilibrium. For example, it has been considered that RER equilibrium took place in 1989 in the case of Morocco. This period was 1991 and 1994-95 for Algeria; 1993-94 for Egypt; 1995 for Iran; 1992 for Jordan; and 1980, 1994, and 1997 for Tunisia.

Some more sophisticated calculations exist, when a variable has a unit root, in using time series techniques introduced by Nelson (1981), where variables are decomposed into a random walk with a drift and a stationary component. Unlike the trend stationary model-based decomposition, this technique allows the steady-state growth path of the series to shift over time. Fluctuations around the shifting permanent path reflects cyclical effects.

15

How Does Exchange Rate Policy Affect Manufactured Exports in MENA Countries?

Mustapha Kamel Nabli
Marie-Ange Véganzonès-Varoudakis*

Recent assessments of economic policies and performance in developing countries have underlined the crucial issue of the management of the real exchange rate (RER). It has been shown that the best performers are countries that have maintained an "appropriate" RER—that is, one close to the equilibrium real exchange rate (ERER) (Williamson, 1985; Harberger, 1986; Razin and Collins, 1997). In particular, all countries that have been successful in promoting manufactured exports have avoided real exchange rate overvaluation.[1]

In fact, RER misalignment—especially overvaluation—is damaging to economic performance because it decreases the profitability of production and the export of tradable goods. In this way, RER misalignment leads to a reduction in economic efficiency and a misallocation of resources. In addition, by increasing uncertainty and raising the risk of macroeconomic collapse, RER misalignment can also hinder growth by deterring domestic and foreign investment and contributing to capital flight. These negative effects of misalignment on growth and export performance have been shown by Edwards (1988), Cottani et al. (1990), and Ghura and Grennes (1993) for different groups of developing countries.

*Centre d'Etudes et de Recherches sur le Développement International and Centre National de la Recherche Scientifique, Université d'Auvergne, France.

Published in Applied Economics (2004), vol. 36, no. 19. Reprinted by permission from Taylor and Francis.

In addition to misalignment, inconsistencies among macroeconomic, trade, and exchange rate policies increase the variability of the RER—which in turn can affect growth. Higher RER volatility sends confusing signals to economic agents. It increases the uncertainty of long-term investments and the profitability of producing tradable goods. The sensitivity of export performance to RER volatility has been highlighted in the case of various economies by Ghura and Grennes (1993), Grobar (1993), Cushman (1993), and Gagnon (1993).

The harmful effect of RER misalignment on exports by the MENA economies is well confirmed by our study. We show that during the past three decades MENA countries experienced substantial RER misalignment, with a net tendency to overvaluation of their RER. This had a significant negative impact on the export growth of manufactured products, though the effect was less significant when total exports are considered. This appears to have resulted in slower economic growth, as manufactured products exports have become a major factor of economic growth in developing economies, many of which have now successfully entered world markets.[2]

The findings bring new empirical evidence to the subject of misalignment and of export growth in the case of MENA countries, on which little previous work has been undertaken. Our results were obtained through the estimation of an export equation on a panel of 53 developing countries (see annex 1), among which 10 are MENA economies. The calculations cover the period 1970–80 to 1999, during which tremendous changes in trade and exchange rate policies are observed.

The first step was to provide an accurate measure of the gap (or misalignment) between RER and its equilibrium level (ERER). The estimates of ERER and of RER misalignment are based on a reduced form approach. RER behavior is modeled using an equation that includes both the role of fundamental factors in the medium to long term (for example,, terms of trade, investment, capital flows, trade openness), and the less persistent impact of short-term variables (for example,, macroeconomic policies, nominal devaluations). The ERER is then computed, using this equation, by eliminating the effect of transitory variables and using estimates of sustainable or long-term values of the fundamental variables. This approach, initiated by Edwards (1989), has been extended by Elbadawi (1994) and Baffes et al. (1997).

The use of this approach also represents a new contribution to the study of exchange rate policy in MENA economies, since the few previous studies were generally based on a time series approach (Mongardini, 1998; Domac and Shabsigh, 1999; Sorsa, 1999; Sundararajan, Lazare, and Williams, 1999; Achy, 2001).[3] In addition to using panel data estimations techniques in comparison to times series econometrics,[4] our calculations allow some comparative analysis among the different regions, as well as among the MENA countries themselves.

The paper is organized as follows. In the second section, panel data calculations of the RER's longterm equilibrium are presented. In the third section, the misalignment and volatility of the MENA countries' RER are discussed and compared to those of other regions. The fourth section presents our estimation of the impact of RER misalignment and of RER volatility on the export performance of the economies. It is illustrated that the misalignment has had a negative influence on the MENA countries' manufactured exports. The fifth section concludes.

Modeling the Longterm Equilibrium of the RER

The longterm equation explaining RER behavior is based on Edwards (1994), who developed a dynamic model of RER determination for a small, open economy with a single nominal exchange rate system. The model allows for both real and nominal factors to play a role in the short run. In the long run, only real factors—the fundamentals—influence the ERER. In the present case, the longterm relationship is specified as follows:[5]

$$\ln (e_t) = c + a_1.\ln (Inv_{i,t}) + a_2.\ln (Open_{i,t}) + a_3.\ln (TOT_{i,t}) + a_4.Capinf_{i,t} + a_5.\ln (DebtServ_t)+ \varepsilon_{i,t}. \tag{1}$$

with:

$e_t =$ 	bilateral RER between the country concerned and the United States, measured as the ratio of the consumption price index in the country (P_{Dt}) to the wholesale price index in the USA (P_{wt}), multiplied by the nominal exchange rate in local currency / US$ (E_t). These price indices are used, respectively, as proxies of the price of nontradable goods (P_{Dt}) and the price of tradable goods ($P_{wt}.E_t$);

$RER_t =$ 	(P_{Dt}) / ($P_{wt}.E_t$);

$- Inv_t =$ 	investment ratio to GDP;

$- Open_t =$ 	indicator of trade openness, measured as the sum of imports and exports, divided by GDP.

As an improved measure of trade openness, we have substituted for $Open_t$, a policy-induced trade openness indicator TP_t, which consists of adjusting $Open_t$ for the "natural trade openness" of the economy, a metric comprising the size of the country and the distance from markets (see Frankel and Romer, 1999). This is Equation (1').

$TOT_t =$ 	external terms of trade, measured as the ratio of export to import prices (in dollars);

$- Capinf_t =$ capital inflows, calculated as the net change in reserves minus the trade balance scaled by GDP;[6]

- $DebtServ_t$ = debt service to total exports;
- c = intercept, a_1 to a_4 = parameters, t = time index, and ε_t = error term.

Following Edwards (1989), it is assumed that, in the long term, an increase in the investment rate (Inv_t) results in an increase in the demand for and relative price of nontradable products—thus increasing Keep as appreciating, JK the real exchange rate. This assumption implies that as the investment rate grows, investment is increasingly constituted of nontradable products (for example,, services and construction), and relatively less of tradable goods (for example,, equipment). This effect can also be due to the multiplier effect of the investment, which raises the aggregated demand mainly for nontradable products.

The RER is positively affected by trade restrictions, which implies a negative sign on the coefficient on the proxy for trade openness, measured as the ratio of imports plus exports to GDP ($Open_t$). The same negative sign is expected for the improved measure of policy-induced trade openness (TP_t).

The impact of the terms of trade (TOT_t) on the RER is more ambiguous, since there are two opposite effects. That is, an increase in the relative price of exported goods to imported goods leads to an appreciation of the RER only if the income effect (which results in higher demand for nontradables) dominates the substitution effect (which is associated with a decline in the relative cost of imported intermediate goods used in the production process of nontradables).

An increase in capital inflows ($Capinf_t$) involves stronger demand for both tradable and nontradable goods. Increased inflows, therefore, lead to a higher relative price of nontradables, and conversely, appreciate the RER—as is necessary for domestic resources to be diverted toward production in the nontradable sector to meet increased demand. On the other hand, a rise in the debt service ($DebtServ_t$), which captures the important impact of debt relief in many MENA countries, contributes to depreciating the RER.

The existence of this long-term relationship implies that the variables of Equations (1) and (1') are cointegrated. It is therefore necessary to determine the order of integration of the series. Table 15A.1 in Annex 15.2 provides the results of the Augmented-Dickey-Fuller (ADF) tests of the data for our sample of 53 developing countries[7] over the time period. The Im et al. (1997) methodology, which provides critical values of ADF tests in the case of heterogeneous panel data, is used. The results indicate that the series are stationary at either the 1 percent or 5 percent level, which allows Equations (1) and (1') to be run.

Hence, Equations (1) and (1') describe the longterm relationship between RER and a number of fundamental variables. The equations were estimated for the panel of 53 developing countries, of which 10 are MENA economies.[8] The results of the regressions—using the White estimator to correct for the heteroscedasticity bias—are presented in Table 15.1. The equations were esti-

Table 15.1. Estimation Results of the Cointegrating Equations (1) and (1′)

Dependant variable: $\ln(e_t)$

Variable	Eq (1)	Eq (1′)
$\ln(Inv_t)$	0.09	0.11
	(2.0)	(2.3)
$\ln(Open_t)$	-0.71	
	(14.4)	
$\ln(TP_t)$		-0.32
		(6.7)
$\ln(TOT_t)$	0.23	0.24
	(4.9)	(4.8)
$Capinf_t$	0.45	0.5
	(4.5)	(4.7)
$\ln(DebtServ_t)$	-0.18	-0.14
	(9.9)	(7.5)
Adjusted R^2	0.63	0.55
Fischer test	25.9	19.1
Haussmann test	20	18.8

Source: Authors' estimations.

Note: Student *t* statistics are within brackets. The number of observations used in eq (1) and (2) are, respectively, 1092 and 1080. Data have been compiled from World Development Indicators, Global Development Finance, Global Development Network, and Live Data Base (World Bank).

mated using the fixed-effect methodology. The estimated regressions explain a fairly large amount of the observed variation of the RER.

Estimated relationships between RER and its fundamentals are consistent with theory (Edwards, 1989): an increase in investment and in capital income, or an improvement of the terms of trade, result in a RER appreciation. This indicates, in the latter case, that the income effect dominates the substitution effect. Conversely, the opening of the economy and the increase in the debt service lead to a RER depreciation.

RER Misalignment

The misalignment (MIS) of the real exchange rate (RER) is measured as the percent difference between the RER and its equilibrium value (ERER):

$$MIS = (RER\ /\ ERER) - 1$$

The estimations of the long-term relationship between the RER and its fundamental determinants have been used to compute the ERER based on Equation (1'). For this purpose, the sustainable, or equilibrium, values of the fundamental variables had to be assessed. The idea is that the deviation of the fundamental variables from their equilibrium—in addition to variations in short-term economic policy variables (see the estimation of the error correction model through equation (A3-1) in annex 3) — leads to a misalignment of the RER. The permanent values of the five fundamental variables—Inv_t, $Open_t$, TOT_t, $Capinf_t$, $DebtServ_t$—were computed using moving averages of the series over a three-year period. This simple method was possible because the series are stationary.[10]

Following this methodology, excessive trade protection, unexpected appreciation of the terms of trade, an increase in investment and in capital flows, or a reduction of the debt service,—in comparison to the "normal" or long-term trend in the economy, lead to an overvaluation of the RER. It can also be shown from the estimation of the error correction model (table A-3 in annex 3) that, in the short term, nominal devaluations (*Dev*), black market premiums (*BMP*), and inflation (*Infl*) explain the deviations of the RER from the ERER.

The results confirm that, during the past three decades, MENA countries have experienced substantial overvaluation of their RER: 29 percent per year on average from the mid-1970s to the mid-1980s, and 22 percent from the mid-1980s to 1999 (see table 15.2). In general, the extent of overvaluation has not significantly decreased—unlike in Latin America, Africa, or Asia. Overvaluation remains higher in MENA than in the other regions, except Communauté Francophone d'Afrique (CFA) Africa (see next section for the experience of individual MENA countries).

On the other hand, exchange rate volatility has generally been lower in the MENA economies than in the other regions of our sample (see table 2). This can surely be explained by the less flexible exchange rate regimes of the MENA countries. This conclusion should, however, be nuanced. In particular during the second subperiod (1985–99), the volatility of the exchange rate in the

Table 15.2. Average Misalignment and Volatility

1975–80 to 1984 (percent per year)	Misalignment	Volatility
MENA	29	7.9
Latin America	20	11.2
Africa (CFA)	61	12.7
Africa (non-CFA)	29	11.3
South Asia	43	13
East Asia	10	5.4
1985 to 1999 (percent per year)	**Misalignment**	**Volatility**
MENA	22	12.4
Latin America	10	12.9
Africa (CFA)	28	14.5
Africa (non-CFA)	13	16
South Asia	15	8.3
East Asia	5	8.6

Source: Author's calculations.

MENA region is not very different from that in Latin America, and is higher than that in Asia.

RER Management and Manufactured Export Performance

Manufactured Exports in the MENA Countries

Table 15.3 presents data on the performance of some MENA countries in terms of manufactured exports. Over the last three decades, the success of these countries in increasing exports and in diversifying their economies varied widely.

Tunisia and Jordan have been the most successful in increasing their export of manufactures. Tunisian manufactured exports rose, on average, from 24.5 percent of total exports in the 1970s to 75 percent in the 1990s (4.6 percent to 21.2 percent of GDP). If Jordan's performance seems less impressive than Tunisia's, its increase in manufactured exports as a percentage of GDP is, in fact, comparable to Tunisia's (although Jordan's level of exports to GDP remains lower). Morocco also significantly increased its exports during the 1970s and 1980s, but these gains slowed in the 1990s.

In Egypt, manufactured exports increased slowly throughout the period, growing from 27.1 percent of total exports in the 1970s to only 36.6 percent in the 1990s (and, in fact, decreasing from 3.1 to 2.4 percent of GDP). The two major oil-exporting countries, Algeria and Iran, showed the most dismal performance, with manufactured exports remaining negligible throughout the period.

Modeling Exports of Manufactured Products

Overvaluation should have had a cost for the MENA countries that we would like to quantify. As seen previously, manufactured exports should have suffered from RER misalignment and volatility. The following model is used to test for these effects:

$$\ln(X_t) = c + b_1.\ GDPgrTP_{i,t} + b_2.\ ln(TOTn_{i,t}) + b_3.\ ln(Inv_{i,t}) + b_4.\ ln(Roads_{i,t}) + b_5.\ ln(H1_{i,t}) + b_6.\ RERVol_{i,t} + b_7.\ ln(RERMis_{i,t}) + \varepsilon_t. \tag{2}$$

Table 15.3. Average Manufactured Exports of Selected MENA Countries

	Algeria		Egypt		Iran		Jordan		Morocco		Tunisia	
	%X	%GDP	%X	%GDP	%X	%GDP	%X	%GDP	%X	%GDP	%X	%GDP
1970–79	3.0	0.6	27.1	3.1	2.9	0.6	25.8	1.9	16.0	2.1	24.5	4.6
1980–89	1.5	0.3	19.2	1.5	4.0	0.3	42.7	5.4	39.4	6.0	49.4	11.7
1990–99	3.3	0.8	36.6	2.4	6.6	1.5	48.9	9.5	52.9	7.5	74.9	21.2

Source: Authors' calculations.

Note: For the first subperiod, four values were missing for *Iran* (1970, 71, 72, and 73). For the third sub-period, two values were missing for *Iran* (1991 and 92) and one for Jordan (1996).

The model explains exports to GDP in logarithmic form by:

- the GDP growth rate of the trade partners $(GDPgrTP_{i,t})$, which can have a "pulling" role in exports
- the logarithm of the terms of trade $ln(TOTn_{i,t})$, the improvement of which increases the profitability of production for export
- the logarithm of the ratio of investment to GDP $[ln(Inv_{i,t})]$, which is conducive to an increase in overall production capacity, and thus to an increase in export capacity
- the availability of core infrastructure, measured by the logarithm of the length of roads $ln(Roads_{i,t})$ in km per km^2, as well as the availability of human capital, approximated by the logarithm of the average number of years of primary schooling of the adult population $[ln(H1_{i,t})]$
- the volatility of relative prices, approximated by the volatility of the RER (RERVol) and calculated as the coefficient of variation of the RER over a five- year period.[11] RER volatility increases uncertainty regarding the profitability of producing tradable goods
- the distortions in relative prices, as measured by RER misalignment (*RERMis*), where overvaluation hampers competitiveness and diverts investment out of the more productive tradable goods sectors. RER misalignment can also disrupt exports by increasing RER uncertainty.

In addition, the heterogeneity of the sample is controlled for by considering country dummy variables. These variables reflect differences in the quality of institutions or different endowments in natural resources—which can be the origin of large discrepancies in the natural propensity to export. The hypothesis of country dummy variables is supported by the data for manufactured exports[12] (see table 15.4 below). A time dummy variable is also introduced for the years 1974–75, corresponding to the first oil shock.

Econometric Results

Equation (2) was estimated on the panel of 53 developing countries from 1970–80 to 1999, for both total (Xtott) and manufactured exports (Xmanuft). Manufactured exports are more sensitive to competitiveness problems. They should consequently be more negatively influenced by RER overvaluation. Because of missing data for some variables, the model was finally estimated on two unbalanced panels of, respectively, 943 and 837 observations.[13] Results are shown in table 15.4.

The estimations confirm the negative impact of exchange rate misalignment on total and manufactured export. The coefficient is rather strong in the case of manufactured exports (–0.72). It remains significant for total exports (–0.10). The weaker elasticity in the latter case can be explained by the fact that total exports include products that are less sensitive to competitiveness,

Table 15.4. Estimation Results of the Exports Equations

Dependent variables: ln($Xmanuf_t$) and ln($Xtot_t$)

Variable	Manufactured exports ln($Xmanuf_t$)	Total eExports ln($Xtot_t$)
$GDPgrTP_{i,t}$	2.83	1.48
	(1.9)	(2.52)
ln($TOTn_{i,t}$)	−1.4	0.1
	(0.81)	(2.49)
ln($Inv_{i,t}$)	0.87	0.30
	(5.8)	(8.69)
ln($Roads_{i,t}$)	0.08	0.10
	(1.4)	(3.48)
ln($H1_{i,t}$)	1.92	0.26
	(11.13)	(5.66)
RERVol	−0.27	−0.1
	(0.80)	(1.21)
Ln(RERMis)	−0.72	−0.10
	(5.75)	(2.75)
Year 1974	0.25	
	(1.65)	
Year 1975	0.34	
	(1.7)	
Intercept		−1.14
		(9.05)
Adjusted R^2	0.81	0.13
Fischer test	31.7	78.3
Haussmann test	12.4	0.20

Source: Authors' estimations.

Note: Student t statistics are within brackets. The number of observations used in the regressions are, respectively, 816 and 964. Data have been compiled from World Development Indicators, Global Development Finance, Global Development Network, and Live Data Base (World Bank).

such as oil products and other primary goods, which are often owned and managed by governments.

For the MENA region as a whole, exchange rate policy helps explain losses in competitiveness and in manufactured exports. During the whole period, RER overvaluation reduced the ratio of manufactured exports to GDP by 18 percent per year on average. Manufactured exports, which averaged 4.4 percent of GDP from 1970 to 1999, could have reached 5.2 percent of GDP if no overvaluation had taken place. These losses were more concentrated in the 1970s and 1980s than in the 1990sdue to the higher overvaluation of the currencies during those two subperiods.

Some countries with a more diversified export base, such as Jordan and Morocco (see table 15.5) faced high losses during the 1970s and 1980s. Because of its high level of manufactured exports, Tunisia still incurred a large loss during the 1990s, despite a relatively low level of misalignment. But in

Table 15.5. Cost of Misalignment on Manufactured Exports, Selected MENA Countries

	DZA			EGY			IRN		
	ExpM[a]	Mis	Cost[b]	ExpM[a]	Mis	Cost[b]	ExpM[a]	Mis	Cost[b]
1970–79	3	1.79	−1.7	27	1.15	−2.9	3	1.42	−0.9
1980–89	1.5	1.59	−0.6	19	1.22	−3.0	4	1.24	−0.7
1990–99	3.3	1.08	−0.2	37	1.09	−2.4	7	1.84	−4.0
1970–99	2.6	1.49	−0.8	27.6	1.15	−2.7	4.5	1.49	−1.8

	JOR			MAR			TUN		
	ExpM[a]	Mis	Cost[b]	ExpM[a]	Mis	Cost[b]	ExpM[a]	Mis	Cost[b]
1970–79	26	1.57	−10.5	16	1.49	−5.7	25		
1980–89	43	1.31	−9.4	39	1.08	−2.4	49	1.03	−1.0
1990–99	49	1.09	−3.1	53	1.10	−3.7	75	1.16	−8.7
1970–99	39.1	1.25	−7.7	36.1	1.21	−3.9	49.6	1.09	−4.8

a. ExpM = manufactured exports as percent of total exports.
b. Cost = cost of overvaluation as percent of total exports.

these countries, RER misalignment either declined significantly or remained low during the 1990s, as the countries saw a continuous rise in diversification of their manufactured exports.

In the major oil-exporting countries, Iran and Algeria, the large overvaluation of the currency certainly contributed to the low diversification of their exports away from oil. But the losses, as measured here, appear small, given the low initial level of manufactured exports, which can be explained by the structure of their economies.

The estimations fail, however, to show a significant impact of RER volatility on either manufactured or total exports of the countries. This finding does not confirm the empirical results of several studies of different groups of economies (see in particular Ghura and Grennes, 1993; Grobar, 1993; Cushman, 1993; Gagnon 1993).

The results also highlight that total, as well as manufactured, exports are positively influenced by the GDP growth rate of the trade partners, the ratio of investment to GDP, and the physical and human infrastructure (measured respectively by the length of the road network and by the level of primary education of the population).[14]

The pulling effect of the trade partners' GDP growth rate is particularly strong in the case of manufactured exports (elasticity of 2.8 against 1.5 for total exports). This result goes in the direction expected. The income elasticity is higher for manufactured products than for other products in the economy.

The same conclusions can be drawn for human capital, which improves the profitability of investment and the competitiveness of manufactured exports much more than in other sectors of the economy. The effect of primary education is particularly strong (elasticity of 1.9, compared to 0.26 for total exports). This makes education a key variable for the competitiveness of the manufacturing sector in the developing world.

Manufactured exports, however, are not sensitive to improvement in terms of trade, which were supposed to provide an incentive to produce for the export sector. This could reflect the fact that the terms of trade measures include prices of exports of agriculture and mining products, which are not included in manufacturing.

Conclusion

In this paper, it is shown that during the 1970s and 1980s MENA countries were characterized by a significant overvaluation of their currencies. Overvaluation decreased in the 1990s, probably due to some degree of flexibilization of the exchange rate regime, or to better macroeconomic management. Misalignment remained, however, higher than in other developing countries (but CFA Africa). This may be explained by the delay in adopting more flexible exchange rates and in reforming the economy.

In fact, although many economies have progressively adopted more flexible exchange rate regimes—leading to a better management of their RER—most MENA countries are still implementing fixed or adjustable-peg exchange rate policies. In addition, if the shift toward a more open economy has begun in several countries of the region, this process needs to be deepened, since the current situation reduces manufactured exports competitiveness and weakens the incentive for exporters to increase their penetration of foreign markets. This is partly the case for oil-exporting countries, which have failed to address the volatility of their economies, and in which diversification of exports is still very low. But this lack of trade openness also explains the low diversification of other MENA countries in the 1970s and 1980s.

The study also illustrates that overvaluation has had a cost for the region in terms of competitiveness. Manufactured exports, in particular, have been affected by the overvaluation of the exchange rate. These findings confirm recent assessments of economic policies and performance in developing countries, which underscore the crucial issue of the management of the real effective exchange rate. The results corroborate the findings of Edwards (1988); Balassa (1990) and Cottani et al. (1990) for different groups of developing countries.

Notes

1. See, for example, Balassa (1990) and Reinhardt (1995) for empirical evidence in both developed and developing countries.

2. In fact, export diversification—through promotion of manufactured exports—is an important factor of sustained growth for different reasons. First, income elasticity of demand is higher for manufac-

tured goods than for primary products. In this way, growth in foreign income is expected to increase the growth prospects of country's manufactured exports. Second, price elasticity of both demand and supply is presumed to be higher for manufactured goods than for primary commodities. This implies a stabilizing effect on the terms of trade and more stable growth of exports over time. Third, development of the manufacturing sector involves substantial prospects for dynamic productivity gains through economies of scale, learning effects, and externalities among firms and industries. See Nishimizu and Robinson (1986) for cross-country evidence at a two-digit industry level of positive correlation between export growth and total factor productivity (TFP) changes.

3. See Sekkat and Varoudakis (2002) for a panel data approach to assessing the misalignment of North African countries.

4. The comparative advantage of panel data regressions compared to time series estimations can be seen first, in the double dimension of the sample (time series-cross section), which improves estimates by adding information, and second, in the country dummy variables, which generally ask for an important degree of freedom, and which improve the results of the estimations.

5. The short-term dynamic of the RER has also been estimated through an error correction model (equation (A3-1) in annex 3. Results are shown in table A.3.

6. An increase in net capital inflows may result from (i) an autonomous augmentation in foreign aid, foreign voluntary lending, or foreign direct investment (FDI); (ii) an increase in borrowing due to the removal of domestic capital controls; (iii) a fall in world interest rates; or (iv) an increase in public borrowing to finance the fiscal deficit.

7. of which 19 are African countries (8 Communauté Francophone d'Afrique and 11 non-CFA), 13 are Latin America countries, 10 are Asian countries, and 11 are MENA countries.

8. The countries were selected based on level of income per capita. To preserve a kind of coherence of the sample, we generally chose intermediate-income countries so they could be compared to countries in the MENA region.

9. The use of the fixed-effect methodology is supported by the data, as shown by the Fischer test of equality of intercepts across countries, and is preferable to the random effect methodology, as revealed by the value of the Haussmann test (see table 15.1).

10. Other attempts have consisted of an "economic" determination of these "sustainable" levels (inspired by Edwards, 1988). We took as a sustainable value for openness the average of the three higher values of the variable, and in the case of capital inflows, zero, if the rate of growth of the economy was inferior to the international interest rate-which meant that borrowing was not sustainable. Those calculations are not shown here because they did not give better results as far as misalignment is concerned.

   Our calculation of misalignment has been adjusted according to a base year, where the RER could be considered close to its equilibrium level. This has been the case especially in periods following devaluation and structural adjustment, when the balance of payments was also close to equilibrium. For example, it has been considered that RER was close to equilibrium in 1989 in Morocco; in 1991 and 1994-95 in Algeria; in1993-94 in Egypt; in1995 in Iran; in 1992 in Jordan; and in 1980, 1994, and 1997 in Tunisia. The method used to determine the probability of the RER being in equilibrium was to identify a period of time when the difference between the observed and the sustainable value of the fundamental variables was very small.

   Some more sophisticated calculations consist-when a variable has a unit root-of using time series techniques introduced by Beveridge and Nelson (1981), where variables are decomposed into a random walk with a drift and a stationary component. This technique, unlike the trend stationary model-based decomposition, allows the steady-state growth path of the series to shift over time. Fluctuations around the shifting permanent path reflect cyclical effects.

11. To compute this indicator, some economists use more or less sophisticated regression techniques, such as the variance of the residual of the regression of the RER on a time trend, or an ARCH modelization of RER behavior. However, from an empirical point of view, all these measures are highly correlated, and the standard deviation or the coefficient of variation measures perform as well as more sophisticated ones (see Kenen and Rodrik, 1986; Grobar, 1993).

12. As shown by the value of the Fischer test of equality of intercepts across countries, and by the value of the Haussmann test as far as the random effect method is concerned (table 15.4).

13. Before proceeding to the estimation of Equation (2), the degree of integration of the series entering into the regression and the existence of a long-term relationship among them have been tested. The results of the ADF tests of the variables of Equation (2) - using Im et al. (1997) critical values - are shown in Table A.2, Annex 2.

14. Surprisingly, in the case of roads, the elasticity for manufactured exports is weakly significant. This may be due to the fact that, in several MENA countries, oil exports represent an important percentage of total exports (as well as of GDP). In this case, it can be assumed that oil exports have led to the construction of good physical infrastructure.

References

Achy, L. 2001. "Equilibrium Exchange Rate and Misalignment in Selected MENA Countries." *EUI Working Papers*, Mediterranean Programme Series, RSC no. 2001/42. European University Institute, Florence, Italy.

Balassa, B. 1990. "Incentive Policies and Export Performance in Sub-Sahara Africa." *World Development* 18(3).

Baffes, J., I. A. Elbadawi, and S. A. O'Connell. 1997. "Single-Equation Estimation of the Equilibrium Real Exchange Rate." Unpublished. Swarthmore College, Swarthmore, PA (May).

Beveridge, S. and C. R. Nelson. 1981. "A New Approach to Decomposition of Economic Time Series into Permanent and Transitory Components with Particular Attention to Measurement of the Business Cycle." *Journal of Monetary Economics* 7.

Cottani, J. A., D. F. Cavallo, and M. S. Khan. 1990. "Real Exchange Rate Behavior and Economic Performance in LDCs." *Economic Development and Cultural Change* 39.

Cushman, D. O. 1993. "The Effects of Real Exchange Rate Risk on International Trade." *Journal of International Economics* 15.

Domac, I. and G. Shabsigh. 1999. "Real Exchange Rate Behavior and Economic Growth: Evidence from Egypt, Jordan, Morocco and Tunisia." IMF Working Paper WP/99/40 (March). International Monetary Fund, Washington, DC.

Edwards, S. 1988. *Exchange Rate Misalignment in Developing Countries.* Baltimore: The Johns Hopkins University Press.

———. 1989. *Real Exchange Rate, Devaluation and Adjustment: Exchange Rate Policy in Developing Countries.* Cambridge, MA: MIT Press.

———. 1994. Real and Monetary Determinants of Real Exchange Rate Behavior: Theory and Evidence from Developing Countries. In *Estimating Equilibrium Exchange Rates,* ed. by J. Williamson. Washington DC: Institute of International Economics.

Elbadawi, I. 1994. "Estimating Long-term Equilibrium Real Exchange Rates." In *Estimating Equilibrium Exchange Rates,* ed. by J. Williamson. Washington DC: Institute of International Economics.

Frankel, J. A. and D. Romer. 1999. "Does Trade Cause Growth?" *The American Economic Review* 89(3).

Gagnon, J. E. 1993. "Exchange Rate Variability and the Level of International Trade." *Journal of International Economics* 34(3-4).

Ghura, D. and T. J. Grennes. 1993. "The Real Exchange Rate and Macroeconomic Performances in Sub-Saharan Africa." *Journal of Development Economics* 42.

Grobar, L. M. 1993. "The Effect of Real Exchange Rate Uncertainty on LDC Manufactured Exports." *Journal of Development Economics* 14.

Harberger, A. 1986. "Economic Adjustment and the Real Exchange Rate. In *Economic Adjustment Exchange Rates in Developing Countries,* ed. by S. Edwards and L. Ahamed. Chicago: University of Chicago Press.

Im, K. S., M. H. Pesaran, and Y. Shin. 1997. "Testing for Unit Roots in Heterogeneous Panels." DAE Working Paper Amalgamated Series, no. 9526. Cambridge University, Cambridge, UK.

Kenen, P. B. and R. Rodrik. 1996. "Measuring and Analysing the Effects of Short-Term Volatility in Real Exchange Rates." *Review of Economics and Statistics* 68.

Mongardini, J. 1998. "Estimating Egypt Equilibrium Real Exchange Rates." IMF Working Paper, WP/98/5 (January). International Monetary Fund, Washington, DC.

Nishimizu, M., and S. Robinson. 1986. "Productivity Growth in Manufacturing." In *Industrialization and Growth: A Comparative Study,* ed. by H. Chenery, S. Robinson, and M. Syruin. World Bank Research Report. Oxford: Oxford University Press.

Razin, O. and S. M. A. Collins. 1997. "Real Exchange Rate Misalignments and Growth." NBER Working Paper no. 6174 (September). National Bureau of Economic Research, Cambridge, MA.

Reinhardt, C. 1995. "Devaluation, Relative Prices, and International Trade." IMF Staff Paper No. 42. International Monetary Fund, Washington, DC.

Sekkat K. and A. Varoudakis. Forthcoming, 2002. "The Impact of Exchange and Trade Policy Reforms on Manufactured Exports in North Africa." *Development Policy Review.*

Sorsa P. 1999. "Algeria: The Real Exchange Rate, Export Diversification, and Trade Protection." IMF Working Paper No. 99/49 (April). International Monetary Fund, Washington, DC.

Sundararajan, V., M. Lazare, and S. Williams. 1999. "Exchange Rate Unification, the Equilibrium Real Exchange Rate, and Choices of Exchange Rate Regime: The Case of Islamic Republic of Iran." IMF Working Paper. WP/99/15 (January). International Monetary Fund, Washington, DC.

Williamson, J. 1985. "The Exchange Rate System." *Policy Analyses in International Economics* 5. Washington, D.C.: Institute for International Economics.

Annex 15.1

List of Countries in the Sample

MENA	AFRICA		ASIA	LATIN AMERICA
	CFA	**Non-CFA**	**South East Asia**	
Bahrain (BHR)	Burkina Faso (BFA)	Botswana (BWA)	Indonesia (IDN)	Argentina (ARG)
Algeria (DZA)	Côte d'Ivoire (CIV)	Gambia, The (GMB)	Korea, Rep.(KOR)	Bolivia (BOL)
Egypt (EGY)	Gabon (GAB)	Kenya (KEN)	Malaysia (MYS)	Brazil (BRA)
Iran (IRN)	Cameroon (CMR)	Madagascar (MDG)	Philippines (PHL)	Chile (CHL)
Jordan (JOR)	Ghana (GHA)	Mozambique (MOZ)	Thailand (THA)	Colombia (COL)
Kuwait (KWT)	Niger (NER)	Mauritius (MUS)	**South Asia**	Costa Rica (CRI)
Malta (MLT)	Senegal (SEN)	Malawi (MWI)	Bangladesh (BGD)	Ecuador (ECU)
Morocco (MAR)	Togo (TGO)	Nigeria (NGA)	India (IND)	Guatemala (GTM)
Syria (SYR)		Tanzania (TZA)	China (CHN)	Mexico (MEX)
Tunisia (TUN)			Sri Lanka (LKA)	Peru (PER)
Other countries			Pakistan (PAK)	Paraguay (PRY)
Israel (ISR)				Uruguay (URY)
				Venezuela, RB (VEN)

Annex 15.2

Table 15A.1. Augmented Dickey-Fuller *(ADF)* Unit Root Tests Equations *(1)* and *(1')*

Variable	ADF statistic	k (1)	Critical value(2)	ADF test
RER				
$\ln(e_t)$	−1.73	1	−1.69**	I(0)
Fundamentals				
$\ln(Inv_t)$	−1.92	1	−1.82*	I(0)
$\ln(Open_t)$	−1.69	1	−1.69**	I(0)
$\ln(TP_t)$	−3.77	1	−1.82*	I(0)
$\ln(TOT_t)$	−2.15	1	−1.82*	I(0)
$Capinf_t$	−2.79	1	−1.82*	I(0)
$DebtSev_t$				
Other variables				
Def_t	−2.43	1	−1.82*	I(0)
p	−2.76	1	−1.82*	I(0)
$Depr_t$	−3.07	1	−1.82*	I(0)
BMP_t	−2.69	1	−1.82*	I(0)

Source: Authors' calculations.
(1) k is the number of lags in the ADF test.
(2) Im et al. (1997) critical values (respectively, *1 and **5 percent level).
Data have been compiled from World Development Indicators, Global Development Finance, Global Development Network, and Live Data Base (World Bank).

Table 15A.2. Augmented Dickey-Fuller *(ADF)* Unit Root Tests Equation *(2)*

Variable	ADF statistic	k (1)k	Critical value(2)	ADF test
$Ln(Xmanuf_{i,t})$	−1.76		−1.69**	
$GDPgrTP_{i,t}$	−3.69	1	−1.82*	I(0)
$\ln(TOTn_{i,t})$	−2.15	1	−1.82*	I(0)
$\ln(Inv_{i,t})$	−1.92	1	−1.82*	I(0)
$\ln(Roads_{i,t})$	−3.65	1	−1.82*	I(0)
$\ln(H1_{i,t})$	−1.86	1	−1.82*	I(0)
$RERVol$	−2.83	1	−1.82*	I(0)
$Ln(RERMis)$	−2.24	1	−1.82*	I(0)

Source: Authors' calculations.
(1) k is the number of lags in the ADF test.
(2) Im et al. (1997) critical values (respectively, *1 and **5 percent level).
Data have been compiled from World Development Indicators, Global Development Finance, Global Development Network, and Live Data Base (World Bank).

Annex 15.3

Short-Term Dynamics of the RER

Since the variables are cointegrated, the short-term dynamic adjustment of the RER toward its equilibrium level can be estimated through an error correction model. The estimated equation is as follows:

$$
\begin{aligned}
\Delta \ln(e_{i,t}) = \quad & -a \, [\ln(e_{i,t-1}) - \ln(e'_{i,t-1})] \\
& + a' \, \Delta \ln(e_{i,t-1}) \\
& + b_1.\Delta\ln(Inv_{i,t}) + b_2.\Delta\ln(Open_{i,t}) \\
& + b_3.\Delta\ln(TOT_{i,t}) + b_4.\Delta\ln(Capinf_{i,t}) \\
& + b_5.\Delta\ln(DebtServ_{i,t}) \\
& + c_1.\Delta\ln(Inv_{i,t-1}) + c_2.\Delta\ln(Open_{i,t-1}) \\
& + c_3.\Delta\ln(TOT_{i,t-1}) + c_4.\Delta\ln(Capinf_{i,t-1}) \\
& + c_5.\Delta\ln(DebtServ_{i,t-1}) \\
& + d_1. \, Depr_{i,t} + d_2. \, Depr_{i,t-1} \\
& + e_1. \, Infl_{i,t} + e_2. \, Inf_{i,t-1} \\
& + f_1. \, Def_{i,t} + f_2. \, Def_{i,t-1} \\
& + g_1. \, BMP_t + g_2. \, BMP_{i,t-1} + \varepsilon_{2t}.
\end{aligned}
\qquad \text{(A3-1)}
$$

In addition to the error correction term—that is, , the lagged error term of the cointegrating equation $(\ln(e_{t-1}) - \ln(e'_{t-1})($, and lagged variables of Equations (1) and (1') in first differences—indicators of fiscal policy (fiscal deficit as percentage of GDP, *Def*) and of exchange rate policy (nominal depreciation, *Depr*, and black market premium, *BMP*), as well as inflation (*Infl*) are included. The assumption is that the adjustment path of the RER toward its equilibrium level may be affected (accelerated or slowed down) by short-term economic policies, including capital controls (for which *BMP* is a proxy), nominal exchange rate depreciation, and fiscal policy, of which inflation can be a consequence. Table 15A.3 below shows the estimates of the error correction model.

Nominal devaluations show a short-term impact on the RER, which is in the expected direction, and significant. The change in the official nominal exchange rate (NER) hence captures the strong temporary effect that devaluation may produce on the RER due to price rigidities.

In addition, these estimations highlight the role of other short-term economic policies through the black market premium (*BMP*) and inflation (*Infl*). These variables (*Infl, BMP*), by leading to a rise in the price of nontradable goods, appreciate the RER and lead to its overvaluation. Although public deficit does not show a significant effect, it can be captured by the inflation variable, the effect of which is strong and which is also supposed to be a proxy for other inappropriate policies.

Table 15A.3. Estimates of the Error Correction Model

Dependant variable: $\Delta\ln(e_t)$

Variable	Eq (1)		Eq (1')	
	Elasticity	Student	Elasticity	Student
ε_{1t-1}	−0.13	(7.29)	−0.2	(9.7)
$\Delta\ln(Inv_t)$	0.04	(1.42)	0.2	(0.78)
$\Delta\ln(Open_t)$	−0.27	(6.97)	−0.5	(14.53)
$\Delta\ln(TOT_t)$	0.1	(2.7)	0.1 5	(4.8)
$\Delta(Capinf)$	0.006	(1.27)	0.25	(3.8)
$\Delta\ln(DebtServ_t)$			0.02	(1.81)
$\Delta\ln(Inv_{t-1})$	0.01	(0.33)	0.03	(1.2)
$\Delta\ln(Open_{t-1})$	0.06	(1.57)	0.02	(0.5)
$\Delta\ln(TOT_{t-1})$	0.02	(0.72)	0.04	(1.4)
$\Delta(Capinf_{t-1})$	0.78	(1.81)	−0.33	(5.1)
$\Delta\ln(DebtServ_{t-1})$			0.04	(2.1)
$\Delta\ln(e_{t-1})$	0.06	(1.64)	0.16	(4.9)
$Depr$	−0. 22	(18.0)	−0.04	(10.9)
$Depr_{t-1}$	−0.05	(8.0)	0.006	(1.4)
$Infl_t$	0.19	(17.8)	0.04	(10.4)
$Infl_{t-1}$	0.05	(7.91)	−0.007	(1.6)
Def_{t-1}	0.05	(0.38)		
Def_t	0.05	(0.44)		
BMP_t	0.006	(2.5)	0.12	(5.5)
BMP_{t-1}	0.21	(0.86)	−0.003	(1.47)
D- W	1.74		2.03	

Source: Authors' estimations.

Note: Student *t* statistics are within brackets. The sample includes, respectively, 640 and 828 observations over the 1970–99 period. * ε_{1t-1} is the lagged error term of the cointegrating Equation (1). Data have been compiled from World Development Indicators, Global Development Finance, Global Development Network, and Live Data Base (World Bank).

•
•
•

16

Public Infrastructure and Private Investment in the Middle East and North Africa

Pierre-Richard Agénor*
Mustapha K. Nabli
Tarik M. Yousef†

According to conventional wisdom, the poor growth and employment performance of the Middle East and North Africa (MENA) region is primarily the result of the "slow, uneven, and hesitant pace" of structural reforms launched in the late 1980s and early 1990s (see World Bank 2003a) and Richards and Waterbury (1996).[1] In particular, governments in the region continue to dominate most economies, with pervasive involvement in production, labor markets, banking systems, and social services. Despite downsizing efforts, the share of MENA's public sectors in output and employment still exceeds averages for developing and industrialized countries. In addition to the size and scope of government intervention, private sector development in the region continues to be stifled by limited progress in building market-oriented institutions and in integrating the region into the world economy (see World Bank 2003b). As a result, the economic recovery of the 1990s was weak, labor productivity remained low, and unemployment rates continued to increase.

---

* School of Social Studies, University of Manchester, United Kingdom, and Centre for Growth and Business Cycle Research. † School of Foreign Service, Georgetown University. The authors are grateful to Nihal Bayraktar for technical support as well as to the editor, three referees, and participants at various seminars for helpful comments on an earlier draft.

World Bank Policy Research Working Paper No. 3661. July 2005. Reprinted by permission from the World Bank.

The absence of dynamic private sectors in MENA's economies has been especially felt in the area of investment. Observers in the early 1990s had taken the view that the public sector has "overinvested" and that public investment competes with, rather than fosters, private investment (see Page 1998 and World Bank 1995). But the decline in public investment rates was not always compensated by a rise in private investment. As a result, capital accumulation rates on a per worker basis stagnated in the past two decades (see Nabli and Keller 2002). Indeed, with the exception of Sub-Saharan Africa, MENA has the lowest private investment ratios among developing regions. Moreover, in countries where public investment levels remained high, the productivity of capital was limited. The very nature of the network utilities that were built to provide infrastructure services (vertically and horizontally integrated state monopolies) often resulted in weak delivery of services such as electricity, natural gas, telecommunications, railroads, and water supply. Common problems included low productivity, high costs, bad quality, insufficient revenue, and shortfalls in maintenance spending (see World Bank 1994 and Kessides 2004). Low productivity of public investment is consistent with recent growth accounting exercises showing that the contribution of physical capital accumulation to growth in MENA countries has declined over time—despite the fact that there has been no attempt in this literature to explicitly separate public and private capital accumulation. [2]

The extent to which public investment (especially in infrastructure) complements or crowds out private investment, and the role of quantity versus quality in the productivity of public investment in MENA, remain largely unknown. To date, there have been few empirical studies focusing on these issues in the region.[3] In an early paper on Egypt, for instance, Shafik (1992) found that public investment tends to crowd out private investment through its effect on credit markets, and to crowd it in through investment in infrastructure. Everhart and Sumlinski (2001), using panel regression techniques and a proxy for the quality of public investment, found no significant effect of public investment on private investment in MENA. Dhumale (2000), using a model that accounts for credit to the private sector and the accelerator effect, found that public investment in infrastructure appeared to have a crowding out effect in oil-exporting countries, and a crowding-in effect in the non-oil-exporting countries. Mansouri (2004) found that public capital had a positive effect on private investment in Morocco.

However, existing studies are lacking in at least three respects. First, they seldom make a clear distinction between the flow effect of public investment, and the stock effect of public capital. But this is crucial, given that the transmission channels are substantially different. Second, these studies do not always account for the simultaneous relationships between public investment and capital, private capital formation, and other variables like output growth, relative prices, and private sector credit. Third, the treatment of dynamics in these studies is sometimes crude, if not inexistent. All three issues are addressed in this paper, which assesses quantitatively the impact of public infrastructure on private capital formation in three MENA countries: Egypt, Jordan, and Tunisia.

The remainder of the paper is organized as follows. The next section provides a brief overview of direct and indirect channels through which public infrastructure (flows and stocks) may affect private investment. The third section describes the vector autoregression (VAR) model that we use to assess the links between public infrastructure and private capital formation. The fourth section examines the data and the construction of our quality measures of the public capital stock in infrastructure. Estimation results and variance decompositions are discussed in the fifth section. In the last section, impulse response functions are computed to assess the dynamic effects of a shock to public infrastructure expenditure and the public capital stock. The last section draws together some policy implications of our analysis.

Public Infrastructure and Private Investment: Transmission Channels

Public infrastructure investment and capital can affect private investment through various channels. For the purpose of this study, and given the empirical technique that we use later on, it is convenient to classify these channels into two broad sets of effects: complementarity and crowding-out effects, and output and relative price effects.

Complementarity and Crowding-Out Effects

The complementarity effect asserts that public capital (as opposed to public investment) in infrastructure may stimulate private physical capital formation because of its impact on private activity. By raising the marginal productivity of private inputs (both labor and capital), it raises the perceived rate of return on, and increases the demand for, physical capital by the private sector.[4] Alternatively, a complementarity effect between public capital in infrastructure and private investment may operate through installation costs. This idea, formalized for instance by Turnovsky (1996) in a growth context, is based on the view that the availability (and quality) of public capital in infrastructure affects some of the costs that firms may incur when investing. For instance, a better road network may reduce expenses associated with the construction of a new factory or the transportation of heavy equipment to a new production site. In large countries, the impact on unit production costs and the productivity of private capital can be substantial (Cohen and Paul 2004).

Of course, the positive effect of public capital on the marginal productivity of private inputs may hold not only for infrastructure but also for public capital in education and health, which may enhance the productivity of labor. Other components of current public spending, related, for instance, to the enforcement of property rights, can also increase the productivity of the economy and exert a positive indirect effect on private investment. But infrastructure capital may have a particularly large effect in countries where initial stocks are low and basic infrastructure services (electricity and communications, for instance) are lacking. Moreover, whereas gains in education and health tend to accrue to individuals, increases in public infrastructure assets tend to have economy-wide spillover effects.

Nevertheless, to the extent that public investment in infrastructure displaces or crowds out private investment, its net positive impact on private capital formation can be highly mitigated. Such crowding-out effects tend to occur if the public sector finances the increase in public investment through an increase in distortionary taxes—which may raise incentives for private agents to evade taxation, or reduce the expected net rate of return to private capital, and therefore the propensity to invest. A similar effect on private capital formation may occur if the increase in public infrastructure investment is paid for by borrowing on domestic financial markets, as a result of either higher domestic interest rates or a greater incidence of rationing of credit to the private sector.[5] Moreover, if an investment-induced expansion in public borrowing raises concerns about the sustainability of public debt over time (that is, the perceived risk of default), and strengthens expectations of a future increase in taxation, the risk premium embedded in interest rates may increase.[6] By negatively affecting expected after-tax rates of return on private capital, the increase in the cost of capital may have a compounding effect on private investment. Private investors may revise downward their investment plans because of anticipated hikes in tax rates to cover the increase in government investment.

Moreover, it is important to note that the productivity and complementarity effects of public infrastructure assets are significant only to the extent that the services derived from them are of sufficient quality. Having roads is a good step, but if these roads are filled with potholes, they may not do much to reduce installation costs. Likewise, an erratic supply of electricity may be tantamount to not having electricity at all. Quality considerations are therefore important when assessing the benefits associated with public capital. This is indeed one of the main features of the empirical methodology developed in this paper.

Indirect Output and Relative Price Effects

Public investment and capital in infrastructure may also affect private capital formation indirectly, through changes in output and relative prices. As noted earlier, public capital in infrastructure may increase the marginal productivity of existing factor inputs (both capital and labor), thereby lowering marginal production costs and increasing the level of private production. In turn, this scale effect on output may lead, through the standard accelerator effect, to higher private investment (see Chirinko 1993). Moreover, if there are externalities associated with the use of some production factors (for instance, learning-by-doing effects resulting from a high degree of complementarity between physical capital and skilled labor), a positive growth effect may also result.

Public infrastructure can also affect private investment indirectly through its "flow" effect on the price of domestic consumption goods relative to the price of imported goods, that is, the (consumption-based) real exchange rate. An increase in public investment in infrastructure, for instance, will raise aggregate demand and domestic prices (in addition to stimulating output). The real exchange rate will tend to appreciate, thereby stimulating demand for these goods and dampening domestic activity. The net effect on output may be positive or negative, depending on the intratemporal elasticity of substitution between domestic and imported goods. If this elasticity is low (as one would expect in the short run), the net effect on output may be positive, so that private investment may indeed increase. At the same time, the appreciation will tend to lower the relative price of imported capital goods, resulting in a drop in the user cost of capital and an increase in private investment. This relative price effect may be particularly important in developing countries where a large fraction of capital goods used by the private sector are imported.

In addition to these effects, changes in domestic prices and the real exchange rate induced by an increase in the flow of public investment in infrastructure may affect private investment through both demand- and supply-side effects on output. On the demand side, the increase in domestic prices may lower private sector real wealth and thus expenditure; if this effect is sufficiently large (relative to the increase in public spending) to entail a fall in domestic absorption, firms may revise their expectations of future demand and lower investment outlays, through a "reverse" accelerator effect. On the supply side, the real appreciation may lead to a shift in resource allocation toward the nontradable goods sector, thereby stimulating investment in that sector and depressing capital formation in the tradable goods sector. The net effect may be a lower growth rate of output, and thus lower investment as a result of an expected reduction in demand growth. At the same time, however, the real appreciation tends to lower the real cost of imported intermediate inputs, thereby stimulating output and private investment.

It is important to note that both the direction and the strength of the various effects described above can vary over time, and depend to a very large extent on the environment in which private investors are operating. For instance, the relationship between public and private investment may be one of substitution in the short run, and one of complementarity in the long run, depending on how "productive" public investment is. In the short term, the crowding-out effect may predominate (because the pool of resources available to finance public and private investment is limited), whereas the complementarity effect may prevail in the long term, as a result of strong supply-side effects. Thus, using dynamic models is essential to study the relationship between public infrastructure and private capital formation, beyond the need to account for gestation lags. At the same time, it is important to control for indirect effects that operate through changes in output, the real exchange rate, and possibly interest rates or credit.

Finally, it is also worth noting that there may be a feedback effect through public investment itself; indeed, to the extent that the rise in private investment stimulates output and leads to higher tax revenue, public investment may increase further, as a consequence of the additional resources at the disposal of the public sector. These dynamic and feedback effects are key reasons for choosing a VAR framework for our empirical analysis, as discussed next.

VAR Specification

The foregoing discussion suggests that it is important, in assessing the link between public infrastructure and private investment, to account for both the flow and stock of public infrastructure, and to control for simultaneous interactions between these variables and output, the real exchange rate, and financial variables (either interest rates or private sector credit). Accordingly, we opted to use a VAR approach. VAR models offer a number of advantages over the specification and estimation of a structural model. First, in developing countries in general, it has proved difficult to estimate robust structural models of private investment (see Agénor 2004). VAR models offer a way of analyzing the dynamic relationship between our two main variables without having to fully specify a structural model of private capital formation. The lumpy nature of much infrastructure investment implies that the full impact of investment in, say, roads or telecommunications, may be felt only after several years; VAR models allow us to take into account delayed responses, even with a parsimonious lag structure. Second, VAR models explicitly recognize the endogeneity of public infrastructure investment and capital—which may result, as noted above, from the feedback effect of private investment on output (through tax revenue). Third, VAR models provide a convenient common framework for examining investment behavior in a cross-country study. Using a uniform single regression model would amount to imposing strong restrictions on specification and the direction of causality among the variables. As a result, models of this type tend to be prone to misspecification errors resulting from "missing variables" bias and the neglect of dynamic feedbacks—a particularly important problem when the purpose of the study is to conduct simulation experiments.

The use of VAR models to study the impact of public investment on private capital formation is by no means new. For instance, Mittnik and Neumann (2001) examined the impact of public investment using impulse response functions derived from a VAR consisting of public investment, private investment, public consumption, and output. Ghali (1998) used a VAR (or, more precisely, a vector error correction model) with real GDP, public investment, and private investment. Ligthart (2000) used an unrestricted VAR in output, public capital, private capital, and employment for Portugal. Belloc and Vertova (2004), using a vector error-correction approach, found a complementarity relationship between public and private investment, and a positive effect of investment on output in six out of seven highly indebted poor countries. Finally, Voss (2002) specified a VAR with ratios of public and private investment to GDP, the growth rates of the relative prices of public and private investment goods, the real interest rate, and the growth rate of GDP.

All these studies, however, suffer from three major limitations in terms of their specification: (i) they do not generally make a distinction between the flow of public investment and the stock of public capital; (ii) they do no always account for potential crowding-out effects; and (iii) they do not account for indirect effects of public investment on private capital formation through the real exchange rate. Belloc and Vertova (2004), for instance, used a trivariate VAR, with no control for factors other than output. As emphasized earlier, the channels through which public infrastructure affects private investment involve both "flow" effects (which operate through aggregate demand, relative prices, and the financial sector), and "stock" effects (which operate through both the demand and the supply sides).

Our VAR improves on existing studies in all three respects. We include the following variables in our specification: the flow of public capital expenditure on infrastructure as a share of GDP, the stock of public capital in infrastructure as a share of GDP, private capital formation as a share of GDP, the ratio of private sector credit to GDP, real GDP growth, and the rate of change of the real exchange rate. The actual growth rate of output is used as a proxy for expected changes in aggregate demand, and captures dynamics associated with the accelerator effect. Changes in private sector credit account for possible crowding-out effects associated with government spending through changes in credit rationing. We chose a credit variable instead of Interest rates, because these rates remained largely under government control for much of the estimation period.[7] Changes in the real exchange rate account for both the relative price effect of an increase in domestic absorption, and indirect effects on the user cost of capital and the price of imported inputs, as discussed earlier.[8]

To assess whether the stock of public capital in infrastructure should be included in the VAR (in addition to the associated flow), we performed an exogeneity test based on estimating both the "unrestricted" and "restricted" VAR models (that is, with and without the public capital stock).[9] To calculate variance decompositions and identify impulse response functions, we use the standard Choleski decomposition. Specifically, to implement this decomposition, the disturbances in the model are assumed to follow the following causal ordering: credit-to-GDP ratio; public infrastructure spending ratio; public infrastructure capital ratio; the rate of change of the real exchange rate; the growth rate of GDP; and the private investment ratio. The reasoning behind this ordering structure is that whereas public expenditure decisions or the public capital stock can affect private sector investment decisions in the short run (within one period), the reverse is not true. Thus, public expenditure on infrastructure does not depend contemporaneously on private investment, an assumption that we take to be consistent with treating public investment as exogenous (at least with respect to private investment) in structural models. Public expenditure on infrastructure naturally precedes the public capital stock. The real exchange rate and output growth are both assumed to respond immediately (within a year) to changes in public investment and the public capital stock. Private sector credit is considered the most "exogenous" variable, with the implicit view being that it is largely under the control of (risk-averse) banks.[10]

Finally, it is important to note that in our VAR model, flows and stocks are entered as ratios, not as levels. Because we use the Perpetual Inventory Method (PIM) to calculate our estimates of capital stocks, there is a recursive (or autoregressive) relation between flows and stocks. However, this relation holds only for the levels of the variables; in our VAR model, we consider the ratios of investment (public and private) to GDP as well as public capital to GDP. An exogenous shock to, say, the public investment-GDP ratio may or may not lead to a change in the same direction of the public capital-GDP ratio, because the response of output is endogenous in the VAR. In particular, if both the public capital stock and GDP increase as a result of the shock (the former arguably in a mechanical fashion, as a result of the autoregressive nature of PIM), their ratio would remain unchanged.

The Data

We begin by examining the data on private and public investment in the three countries in our sample. Next, we consider the evolution of public capital expenditure on infrastructure, and describe how these flows are converted into stocks. We then explain how our basic indicators of the quality of public capital in infrastructure are constructed, and how they are used to derive a composite indicator.

Overall Trends

Figure 16.1 shows the evolution of public and private investment ratios to GDP since the mid-1960s in Egypt, the mid-1970s in Jordan, and the early 1970s in Tunisia. The share of public investment in GDP has displayed substantial volatility over time in all three countries, but has been on a downward trend in Egypt and Jordan since the late 1980s. Private investment ratios have

Figure 16.1. MENA Countries: Public and Private Investment

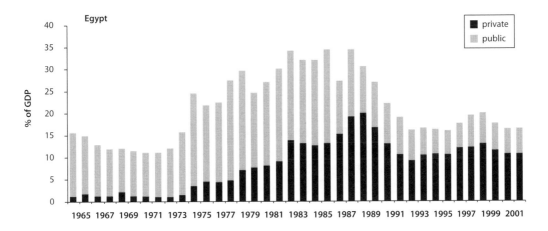

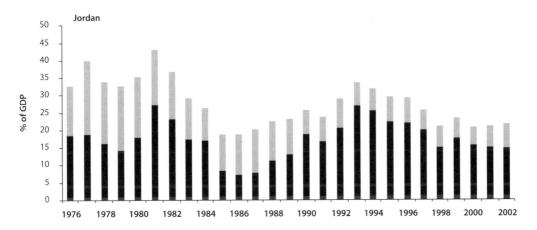

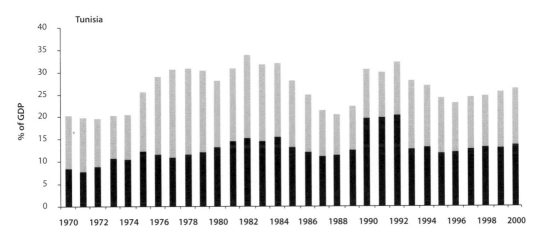

at the same time been subject to large fluctuations, most significantly during the 1980s and 1990s—a period characterized also by large fluctuations in GDP in the region as a whole. In Egypt, following a steady increase from the mid-1960s to the late 1980s, the share of private investment in GDP has averaged 10 percent. In Jordan and Tunisia, private investment ratios have declined significantly since the peaks of the early 1990s, fluctuating in recent years between 12 and 15 percent.

Flows and Stocks of Public Infrastructure

National Accounts data on public investment in infrastructure are generally not available. For the purpose of our study, we used government budget data published in the IMF's *Government Finance Statistics (GFS) Yearbook* to build an estimate. Specifically, as discussed in the Annex, we calculated capital expenditure on "core" infrastructure by adding capital outlays on fuel and energy, water transportation, and transportation and communications. Of course, all capital expenditures on these categories do not necessarily represent "investment," as conventionally defined; some components of these outlays may be related to current spending, such as maintenance operations. However, we did not have sufficient information to refine the GFS estimates.

The data indicate that the evolution of total capital expenditure as a proportion of GDP, and capital expenditure on infrastructure, both as a share of total public expenditure (including current spending), and as a share of total capital expenditure only, display a declining trend since the early 1980s for Jordan and the late 1980s for Tunisia. But for all three countries, the behavior of the ratio of total capital expenditure to GDP is consistent with the evolution of total public investment illustrated in Figure 16.1. As a proportion of total capital outlays, the share of capital expenditure on infrastructure has averaged 30 percent for Jordan, and almost 40 percent for Tunisia, in recent years. For Egypt, by contrast, there are large fluctuations during the past 40 years, but no clear trends. In recent years, the share of capital expenditure on infrastructure in total capital outlays has fluctuated between 45 and 50 percent.

Using our flow data on infrastructure spending, we calculated the stock of public capital in infrastructure, using the perpetual inventory method and the GDP deflator to estimate real values in constant local prices. This procedure is, of course, subject to limitations.[11] Differences in the efficiency of the public sector and the price of infrastructure capital, in particular, mean that the same level of capital spending on infrastructure may yield very different results across countries. We account for quality ex post by using various indicators, as discussed below. More generally, the use of perpetual inventory methods to calculate stocks from expenditure flows may introduce systematic errors in stock estimates. At the same time, however, it should be noted that adequate price variables for public infrastructure are difficult to construct (given that infrastructure services are often provided free of charge), and that errors in estimating initial stocks (a common problem with this methodology) tend to become less significant over time. In addition, the alternative of using actual stocks of infrastructure (such as roads, electricity production, or water supply) was not feasible because of lack of data; the only complete series that we had at our disposal was that of electricity production, but it was felt that using it as a the sole indicator of quality of the overall stock of infrastructure was not warranted.

Quality Indicators

In assessing the impact of the public capital stock in infrastructure on private investment, it is important to account not only for the absolute amount of that stock, but also for the quality (or efficiency) with which public capital is used.[12] A common procedure for estimating the quality of public infrastructure capital is to calculate the index proposed by Hulten (1996) His composite measure of public capital efficiency is based on four basic indicators: mainline faults per 100 telephone calls for telecommunications; electricity generation losses as a percent of total electricity output; the percentage of paved roads in good condition; and diesel locomotive utilization as a percentage of the total rolling stock. In practice, researchers have found that these individual quality indicators tend to be highly correlated with the quantities of each type of infrastructure.[13] Thus, much of the variation in infrastructure quality may be well captured by variations in its quantit,

The individual quality indicators proposed by Hulten (1996) are subject to limitations. For instance, electric power losses include both "technical" losses, reflecting the quality of the power grid, and outright theft; in general, the breakdown between the two components is not available. Moreover, these series tend to fluctuate significantly over time, and these fluctuations are not always easy to interpret as changes in quality as opposed to, say, measurement errors or "abnormal" shocks (due, say, to bad weather). More importantly in the present case, these indicators were not all available for our group of countries, and when they were, many data points were missing. Despite using a combination of local and international sources—including the *World Development Indicators* of the World Bank and Canning's (1998) database on physical infrastructure stocks—we were unable to "piece together" complete series, with a sufficient amount of overlapping with our private investment series.

We therefore followed another approach, which consisted in, first, defining two alternative quality indicators and, second, combining them to create a composite indicator. Our first individual indicator is an "ICOR-based" measure. Aggregate ICORs (calculated as the ratio of total domestic investment divided by the change in output) are commonly viewed as a measure of the efficiency of investment. Here we apply this idea to public infrastructure only, by defining an ICOR coefficient as public capital expenditure on infrastructure divided by the change in GDP. We then invert this measure and take a three-year moving average, in order to smooth out the behavior of the series over time.

Our second indicator is an "excess demand" measure. Our premise is that, if growth in the demand for infrastructure services tends to exceed growth in supply, pressure on the existing public capital stock will intensify and quality will deteriorate. To construct these indicators, we proceeded in two steps. First, we calculated individual indicators of "excess demand" for three categories of infrastructure services: electricity generation; the number of telephone mainlines; and the percentage of paved roads in the road network. To estimate demand for infrastructure service h, we applied the annual growth rate of real GDP per capita to the stock of public capital in h at the base period. We used elasticity values of unity in each case.[14] To estimate supply of infrastructure service h, we used the actual stock of h. We then calculated individual indicators of excess demand for each component of infrastructure services by taking the ratio of supply to "predicted" demand. This ratio gives, therefore, an indicator of adequacy between supply and demand; a fall in the ratio would indicate excessive pressure on existing infrastructure, and therefore, a deterioration in quality. Second, we calculated a "composite" excess demand indicator for each country. To do so, we used the same procedure as Hulten (1996) did to calculate his quality index, that is, we standardized each of the three series (by subtracting the mean and dividing by the standard error) and calculated the unweighted, arithmetic average of the standardized series.

Continuous annual time series for all three of the infrastructure services referred to earlier were not available for the whole estimation period. For instance, data on roads (in terms of kilometers per capita) were available only since 1990. We therefore calculated the composite indicator with all the information available in the base period to begin with, and added additional series as they became available. Again, a three-year moving average was used, in order to smooth out spikes possibly associated to measurement errors or random events.

The evolution of both indicators is displayed in figures 16.2, 16.3, and 16.4. Results for the ICOR-based indicator suggest that, whereas quality seems to have improved in recent years in Tunisia, it has deteriorated in Egypt and Jordan. By contrast, results for the composite excess demand indicator suggest that quality improved in all three countries in recent years.

Differences in the behavior of our two quality indicators may appear problematic, given that there is no strong a priori reason for choosing among them. We thus follow the logic of the approach proposed by Calderón and Servén (2004b), who define several standard quality indicators—based on electricity losses, percentage of paved roads, and telephone faults, given that they use stocks of electricity, roads, and telephones in their regressions—and

Figure 16.2. Egypt: Variance Decomposition of Private Investment in Percent of GDP

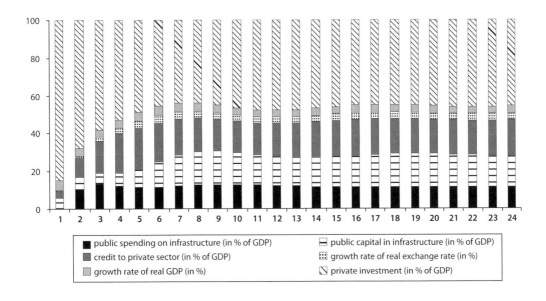

Figure 16.3. Jordan: Variance Decomposition of Private Investment in Percent of GDP

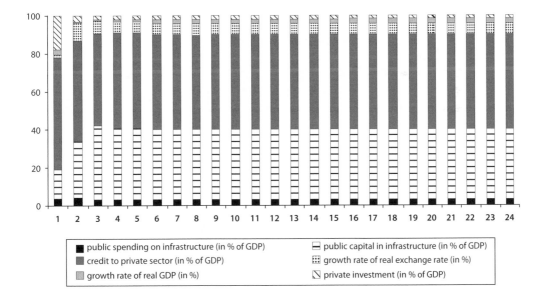

use principal components analysis to "summarize" the information contained in all of these series. Specifically, we applied principal components analysis to the two quality series that we defined earlier.[15] The results show that the first principal component explains 64 percent of the total variance of the underlying variables for Egypt, 68 percent for Jordan, and 55 percent for Tunisia. After

Figure 16.4. Tunisia: Variance Decomposition of Private Investment in Percent of GDP

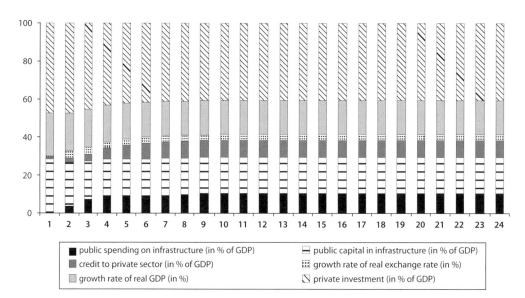

renormalization, we use a weighted average of the two principal components, using as weights the proportion of total variance explained by each component, as our quality indicate

Estimation and Variance Decompositions

As noted earlier, our VAR model consists of public capital expenditure on infrastructure as a share of GDP; private investment as a share of GDP; the growth rate of real GDP; the ratio of private sector credit to GDP; the rate of change of the real exchange rate; and possibly the public capital stock in infrastructure. Prior to estimation, we examined the stationarity properties of each of these variables with Augmented Dickey-Fuller and Phillips-Perron unit root tests. The results (which are available upon request) indicated that all series are either stationary or trend stationary. As a result, we included an exogenous time trend in the VAR.

The first step in the estimation was to verify that the public capital stock in infrastructure "belongs" to the VAR. To do so, we applied the exogeneity test described earlier. The results indicated that the null hypothesis (exclusion of the public capital stock from the VAR) was soundly rejected by the likelihood ratio test. Moreover, because the crowding-out effects associated with changes in public investment flows could be quantitatively small, we also tested for whether the flow of public capital spending on infrastructure, as opposed to the stock of public capital, should be excluded from the VAR. The results, based on the likelihood ratio tests, again led to a rejection of the null hypothesis.

We then chose the optimal lag length, using the Akaike criterion. Given the relatively small size of the sample, we were able to compare models with only one and two lags.[16] The Akaike criterion suggested a lag of two years for Egypt, and one year for Jordan and Tunisia. Admittedly, lags of this order may not be sufficient to properly account for the long gestation periods associated with some types of public investment, but insufficient degrees of freedom prevented us from experimenting with higher-order systems. Nevertheless, it should be noted that we introduce explicitly the stock of capital in infrastructure itself, and that our hypothesis is that the (quality-adjusted) stock produces a proportional flow of services. Simulations related to changes in the public capital stock are therefore unaffected by the problem of gestation lags.

The extent to which exogenous changes (or innovations) in public infrastructure, and other variables in the VAR model, affect the behavior of private capital formation can be gauged by computing the proportion of the variance of the forecast error for the private investment-to-GDP ratio that can be attributed to variations in each variable at different forecast horizons. Figures 16.2, 16.3, and 16.4 show these variance decompositions, at a horizon of up to 24 periods. For Egypt, shocks to the private investment ratio account for more than 80 percent of its variance in the short run, and close to 50 percent in the long run. The fraction explained by the credit-to-GDP ratio increases from about 3 percent in the short term to 17 percent in the long term. So does the share of public capital spending on infrastructure, the share of which rises from 3 percent to almost 11 percent. The share of public capital also grows over time, to about 13 percent.

For Jordan, the credit-to-GDP ratio and the ratio of public capital to GDP play an important role in explaining the variability of the private investment ratio, in both the short and the long term. By contrast, all the other variables have a negligible role. By contrast, for Tunisia, the credit-to-GDP ratio appears to play a negligible role; in both the short and the long term, it explains barely 3 percent of variations in the private investment ratio. Public expenditure on infrastructure and public capital, instead, explain about a third of these fluctuations in the long term. Shocks to private investment itself explain a large fraction of the variance of that variable, even in the long term. Overall, therefore, the variance decompositions suggest that public capital in infrastructure matters more than public spending on infrastructure (particularly so for Jordan), although other shocks (such as credit for Jordan), as well as "own" innovations (for Egypt and Tunisia), also appear to have mattered to a considerable degree.

Impulse Response Analysis

We now examine the impulse response functions associated with shocks to public spending on infrastructure and our quality-adjusted measure of public capital. As noted earlier, this analysis is important because it allows us to assess to what extent flows and stocks of public infrastructure affect private investment, taking into account crowding-out effects and the possibility that indirect effects may occur through changes in the growth rate of output and the real exchange rate.

Shock to Public Spending on Infrastructure

The left-hand side of figure 16.5 shows the response over a 10-year horizon of the private investment rate to a one-standard-deviation innovation in the ratio of public capital expenditure on infrastructure in GDP. The solid lines in the figure represent the impulse response functions themselves, whereas the dotted lines are the associated 95 percent upper and lower confidence bands.[17]

The results indicate that the shock to the public capital expenditure ratio has a statistically significant effect on the private investment rate in none of the three countries. Moreover, in the case of Egypt and Jordan, the shock has no effect on the growth rate of output, the real exchange rate, or the credit ratio. By contrast, in the case of Tunisia, the real exchange rate appreciates, and output falls significantly, in the second period. Thus, the lack of significance of a public spending shock on private investment in Tunisia may result from the fact that the resulting increase in aggregate demand (which tends to raise domestic prices) is offset by an adverse real wealth effect on private consumption expenditure, at the same time as the real appreciation leads to a contraction in output. In turn, this contraction in activity may offset the initial positive impact of public expenditure on private investment through a "reverse" accelerator effect.

Shock to Public Capital in Infrastructure

The right-hand side of figure 16.5 displays the response of the private investment ratio to a one-standard-deviation innovation in the ratio of public infrastructure capital to GDP. The results show that the shock has a positive and statistically significant effect on private capital formation in the first two periods for Tunisia, and the first three periods for Jordan. In the case of Egypt, there is no significant effect. Moreover, in the case of Jordan, the growth rate of output increases significantly in the first three periods, which seems to occur without any significant pressure on domestic prices (and thus no tendency for the real exchange rate to appreciate); thus, the rise in the investment ratio may also reflect an indirect accelerator effect.

Overall, therefore, our results indicate that there are significant—albeit relatively small, in absolute terms, and short-lived—"stock" effects only of public infrastructure; there is no evidence of a "flow" effect in none of the countries in our sample. To assess whether the increase in the quality-adjusted infrastructure public capital stock reflects an increase in the stock itself (that is, the "raw" quantity of capital) or a change in quality, we re-estimated the

Figure 16.5. MENA Countries: Response of Private Investment in Percent of GDP to One Standard Deviation Innovation in Public Spending on Infrastructure or in Public Capital Stock in Infrastructure, Both in Percent of GDP

(+/−2 standard errors)

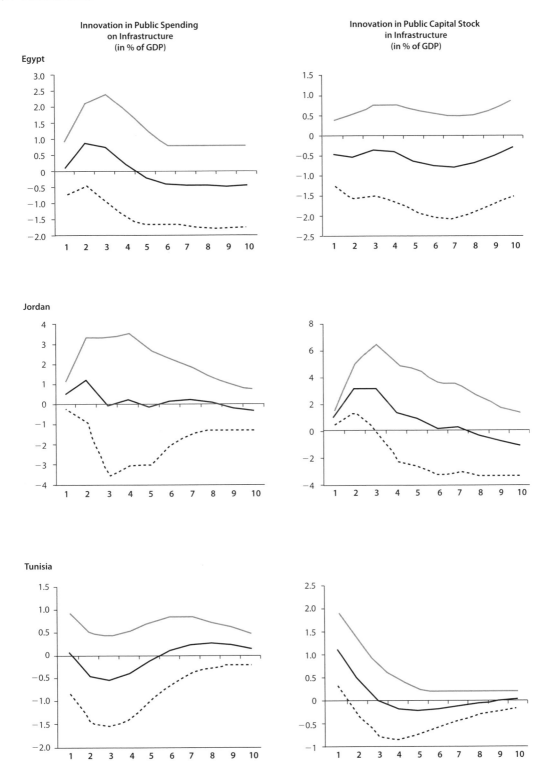

VAR model for each country with the unadjusted capital stock. The results showed no significant effects associated with an innovation in the capital stock in Jordan and Tunisia. Moreover, in the case of Jordan, the private investment ratio actually fell slightly on impact. Our interpretation of these results is thus that quality matters for both countries. Increasing the quantity of infrastructure, by itself, does not have a significant effect on the ratio of private investment to output.

Policy Implications

Our empirical results have potential useful policy implications not only for the three countries in our sample but possibly also for the MENA region in general. As concluded in a recent report by the World Bank (2004), stimulating growth and job creation in MENA will require comprehensive policy reforms. A key issue in this context, as noted earlier, is the role of the public sector. Although our study is subject to some limitations (owing in part to the paucity of data and the "black box" nature of VARs) we tentatively view it as bringing to the fore two main policy messages: the first is that the quality of public investment, specifically in infrastructure, matters. The second is that the weak effect of public capital on private investment may reflect the fact that the complementarity effect, while potentially important, may not "kick in," because of an unfavorable environment for private sector activity.

Regarding the first message, an implication of our results is indeed that it may be more important, in some countries, to improve the quality of the existing infrastructure than to engage in further investment. Reducing unproductive public capital expenditure and improving quality must be accompanied by policy reforms aimed at limiting investment to infrastructure capital that crowds in the private sector and/or corrects for fundamental market failures.[18] To do so requires redefining the role of the public sector as a catalyst for, rather than a provider of, the majority of infrastructure services. This will entail privatization and greater involvement of the private sector in infrastructure investment. Such involvement will allow commercial discipline to be introduced in the delivery of services, thereby improving efficiency and the quality and coverage of services, lowering costs, and reducing the burden on the public budget.

Private sector involvement in the delivery of basic infrastructure has indeed increased in developing countries. According to a comprehensive report by the International Finance Corporation (2003), during the 1990s, more than 130 developing countries pursued (through a variety of schemes) private participation in that sector. During the period 1990-2001, for developing countries in general, private participation accounted for 25 percent of total investment in infrastructure. However, the same report notes that in MENA, investment in infrastructure projects with private participation fell (in 2001 U.S.

dollars) from US$3.6 billion in 1993 to US$2.8 billion in 2001. Cumulative investment in the region for the period 1990–2001 amounted to US$22.8 billion, which was less than that in Sub-Saharan Africa (US$23.4 billion) and South Asia (US$39.6 billion), and substantially less compared to East Asia and the Pacific (US$210.6 billion), Europe and Central Asia (US$97.1 billion), and Latin America and the Caribbean (US$360.6 billion).[19]

The second policy message of our study—which is somewhat more speculative in nature, given that we did not estimate a "structural" model—is that the lack of a strong and persistent effect of public infrastructure capital on private investment (even after adjusting for quality) may reflect the unfavorable environment in which the private sector has operated in the region. Indeed, a key conclusion of recent research by the World Bank (2003b) is that the unfavorable investment environment in MENA accounts to a significant degree for the lack of a strong response from the private sector in the last decade. While infrastructure (in the form of the provision of critical telecommunications, transport, and energy services) is important, other improvements in the environment in which domestic investment is conducted may be equally important. These include, inter alia, the need to provide financing on adequate terms, and guarantee a secure and efficient judicial system. Without renewed effort to tackle these issues, private investment may not achieve its potential to stimulate growth and job creation in the region.

Notes

1. See World Bank (2004) for a review of employment and growth outcomes in the 1990s and their links to trends in physical and human capital accumulation, and Agénor et al. (2004). Elbadawi (2004) emphasized the role of conflict and instability, whereas Hakura (2004) found that excessive government intervention and poor institutions were key factors hampering growth.

2. The same observation applies to growth in total factor productivity, which has been either negative or below international levels since the 1980s (Nabli and Keller 2002). The efficiency of public spending on education has also been low, limiting the contribution of advances in educational attainment in the region to growth (see Pritchett 1999 and World Bank 2004).

3. Appendix A of the Working Paper version of this article provides a broad review of empirical studies linking public investment to private capital formation and growth in developing countries.

4. Greater availability of public capital in infrastructure could in principle also reduce the demand for private inputs, at a given level of output (net substitution effect). But if inputs are gross complements (as is the case in general), higher availability of public capital will always increase the marginal productivity of private inputs. Moreover, public and private physical capital are likely to have a high degree of complementarity, that is, a small elasticity of (net) substitution.

5. Note that any component of government expenditure (not only infrastructure investment), as long as it is financed through domestic borrowing, may lower private investment by driving interest rates up or increasing the incidence of credit rationing.

6. In a small, open economy with open capital markets facing a fixed world interest rate, crowding-out effects through a rise in domestic interest rates cannot occur. But for small developing countries, the supply curve of foreign capital is upward-sloping rather than horizontal. In such conditions, and if the risk premium faced on world capital markets is positively related to the debt-to-GDP ratio, an increase

in domestic public debt, induced by a rise in public investment in infrastructure, may lead to both lower credit to the private sector and higher domestic interest rates.

7. Mansouri (2004), in his study on Morocco, uses the real deposit rate as a proxy for the cost of borrowing. However, this is a debatable assumption, given that official nominal interest rates remained under control during much of his estimation period.

8. In principle, we should use changes in the ratio of the price of imported investment goods to the domestic price of these goods (or the national accounts deflator of private investment), as for instance in Mansouri (2004). However, sufficiently long time series were not available for our sample.

9. Let Ω_U and Ω_C denote the variance-covariance matrices of the residuals associated with the unrestricted and restricted models, respectively, and define the likelihood ratio statistic, λ, as

$$\lambda = (T\text{-}c)\ (\log|\Omega_C| - \log|\Omega_U|),$$

where $|\Omega_C|$ (respectively $|\Omega_U|$) is the determinant of Ω_C (respectively Ω_U), T the number of observations, and c the number of parameters (equal to the number of lags times the number of variables, plus one for the constant term) estimated in each equation of the unrestricted system. This statistic has a χ^2 distribution with degrees of freedom equal to the number of restrictions in the system, which is in turn equal to one times the number of lags.

10. Of course, this ordering may be viewed as somewhat arbitrary. However, in the actual estimation we conducted sensitivity tests and verified that the results are largely independent of the causal ordering described above.

11. See Hulten (1990) for a detailed discussion of the conceptual and measurement problems involved in constructing capital series. To calculate the public capital stock, we used a uniform depreciation rate of 2.5 percent. By comparison, Nehru and Dhaneswar (1993) used a uniform rate of 4 percent, whereas Larson et al. (2000) use alternative values of 4 and 6 percent, to estimate aggregate stocks of capital. However, sensitivity analysis showed that our empirical results are not unduly sensitive to our particular choice.

12. According to the World Bank (1994, p. 1), technical inefficiencies in roads, railways, power, and water in developing countries caused losses equivalent to a quarter of their annual investment in infrastructure in the early 1990s. See Estache (2004) for a further discussion.

13. Calderón and Servén (2004a, p. 19) found a high degree of correlation between the individual quality indicators listed above and the related quantities of infrastructure (that is, between power generation capacity and power losses, or between road density and road quality, the latter measured by the proportion of paved roads in). In a companion study (Calderón and Servén (2994b, p. 11) they obtained the same result with their two synthetic indicators of quantity and quality of infrastructure. Esfahani and Ramírez (2003, p. 446) also noted the existence of a close correlation between stocks of infrastructure capital and quality in their sample.

14. In their estimation of demand functions for infrastructure services based on panel data, Fay and Yepes (2003, p. 8) found long-term elasticities of 0.375 for electricity, 0.5 for telephone mainlines, and 0.14 for paved roads. These estimates differ quite significantly from our values of unity. However, the Fay-Yepes estimates refer to low- and middle-income countries in general, so there is no indication that they are adequate for MENA countries in particular-or, for that matter, the three countries in our sample. Moreover, in their regressions, there is no price (or user cost) variable, so their estimated income elasticities may be biased.

15. See, for instance, Jackson (1991) for a description of principal components analysis. The first step in this analysis is to put all of the data in standard units. By doing so, all of the transformed variables have unit variances and the resulting covariance matrix is actually the correlation matrix of the original variables.

16. Specifying a maximum lag length that is too short may impose unwarranted zero restrictions. At the same time, imposing a lag length that is too long may result in inefficient parameter estimates, because the model is over-parameterized.

17. The impulse responses and their associated confidence intervals are computed using Monte Carlo simulations employing 1,000 draws. A complete set of results for all the variables in the VARs are available upon request.

18. The existence of market failures is not, of course, an automatic justification for government involvement; such failures only provide a presumption of the need for government intervention. Moreover, even when it is required or desirable, intervention can take many forms; direct public provision is only one of them, and not necessarily the best one. In practice, one has to take into account possible government failures, and compare the costs and benefits of both options.

19. In MENA as elsewhere, a large share of these investments focused on telecommunications (44 percent for all developing countries) and electricity (28 percent). See International Finance Corporation (2003) Harris (2003), and Kessides (2004), for more details.

References

Agénor, Pierre-Richard. 2004. *The Economics of Adjustment and Growth.* 2nd ed. Boston, MA: Harvard University Press.

Agénor, Pierre-Richard, Mustapha K. Nabli, Tarik Yousef, and Henning T. Jensen. "Labor Market Reforms, Growth, and Unemployment in Labor-Exporting Countries in the Middle East and North Africa." 2004. Policy Research Working Paper 3328. The World Bank, Washington, DC. (June) *Journal of Policy Modeling.* Forthcoming.

Belloc, Marianna, and Pietro Vertova. 2004. "How Does Public Investment Affect Economic Growth in HIPC? An Empirical Assessment." Working Paper 416. University of Siena, Italy. (January)

Calderón, César, and Luis Servén. 2004a. "Trends in Infrastructure in Latin America, 1980-2001." Policy Research Working Paper 3401. The World Bank, Washington, DC. (September)

———. 2004b. "The Effects of Infrastructure Development on Growth and Income Distribution," Policy Research Working Paper 3400. The World Bank, Washington, DC. (September)

Canning, David. 1998. "A Database of World Infrastructure Stocks, 1950-95." *World Bank Economic Review* 12 (September): 529-47.

Chirinko, Robert S. 1993. "Business Fixed Investment Spending: A Critical Survey of Modelling Strategies, Empirical Results, and Policy Implications." *Journal of Economic Literature* 31 (December):1875-911.

Cohen, Jeffrey P., and Catherine J. M. Paul. 2004. "Public Infrastructure Investment, Interstate Spatial Spillovers, and Manufacturing Costs." *Review of Economics and Statistics* 86 (May): 551-60.

Dhumale, Rahul. 2000. "Public Investment in the Middle East and North Africa: Towards Fiscal Efficiency." *Development Policy Review,* 18 (June): 307-24.

Esfahani, Hadi, and Maria T. Ramírez. 2003. "Institutions, Infrastructure, and Economic Growth." *Journal of Development Economics* 70 (April): 443-77.

Estache, Antonio. 2004. "Emerging Infrastructure Policy Issues in Developing Countries: A Survey of the Recent Economic Literature." Policy Research Working Paper 3442. The World Bank, Washington, DC. (November)

Everhart, Stephen S., and Mariusz A. Sumlinski. 2001. "The Impact on Private Investment of Corruption and the Quality of Public Investment." Discussion Paper 44. International Finance Corporation. (October)

Fay, Marianne, and Tito Yepes. 2003. "Investing in Infrastructure: What is Needed from 2000 to 2010?" Policy Research Working Paper 3102. The World Bank, Washington, DC. (July)

Ghali, Khalifa A. 1998. "Public Investment and Private Capital Formation in a Vector Error-Correction Model of Growth." *Applied Economics* 30 (June): 837-44.

Hakura, Dalia S. 2004. "Growth in the Middle East and North Africa." Working Paper 04/56. International Monetary Fund, Washington, DC. (April)

Harris, Clive. 2003. "Private Participation in Infrastructure in Developing Countries: Trends, Impacts, and Policy Lessons." Working Paper 5. World Bank, Washington, DC. (June)

Hulten, Charles R. 1990. "The Measurement of Capital." In *Fifty Years of Economic Measurement,* ed. Ernst R. Berndt and Jack E. Tripplett. Chicago, IL: University of Chicago Press.

_____. 1996. "Infrastructure Capital and Economic Growth: How Well you Use it May Be More Important Than How Much You Have." NBER Working Paper 5847. National Bureau of Economic Research, Cambridge, MA. (December)

International Finance Corporation. 2003. *Private Participation in Infrastructure: Trends in Developing Countries in 1990-2001.* Washington, DC: International Finance Corporation.

Jackson, J. Edward. 1991. *A User's Guide to Principal Components.* New York: John Wiley and Sons.

Kessides, Ioannis N. 2004. *Reforming Infrastructure: Privatization, Regulation, and Competition.* Washington, DC: World Bank,.

Larson, Donald F., Rita Butzer, Yair Mindlak, and Al Crego. 2000. "A Cross-Country Database for Sector Investment and Capital." *World Bank Economic Review* 14 (May): 371-91.

Ligthart, Jenny E. 2000. "Public Capital and Output Growth in Portugal: An Empirical Analysis." Working Paper 00/11. International Monetary Fund, Washington, DC. (January)

Mansouri, Brahim. 2004. "Déséquilibres Financiers Publics, Investissement Privé et Croissance au Maroc." Unpublished. Marrakesh: Cadi Ayyad University. (March)

Mittnik, Stefan, and Thorsten Neumann. 2001. "Dynamic Effects of Public Investment: Vector Autoregressive Evidence for Six Industrialized Countries." *Empirical Economics* 26 (June): 429-36.

Nabli, Mustapha K., and Jennifer Keller. 2002. "The Macroeconomics of Labor Market Outcomes in MENA over the 1990s: How Growth has Failed to Keep Pace with a Burgeoning Labor Market." Unpublished. World Bank, Washington, DC. (April)

Nehru, Vikram, and Ashok Dhareshwar. 1993. "A New Database on Physical Capital Stock: Sources, Methodology, and Results." *Revista de Analisis Economico* 8 (June): 37-59.

Page, John. 1998. "From Boom to Bust-And Back? The Crisis of Economic Growth in the Middle East and North Africa." In *Prospects for Middle Eastern and North African Economies: From Boom to Bust and Back?* ed. Nemat Shafik. New York: St. Martin's Press.

Pritchett, Lant. 1999. "Has Education Had a Growth Payoff in the MENA Region?" Discussion Paper 18, MENA Region. World Bank, Washington, DC. (June)

Richards, A., and J. Waterbury. 1996. *A Political Economy of the Middle East.* 2nd ed. Boulder, CO: Westview Press.

Shafik, Nemat. 1992. "Modeling Private Investment in Egypt." *Journal of Development Economics* 39 (June): 263-77.

Turnovsky, Stephen J. 1996. "Fiscal Policy, Adjustment Costs, and Endogenous Growth." *Oxford Economic Papers* 48 (July): 361-81.

Voss, Graham M. 2002. "Public and Private Investment in the United States and Canada." *Economic Modeling* 19 (August): 641-64.

World Bank. 1994. *Investing in Infrastructure.* World Development Report. New York: Oxford University Press.

———. 1995. *Claiming the Future: Choosing Prosperity in the Middle East and North Africa.* Washington, DC: World Bank.

———. 2003a. *Jobs, Growth and Governance in the Middle East and North Africa-Unlocking the Potential for Prosperity.* Washington, DC: World Bank.

———. 2003b. *Trade, Investment and Development in the Middle East and North Africa.* Washington, DC: World Bank.

———. 2004. *Unlocking the Employment Potential in the Middle East and North Africa: Toward a New Social Contract.* Washington, DC: World Bank.

Annex 16A. Data Sources and Definitions

This annex provides a brief description of the data used in this study. The actual dataset is available upon request.

Gross fixed capital formation by the private sector in percent of GDP: For Egypt, the data source is International Finance Corporation (IFC) for 1982-99, and World Development Indicators (WDI) for 2000-02. For 1965-81, the shares of total public and private investment are applied to total fixed capital formation to construct the private fixed capital formation investment series. For Egypt, series on total public and private investment for 1965-81 were provided by the Bank's desk economist. For Jordan and Tunisia, data source is WDI.

Claims on private sector in percent of GDP: data source is IFS.

Growth rate of the real effective exchange rate (REER): defined as the log difference of the REER. For 1980-2002, data source is IFS. Before 1980, the REER is calculated as the ratio of the nominal exchange rate times the unit value of imports, divided by the consumer price index.

Growth rate of real GDP: defined as the log difference of real GDP. Data source is WDI.

Gross fixed capital formation by the public sector as percent of GDP: For Egypt, data source is IFC for 1982-99, and WDI for 2000-02. For 1965-81, the shares of total public and private investment are applied to total fixed capital formation to construct the series. Series on total public and private investment for 1965-81 were provided by the Bank's desk economist. For Jordan and Tunisia, data source is WDI.

Public capital expenditure infrastructure: Data source is the IMF's Government Finance Statistics (GFS). It is obtained by adding fuel and energy; railway, air, pipeline, and other transportation; water transport; transportation and communication; and other transportation and communication. This series is deflated by the GDP deflator to calculate a series at constant prices.

Public infrastructure capital stock at constant prices: calculated using the perpetual inventory method, using a uniform depreciation rate of 2.5 percent.

Adjusted public infrastructure stock at constant prices: obtained by multiplying the raw stock data by the composite quality index for public infrastructure, normalized at unity in the first period of estimation.

Composite quality index: defined as the weighted average of the two principal components, using as weights the proportion of total variance explained by each component. The principal components are calculated over the two separate indicators (ICOR-based and "excess demand" measures) described in the text.

17

Governance, Institutions, and Private Investment

An Application to the Middle East and North Africa

Ahmet Faruk Aysan*
Mustapha Kamel Nabli
Marie-Ange Véganzonès-Varoudakis†

During the 1980s and 1990s, private investment in the Middle East and North Africa (MENA), on average, showed a decreasing trend. With the liberalization of economies and the acceleration of reforms, private investment increased throughout much of the world in the 1990s. The Middle East and North Africa countries did not follow this pattern. While private investment to GDP declined by 2.4 percent in the region, this rate increased by 4.8 percent in Latin America and the Caribbean (LAC), 15.8 percent in Africa (AFR), 23.4 in South Asia and 14 percent in East Asia (EAP), despite the financial crisis.

This paper addresses the issue of the low level of private investment in the MENA region, with special emphasis on the role of governance. In fact, the MENA countries have on average been characterized by a clear deficit of "good" governance institutions, particularly as regards democratic institutions such as political rights, civil liberties, and freedom of the press. Similarly, the quality of the administration has also been of some concern. These defi-

*Boğaziçi University, Istanbul, Turkey. †Centre d'Etudes et de Recherches sur le Développement International and Centre National de la Recherche Scientifique, Université d'Auvergne, France.

Published in *The Developing Economies* XLV-3 (September 2007), 339–77. Used by permission from Blackwell Publishing Ltd.

Figure 17.1. Private Investment by Region
(% GDP)

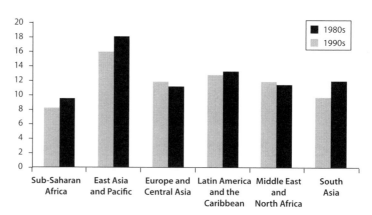

Source : Authors' calculations.

Figure 17.2. Private Investment in MENA Countries
(% GDP)

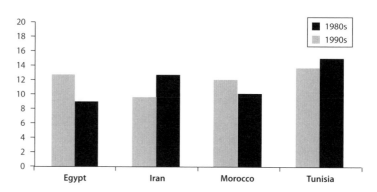

Source : Authors' calculations.

ciencies have been reported as being responsible for the slow economic activity in MENA (see El Badawi 2002; and World Bank 2003).

These results are in line with a growing literature on governance that suggests that successful market-based economies need "good" governance institutions.[1] However, the channels investigated to date concern more the impact of governance on economic growth,[2] GDP per capita,[3] and volatility of economic activity[4]; little has been empirically done to analyze the effects of institutions on private investment. As far as private investment is concerned, the literature on the role of governance has essentially focused on the effect of the rule of law—more specifically, on the security of property rights, which is the best documented effect and the best supported by empirical evidence.[5] Other components of governance are not as well documented and the empirical validation is not as successful. This is not only the case for corruption and bureaucratic quality,[6] but also for democratic participation, research into which lacks theoretical and empirical precision.[7] A few studies have, however, addressed more successfully the links among political instability, policy uncertainties, and firms' decisions to invest.[8]

Governance, however, is part of the investment climate of a country. Investment decisions are mainly driven by profitability motives (Jorgenson 1963). The forward-looking nature of investment underlines the importance of a stable and secure environment—in particular the security of property rights. At the same time, "good" governance institutions are viewed as reducing uncertainty and promoting efficiency (see North 1981). In this respect, and as reported by World Bank (2003), better governance improves the investment climate by improving bureaucratic performance and predictability. This in turn reduces uncertainty, as well as the cost of doing business. Better governance also contributes to the effective delivery of public goods that are necessary for productive business. Cross-country correlations using broad proxies for investment climate quality suggest a positive link between the investment climate and private investment decisions.[9]

As a part of the reflection on the channels through which governance may affect economic performance, one strand of the literature has recently reconsidered the role of economic policies in explaining cross-country economic achievements. This research has also been important to our interest in the determinants of private investment. Recent work on the role of both governance and economic policies has found that governance institutions are the dominant factor, with little, if any, independent influence by policies.[10] However, these results stem from endogeneity and specification problems, as pointed out by Sachs (2003). In fact, economic policies are likely to affect cross-country variations in governance quality. There is, in particular, some evidence that greater openness to trade and stronger competition are conducive to better governance.[11] Given these conditions, economic policies may explain economic performances through their impact on governance.[12] In the case of private investment, we show that both direct and indirect effects can be brought together if the model chosen is well specified.[13] We estimate in particular a simultaneous model of private investment and of various forms of governance institutions, where economic policies concurrently explain both variables.

In this paper, we also address other shortfalls of the empirical literature on governance and economic performances. We intend, in particular, to categorize what types of governance institutions are more detrimental to entrepreneurial investments. To this end, we introduce a large set of governance variables that are not typically used in the literature on determinants of private investment. Since these indicators are likely to be correlated, we process a few aggregated indicators, using the principal component analysis methodology.

Based on the existing literature, we categorize so-called governance institutions in three broad clusters: "Administrative Quality" (QA), "Public Accountability" (PA), and "Political Stability" (PS). We also generate a global indicator of governance (GOV) that summarizes these three aspects[14]. This method allows a second step to evaluate the contribution of the initial indicators to the private investment decision. This information will be useful in understanding which factors explain the low investment performance of the region. In this paper, human development and economic policy variables have been similarly processed.

Our empirical approach relies also on panel data (cross-section-time series analysis) that is suitable—contrary to previous studies—to jointly assessing the impact of economic policies and governance institutions on private investments. The time series dimension captures the variability of policies through time, and the cross-section dimension covers the governance variables, which tend to evolve slowly. This paper also acknowledges the deficiencies of existing data on governance as subjective and outcome-based, rather than representing the quality of actual institutions. However, this paper points out that these deficiencies do not constitute a severe problem in analyzing the effects of governance on private investment. Whether actual or not, what is important for private investors is the perceived quality of governance at the time of investment.

This paper also benefits from a newly constructed data set on private investment. The ultimate purpose of this paper is to determine which factors are central in the decision-making process of private entrepreneurs to invest. However, because of the lack of comparable data on private investment, most of the earlier studies use aggregate investment as a proxy for private investment. Later, the International Finance Corporation (IFC) of the World Bank launched a project that addressed the private investments of various developing countries from 1970 to 1999. Studies using this disaggregated data on private investment show that private and public investment can have very different determinants (Aizenman and Marion 1999). Therefore, disaggregated data need to be utilized in order to capture the investment-conducive factors in today's globalized economies. Building on the IFC series, our new data set covers 99 countries (60 for high-quality data) over the period 1970-2002 (see Annex 17.1).

Finally, as previously mentioned, our empirical model allows for the simultaneous estimation of private investments and of various types of governance institutions. This model is also justified by the fact that—in addition to economic policies—changes in private investment can influence the quality of governance. Moreover, some hidden factors are likely to affect private investment and governance institutions in parallel. Our empirical results show that governance institutions play a significant role in private investment decisions. This result is particularly true in the case of "Administrative Quality" (QA), in the form of control of corruption, bureaucratic quality, investment-friendly profile of administration, and law and order. Similarly, "Political Stability" (PS) significantly generates higher private investment. Evidence in favor of "Public Accountability" is also found.

This paper is organized as follows: The second section introduces our classification of governance institutions to determine which institutions are detrimental to entrepreneurial investments. The third section presents the other determinants of private investment that will be taken into consideration in our empirical analysis, and highlights the importance of these factors for the MENA countries. The fourth section presents the characteristics of the data used. The fifth section introduces the private investment model tested and the results of the estimations. The sixth section uses this model to determine which factors would boost the level of MENA's private investments in the future. The last section presents the conclusions.

Governance Institutions: An Attempt at Classification

A first step in our analysis of the link between governance and private investment has been to differentiate and categorize the numerous different dimensions of governance, to better understand which institutions are investment-conducive. Existing literature on the classification of governance institutions provides some alternatives. Various authors have aggregated certain indices to capture better the common features of the existing data.

Kaufmann, Kraay, and Mastruzzi (2003) categorize governance institutions in six broad groups. Their measures of governance are based on 194 variables drawn from 17 different sources in order to measure six different aspects of governance. "Government Effectiveness" and "Regulatory Quality" summarize the ability of the government to formulate and implement sound policies. The respect of citizens and the state for the institutions that govern their interactions is categorized as "Rule of Law" and "Control of Corruption." "Political Stability and Absence of Violence" measures perceptions of likelihood that the government in power will not be destabilized, and indicate the continuity of policies. "Voice and Accountability" captures the process by which citizens of a country are able to participate in the selection of their government (see Annex 17.2 for more details on these indicators). The World Bank (2003) has used two indices on "Public Accountability" and "Administrative Quality" by aggregating the existing relevant data sets for these features of governance.

Our choice of indicators has been limited by the lack of annual data available for a large sample of countries over long periods of time. Considering the existing classifications of governance data, this paper categorizes the governance variables that are likely to affect individual investors' decision into three broad clusters: "Administrative Quality" (QA), "Public Accountability" (PA), and "Political Stability" (PS).

Quality of Administration

The first set of candidates is intended to provide information on the ability of government to deal with investors and to provide them with an investment-friendly and reliable context in which to conduct their investment projects. Following World Bank (2003), we have defined the first governance variable as the "Quality of Administration." This variable incorporates four indicators from the International Country Risk Guide (ICRG, 1999), namely: (i) "Control over Corruption;" (ii) "Quality of Bureaucracy;" (iii) "Investment Profile;" and (iv) "Law and Order" (see definitions of variables in Annex 17.3). These institutions are part of the investment climate of a country. They promote investments by reducing the costs and risks of doing business.

Corruption often has adverse effects on economic activities. This fact is well documented and is often described as one of the major constraints facing enterprises in the developing world (World Bank 2002). In his cross-country analysis, Mauro (1995) shows that corruption reduces growth. Gupta, Davooli, and Alonso-Terme (2002) stress that corruption exacerbates income inequality and poverty. Mo (2001) documents a causal chain of interest for our work, linking corruption to low growth through reduced human and physical capital. In fact, for private investors, corruption increases investment and operation costs, as well as uncertainties about the timing and effects of the application of government regulations. Corruption also raises the investment and operational costs of public enterprises, leading to insufficient and low-quality infrastructures that are detrimental to private investment. (see Tanzi and Davooli 1997). The same conclusions have been reached about the effects of bureaucratic quality on economic activity (see Evans and Rauch 2000).

The "Quality of Bureaucracy" index of ICRG summarizes the ability of the government to formulate and implement sound policies. Moreover, the "Quality of Bureaucracy" index indicates that "countries where the bureaucracy has the strength and expertise govern without drastic changes in policy or interruptions in government services. In these low-risk countries, the bureaucracy tends to be somewhat autonomous from political pressure and to have an established mechanism for recruitment and training." (ICRG, 1999)

The "Investment Profile" is a measure of the "government's attitude to inward investment as determined by the assessment of four subcomponents: risk to operations, taxation, profit repatriation, and labor costs." Because investors are making long-term decisions, risks to operations and other uncertainties about future policies are detrimental to investment decisions. Taxation and labor costs have also a first-order implication on costs, and therefore on decisions to invest. Although government regulations and taxation are reasonable and warranted in order to protect the general public, and to generate revenues to finance the delivery of public services and infrastructures, overregulation and overtaxation deter investments by raising business startup and operating costs.

In the "Law and Order" index, the "Law" subcomponent provides an "assessment of the strength and impartiality of the legal system," while the "Order" subcomponent concerns the "popular observance of the law." Although many aspects of the business environment affect investments, the security of property rights is the most important and the better documented issue. Because of the forward-looking nature of investment, investors need institutions that preserve the right of private property, ensure equitable and consistent rule of law in protecting this right, and offer effective incentives to respect and enforce it. A reliable judiciary, in particular, reduces transaction costs for businesses and sends positive signals to investors that rules of law will be equitably and consistently protected and enforced. On the empirical side, the issue of property rights and of rule of law has been widely covered by the literature, and the results of cross-country analysis are robust to various tests and specifications.[15]

Public Accountability

The second set of indicators measures "Public Accountability." This index consists of two indicators from Freedom House (FH): "Civil Liberties" and "Political Rights."

Public accountability is part of the investment climate of an economy. Because fixed capital investments are generally irreversible, private investment decisions are highly sensitive to the perception of the credibility and tenacity of the political regime, as well as of policies.[16] An open and participatory political system provides stability of social institutions and ensures broad public support for policies, which are in this case more sustainable in the long run. Public accountability is a guarantee of transparency and of better availability of information, which also help governments build credibility. Public accountability provides access to policy makers and can hold them responsible for failures in implementing policies. In particular, freedom of press, free political parties, and open elections contribute to government's legitimacy and give voice to citizens in the decision-making process. On the empirical side, the literature on democratic participation has focused on the effects of transparency and accountability on growth, using data on civil liberties, political rights, and freedom of the press from various sources. The empirical validation has, however, produced mitigated success.[17] The work of Pastor and Sung (1995) is one of the few to show a positive effect of various indicators of democratic institutions on private investment in the developing world.

Political Stability

The last set of variables is intended to measure "Political Stability." Political instability increases the uncertainty in the economy and deters risk-averse entrepreneurs from taking action for profitable investment opportunities. The political stability index includes the following variables from ICRG (1999):

"Government Stability," "Internal Conflict," "External Conflict," and "Ethnic Tensions." Various authors, using different indicators of political uncertainties, have brought empirical evidence that institutions associated with political instability hamper aggregate investment.[18]

All the political and governance indicators have been aggregated by using principal component analysis (PCA) to account for the multicollinearity issue in using these potentially correlated variables in the same regression equation. In addition, we have generated a global indicator of governance (GOV), which summarizes the information contained in the three previous indicators (QA, PA, and PS). Results of PCA are given in Annex 17.4.

Other Determinants of Private Investment

Although the importance of private investment has been widely discussed in the literature, there is less evidence on what induces private firms to invest in developing countries. In fact, developing countries do not operate in a competitive environment, and face constraints that are not accounted for in the neoclassical model. This partly explains why most economists do not agree on the subject of the determinants of investment in developing countries.[19] This phenomenon is also the case for MENA economies, for which the empirical literature is deficient.[20] In this paper, we address some of these constraints, in particular the ones linked to economic policy and to the quality of governance institutions.

The Neoclassical Accelerator Model

In the macroeconomics literature, the neoclassical flexible accelerator model is the most widely accepted model of investment. This model is based on the neoclassical idea of the theory of the firm (Jorgenson 1963), which postulates that enterprises decide to invest so as to generate more profit in the future. The investment function is derived from the optimization problem of the firms, which maximize current and expected profits by equating the production prices to their marginal costs. Firms will invest so long as the marginal benefit of doing so outweighs the additional cost. The net investment is the gradual adjustment of the actual capital stock to its desired level, which is derived from maximization of profit. The determinants of investment in the neoclassical flexible accelerator model include the expected aggregate demand (the accelerator), the user cost of capital, the wage rate, and the initial capital stock.

This model postulates, however, that firms operate in competitive markets, which contradicts the structural and institutional factors prevailing in developing countries. Even though the empirical tests of the model appear to be successful for several developed countries, the firms in developing countries face certain constraints that are not accounted for in the conventional neoclassical theory.[21] Some of these constraints (in particular those of specific interest for the MENA region) are discussed below.

Structural Reforms

Among the most common constraints faced by developing countries is the deficit of economic reforms. This is the case in the MENA countries, which have lagged behind other regions in terms of reforming their economy (Nabli and Véganzonès-Varoudakis 2007). Structural reforms constitute an important determinant of the actual and future profitability of private investment. We have considered trade policy and financial development as part of our structural reforms index.

By providing more opportunities and incentives for firms to invest, financial development is an important part of private investment decisions. A developed financial system mobilizes and allocates resources to enterprises. A developed financial system is also expected to be more efficient due to increasing technological specialization, which leads to a better selection of projects and more advanced diversification of risks. This allows firms to finance more investment projects, and increases the productivity of new investments (see Levine 1997 for a synthesis). In addition, given the lack of well-functioning financial markets, the neoclassical assumption of the flexible accelerator model regarding the availability of credit supply by the banking sector cannot be taken for granted in developing countries. This discrepancy also occurs because of public deficits and public debt, which can lead to financial repression and to the eviction of private investment. On the empirical side, the impact of financial development on private investment is now well documented.[22] In his survey of investment functions in developing countries, Rama (1993) presents the positive effect of financial development on private investment in 21 of the 31 papers surveyed.

Trade reforms constitute another factor that can stimulate private investment decisions. Trade openness increases competitiveness and provides access to enlarged markets (Balassa 1978; Feder 1982). Trade openness can be at the origin of economies of scale and of productivity gains. In addition, trade openness influences the availability of external credit—considering the general consensus on the role of tradable goods in providing positive externalities in the form of collateral for external financing (Caballero and Krishnamurthy 2001).

All these factors create favorable conditions for enterprises to invest. However, as mentioned in the introduction, economic reforms are also expected to affect private investment through their impact on the quality of governance institutions. There is, in particular, some evidence that greater openness to trade and stronger competition are conducive to governance improvement.[23] Opening up markets may help to weaken vested interests and reduce rents derived from prevailing economic and institutional arrangements. Trade openness may also lead to demands for governance institutions more suited to an increasingly varied and complex range of transactions (see IMF 2003).

Human Capital

Human capital is part of the investment climate of an economy and is generally considered as complementary to physical capital. Here, we have considered health and education as part of the human capital index. Human capital stimulates private capital formation by raising the profitability of investment. Human capital can also be at the origin of positive externalities.[24] Because skilled workers are better at dealing with change, a skilled work force is essential for firms to adopt new and more productive technologies.[25] Besides, new technologies generally require significant organizational changes, which are handled better by a skilled workforce.[26] Human capital also gives the opportunity to enterprises to expand or enter new markets.

Moreover, human capital entails better governance institutions. Better educated people with higher life expectancy become more competent bureaucrats and—in addition to better monitoring of the functioning of government officials—demand better quality of bureaucracy (Galor et al. 2005). In addition, educational attainment reduces political instability by generating more avenues to reconcile opposing parties. This idea constitutes one of the classical approaches in the literature to highlight the importance of education in bringing better governance institutions (Lipset 1959). From the democratic accountability point of view, a more educated society is more likely to be enfranchised in terms of civil rights and liberties (Acemoglu and Robinson 2001). These considerations justify that human capital also appears as an explanatory factor in private investment decisions, through its impact on the quality of governance institutions.

Although educational attainment has improved in the majority of developing countries, many firms still rate inadequate skills and education of workers as severe obstacles to their operations (see World Bank 2002). This is the case in the MENA region, where progress is still needed in order to catch up with South East Asia and Latin America.[27] To meet this challenge, and as pointed out by World Bank (2003), MENA countries have to gear up their educational systems, both to improve basic education and to equip the labor force with skills appropriate for enterprises to invest efficiently.

Some Considerations on the Data Used

A New Data Set on Private Investment

Data on the breakdown of investments as either private or public are scarce. The best available data set on private investment was provided by the International Finance Corporation of the World Bank.[28] However, this data set covers only the period from 1970 to 1999. It also has some limitations for certain countries in terms of the quality of the breakdown of public and private investment. This is most often because of the status of state-owned enterprises, for which investment data are not always available, and which are in this case included in the private investment series.

Considering these pitfalls of existing data, we have re-examined the IFC data set and updated the private investment series for the available years after 1999. More important, we have carefully checked the IFC private investment series and compared them to the national sources, where available, as well as to the World Bank and International Monetary Fund series. This has been done in close collaboration with the country economists of these two institutions. We have thus been able to generate high-quality data for the majority of our sample countries, as well as for other countries, which can be considered as relatively accurate. This private investment series, which covers 60 countries, has been used in the empirical analysis (see in Annex 17.1 the list of countries). We have also generated a broader set of private investment series, which includes countries for which the distinction between private and public investment is not as satisfactory, but which can be used for robustness analysis. This data set covers 99 countries.

Nature of Data on Governance

The data usually used in governance are produced by independent, private firms, which provide consulting services to international investors such as the International Country Risk Guide, the Heritage Foundation (HF), Freedom House, or the Fraser Institute (FI). To a certain extent, these indices provide very similar information on various aspects of governance. These data sets have certain common features. First of all, they can be considered to be subjective. They measure perceptions of governance quality rather than actual quality. They also measure outcomes rather than actual rules (see Glaeser et al. 2004). Finally, given that governance institutions do not change easily in theory, institutional indices are supposed to be rather persistent, even though they are relatively volatile in existing data sets.

All these factors appear counter to using the governance indices commonly used in the literature. In fact, these characteristics are very useful in determining investor perceptions of the quality of governance at the time of their investment. Indeed, what we are more concerned about is not actual governance quality per se, but its perception by the private sector, since our ultimate aim is to identify the determinants of private investment. This paper strongly shows that, in addition to the conventional determinants of private investment, governance institutions—whether perceived or real—are detrimental to investors' decision to invest. Hence, we allow the possibility that perceived institutions differ from actual institutions. It is quite possible that in our framework, even though quality of actual governance is not high, private investors tend to perceive that their investment projects are protected by good institutions or vice versa.

To illustrate this idea, it can be noticed that following economic crises, governance indices of crises-hit countries can vary enormously. It is hard to believe that institutions change drastically in a short period of time, but it is reasonable to argue that perceptions of governance institutions, in the eyes of beholders, that is, investors, are altered through the crises. Investors modify their expectations of institutions when new information is revealed in a crises-hit economy.

One explanation for these drastic upheavals in the governance indices of crises-hit countries is that investors definitely have incomplete and asymmetrical information on the quality of governance institutions in the economy. During normal times, when business runs as usual, information on the quality of governance is not widely noticed. However, with the advent of crises or new information, governance institutions face a real examination. Hence, the manner in which countries handle new conditions can influence the perception of governance by private investors. This information also accumulates over time and provides a basis for long-term perceptions of governance quality throughout the countries.

The advanced countries of today have built their investor-friendly and persistent governance institutions over long periods of time, after successfully passing certain historical tests. However, in the short term, investors make their judgments on the quality of governance based on a numerous factors. These factors certainly include some historical episodes experienced by the country that can provide insight into the future potential performance of existing governance institutions. Debt repudiation or the state's appropriation of private property in the past, for example, definitely are taken into account when entrepreneurs assess the quality of a country's governance. However, in addition to this type of backward-looking behavior, entrepreneurs' perception of the quality of governance is also shaped by existing conditions and those anticipated in the future. In this regard, we argue that existing indices measuring the quality of governance capture investors' concerns about the institutions quite well.

The Econometric Analysis

The Model Tested

The primary purpose of the model tested is to disentangle the effects of governance on private investment. More important, in this paper we want to make a horse race among the different types of governance variables commonly used in the literature, to distinguish the ones most vital in accelerating private investment in our sample of developing countries.

In the empirical model, endogenous variables are the share of private investment and the various measures of governance, namely: QA, PA, PS, and GOV. These endogenous variables are simultaneously determined by influencing each other. In order to account for this reverse causality, we establish a system of equations to estimate the share of private investment (PI) in GDP and quality of governance institutions (QI) simultaneously. In the private investment equation, a lower ranking for quality of governance institutions is expected to reduce private investment. In the governance equation, private investment enters on the right side with an expected positive sign. This simultaneous system of equations also enables us to take into account other factors that affect both private investment and governance institutions.

This system of equations is estimated using three-stage least squares (3SLS) by controlling other determinants of endogenous variables. Three-stage least square estimation allows us to use the links between endogenous variables efficiently. Because endogenous variables appear as regressors in other equations, they have to be instrumented out using exclusion restrictions. Initially, 3SLS regressions are run separately for QA, PS, and PA. However, to complete the analysis, we have substituted, in this system of equations, the aggregate GOV, which is calculated as the principal component analysis of all the initial indicators, and which provides a summary of the three measures of governance.

The model estimated is the following:

$$PI_{it} = \alpha_0 + \alpha_1 QI_{it} + \alpha_2 X_{1i} + \varepsilon_{1it} \tag{1}$$

$$QI_{it} = \gamma_0 + \beta_1 PI_{it} + \beta_2 X_{2i} + \varepsilon_{2it} \tag{2}$$

where

PI_{it} is the share of private investment in GDP
QI_{it} represents the various indexes of governance (*QA, PA, PS,* and *GOV*)
X_{1i} and X_{2i} are the other control variables in private investment (*PI*) and governance (*GOV*) equations respectively
ε_{1it} and ε_{2it} are the error terms of each equation. *i* indicates the country and *t* represents the time of the variable.

The determinants of private investment in the neoclassical flexible accelerator model include the expected aggregate demand (the accelerator) and the user cost of capital. Hence, the private investment equation in our specification incorporates real interest rate to capture the user cost of capital. It also accounts for the GDP growth rate in last year to control for the accelerator effect. These two variables are excluded from the governance equation (*QI*) in order to identify the system.

Both of the equations, on the other hand, take into account the GDP per capita, as well as the variations in structural reform (*SR*) and human capital (*H*). Structural reforms are proxied through trade policy (*TP*), and financial development. Financial development is proxied by private credit by banks and other depository institutions. Trade policy is constructed as commercial openness (calculated by aggregating the export and import in total GDP), from which we have subtracted the exports of oil and mining products, as well as the "natural trade openness" constructed by Frankel and Romer (1999). The trade policy and financial development variables form the structural reform indicators, after implementation of the principal component analysis (see Annex 17.4 for results of PCA). Structural reform is expected to stimulate private investment, as well as institutional change for the better.

Human capital (H) is expressed through life expectancy at birth, and average years of primary, secondary, and higher schooling in the total population over 15 years old. These variables are also aggregated with principal component analysis. Human capital is widely considered to enhance private investment and to lead to better governance institutions. Therefore, the human capital variable is expected to have positive coefficients in both of the equations.

GDP per capita is controlled in the investment equation to account for the neoclassical Solow growth model. Countries with lower GDP per capita are expected to gradually catch up with their more developed counterparts by having more capital investment over time. Moreover, GDP per capita accounts for possible externalities, such as greater market size, on demand and supply of good and services, and finally on private investment. GDP per capita in governance equations represents the idea that more developed countries can afford to have better governance institutions (Azariadis and Lahiri 2002). Hence, a positive relationship is expected between GDP per capita and governance quality.

Oil export as a percentage of total merchandise export also enters into both equations. The typical natural curse hypothesis is taken into account by incorporating this variable into the investment equation. When a country relies more on natural resources extraction in its exports, there can be less incentive to invest in other products. This result, for example, may stem from the increase in the cost of labor (Rodriguez and Sachs 1999). This variable also has an implication for the quality of governance institutions. Countries with less reliance on natural resources are expected to form better governance institutions. The natural resource-abundant countries do not need to mobilize the society to enhance aggregate income. The ruling class can control the economy by collaborating with a small number of people in the society. Therefore, the production structure of the country does not generate good governance institutions in favor of society (Ross 2001; Bellin 2001). Under these circumstances, the elite are also less inclined to provide better governance by considering the future effects of today's enfranchisements (Acemoglu and Robinson 2001) and engage in more rent-seeking activities.[29] Hence, the share of oil exports in merchandise exports is expected to reduce the quality of governance institutions.

The tenure of the system from Keefer et al. (2001) is excluded from the investment equation to identify the system of equations. Tenure of the system reports the number of years that an administrative system—regardless of whether autocratic or democratic—lasts in the country. The underlying idea to include this variable in the governance equation is to account for the fact that institutions settle over time. The longer time passes with the existing system, the better institutions are established. This exclusion restriction is quite reasonable considering that tenure of the system has a direct impact on the governance institutions, whereas its influence on private investment is more likely to be realized through its effect on these institutions.

Finally, a regional dummy for the MENA countries appears as a right-hand-side variable in both of the equations. One of our primary purposes is to understand the position of MENA countries among the other countries and to see whether MENA substantially diverges from the rest of the world in terms of private investment and of governance performance.

Estimation Results

Equations (1) and (2) have been estimated on an unbalanced panel of 31 developing countries over 1980-2002, using the 3SLS estimations technique. Four sets of regressions have been conducted, each one with a different indicator of governance. Table1 presents the estimation's results of equations (1) and (2) when QA, PS, PA, and GOV are taken into consideration, respectively.

Administrative Quality. In Table 17.1—when QA is used as a measure of governance—estimation results produce quite interesting conclusions. One of the most interesting outcomes concerns the QA index, which gives a positive and significant coefficient at the 5 percent level in the investment Equation (1). This result confirms that a low level of corruption, good-quality bureaucracy, clear security of property rights, reasonable risk to operations, sound taxation and regulation, as well as more effective law and order, are of first importance for enterprises' decisions to invest. This result makes a real contribution to the empirical literature on governance by validating, over a relatively long period of time, the role of a large set of governance variables on private economic performance.

Our result is unambiguous and robust to the introduction of other explanatory variables. This is the case of structural reforms and human capital. The roles of these variables in explaining cross-country economic achievement have recently been questioned (Easterly and Levine 2003). Our regression results indicate the significant impact of these variables on private investment decisions. Hence, our estimations stress that, although the quality of governance constitutes a major factor in private sector decisions, the role of economic policies cannot be disregarded. Our result also confirms that firms in developing countries face constraints that are not accounted for in more developed economies and that deficiencies in trade policy, financial development, and education have a long-term impact on private investment decisions and growth.

Another conclusion of our model consists in validating the neoclassical theory of the firm in the case of developing countries. The accelerator variable has the expected positive sign, which implies that anticipations of economic growth induce more investment. Similarly, the interest rate appears to exert a negative and significant effect on private investment, which is consistent with the user cost of capital theory. Both variables are highly significant, indicating that at the final stage, supply and demand considerations constitute major factors for entrepreneurs to undertake a new investment project. However, our model fails to verify the Solow hypothesis of decreasing return to scale of physical capital accumulation. The coefficient of the GDP per capita variable, although negative, is not significant.

Table 17.1. Estimation Results

Explanatory variables	Endogenous variables		Endogenous variables		Endogenous variables	
	Priv Inv (1)	QA (2)	Priv Inv (3)	QA (4)	Priv Inv (5)	PS (6)
QA	1.99		2.07			
	(1.98)**		(2.06)**			
PS					3.51	
					(1.67)*	
PA						
GOV						
Private investment		0.1				−0.065
		(2.16)**				(−1.61)
Structural reforms	1.64	0.11	1.64	0.31	1.07	0.5
	(4.73)***	(−1.04)	(4.75)***	(9.37)***	(−1.45)	(4.86)**
Human capital	0.62	−0.02	0.57	0.04	−0.1	0.25
	(2.82)***	(−0.46)	(2.63)***	(−1.08)	(−0.2)	(5.21)***
Oil exports	−0.03	0.0003	−0.03	−0.003	−0.05	0
	(−2.66)***	(−0.11)	(−2.91)***	(−1.65)*	(−2.86)***	(−0.10)
GDP per capita	0	0.0001	0	0.0001	0	0.0002
	(−0.28)	(3.54)***	(−0.01)	(4.1)***	(−0.42)	(4.04)***
MENA dummy	−1.2	0.15	−1.1	0.06	−2.3	0.34
	(−1.21)	(−0.84)	(−1.11)	(−0.38)	(−1.75)*	(1.84)*
Rear	−0.02		−0.036		−0.05	
	(−2.06)**		(−3.39)**		(−2.53)**	
Growth	0.22		0.2		0.22	
	(3.29)***		(2.88)**		(3.09)***	
Ten syst		0.02		0.017		0.013
		(4.36)***		(6.19)***		(3.71)***
Constant	11.8	−1.53	11.8	−0.52	14	−0.2
	(16.95)***	(−3.20)***	(16.92)***	(−6.52)***	(7.48)***	(−0.4)
Numb obs	349	349	349	349	349	349

Note: (*) indicates significance at 10%; (**) indicates significance at 5%; (***) indicates significance at 1%. See sources of data in footnote 30.

Finally, estimation of Equation (1) confirms the natural curse hypothesis. The coefficient of the oil export variable as a percentage of total merchandise export is significant and negative. Identically, the regional dummy for MENA countries exhibits a negative coefficient. MENA countries seem to be diverging from the rest of the world in terms of private investment, which is the key determinant of long-term growth. However, this dummy variable is not significant at the conventional levels. This result is likely to stem from the oil export variable in the system, which significantly reduces private investment.

In the QA equation (table 17.1, column 2), our estimations reveal the positive impact of several factors on the quality of administration. This is the case with GDP per capita, which means that more developed countries entail bet-

Endogenous variables		Endogenous variables		Endogenous variables	
Priv Inv (7)	PA (8)	Priv Inv (9)	GOV (10)	Priv Inv (11)	GOV (12)
4.43					
(−1.6)					
		2.25		2.26	
		(1.99)**		(2.00)**	
	−0.08		0.014		
	(−1.53)		(−0.667)		
3.27	−0.05	1.98	0.1	1.98	0.13
(4.86)***	(−.40)	(8.06)***	(−1.2)	(8.07)***	(−1.46)
−0.05	0.21	0.36	0.124	0.35	0.133
(−0.10)	(3.49)***	(−1.4)	(3.27)*	(−1.36)	(4.36)***
−0.05	−0.001	−0.035	0	−0.038	−0.001
(−2.90)***	(−0.19)	(−2.97)***	(−0.13)	(−3.14)***	(−0.49)
−0.01	0	0	0.0003	0	0.0003
(−1.12)	(6.56)***	(−0.84)	(8.72)***	(−0.81)	(8.84)***
3.72	−1.14	−0.34	−0.28	−0.32	−0.29
(−1.11)	(4.91)***	(−0.31)	(−1.91)**	(−0.29)	(−2.09)**
−0.05		−0.037		−0.035	
(−3.13)***		(−2.87)***		(−3.21)***	
0.29		0.22		0.21	
(3.04)***		(3.53)***		(3.58)***	
	0.11		−0.015		−0.016
	(2.54)***		(5.75)***		(6.44)***
11.1	−0.73	12.2	−0.82	12.2	−0.66
(16.34)***	(−1.19)	(15.55)***	(−2.14)	(15.61)***	(−9.39)
349	349	349	349	349	349

ter governance institutions. Also, private investment helps improve the administrative quality significantly at a 5 percent level. This last result justifies the use of the 3SLS estimation technique in order to address—among other things—the two-way causality. Tenure of system also predicts better administrative quality at less than 1 percent significance level.

Our estimations fail, however, to validate the negative impact of the share of oil exports in merchandise exports. This result contradicts the fact that countries with less reliance on natural resources form better governance institutions. More important, structural reforms and human capital do not appear to immediately improve administrative quality. However, when estimating the system by eliminating private investment from Equation (2), structural reforms appear to be positive and highly significant, other results being unchanged[31] (see table 17.1, column 4). This result seems to be due to the fact that the structural reforms index is correlated with private investment. Hence, the positive impact of private investment on administrative quality appears to be mainly due to the structural reforms that stimulate firms' decisions to invest. This result confirms that, in addition to the direct link highlighted previously, economic reforms affect private investment through their impact on institutional quality. This two-channel causality brings new empirical evidence on the link between institutions and private economic activity.

Political Stability. When PS is taken into consideration (columns 5 and 6, Table 17.1), the first interesting result is that this factor—similar to QA—appears to have a significant and positive impact on firms' decisions to invest. This conclusion is in line with the findings of various authors who have been able to show—using various indicators of political stability—that a sound and stable political environment provides enterprises with more predictable conditions to invest.

Besides, our new set of estimations validates most of the conclusions drawn previously for QA with a few exceptions. First, structural reforms and human capital are still validated as important factors for private investment decisions. This time, however, they play their roles indirectly only, through improving political stability. This conclusion constitutes quite interesting empirical evidence. Structural reforms, by leading to better economic performances, lower the discontent of the population and produce a more stable political environment. Education goes in the same direction.

Another small difference can be seen in the MENA dummy variable, which is now significant in both equations, though at the 10 percent level: MENA countries underperform in private investment while appearing to be better in reaching more stable political systems. This finding is quite understandable considering that MENA countries display high government stability, which is one of the main components in the aggregate political stability indicator.

Other conclusions, such as the neoclassical investment model and the natural curve hypothesis in Equation (1) of private investment, the positive impact of the tenure of the system and the greater political stability of richer countries in equation (2) of institutional quality, hold in the case of the PS index.

Public Accountability. Columns 7 and 8 of table 17.1 report the regression results when PA is controlled to gauge the quality of institutions. Results are this time slightly different. In fact, our estimations fail to find strong evidence that PA is detrimental to private investment. Although some empirical evidence can been found in the literature (see in particular Pastor and Sung 1995), this result may be explained by the unresolved debate on the potential role of democratic institutions on growth (see Glaeser et al. 2004), as well as by some deficiencies in the specification of our model. For comparison purposes in this paper, we have estimated the same model for each of our indicators of governance. Hence, our results are likely to stem from the fact that the underlying mechanisms to shape PA are different from the mechanisms of QA and PS. It is shown in the next section that the specification including PA in the aggregated governance indicator (Gov) indicates the role of this factor in the private investments decisions.

This set of estimations, however, seems to still validate that structural reforms encourage private investment decisions. This time, the link appears to be only direct, and the coefficient of the structural reform indicator in the institutional quality equation [Equation (2)] appears insignificant. Besides, as for PS education and health of the population seem to encourage private investment by participating in the democratization process of the country. An interesting result also concerns the MENA dummy variable in the PA equation: Its coefficient is now significant and negative. This finding confirms the deficit in democratic institutions of the MENA region, as already stressed by several authors (see, in particular, World Bank 2003). Moreover, following our estimations, richer countries exhibit better democratic institutions, and natural resources exporters still show low private investment performances. The initials results for real interest rate, economic growth and tenure of system remain unaltered as well.

Governance. Our last set of estimations takes into consideration the aggregate indicator of governance, which summarizes the information contained in the three previous indicators. Results of the regressions are reported in columns (9) to (12) of table 17.1. This last set of estimations confirms most of the results obtained before. The aggregate indicator of governance appears to have a positive and significant coefficient that validates the importance of this factor for the firm's decisions to invest. Structural reforms are highly significant in enhancing private investment. The effects of human capital work indirectly by affecting aggregate governance. Overall, MENA countries underperform in terms of governance institutions. This result indicates the need for institutional reform in the MENA region, especially considering the positive and persistent role of governance institutions in private investment.

Other results remain the same as well, which confirms the robustness of our previous results. An interesting point, however, can be seen in the fact that since PA is included in the aggregate indicator of governance,[32] this factor now actively plays a role in the firm's decisions to invest. Even though this result has to be considered with caution, it can be seen as further evidence for the literature on the positive role of democratic institutions in the economic performance of the countries.

Governance Institutions: How Much Can They Improve Private Investment in MENA?

In this section, we use the model estimated previously to determine which factors would improve investment performance in our MENA countries. We evaluate, in particular, the contribution of administrative quality, political stability, and public accountability, which have been revealed to be of primary importance in firms' decisions to invest. We also consider the role of structural reforms and human capital. For this purpose, we simulate how much private investment the region would have achieved if governance institutions, structural reforms, and human capital had been improved by one standard deviation. This simulation has been done for two time periods, the 1980s and the 1990s, respectively. For the calculations, we use the last set of estimations, which summarize the effects of the three subcomponents of governance (see table 17.1, columns 9 and 10).

A first step consisted in calculating the coefficients of the initial variables that explain the composite indicators of governance (GOV), structural reforms (SR) and human capital (H). The calculation is based on the estimated coefficients of these aggregate indicators in the regression (table 17.1, column 9), as well as on the weights of each principal component in the aggregate indicator combined with the loading of the initial variables in each principal component (Annex 17.4).[33] In the case of human capital calculations, we consider the indirect impact on private investment through the improvement of the quality of governance institutions. We use in this case the coefficient of the human capital indicator in the governance equation (table 17.1, column 10) combined with the estimated coefficient of the governance indicators in the investment equation (table 17.1, column 9). Coefficients of the initial variables are presented in Annex 5 and contributions to private investment appear in tables 17.2 and 17.3. In tables 17.2 and 17.3, the contribution of the QA index has been calculated by aggregating the contributions of its four subcomponents.[34] The same thing has been done for PS,[35] PA,[36] SR,[37] and H.[38]

These simulations show quite interesting results (see table 17.2). A first set of conclusions concerns the potentially significant impact of improved governance institutions in the region. An amelioration of one standard deviation of the QA would have increased private investment by 1.4 percent of GDP dur-

Table 17.2. Private Investment to GDP

(Increase with an improvement in)

	Structural reforms[a]	GOV[a]	QA	PA	PS	Human capital[b]	Total contributions[c]
1980	2.3	3.5	1.4	1.1	0.9	0.4	6.1
1990	3.0	3.4	1.4	1.2	0.8	0.5	6.8

Source: Authors' calculations.
Note: a. Direct impact on private investment calculated from equation (9), table 17.1.
b. Indirect impact on private investment calculated from equations (9) and (10), table 17.1.
c. Sum of direct and indirect impact.

ing the 1980s and the 1990s. This augmentation is of 1.1 to 1.2 percent of GDP in the case of PA and of 0.8 to 0.9 percent of GDP for an amelioration of the PS. In total, private investment could have been higher by 3.4 to 3.5 percent of GDP if governance institutions had been reformed in an appropriate way.

Our calculations also point out that governance deficiencies have not been the only reasons for low private investment performance in MENA. Reforming the economy in other dimensions is necessary to boost private investment in the region. This has been the case over the whole period, but more importantly during the 1990s, when private investment could have been increased by 3 percent of GDP if structural reforms had been improved by one standard deviation (2.3 percent in the 1980s).

On average, private investment could have reached 17.7 and 18 percent of GDP in the 1980s and the 1990s (compared to 11.6 and 12 percent observed) if governance institutions and structural deficiencies had been improved at the same time (see table 17.3). If we add the indirect impact of human capital (0.4 to 0.5 percent of GDP, through the amelioration of governance institutions), private investment in Egypt could have been stimulated by 48 and 77 percent during the 1980s and the 1990s, and could have reached 18.7 and 15.7 percent of GDP (compared to 12.6 and 8.9 observed), respectively. This percentage increase would have been of 64 and 54 percent in Iran (with a private investment ratio of 15.7 and 19.5 percent of GDP in this case), 51 and 68 percent in Morocco (with a ratio of private investment of 18.1 and 16.9 percent of GDP), and 45 percent in Tunisia (19.7 and 21.7 percent of GDP for the private investment ratio). These figures are in line with the performances of the East Asian economies that achieved, on average for our sample of countries, an investment ratio of 17.5 and 19.9 percent of GDP during the two subperiods.[39]

Our simulations also give a more precise diagnostic of which specific governance institutions would improve private investment performance in MENA. Contributions are calculated for each indicator of governance, as well as for structural reforms and human capital. Interesting conclusions relate to the impact of the different governance institutions. PA appears to be of primary importance in enhancing the confidence of private investors in MENA. An improvement of one standard deviation of civil liberties and political

Table 17.3. Private Investment to GDP

	1980s		1990s	
	Observed	Predicted	Observed	Predicted
Egypt (% GDP)	12.6	18.7	8.9	15.7
% increase		(48)		(77)
Iran (% GDP)	9.6	15.7	12.7	19.5
% increase		(64)		(54)
Morocco (% GDP)	12.1	18.1	10.1	16.9
% increase		(51)		(68)
Tunisia (% GDP)	13.6	19.7	14.9	21.7
% increase		(45)		(43)
Average (% GDP)	12.0	18.0	11.6	18.5

Source: Authors' calculations.

rights would have respectively increased private investment decisions by approximately 0.5 and 0.6 percent of GDP during the 1980s and the 1990s (see table 17.4). This result clearly shows that democratic institutions matter for the region. This finding can be linked to the significant deficit of democratic institutions in MENA countries (see World Bank 2003). This aspect gives to the region a significant scope for improving private investment performances in the future.

On QA, bureaucratic quality and corruption constitute other key factors for private investment decisions in the region. An improvement in the quality of the bureaucracy and a reduction of the level of corruption, both by one standard deviation, would have stimulated firms' investment by 0.4 to 0.5 percent of GDP for each factor. These findings confirm some conclusions of the literature, specifically on the role played by corruption in increasing the cost and risk of doing business. Besides, our calculations add to the subject by quantifying the importance of these two factors for the countries of our interest.

On the side of PS, attention should be given in the region to the reduction of internal and external conflicts, as well as of ethnic tensions. Narrowing the gap with politically more stable developing countries by one standard deviation would have helped private investment decisions, which could have been higher by 0.2 to 0.3 percent of GDP, depending on the factor. Our findings corroborate that institutions associated with political instability have a disruptive effect on aggregate investment. This result makes political stability a significant factor in reducing uncertainty and creating a friendly business environment in MENA.

Another striking feature of this set of calculations relates to the critical role of financial development and trade policy within the MENA region. A more developed financial system in the region would have helped private firms realize their investment projects—which could have been higher by 1.2 to 1.7 percent of GDP. A more open trade policy would also have stimulated private

Table 17.4. Private Investment to GDP

(Increase with an improvement in)

	SR	trade pol	priv cred	QA	corrup tion	bur qual	inves prof	law ord	PA	pol rights	civ lib	PS	gov stab	int confl	ext confl	ethn tens
1980	2.2	1.0	1.2	1.4	0.45	0.53	0.19	0.28	1.1	0.53	0.57	0.9	0.10	0.27	0.30	0.27
1990	3.0	1.3	1.7	1.4	0.42	0.44	0.25	0.26	1.2	0.62	0.56	0.8	0.12	0.25	0.20	0.22

Source: Authors' calculations

investment by 1 to 1.3 percent of GDP. These results have to be related to the deficit of the region in these two fields of activity (see Nabli and Véganzonès-Varoudakis 2007). These findings reveal that structural reforms represent another important question that MENA governments have to address if the region wants to catch up with more successful developing economies.

Conclusion

This paper empirically shows, for a panel of 31 developing countries studied during the 1980s and the 1990s, that governance institutions constitute an important part of the investment climate of developing economies. This result strongly holds for the QA and confirms that a low level of corruption, good-quality bureaucracy, a reliable judiciary, strong security of property rights, a reasonable risk to operations, and sound taxation and regulation contribute significantly to firms' decisions to invest. Our estimations also verify that PS, by providing a sound and predictable environment to enterprises, contributes as well to a friendly business environment. These results add significantly to the literature on governance by validating the role of a large set of institutional variables on private economic performances over a relatively long period of time.

Our findings are unambiguous and robust to the introduction of other explanatory variables. This is the case for structural reforms—in the form of trade openness and financial development—and for human capital, which appear to play significant roles in private investment decisions. This result shows that firms in developing countries face constraints that are not accounted for in more developed economies. It also shows that—contrary to recent works, which make governance institutions the dominant factor, with little independent influence of economic policies (see Rodrick, Subramanian, and Trebbi 2002 and Easterly and Levine, 2003)—economic policies and governance institutions both contribute to firms' decisions to invest. We show as well that structural reforms and human capital contribute to firms' decisions to invest by also improving the quality of governance. These conclusions have been reached by estimating a simultaneous model of private investment and governance quality, whereby economic policies and human capital concurrently explain both variables. These conclusions can be considered an important contribution to the empirical literature on governance.

Our estimations find, in addition, some evidence that PA is detrimental to private investment. Although our results have to be considered with caution, they can be regarded as contributing some empirical evidence to the unresolved debate on the potential role of democratic institutions on growth (see Glaeser et al. 2004 and Pastor and Sung 1995 for more conclusive studies).

In MENA, improved governance institutions would greatly stimulate private investment. This is the case for all components of governance, with special attention to civil liberties and political rights, corruption and bureaucratic quality, and conflicts and ethnic tensions. By reforming substantially their governance institutions during the 1980s and the 1990s, (that is, by increasing by one standard deviation all components of governance), MENA countries could have boosted private investment by 3.4 to 3.5 percent of GDP. This result makes governance a key variable for improving the investment climate in the region.

Governance deficiencies, however, are not the only issues that MENA could address to encourage private investment in the region. Reforming the economy constitutes another powerful instrument that would also stimulate firms' investment decisions. A more developed financial system would have permitted the private sector to implement more investment projects. One standard deviation increase during the 1980s and the 1990s would have raised the private investment ratio by 1.2 to 1.7 percent of GDP. Similarly, a more open trade policy would have stimulated private investment decisions by 1 to 1.3 percent of GDP during the same period. This makes structural reforms an important issue that MENA governments also have to address if the region wants to catch up with more successful developing economies.

Notes

1. See in particular Rodrik (1999) and Frankel (2002).

2. See, for example, Knack and Keefer (1995); Acemoglu, Johnson, and Robinson (2001); Rodrik, Subramanian, and Trebbi (2002).

3. See Hall and Jones (1999; Acemoglu, Johnson, and Robinson (2001); Easterly and Levine (2003); and Rodrik, Subramanian and Trebbi (2002).

4. See, for example, Acemoglu, Johnson, Robinson, and Taicharoen (2003).

5. See North (1990); Knack and Keefer (1995); Calderon and Chong (2000); Easterly and Levine (2003); Rodrik, Subramanian, and Trebbi (2002); and Saleh (2004).

6. See, in particular, Keefer (2002).

7. This shortcoming is a more general concern in the literature on democracy and development (see De Haan and Siermann[1996]; Przeworski and others[2000]). The work of Pastor and Sung (1995) is, however, one of the few to show a positive effect of various indicators of democratic institutions on private investment in the developing world.

8. See, in particular, Rodrik (1991); Alesina and Perotti (1996); Le (2004); and Brunetti and Weder (1994).

9. World Bank (2003) has investigated the correlation between private investment and the ICRG (1999) index of "investment profile." This index is based on measures of contract enforceability, expropriation, profit repatriation, risk of operation, taxation, and payment delays.

10 See, in particular, Rodrik, Subramanina, and Trebbi (2002) and Easterly and Levine (2003).

11. For the positive spillover from trade openness on institutions, see Berg and Krueger (2003); Islam and Montenegro (2002); and Wei (2000). For the role of domestic competition, see Ades and Di Tella (1999); Djankov et al. (2001); and the World Bank (2002).

12 This impact might also be explained by the fact that the measure of institutional quality is most often subjective and an amalgam of policy and institutional factors.

13. In trying to gauge the exogenous contribution of institutions, recent research has given particular attention to the possible role played by geographical and historical influences on institutional formation (see Acemoglu, Johnson, and Robison[2001] and Engelman and Sokoloff 2002).

14. Various methods of aggregation have been used to categorize different types of institutions. See, in particular, Acemoglu, Johnson, Robinson, and Taicharoen (2003); Kaufmann et al. (2003); and the World Bank (2003).

15. See Calderon and Chong (2000) and Acemoglu, Johnson, and Robinson (2001) in the context of growth; see North (1981); Knack and Keefer (1995); Calderon and Chong (2000); Easterly and Levine (2003); Rodrik, Subramanian, and Trebbi (2002); and Saleh (2004) in the context of investment.

16. See, in particular, Rodrik (1991) and Serven and Solimano (1993).

17. See De Haan and Siermann (1996); Prszeworski and Limongi (1993); and Prszeworski et al. (2000).

18. See, in particular, Rodrik (1991); Alesina and Perotti (1996); Le (2004); and Brunetti and Weder (1994). In the growth context, see also Alesina et al. (1996); Svensson (1998); and Olson et al. (2000).

19. See, for example, Greene and Villanueva (1991); Blejer and Khan (1984); and Serven (1997).

20. See Shafik (1992) on Egypt; Schmidt and Muller (1992) on Morocco, as well as Bisat, El-Erian, El-Gamal, and Mongelli (1996); and Aysan, Sang, and Véganzonès-Varoudakis (forthcoming) on MENA.

21. See, in particular, Shafik (1992) and Agenor and Montiel (1999) for a discussion and additional references.

22. See, for example, McKinnon (1973) and Shaw (1973).

23. For the positive spillover from trade openness on governance quality, see Berg and Krueger (2003); Islam and Montenegro (2002);and Wei (2000). For the role of domestic competition, see Ades and Di Tella (1999); Djankov et al. (2001); and World Bank (2002).

24. See Lucas (1988), Psacharopoulos (1988) and Mankiw, Romer, and Weil (1992).

25. See, in particular, Acemoglu and Shimer (1999).

26. See Bresnahan, Brynjolfsson and Hitt (2002).

27. See Nabli and Véganzonès-Varoudakis (2007).

28 See Aizenmann and Marion (1999) and Everhart and Sumlinski (2001).

29. Aysan (2006) points out that this variable captures the "rentier effect." He notes that "it is easier for the elite to control and capture the rents from 'point source' resources. Resource rents are generally high in oil production. Around 80 percent of oil income is considered to be resource rent (Gylfason 2001), while such rents are much lower for other types of products in industry or in agriculture. A small work force is required to extract oil resources. Most of the time, oil is extracted by foreign firms with sophisticated technical skills (Isham et al. 2002). As a result, the ruling elite can exclude the majority of the population in extracting oil reserves. In other words, there exists no incentive on the part of the elite to incorporate the society into increasing aggregate production. Given the lack of economic preconditions, the citizens cannot generate pressure for increased literacy and political influence. This lack of political influence further feeds the vicious cycle by not effectively and peacefully revealing public interest and preferences."

30. Sources of data are as follows: The private investment series have been processed from various national and international sources (International Finance Corporation [IFC], World Development

Indicators [WDI], and Life Data Base [LDB]—see section 4.1 for more details); the "Administrative Quality" and "Political Stability" indexes use ICRG (1999) data; the components of the "Public Accountability" indicator come from Freedom House (2002); the "Structural Reforms" index uses data from WDI, but the oil export series entering the trade policy indicator comes from the United Nations; in the "Human Capital' indicator, the numbers of years of schooling are from Barro and Lee (1994) and from Barro (2000a and b), and the life expectancy series is from WDI. All aggregated indicators have been generated after implementing the PCA methodology (see Annex 17.4 for more details). Interest rates have been calculated from IFS, and tenure of the system comes from Keefer and others (2001). All other data are from WDI.

31. Oil export also becomes significant in the "Administrative Quality" equation at a 10 percent level.

32. PA contributes significantly and with the right sign to GOV (see the results of the PCA in Annex 17.4).

33. For more details on the methodology, see Nagaraj, Varoudakis, and Véganzonès (2000).

34. Theses subcomponents are corruption, bureaucracy quality, investment-friendly profile of administration and law and order (see section 2).

35. Political Stability has been proxied by aggregating the following indicators: government stability, internal and external conflicts, and ethnic tensions.

36. Public Accountability has been calculated by using civil liberties and political rights.

37. The Structural Reform indicator contains trade policy and financial development.

38. Human Capital is defined from life expectancy, and years of primary, secondary, and tertiary education.

39. For comparison purposes, we have benchmarked the effort represented by the improvement of one standard deviation of each initial indicator entering the governance (GOV), structural reforms (SR) and human capital (H) indicators to the reforms achieved by the East Asian economies. These calculations are shown in Table A.6., Annex 17.6. Figures of the table are the level of reforms potentially reached by our MENA countries divided by the ones achieved by the East Asian economies. For example, the value 1 means that an improvement of one standard deviation has increased the reform indicator in MENA to the level of the East Asian economies. As well, the value 1.2 means that the level reached by MENA is 20 percent higher than the one observed in East Asia. Most of the time, the effort considered in the simulations gives to our MENA countries an advance in "Administrative Quality," "Political Stability" and "Public Accountability" (during the 1990s, in this case). MENA, however, would not catch up with East Asia in terms of structural reforms (except in the case of Tunisia).

References

Acemoglu, Daron, and Robert Shimer. 1999. "Efficient Unemployment Insurance." *Journal of Political Economy* 107 (5): 893–928.

Acemoglu, Daron, and James A. Robinson. 2001. "A Theory of Political Transitions." *American Economic Review* 91 (4): 938–63.

Acemoglu, Daron, Simon Johnson, and James A. Robinson. 2001. "The Colonial Origins of Comparative Development: An Empirical Investigation." *American Economic Review* 91 (5): 1369–401.

Acemoglu, Daron, Simon Johnson, James Robinson, and Yunyong Taicharoen. 2003. "Institutional Causes, Macroeconomic Symptoms, Volatility, Crises and Growth." *Journal of Monetary Economics* 89 (September): 49–123.

Ades, Alberto, and Rafael Di Tella. 1999. "Rents, Competition and Corruption." *American Economic Review* 89, no. 4: 982–93.

Aizenman, Joshua, and Nancy P. Marion. 1999. "Volatility and Investment: Interpreting Evidence from Developing Countries." *Economica* 66(262): 157–79.

Agenor, Pierre-Richard, and Peter J. Montiel. 1999. *Development Macroeconomics.* Princeton, NJ: Princeton University Press.

Alesina, Alberto, and Roberto Perotti. 1996. "Income Distribution, Political Instability, and Investment." *European Economic Review* 40(6): 1203–28.

Alesina, Alberto, Sule Ozler, Nouriel Roubini, and Phillip Swagel. 1996. "Political Instability and Economic Growth." *Journal of Economic Growth* 1 (2): 189–211.

Aysan, Ahmet Frank. 2006. "The Role of Efficiency of Redistributive Institutions on Redistribution: An Empirical Assessment." Boğaziçi University Research Papers, ISS/EC 2006-14. Istanbul: Boğaziçi University.

Aysan, Ahmet F., Gaobo Pang, and Marie-Ange Véganzonès-Varoudakis. Forthcoming. "Uncertainty, Economic Reforms and Private Investment in the Middle East and North Africa." *Applied Economics.*

Azariadis, Costas, and Amartya Lahiri. 2002. "Do Rich Countries Choose Better Governments?" *Contributions to Macroeconomics* 2 (1): Article 4.

Balassa, Bela. 1978. "Exports and Economic Growth-Further Evidence." *Journal of Development Economics* 5(2): 181–89.

Barro, Robert J. 2000a. "International Data on Educational Attainment: Updates and Implications." CID Working Paper 42. Harvard University, Cambridge, MA.

———. 2000b. "International Measures of Schooling Years and Schooling Quality." *American Economic Review* 86(2): 218–23.

Barro, Robert J., and Jong-Wha Lee. 1994. "Panel Data Set Cross Countries." National Bureau of Economic Research, http://www.nber.org/pub/barro.lee/

Bellin, Eva. 2001. "The Politics of Profit in Tunisia: Utility of the Rentier Paradigm?" *World Development* 22 (3): 427–36.

Berg, Andrew, and Ann Krueger. 2003. "Trade, Growth, and Poverty—A Selective Survey." IMF Working Paper 03/30. International Monetary Fund, Washington, DC.

Bisat, Amer, Mohamed A. El-Erian, Mahmoud El-Gamal, and Francesco P. Mongelli. 1996. "Investment and Growth in the Middle East and North Africa." IMF Working Paper WP/96/124. International Monetary Fund, Washington, DC.

Blejer, Mario, and Mohsin Kahn. 1984. "Government Policy and Private Investment in Developing Counties." IMF Staff Papers 31 (2): 79–403. International Monetary Fund, Washington, DC.

Bresnahan, Timothy, F. Erik Brynjolfsson, and Lorin M. Hitt. 2002. "Information, Technology, Workplace Organization and the Demand of Skilled Labor: Firm-Level Evidence." *Quarterly Journal of Economics* 117 (1): 339–76.

Brunetti, Aymo, and Beatrice Weder. 1994. "Political Credibility and Economic Growth in Less Developed Countries." *Constitutional Political Economy* 5 (1):23–43.

Caballero, Ricardo, and Arvind Krishnamurthy. 2001. "A Dual Liquidity Model for Emerging Markets." NBER Working Paper 8758. National Bureau of Economic Research, Cambridge, MA.

Calderon, Cesar, and Alberto Chong. 2000. "Causality and Feedback between Institutional Measures and Economic Growth." *Economic and Politics* 12 (1): 69–81.

De Haan, Jakob, and Clemens L. J. Siermann. 1996. "New Evidence from Historical Accounts and Contemporary Data." *Land Economics* 75 (3): 341–59.

Djankov, Simon, Rafael La Porta, Florencio Lopez-de-Silanes, and Andrei Sheifer. 2001. "The Regulation of Entry." CEPR Discussion Paper No. 2953. (September)

Easterly, William, and Ross Levine. 2003. "Tropics, Germs, and Crops: How Endowments Affect Economic Development." *Journal of Monetary Economics* 50 (1): 3–39.

El Badawi, Ibrahim A. 2002. "Reviving Growth in the Arab World." Working Paper Series 0206. Arab Planning Institute, Safat, Kuwait.

Engelman, S., and K. Sokoloff. 2002. "Factor Endowments, Inequality, and Paths of Development among New World Economies." *Economia* 3 (1): 41–109.

Evans, Peter, and James Rauch. 2000) "Bureaucratic Structure and Bureaucratic Performance in the Less Developed Countries." *Journal of Public Economics* 75 (1): 49–71.

Everhart, Stephen, and Mariuzs Sumlinski. 2001. "Trends in Private Investment in Developing Countries, Statistics for 1970–2000, and the Impact on Private Investment of Corruption and the Quality of Public Investment." IFC Discussion Paper 44, Washington, DC.

Feder, G. 1982. "On Exports and Economic Growth." *Journal of Development Economics* 12 (1–2): 59–73.

Frankel, Jeffrey. 2002. "Promoting Better National Institutions: The Role of the IMF." Paper presented at the Third Annual IMF Research Conference, Washington, DC. November 7–8.

Frankel, J.A., and D. Romer, 1999. "Does Trade Cause Growth?" *The American Economic Review* 89 (3): 379–99. Fraser Institute, *Economic Freedom in the World*, Vancouver, Canada.

Freedom House. 2002. Freedom in the World 2001. 2002. http://www.freedomhouse.org. Accessed 2003.

Galor, Oded, Omer Moav, and Dietrich Vollrath. 2005. "Land Inequality and the Emergence of Human Capital Promoting Institutions." *Development and Comp Systems* 0502018. Economic Working Paper Archive at WUSTL.

Gylfason, T. 2001. "Natural Resources, Education, and Economic Development." *European Economic Review* 45 (No. 6): 847–59.

Glaeser, Edward L., Rafael La Porta, Florencio Lopez-de-Silanes, and Andrei Shleifer. 2004. "Do Institutions Cause Growth?" NBER Working Paper 10568. National Bureau of Economic Research, Cambridge, MA.

Greene, Joshua, and Delano Villanueva. 1991. "Private Investment in Developing Countries." IMF Staff Papers 38 (March):33–58. International Monetary Fund, Washington, DC.

Gupta, Sandeev, Hamid Davooli, and Rosa Alonso-Terme. 2002. "Does Corruption Affect Income Inequality and Poverty?" *Economics of Governance* 3 (1): 23–45.

Hall, Robert, and Charles Jones. 1999. "Why Do Some Countries Produces So Much More Output per Workers than Others?" *Quarterly Journal of Economics* 114 (1): 83–116.

Heritage Foundation. 2003. Index of Economic Freedom. Available online at http://www.heritage .org/research/ features/index *(The Wall Street Journal).*

ICRG. 1999. *Brief Guide to the Rating System.* Political Risk Service Group, New York.

International Finance Statistics Database (IFS). The International Monetary Fund, Washington, DC.

International Monetary Fund. 2003. World Economic Outlook. *Growth and Institutions.* World Economic and Financial Surveys, Washington, DC.

Isham, J., M. Woolcock, L. Pritchett, and G. Busby. 2005. "The Varieties of Rentier Experience: How Natural Resource Export Structures Affect the Political Economy of Economic Growth."

Islam, Roumeen, and Claudio Montenegro. 2002. "What Determines the Quality of Institutions?" Policy Research Working Paper 2764 (January). World Bank, Washington, DC.

Jorgenson, Dale W. 1963. "Capital Theory and Investment Behavior." *American Economic Review* 53 (2): 247–59. (May)

Kaufmann, Dani, Aart Kraay, and Maximo Mastruzzi. 2003. "Governance Matters III, Governance Indicators for 1996–2002." Policy Research Working Paper 3106. World Bank, Washington, DC.

Keefer, Philip. 2002. "The Political Economy of Corruption in Indonesia." World Bank, Washington, DC.

Keefer, Philip, Thorsten Beck, George Clarke, Alberto Groff, and Patrick Walsh. 2001. "New Tools in Comparative Political Economy: The Database of Political Institutions." *World Bank Economic Review* 15 (1): 165–76.

Knack, Stephen, and Philip Keefer. 1995. "Institutions and Economic Performance: Cross-Country Tests Using Alternative Institutional Measures." *Economics and Politics* 7 (3): 207–27.

Le, Quan V. 2004. "Political and Economic Determinants of Private Investment." *Journal of International Development* 16(4): 289–604.

Levine, Ross. 1997. "Financial Development and Economic Growth: Views and Agenda." *Journal of Economic Literature* 35 (2): 688–726.

Life Data Base (LDB). World Bank, Washington, DC.

Lipset, Seymour Martin. 1959. "Some Social Requisites of Democracy: Economic Development and Political Legitimacy." *American Political Science Review* 53 (1): 69–105.

Lucas, Robert. 1988. "On the Mechanics of Development." *Journal of Monetary Economics* 22 (1):1–175.

Mankiw, Gregory, David Romer, and David Weil. 1992. "A Contribution to the Empirics of Economic Growth." *Quarterly Journal of Economics* 106 (3): 407–37.

Mauro, Paolo. 1995. "Corruption and Growth." *Quarterly Journal of Economics* 110 (3): 681–712.

McKinnon, Ronald I. 1973. *Money and Capital in Economic Development*. Washington, DC: Brookings Institution.

Mo, Park Hung. 2001. "Corruption and Economic Growth." *Journal of Comparative Economics* 29 (1): 66–79.

Nabli, Mustapha, and Marie-Ange Véganzonès-Varoudakis. 2007. "Reform Complementarities and Economic Growth in the Middle East and North Africa." *Journal of International Development* 19(1): 17–54.

Nagaraj, Ratapolu, Aristomène Varoudakis, and Marie-Ange Véganzonès. 2000. "Long-Run Growth Trends and Convergence across Indian States: The Role of Infrastructures." *Journal of International Development* 12 (1): 45–70.

North, Douglas C. 1981. *Structure and Change in Economic History*. New York: W. W. Norton.

———. 1990. *Institutions, Institutional Change, and Economic Performance*. Cambridge: Cambridge University Press.

Olson, Mancur, Naveen Sarna, and Anand V. Swamy. 2000. "Governance and Growth: A Simple Hypothesis Explaining Cross-Country Differences in Productivity Growth." *Public Choice* 102 (3–4): 341–64.

Pastor, Manuel, and Jae Ho Sung. 1995. "Private Investment and Democracy in the Developing World." *Journal of Economic Issues* 29 (1): 223–321.

Przeworski, Adam, and Fernando Limongi. 1993. "Political Regimes and Economic Growth." *Journal of Economic Perspectives* 7 (3): 51–69.

Przeworski, Adam, Michael Alvarez, Jose Antonio Cheibub, and Fernando Limongi. 2000. *Democracy and Development: Political Institutions and Well-Being in the World, 1950–1990*. New York: Cambridge University Press.

Psacharopoulos, George. 1988. "Education and Development: A Review." *World Bank Research Observer* 3 (1): 99–116..

Rama, Martin. 1993. "Empirical Investment Equations in Developing Countries." In *Striving for Growth after Adjustment*, ed. L. Servén and A. Solimano. World Bank: Washington, DC.

Rodriguez, Francisco, and Jeffrey D. Sachs. 1999. "Why Do Resource Abundant Economies Grow More Slowly?" *Journal of Economic Growth* 4 (3): 277–303.

Rodrik, Dani. 1991. "Policy Uncertainty and Private Investment in Developing Countries." *Journal of Development Economics* 36 (2): 229–42.

———. 1999. "Institutions for High-Quality Growth: What They Are and How to Acquire Them." Paper presented at the IMF Conference on Second Generation Reforms, Washington, DC. November 8–9.

Rodrik, Dani, Arvind Subramanian, and Francesco Trebbi. 2002. "Institutions Rule: The Primacy of Institutions over Geography and Integration in Economic Development." NBER Working Paper 9305. National Bureau of Economic Research, Cambridge, MA.

Ross, Michael. 2001. "Does Oil Hinder Democracy?" *World Politics* 53 (3): 325–61.

Sachs, Jeffrey. 2003. "Institutions Don't Rule: A Refutation of Institutional Fundamentalism." NBER Working Paper 9490. National Bureau of Economic Research, Cambridge, MA.

Sachs, Jeffrey, and Andrew Warner. 1997. "Natural Resource Abundance and Economic Growth." Center for International Development. Harvard University, Cambridge, MA. Available online at http://www.cid.harvard.edu//ciddata/ciddata.html. Accessed 2003.

Saleh, Jahangir. 2004. "Property Rights Institutions and Investment." Policy Research Working Paper Series 3311. World Bank, Washington, DC.

Schmidt-Hebbel, Klaus, and Tobias Muller. 1992. "Private Investment under Macroeconomic Adjustment in Morocco." In *Reviving Private Investment in Developing Countries,* ed. Alay Chhibber, Mansoor Dailami, and Nemat Shafik. Amsterdam: North Holland.

Serven, Luis. 1997. "Uncertainty, Instability, and Irreversible Investment: Theory, Evidence, and Lessons for Africa." Policy Research Working Paper Series 1722. World Bank, Washington DC.

Servén, Luis, and Andrés Solimano. 1993. "Private Investment and Macroeconomic Adjustment: A Survey." In *Striving for Growth after Adjustment*, ed. Luis Servén and Andrés Solimano. Washington, DC: World Bank.

Shafik, Nemat. 1992. "Modeling Private Investment in Egypt." *Journal of Development Economics* 39 (2): 263–77.

Shaw, E. 1973. *Financial Deepening in Economic Development*. New York: Oxford University Press.

Svensson, Jakob. 1998. "Investment, Property Rights and Political Instability: Theory and Evidence." *European Economic Review* (Elsevier) 42 (7): 1317–41.

Tanzi, Vito, and Hamid Davooli. 1997. "Corruption, Public Investment, and Growth." IMF Working Papers 97/139. International Monetary Fund, Washington, DC.

Transparency International. 2002. *Global Corruption Report 2003*. Berlin, Germany.

Wei, Shang-Jin. 2000. "Natural Openness and Good Government." NBER Working Paper 7765. National Bureau of Economic Research, Cambridge, MA.

World Bank. 2002. *World Development Report 2002: Building Institutions for Market*. New York: Oxford University Press.

———. 2003. *Better Governance for Development in the Middle East and North Africa: Enhancing Inclusiveness and Accountability.* MENA Development Report. World Bank, Washington, DC.

World Development Indicators Database (WDI). 2005. World Bank, Washington, DC.

Annex 17.1. List of Countries

List of Countries with High Quality Data (60 countries)

Argentina	Kenya*
Bangladesh*	Lithuania
Barbados*	Malawi*
Belize	Malaysia*
Benin*	Mauritius*
Bolivia*	Mexico
Brazil*	Moldova
Bulgaria	**Morocco***
Cambodia	Namibia
Chile*	Pakistan*
China*	Panama
Colombia*	Papua New Guinea*
Comoros	Paraguay*
Costa Rica*	Peru*
Cote d'Ivoire	Philippines*
Croatia	Poland*
Dominican Rep.	Romania
Ecuador*	Serbia and Montenegro
Egypt*	Seychelles
El Salvador	South Africa*
Estonia	St Lucia
Ethiopia	St. Vincent and the Grenadines
Guatemala*	Thailand*
Guinea-Bissau	Trinidad & Tobago*
Guyana	**Tunisia***
Haiti	Turkey*
Honduras*	Uruguay*
India*	Uzbekistan
Indonesia*	Venezuela*
Iran	Yugoslavia (FR)

Because of the lack of corresponding data for some countries, only counties marked with * are included in the final regressions.

Annex 17.2. Classification of Governance Institution by Kauffmann, Kraay, and Mastruzzi (2003)

Kaufmann, Kraay and Mastruzzi (2003) categorize governance institutions in six broad groups. Their measures of governance are based on several hundred variables measuring perceptions of governance, drawn from 25 separate data sources constructed by 18 different organizations. Their aggregate governance indicators aim to measure six different aspects of governance:

1. Government Effectiveness
2. Regulatory Quality
3. Rule of Law
4. Control of Corruption
5. Political Stability and Absence of Violence
6. Voice and Accountability

"Government Effectiveness" and "Regulatory Quality" clusters summarize various indicators of the ability of the government to formulate and implement sound policies. "Government Effectiveness" is composed of a single grouping of responses on the quality of public service provision, the quality of bureaucracy, the competence of civil servants, independence of civil service from political process, and credibility of government's commitment to policies. These are considered requisite conditions enabling governments to produce and implement sound policies and deliver more efficient redistribution. "Regulatory Quality" measures governance by extracting information from policy outcomes. It includes measures of market-unfriendly policies such as excessive regulation of economy, price controls, or inadequate bank supervision.

The respect of citizens and the state for the institutions which govern their interactions is categorized as "Rule of Law" and "Control of Corruption." The "Rule of Law" cluster includes several indicators which measure the extent to which agents have confidence in, and abide by, the rules of society, such as perception of incidence of crime, effectiveness and predictability of the judiciary, and enforceability of contracts. They also provide a cluster for "Control of Corruption," measuring perceptions of corruption, conventionally defined as the exercise of public power for private gain. The presence of corruption is often a manifestation of lack of respect for the rules which govern the interaction between state and citizens, and hence represents inefficiency in governing redistribution.

The quality of institutions is very much related to how authority figures are selected and replaced. The "Political Stability and Absence of Violence" cluster combines several indicators which measure the perceived likelihood that the government in power will be destabilized or overthrown by unconstitutional and violent means such as domestic violence and terrorism. This index indicates the continuity of policies and its effects on the efficiency of redistribution.

The "Voice and Accountability" cluster is the closest to measures of democracy indicators. Kaufmann, Kraay, and Mastruzzi include this cluster as an indicator of governance, in an attempt to capture the process by which citizens of a country are able to participate in the selection of governments. This cluster includes a number of indicators measuring various aspects of the political process, civil liberties and political rights, as well as various indicators measuring the independence of the media, in an attempt to quantify the accountability of those in a position of authority.

Annex 17.3. Our Governance Indicators

Quality of Administration

The QA index is composed of four indicators from ICRG, defined in the following manner:

(i) **Control over Corruption** "is a measure of corruption within the political system. Such corruption is a threat to foreign investment for several reasons: it distorts the economic and financial environment; it reduces the efficiency of government and business by enabling people to assume positions of power through patronage rather than ability, and, last but not least, introduces an inherent instability into the political process."

(ii) **Quality of Bureaucracy** indicates "countries where the bureaucracy has the strength and expertise to govern without drastic changes in policy or interruptions in government services. In these low-risk countries, the bureaucracy tends to be somewhat autonomous from political pressure and to have an established mechanism for recruitment and training. Countries that lack the cushioning effect of a strong bureaucracy receive low points because a change in government tends to be traumatic in terms of policy formulation and day-to-day administrative functions."

(iii) **Investment Profile** "is a measure of the government's attitude to inward investment as determined by an assessment of four sub-components: the risk to operations, taxation, repatriation and labor costs."

(iv) **Law and Order** "are assessed separately. The Law sub-component is an assessment of the strength and impartiality of the legal system, while the Order sub-component is an assessment of popular observance of the law."

Public Accountability

The second set of candidates measures PA." This index includes two indicators from Freedom House (FH): "Civil Liberties" and "Political Rights."

The "Civil Liberties" index mainly addresses the following questions:

- Are there free and independent media, literature, and other forms of cultural expressions?
- Is there open public discussion and free private discussion?
- Is there freedom of assembly and demonstration?
- Is there freedom of political or quasi-political organization?
- Are citizens equal under the law, do they have access to an independent and nondiscriminatory judiciary, and are they respected by the security forces?
- Is there protection from unjustified imprisonment, exile or torture, whether by groups that support or oppose the regime?
- Is there freedom from war or insurgency situations?
- Are there free trade unions and peasant organizations or the equivalent,

and is there effective collective bargaining?
- Are there free professional and other private organizations?
- Are there free businesses or cooperatives?
- Are there free religious institutions, and free private and public religious expression?
- Is there personal and social freedom, which include aspects such as gender equality, property rights, freedom of movements, choice of residence, and choice of marriage and size of family?
- Is there equality of opportunity—which includes freedom from exploitation by or dependency on landlords, employers, union leaders, bureaucrats, or any other type of denigrating obstacle—to a share of legitimate economic gains?
- Is there freedom from extreme government indifference and corruption?

The "Political Rights" index addresses the following questions:

- Is the head of state, head of government, or other chief authority elected through free and fair elections?
- Are the legislative representatives elected through free and fair elections?
- Are there fair electoral laws?
- Are the voters able to endow their freely elected representatives with real power?
- Do the people have the right to freely organize into different political parties or other competitive political groupings of their choice, and is the system open to the rise and fall of those competing parties or groupings?
- Is there a significant opposition vote, a de facto opposition power, and a realistic possibility for the opposition to increase its support or gain power through elections?
- Are the people free from domination by the military, foreign powers, totalitarian parties, religious hierarchies, economic oligarchies, or any other powerful groups?
- Do cultural ethnic, religious, and other minority groups have reasonable self-determination, self-government, autonomy, or participation through informal consensus in the decision-making process?
- For traditional monarchies which have no parties or electoral process, does the system provide for consultation with the people to encourage discussion of policy, and to allow the right to petitions the rulers?

Political Stability
The PS index includes the following variables from ICRG:

- **Government Stability** "is a measure both of the government's ability to carry out its declared program(s), and its ability to stay in office. This will depend on the type of governance, the cohesion of the government and governing party or parties, the closeness of the next election, the government's command of the legislature, popular approval of government policies, and so on."

- **Internal Conflict** "is an assessment of political violence in the country and its actual or potential impact on governance. The highest rating is given to those countries where there is no armed opposition to the government and the government does not indulge in arbitrary violence, direct or indirect, against its own people. The lowest rating is given to a country embroiled in an ongoing civil war."

- **External Conflict** "is an assessment both of the risk to the incumbent government and to inward investment. It ranges from trade restrictions and embargoes, whether imposed by a single country, a group of countries, or the international community as a whole, through geopolitical disputes, armed threats, exchanges of fire on borders, border incursions, foreign-supported insurgency, and full-scale warfare."

- **Ethnic Tensions** "measures the degree of tension within a country attributable to racial, nationality, or language divisions. Lower ratings are given to countries where racial and nationality tensions are high because opposing groups are intolerant and unwilling to compromise. Higher ratings are given to countries where tensions are minimal, even though such differences may still exist."

Annex 17.4. Principal Component Analysis

Table A17.4.1. The Administrative Quality Indicator

Component	Eigenvalue	Cumulative R²
P1	2.23	0.56
P2	0.83	0.76
P3	0.51	0.89
P4	0.43	1

Loadings	P1	P2	P3	P4
Corruption	0.49	−0.57	0.06	0.65
Bureaucracy Quality	0.54	−0.08	0.64	−0.54
Investment Profile	0.41	0.81	0.08	0.40
Law and Order	0.54	−0.02	−0.76	−0.36

$QA = P1*(0.5577/0.7640) + P2*(0.2063/0.7640)$

Table A17.4.2. The Political Stability Indicator

Component	Eigenvalue	Cumulative R²
P1	2.24	0.56
P2	0.70	0.74
P3	0.69	0.91
P4	0.36	1.00

Loadings	P1	P2	P3	P4
Government Stability	0.45	0.65	0.57	0.22
Internal Conflicts	0.58	−0.06	−0.08	−0.81
External Conflicts	0.48	0.18	−0.75	0.41
Ethnic Tensions	0.47	−0.73	0.33	0.36

$PS = P1* (0.5604/0.7356) + P2* (0.1752 /0.7356)$

Table A17.4.3. The Public Accountability Indicator

Component	Eigenvalue	Cumulative R²
P1	1.88	0.94
P2	0.12	1

Loadings	P1	P2
Political Rights	0.71	0.71
Civil Liberties	0.71	−0.71

$PA = P1$

Table A17.4.4. The Governance Indicator

Component	Eigenvalue	Cumulative R²
P1	3.94	0.39
P2	1.64	0.56
P3	1.2	0.68
P4	0.91	0.77
P5	0.69	0.84
P6	0.47	0.89
P7	0.43	0.93
P8	0.33	0.96
P9	0.26	0.99
P10	0.13	1

Loadings	P1	P2	P3	P4	P5	P6	P7	P8	P9	P10
Corruption	0.25	−0.15	0.61	0.19	0.00	0.53	0.46	0.06	−0.05	0.03
Bureaucracy Quality	0.30	−0.13	0.35	0.51	−0.10	−0.68	−0.13	0.12	−0.10	0.03
Investment Profile	0.33	−0.03	−0.43	0.40	0.11	0.02	0.31	−0.63	0.18	−0.08
Law and Order	0.37	−0.31	0.13	−0.12	0.06	0.20	−0.58	−0.05	0.59	−0.05
Political Rights	0.26	0.63	0.08	0.07	0.06	0.09	−0.15	0.11	−0.06	−0.69
Civil Liberties	0.26	0.63	0.04	0.03	0.07	0.08	−0.13	−0.01	0.06	0.71
Government Stability	0.31	−0.20	−0.52	0.24	0.16	0.21	0.01	0.67	−0.16	0.06
Internal Conflicts	0.41	−0.18	−0.03	−0.30	−0.16	0.10	−0.27	−0.31	−0.71	0.03
External Conflicts	0.33	0.07	−0.14	−0.33	−0.73	−0.15	0.34	0.16	0.26	−0.02
Ethnic Tensions	0.31	−0.04	0.08	−0.52	0.61	−0.36	0.34	0.07	0.06	−0.02

GOV = P1*(0.3937/0.7696) + P2*(0.1641/0.7696) + P3*(0.1204/0.7696) + P4*(0.0915/0.7696)

Table A17.4.5. The Structural Reform Indicator

Component	Eigenvalue	Cumulative R²
P1	1.49	0.75
P2	0.59	1

Loadings	P1	P2
Trade Policy	0.71	0.71
Private Credit	0.71	−0.71

SR = P1

Table A17.4.6. The Human Capital Indicator

Component	Eigenvalue	Cumulative R^2		
P1	3.14	0.78		
P2	0.38	0.88		
P3	0.31	0.96		
P4	0.18	1		

Loadings	P1	P2	P3	P4
Life Expectancy	0.52	−0.33	0.03	−0.79
H1	0.50	−0.41	0.55	0.53
H2	0.50	−0.05	−0.80	0.32
H3	0.48	0.85	0.23	−0.03

$H =$ **P1**

Annex 17.5. Short-Term Coefficients of the Disaggregated Indicators

Table A17.5.1. Direct Effect on Private Investment[a]

Index	Variables	Short-term coefficients	
		Standardized variables	Level variables
GOV	Corruption	0.49	0.45
	Bureaucracy Quality	0.54	0.52
	Investment Profile	0.32	0.15
	Law and Order	0.29	0.23
	Political Rights	0.64	0.32
	Civil Liberties	0.63	0.39
	Government Stability	0.14	0.06
	Internal Conflict	0.29	0.11
	External Conflict	0.27	0.12
	Ethnic Tensions	0.22	0.15
SR	Trade Policy	1.40	0.05
	Private Credit	1.40	0.07

Source: Authors' calculations.
Note: a. Direct impact is calculated using the estimated coefficient of the aggregated indicators (GOV and SR, see equation (9), Table (17.1)), as well as the weights of each principal component in the aggregate indicators, combined with the loading of the initial variables in each principal component (see Annex 17. 4).

Table A17.5.2. Indirect Effect on Private Investment[a]

Index	Variables	Short -term coefficients		
		Standardized variables[b]	Level variables[b]	Level variables[c]
H	Life Expectancy	0.06	0.01	0.01
	Primary Education	0.06	0.04	0.09
	Secondary Education	0.06	0.09	0.19
	Tertiary Education	0.06	0.51	1.14

Source: Authors' calculations.
Note: a. Indirect impact is calculated using the coefficient of the human capital indicator in the governance equation (column 10, Table 17.1), multiplied by the coefficient of the governance indicator in the investment equation (column 9, Table 17.1), in addition to the weights of each principal component in the aggregate indicators, combined with the loading of the initial variables in each principal component (see Annex 17.4).
b. Coefficient entering the governance equation (2).
c. Coefficient entering the private investment equation (1).

Annex 17.6

Table A17.6. Level of Variables with an Increase of One Standard Deviation Compared to the Actual Level in East Asia

	SR		QA				PA		PS				H			
	trade pol	priv cred	corrup tion	bur qual	inves prof	law ord	pol rights	civ lib	gov stab	int confl	ext confl	ethn tens	life exp	lary	liary	lllary
1980s																
Egypt	1.0	1.0	1.0	1.2	1.0	1.2	0.9	1.1	1.3	1.2	1.0	2.0	1.0	0.8	1.6	1.3
Iran	0.4	1.2	1.4	0.8	1.1	0.9	0.7	0.7	1.1	0.8	0.4	1.4	1.1	0.9	1.5	1.0
Morocco	0.9	0.9	1.1	1.4	1.1	1.0	1.2	1.0	1.5	1.1	0.9	1.9	1.1	0.3	0.5	0.7
Tunisia	1.1	1.6	1.4	1.3	1.1	1.0	0.7	1.0	1.2	1.2	0.8	2.8	1.1	0.9	1.4	1.1
1990s																
Egypt	0.9	0.9	1.2	1.3	1.3	1.2	1.1	1.1	1.4	1.1	1.1	1.9	1.1	1.0	1.5	1.6
Iran	0.6	0.8	1.5	1.4	1.1	1.3	1.1	0.9	1.4	1.3	1.0	1.8	1.1	1.0	1.5	1.4
Morocco	1.0	1.0	1.3	1.3	1.4	1.5	1.3	1.3	1.5	1.3	1.1	1.7	1.1	0.3	0.4	0.7
Tunisia	1.3	1.3	1.3	1.3	1.4	1.3	1.1	1.2	1.4	1.4	1.1	1.8	1.2	1.0	1.3	1.4

Source: Authors' calculations.

Note: Figures represent the level potentially reached by the MENA countries when increasing the control variables by one standard deviation divided by the levels achieved by the East Asian economies. For example, the value 1 means that an improvement of one standard deviation has increased the reform indicator in MENA to the level of the East Asian economies. Similarly, the value 1.2 indicates that the level reached by MENA is 20 percent higher than the level observed in East Asia.

Index